C
for
Engineers

D0870179

Brian Bramer B.Tech., Ph.D., C.Eng., M.I.E.E., M.I.E.E.E.
Principal Lecturer in Computing Science
Department of Computing Science
De Montfort University
Leicester

Susan Bramer B.A.
Lecturer in Computing Science
Department of Computing Science
De Montfort University
Leicester

A member of the Hodder Headline Group
LONDON • SYDNEY • AUCKLAND
Copublished in North, Central and South America by
John Wiley & Sons, Inc., New York • Toronto

First published in Great Britain 1997 by
Arnold, a member of the Hodder Headline Group
338 Euston Road, London NW1 3BH

Copublished in North, Central and South America by
John Wiley & Sons, Inc., 605 Third Avenue,
New York NY 10158–0012

British Library Cataloguing in Publication Data
A catalogue record for this book is available from the British Library

Library of Congress Cataloging-in-Publication Data
A catalog record for this book is available from the Library of Congress

ISBN 0 340 67769 4
ISBN 0 470 23721 X (Wiley)

Printed and bound in Great Britain by
J W Arrowsmith Ltd, Bristol

Contents

Preface   viii

Sources of information   x

1 Computer systems: an overview   1
   1.1 The ANSI C standard   1
   1.2 Computer hardware and software   2
   1.3 Instruction and data storage   4
   1.4 Low- and high-level languages   6

2 Program design, coding and testing   8
   2.1 General requirements for software systems   8
   2.2 System analysis   9
   2.3 Programming paradigms   9
   2.4 Program design - stepwise refinement   10
   2.5 Testing   15

3 Outline structure of a C program   16
   3.1 Program modules and objects   16
   3.2 Program creation, compilation and execution   18
   3.3 Editing, compiling and executing the program   20

4 Starting to program in C   21
   4.1 Program to display a message on the display screen   21
   4.2 Program to calculate the area of a rectangle   22
   4.3 Types, constants and variables   22
   4.4 Statements and expressions   25
   4.5 Function calling, function parameters and the function result   26
   4.6 The standard input/output streams *stdout*, *stderr* and *stdin*   30
   4.7 Review of Program 4_3   30

5 Using standard library functions   31
   5.1 Introduction to the *printf* function   31
   5 2 Introduction to mathematical functions (sqrt, sin & cos)   32
   5.3 Numeric keyboard input using the *scanf* function   35
   5.4 The type qualifier *const* and *named constants*   37
   5.5 The preprocessor #define directive and *symbolic constants*   38

6 Program layout, documentation and debugging   40
   6.1 The C character set   40
   6.2 Programming style: documentation and layout   40
   6.3 Defining new type names using *typedef*   43
   6.4 Detection of compile, link and run-time errors   43

7 Integral data types   48
   7.1 Integral numeric data types   48
   7.2 Integer number constants   49
   7.3 Printing and reading integral types   50
   7.4 The enumerative type   51

8 Real number types   **53**
    8.1 Real number constants   53
    8.2 The accuracy of real number calculations   54
    8.3 Conversion between real types   55
    8.4 Printing and reading real numbers   55

9 Expressions and operators   **59**
    9.1 Type conversion in expressions   59
    9.2 Operator *precedence* and *associativity*   61
    9.3 Arithmetic operators   62
    9.4 The *bitwise* operators   64
    9.5 Casting or conversion operators   65
    9.6 The *sizeof* operator   65

10 Assignment operators   **68**
    10.1 The = assignment operator   68
    10.2 Type conversion across assignment   69
    10.3 Increment and decrement operators   71
    10.4 The compound assignment operators   74

11 The *if* statement   **76**
    11.1 The *if* statement   76
    11.2 Relational operators   77
    11.3 Logical operators   79
    11.4 Testing *scanf* for successful conversion   79
    11.5 Compound statements   80
    11.6 Nested *if* statements   81
    11.7 The conditional operator *?*   83
    11.8 Using diagnostic aids in <assert.h>   84

12 The *while* and *do* statements   **85**
    12.1 The *while* statement   85
    12.2 The *do* statement   88
    12.3 The *null* or empty statement   91
    12.4 Infinite loops   92

13 The *for* statement   **93**
    13.1 The *for* statement   93
    13.2 Program to evaluate capital growth at a given interest rate   94
    13.3 The sequence operator , (comma)   96
    13.4 Program to evaluate the factorial of an integer number   97

14 Further control statements   **101**
    14.1 The *continue* statement   101
    14.2 The *break* statement   101
    14.3 The *goto* statement   102
    14.4 The *switch* statement   102

15 More on input and output   **106**
    15.1 Validation of numeric data input   106
    15.2 Plotting a graph on a text display screen   108
    15.3 Plotting a graph on a graphics display screen   111

16 Functions **115**
16.1 Function *definition* 115
16.2 The *return* statement 116
16.3 A function to square a number 117
16.4 Function *prototypes* 119
16.5 Function to raise a *float* to an positive *integer* exponent 120
16.6 Function declarations in the original C 122
16.7 Passing parameters using *pass by value* 122
16.8 Passing parameters *by reference* 123
16.9 Function to swap the values of two variables 125
16.10 Function to maintain a running mean 126
16.11 Summary: *pass by reference* 128
16.12 Efficiency: parameter passing and function result 128
16.13 Using preprocessor macros to generate *inline functions* 129

17 Towards larger programs **133**
17.1 Information hiding and the scope of identifiers 133
17.2 Declarations and definitions 133
17.3 Local identifiers and local scope 134
17.4 External identifiers and file scope 134
17.5 *Automatic* and *static* storage classes 137
17.6 Evaluating Fibonacci numbers using *static* local variables 137
17.7 The type qualifiers *const* and *volatile* 139
17.8 Summary: identifier scope 140
17.9 Storage classes 140

18 Multi-file programs **142**
18.1 Modular programming and multi-file programs 142
18.2 External linkage and external variables and functions 143
18.3 Internal linkage and *static* external variables and functions 145
18.4 Constructing and using header files 146
18.5 Conditional selection 149
18.6 Random number generators 150
18.7 Simulation of the flow of patients through a doctor's surgery 153
18.8 Side effects 155
18.9 ADTs - abstract data types 156
18.10 Summary: external identifiers, internal and external linkage 157

19 One-dimensional arrays **158**
19.1 Defining and initialising arrays 158
19.2 Accessing the elements of an array 159
19.3 Program to calculate the average of a sequence of real numbers 160
19.4 Arrays as function parameters 162
19.5 Summary: arrays as function parameters 168
19.6 Using *#define* and *enum* to specify the array size 169
19.7 Using an array to implement a stack ADT 170
19.8 Implementing ADTs (abstract data types) 173
19.9 Simulation of the flow of patients through an outpatient clinic 174

20 Characters and strings   **177**
    20.1 The character type *char*   177
    20.2 Printing and reading characters   179
    20.3 Direct character I/O from the operating system   182
    20.4 The standard library <ctype.h>: functions to test characters   183
    20.5 String constants   184
    20.6 Defining and manipulating arrays of characters   185
    20.7 String input and output   186
    20.8 Program using functions to process strings   188
    20.9 Array processing functions in <string.h>   195

21 Pointers   **197**
    21.1 Variables and addresses   197
    21.2 Defining and using pointers   198
    21.3 Arrays and pointers   200
    21.4 *const* qualified pointers   206
    21.5 The *null pointer*   206
    21.6 Pointers to pointers   207
    21.7 The generic pointer type *void* *   208
    21.8 Arrays of pointers   209
    21.9 Passing parameters to function *main*   209
    21.10 Pointers and the *sizeof* operator   211

22 Functions and pointers   **212**
    22.1 Pointers as function parameters   212
    22.2 Functions that return a pointer as the function result   212
    22.3 String processing functions using pointers   213
    22.4 Pointers should only contain valid addresses   221
    22.5 When is an actual parameter an array or a simple variable?   222

23 Input and output functions   **223**
    23.1 Standard input/output streams   223
    23.2 Opening, closing, deleting and renaming files   224
    23.3 Character and string input and output   225
    23.4 The *fprintf*, *printf* and *sprintf* functions   227
    23.5 The *fscanf*, *scanf* and *sscanf* functions   228
    23.6 Binary (unformatted) input and output   228

24 Structures   **230**
    24.1 Declaring and initialising structures   230
    24.2 Accessing the members of a structure   231
    24.3 Pointers to structures   232
    24.4 Structures as function parameters   232
    24.5 Structures as members of structures   233
    24.6 An ADT (abstract data type) to store student records   233
    24.7 An ADT to store complex numbers   245
    24.8 Unions   249
    24.9 Bitfields   251

25 Dynamic storage allocation   **255**
25.1 Functions to allocate memory dynamically   255
25.2 Using dynamic storage allocation to implement a stack   257
25.3 Linked lists   262

26 Multi-dimensional arrays   **266**
26.1 Declaring and accessing multi-dimensional arrays   266
26.2 Multi-dimensional arrays as function parameters   267
26.3 Functions to read, write and multiply a two-dimensional matrix   268
26.4 Dynamically allocating multi-dimensional arrays   273
26.5 Two-dimensional arrays using an array of pointers to row data   280
26.6 Efficiency considerations when manipulating matrices   283

27 Evaluating mathematical series   **284**
27.1 Truncating infinite series   284
27.2 Program to evaluate the sine function sin(x)   285
27.3 Rounding errors   287
27.4 Evaluation of square root using Newton-Raphson method   291

28 Advanced use of functions   **294**
28.1 Recursive functions   294
28.2 Pointers to functions   295
28.3 Passing pointers to functions as function parameters   296
28.4 Returning pointers to functions as a function result   299
28.5 Functions with a variable number of parameters   302

29 Accessing operating system facilities   **305**
29.1 Hardware and software interrupts   305
29.2 Accessing MS-DOS operating system facilities   306
29.3 Using the RS232 serial port via MS-DOS   309
29.4 Using a Microsoft compatible mouse under MS-DOS   315
29.5 Invoking processes   317

30 Using assembly language from C   **319**
30.1 Separate assembly language functions   319
30.2 In-line assembly language statements   322
30.3 Interfacing other high-level languages with C   323

31 Low-level hardware programming   **324**
31.1 Setting up pointers to 'point to' locations in physical memory   324
31.2 Directly accessing video RAM of an IBM PC compatible computer   325
31.3 Accessing input/output device registers   328
31.4 Polled and interrupt I/O programming   328
31.5 Directly accessing the serial ports of an IBM PC compatible   328
31.6 Interrupt control of the serial ports of an IBM PC compatible   332

Appendix A The ASCII character code   **342**

Appendix B Answers to the exercises   **343**

Appendix C The standard library   **380**

Appendix D Table of C operators   **394**

References   **395**

Index   **396**

Preface

This book is intended as a learning text for students of Computer Science, Electronic Engineering, Information Technology and other courses, in a module which introduces programming in the C language. In addition, the book may also be used for self-instruction by programmers who wish to program in C.

This learning text would normally accompany a course of practical/tutorial sessions which may be backed by lectures. Each chapter is a self-contained unit that can be read by the student and many include exercises to be attempted during tutorial/practical sessions (answers to the exercises are given in Appendix B). To complete each chapter there are problems that should be attempted and may be used by instructors as a means of assessment. Certain sections (indicated by *) contain advanced topics or specialised material which may be skipped on the first reading.

Good programming practice is encouraged throughout by the use of modular and structured programming techniques. To illustrate and support concepts introduced within the text a large number of sample programs are presented (associated with each program is a discussion which dissects the program code line by line). Except for a few programs which contain machine or compiler specific code the programs should run under any modern compiler. The programs have been tested on IBM PC compatible microcomputers under DOS (using Turbo C/C++ V3.0, Microsoft C/C++ V10.00 and DJ's port of GNU C/C++ V2.6.3) and Windows 95 (using Borland C/C++ V4.51 and Microsoft Visual C++ V4.00). In addition the programs have been tested under UNIX on Apollo Domain DN4500, Hewlett Packard 720 and DEC Alpha 3000 workstations and IBM PC compatibles (using LINUX). The disk which accompanies this text contains a series of subdirectories entitled C4, C5, C6, etc., which correspond to the chapter numbers. Each subdirectory contains the programs presented in the chapter plus sample answers to the exercises. See the README file on disk for a description of the file naming conventions used.

This book is a self-contained text and makes no assumptions about previous programming experience. In a formal course other modules could provide support in the area of Software Engineering, object orientated analysis and design and assembly language programming (to support the chapters on pointers and the chapters on accessing low-level system dependent facilities).

Although this book is suitable for a wide range of courses, particular support is given to students on mathematical, engineering or physical science based courses. For example, the text introduces mathematical library functions at an early stage (Chapter 5), contains a chapter devoted to the problems associated with evaluating mathematical series (Chapter 27) and describes techniques to access low-level system dependent facilities (Chapters 29 and 31). The majority of programs, however, deal with the general problems of storing and manipulating different types of data and are applicable to a range of subject areas.

Outline of the book

Chapter 1 provides a general introduction to computer systems, information representation, and computer hardware and software fundamentals. Chapter 2 contains a general discussion of the problems faced when implementing large complex software systems and presents an introduction to program design, coding and testing.

Chapter 3 introduces functions, discussing their place in modular programming, and describes the role of the editor, preprocessor, compiler, linker and run time system. Chapter 4 describes, by means of a simple program, the outline structure of a program and the role of constants, variables, expressions, statements, etc. Input/output and mathematical functions are introduced in Chapter 5 together with sample programs which read data, perform a calculation and print results. Chapter 6 discusses program layout and the detection of compile, link and run time errors (program listings are presented which contain typical errors).

Chapters 7 and 8 discuss integral and real data types and describe functions to perform input/output operations. Chapters 9 and 10 introduce the *operators* which are used to build up expressions and the concept of operator *precedence* and *associativity*.

Conditional statements and program loop control statements, which are important tools in the implementation of well structured programs, are described in Chapters 11 to 14. Chapter 15 discusses input data verification and display output using graphs.

Functions, which are critical to the implementation of modular programs, are described in Chapter 16. Chapter 17 discusses *data hiding* and describes how it may be achieved in C programs. Chapter 18 continues the discussion by considering multi-file programs.

Chapters 19 and 20 introduce arrays (Chapter 20 dealing specifically with strings). Chapter 21 introduces basic pointer operations and Chapter 22 discusses the use of pointers with functions. Chapter 23 describes the input/output facilities, providing more details of the functions which have been used in earlier chapters. Structures are introduced in Chapter 21 and used to build a simple student records system. Chapter 25 introduces dynamic storage allocation which is then used in Chapter 26 which discusses multi-dimensional arrays.

Chapter 27 discusses the problems of accuracy and the implementation of algorithms to evaluate mathematical functions such as sin(x), sqrt(x), etc. Chapters 29, 30 and 31 describe techniques to access low-level system dependent facilities.

Updates for the second edition

The text of the first edition has been updated to reflect experience gained in classroom use. Some sections have been moved (e.g. the chapter on pointers now immediately follows the chapters on arrays and strings) or enhanced (e.g. the chapter on multi-dimensional arrays has been extended to discuss dynamic memory allocation techniques). In addition, the number of programs and exercises has been increased (approximately twice as many exercises with sample answers).

Recommendations to tutors

It is recommended that the sample programs and exercises are obtained from the disk which accompanies this text and tested with the target compiler. This should give an indication of any problem areas. The language is still evolving and compilers differ in implementation details or totally lack more modern facilities. Students can then be provided with information to enable them to overcome any problems.

Files for the preparation of OHPs (for HP3/4 laserjet printers) and copies of the programs and exercises may be obtained using a WWW browser from the URL http://www.cms.dmu.ac.uk/~bb/bb.html. Tutors may obtain sample answers to the problems by email from bb@dmu.ac.uk.

Acknowledgements and dedications

We wish to acknowledge the assistance of colleagues who helped with the preparation of this book. This book is dedicated to our lovely daughters Elinor and Isobel who are still helping!

Brian Bramer, Susan Bramer, 1996

Sources of information

Association of C and C++ Users, UK

ACCU is an organisation for the development and use of the C and C++ languages. It publishes CVu (the Journal of the ACCU) and Overload (the magazine of the C++ special interest group). Both journals are useful sources of information about the language, in particular the latest developments of C++. For membership details use email to contact the internet information address info@accu.org.

The C Users Group, USA

'The C Users Journal' is published monthly and contains many useful articles on the C and C++ languages and related topics. In particular there are regular articles on the development of the C++ draft standard. Subscribers are automatically enrolled as members of 'The C Users Group'. Subscription details may be obtained from The C Users Journal, 1601 W23rd, Suite 200, Lawrence, KS 66046-9950, USA.

The C++ Report comes out nine times per year and covers analysis, design and implementation issues. For information send email to PO0976@pslink.com.

World Wide Web Information

There is a wide range of information on C/C++ available via the WWW. If you have a WWW browser try going http://uu-gna.mit.edu:8001/uu-gna/text/cc/index.html or http://info.desy.de/general/users.html and look for C/C++ on the panel. A Newsgroup such as comp.lang.c can be contacted using a WWW browser by going news:comp.lang.c. If using ftp open sunsite.doc.ic.ac.uk and look in directory \usenet\usenet-by-group\comp.lang.c. A booklist and source of information is available by ftp from ftp.demon.co.uk in file /pub/books/reviews/cppbl.txt.

The GNU C/C++ compilers are free software which may be used under the terms of the GNU General Public License as published by the Free Software Foundation. Versions are available for the majority of computer systems including IBM PC compatibles running DOS, OS/2, etc. The software may be obtained by anonymous ftp from the major internet mirror sites including the following (see readme files for installation details):

emx V0.9a port of GNU C/C++ for DOS and OS/2 (developed by Eberhard Mattes)
    src.doc.ic.ac.uk in /pub/packages/os2/unix/emx09a
    ftp_os2.nmsu.edu in /os2/unix/emx09a

djgpp port of GNU C/C++ for DOS (developed by DJ Delorie)
    src.doc.ic.ac.uk in /pub/packages/ibmpc/simtel/vendors/djgpp
    oak.oakland.edu in /pub/simtel/vendors/djgpp

The majority of sample programs in this book have been compiled and executed under both the above versions of GNU C/C++.

1

Computer systems: an overview

1.1 The ANSI C standard

C was designed in the 1970s by Denis Ritchie (Kernighan & Ritchie 1978) as a *system implementation* language for the UNIX operating system (a *system implementation* language has 'high-level' program and data constructs plus 'low-level' facilities such as bit-manipulation and the ability to access memory directly). Prior to that time operating systems and other low-level programs had been implemented in assembly language which, although efficient when written by a **good** programmer, is very difficult to write and is processor dependent. Using C to implement UNIX enabled it to be portable across a wide variety of computer systems based on different processors. Assembly languages, however, are still used to implement hardware dependent operations which cannot be done in C or functions where speed is critical (Chapter 30 will discuss linking assembly language functions to C).

In 1989 ANSI (American National Standards Institute) approved an updated C standard (Kernighan & Ritchie 1988) which remedied many of the deficiencies in the original C. In particular ANSI C provides *function prototypes* which enable the compiler to cross check the definition of a function with its use (i.e. the number and type of parameters) and specifies a standard library with an extensive set of functions for input/output, string manipulation, etc. In addition, features which were either loosely specified or not specified at all in the original C were specified precisely. The programs in this book will adhere to the ANSI C standard which is supported by the majority of modern C compilers (updates from the original C will be noted where appropriate).

The C language was designed to be used by professional programmers who, it is assumed, know what they are doing and as such lacks many of the restrictions and checks of more modern languages such as Pascal and Modula 2, e.g. lack of rigorous type checking, array bound checking, etc. C is, however, a very powerful and flexible language allowing fast program development and is used extensively in industry and commerce to implement programs to solve problems in a wide range of application areas.

To understand many of the low level facilities of C an appreciation of computer hardware and information storage is useful. The remainder of this chapter introduces these topics and may be skipped by readers who already have this knowledge.

1.1.1 The C++ language

The C++ programming language (Stroustrup 1993, Bramer & Bramer 1996), originally a superset of C language with enhancements to support object orientated programming techniques, has now evolved into a separate language. In traditional programming languages the data and associated functions are distinct, in that the data is declared and then the functions are implemented. Object orientated programming languages contain facilities which support the encapsulation of a set of data types and associated functions into integrated entities called objects.

1.2 Computer hardware and software

1.2.1 Computer hardware

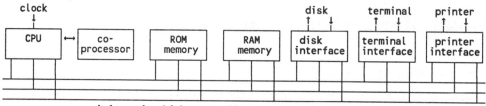

information highways: address, data and control buses

Fig. 1.1 Typical microcomputer configuration using a common bus system

Fig. 1.1 is a simplified representation of the hardware (physical components) of a simple single processor computer system comprising:

1   CPU (Central Processing Unit), e.g. microprocessor integrated circuit chip.
2   Co-processor (if fitted), e.g. for real number calculations or graphics.
3   Main or primary memory:
    (a) ROM (Read Only Memory) which contains permanent programs, e.g. power-up test programs and the 'bootstrap loader' which loads the operating system off disk;
    (b) RAM (Random Access read/write Memory) which is used to hold programs being executed and data being processed.
4   Disk interface which controls a floppy disk and/or hard disk as secondary memory for saving programs and data as files.
5   Terminal interface which controls the display screen and the keyboard.
6   Input/output interface devices for connecting external devices such as printers, modems, data acquisition subsystems, etc.

In Fig. 1.1 an *information highway* or *bus system* connects the components of the system:

Address bus: carries the address of the memory location or I/O device being accessed.

Data bus: carries the data signals.

Control bus: carries the control signals between the CPU and the other components of the system, e.g. signals to indicate when a valid address is on the address bus and if data is to be read or written.

A program consists of a sequence of instructions and associated data stored in main memory. In outline the CPU consists of two major components:

The control unit which *fetches* instructions from the main memory, decodes them to determine the operation required and then sets up instruction *execution*, e.g. to add two numbers together.

The arithmetic/logic unit (ALU) which, under the direction of the control unit, performs operations upon numeric and other data.

Each instruction that the computer hardware can execute has a particular binary pattern, with sequences of such binary patterns in the memory of the computer forming a program. Programs in this form are in a language called *machine code*, i.e. the language that the hardware of the computer understands. Before a program written in the C language can be executed it must be converted into machine code using a program called a compiler.

During program execution main memory is used to store the machine code and data. The majority of modern computer systems use a memory store built up of bytes of storage with each byte having an assigned location address. Fig. 1.2 shows such a memory organisation with the first byte of memory having address 0, the next 1, the next 2, etc.

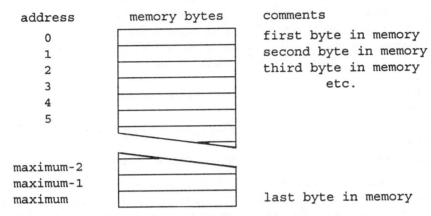

Fig. 1.2 The organisation of computer primary memory

In C there is a range of *data types* used to represent different types of data, e.g. characters, integer numbers, real numbers, etc. A program starts with *declarations* which specify the names and *data types* of *variables* which will be used to store data, e.g. a variable called x may be used to hold an integer numeric value. Knowing the *data type* of each variable enables the compiler to allocate memory to store the variable and to convert between different data types in calculations. For example, character data requires one byte of storage, an integer number two or four bytes and a real number four or eight bytes. The place in memory where the variable is stored is called its *address* which is used by the program to reference the variable in operations (generally the programmer need not be concerned with the actual values of addresses but it helps to know what an address is and what it is used for).

Information, such as program text, is held on disk (secondary memory) in a file structure which is organised and controlled by the operating system (see next section). Facilities are provided which enable the user to enter a program from the keyboard, correct any errors and save the result as a named file. The file can then be compiled, linked and executed.

1.2.2 Computer software

Before a computer can process information (i.e. carry out calculations or read a character from a keyboard) it requires a program. A program is a series of instructions stored in the main memory that are executed sequentially by the processor. The programs of a computer system are called its software:

System software includes the operating system which manages the overall operation of the computer system and software to support program execution, user interaction, etc.

Application programs for solving end-user problems, e.g. word processors, spreadsheets, accounting programs, CAD design tools, etc.

When a computer is switched on the operating system is read from disk into main memory (by a *bootstrap loader* in ROM). The *bootstrap loader* then passes control to the operating system which, after initialisation, prompts the user for command input. The facilities provided by the operating system and support software include:

1 Control of the disk file system, e.g. opening/closing/reading/writing.
2 Editors for the creation and modification of programs and data.
3 An assembler which translates programs from assembly language (see Section 1.4.1) into object code (object code contains machine code instructions plus information for the linker).
4 Compilers which translate programs from high-level languages (see Section 1.4.2) into object code.
5 A linker which links various object code program modules into a complete executable machine code program.
6 Execution and debugging of systems, application and user programs.

A native compiler (or assembler) produces code suitable for execution on the host computer or systems with a compatible processor. A cross compiler (or assembler) executing on one computer (the host) generates code suitable for another computer (the target) usually with a different processor. The resultant output object code is then linked (on the host) with libraries to provide I/O facilities, etc. (Bramer 1990).

1.3 Instruction and data storage

Within the computer hardware **memory** is used to store the instructions of the program being executed and the data to be processed. The data is the information to be processed by the computer system and may be simple numbers for mathematical calculations, text such as names and addresses or more complex structures such as pictures or drawings.

1.3.1 Representation of integer numbers

Within modern computer systems the basic element of storage is the *binary digit* (or *bit*) which can represent a 0 or a 1. The reason for this is that it is very easy to build electronic switches where an off/on condition is used to represent a 0/1 binary value. Although a single bit can only have two states, 0 or 1, a sequence of bits can be used to represent a larger range of values. Such a sequence is called a word of storage and is usually 8, 16, 32, 64 or 128 bits in length. An 8-bit word, for example, can represent an unsigned positive number in the range 0 to 11111111 binary (0 to 255 decimal):

bit	7	6	5	4	3	2	1	0
bit value	2^7	2^6	2^5	2^4	2^3	2^2	2^1	2^0

In the diagram above the least significant or rightmost bit, bit 0, represents 2^0 or 1 and the most significant or leftmost bit, bit 7, represents 2^7 or 128 decimal (the convention for identifying the bits within a word is that the rightmost or least significant bit is numbered 0). The combinations of 1s and 0s of the 8-bit word thus represent an unsigned value in the range 0 to 11111111 binary (0 to 255 decimal). The general term given to an 8-bit storage word is a **byte** which is used by the majority of modern computer systems as their fundamental unit of storage. To represent values that are too large to store in 8 bits a number of bytes may be used. For example, a 16-bit number (made up from two bytes) can represent an unsigned value in the range 0 to 65535 decimal.

Many commercial and scientific calculations require the use of signed numbers and the majority of modern computer systems use *twos complement binary arithmetic* in which the most significant bit is used to store the sign (1 for a negative number and 0 for a positive number). Using twos complement binary arithmetic an 8-bit number can represent values in the range -128 to +127 and a 16-bit number values in the range -32768 to +32767. In C the *data types* used to represent integer numbers are short int, int and long int which may be *signed* or *unsigned* (the programmer would use the most appropriate for the application). In practice short int and int are at least 16-bit and long int is at least 32-bit (Table 1.1 shows the numeric values which can be represented).

In practice it would be both difficult and error prone to enter data directly in binary form, so hexadecimal (base 16) or decimal is more commonly used.

data size	unsigned range	signed range
8-bit	0 to 255	-128 to +127
16-bit	0 to 65535	-32768 to +32767
32-bit	0 to 4294967295	-2147483648 to 2147483647

Table 1.1 Numeric range of 8-, 16- and 32-bit unsigned and signed numbers

1.3.2 Representation of real numbers

Integer numbers are suitable for whole number calculations (i.e. no fractional component) and where a limited number range is acceptable. The majority of scientific and engineering applications use numbers with fractional components which can vary in size from very small to very large values, e.g. from the size of atomic particles to intergalactic distances. C provides float, double and long double real number *data types* which are represented internally in floating point format.

In the floating point number system the real value is represented by a signed fractional component called the mantissa and a signed exponent. For example, decimal floating point numbers (using base 10) can be represented:

$$\text{mantissa} * 10^{\text{exponent}} \quad \text{where} \quad 0.1 <= \text{mantissa} < 1.0$$

To maintain accuracy the absolute value of the mantissa is maintained within the range shown (this process is called normalisation), e.g. 6520000.0 would be $0.652*10^7$ and -0.00000000652 would be $-0.652*10^{-8}$. In practice many printers cannot print superscripts so the above examples would be printed as 0.652E7 and -0.652E-8 where the E indicates an exponent of 10.

Within computer systems the fractional component is held as a binary fraction and the exponent is a power of 2 (or possibly 16). Typically the number would be stored in 32 bits with 24 bits to hold the signed mantissa and 8 bits for the signed exponent. In this case the accuracy of the mantissa is 23 binary bits (which is equivalent to 6 or 7 decimal figures of accuracy), and the range of the exponent would be -128 to +127. Greater accuracy can be obtained by using 64-bit storage in which 53 bits may be used to store the signed mantissa (giving 15 to 17 decimal figures of accuracy) and 11 bits for the exponent.

1.3.3 Character data

Character data is used within a computer to represent text (such as names and addresses) and consists of the usual printable characters, e.g. the alphabet A-Z and a-z, digits 0-9 and other characters such as +, -, *, /, !, $, % and &.

Each character is stored in a byte of memory and represented by a particular binary pattern or character code. To enable different computers, terminals and printers to be connected together there are a number of standard character codes. The most commonly used character code is ASCII (American Standard Code for Information Interchange), which is listed in Appendix A. The character A, for example, is represented by the binary pattern 01000001 (41 hexadecimal), and B by 01000010 (42 hexadecimal). The majority of computer users do not need to know or even be aware of these codes as the keyboard and display equipment converts between the characters and the internal codes, i.e. if the user hits the key A on the keyboard the binary value 01000001 is sent to the computer.

In C, characters are represented by a *data type* called char which is stored in a *byte*. A point to note is that C makes no guarantee about the character set used to store the char data type or even the way the characters are ordered, i.e. in ASCII the alphabet is consecutively ordered with A represented by decimal 65, B by 66, C by 67, up to Z which is 90 (but a particular machine may use some other character code, e.g. EBCDIC).

1.3.4 Instruction representation

A computer program is made up from a sequence of instructions which are represented by binary patterns. For example, the binary pattern 0100 0010 0100 0011 (4243 hexadecimal), when executed by the Motorola MC68000 microprocessor, would set the lower 16 bits of the data register D3 to 0. Each instruction that the computer hardware can execute has a particular binary pattern, with sequences of such binary patterns in the memory of the computer forming a program. Programs in this form are in a language called *machine code*, i.e. the language the hardware of the computer understands. It is clear that if humans had to write programs in machine code, programming would be a very error prone and time consuming task.

1.4 Low- and high-level languages

1.4.1 Assembly languages

In assembly languages each machine instruction is represented by a meaningful mnemonic (ADD, SUB, DIV) and data specified in binary, hexadecimal, decimal and character form. For example, the MC68000 instruction which clears the lower 16 bits of data register D3 (0100001001000011 in machine code) would be written in 68000 assembly language:

```
CLR.W       D3
```

where CLR.W is the instruction or operation-code mnemonic and D3 is the position of the data being operated upon (called the operand). The computer hardware can *only* *understand* machine code, so before it can be executed an assembly language program has to be converted into machine code. This is done by a program called an assembler which takes each assembly language statement and converts it on a one-to-one basis into the equivalent machine code instruction which can then be executed.

Assembly language programming is difficult because it is only one level above machine code and hence orientated to a particular computer (each type or model of central processing unit has its own machine code language). For example, a program which had been implemented in assembly language on an MC68000 microcomputer would have to be totally rewritten if transferred to an Intel 8086 based system. Even with the above disadvantages assembly language programming is still required in many industrial applications, e.g. time critical functions in a real-time control system.

Machine code and assembly languages are described as low-level languages in that they are orientated towards the computer hardware. High-level languages on the other hand are problem orientated and computer independent.

1.4.2 High-level problem solving languages

High-level languages are written in an English or mathematical notation which is orientated towards solving practical problems. Some examples of high-level languages are:

FORTRAN FORmula TRANslation: a language widely used for mathematical, scientific
and engineering applications;
PASCAL   a general purpose problem solving language;
C   a systems implementation language;
Ada   a systems implementation language designed for real-time applications;
Smalltalk an object oriented programming language;
C++   an object oriented programming language (evolved from C).

After the program source code has been entered into the computer it has to be converted into machine code by a program called a compiler. Each statement in a high-level language can be converted into a number of machine code instructions. For example, consider the following statement in C (where x is a *variable*):

```
x = 7 + 2 * (267 - 23);
```

The equivalent in 68000 assembly language is (the variable is in data register D0):

```
MOVE.L      #267,D0
SUB.W       #23,D0
ADD.W       D0,D0
ADD.W       #7,D0
```

and in 68000 machine code (hexadecimal byte values):

```
20 3C 00 00 01 0B 04 40 00 17 D0 40 06 40 00 07
```

In general the compilation process is not 100% efficient so a program written in a high-level language will take more memory and run more slowly than an equivalent assembly language program written by a good programmer. However, the advantages of working in a language which is orientated towards solving problems rather than the computer hardware means the majority of application programs are written in high-level languages.

An additional advantage of using high-level languages is that such languages are less computer dependent than assembly languages (depending upon the quality of the international standard of the language and the particular implementation).

2

Program design, coding and testing

2.1 General requirements for software systems

As end-user requirements become more exacting system software grows in complexity and size. Systems consisting of 200,000 to 500,000 lines of code, once beyond imagination, are now commonly found in a single product. In general, software systems have a number of overall requirements:

Correctness and reliability, which outweigh all the other requirements. Faults in programs can range in effect from being costly, for example, incorrectly ordered stock for a supermarket, to disastrous, for example, a fault that could lead to an explosion in a computer controlled chemical process.

Flexibility and reusability. To be commercially viable, components of software systems must be capable of being used across a range of products and computer systems (Bramer 1990). When implementing a new software system complete subsystems often have to be coded and tested even though similar subsystems exist in current programs. This is because the required subsystem is often interdependent with other subsystems in the product. Unravelling the interdependence often costs more than reimplementation.

Efficiency. As a software system grows in size and complexity it also tends to run slower. Slow response time may be annoying to an engineer using a CAD system but it could prove disastrous in a jet aircraft travelling at Mach 2. This may force sections of a system to be coded in assembly language, but efficiency must never be pursued at the expense of correctness and only in extreme cases at the expense of flexibility. Today it is generally simpler and cheaper to purchase faster hardware than to spend time gaining marginal improvements in software efficiency.

Maintainability. This deals with the problem of updating and improving software regardless of complexity. Modifying systems consisting of hundreds of thousands of lines of code written by software engineers who have since moved on is a daunting task. Will new staff be able to understand the code as originally written? If not, product maintenance will be very costly, time consuming and prone to error.

In an era of increasing system size and complexity an important issue is productivity. A software system consisting of 500,000 lines of code may take 150 man-years to implement. Without use of modern techniques and tools such systems may never become operational. CASE (Computer Aided Software Engineering) tools aid with software specification, design, debugging, integration, performance analysis, verification, and maintenance. The functionality offered by software development tools depends to a large extent on the complexity and size of the project and hence the funds available to purchase tools and support software and hardware. In practice this can range from a simple editor, compiler and run-time system on a PC to a CASE system running on a high powered professional workstation.

2.1.1 Documentation

Documentation is vitally important if a program is to be understood, not only by others, but by the original programmer at a later stage. A major aim when writing a program (apart from making it work) is to make it readable. The program code should be documented, as it is written, by inserting comments at appropriate places.

2.2 System analysis

The object of the analysis phase is to find out exactly what the end-user wants the final program to do (the programmer himself may be the end-user). A problem is that often users do not know what they want because they do not know the capabilities of modern computer systems. In many application areas full time professional analysts are employed to discover the real requirements and analyse complex problems. From the analysis phase, a requirements specification is drawn up, which specifies exactly what the program will do. When complete, the finished program can be checked against this document.

All the exercises and problems presented in this book are in effect specifications of programs to be written. It may appear from these specifications that the end product is obvious, and no analysis was required. Even simple problems, however, do require some analysis if only to find out what type of data is to be processed and how much there will be, e.g. will a file contain 100 items or 1000000000 (which will not fit onto a floppy disk)?

2.3 Programming paradigms

Over the past twenty or thirty years software engineering techniques have been developed to support reusability and assist the problems of system maintenance. The following outlines the common programming paradigms developed to date.

Procedural programming. A program is seen as a set of independent algorithms. Each algorithm is implemented as a procedure (or subroutine or function depending upon the language) which is kept as independent as possible with implementation details hidden inside the procedure. The procedure communicates with the outside world via parameters which pass information in and out. Using procedures simplifies testing and maintenance (one knows where to look for a particular problem) and once implemented a procedure can be reused in other systems. Examples of languages which support the procedural paradigm are Fortran, Algol, Pascal, Ada, C, C++, etc.

Modular programming. A program is seen as a number of data sets with associated procedures which organise and operate upon the data. A *module* contains a data set together with its associated procedures. Implementation details are hidden within the module with users of the module accessing facilities via a public interface (e.g. the definition module of a Modula 2 program or the header file of a C/C++ program, see Section 18.4). Using modules to hold data and associated procedures simplifies testing and maintenance (one knows where to look for particular problems) and once implemented a module can be reused in other systems.

Data abstraction. In Software Engineering terminology the components of a module are collectively known as an *abstract data type* (sometimes called a *user defined type*), a concept for grouping data and associated operations into an integrated entity. Although languages such as Modula 2 and C enable the implementation of abstract data types they cannot be treated like the fundamental types of the language, e.g. objects declared in declaration statements and operated upon by operators such as *, +, -, /, etc. Languages such as Ada and C++ enable the definition of abstract data types which can then be treated (almost) as though they were fundamental types, e.g. one can write expressions such as a = b * c + e where a, b, c and e are abstract data types.

Object-oriented programming. In effect a module is a 'black box' which implements an abstract data type. The problem is that a 'black box' can be restrictive in that it is difficult to adapt to meet some new requirement. Object-oriented programming languages support the implementation of abstract data types as encapsulated entities but also enable new types to inherit selected properties (data and operations) of existing types and add their own. The inheritance mechanism extends reusability in that it enables the creation of a new data type which contains common characteristics from the base types plus extra characteristics of its own. Once a type has been defined objects (variables) may be created which have the properties of the type. Examples of object-oriented languages are Smalltalk, C++ and Eiffel.

2.4 Program design - stepwise refinement

It is recognised that human beings can only carry between five and ten separate operations in their heads at a time. If a program is more than 10 or 20 lines of code (depending upon experience and complexity of problem), any attempt to design and code the entire program in one go will lead to a badly conceived and incorrect program. One design technique is stepwise refinement, whereby a task is visualised initially at a very simple level and subsequently refined in more and more detail. This section introduces the simple techniques which would be used when designing the sample programs and exercises in the early chapters of this book, the design being carried out using *pseudo code* or *structured English*.

2.4.1 Design exercise - a simple calculator

Design a calculator where numeric values may be entered as decimal or hexadecimal numbers, simple arithmetic performed and the result displayed in decimal. The initial specification of the calculator program is:

1   16-bit integer arithmetic (maximum numeric range is -32768 to 32767).
2   Entry of numeric data may be in decimal and hexadecimal.
3   Operations: add, subtract, multiply and divide using straight left to right evaluation.
4   Display the results as a signed decimal number on entry of an = character.

The approach to be taken is to design (and code and test) small parts of the problem at a time. This is a very useful method, particularly when controlling new equipment or experiments, where it is sometimes a major problem to control just one solenoid or valve or motor. It is often difficult to get general purpose input/output interfaces to do exactly what is required (even if the requirements are quite simple) and 'talking' to external equipment complicates things further. Once the problems of controlling the elementary components of a system have been overcome the software produced can then be used to form modules of the complete system. In the case of the calculator program nothing can be done until numeric values can be written to the screen and read from the keyboard and these are the first problems to be tackled.   Once input/output functions have been implemented the real working parts of the calculator program can be designed, implemented and tested.

It is assumed that the following input/output subroutines are available (if not available one would have to start programming I/O devices to read and write characters):

`write_character(character_out)`	write character to the screen
`read_character(character_in)`	read a character from the keyboard
`newline`	write a newline to the screen.

Calculator stage 1 refinement

Implement and test a subroutine to write a 16-bit decimal number to the display screen.

```
main program (* to test write_decimal *)
write_decimal(0)
newline
write_decimal(-10)
newline
write_decimal(10)
newline
write_decimal(30000)
newline
write_decimal(-30000)
stop

(* write number as a signed 16-bit decimal integer, suppress leading 0's *)
SUBROUTINE write_decimal(number)
IF number = 0
    write_character('0')
ELSE
    IF number < 0
        write_character('-')
        number = -number
    END IF
    print_0 = FALSE        (* used to suppress leading zeros *)
    divisor = 10000
    LOOP                                (* print next digit *)
        quotient = number / divisor
        IF quotient <> 0 OR (quotient = 0 AND print_0)
            print_0 = TRUE
            character = quotient + ASCII '0'
            write_character(character)
        END IF
        number = REMAINDER OF number / divisor
        divisor = divisor / 10
    UNTIL divisor = 0
END IF
RETURN
```

Only minimal testing of `write_decimal` is performed. When `read_decimal` is implemented (next stage) more extensive testing of both routines can be carried out.

Calculator stage 2 refinement

Implement and test a subroutine to read a signed decimal number from the keyboard. Call routine when a digit is read from the keyboard and terminate on a non-digit character.

```
main program
number = 0
REPEAT
    read_character(character)
    IF character IN ['0' - '9'] THEN
        read_decimal(number, character)
    newline
    write_decimal(number)
    newline
FOREVER

(* read a decimal number from the keyboard (exit on non-digit)
    on entry : character contains first digit character
    on exit  : number    contains the decimal value read
               character last character read              *)
read_decimal(number, character)
number = 0
REPEAT
    write_character(character)
    number = number * 10 + (character - ord ('0'))
    read_character(character)
UNTIL character NOT IN ['0' - '9']
RETURN
```

The specification called for hexadecimal input in addition to decimal. It would be reasonable to implement and test this while the problem of implementing read_decimal was fresh in one's mind.

Calculator stage 3 refinement

Implement and test a subroutine to read a hexadecimal number from the keyboard. Call routine when a '$' is read from the keyboard and terminate on a non-hex-digit character. Allow hex digits preceded by $ character.

```
main program
number = 0
REPEAT
    read_character(character)
    IF character IN ['0' - '9'] THEN
        read_decimal(number, character)
    ELSE
        IF character = '$' THEN
            read_hexadecimal(number, character)
    newline
    write_decimal(number)
    newline
FOREVER
```

```
(* read a hexadecimal number (exit on non-hex character)
     on exit  : number    contains the hexadecimal value read
                 character last character read                    *)
read_hexadecimal(number, character)
number = 0
read_character(character)
WHILE character IN ['0' - '9', 'A' -  'F'] DO
    write_character(character)
    IF character in ['0' - '9'] THEN
        tempnum = character - ord ('0')
    ELSE
        tempnum = character - ord ('A') + 10
    number = number * 16 + tempnum
    read_character(character)
RETURN
```

At this point basic numeric input/output is complete (extensions can be added later) and it is time to start implementing the operations of the calculator.

Calculator stage 4 refinement

Implement and test a subroutine to allow entry of + - * / operators, do calculations and print result when '=' is entered.

```
main program
REPEAT
        result = 0                       (* result of overall calculation *)
        number = 0                       (* current number being typed *)
        operator_character = '+'              (* initial operator *)
        REPEAT
           read_character(character)
           IF character IN ['0' - '9'] THEN
               read_decimal(number, character)
               calculate(result, number, operator_character)
           ELSE
               IF character = '$' THEN
                   read_hexadecimal(number, character)
                   calculate(result, number, operator_character)
               ELSE
                   IF character IN  ['+' '-' '*' '/'] THEN
                        operator_character = character
                        write_character(character)
        UNTIL character = '='
        write_character(character)
        write_decimal(result)
        newline
FOREVER
```

```
(* perform the operation - result = result operator number *)
SUBROUTINE calculate(result, number, operator character)
CASE operator_character OF
    '+' THEN result  = result + number
    '-' THEN result  = result - number
    '*' THEN result  = result * number
    '/' THEN result  = result / number
number = 0
operator_character = '+'
RETURN
```

Calculator stage 5 refinement

Examine program and tidy up. A larger program would require this at several stages.

2.4.2 Design exercise - discussion

The refinement of each stage can stop when the design is of sufficient detail that it can be translated directly into program instruction statements, or calls to existing modules. The design process is generally iterative and modifications to existing stages may be needed. This can occur when a new situation arises that requires a backtrack in the design process. If possible, modifications should be carried out at the design stage; once a program has been coded, modification becomes much more expensive. Possible extensions to the calculator program are:

1   To add a write_hexadecimal subroutine to display the result in hexadecimal as well as decimal.
2   To abort the calculation when the ESC key is pressed.
3   To check for overflow on operations such as + and * and display an error message.
4   Extend the calculation part of the program to take account of operator precedence (* and / usually have a higher priority than + and -) and to make use of () to change the order of evaluation. Ensure that multiple operators may not be entered (5 +* 8) or an operator missed entirely.
5   Allow the entry of the DEL or backspace key to delete the last character entered.
6   Extend the read_decimal and write_decimal subroutines to accept real numbers with fractional components (hexadecimal I/O can still be integer only, reading and printing the whole number part of the real).

In practice, critical situations may occur where there is no means of recovering from an error condition, and the program would terminate with a **fatal error** or **unrecoverable error** message to the user. Such critical situations should be discovered during the specification and design phases, and some means to recover from them found.

The approach taken above was one of incremental design and implementation in which a few modules at a time are designed, implemented and tested. Another approach is to design the whole system to the point where it can be coded and then implement and test. Problems can occur during implementation when it is realised that critical issues have been overlooked at the analysis stage. Although the use of prototyping tools can help overcome some of these problems there is no easy answer and reference should be made to Software Engineering texts for detailed discussion (Martin & Odell 1995).

2.4.3 Implementation of the calculator program in C

The implementation of the calculator program entails the mapping of the structures of the program into the C equivalent, i.e.

IF structures map directly into the C **if** statement (Chapter 11)
WHILE structures map directly into the C **while** statement (Section 12.1)
REPEAT .. UNTIL structures will map into the C **do .. while** statement by inverting the terminating condition (Section 12.2)

CASE structures will map into the C **switch** statement (Section 14.4)

The input/output subroutines can be provided by C functions:

`write_character(character)` by `putchar(character)`
`read_character(character)` by `character = getchar()`
    (`getchar` usually echoes the character; however, most systems have a variation which does not echo, e.g. `getch` under Turbo C and Microsoft C)
`newline` by `putchar('\n')`

2.5 Testing

Although methods of thorough testing are beyond the scope of this book, the subject is introduced in this section. Unless a program has been formally proved, confidence in it can only be determined by thorough testing. Two approaches are:

Black box testing. All reasonable combinations of input to a module are tried out, the results are predicted **in advance** and compared with the actual results. Such test data should, if possible, be devised at the program specification and design stage before any coding is carried out.
White box testing. Test data is devised to follow every possible path through the module. Again, results must be predicted in advance; it is easy to convince oneself that incorrect results are correct once a program has produced them.

In practice, a combination of these methods is often used. For example, white box testing (together with the display of internal variables) is often used when homing in on a fault. When testing any particular input value, it is important to test:

    (a) normal values;
    (b) ends of ranges;
    (c) other special values (e.g. 0 often causes trouble);
and (d) possible invalid values.

Suppose, for example, valid numerical data input to a module should be -7 to +7 inclusive. A suitable set of test data could be -7, -1, 0, +1, +7, -8 and +8 where the latter two values should be rejected as invalid input.
    Initial testing is best planned as soon as the specification is complete. It is often useful to arrange for someone else to test one's programs. The situation that is not considered when testing will often have been left out during the design and implementation stages as well.

3

Outline structure of a C program

This chapter will describe, in outline, the structure of a C program and then go on to discuss the programming environment in terms of program creation, compilation, linking and execution.

3.1 Program modules and objects

A large software system can consist of many individual programs, each of which may contain 200,000 lines or more of program statements. Attempting to design, code and test a large program as a single entity is virtually impossible, so it is broken down into logical components called modules (implemented as *functions* in C and C++) and/or objects (implemented as *classes* in C++; a *class* is an integrated entity containing data structures and functions which operate on them, i.e. an *object* in object oriented terminology).

During the program specification and design stages logical tasks or sequences of tasks and associated data sets, which will become modules or objects, are identified and specified. Once a specification of the logical steps performed by each module or object has been drawn up the individual *functions* can be designed, coded and tested.

3.1.1 Identifiers

A large program may contain hundreds of variables (used to store data) and functions each of which has its own name or *identifier*. The *identifiers* can be of any length and are constructed from upper and lower case alphabetic letters, digits and the _ (underscore) character, with the proviso that the first letter must be alphabetic, e.g.:

```
test   Test   TEST   read_voltage   print_results   set_temperature   test_set_4
```

Note that C is case sensitive, i.e. in the above examples the names test, Test and TEST are different identifiers, and certain identifiers are reserved as keywords which have a particular meaning in the language, e.g. do, while, int, float, etc.

The programmer selects names that have some meaning within the overall context of the program, e.g. the function read_voltage may read a voltage from an experiment via an analogue to digital converter. To support program development there is a large number of functions available in *standard libraries* (see Section 3.1.3).

3.1.2 Function call and return

A function *calls* (transfers control to) another function by naming it in a *program statement* (discussed in the next chapter) and passes any information required in the form of *parameters* (also called *arguments*). When the task is complete the function returns control to the calling function together with any results. Functions may call other functions or even themselves (recursion).

3.1.3 Standard libraries

Facilities such as input/output (file open, close, read, write) and string processing are provided by *standard libraries* which contain functions for use by the C program. Associated with each of the *standard libraries* is a *standard header file* which contains information about the library functions. For example, the standard header file <math.h> contains details of the standard mathematical library which contains functions such as sqrt (square root), sin (sine), cos (cosine), etc.   A C program starts with *preprocessor* directives to include the contents of specified *header files,* which are used by the compiler to check function use (details later).

3.1.4 The function *main*

When a C program is executed the operating system *calls* (transfers control to) a function called main which can then use other functions to read data (e.g. scanf), process information (mathematical functions such as sin and cos), write results (e.g. printf), etc. Every program must therefore have one (and only one) function called main. When execution is complete main returns control to the operating system.

```
preprocessor directives
int main(void)
{
    definitions
    statements
}
```

Fig. 3.1 Outline structure of a C program consisting of the function main

Fig. 3.1 shows the outline structure of a simple C program which consists of:

preprocessor directives, e.g. to define a macro or include a header file (details later)

int main(void) indicates that the function main follows

{ indicates the start of the function main

definitions   define *variables* used within main

statements   specify the computing operations to be carried out

} matches the { and indicates the end of the function main

The operations specified in the statements act on *variables* which are used to store data. Such variables may be:

fundamental types which are the basic data types of programs, e.g. characters, integer numbers, real numbers;

or   *derived types* which are constructed from the *fundamental types* to suit the particular application, e.g. arrays and structures.

Before a variable can be used its name or *identifier* and *type* must be defined in a *definition* (discussed in the next chapter).

3.2 Program creation, compilation and execution

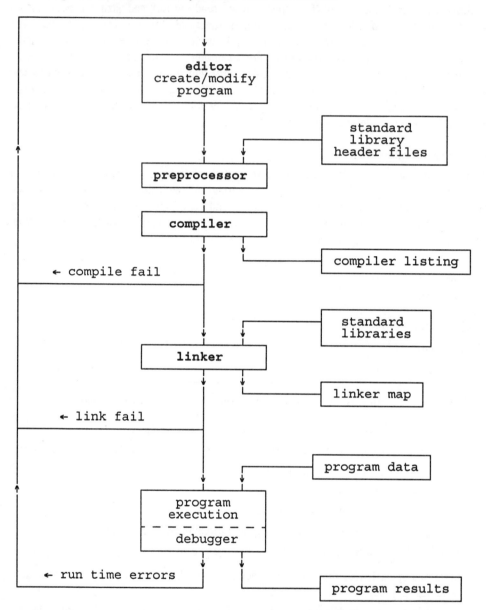

The above diagram shows the sequence of events required to implement a C program:

Editor. The editor is used to create the program text or modify existing programs.

Preprocessor. The program starts with preprocessor directives which enable macro substitution, conditional compilation and the inclusion of other text files into the program, e.g. *header files* which supply details about library functions. The preprocessor reads the program source file, expands any macros, includes any header files and writes the result to an intermediate text file which is read by the compiler.

Compiler. The compiler converts the file from the preprocessor into object code (possibly with an intermediate assembly language stage) which contains executable machine code instructions plus information for the linker, e.g. details of standard functions required. Some compilers can generate a combined compiler/assembler listing which shows the original C code and the generated assembly language statements.

Linker. Except for very specialist programs (e.g. an embedded controller) the majority of programs require standard library functions. The linker adds object code files, either standard libraries or other files supplied by the user, to form the executable program file (in machine code to be executed under the control of the operating system).

Program execution. The user issues commands to the operating system to run the program. During program execution data may be entered, from either the keyboard or files, and results output, to either the display screen or files.

Debugger. Many C environments contain an optional debugger which assists in error detection, e.g. at run time program execution can be traced, breakpoints inserted (to halt the program at a particular point), variables examined, etc. When the program works correctly the debugger is removed and the program runs by itself.

The editor, compiler, assembler, linker and debugger may be separate programs (to be invoked separately by the user) or components of an integrated environment, e.g. Borland's C/C++ IDE (Integrated Development Environment) or Microsoft's C/C++ PWB (Programmer's WorkBench). An integrated environment contains an editor, enabling the user to type in the program, and, by hitting a keyboard key or mouse button, invoke the compilation/link process. If compilation or link fails control returns to the editor with error messages, enabling the user to identify the cause. If the compilation/link completes without errors the user can progress to program execution (which may be run under the control of the debugger).

Few programs work correctly first time and an iterative error correction process is required. For example, errors may be reported at various points during the above process:

During compilation: a *syntax* error indicates that the program does not conform to the rules of the language, e.g. the structure of a statement is incorrect.

During linking: multiple definitions of a reference (two functions of the same name) or undefined reference (a function called in the program was not found).

At execution time: the program crashes with a *run time* error (e.g. division by 0) or the program does not do what the specification required (the results are incorrect).

If errors occur the program text has to be modified (using the editor) and the compilation, link and execute cycle invoked again. This iterative process continues until the program runs correctly (error correction is discussed further in Chapter 6).

At each stage in the process information is stored and passed between the editor, compiler, linker, etc. using files on disk. The precise naming convention used for the files depends upon the operating system and compiler being used but normally a filename is made up from two components, the name (up to eight characters under MS-DOS) and an extension (up to three characters under MS-DOS) separated by a period (.). For example, the filename of the file used to store the source code of Program 4_1 when using Turbo C or Microsoft C under MS-DOS could be p4_1.c and the object code file generated by the compiler would then be p4_1.obj (such compilers can compile both C and C++ programs with C++ programs having the extension .cpp). Refer to the compiler manuals for details.

3.3 Editing, compiling and executing the program

The sequence of commands required to edit, compile and run a program depends upon the operating system, editor, compiler and linker being used. For example, using an IBM PC compatible computer running the MS-DOS operating system using the MS-DOS editor and the Turbo C/C++ V3.00 compiler (user input shown in **bold**):

```
c:> edit prog.c          edit source file prog.c
c:> tcc -w prog.c        compile the C program (all warnings on)
                            the compiler will display any errors or warnings
c:> prog                 if OK execute the program in file prog.exe
```

or using the Turbo C/C++ V3.00 IDE (integrated development environment):

```
c:> tc prog.c            invoke Turbo C/C++ IDE
```

Using a Hewlett Packard 700 workstation running the UNIX operating system:

```
$ ved prog.c             use HP visual editor editor to type in program
$ cc -Aa prog.c -lM      compile the program into file a.out (default)
                           -Aa compilers ASCI C, -lM link maths library
$ a.out                  execute the program in file a.out
```

Alternatively, if one is using a Windows based development system (such as Microsoft's Visual C++ or Borland C++) one would select the appropriate icon to invoke the corresponding integrated development environment.

When a program is executed the standard output stream stdout (discussed in Chapter 5) usually writes to the computer display screen (if nothing appears on the screen check that program output has not been redirected to a disk file). Under UNIX and MS-DOS program output can be redirected at execution time (see Programs 15_1 and 15_2):

```
$ prog > result          execute program and print to the file result
```

The standard input stream stdin (discussed in Chapter 5) usually reads from the keyboard.

It is sometimes necessary to interrupt program execution (e.g. if it is looping). How this is achieved is system dependent (e.g. UNIX uses the CTRL/C or CTRL/Q key and Windows 95 and OS/2 use ALT/ESC) and may require a reboot of the operating system (e.g. with MS-DOS).

Problem for Chapter 3

From manuals determine what C program development environment you are using. Is it an integrated environment or is the editor a separate program?

On the next page is Program 4_1 which prints a message on the display screen:

(a) Using the editor type in the program (exactly as it is).
(b) Compile and link the program.
(c) If errors occur use the editor to modify the program to remove the cause.

Repeat the process until the program compiles and links without error. Execute the program. Do the following appear on the screen?

```
Hello reader of 'C for Engineers'
```

4

Starting to program in C

Chapter 3 introduced the outline structure of a C program. This chapter presents a simple C program and then discusses *types*, *constants*, *variables*, *statements*, *expressions*, etc. which contribute towards the complete program. At this stage much of the description will be at an introductory level and later chapters will provide detail.

4.1 Program to display a message on the display screen

```
/* Program 4_1 - to print a message to the display screen  */

#include <stdio.h>                            /* preprocessor directive */

int main(void)                                /* start of function main */
{
    printf("Hello reader of 'C for Engineers'\n");     /* print message */
    return 0;                                 /* terminate program */
}
```

Program 4_1 A C program to print a message to the display screen

Program 4_1 (in file c4\p4_1.c on the disk which accompanies this text) is a simple C program that contains the following *program statement* which prints a message to the display screen:

```
    printf("Hello reader of 'C for Engineers'\n");          /* print message */
```

printf is the standard library function (declared in header file <stdio.h>) which is used to print information to the display screen. The information to be printed is passed to the function printf as a *control string* enclosed in " marks (printf and the *control string* will be discussed in Chapter 5). A run of Program 4_1 gave:

```
Hello reader of 'C for Engineers'
```

followed by a *newline* (the character sequence \n is the C notation for the *newline character* which moves the cursor to the start of the next line on the screen).

In addition to program code Program 4_1 contains *program comment*, text enclosed within /* and */, which is effectively ignored by the compiler. *Program comment* enables the human reader to gain a better understanding of the purpose and structure of the program than is available from the program code alone. For example, Program 4_1 begins with a comment which briefly describes the objective of the program and further comments expand on the role of particular lines of code.

Exercise 4.1 (*see Appendix B for sample answer*)

Modify Program 4_1 to print your name and address to the display screen.

4.2 Program to calculate the area of a rectangle

```
/* Program 4_2 - to calculate the area of a rectangle                    */

#include <stdio.h>                              /* preprocessor directive */

int main(void)                                 /* start of function main */
{
    float width,                               /* define variable width */
          length,                             /* define variable length */
          area;                                /* define variable area */

    width = 2.0f;                              /* initialise the width */
    length = 4.0f;                            /* initialise the length */
    area = width * length;                 /* calculate rectangle area */
    printf("rectangle %f by %f, area = %f\n",
           width, length, area);                   /* print result */
    return 0;                              /* terminate program */
}
```

Program 4_2 To calculate the area of a rectangle

Program 4_2 (in file c4\p4_2.c on the disk which accompanies this text) is a C program which calculates the area of a rectangle from the width and length using the relationship area = width * length (details will be discussed later in this chapter). After calculating the area the result is printed on the display screen, e.g. a run using Turbo C V3.00 gave:

```
rectangle 2.000000 by 4.000000, area = 8.000000
```

Section 4.1 introduced *program comment*, text enclosed within /* and */, which enables the human reader to gain a better understanding of the purpose and structure of the program than is available from the program code alone. In the early chapters comments will often be used to explain what is happening in the code. In general, however, it is recommended that comments should explain *why* the code is there, e.g. in Program 4_2 the comment calculate rectangle area explains *why*, a comment such as multiply width by length would not. Once one becomes familiar with C the purpose of the line should be clear from well written code.

4.3 Types, constants and variables

Chapter 1 explained that data is the information to be processed by the computer system, e.g. numbers for mathematical calculations, text such as names and addresses or more complex structures such as pictures or drawings. Each data element in a program is of a particular *type* which determines what data or information may be stored within it.

4.3.1 Types

The fundamental integral types (which store whole number data) are (see Chapter 7):

type	numeric range
char	integer character code range 0 to + 127
signed char	signed integer range -128 to +127
unsigned char	unsigned integer range 0 to 255
short int	signed integer minimum range -32768 to 32767
unsigned short int	unsigned integer minimum range 0 to 65535
int	signed integer minimum range -32768 to 32767
unsigned int	unsigned integer minimum range 0 to 65535
long int	signed integer minimum range -2147483648 to 2147483647
unsigned long int	unsigned integer minimum range 0 to 4294967295

The fundamental types used to store real numbers are (see Chapter 8):

type	information stored
float	single precision real number, minimum precision 6 decimal digits
double	double precision real number, minimum precision 10 decimal digits
long double	double precision real number, minimum precision 10 decimal digits

The number of bytes used to store a particular type is implementation dependent (so long as the minimum range is maintained). Typically, on IBM PC compatible microcomputers, type char is one byte (8 bits), short int is two bytes, int is two or four bytes, long int is four bytes, float is four bytes, double is eight bytes and long double is ten bytes.

The fundamental types may be used by the programmer to construct *derived types* to suit the particular application:

arrays	a group of elements of a given type
functions	take parameters of given types and return an object of a given type
pointers	which *point to* (contain the address of) a given type
constants	are fixed values of a given type
enumerations	allow the definition of an integral type with associated constants
structures	a group in which the elements are of dissimilar types, e.g. a record
unions	an overlap of different structures.

An example of a *derived type* is a *string* which is an 'array of type char' (a sequence of characters).

In C++ (Bramer & Bramer 1996), classes enable the creation of user defined *types* containing data structures and associated operators. The user specifies the data (fundamental types or *derived types*) to be stored within the *class*, and functions and operators which manipulate and operate upon the data. In effect, *class*, allows the user to create an integrated entity containing data, functions and operators: an *object*, in object oriented terminology.

4.3.2 Constants

Some of the data in a program never changes, e.g. Program 5_1, given the radius of a circle, calculates its area using the following relationship:

area = π * radius^2

The value π is a *mathematical constant* (which is defined as the ratio of the circumference of a circle to its diameter), i.e.:

$$\pi = \frac{\text{circumference of circle}}{\text{diameter of circle}} = 3.14159265358979323846264643...$$

Data values which never change during program execution are called *constants* and may be expressed literally (the value of π may be written as `3.1415926`, see Program 5_1 lines 12 and 14) or by giving it a symbolic name or *identifier* (such as PI or pi) which is given the data value when it is defined. The symbolic name can then be used throughout the program making it more readable, e.g. in Program 5_3 the name `PI` is defined in line 9 and then used in lines 16 and 18.

A program may contain hundreds or thousands of constants. Consider Program 4_2 (a very short program) which contains the following constants:

1 `2.0f` and `4.0f` are single precision real number constants of *type* `float`
2 `"rectangle %f by %f, area = %f\n"` is a *string* constant of type 'array of `char`' (a string is a sequence of characters delimited by " marks)
3 `0` is an integer number constant of *type* `int`.

The compiler determines the *type* of the constant from its format, i.e.:

`int`   a whole number, e.g. `1, 0, -5, 0xff, 123, -6785`, etc.
`long int` a whole number with `L` suffix, e.g. `1L, 0L, -5L, 0xffL, 123L, -6785L`, etc.
`double`   number with decimal point and/or exponent, e.g. `1.0, 134.56, 5e6, 4.0e-6`, etc.
`float`   number with decimal point/exponent and an `f` suffix, e.g. `134.56f, 5e6f`, etc.
`char`   a character enclosed in ' marks, e.g. `'a', '6', '\n', '\a'`, etc.
`string`   a sequence of characters enclosed in " marks, e.g. `"hello sam"`.

The constants `'\n'` and `'\a'` are of type `char` and are single characters not two, the sequence \n being the C notation for the *newline character* (which moves to the start of the next line on the screen or page) and \a being the *alarm* character (which gives an audible alarm tone). Note that there is no `string` type as such, a *string* being the derived type 'array of `char`'. Strings can, however, be used without understanding arrays.

4.3.3 Variables

The previous section explained that *constants* are data values which do not change throughout the execution of a program. Other data in the program will be subject to change, e.g. if a program is summing a sequence of numbers the running total will change every time the next item is added to it. A data value which changes is called a *variable*.

When programming, a *variable* can be thought of as a *data store* or *data container* and the compiler will allocate an area in RAM memory to hold the value. To enable a particular variable to be referred to in the program (to store a value in it) each variable is given a name or *identifier* (see Section 3.1.1 for details of construction rules), e.g.:

`radius    area    Area    circle_area    Voltage    output_current    Minimum_temperature`

Each variable name or identifier is associated with a particular area in memory of suitable size for its data type, e.g. a character would be allocated one byte and an integer number two or four bytes. Although programmers tend to talk about the 'value of a variable', in more precise terms it should be considered as 'the value contained in the variable' or, even better, 'the value contained in the memory address associated with the variable name'.

4.3.4 Declarations and definitions

Before a variable can be used in a program its name and *type* must be *declared* so that the compiler knows what kind of entity the name refers to.

In a *declaration* the *type* is specified followed by a list of variable names separated by commas with a semi-colon terminating the declaration, e.g. in Program 4_2:

```
float width,                             /* define variable width */
      length,                            /* define variable length */
      area;                              /* define variable area */
```

This declares variables width, length and area to be of type float. For reasons of clarity the names were on separate lines but the declaration could have been written:

```
float width, length, area;               /* define variables */
```

These *declarations* are also *definitions* in that they define an entity for the name to refer to, i.e. the compiler allocates storage in memory (four bytes to store each float). Do not worry about the subtleties of *declarations* and *definitions* at this stage; this becomes important in multi-file programs where a variable is *defined* in one file (with storage allocated) and *declared* in another (to allow it to access the storage allocated in the first file): see Chapters 17 and 18.

When a variable is defined it may be given an *initial value*, otherwise its value is either zero or *undefined* depending on context (details in Chapters 17 and 18). For example:

```
char char_a = 'a';
int temperature, min_temperature = 50, max_temperature;
float radius = 2.0f, circle_area, sphere_area, sphere_volume;
```

In these definitions the following variables are given initial values:

char_a	initial value 'a'	type char	(character)
min_temperature	initial value 50	type int	(integer number)
radius	initial value 2.0f	type float	(single precision real number).

A variable defined with an initial value may be *assigned* a new value (see next section).

4.4 Statements and expressions

Program *statements* specify the computing operations to be carried out, e.g. print the value of a variable or add two variables and assign the result to another. In Program 4_2 there are five statements (each terminated by a ;):

```
width = 2.0f;                            /* initialise the width */
length = 4.0f;                           /* initialise the length */
area = width * length;                   /* calculate the area */
printf("rectangle %f by %f, area = %f\n", width, length, area);
return 0;                                /* terminate program */
```

The first three are *assignment statements* which assign a value to a variable, the third passes results to the *output stream* stdout to be printed on the display screen, and the return terminates the function main and returns control to the operating system. The assignment statements contain *expressions* which are built up from:

    (a) *operators*   + add, - subtract, * multiply, / divide (details in Chapter 9),

and (b) *operands*   data to be operated upon such as variables and constants.

In an assignment statement the value of the expression to the right of the = is evaluated and assigned to the variable on the left (= is the *assignment operator*), i.e.:

```
width = 2.0f;                                    /* initialise the width */
```

In this case the expression to the right of the = is a constant, the value of which is assigned to the variable `width`. Consider:

```
area = width * length;                            /* calculate the area */
```

The value of the expression `width * length` is evaluated (multiplying the value of `width` by `length`) and the result assigned to variable `area` (`width` and `length` are unchanged). When a variable name is used in a statement the memory location assigned to the variable is accessed either to read the current contents (e.g. `width`) or to write a new one (e.g. `area`).

In C terminology the expression to the left of an = is generally referred to as an *lvalue* (left value) which is the general name for an *expression referring to a region of storage in memory*. Compilers often use the term in error reports, see Chapter 6.

One problem, particularly when learning to program, is that assignment statements resemble mathematical equations (where = means *equals*); however, they are distinct and should not be confused, for example:

```
radius = radius + 1;
```

is a meaningless mathematical equation but an acceptable assignment statement, i.e. the constant 1 is added to the value of `radius` and the result assigned to `radius`. Languages such as Pascal and Modula 2 attempt to get around this by using := as the assignment operator (:= can be considered as a 'becomes equal to' operator). Similarly in C the assignment operator = can be read as 'becomes equal to'.

4.5 Function calling, function parameters and the function result

Chapter 2 described how a large program can consist of many tens of thousands of lines of code which is broken down into logical components called modules, which, in C, are implemented as *functions*.

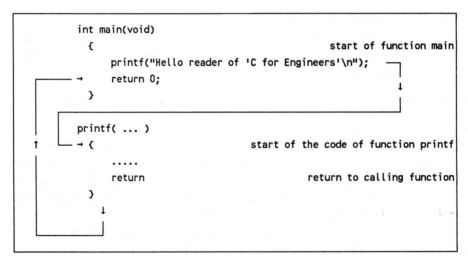

Fig. 4.1 Execution flow of Program 4_1 on the call to function `printf`

Fig. 4.1 shows the flow of instruction execution of Program 4_1 on the call to printf. A function calls (transfers control to) another function, which will carry out a specific task, by naming it in a *program statement*. The parameters, enclosed in (), pass information to the called function. The *function result* (if any) is returned via the function name (as the contents of a variable are accessed via the variable name, see sqrt below). When the call to printf is executed in Program 4_1 the parameter "Hello reader of 'C for Engineers'\n" is passed to the function which prints the information to the display screen. When complete the last instruction of printf returns control to the statement following the printf call in function main (return in this case).

Although some functions are 'stand alone', in that no data is passed in or out, the majority:

(a) require data from the calling function in the form of parameters, e.g. printf,

and (b) return a *function result*, e.g. the square root of a number.

When a function is defined the first line (called the *function header*) specifies the function name, the *type* of the *function result* and any parameters. For example, the *function header* of function sqrt in the standard mathematical library header file <math.h> is:

    double sqrt(double value)

indicating that:

(a) the function returns a *function result* of type double (double precision real),
(b) the function name is sqrt,

and (c) it has one parameter of type double (double precision real).

```
/* Program 4_3 - to evaluate the square root of a number                   */

#include <stdio.h>                          .        /* standard stream I/O library */
#include <math.h>                                    /* standard maths library */

int main(void)                                       /* start of function main */
{
    double number, root;                                /* define variables */
    number = 16.0;                                      /* initialise number */
    root = sqrt(number);                            /* calculate square root */
    printf("number = %f, root = %f\n", number, root);       /* print result */
    return 0;                                        /* terminate program */
}
```

Program 4_3 To evaluate the square root of a number

Program 4_3 evaluates the square root of a number by calling the function sqrt. The sequence of events (simplified) is:

1 variable number is assigned the value 16.0
2 the function sqrt is called with the parameter 16.0 (control transferred to sqrt)
3 the code of sqrt is executed evaluating the square root of 16.0, i.e. the solution is 4.0
4 the final instruction of sqrt returns control to the calling function, returning the solution as a function result (in effect the identifier sqrt now has the value 4.0)
5 the value returned via the name sqrt is assigned to the variable root (the value 4.0).

A simplified view of the overall flow of instruction execution in Program 4_3 would be:

1 the operating system sets up the program environment and calls the function `main`
2 storage is allocated in main memory for the variables `number` and `root`
3 execute assignment `number = 16.0`
4 execute `root = sqrt(number)`, i.e.:
    4.1 call function `sqrt`
    4.2 evaluate the square root of `number`
    4.3 return to calling function (`main` in this case)
    4.4 assign the function result from `sqrt` to variable `root`
5 execute `printf("number = %f, root = %f\n", number, root);`, i.e:
    5.1 call function `printf`
    5.2 print results on display screen (details in next chapter)
    5.3 return to calling function (`main` in this case)
6 execute statement `return 0` (see next section)
7 deallocate variable storage and return to the operating system.

Because the result of a particular function is returned via its name an expression may contain a number of function calls in addition to variable names, constants, etc. For example, the **mathematical equation** for `sin(2θ)` is:

```
sin(2θ)= 2 sin(θ) cos(θ)
```

The **program statements** to evaluate sin 2θ of a `double` precision real variable `angle` are:

```
angle = 3.14159 * 25.0 /180.0;              /* angle 25° in radians */
x = 2.0 * sin(angle) * cos(angle);          /* calculate sin 2θ */
```

The functions `sin` and `cos` are called (C does **not** specify in which order) returning the *function results* sin = 0.422618 and cos = 0.906308 (both of type `double`). Then the complete expression is evaluated and the result assigned to variable `x`, i.e. the `angle` is 25°, hence the value of sin 2θ would be 0.766044 (more details in Program 5_2).

The function `sqrt` has one parameter and returns a value but this is not always the case. For example, the mathematical function `pow(x,y)`, which evaluates x^y, has two parameters both of type `double` and returns a `double` function result, e.g.:

```
z = pow(number, 3.0);              /* cube number and assign result to z */
```

Other functions may have no parameters and/or return no function result, e.g.:

1 The function `srand` (in header file `<stdlib.h>`) has one `int` parameter which seeds a pseudo random number generator and returns no function result.
2 the function `rand` (in header file `<stdlib.h>`) has no parameters and returns the next number in the pseudo random number sequence as an `int` function result, e.g.:

```
srand(25);                 /* seed the random number generator */
i = rand();                /* get next pseudo random number   */
j = rand();                /* get next pseudo random number */
```

Note that although `rand` has no parameters the `()` are still required to tell the compiler that this is a function call, otherwise it would take `rand` as a variable name. Even if a function returns a result it does not have to be used.

4.5.1 The function *main*

When a program is executed the operating system sets up the program environment and then calls the function `main`. When `main` terminates it returns a *function result* of type `int` which the operating system can use as a test of successful program completion (0 indicating success and non-zero some error condition). The test would be used if a sequence of programs are to be executed where the choice of later programs depends upon the success of those preceding. In Program 4_3 the *function header* of function `main` was:

```
int main(void)
```

indicating that:

      (a) the function returns a *function result* of type `int` (integer),
      (b) the function name is `main`,
and (c) it has no parameters; any parameters are enclosed in `()` and the keyword `void` indicates that there are no parameters.

Following the *function header* is a *compound statement* (a sequence of statements enclosed within `(` and `)` braces) which contains the program code of `main` (discussed in Chapter 16).

    The `return` statement is used to terminate a function and return the function result, e.g. in Program 4_3 the final statement indicates successful program completion:

```
return 0;                                   /* terminate program */
```

4.6 The standard input/output streams *stdout, stderr* and *stdin*

In general, when a C program starts, three standard input/output streams are automatically set up and opened ready for use (details of use in next chapter):

`stdout`   the standard output stream (usually prints to the computer display screen)
`stderr`   the standard error stream (usually prints to the computer display screen)
              (on a windowed system `stdout` and `stderr` could be to separate windows)
`stdin`   the standard input stream (usually reads from the computer keyboard).

The `printf` function is used to send information to `stdout` and the `scanf` function used to read information from `stdin` (discussed in Chapter 5).

    Associated with the I/O streams are status and error indicators which may be used to test the state of the stream (using an **IF statement**, see Chapter 11). For example, it is possible to check to see if a conversion failed when reading numeric input due to entry of a faulty character, e.g. an integer number entered as `12a34`. Thus it is possible for all input to be verified and action taken in case of error, for example, an error message may be printed and the user prompted for more input (see Program 13_2 and Section 15.1).

    In addition, it is possible to check to see if the user entered *end of file* to indicate the end of data input. Keyboard entry of *end of file* is system dependent, e.g.:

        under MS-DOS it is CTRL/Z or newline followed by CTRL/Z
        under UNIX   it is newline followed by CTRL/D.

4.7 Review of Program 4_3

In summary the sequence of statements in Program 4_3 is:

1   `#include <stdio.h>` is a *preprocessor directive* to include a copy of the standard header file stdio.h at this point in the program (stdio.h provides the compiler with information about the standard input/output streams stdout and stdin)

2   `#include <math.h>` includes a copy of the standard header file math.h which provides information about the standard mathematical functions

3   `int main(void)` is the *function header* for the function main

4   `(` indicates the start of the function main

5   Variables number and root are defined as type double (double precision real)

6   `number = 16.0;` is an *assignment statement* which assigns the value 16.0 to the variable number

7   `root = sqrt(number);` is an *assignment statement* which calls the function sqrt to evaluate the square root of number and assigns the result to the variable root

8   `printf(" ....");` is a *statement* which calls the function printf to print the results of the program to the standard output stream stdout (stdout is described in Chapter 5)

9   `return 0;` terminates the function main and returns a function result of 0 (success) to the operating system

10 `)` indicates the end of the function main.

In Program 4_3 blank lines were inserted to improve the overall layout of the program.

Problem for Chapter 4

Enter Program 4_3 (or obtain from file c4\p4_3.c on the disk which accompanies this text) and get it working. Then, **one at a time** put errors in the program, compile/link and execute (if possible) and comment on the result (Chapter 6 discusses error detection), e.g.:

    (a) miss root from the variable definitions
    (b) miss the = from an assignment statement
    (c) miss the ; from the end of a statement
    (d) miss a " in the call to printf
    (e) mistype the name of function sqrt
    (f) miss out the line number = 16.0; completely
    (g) miss out the line return 0; completely
    (h) miss out the line #include <math.h> completely.

5

Using standard library functions

Higher-level facilities such as input/output (file open, close, read, write) and mathematical functions (sin, cos, sqrt, etc.) are provided by *standard libraries* which contain functions which must be explicitly called by the C program. This chapter introduces the basic keyboard input (scanf) and screen output (printf) functions and the mathematical functions sqrt, sin and cos. This is at an introductory level and further details are provided later.

5.1 Introduction to the *printf* function

The standard library function printf is used to print information to the standard output stream **stdout** (usually the display screen), e.g.:

```
printf("Hello John Doe how are you ?\n");
```

will print the string enclosed in " delimiters, i.e.:

```
Hello John Doe how are you ?
```

followed by a *newline*. In this case there is a single parameter to printf, called the *control string*, which contains the characters to print and the character sequence \n which is the C notation for the *newline character* (which moves the cursor to the start of the next line on the screen). Now consider the call to printf in Program 4_3:

```
printf("number = %f, root = %f\n", number, root);        /* print result */
```

This call to printf has three parameters (separated by commas - ignore the comma inside the string which is part of the text to be printed) which are used to pass information into the function:

1   The *control string* "number = %f, root = %f\n" which controls the printing of information onto the screen.
2   The variable number, the numeric value of which is to be printed on the screen.
3   The variable root, the numeric value of which is to be printed on the screen.

In addition to the characters to be printed the control string contains the *conversion specification* %f (also called a *format control*). The effect of the %f conversion specifications is to print the value of the following parameters (variables number and root) as signed decimal real numbers, i.e. %f **converts** the value of the parameter into a sequence of characters to be printed on the screen. The effect of the above call to printf in Program 4_3 is:

1   to print the text string "number = "
2   the first %f prints the value of the second parameter (variable number, i.e. 16.0)
3   to print the text string ", root = "
4   the second %f prints the value of the third parameter (variable root, i.e. 4.0)
5   "\n" to print a newline character (move to start of next line).

There are corresponding conversion specifications for integers (%d), characters (%c), etc.

5.2 Introduction to mathematical functions (sqrt, sin & cos)

```
 1 /* Program 5_1 - from circle radius calculate area and recalculate radius */
 2
 3 #include <stdio.h>                                /* standard I/O library */
 4 #include <math.h>                                 /* standard maths library */
 5
 6 int main(void)
 7 {
 8     float radius = 2.0f,              /* radius of circle, initial value 2.0 */
 9            area,                                    /* area of circle */
10            radius_check;                            /* check of radius */
11
12     area = 3.1415926f * radius * radius;           /* calculate area */
13     printf("radius = %f, area = %f", radius, area);
14     radius_check = sqrt(area / 3.1415926f);        /* recalculate radius */
15     printf(", radius check = %f \n", radius_check);
16     return 0;
17 }
```

Program 5_1 Calculate circle area then recalculate radius

Program 5_1 (in file c5\p5_1.c on the disk which accompanies this text), given the radius of a circle, calculates its area and then recalculates the radius to check the result, i.e.:

$$\text{area} = \pi * \text{radius}^2$$

$$\text{radius} = (\text{ area } / \pi)^{1/2}$$

The line numbers down the left hand side of Program 5_1 are **not** part of the program but are there to enable identification of particular lines when discussing the programs within the text of this book. For example, the sequence of statements in Program 5_1 is:

line

3   #include <stdio.h> includes the standard header file <stdio.h>

4   #include <math.h> includes the header file <math.h> which provides information about the sqrt function used in line 14 (without this the program would not work, discussed in the next section)

8   defines variable radius and initialises its value to 2.0f

9   defines variable area

10 defines variable radius_check

12 area = 3.1415926f * radius * radius; calculates the circle area and assigns the result to variable area

13 printf("radius = %f, area = %f", radius, area); print the values of radius and area

14 radius_check = sqrt(area / 3.1415926f); call sqrt function to calculate the radius from the area and assigns the result to the variable radius_check

15 printf(", radius check = %f \n", radius_check); prints the value of radius_check.

C library functions which print to the screen or disk files append new information directly on to the end of any existing information. When executed Program 5_1 prints:

radius = 2.000000, area = 12.566370, radius check = 2.000000

followed by a *newline* (at the end of the second printf call).

5.2.1 Using the mathematical function *sqrt* (square root)

In C facilities such as I/O and mathematical functions are provided by standard libraries. An implication of this is that C knows nothing about the library functions in terms of their names, number and type of parameters (data to be passed to and from the function) and function result returned (if any). The compiler, however, requires this information before it can check that a function call in the program is correct. Associated with each of the *standard libraries* is a *standard header file* which contains *function prototypes* and other information which gives details about the library functions (*function prototypes* will be discussed in Section 16.4). A C program starts with *preprocessor* directives to include specified header files which can then be used by the compiler to check function calls.

The preprocessor directive #include <math.h> in Program 5_1 reads the header file <math.h> which contains the *function prototypes* of all the mathematical functions. This informs the compiler that sqrt has one parameter of type double (double precision real) and returns a function result of type double. The operations performed by the function call:

```
radius_check = sqrt(area / 3.1415926f);
```

are:

1   the *expression* area / 3.1415926f is evaluated as a float (i.e. both operands are float)
2   the result is converted to a double to be passed as a parameter to sqrt
3   sqrt is called with the double parameter
4   sqrt evaluates the square root of the parameter
5   sqrt terminates and returns control to main with the function result which is a double
6   the double function result is converted to a float and assigned to radius_check.

Unlike more modern languages, such as Pascal, Modula 2 and C++, C does not have to know about a function before the function is called (to maintain compatibility with the original C which did not have function prototypes). How a particular parameter is passed on function call when C has no *function prototype* depends upon its data type (parameter passing will be covered in detail in Chapter 16). In the case of a parameter of type float it is converted to a double. This happens to be suitable for the sqrt function but would cause problems if the function expected some other type such as an int. In addition, if a function prototype is missing C assumes that any function result is of data type int.

Thus if, in Program 5_1, the #include <math.h> had been missed sqrt would have been called correctly with a parameter of type double but the function result returned from sqrt would have been assumed to be of type int (to be converted to float before assigning to radius_check). This would result in unpredictable behaviour which can range from rubbish returned from the function call to a crash of the program, e.g. a segmentation or memory fault. Missing #include directives is a fairly common error and a modern compiler will issue a warning message if a function prototype is not available when a function is called (see example in Chapter 6).

Exercise 5.1 *(see Appendix B for sample answer)*

1   Enter Program 5_1 compile, link and execute it. Repeat with the preprocessor directive #include <math.h> removed; what happens?
2   Replace line 15 with the following (see sample answer for further discussion):

```
printf(" converted %d \n", printf(", radius check = %f \n", radius_check));
```

5.2.2 Using the mathematical functions *sin* (sine) and *cos* (cosine)

```
 1 /* Program 5_2 - calculate sin(2A) = 2 * sin(A) * cos(A)                    */
 2 /*                        cos(2A) = cos(A) * cos(A) - sin(A) * sin(A)        */
 3
 4 #include <stdio.h>
 5 #include <math.h>
 6
 7 int main(void)
 8 {
 9     float angle = 25.0f, sin_2a, cos_2a;                    /* define variables */
10
11     angle = 3.14159f * angle / 180.0f;                     /* angle in radians */
12     sin_2a = 2.0f * sin(angle) * cos(angle);                      /* sin 2A */
13     cos_2a = cos(angle) * cos(angle) - sin(angle) * sin(angle);   /* cos 2A */
14     printf("angle A = %f, sin(A) = %f, cos(A) = %f \n",
15               angle, sin(angle), cos(angle));
16     printf("  sin(2A) = %f and %f ", sin_2a, sin(2.0f * angle));
17     printf("and cos(2A) = %f and %f \n", cos_2a, cos(2.0f * angle));
18     return 0;
19 }
```

Program 5_2 To evaluate sin 2Θ and cos 2Θ

The **mathematical equations** for sin(2Θ) (see Section 4.5) and cos(2Θ) are:

$$\sin(2\Theta) = 2\sin(\Theta)\cos(\Theta)$$
$$\cos(2\Theta) = \cos^2(\Theta) - \sin^2(\Theta)$$

Program 5_2 evaluates sin(2Θ) and cos(2Θ) using the sin and cos functions from the mathematical library <math.h>. Both functions take a double precision parameter, the angle in radians, and return a function result of type double. The program evaluates the values of sin(2Θ) and cos(2Θ) using the above equations, and then prints the values together with function results from sin and cos called with the angle 2Θ. The program sequence is:

9   define variables and initialise the angle to 25°
11   convert the angle from degrees to radians (for sin and cos)
12-13   calculate sin(2Θ) (variable sin_2a) and cos(2Θ) (variable cos_2a) using above equations (Section 4.5 explained how an expression may contain a number of function calls in addition to variable names, constants, etc.)
14-15   print the value of angle, sin(angle) and cos(angle)
16   print sin_2a calculated in line 12 and the value returned by sin(2 * angle)
17   print cos_2a calculated in line 13 and the value returned by cos(2 * angle).

In the calls to printf some of the parameters are variables and some are expressions, e.g. in the call to printf in line 16 the second parameter sin_2a is a variable and the third parameter sin(2.0f * angle) is an expression. This is an example of the general rule of C that anywhere where it is permissible to use the value of a variable (of some type) an expression (of the same type) may be used.

A run of the program on an IBM PC compatible under Turbo C/C++ Version 3.00 gave:

```
angle A = 0.436332, sin(A) = 0.422618, cos(A) = 0.906308
  sin(2A) = 0.766044 and 0.766044 and cos(2A) = 0.642788 and 0.642788
```

5.3 Numeric keyboard input using the *scanf* function

```
 1 /* Program 5_3 - read radius of circle from the keyboard              */
 2 /*                 calculate circle area and recalculate radius        */
 3
 4 #include <stdio.h>
 5 #include <math.h>
 6
 7 int main(void)
 8 {
 9     const float PI = 3.1415926f;                        /* constant PI */
10     float radius = 2.0f,                             /* radius of circle */
11           area,                                        /* area of circle */
12           radius_check;                               /* check of radius */
13
14     printf("Enter radius of circle (real number) ? ");
15     scanf("%f", &radius);                                 /* read radius */
16     area = PI * radius * radius;                      /* calculate area */
17     printf("radius = %f, area = %f", radius, area);
18     radius_check = sqrt(area / PI);                 /* calculate radius */
19     printf(", radius check = %f \n", radius_check);
20     return 0;
21 }
```

Program 5_3 Using *scanf* to read a real number from the keyboard

A problem with Program 5_1 is that if the area of another circle is required the program has to be modified, recompiled and linked. Program 5_3 is similar to Program 5_1 except that the circle radius is read from the keyboard. The lines which contain updated code are:

9   const float PI = 3.1415926f; defines PI with the value 3.1415926f (see Section 5.4)
14 prompts the user to enter the radius of the circle on the keyboard
15 scanf("%f", &radius); reads a real number of type float from the keyboard and returns the value in the variable radius (discussed below).

The standard library function scanf reads information from the keyboard. The "%f" conversion specification in line 15 instructs scanf to read a float real signed decimal number from the keyboard and return the value in the second parameter, &radius. A run of Program 5_1 gave (user input in **bold** with the Enter or carriage return key shown as ↴):

Enter radius of circle (real number) ? 6↴
radius = 6.000000, area = 113.097328, radius check = 6.000000

When scanf is expecting a float real number to be entered it may be typed on the keyboard as 6, 6.0, 6.0e0, 0.6e1, etc. In the latter cases e represents the power of 10.

5.3.1 The *scanf* control string

The function scanf, which reads characters from the standard input stream **stdin** (usually the keyboard), is called with the following parameters:

(a) the *control string* which controls the reading of characters from the keyboard and their conversion into values to be assigned to variables of various data types,

and (b) other parameters; in the main a list of addresses of (or *pointers* to) variables.

The control string may contain:

1 **Conversion specifications** beginning with % which specify how characters in the input stream are matched and converted (%d for decimal `int` and %f for `float`, more details in Chapters 7 and 8). If converted successfully the value is returned in the variable **whose address** is given by the corresponding parameter.

2 **Spaces** which cause the input stream to be read up to the next non-**white space** character (**white space** is the C term for spaces, tabs and newlines).

3 Characters other than **white space** and conversion specifications; the next character in the input stream must match this character.

For example, line 15 of Program 5_3:

```
scanf("%f", &radius);                                    /* read radius */
```

The *control string* is `"%f"` which tells `scanf` to convert a real number and return the value in the next parameter `&radius` (the & is discussed in Section 5.3.2) which must be a `float` variable. When executed a sequence of digit characters is read from the keyboard and converted into a number in internal `float` format the value of which is returned in `radius`.

Apart from character input **white space** in the input text stream is skipped, `scanf` reads across spaces, tabs, newlines, etc. to find its input, e.g. in line 15 of Program 5_3 any spaces or newlines typed before the number will be ignored.

It is important to note that text streams normally operate on a line by line basis with each line consisting of zero or more characters terminated by the newline character. As characters are typed on the keyboard they are automatically echoed to the screen and the line is formed in an input buffer and only when newline (or *end of file*) is entered is it passed to `scanf`. The `scanf` function then processes the line carrying out conversions as specified by the control string. If all the conversions specified cannot be satisfied by the current line of text `scanf` will request another line, e.g. if a control string `"%f%f"` specifies two numbers are to be entered and the user only enters one.

5.3.2 Parameters to the *scanf* function

Parameters in C are passed into a function *by value*, i.e. copies of the *actual parameters* are made in temporary variables and these are passed. Consider:

```
sin_a = sin(angle);
radius_check = sqrt(area / 3.1415926f);
```

In the first statement a **copy** of the value of variable `angle` is passed to `sin`. In the second statement the value of the expression `area / 3.1415926f` is evaluated and passed to `sqrt`.

Pass by value prevents code within the function inadvertently accessing the *actual parameters* and corrupting them. Now consider line 15 of Program 5_3:

```
scanf("%f", &radius);
```

To be able to return the number read from the keyboard `scanf` needs to be able to access the original memory area allocated to the variable `radius`. An & before a variable name tells the compiler that the *memory address* of the variable (called a *pointer* in C) is to be passed to the function at execution time. In line 15 `scanf` uses the address passed by the second parameter to access the memory area allocated to `radius`. This method of passing parameters is known as *pass by reference* (more discussion in Section 16.8).

It is important that the conversion specifications match the type of the corresponding parameters, e.g. %f for float, %d for decimal int, etc. Using incorrect conversion specifications results in incorrect values being returned (e.g. attempting to return a float value into an int) and possibly a crash of the program.

5.3.3 The function result of *scanf*

In addition to returning values read from the keyboard (into the parameters) function scanf also returns, as an int function result, the number of successful conversions which should be checked by the program (using an **IF statement**; see Chapter 11, Program 11_2):

1   If no conversions occurred 0 is returned.
2   If a matching failure occurs (e.g. a non-numeric character in a decimal number) conversion stops and the number of successful conversions is returned (the faulty character is left in the input stream where the program can read it and take action, see Program 13_2).
3   If *end of file* occurs before any conversions the value EOF (defined in <stdio.h>) is returned. How *end of file* is entered is system dependent; see Section 4.6.

In practice input should be verified and action taken in case of error, e.g. an error message printed and the user prompted for more input (further discussion in Section 15.1).

5.4 The type qualifier *const* and *named constants*

In Program 5_1 the value of π was specified twice, in lines 12 and 14, as the float constant 3.1415926f. A good optimising compiler may realise that this is the same value and generate one copy of it, otherwise two copies will be generated, wasting memory. In Program 5_1 this is not a problem but many programs make extensive use of constants and generating a separate copy at each point in the program would be very inefficient as well as a source of errors due to mistyping.

In line 9 of Program 5_3 π is defined as the *named constant* PI (in effect a non-modifiable variable) which is then used in lines 16 and 18. The *type qualifier* const (new in ANSI C) tells the compiler that the following objects are to be treated as constants and may not be altered (therefore they must be initialised at definition). If the compiler knows something is a constant it can optimise the code more efficiently and generate errors if the programmer attempts to alter its value (see Section 6.4). It is recommended that *named constants* are defined before variables so that the definitions stand out in the program.

Using *named constants* can improve program maintainability and readability by using relevant names for constants within the program and also assist the compiler with optimisation. In practice some naming convention should be adopted to make the identification of variables, constants, etc. easier when reading a program. For example, the convention used in this book is to use lower case letters for the names of variables and functions, upper case letters for the names of constants and an upper case letter followed by lower case letters for the names of new *types*. The precise convention is not critical so long as one is consistent (and that is not always easy in a large program).

5.5 The preprocessor #define directive and *symbolic constants*

An alternative method of defining constants is to use the preprocessor #define directive to define *symbolic constants* (it may also be used to define macros with parameters, see Section 16.13):

#define IDENTIFIER replacement_text

The preprocessor, when it reads the program source code file, replaces all occurrences of IDENTIFIER with the replacement_text. Remember that each preprocessor directive should be on a separate line and **not** terminated with a ;.

```
 1 /* Program 5_4 - read radius of circle from the keyboard          *
 2 *                 calculate circle area and recalculate radius    */
 3
 4 #include <stdio.h>
 5 #include <math.h>
 6 #define PI   3.1415926f                                /* constant PI */
 7
 8 int main(void)
 9 {
10     float radius = 2.0f,                          /* radius of circle */
11           area,                                     /* area of circle */
12           radius_check;                            /* check of radius */
13
14     printf("Enter radius of circle (real number) ? ");
15     scanf("%f", &radius);                              /* read radius */
16     area = PI * radius * radius;                   /* calculate area */
17     printf("radius = %f, area = %f", radius, area);
18     radius_check = sqrt(area / PI);              /* calculate radius */
19     printf(", radius check = %f \n", radius_check);
20     return 0;
21 }
```

Program 5_4 A version of Program 5_3 using #define instead of const

Program 5_4 is a version of Program 5_3 in which line 9 (using const) has been replaced with the following #define directive (line 6):

#define PI   3.1415926f   /* constant PI */

The identifier PI is called a *symbolic constant* and by convention is in upper case. When the preprocessor reads the program file all occurrences of symbolic constants are replaced with the corresponding replacement_text using literal substitution (the compiler then reads the resultant file). After preprocessing the compiler would see lines 16 and 18 as:

    area = 3.1415926f * radius * radius;
    radius_check = sqrt(area / 3.1415926f);

In effect as though the programmer had used the float constant 3.1415926f in the program source code. Thus the compiler knows nothing about symbolic constants.

Remember that the preprocessor performs literal substitution and an error in a preprocessor directive will appear at compile time in a line of code that may look perfectly OK. For example, if a ; has been typed on the end of the #define in line 6 by mistake:

#define PI   3.1415926f;   /* constant PI */

After preprocessing Program 5_4 the compiler would see lines 16 and 18 as:

```
area = 3.1415926f; * radius * radius;
radius_check = sqrt(area / 3.1415926f;);
```

and generate error messages due to the incorrect placing of the ; characters. For example, Turbo C V3.00 gave the following messages when compiling a version of Program 5_4 with the above error:

```
Error x.c 16: Illegal use of floating point in function main
Error x.c 18: Function call missing ) in function main
Error x.c 18: Expression syntax in function main
```

The problem is that the line of code where the error was found (lines 16 and 18 in this case) looks correct; the error being in the #define directive in line 6. Because such errors can be quite difficult to find most compilers provide some means of examining the output of the preprocessor to track down such errors, e.g. using Turbo C V3.00 program CPP.EXE.

The #define directives are normally placed at the start of a file following the #include directives, and have file scope, i.e. from the #define to the end of the current file. However, the #undef directive may be used to 'undefine' an identifier:

```
#undef PI                                         /* undefine PI macro */
```

It must be emphasised that the compiler knows nothing about symbolic constants and can perform no optimisation. In ANSI C the preferred technique is to use the const qualifier to define *named constants* (which the compiler knows about). However, *symbolic constants* are still seen in older programs and are used extensively in header files to define constants relevant to the library concerned, e.g. to define symbolic constants such as INT_MIN, INT_MAX, etc. in <limits.h> (see Section 7.1).

Exercise 5.2 *(see Appendix B for sample answer)*

Type in Program 5_3 (or get from disk file c5\p5_3), compile and link and then execute with various data (in particular enter invalid characters). Extend the program to evaluate sphere surface area = 4π * radius^2 and volume = $\frac{4}{3} \pi$ * radius^3 and then recalculate the radius from the sphere volume (note that the mathematical function pow(x,y) evaluates x^y).

Remove the & from before variable name radius in the call to scanf in line 15 of Program 5_3. Compile, link and execute the program. What happens?

Put a ; on the end of the #define directive in line 6 of Program 5_4. Compile and examine the error messages. Have a look at the output of the preprocessor.

Problem for Chapter 5

Type in Program 5_2 (or get from disk), compile, link and execute (a run of the program is given at the end of Section 5.2.2). Modify the program to read the angle from the keyboard using the scanf function.

The program calls the functions sin and cos several times with the same parameter (variable angle). Modify the program to evaluate the sin and cos of angle only once and then extend it to evaluate tan(2θ), i.e.:

```
tan(2θ) =  2 tan(θ) / (1 - tan²(θ))
```

tan(θ) may be evaluated using the maths function tan(amgle) (where angle is in radians).

6

Program layout,
documentation and debugging

6.1 The C character set

```
a b c d e f g h i j k l m n o p q r s t u v w x y z
A B C D E F G H I J K L M N O P Q R S T U V W X Y Z
0 1 2 3 4 5 6 7 8 9
! " # % & ' ( ) * + ,  - . / : ; < = > ? [ \ ] ^ _ { | } ~
space, horizontal and vertical tab, form feed, newline
```

Table 6.1 The C character set

The ANSI C standard talks about two character sets:

(a) the character set used to code the program,

and (b) the character set used at execution time.

When the program is compiled and executed on the same machine these two character sets are the same. They **may** differ when using a cross compiler, where the program is compiled and linked on a host machine and executed on a target machine (which may use a different character set). In such cases the compiler and system documentation will discuss any problems.

The ANSI standard requires an alphabet of 96 characters, as shown in Table 6.1, which are available on the majority of computer systems and terminals. Note:

1 If some of the character set is missing (e.g. # [\ ] ^ { | } ~ are not available on some terminals) this can be overcome by the use of **trigraphs**, see compiler manual.

2 The C language is *case sensitive*, hence the names printf, PRINTF and Printf will be treated by the compiler as different identifiers (if the linker prints the error messages *undefined reference* or *unresolved reference* check that the names of functions are spelt correctly and in the correct combination of upper and lower case).

3 C is a free format language and the compiler (not preprocessor) does not worry about the layout of the program. In particular the characters **space**, **tab** and **newline** are called **white space** and have no special effect on the program (discussed below).

6.2 Programming style: documentation and layout

Good program layout and documentation is important for various reasons, including:

(a) the simplification of error detection and correction by the original programmer,

and (b) improving the maintainability of the program by clarifying the objectives and operation of the program.

One aim when writing a program (apart from making it work) is to make it readable. The program code should be documented, as it is written, by inserting comments at appropriate places. General guidelines on comments are:

1   The source file should begin with a general description of its overall function and use, e.g. that it contains a program, or a header file, or an implementation of functions, etc.   Additional details such as the specialist support libraries required, who implemented it, when modifications were made, etc. are useful, particularly when a large team is working on a program consisting of many source files.

2   Every function and class should begin with a general description followed by details of how it is used, e.g. global variables accessed, parameters passed in and out, function result returned (if any), etc. This can take the form of a 'written contract' between the function and its caller, e.g. *pre conditions* indicating what is required by the function and *post conditions* indicating what facilities are supplied by the function.

3   If the name of a variable does not make its use clear add a comment to the line (so far the programs have been so simple that often the variable name alone is sufficient).

4   Place comments before or within any section of program code which is complex or may be difficult to follow.

In C a comment starts with /* (no space between the characters) and is terminated by */. When compiled the comment is **replaced by a space** and so becomes **white space** (see below). Comments may not appear within strings and comments may not appear within comments, i.e. in /* --- /* --- */ --- */ the first */ will terminate the comment.

6.2.1 Program layout

Within certain limits C does not care how a program looks. For example consider the following version of Program 5_3 (which will compile, link and execute correctly):

```
/* Program 5_3a */
#include <stdio.h>
#include <math.h>
int main(void){const float PI=3.1415926f;float radius,area,radius_check;
printf("Enter radius of circle (real number) ? ");scanf("%f",&radius);area
=PI*radius*radius;printf("radius = %f, area = %f",radius,area);radius_check=
sqrt(area/PI);printf(", radius check = %f \n",radius_check);return 0;}
```

Not only do the comments fail to indicate what the program does but the code layout is a mess with several statements or parts of statements per line. With certain exceptions, C ignores spaces, tabs and newlines treating them as **white space**. Exceptions include:

(a) *preprocessor directives* must be on separate lines (newline is the terminator),

(b) **white space** separates keywords, identifiers, etc. (e.g. between `float` and `radius`),

and (c) **white space** must not occur in the middle of *keywords, identifiers, strings* and *character constants*.

Space characters within a string are part of the string (not **white space**) and a string cannot contain a newline character. For example, the following statement would generate the error message *unterminated string* (or similar):

```
    printf("Enter radius of
circle (real number) ? ");
```

If a very long string is required use can be made of the string joining feature (new in ANSI C) by which adjacent strings (separated by **white space**) are concatenated:

```
printf("Enter radius of "
       "circle (real number) ? ");
```

The two strings are joined to form `"Enter radius of circle (real number) ? "`.

If a line becomes too long it is generally possible to replace a space character by a newline. For example, line 9 of Program 5_2 could be written:

```
float angle = 25.0f,
      sin_2a,
      cos_2a;
```

There are occasions where inserting a newline is not possible. For example, preprocessor directives must be on one line and terminated by a newline, yet macro definitions can be very long (see Section 5.5 and Section 16.13). To overcome this problem the sequence **backslash newline** (no spaces following the \) becomes *invisible* to the C system, e.g. the preprocessor will accept:

```
#include \
    <stdio.h>
```

General guidelines on program layout or style are:

1 Place at least one blank line following preprocessor directives, between functions and between declarations/definitions and statements within a function.
2 Write one statement per line.
3 Use spaces to make definitions and statements readable, e.g. around operators in assignment statements, following commas in definitions and function calls, etc.
4 Variable, function, and type names should be chosen to indicate their use in the program. In addition, some naming convention should be adopted, e.g. lower case letters for the names of variables and functions, upper case letters for the names of constants and an upper case letter followed by lower case letters for the names of new *types*; see next section.
5 If making the program slightly longer improves its readability do it! Some programmers have an unfortunate tendency to write terse, cryptic and unreadable code (possibly thinking that this is a sign of a good programmer).
6 Use indentation to show the logical structure of the code. For example, in the programs so far the definitions and statements within `main` have been indented four spaces to highlight the beginning and the end of the function. More examples of indentation will be shown when control structures are introduced in Chapter 11.
7 Use some pattern to separate functions, making a new one immediately visible, e.g. a comment consisting of a complete line of `/****************************************/`.

Companies often have their own *house style* of program layout to ensure consistency across the organisation. The precise form of the style is not critical but once a style has been chosen it should be used consistently.

6.3 Defining new type names using *typedef*

A major aid in program readability is the use of identifiers which are meaningful within the context of the program, e.g. the identifiers radius, area, radius_check, angle, PI, etc.

The keyword *typedef* enables the user to declare a new (more meaningful) name for an existing type (without creating a new type), e.g.:

```
typedef float Object_area;
typedef float Object_volume;
typedef int   Loop_counter;
```

The identifiers Object_area and Object_volume are synonyms or alternative names for the type float, and Loop_counter is a synonym for int.   Once a new type name has been specified it can be used to define variables, e.g.:

```
Object_area    circle_area, sphere_area, cylinder_area;
Object_volume  sphere_volume, cylinder_volume;
Loop_counter   counter_1, counter_2;
```

Note that *typedef* does not create a new type, just an alternative name.   The variables circle_area, sphere_area, etc. are of type float, having the same properties and obeying the same rules as other float variables.   It can, however, help the overall semantics and readability of the program to use meaningful names such as Object_area and Object_volume instead of float.   To make type identifiers stand out in a program it is wise to have a convention for assigning names, e.g. to start the names with a capital letter (as above).

The keyword *typedef* obeys the same scope rules as declarations, therefore new type names may be specified within compound statements or a program source file may start with the specification of new types that will be used within the functions in the file (scope will be discussed in Chapter 17).

6.4 Detection of compile, link and run-time errors

At the simplest level errors in programs tend to be either syntactic or semantic:

syntactic: the program constructs or statements do not conform to the syntax (rules) of the programming language being used;

semantic: the program does not do what the specification states, i.e. the program gives run-time errors or prints incorrect results.

```
Error p6_1.c 11: Cannot modify a const object in function main
Error p6_1.c 13: Statement missing ; in function main
Warning p6_1.c 14: Possible use of 'radius' before definition in function main
Error p6_1.c 14: Statement missing ; in function main
Error p6_1.c 16: Undefined symbol 'areax' in function main
Warning p6_1.c 16: Call to function 'sqrt' with no prototype in function main
Error p6_1.c 17: Unterminated string or character constant in function main
Error p6_1.c 18: Function call missing ) in function main
Warning p6_1.c 19: Function should return a value in function main
Warning p6_1.c 19: 'radius_check' is assigned a value that is never used in main
```

Fig. 6.1 Turbo C/C++ V3.00 compiler error listing of Program 6_1

```
 1 /* Program 6_1   - read radius of circle from the keyboard    *
 2 *                    calculate circle area and check radius    */
 3
 4 #include <stdio.h>
 5
 6 int main(void)
 7 {
 8     const float PI = 3.1415926f;
 9     float radius, area, radius_check;
10
11     PI = 10.0f;
12     printf("Enter radius of circle (real number) ? ")
13     scanf("%f", radius);
14     area = PI * radius  radius;
15     printf("radius = %d, area = %f", radius, area);
16     radius_check = sqrt(areax / PI);
17     print(", radius check = %f \n, radius_check);
18     return 0;
19 }
```

Program 6_1   Version of Program 5_3 with errors

Program 6_1 shows a modified version of Program 5_3 with a number of deliberate errors. Fig. 6.1 (previous page) shows a Turbo C++ V3.00 compiler error listing of Program 6_1 reporting errors in the following lines (see also Figs 6.2 and 6.3):

11 PI = 10.0f; attempting to alter a *const qualified* object. In C terminology an *object* is a named region of storage and an lvalue is an expression (on the left side of an =) referring to an *object*, see error message for line 11 in Fig. 6.2.

14 area = PI * radius radius; the * operator has been missed

16 radius_check = sqrt(areax / PI); the name areax is mistyped

17 printf(", radius check = %f \n, radius_check); missing " string delimiter.

Errors are also reported in lines 13 and 18 which are correct. The messages are due to:

line

13 the missing ; on the end of line 12

18 the missing " in line 17.

In addition to error messages the compiler may generate warnings indicating that although the syntax of the code is correct, and the program may be linked and executed, it suspects that something may be wrong. C was designed for professional programmers who may use unorthodox techniques deliberately and the compiler will generate warnings in case the use was unintentional. For example, in Fig. 6.1 there are warnings referring to lines:

14 because an error was reported on line 13 (due to an error on line 12) the compiler thinks that the variable radius has not been assigned a value

16 The #include <math.h> preprocessor directive is missing and hence there is no *function prototype* for the function sqrt. The compiler is unable to check the number and type of parameters and the result returned. It will be assumed that an int is returned and hence a run-time error will occur (faulty results or a program crash).

19 due to the error reported in line 18 the compiler thinks that return is missing.

Note that there are three other errors in Program 6_1 which the compiler has not found:

In line 13 the & is missing before the variable radius (this type of error is very difficult for the compiler to find). Section 5.3, on scanf, described how an & before a variable name tells the compiler that the *memory address* of the variable is to be passed as a parameter. In this case, because the & is missing, the **value** of radius (which could be anything as it has not been initialised) is passed to scanf which would use it as an address. What precisely happens is implementation dependent and can range from a run-time error message, incorrect program results or a crash of the program.

In line 15 the %d integer number conversion has been specified and the corresponding parameter is of type float. Rubbish will probably be printed on the screen (see Section 8.4 for an example of incorrect conversion specifications).

In line 17 the function name printf has been mistyped as print. When the error on this line is corrected the compiler will indicate that there is no prototype for function print. If linked the linker would print an *undefined reference* or *unresolved reference* error message (assuming there is no function of that name).

The format and content of the error messages varies from compiler to compiler. Figs 6.2 and 6.3 show the error reports from the HP700 UNIX based C compiler and the GNU C/C++ compiler V2.6.3 (DJ.Delorie's port for DOS) respectively. Note that the GNU C compiler has only found the unterminated string in line 17 of Program 6_1. If this was corrected and the program compiled again errors in other lines would then be reported.

```
cc: "x.c", line 13: error 1000: Unexpected symbol: "scanf".
cc: "x.c", line 14: error 1000: Unexpected symbol: "radius".
cc: "x.c", line 17: error 1004: Unexpected end of line.
cc: "x.c", line 18: error 1000: Unexpected symbol: "return".
cc: "x.c", line 11: error 1549: Modifiable lvalue required for assignment operator.
cc: "x.c", line 12: error 1533: Illegal function call.
cc: "x.c", line 16: error 1588: "areax" undefined.
cc: "x.c", line 17: error 1588: "print" undefined.
```

Fig. 6.2 HP700 UNIX based C compiler cc error listing of Program 6_1

```
P6_1.c:17: unterminated string or character constant
P6_1.c:17: possible real start of unterminated constant
```

Fig. 6.3 GNU C/C++ V2.6.3 compiler error listing of Program 6_1

6.4.1 Debugging compile time errors and warnings

The format and content of the error messages varies from compiler to compiler and can often be very obscure. With practise the programmer learns to interpret the messages of the particular compiler in use, e.g. see Figs 6.1, 6.2 and 6.3. An error may generate an error message further on in the code, or even several error messages. In particular, a missing ; or } in a function can generate all sorts of spurious error messages, often in functions further down the code, and be very difficult to track down. One approach is to correct the obvious errors and recompile. This may remove some spurious error messages enabling the programmer to narrow down the cause of any remaining errors. In a large program it may be necessary to separate the functions into different files to be compiled independently. This not only tends to narrow down the cause of errors but is good programming practice (Chapter 18 will cover multi-file programs).

The level of warnings generated can generally be selected at compile time from none at all to warning about anything in the least bit questionable. It is wise to have the level set as high as possible; the warnings can always be ignored. For example, if Program 5_3 is compiled with the Microsoft C compiler version 7.00 with warning level 4 (/W4 option) it will generate the following warning:

```
   18    radius_check = sqrt(area / pi);              /* calculate radius */
***** P5_2.C(18) : Warning C4136: conversion between different floating types
```

The function result of sqrt is of type double which is converted to a float before being assigned to radius_check. The warning indicates that the conversion between different floating types may result in a loss of precision, i.e. double has a precision of 15 decimal digits and float a precision of 7 decimal digits (more discussion in Chapter 8). In the case of Program 5_3 the warning can be ignored as the precision of float is sufficient. However, a float variable may inadvertently be used in a sequence of calculations which should be carried out in double precision and the warning would be very useful.

6.4.2 Debugging execution time errors

The compiler can only detect errors in the syntax of the language and is limited in its generation of warnings. The linker will detect undefined references (missing functions) or multiple definitions of a reference (more than one copy of a function). Even if the program compiles and links it may still contain run-time errors which cause it to fail or give faulty results when executed.

When coding a program the programmer works from a design which was derived from a specification. It is possible that the resultant program code does not do what the design states it should (it is assumed that the specification and design were correct). For example, consider the statement in line 12 of Program 5_1 which calculates the area of a circle:

```
area = 3.1415926f * radius * radius;
```

The programmer, when typing in the statement hits the 2 key instead of the 3, i.e.:

```
area = 2.1415926f * radius * radius;
```

To the compiler the statement is valid and would compile without errors or warnings. At execution time, however, the value of area would be incorrect and the results of any succeeding calculations which used the value would also be incorrect. In a short program this error is fairly easy to find but in a large program could be very difficult. If the cause of a run-time error is not obvious the program has to be debugged at run-time, e.g. printing intermediate results of calculations or using run-time debugging tools, see Section 7.8 on the assert function. The thing to remember is that proficiency in program implementation and testing is achieved by experience and there is no short-cut or magic formula. Ideally, test data should be planned and results predicted before coding begins.

Exercise 6.1 (see Appendix B for sample answer)

Program 4_1 uses the return 0; statement to return a success indicator to the operating system. Write a batch file to execute the program and report success or failure. Test it with Program 4.1 and a modified version which reports failure, e.g. use return 1;.

Problem for Chapter 6

The program below (in file c6\prob6.c on the disk which accompanies this text), when given the radius r and height h of a cylinder, evaluates the volume = $\pi r^2 h$, curved surface area = $2\pi rh$ and total surface area = $2\pi r(r + h)$. It contains a number of errors, both in the syntax of individual statements (the rules of the C language are not observed) and the overall semantics (the program does not do what is required). Correct the errors and check the results of a run of the program, e.g. (user input in bold with newline shown as ↲):

```
Enter radius of cylinder (real number) ? 3↲
Enter height of cylinder (real number) ? 4↲
volume = 113.097328, radius check = 3.000000
curved area = 75.398224, radius check = 3.000000
total area = 131.946884, height check = 4.000000
```

```
 1 /* Problem 6 - Calculate surface areas and volume of a cylinder */
 2
 3 #include <stdio.h>
 4
 5 int main(void)
 6 {
 7     const float PI = 3.1415926f,                    /* constant PI */
 8                  TWO_PI = PI * 2.5f;                 /* constant 2PI */
 9     float radius = 2.0f,                        /* radius of cylinder */
10           height = 5.0f,                        /* height of cylinder */
11           curved_area,                        /* curved surface area */
12           total_aea,                            /* total surface area */
13           volume,                                     /* and volume */
14           radius_check,                            /* check radius */
15           height_check;                            /* check height */
16
17     printf("Enter radius of cylinder (real number) ? ");
18     scanf("%f", &radius);                            /* read radius */
19     printf("Enter height of cylinder (real number) ? );
20     scanf("%f", height);                            /* read height */
21
22     /* calculate volume and then check radius */
23     volume = PI * radius * height;
24     radius_check = sqt(volume / (TWO_PI  height));
25     printf("\nvolume = %f, radius check = %f", volume, radius_check);
26
27     /* calculate curved area and then check radius * /
28     curved_area = TWO_PI * radius * height;
29     radius_check = curved_area * radius / (TWO_PI * height);
30     printf("\ncurved area = %f, radius check = %f, curved_area radius_check);
31
32     /* calculate total area and then check height */
33     total_area = PI * height * (radius + height);
34     height_check = (total_area / TWO_PI - radius;
35     printf("\ntotal area = %f, height check = ", total_area, height_check);
```

Problem for Chapter 6 A program with a number of semantic and syntax errors

7

Integral data types

In many languages integer, character and logical (or boolean) data is represented using separate data types with their own rules. In C these are not separate data types but are all represented using integral types (boolean data will be introduced in Chapter 11).

7.1 Integral numeric data types

The integer data types may be *signed* (take positive or negative values) or *unsigned* (only positive values). The following table shows the integer data types (including characters) together with their minimum numeric ranges as specified by the ANSI standard:

data type	numeric range
char	integer character code range 0 to + 127　　see Section 20.1
signed char	signed integer range -128 to +127　　see Section 20.1
unsigned char	unsigned integer range 0 to 255　　see Section 20.1
short int	signed integer minimum range -32768 to 32767
unsigned short int	unsigned integer minimum range 0 to 65535
int	signed integer minimum range -32768 to 32767
unsigned int	unsigned integer minimum range 0 to 65535
long int	signed integer minimum range -2147483648 to 2147483647
unsigned long int	unsigned integer minimum range 0 to 4294967295

The number of bits used to represent short int, int and long int is implementation dependent so long as the minimum range is maintained and the longer types provide at least as much storage as the shorter. The intention is that int is implemented as the most convenient size for the target processor (in terms of instruction set, execution speed, etc.) with short int and long int provided to meet any special requirements. It is therefore possible for the three types to be different sizes (e.g. 16, 32 and 64-bit) or all the same size (e.g. 32-bit) depending upon the processor (typically short int and int are 16-bit and long int is 32-bit). The standard header file <limits.h> (see Appendix C.5) provides details on the integral types enabling programs to determine if the specific implementation can support the application (see Chapter 9; Program 9_2). It is also worth remembering that the order in which multi-byte integers are stored depends on the machine architecture, e.g. little-endian (Intel 8086 family) or big-endian (Motorola 68000 family).

In a declaration short int, int and long int may be prefixed with the type specifier signed which is redundant for these types, i.e. signed int is the same as int (the type specifier signed is mainly used to force the char type to be signed, see Section 20.1).

When implementing programs int is the basic 'working' integer data type where the size would not exceed the maximum for a 16-bit signed number (e.g. a counter in a short loop) otherwise the long int data type should be used. Care should be taken when signed and unsigned types are used in expressions as the conversion between the types is implementation dependent (see Section 9.1). In practice try to avoid mixing the types, i.e. select a type for a particular set of operations and keep to it. For example, use signed types for 'normal' arithmetic work and unsigned types for operations that are naturally unsigned, e.g. memory mapped I/O register addresses (see Section 31.1).

In C characters may be stored in any integral type and the type char is, in effect, a byte size int (see Section 20.1). In many applications it is used to store byte sized data (other than character codes) in char variables specifying signed or unsigned as required.

type	numeric range
signed char unsigned char	signed integer range -128 to +127 unsigned integer range 0 to 255

In practice these types may be treated as *signed byte* and *unsigned byte* types. For example, when sampling data from an 8-bit A to D (analogue to digital) converter, it would be very wasteful of memory to store a large amount of such data in int or even short int variables (both of which may be 32-bit in a particular implementation).

7.2 Integer number constants

The rules for integer constants are (char constants will be discussed in Section 20.1):

1   Decimal value: an integer constant which consists of a sequence of digits and which does **not** start with 0 (zero, see octal below).
2   Octal value: an integer constant which consists of a sequence of digits and which starts with **0 (zero)**. It may not contain the digits 8 or 9. **Be careful**, it is easy to type in a value 0356 meaning it to be decimal and forgetting that the preceding 0 makes it octal.
3   Hexadecimal value: an integer constant which starts with **0x or 0X** and which consists of digits and the letters a to f (or A to F) which represent the values 10 to 15.

An integer constant may be suffixed with the letter:

u or U   specifying that the value is unsigned
l or L   specifying that the value is long (recommend using L so not to confuse with 1).

Below are three groups of numbers each consisting of a decimal, octal and a hexadecimal constant which are equal in value (i.e. 10 decimal equals 012 octal equals 0xa hexadecimal):

    10 = 012 = 0xa   1024 = 02000 = 0x400   30010 = 074472 = 0X753A

When an integer constant is specified the data type it becomes is determined as follows:

1   A plain decimal will be the first of int, long int or unsigned long int which can represent the value.
2   A plain octal or hexadecimal will be the first of int, unsigned int, long int or unsigned long int which can represent the value.
3   A constant suffixed by u or U will be the first of unsigned int or unsigned long int which can represent the value.
4   A constant suffixed by l or L will be the first of long int or unsigned long int which can represent the value.
5   A constant suffixed by u or U **and** l or L will be unsigned long int.

In order to know what type a constant may become it is necessary to know something about the way integers are represented on the target system. Some compilers will issue a warning if a constant is promoted to long without the l or L suffix.

7.3 Printing and reading integral types

conversion specification	parameter type	converted to
%c	int	single character (printed as a character)
%d or %i	int, short, char	signed decimal notation
%u	int, short, char	unsigned decimal notation
%o	int, short, char	unsigned octal notation
%x or %X	int, short, char	unsigned hexadecimal notation
%ld %lu %lx %lo	long int	as above but for long int
%		printed as a %

Table 7.1 *printf* conversion specifications for integral data types

Table 7.1 lists the printf conversion specifications for integral types. Note that %d, %i, %o and %x are used for int, short int and char (when printing the character in integer form). If # follows the % when using the octal (%o) and hexadecimal (%x) conversion specifications a leading 0 or 0x will be printed (by default they are not printed).

When information is printed on a line its position is called the *field* and the number of characters printed the *field width*. When using conversion specifications printf prints sufficient characters to display the value unless a minimum field width is specified following the %. Unless otherwise specified (see Appendix C.12.6) the value is printed right justified and padded with sufficient spaces on the left to fill the *field width*, e.g.:

%d   print an integer using a field width sufficient to print the value, e.g. two characters for 15 and three for 150

%3c   print a character with a minimum field width of 3

%7d   print an integer with a minimum field width of 7 (if the value is too large to fit into seven characters the field width is increased as required).

conversion specification	parameter type	converted to
%c	char *	single character (as a character)
%d	int *	optionally signed decimal integer
%i	int *	optionally signed decimal, octal (with leading 0) or hexadecimal (leading 0x or 0X) integer
%u	int *	unsigned decimal integer
%o	int *	optionally signed octal int (optional leading 0)
%x or %X	int *	optionally signed hexadecimal int (optional 0x)
%hd %hu %ho %hx	short int *	as above, but for data type short int
%ld %lu %lo %lx	long int *	as above, but for data type long int

Table 7.2 *scanf* character conversions for integral data types
    the * following the parameter type indicates that a *pointer* is required,
    i.e. an & before the variable name to pass an address

The function scanf is called with the following parameters (see Section 5.3):

    (a) the *control string* which controls the reading of characters from the keyboard and their conversion into values to be assigned to variables of various data types,

and (b) other parameters; in the main a list of addresses of (or *pointers* to) variables.

The control string may contain **conversion specifications** which specify how characters in the input stream are matched and converted. If converted successfully the value is returned in the variable whose **address** is given by the corresponding parameter. Table 7.2 presents the scanf conversion specifications for integral data types. It should be noted that short int, int and long int use **different** conversion specifications. If a numeric value is to be stored in a char variable it should be read into an int and then assigned to the char.

```
 1 /* Program 7_1 - read and print integer in decimal, octal and hexadecimal */
 2
 3 #include <stdio.h>                          /* standard stream I/O library */
 4
 5 int main(void)
 6 {
 7     int data;                               /* holds integer read */
 8
 9     printf("Please enter an integer number ? ");
10     scanf("%d", &data);                     /* read next integer */
11     printf(" decimal %8d octal %#8o hexadecimal %#8x\n", data, data, data);
12     return 0;
13 }
```

Program 7_1 Read and integer and print value in decimal, octal and hexadecimal

Program 7_1 calls scanf to read an integer from stdin and then printf to print its value in decimal, octal and hexadecimal to stdout:

7   define variable data to be of type int
9-10   prompt user to enter an integer number and call scanf to read an integer into data
11   call printf to print the value of data in decimal (%8d conversion specification), octal (%#8o) and in hexadecimal (%#8x); all are printed using a field width of 8.

A run of Program 7_1 gave:

```
Please enter an integer number ?  15 ↲
decimal        15 octal        017 hexadecimal        0xf
```

7.4 The enumerative type

Consider an application where the value of a variable represents a particular component, e.g. bolt = 0, washer = 1, nut = 2, etc.:

```
int component_1, component_2;
scanf("%d", &component_1);
if (component_1 == 1) printf("\n component %d is a washer ", component_1);
```

A problem is that one has to remember that 0 represents bolts, 1 washers, etc. It would be preferable to be able to use names such as BOLT and NUT directly in the program. The enumeration type provides a compact way of doing this and improves program readability.

```
enum Component {BOLT, WASHER, NUT, LOCK_NUT, NYLON_NUT};
```

A new unique integral type enum Component is defined together with the set of mnemonic identifiers, called enumerators, {BOLT, WASHER, NUT, LOCK_NUT, NYLON_NUT} which it may take. The identifier Component is called the enumeration *tag* or name (the convention used in this book is to begin type identifiers with a capital letter so that they stand out in a program). Once the new type has been defined variables of that type can be defined, e.g.:

```
enum Component component_1, component_2;
```

The variables component_1 and component_2 are of type enum Component. An alternative and possibly more elegant way to define an enumeration is to use *typedef* (see Section 6.3), e.g. a fragment of code processing components such as bolts, washers, etc. can be written:

```
typedef enum {BOLT, WASHER, NUT, LOCK_NUT, NYLON_NUT} Component;
Component component_1, component_2;

scanf("%d", &component_1);
if (component_1 == WASHER) printf("\n component %d is a washer", component_1);
component_2 = LOCK_NUT;
```

This defines a type Component and then variables component_1 and component_2 of that type. Note that a new type has not been created, the type Component is another representation of int. The enumerators are constants of type int with, by default, the first having the value 0 and each succeeding one the next integer value. In the above example BOLT = 0, WASHER = 1, NUT = 2, LOCK_NUT = 3 and NYLON_NUT = 4. The enumerators can be initialised, e.g.:

```
enum Component {BOLT = 10, WASHER = 20, NUT = 30, LOCK_NUT, NYLON_NUT};
```

to initialise BOLT = 10, WASHER = 20, NUT = 30, LOCK_NUT = 31 and NYLON_NUT = 32. The enumerative type is really an int and I/O is performed using the normal int conversion specifications with the values 10, 20, 30, 31 and 32 in a data file representing the components Bolts, Washers, Nuts, Lock_nuts and Nylon_nuts respectively. The enumerators used in enumerations must be unique to each other and variable names but different enumerators may have the same numeric value.

All operations performed on enumerative types are int and C provides no range checking, therefore the semantically meaningless operations may be performed, e.g.:

```
component_2 = component_1 * LOCK_NUT + 250;
```

Enumerators may be used in any expression where an int constant may be used, not just those involving variables of the particular enumeration type. In addition it is possible to use enum to specify general purpose int constants, e.g.:

```
enum {BELL = '\a', NEWLINE = '\n', ARRAY_SIZE = 100};

putchar(BELL);                              /* write character to stdout */
```

In this case, because the identifier or *tag* of the enumeration is not specified, it is not possible to declare variables of this type. The identifiers BELL, NEWLINE, and ARRAY_SIZE may be used as general purpose int constants to improve program readability.

Exercise 7.1 (*see Appendix B for sample answer*)

Fred Smith, a decorator, measures the length, width and height of a room and calculates the area of the walls then subtracts a third. Implement a program which, given the room dimensions (each to the nearest metre), calculates the cost at £10 per square metre (use integer arithmetic throughout). Change the program to calculate the cost from two-thirds of the wall area; comment on any differences in the result obtained from the first program.

Problem for Chapter 7

Implement and test a program which reads a temperature in Celsius from the keyboard, converts it to Fahrenheit and prints the result:

```
temperature°F = 32 + 9 * temperature°C / 5
```

8

Real number types

Real number types are required in many mathematical, scientific and engineering applications to hold numeric values that may not be represented in integer (whole number) form. For example, numeric values that:

(a) have fractional components: π has the value 3.141592653589793238462643, e = 2.718281828459045235360287 (the base of natural logarithms),

(b) are less than one: the permittivity of free space ϵ_0 = 8.854 * 10^{-12} and the permeability of free space μ_0 = 4π * 10^{-7},

or (c) are very large: the resistivity of mica is of the order of 5.0 * 10^{11} ohm metres.

The notation for numbers such as 8.854 * 10^{-12} or 5.0 * 10^{11} is 8.854e-12 and 5.0e11 respectively (called exponential or scientific notation where e represents the power of 10).

Within the computer hardware real numbers are implemented in floating point format which has two important attributes:

Precision specifies the maximum number of decimal places that the floating value carries, e.g. the value of π above is accurate to 25 decimal digits.

Range specifies the minimum and maximum values that can be represented, e.g. in Turbo C/C++ V3.00 the type float has the range 1.17e-38 to 3.4e+38.

C has three real number types:

float: single precision floating point (minimum precision of 6 decimal digits), used for fast real calculations where accuracy is of secondary importance,

double: double precision floating point with a minimum precision of 10 decimal digits, used where accuracy is important and speed less so,

long double: extended precision floating point (implementation dependent), takes advantage of very high precision floating point hardware (if available).

Section 8.2 will discuss the precision of real number types and the effect this has on the accuracy of calculations (Chapter 27 will discuss the effects of accuracy when evaluating mathematical series).

8.1 Real number constants

If a constant contains a decimal point or an exponent it is a real number of type double. To specify float or long double real constants an f (or F) or l (or L) suffix is appended, e.g.:

float	1.0f	5e11f	3.141592653589793238462643F	8.854e-12f
double	1.0	5e11	3.141592653589793238462643	8.854e-12
long double	1.0l	5e11l	3.141592653589793238462643L	8.854e-12l

A constant may be specified to greater precision than the type can hold; if so the value is rounded or truncated (dependent on the implementation).

8.2 The accuracy of real number calculations

The accuracy to which real number calculations can be carried out using a particular real type is determined by the **precision**, i.e. the maximum number of decimal places that the floating value carries. In practice, the number of bits used to represent real types is implementation dependent so long as the minimum precision is maintained and each type must give at least the same range and precision as the previous type. It is therefore possible for the real types to be three distinct sizes or all the same length (float is typically 32-bit, double 64-bit and many compilers implement long double as double).

The standard header file <float.h> provides details on the range and precision of real numbers enabling programs to determine if the specific implementation can support the application. Table 8.1 shows the range and precision of the real types under Turbo C/C++ V3.00 running on an IBM PC compatible (in fact the table is the result of the program which is the answer to the first problem of Chapter 9).

	float	double	long double
size in bytes	4	8	10
range minimum	1.175494e-38	2.2250738585e-308	3.3621031431e-4932
range maximum	3.402823e+38	1.7976931348e+308	1.1897314953e+4932
precision digits	6	15	19
precision epsilon	1.192092e-07	2.2204460493e-16	1.0842021725e-19

Table 8.1 Range and precision of the real types under Turbo C/C++ V3.00

In addition to the number of digits of precision for each real type <float.h> contains a value *epsilon* which is an indicator of the precision to which calculations can be carried out (see Table 8.1). *Epsilon* is specified as (!= means *not equal*):

   1.0 + epsilon != 1.0

The value of *epsilon* is the smallest number which when added to 1.0 changes the value, i.e. adding any smaller value to 1.0 still gives 1.0. The higher the precision of the real type the smaller is *epsilon*, and programs can check this value to see if calculations can be carried out to the required precision, i.e. using floating point numbers with a precision of 4 digits *epsilon* would be 0.001. For example, consider calculating the roots of the equation:

$$x^2 + 0.4002x + 0.00008 = 0$$

using the formula:

$$x = \frac{-b \pm \sqrt[2]{(b^2 - 4ac)}}{2a}$$

The true root is -0.0002. However, when using four-digit arithmetic the root would be -0.0001625 (an error of 25%):

using eight-digit arithmetic $x = \dfrac{-0.4002 + \sqrt[2]{(0.16016004 - 0.00032)}}{2.0} = -0.0002$

using four-digit arithmetic $x = \dfrac{-0.4002 + \sqrt[2]{(0.1602 - 0.0003)}}{2.0} = -0.0001625$

The four-digit arithmetic assumed that numbers were rounded to the nearest digit.

The type chosen in practice is application dependent, i.e. on the precision and range of the data to be processed. For example, there is no point in sampling experimental data accurate to 3 decimal digits (e.g. measurements made using a good analogue meter) and then processing it using double variables and printing the results to 10 or 12 digits. In fact results so presented would be totally misleading (Chapter 27 discusses numeric errors).

8.3 Conversion between real types

Unlike Pascal or Modula 2, C is not a 'strongly typed' language, allowing mixtures of types (reals, integers, etc.) in expressions. When a mixture of types is used in an expression a set of rules known as the **usual arithmetic conversions** are used to determine what type the overall result will be (see Chapter 9). In the case of real types the rule is:

**when two different real types are used in an expression the
lower precision value is implicitly converted to the higher precision type
and the arithmetic performed at that precision**

If a lower precision real is assigned the value of a higher precision real the value of the longer real is converted to shorter by truncation or rounding (implementation dependent). For example, a double with 15 digits of precision may be assigned to a float with 7 digits of precision and a significant amount of information lost (more details in Section 10.2). A modern compiler may issue a warning message in such cases, e.g. Microsoft C V7.00:

***** p5_3.c(18) : warning C4136: conversion between different floating-point types

In addition, if a lower precision real is assigned the value of a higher precision real the value may be outside the range that can be held, i.e. under Microsoft C on an IBM PC compatible float has the range $1.175*10^{-38}$ to $3.4*10^{38}$ and double the range $2.2*10^{-308}$ to $1.79*10^{308}$. If the value cannot be held the behaviour is *undefined* (the program may give a run-time error or carry on with a faulty value, see Program 10_1).

8.4 Printing and reading real numbers

conversion specification	parameter type	converted to
%f	float, double	signed decimal real number in form [-]mmm.ddd number of ds specified by precision (default 6 a precision of 0 suppresses the decimal point
%e	float, double	signed decimal real number in form [-]m.ddddd±xx the number of ds is specified by the precision (default 6) 0 precision suppresses decimal point
%g	float, double	%e is used if the exponent is less than -4 or greater than the precision otherwise %f is used
%Lf %Le %Lg	long double	as above but for long double real

Table 8.1 *printf* conversion specifications for real data types

When printing real number types the following formatting defaults apply:

1 **Field width**: only sufficient characters are generated to print the value, i.e. no spaces are padded in front of or behind the number. If the field width is specified allowance must be made for any sign, the decimal point, fractional component and any exponent (by default the value will be printed right justified in the field). If the specified field width is insufficient to print the value it will be extended as required.

2 The **precision** (the number of digits printed following the decimal point) is 6. This may be changed in the conversion specification (see below). Do not confuse the precision used when printing with the precision of the real number when stored in floating point format.

Table 8.1 (previous page) presents the `printf` conversion specifications for real number data types. Note that %f, %e and %g are used for **both** float and double. For example (for clarity ▲ indicates a printed space):

%f   print a float or double; precision is 6 using a sufficient field width to print the value, e.g. 3.141592

%12f   print a float or double; precision is 6 with a field width of 12, e.g. ▲▲▲▲3.141592

%12.2f   print a float or double; precision is 2 (two digits following decimal point) with a field width of 12, e.g. ▲▲▲▲▲▲▲▲3.14

%.2Lf   print a long double; precision 2 using sufficient field width to print the value, e.g. 3.14

%12.2e   print a float or double in e format; precision is 2, e.g. ▲▲▲3.56e+005.

Table 8.2 presents the `scanf` conversion specifications for real number data types. It should be noted that float, double and long double use **different** conversion specifications. A very common error is to use %f, %e or %g with a double variable (as with `printf`). This will work if, in the particular implementation, float and double are actually the same size (the code is then non-portable) otherwise rubbish is returned or the program crashes.

The reason why %f works for both float and double in the case of `printf` is that the parameters are passed *by value* where float parameters are converted to double before being passed (long double are passed as long double). The function `scanf` *passes by reference* where the original parameter is accessed via its address and thus the type and size of the parameter (float, double or long double) must be specified.

conversion specification	parameter type	converted to
%f %e %g	float *	signed decimal real number type float
%lf %le %lg	double *	signed decimal real number type double
%Lf %Le %Lg	long double *	signed decimal real number type long double

Table 8.2 *scanf* character conversions for real data types
        the * following the parameter type indicates that a *pointer* is required,
        i.e. an & before the variable name to pass an address

```
 1 /* Program 8_1 - reading and printing integer and real numbers          */
 2
 3 #include <stdio.h>                            /* standard stream I/O library */
 4
 5 int main(void)
 6 {
 7     const double PI = 3.1415926535897932;                   /* constant pi */
 8     const double PERMITTIVITY = 8.854e-12;             /* small constant */
 9     const double RESISTIVITY = 5.0e10;                  /* large constant  */
10     double data;                               /* define double variable */
11     int idata, field = 15;                    /* define integer variables */
12     char ch;                                  /* define character variable */
13
14     /* print pi in various ways using %f */
15     printf("%f,%15f,%15.8f,%.8f,\n", PI, PI, PI, PI);
16     printf("%12f,\n", PI);                     /* print PI right justified */
17     printf("%-12f,\n", PI);                     /* print PI left justified */
18     printf("%*f,\n", field, PI);      /* using variable to specify field width */
19     /* print using %e and %g */
20     printf("%e,%g,%g,%g,\n", PI, PI, PERMITTIVITY, RESISTIVITY);
21
22     /* read a char, int and double and print the values   */
23     printf("Enter a character, an integer and a real number ? ");
24     scanf("%c%d%lf", &ch, &idata, &data);
25     printf("character %c, integer %d, double %f,\n", ch, idata, data);
26     return 0;
27 }
```

Program 8_1 Using the functions *printf* and *scanf*

Program 8_1 uses printf to display real values:

7-12   define variables of various types
15   call printf to print the value of PI with various field widths and precision
16-17   call printf to print the value of PI right and left justified in a field width of 12
18   call printf to print the value of PI with the field width specified as the parameter
        field (discussed below)
20   call printf to print real values using the %e and %g conversion specifications
24   call scanf to read a char, int and a double (using %c, %d and %lf conversion
        specifications)
25   call printf to print the values read.

A run of Program 8_1 gave (user input in bold):

```
3.141593,       3.141593,       3.14159265,3.14159265,
    3.141593,
3.141593    ,
        3.141593,
3.141593e+00,3.14159,8.854e-12,5e+10,
Enter a character, an integer and a real number ? a 25 5.18↵
character a, integer 25, double 5.180000,
```

Information is normally printed right justified in the field (padded with spaces on the left). Following the % with a - sign instructs `printf` to print left justified in the field padding with spaces on the right (as in line 17 of Program 8_1). Appendix C.12.6 presents full details of the various ways in which `printf` may display information.

It may be necessary to calculate the field width at run-time to suit the data to be displayed. In such cases a variable (such as `field` in Program 8_1) may be used to specify the field width; following the % with an * instructs `printf` to use the next parameter to be processed as the field width (followed by the parameter to be printed), i.e. line 18 of Program 8_1:

```
printf("%*f,\n", field, PI);          /* using variable to specify field width */
```

The first parameter is the *control string*, the second parameter `field` specifies the field width to be used in the `%*f` conversion and the third parameter `PI` is the thing to be printed.

When using `printf` (or `scanf`) it is **very** important that the parameters following the control string correspond, one to one, with the conversion specifications within the control string. The programmer must ensure that the conversion specification specifies the correct type for its corresponding parameter otherwise printing (or reading) will be incorrect, e.g. if line 25 of Program 8_1 were replaced with:

```
printf("character %d, integer %f, double %c,\n", ch, idata, data);
```

This would compile and link correctly but print incorrectly at run-time. For example, the result printed with Turbo C compiler version 3.00 on an IBM PC compatible was:

```
character 97, integer -0.000000, double ¶
```

The real and integer variables have been printed incorrectly and the character has been printed as its equivalent integer value, i.e. the ASCII character code of the character a.

Exercise 8.1 *(see Appendix B for sample answer)*

The area of a triangle whose sides are of length a, b and c is given by:

```
area = √ (s * (s - a) * (s - b) * (s - c))      where s = (a + b + c) / 2
```

Implement and test a program which, given the length of the sides, calculates the area.

Problems for Chapter 8

1   Modify the problem for Chapter 7 (Celsius to Fahrenheit) to use real numbers.

2   Implement a program to find the roots of the quadratic equation $ax^2 + bx + c = 0$, i.e.:

$$x = \frac{-b \pm \sqrt{(b^2 - 4ac)}}{2a}$$

Check the values of the roots by substituting into the quadratic equation; it should give 0.0. Test the program with various data including:

```
a = 1.0     b = -2.0     c = 1.0     roots = 1.0 and 1.0
a = 2.0     b = -6.0     c = 4.0     roots = 2.0 and 1.0
a = 2.0     b = 6.0      c = 2.0     roots = -0.381966 and -2.618034
a = 61.0    b = 159.0    c = 87.0    roots = -0.781449 and -1.825108
```

The problem for Chapter 11 will discuss what happens when $(b^2 - 4ac)$ is negative and the roots are complex numbers with a real and an imaginary component.

9

Expressions and operators

Section 4.4 introduced *program statements* which specify the computing operations to be carried out, e.g. to print the value of a variable or to add two variables and assign the result to another. For example, in an *assignment statement* the value of the *expression* to the right of the = is evaluated and the result assigned to the variable on the left:

```
r_check = sqrt(area / 3.1415926f);            /* calculate radius */
sin_2a = 2.0f * sin(angle) * cos(angle);      /* sin 2A */
```

A general rule of C is that anywhere where it is permissible to use the value of a variable (of some type), an expression (of the same type) may be used. For example, the expression sin(2.0f * angle) is used as a parameter in the following call to printf:

```
printf(" sin(2A) = %f and %f \n", sin_2a, sin(2.0f * angle));
```

The **expressions** which are used to form statements are built up from:

    (a) *operators*   + add, - subtract, * multiply, / divide (details in Section 9.3),
and (b) *operands*   data to be operated upon such as variables and constants.

For example, a simple expression would consist of two operands and an operator (called a *binary* operator because it has two operands), e.g.:

```
i + j
```

The evaluation of the expression produces a result of the same type as the type of the highest precision operand after any integral promotions (discussed in the next section). This result may now be:

    (a) assigned to a variable, e.g. k = i + j,
    (b) used as part of another expression, e.g. m * (i + j),
or (c) passed as a parameter to a function, e.g. sqrt(i + j).

When terminated by ; an expression becomes a statement:

```
k = i + j;                      /* an assignment statement */
m * (i + j);           /* does nothing useful but is a valid statement */
```

9.1 Type conversion in expressions

Because expressions can contain a mixture of types there are a number of rules which cover the *conversion* between types. In arithmetic expressions involving integer and real types the conversions are:

1   The *integral promotions*.
2   Conversion between integer types.
3   Conversion between floating point types (described in Section 8.3).
4   Conversion between integral and floating point types.

The conversion process is given various names including *automatic conversion, implicit conversion, promotion, coercion* and *widening*.

9.1.1 The integral promotions

In C integer arithmetic is carried out at a minimum precision of int. If an expression contains a char, short int, an *enumeration type* (see Section 7.4) or a *bitfield* (see Section 24.9) the following *integral promotion* is applied:

(a) if int can hold all the values of the original type it is converted to an int , else (b) it is converted to an unsigned int.

9.1.2 The *usual arithmetic* conversions

If the operands of an expression have different types a conversion will be carried out under the following rules:

```
IF either operand is long double the other is converted to long double
else
    IF either operand is double the other is converted to double
    else
        IF either operand is float the other is converted to float
        else
            the integral promotions are applied on both operands then
            IF either operand is unsigned long int
                the other is converted to unsigned long int
            else
                IF one operand is long int and the other unsigned int
                    IF long_int can represent all values of unsigned int
                        convert the unsigned int to long int
                    else convert both operands to unsigned long int
                else
                    IF either operand is long int
                        the other is converted to long int
                    else
                        IF either operand is unsigned int
                            the other is converted to unsigned int
                        else both operands are of type int
```

In general, so long as there are no unsigned operands, the lower precision operand is converted or promoted to the higher, the operation performed and the result of the expression is of the higher type.

Mixing signed and unsigned types is little trouble so long as the values are positive and can be represented in the new type. If, when converting to a signed type, the value is too large to be represented the result is implementation dependent. If, when converting from a signed type to an unsigned type, the value is negative the result is the least unsigned integer congruent to the signed integer (modulo 2^n where n is the number of bits used to represent the unsigned type). In two's complement arithmetic the conversion is conceptual and has the effect of copying the bit pattern of the signed type to the unsigned type. In practice avoid mixing signed and unsigned types and in particular don't try to convert a negative number to an unsigned type. Select a type for a particular set of operations and keep to it. In general use signed types unless the operations are naturally unsigned, e.g. memory mapped I/O register addresses.

In addition to conversion when using operators such as +, -, *, etc., there is conversion across assignment operators (covered in Section 10.2).

9.2 Operator *precedence* and *associativity*

Operators are used in expressions where they operate upon *operands* (data to be operated upon such as variables and constants). To determine exactly how an expression is evaluated *operators* have rules of *precedence* and *associativity*.

Precedence determines the priority of the operators. Consider whether the expression:

i + j * k   should be evaluated as   i + (j * k)   or   (i + j) * k

The * has a higher precedence than + (see Table 9.1, below) so the former is the correct result. Note that the () can be used to alter the order of evaluation, e.g. x = (i + j) * k.

Associativity determines how operators of the same precedence are grouped. For example, is the expression i * j / k (where * and / have the same precedence) evaluated as (i * j) / k or i * (j / k). Unary operators (which have one operand) and assignment operators associate from right to left; all the others associate from left to right, i.e. the expression i * j / k is evaluated as (i * j) / k.

Expressions inside parentheses () are evaluated first. Hence, parentheses may be used to change the order in which operations are performed by overriding the normal rules of precedence and associativity: see Program 9_1 (next page). Even if the rules are not being overridden the use of parentheses can make a complex expression more readable by making the order of evaluation 'obvious' to the reader.

Table 9.1 shows the precedence and associativity of all the operators of C (Appendix D contains an extended copy of this table). As the operators are covered in the following chapters this table will be referred to.

precedence		operators	associativity
highest	15	. -> [] ()	left to right
	15	unary	lvalue++ lvalue--	right to left
	14	unary	! ~ + - * & ++lvalue --lvalue	right to left
	14	unary	(typecast) sizeof	right to left
	13	multiplicative	* / %	left to right
	12	additive	+ -	left to right
	11	bitwise shifts	<< (left) >> (right)	left to right
	10	relational	< <= > >=	left to right
	9	equality	== !=	left to right
	8	bitwise AND	&	left to right
	7	bitwise XOR	^	left to right
	6	bitwise OR	|	left to right
	5	logical AND	&&	left to right
	4	logical OR	||	left to right
	3	conditional	?:	right to left
	2	assignment	= += -= *= /= %= &= ^= |= <<= >>=	right to left
lowest	1	sequence	,	left to right

Table 9.1 Precedence and associativity of operators

```
 1 /* Program 9_1  test precedence and associativity of operators */
 2
 3 #include <stdio.h>
 4
 5 int main(void)
 6 {
 7     int i = 10, j = 2, k = 5;
 8     printf(" i + j * k;    = %d \n", i + j * k);
 9     printf(" (i + j) * k; = %d \n", (i + j) * k);
10     printf(" i + (j * k); = %d \n", i + (j * k));
11     printf(" i * j / k;    = %d \n", i * j / k);
12     printf(" (i * j) / k; = %d \n", (i * j) / k);
13     printf(" i * (j / k); = %d \n", i * (j / k));
14     return 0;
15 }
```

Program 9_1 Test precedence and associativity of operators

A run of Program 9_1 gave:

```
i + j * k;    = 20
(i + j) * k; = 60
i + (j * k); = 20
i * j / k;    = 4
(i * j) / k; = 4
i * (j / k); = 0
```

9.3 Arithmetic operators

Arithmetic operators are either **unary operators** which have one operand, e.g. the - sign in z = -x, or **binary operators** which have two operands, e.g. the * in z = x * y (don't confuse this term with the binary number system used to store data within the computer).

The **binary arithmetic** operators are addition +, subtraction -, multiplication *, division / and modulus or remainder % (which may not be used with real operands). For example, consider (x and y are int variables having the values 11 and 3 respectively):

expression	operation	result	comment
x + y	11 + 3	14	
x - y	11 - 3	8	
x * y	11 * 3	33	
x / y	11 / 3	3	result truncated
x % y	11 % 3	2	the remainder of 11/3

The following are system dependent:

1 The action taken on **overflow** and **underflow**.
2 The direction of truncation for / with negative operands.
3 The sign of the result of % with negative operands.

The **unary arithmetic** operators are - and + where:

- returns the negative value of the operand, e.g. -x
+ has almost no effect except that an integral operand undergoes integral promotion (it was added for symmetry with unary -).

The precedence and associativity of all the C operators are shown in Table 9.1. Table 9.2 summarises the precedence and associativity of arithmetic operators and () with examples in Table 9.3.

precedence	operators		associativity
highest		()	left to right
↑	unary	+ -	right to left
	multiplicative	* / %	left to right
lowest	additive	+ -	left to right

Table 9.2 Precedence and associativity of arithmetic operators and ()

example expression	order of evaluation
x + y - j + k	((x + y) - j) + k
y * (i + -x)	y * (i + (-x))
x + y * 2 - k	(x + (y * 2)) - k
x * y + -i / 9 * k - 8	((x * y) + (((-i) / 9) * k)) - 8
x + i / k	x + (i / k)

Table 9.3 Examples of the precedence and associativity of arithmetic operators

Take care when mixing types. Consider x + i / k where x is a float and i and k are int. Although x is a float the sub-expression (i / k) would be evaluated as an int (losing any fractional component) then converted to a float to be added to x (this problem may be overcome by the use of a *casting* or *conversion* operator, see Section 9.5).

Note that the order in which the operands of an operator are evaluated is not specified, e.g.:

    x = sin(angle) * cos(angle);

The sin function may be called before cos or vice versa (selected to be the most efficient for the architecture of the computer concerned). In this case it does not matter but a situation may arise where two functions are accessing and modifying a common data set (called a *side effect*, see Section 18.8) and the order of evaluation is critical. A program which works on one machine may fail when transported to another. In such circumstances the algorithm should be broken down into several statements to ensure the correct order of evaluation of the algorithm as a whole (this may also serve to make the code more readable).

Exercise 9.1 (*see Appendix B for sample answer*)

(a) Implement and test a program which, given the number of seconds since midnight, prints the time in the format hh:mm:ss where hh, mm and ss is the time in hours, minutes and seconds respectively (e.g. 01:36:07, two-digit values with leading zeros).

(b) Implement and test a program which, when given a distance in metres, converts it into feet and inches (there are 3.280839895 feet/metre and 12 inches in a foot).

9.4 The *bitwise* operators

C can be used as a replacement for assembly language in many applications, and therefore has a number of bit level operators. The following truth table shows the logical operations AND, OR (inclusive or) and EOR (exclusive or) on two bits A and B:

A	B	AND	OR	EOR
0	0	0	0	0
0	1	0	1	1
1	0	0	1	1
1	1	1	1	0

The C bitwise logical operators & (and), | (or) and ^ (exclusive or) have two integral operands and perform the specified operation upon the corresponding bits in each operand.

```
k = i & j;                  /* logical AND, i & j, assign result to k */
k = i | j;              /* logical inclusive OR, i | j, assign result to k */
k = i ^ j;              /* logical exclusive OR, i ^ j, assign result to k */
```

For example, assuming that i and j are byte sized variables having the values 00001010 and 01001100 respectively, the following table shows the result of &, | and ^ operations.

operation	operator	example operation	result
AND	i & j	00001010 & 01001100	00001000
inclusive OR	i | j	00001010 | 01001100	01001110
exclusive OR	i ^ j	00001010 ^ 01001100	01000110

The operators << left shift and >> right shift have two operands; the value of the bit pattern in the left hand operand is shifted by the number of bits specified by the second operand:

```
k = i >> 3                  /* k assigned the value of i shifted right 3 bits */
k = i << j              /* k assigned i shifted left by number of bits specified by j */
```

If, in the first example, i was 01001100, k would be assigned the value 00001001. Note:

<< the bit pattern is shifted left, 0s are shifted in from the right
>> the bit pattern is shifted right, the value shifted in from the left may be 0s (logical shift) or a copy of the sign bit (arithmetic shift); it is implementation dependent.

Bits shifted out are lost. Note that shifting by more bits than there are in the data word gives an implementation dependent result.

The final bitwise operator is unary ~ (not or one's complement) which inverts the value of every bit in the operand, i.e. 0 becomes 1 and 1 becomes 0:

```
i = ~i                      /* form one's complement of i */
```

If the value of i was 00001010 the one's complement would be 11110101. Consider:

```
k = k & 0xf                 /* clears all except the lower 4 bits of k to 0 */
k = k & ~0xf                /* clears the lower 4 bits of k to 0 */
```

Section 24.9 discusses the use of *bitwise* operators to store bit fields within a variable.

9.5 Casting or conversion operators

When evaluating an expression or part of an expression it often turns out not to have the required type. For example, consider the following where x is a float and i and k are int:

    x + i / k

Although x is a float the sub-expression (i / k) would be evaluated as an int (losing any fractional component) then converted to a float to be added to x.

   A **casting** or **conversion** operator, which forces the result of an expression to have a particular type, associates from **right to left** and takes the form:

       (type) expression

Thus the above example would be written:

    x + (float) i / k

As a cast is a higher priority than / (see Table 9.1) it forces the value of i to be converted to a float. When the expression (float) i / k is evaluated the value of (float) i is a float thus k is converted to a float and the expression i / k is then evaluated as a float to be added to x. The above expression could also be written in either of the following ways:

    x + i / (float) k
    x + (float) i / (float) k

Note that the following would not work:

    x + (float) (i / k)   /* error!! */

The expression (i / k) is evaluated as an int and the result forced to a float by the cast.

   A float variable may be used in an int expression (if the value will fit) discarding any fractional component, e.g. if x is a float and i and k are int:

    i + (int) x / k

Casts can also be used to remove compiler warning messages generated when assigning higher precision types to lower, for example:

    long int j = 20;
    int i = j;

generated the following warning when compiled under Turbo C/C++ V.3.00:

Warning x.c 2: Conversion may lose significant digits in function main()

This warns that the long int value of j is converted to an int before being assigned to i and information could be lost. Explicit casting removes the warning, i.e.:

    int i = (int) j;

The cast indicates to the compiler that an int is required and so a warning is not issued.

9.6 The *sizeof* operator

It is sometimes necessary to determine the amount of memory required to store a data structure. For example, when meeting a C system for the first time a useful exercise is to determine the number of bits used to represent types such as int, long int, float, double, etc. C provides the unary operator sizeof which returns (as an integer) the number of bytes required to store a type or the result of an expression:

```
sizeof (type_name)
sizeof unary_expression
```

where the type_name may be a type such as int or float, or an array (see Chapter 19) or a structure (see Chapter 24) and the value returned is of type size_t (defined in <stdlib.h>), typically an unsigned int which can be cast as required. For example:

```
sizeof (long int)     number of bytes required to hold a long int
sizeof x              number of bytes required to hold the variable x
sizeof (x + y)        number of bytes required to hold the result of an expression
```

Be careful not to write the latter as:

```
sizeof x + y          /* error! */
```

sizeof has a higher priority than + so this expression adds the size of x (in bytes) to the value of y. Although sizeof has been written as though it is a function call it is an operator. In addition, if type_name is a *pointer type*, sizeof returns the size of the *pointer type*, **not** the size of the type pointed to (see Section 21.10).

```
 1  /* Program 9_2, display integral sizes and ranges */
 2
 3  #include <stdio.h>
 4  #include <limits.h>
 5
 6  int main(void)
 7  {
 8      printf("\nchar               size %2d bytes, range %11d to %11d ",
 9                 (int) sizeof(char), CHAR_MIN, CHAR_MAX);
10      printf("\nsigned char        size %2d bytes, range %11d to %11d ",
11                 (int) sizeof(signed char), SCHAR_MIN, SCHAR_MAX);
12      printf("\nunsigned char      size %2d bytes, range %11d to %11d ",
13                 (int) sizeof(unsigned char), 0, UCHAR_MAX);
14      printf("\nshort int          size %2d bytes, range %11d to %11d ",
15                 (int) sizeof(short int), SHRT_MIN, SHRT_MAX);
16      printf("\nunsigned short int size %2d bytes, range %11u to %11u ",
17                 (int) sizeof(unsigned short int), 0, USHRT_MAX);
18      printf("\nint                size %2d bytes, range %11d to %11d ",
19                 (int) sizeof(int), INT_MIN, INT_MAX);
20      printf("\nunsigned int       size %2d bytes, range %11u to %11u ",
21                 (int) sizeof(unsigned int), 0, UINT_MAX);
22      printf("\nlong int           size %2d bytes, range %11ld to %11ld ",
23                 (int) sizeof(long int), LONG_MIN, LONG_MAX);
24      printf("\nunsigned long int  size %2d bytes, range %11lu to %11lu ",
25                 (int) sizeof(unsigned long int), 0L, ULONG_MAX);
26      return 0;
27  }
```

Program 9_2 Displays the size (in bytes) and numeric range of the integral data types

Program 9_2 displays the size (in bytes) and numeric range of the integral types (the names CHAR_MAX, CHAR_MIN, etc. are defined in <limits.h>, see Appendix C.5). The table below presents the results of Program 9_2 when run on an IBM PC compatible using Turbo

V3.00 or Borland V4.51. Presented alongside are the results given by Microsoft Visual V4.0 and GNU V2.6.3 on an IBM PC compatible and the cc compiler on a Hewlett Packard 700 workstation (notice how the field width has been specified in Program 9_2 to tabulate the results):

IBM PC compatible Turbo C V3.00/Borland V4.51				IBM PC GNU and MS Visual C 4.0 HP 700 UNIX compiler cc		
type	size	number range		size	number range	
char	1	-128 to	127	1	-128 to	127
signed char	1	-128 to	127	1	-128 to	127
unsigned char	1	0 to	255	1	0 to	255
short int	2	-32768 to	32767	2	-32768 to	32767
unsigned short int	2	0 to	65535	2	0 to	65535
int	2	-32768 to	32767	4	-2147483648 to	2147483647
unsigned int	2	0 to	65535	4	0 to	4294967295
long int	4	-2147483648 to	2147483647	4	-2147483648 to	2147483647
unsigned long int	4	0 to	4294967295	4	0 to	4294967295

The size of int and unsigned int was two bytes (16 bits) using the Turbo and Borland compilers and four bytes (32 bits) using the MS Visual, GNU and HP compilers (char, short int and long int were similar in all examples).

Exercise 9.2 *(see Appendix B for sample answer)*

Implement and test a program which reads up to six real numbers from the keyboard and calculates the average, i.e.:

$$\text{average of } x = \sum_{i=1}^{n} x_i \ / \ n$$

where Σ indicates summation, x_i are the numbers and n is the number of elements. If less than six numbers are entered terminate with an invalid character, e.g.:

    10.0 20.0 30.0 $

Remember that scanf returns the number of successful conversions as an int function result (see Section 5.3.3).

Problems for Chapter 9

1   Implement and test a program which prints the number of bytes used to store real types together with their precision and range (from <float.h>, see compiler manuals).

2   Write and test a program using integer arithmetic to calculate the minimum number of bank-notes and coins needed to pay out a specified amount in cash, assuming that the amount is given as a multiple of the smallest unit of currency. For example, in the UK assume that the amount is specified in pence and that there are notes to the value of £50, £20, £10 and £5 and coins to the value of £1, 50p, 20p, 10p, 5p, 2p and 1p.

10

Assignment operators

10.1 The = assignment operator

Chapter 9 discussed operators and their use when building expressions, e.g.:

```
i + j * k
```

The above expression produces a result of the same type as the type of the highest precision operand after any integral promotions. This result may now be:

(a) assigned to a variable, e.g. x = i + j * k,
(b) used as part of another expression, e.g. (i + j * k) / x,
or (c) passed as a parameter to a function, e.g. sqrt(i + j * k).

The assignment operator = is a binary operator in which the result of the expression on the right (called an rvalue - right value) is assigned to the **variable** on the left (called an lvalue which is the general name for an *expression referring to a region of storage in memory*):

```
i = j * k
```

This is an **expression** which:

(a) evaluates j * k and assigns the result to i (after any conversion - see next section), and (b) has an overall result, which is the **value** assigned to i and is of the **type** of i.

For example, if j and k are variables of type int having values of 5 and 10 respectively, the expression j * k would be evaluated having a result of 50 and type int; then:

1   If i is an int the value 50 would be assigned to i and the result of the expression would be 50 and have the type int.
2   If i is a float the result of j * k would be converted to a float and the value 50.0 assigned to i. The result of the expression would be 50.0 and have the type float.

The result of an expression involving assignment may be used in a similar way to the result of any other expression, e.g. the result assigned to another variable:

```
x = i = j * k
```

Assignment associates from **right to left**, thus the grouping of the above expression is:

```
x = (i = (j * k))
```

Such an expression is made into an *assignment statement* by a ; terminator:

```
x = i = j * k;
```

In addition, C has increment and decrement operators (discussed in Section 10.3) and *compound assignment* operators (discussed in Section 10.4), e.g.:

```
i++          /* increment i by 1 */
i--          /* decrement i by 1 */
i += 1       /* increment i by 1 */
i *= 10      /* multiply i by 10 */
```

10.2 Type conversion across assignment

Consider the expression:

```
i = j
```

If i and j are of different types, the value of the right hand side (which may be the result of an expression) is converted to the type of the left, which is the type of the result. If the conversion is from a lower precision type to a higher the *usual arithmetic* conversions apply: see Section 9.1. Problems can occur when there is a conversion from a higher precision to a lower, e.g. assigning a float to an int. In such cases the following applies:

(a) longer integers are converted to shorter by **discarding** the high-order bits;
(b) real to integer conversion causes truncation of any fractional components;
(c) longer reals are converted to shorter by truncation or rounding (implementation dependent), e.g. double to float.

Thus if the value of the higher precision cannot be stored in the lower, information is lost (a modern compiler may issue a warning under such circumstances). If, in (b) and (c) above, the value is outside the range that can be held the behaviour is *undefined* (the program may give a run-time error or carry on with a faulty value).

Note that assignments will not perform integral promotions if the operands are of the same type, e.g. in the following examples char_1 and char_2 are of type char:

```
char_2 = char_1;
```

The value of char_1 will be assigned to char_2 (without being promoted and then the high-order bits being dropped). But integral promotion will take place in a statement such as:

```
char_2 = char_1 + 1;
```

The value of char_1 will be promoted to int, char_1 + 1 evaluated and the high-order bits of the int result dropped to convert to a char to be assigned to char_2.

Program 10_1 (next page) shows some examples of expressions using mixtures of types. Consider lines:

5-8	define variables, before main, making them external (discussed in Section 17.4)
12-13	prompt for entry of an int and long int and read in the values
14-15	prompt for entry of a float and double and read in the values
17	long_i = long_i + int_i; convert the value of int_i to long int, add long_i and assign value to long_i
18	drop the high-order bits of long_i and assign result to int_j
19	print values of int_j and long_i
20	float_value = float_value + int_i; convert the value of int_i to float, add to float_value and assign the float result to float_value
21	double_value = double_value - float_value; convert the value of float_value to double, subtract from double_value and assign the result to double_value
22	float_value = double_value + float_value; convert the value of float_value to double, add to double_value and round or truncate the double result to float to assign to float_value
23	int_i = float_value; convert float_value to int and assign to int_i
24-25	print results of above calculations and flush the output stream stdout (see below)
26	multiply double_value by a very large float constant and attempt to round or truncate the double result to a float (may cause overflow - see below).

```
 1 /* Program 10_1 - conversions between types    */
 2
 3 #include <stdio.h>                          /* standard stream I/O library */
 4
 5 int int_i, int_j;                                    /* define 2 ints */
 6 long int long_i;                                 /* define a long int */
 7 float float_value;                                  /* define a float */
 8 double double_value;                               /* define a double */
 9
10 int main(void)
11 {
12     printf("\nEnter an int and long int ? ");
13     scanf("%d%ld", &int_i, &long_i);
14     printf("\nEnter a float and double ? ");
15     scanf("%g%lg", &float_value, &double_value);
16
17     long_i = long_i * int_i;                    /* long int expression */
18     int_j = long_i;                                  /* int expression */
19     printf("int %d, long int %ld", int_j, long_i);
20     float_value = float_value + int_i;             /* float expression */
21     double_value = double_value - float_value;    /* double expression */
22     float_value = double_value + float_value;       /* double to float */
23     int_i = float_value;                             /* float to int */
24     printf("\nint %d, float %f, double %f\n", int_i, float_value, double_value);
25     fflush(stdout);                                 /* flush stdout */
26     float_value = double_value * 3.0e+38F;          /* overflow ?? */
27     printf("float %f\n", float_value);
28     return 0;
29 }
```

Program 10_1 Conversion between real and integral types

In lines 18, 22, 23 and 26 of Program 10_1 there is conversion from higher to lower precision types, i.e. in line 22 a double with a precision of 15 decimal digits may be converted to a float with 7 digits, e.g. Microsoft C V7.00 gave the following warnings:

```
p10_1.cpp(18) : warning C4135: conversion between different integral types
p10_1.cpp(22) : warning C4136: conversion between different floating-point types
p10_1.cpp(23) : warning C4051: type conversion; possible loss of data
p10_1.cpp(26) : warning C4136: conversion between different floating-point types
```

These warn that the conversions between the different integral and floating types result in a loss of precision (which may be critical or not depending upon the application).

When an expression is evaluated it is possible that the destination may be unable to hold the value at all. For example, consider line 26 of Program 10_1:

```
float_value = double_value * 3.0e+38F;
```

The constant 3.0e+38F is a large value, near to the maximum that can be stored in a typical 32-bit float. If double_value is of any size the expression double_value * 3.0e+38F evaluated as a double may cause overflow when converted to float before being assigned to float_value. The following is a run of the program under Turbo C V3.00 (user input in **bold** with newline shown as ⤶):

```
Enter an int and long int ? 5  25000 ↵
Enter a float and double ? 3.25   10.5 ↵
int -6072, long int 125000
int 10, float 10.500000, double 2.250000
Floating point error: Overflow.
Abnormal program termination
```

This shows that when the value of long_i is assigned to int_j in line 18 the high-order bits of the long int value 125000 are discarded to yield the int value -6072, i.e. 125000 has the value 0x1e484 which, when the high-order bits are discarded to yield a 16-bit value, gives e848 which, as a two's complement signed int, has the value -6072.

The program terminates with a run-time error indicating that a floating-point overflow occurred, i.e. the result of double_value * 3.0e+38F was too large to assign to a float (maximum value 3.402823466e+38F). Note the use of function fflush on line 25 to flush the output stream stdout. If this had not been done it is possible that any characters in the stream could have been lost when the program terminated (again system dependent).

Although, in the above run, the program terminated with a run-time error this is not always the case and in such circumstances **undefined behaviour** occurs. The action taken is implementation dependent, varying from program termination with an error message (as above) to continuing execution with an incorrect value stored in the variable in question. It is up to the programmer to prevent **undefined behaviour**:

During the analysis and design phase: by careful analysis of the program data in terms of its precision and range and then selecting appropriate types to store the data.

During implementation: when information from <limits.h> and <float.h> can be used to determine the precision and range of real types and run-time action taken and/or messages printed if undefined behaviour is likely to result.

Exercise 10.1 (see Appendix B for sample answer)

Enter Program 10_1 (or get file C10\p10_1.c off the disk which accompanies this text). Compile and generate an assembly listing, e.g.:

Turbo C: use tcc -A -S -f287 filename.c to generate an assembly listing filename.asm

Examine the assembly listing to see if the conversions are as expected. Make sure the compiler is generating ANSI standard C (/Za with Microsoft C V7.0) and that optimisation is off (/Od with Microsoft C) otherwise the code may be optimised out of all recognition.

10.3 Increment and decrement operators

Adding one to or subtracting one from the value of a variable is a very common programming requirement (many machines have special instructions for this purpose). In C the increment operator ++ adds one and the decrement operator -- subtracts one, and can either prefix or postfix the operand (Table 9.1 and Appendix D show the precedence and associativity of these operators). Thus the following statements increment i by 1:

```
i = i + 1;
i++;
++i;
```

In these increment statements it does not matter if prefix or postfix is used but in more complex expressions it is critical and the following rules are used:

postfix (e.g. i++ or i--) the value of the operand is used in the expression **then** it is incremented or decremented.

prefix (e.g. ++i or --i) the value of the operand is incremented or decremented and the **new** value used in the expression.

For example, assuming i = 10 consider the statements:

k = i++; after assignment k would = 10 and i = 11
k = ++i; after assignment k would = 11 and i = 11

Now, assuming i = 10 and j = 2 consider the expressions (which may be part of a larger expression):

i * j++   result = 20, j = 3 (incremented after evaluation)
i * ++j   result = 30, j = 3 (incremented before evaluation)
i * j--   result = 20, j = 1 (decremented after evaluation)
i * --j   result = 10, j = 1 (decremented before evaluation)

Remember, in addition to evaluating the expression, the value of the variable in memory is altered (this is called a *side effect*, see Section 18.8). **Do not** use a variable more than once in an expression if one (or more) of the references has one of these operators attached to it. The standard does not specify the order in which the operands of an operator are evaluated and there is no guarantee when an affected variable will change its value. Consider:

```
(i * j++) + (i * j)
```

will the value of j in (i * j) be that before or after the increment in (i * j++)?

```
1  * Program 10_2 - test increment and decrement operators */
2
3  #include <stdio.h>
4
5  int main(void)
6  {
7      int i = 10, j;
8
9      j = 2;  printf(" i = %d, j = %d, i * j++ = %d \n", i, j, i * j++);
10     j = 2;  printf(" i = %d, j = %d, i * ++j = %d \n", i, j, i * ++j);
11     j = 2;  printf(" i = %d, j = %d, i * j-- = %d \n", i, j, i * j--);
12     j = 2;  printf(" i = %d, j = %d, i * --j = %d \n", i, j, i * --j);
13     j = 2;  printf(" (i * j++) + (i * j)   = %d \n", (i * j++) + (i * j));
14     j = 2;  printf(" (i * j)   + (i * j++) = %d \n", (i * j) + (i * j++));
15     j = 2;  printf(" (i * j++) + (i * j--) = %d \n", (i * j++) + (i * j--));
16     j = 2;  printf(" (i * j--) + (i * j++) = %d \n", (i * j--) + (i * j++));
17     j = 2;  printf(" (i * ++j) + (i * j)   = %d \n", (i * ++j) + (i * j));
18     j = 2;  printf(" (i * j)   + (i * ++j) = %d \n", (i * j) + (i * ++j));
19     j = 2;  printf(" (i * ++j) + (i * --j) = %d \n", (i * ++j) + (i * --j));
20     j = 2;  printf(" (i * --j) + (i * ++j) = %d \n", (i * --j) + (i * ++j));
21     return 0;
22 }
```

Program 10_2 Test of increment and decrement operators

Program 10_2 tests some expressions involving increment and decrement operators and prints the results, i.e. in lines:

9-12   expressions containing one reference to the variable altered using ++ or --
13-20   expressions containing two references to the variable altered using ++ or --.

The following tables show the results from GNU C V2.6.3 compiler, Microsoft C V7.00, Turbo C V3.00 and Borland V4.51 on an IBM PC compatible, Whitesmiths Version 3.2 cross compiler executing on a MC68000 based target microcomputer and Apollo DN4500, DEC Alpha and Hewlett Packard 700 UNIX based workstations.

IBM PC GNU C for DOS	IBM PC Turbo C & Borland C MC68000 Whitesmiths C HP 700 UNIX C
i = 10, j = 3, i * j++ = 20	i = 10, j = 3, i * j++ = 20
i = 10, j = 3, i * ++j = 30	i = 10, j = 3, i * ++j = 30
i = 10, j = 1, i * j-- = 20	i = 10, j = 1, i * j-- = 20
i = 10, j = 1, i * --j = 10	i = 10, j = 1, i * --j = 10
(i * j++) + (i * j) = 40	(i * j++) + (i * j) = 50
(i * j) + (i * j++) = 40	(i * j) + (i * j++) = 40
(i * j++) + (i * j--) = 40	(i * j++) + (i * j--) = 50
(i * j--) + (i * j++) = 40	(i * j--) + (i * j++) = 30
(i * ++j) + (i * j) = 60	(i * ++j) + (i * j) = 60
(i * j) + (i * ++j) = 50	(i * j) + (i * ++j) = 50
(i * ++j) + (i * --j) = 50	(i * ++j) + (i * --j) = 50
(i * --j) + (i * ++j) = 30	(i * --j) + (i * ++j) = 30

IBM PC Microsoft C Apollo DN4500 UNIX C	DEC Alpha UNIX C
i = 10, j = 3, i * j++ = 20	i = 10, j = 3, i * j++ = 20
i = 10, j = 3, i * ++j = 30	i = 10, j = 3, i * ++j = 30
i = 10, j = 1, i * j-- = 20	i = 10, j = 1, i * j-- = 20
i = 10, j = 1, i * --j = 10	i = 10, j = 1, i * --j = 10
(i * j++) + (i * j) = 50	(i * j++) + (i * j) = 40
(i * j) + (i * j++) = 50	(i * j) + (i * j++) = 40
(i * j++) + (i * j--) = 50	(i * j++) + (i * j--) = 40
(i * j--) + (i * j++) = 30	(i * j--) + (i * j++) = 40
(i * ++j) + (i * j) = 60	(i * ++j) + (i * j) = 60
(i * j) + (i * ++j) = 60	(i * j) + (i * ++j) = 60
(i * ++j) + (i * --j) = 40	(i * ++j) + (i * --j) = 40
(i * --j) + (i * ++j) = 40	(i * --j) + (i * ++j) = 40

The order of evaluation of operands in expressions such as (i * ++j) + (i * --j) differed from compiler to compiler giving different results for the same expressions. Also note that in a function call such as in line 9:

```
printf(" i %d, j %d, i * j++ %d \n", i, j, i * j++);
```

the order in which the parameters are evaluated is not specified by the standard. All the compilers have evaluated the third parameter i * j++, before the second j, i.e. the value of j is printed as 3 (after being incremented). The moral is don't write code that is dependent upon the order of evaluation. Break the code down into separate statements so that the order of evaluation will be as required by the specification.

Note that the increment and decrement operators can only be applied to variables, i.e. not constants, expressions, function calls, etc. For example, the following are illegal:

```
5++       (i + j)--     ++sqrt(x)                          /* invalid!!! */
```

If incrementing (or decrementing) a variable any of the following can be used:

```
i = i + 1;                                       /* add one to i */
i =+ 1;                          /* add one to i, see next section */
++i;                                             /* add one to i */
i++;                                             /* add one to i */
```

Programmers who use more modern languages would tend to use the first and professional C programmers the last. It really does not matter so long as one is consistent.

10.4 The compound assignment operators

The original C was developed before the days of optimising compilers and contains a number of operators by which the programmer could indicate, at the program source code level, possible optimisation. For example, using i++ could enable the compiler to use a fast increment instruction rather than a general add instruction.

The compound assignment operators were another means of improving program performance before the days of optimising compilers. Today they should be restricted as their use can lead to code which is difficult to read (especially for programmers who are not specialists in C or C++).

The compound operators provide a shorthand form for use in statements where the variable on the left hand side of an assignment is repeated immediately on the right, e.g.:

```
i = i + 20;                             /* add 20 to the variable i */
j = j * k;                              /* multiply variable j by k */
x = x / 10.0;                           /* divide variable x by 10.0 */
```

can all be written in shorthand form:

```
i += 20;                                /* add 20 to the variable i */
j *= k;                                 /* multiply variable j by k */
x /= 10.0;                              /* divide variable x by 10.0 */
```

The compound assignment operators are:

```
+=    -=    *=    /=    %=    <<=    >>=    &=    ^=    |=
```

An expression of the form: variable operator = expression

is equivalent to: variable = (variable) operator (expression)

Note the (). The () around expression indicate that

k *= j + i;   is equivalent to   k = k * (j + i);

whereas the longhand form of writing the expression:

k = k * j + i;   is equivalent to   k = (k * j) + i;

The () around variable indicate that if it is an expression it is evaluated only once, e.g. to add 20 to element row i column j of the two-dimensional array c (see Section 26.1):

```
c[i][j] +=  20.0f;
```

is more efficient than

```
c[i][j] = c[i][j] + 20.0f;
```

because the subscript calculation [i][j] is only performed once (a modern optimising compiler may well do this anyway).

Take care not to confuse compound operators such as += with the = and + operators, e.g. the following expression assigns i the value +20:

```
i =+20;                                      /* add 20 to the variable i, error?? */
```

Use the compound assignment operators sparingly as their use can lead to code which is difficult to read. Modern compilers have reduced the requirement for such shorthand techniques and program readability and maintainability is of paramount importance. They can, however, be used to good effect within loops accessing array elements (see line 59 of Implementation File matrix1.c in Chapter 26).

Exercise 10.2 (see Appendix B for sample answer)

A company employs five grades of staff with grades C, D and E paid weekly and A and B paid monthly. Write a program which reads the number of staff in each grade, their pay rates (weekly or monthly), and prints the pay bills for the weekly and monthly staff and the total annual pay bill.

Problems for Chapter 10

1   Enter Program 10_2 (or get from disk file c10\p10_2.c). Using as many C systems as possible compile, link and execute. Compare the results! Try some variations!

2   Implement and test a program which evaluates the reactance of a series circuit consisting of an inductor L and capacitor C at frequency f:

```
reactance = 2πfL - 1 / (2πfC)
```

The program should read the values of L, C and f, evaluate the reactance and print the result, e.g. if L = 0.2 Henries, C = 2μfarads and f = 50Hz the reactance is -1528.717Ω.

3   Implement and test a program which evaluates the period of oscillation in seconds of load W attached to a vertical spring of stiffness k:

$$\text{period of oscillation} = 2\pi \sqrt{\left(\frac{W}{k\,g}\right)}$$

where standard gravity g is 9.80665 metres/sec^2 or 32.2 ft/sec^2. It can be assumed that the spring is perfectly elastic, obeys Hooke's Law (stress is proportional to strain) and its mass is negligible compared to the weight W. The program should read the values of W and k, evaluate the period and print the result, e.g. if W = 150 lbs and k = 350 lbs/inch the period equals 0.209 seconds.

4   Modify the answer to Exercise 10.2 whereby grade E is paid an hourly rate and the number of hours worked per week must be entered for each person.

11

The *if* statement

Although program flow is normally sequential it is often necessary to select alternative paths through a program. This is achieved by the use of the if statement which is described in this chapter, together with related topics.

11.1 The *if* statement

The first form of the if statement is shown below together with a diagrammatic representation; expression is evaluated and only if it is *true* is statement executed. After the if, execution continues with next statement.

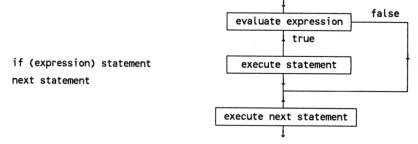

```
if (expression) statement
next statement
```

For example, the following code prints the message "x is 0" only if the value of the int variable x is zero; execution then continues with the statement following the if (== is the *relational operator* which tests for equality - discussed in Section 11.2):

```
if (x == 0) printf("x is 0\n");
```

In the second form of the if statement expression is evaluated and if it is *true* statement1 is executed, if *false* statement2 is executed. Execution then continues with next statement.

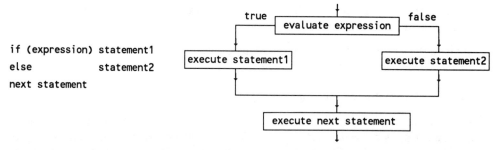

```
if (expression) statement1
else            statement2
next statement
```

The if statement is used extensively in programs, e.g. when reading data the function scanf returns as an int function result the number of successful conversions. This can be used to see if an error occurred during a read (e.g. a letter found in an integer value) and if so the program can attempt to recover from the error and continue. Section 15.1 discusses the validation of input data.

```
 1 /* Program 11_1 - read a number and test if zero or non-zero  */
 2
 3 #include <stdio.h>                              /* standard stream I/O library */
 4
 5 int main(void)
 6 {
 7     int i;
 8
 9     scanf("%d", &i);                            /* read number */
10     if (i == 0)  printf("value was zero = %d\n");
11     else         printf("value was non-zero = %d\n");
12     return 0;
13 }
```

Program 11_1   Read an integer number and test if zero

Program 11_1 reads an integer number from stdin and tests, using an if statement, if it is zero or non-zero.

Note the ; on the end of line 10 which is required to terminate the printf statement and, if missed, will generate an error, e.g. using Turbo C V3.00:

```
Error p11_1.c 11: Statement missing ; in function main()
```

Exercise 11.1 *(see Appendix B for sample answer)*

Enter Program 11_1 (or obtain from disk file c11\p11_1.c), compile, link and execute it with various data (including invalid characters; Section 11.4 shows how to deal with input errors). Remove the ; on the end of line 10; what happens when it is compiled?

Replace the == operator in line 10 of Program 11_1 with the = operator. What happens when the program is compiled, linked and executed? This is discussed in the next section.

11.2 Relational operators

Unlike more modern languages C has no separate boolean or logical data type with its own rules. Logical expressions are evaluated using integral data types and *true* and *false* are represented by non-zero and zero respectively, i.e:

```
    if (expression) statement
```

If the value of expression is non-zero it is treated as *true* and statement executed otherwise if it is zero it is *false* and statement is skipped.

operator	condition tested	example	testing
==	equal	z == 1	is the value of z equal to 1 ?
!=	not equal	ch != '0'	ch not equal to the character '0' ?
<	less than	x < 1.0	x less than 1.0 ?
>	greater than	x > y	x greater than y ?
<=	less than or equal	x <= 1.0	x less than or equal to 1.0 ?
>=	greater than or equal	x >= y	x greater than or equal to y ?

Table 11.1   Relational operators

Table 11.1 presents a list of the *relational operators* (see Table 9.1 or Appendix D for their precedence and associativity) which compare two operands and produce an int result:

0 if the relationship was *false*

1 if the relationship was *true*.

Lines 10 and 11 of Program 11_1 could have been written using the != operator:

```
if (i != 0) printf("value was non-zero = %d\n");
else        printf("value was zero = %d\n");
```

Often one form (== or !=) will make the logic of the code clearer. It could have been written:

```
if (i) printf("value was non-zero = %d\n");
else   printf("value was zero = %d\n");
```

If i is non-zero (*true*) the first printf statement is executed, otherwise the second (following the else). The use of such *shorthand* techniques is not recommended as they can make the logic of the code difficult to follow.

It is wise to avoid comparing real numbers for equality (using ==) or inequality (using !=), e.g. if x and y are of type float:

```
if (x == y) printf("x equals y");        /* dangerous */
if (x != 1.0f) printf("x is not 1.0");   /* for real */
if (y == 5.0f) printf("y equals 5.0");   /* numbers */
```

Even if a sequence of calculations should, theoretically, result in two equal (or unequal) real values the limited precision of real number computations introduces rounding errors which lead to inaccuracy in the result (see Section 8.2 and Chapter 27). Therefore expressions (such as the above) which directly compare two real numbers should be avoided. An alternative is to subtract the values to be compared and see if the absolute value of the result is less than the accuracy required, i.e.:

```
if (fabs(x - y) < 1.0e-6) printf("x equals y");      /* safer for reals */
```

The function fabs returns the absolute value of x - y which is tested to see if it is less than 1.0e-6 (the 'accuracy' required). The problem is in determining the required accuracy, e.g. when x and y are very small or very large numbers. In this case an alternative technique would be to examine x - y relative to the value of x or y, e.g.:

```
if (fabs(x - y) < fabs(1.0e-6 * x)) printf("x equals y");   /* safer for reals */
```

There is no easy answer to such problems and each algorithm must be examined with care to determine the coding techniques to be used (Chapter 27 will discuss the effects of accuracy).

Note the use of operator == in line 10 of Program 11_1, i.e. if (i == 0). A common mistake is to use a single = which changes the expression to an assignment operation, i.e.:

```
if (i = 0)  printf("value was zero = %d\n");          /* error!! */
```

This expression assigns the value 0 to the variable i, thus overwriting the value read from the keyboard. The integral result of the expression, i = 0, is then used for the if conditional test and being zero is taken as false and the statement in line 11 executed. Such errors can be very difficult to find. Modern compilers, however, will issue a warning if an assignment is found within a conditional, e.g. using Turbo C V3.00:

```
Warning p11_1.c 10: Possibly incorrect assignment in function main()
```

11.3 Logical operators

Logical expressions such as i == 0 may be combined using the logical operators && (AND) and || (OR) both of which are binary operators: see Table 11.2.

operation	operator	use	operation performed
AND	&&	a && b	if a AND b are true (non-zero) result is true
OR	||	a || b	if a OR b is true (non-zero) result is true
NOT	!	!a	unary operator performs logical inversion

Table 11.2 Logical operators

The logical NOT operator ! can be used to invert the result of a logical expression. Unlike arithmetic operators (see Section 9.3) C guarantees that the operands of binary logical operators are evaluated from **left to right** (after any precedence), i.e. in the above table the operand a will be evaluated first. In addition, if the final result of the expression can be determined from the value of a the operand b is not evaluated, i.e.:

    a && b   if a is false (zero) b is not evaluated
    a || b   if a is true (non-zero) b is not evaluated

Consider the following expressions:

    if (sqrt(x) > y) ......
    if (i/j <= k) ....

A run-time error would occur in the first statement if x was less than 0 and in the second statement if j was zero. The statements could be rewritten thus:

    if ((x >= 0) && (sqrt(x) > y)) ......
    if ((j != 0) && (i/j <= k)) ....

In both cases the second operand would not be evaluated if the first was false, i.e. x was less than 0 or j was 0. Note that the above statements could have been written:

    if (x >= 0 && sqrt(x) > y) ......
    if (j != 0 && i/j <= k) ....

because the relational operators have a higher precedence than && and ||. However, the extra parentheses in the first example make the expressions more readable. It is very easy to write logical expressions which are very difficult to read. In practice write expressions in a way that is natural to the application and achieves the most readable code.

Exercise 11.2 (*see Appendix B for sample answer*)

A car park charges £1/hour for cars, £3/hour for trucks and £5/hour for buses. Implement a program which, given the vehicle type (as a character, e.g. c for car, t for truck and b for bus) and the time parked, calculates the charge (part of an hour counts as a full hour). What happens when invalid data is entered (discussed in next section)?

11.4 Testing *scanf* for successful conversion

Previous programs in this book have assumed that read operations were performed without error, e.g. line 9 of Program 11_1 which attempts to read an integer numeric value from stdin into the variable i:

    scanf("%d", &i);   /* read number */

It is very easy, however, when typing in the number, for the user to enter a letter instead of a digit which would give an error condition which the program should deal with.

In addition to returning values read from the keyboard (e.g. into parameter i) function scanf also returns as an int function result the number of successful conversions:

(a) If no conversions occurred 0 is returned.
(b) If a matching failure occurs (e.g. a non-numeric character in a decimal number) conversion stops and the number of successful conversions returned (the faulty character is left in the input stream where the program can read it and take action).
(c) If *end of file* occurs before any conversions the value EOF (defined in <stdio.h>) is returned.

For example:

```
if (scanf("%d", &i) == 1) printf("value %d read OK\n", i);
else                      printf("data input error\a\n");
```

The function scanf attempts to read one integer value (%d conversion specification); if successful it will return a function result of 1 (one successful conversion) else 0 (conversion failed) or EOF (*end of file* entered). The if statement checks the value returned by scanf and prints an appropriate message. Note that if the conversion failed the value of i is unchanged. In practice, the program would attempt to recover from the error by reading the faulty character from the input stream and prompting the user for more input, see Program 13_2 and Section 15.1.

11.5 Compound statements

The simple programs presented so far have consisted of individual program statements which are executed sequentially. However, it is often necessary to group a number of statements together into a *compound statement*, e.g. to be executed under some condition as part of an if statement. In C a compound statement is enclosed in braces {}:

```
{
  definitions
  statement
  statement
  ....
}
```

A compound statement (sometimes called a *block*) **may** define *local* types (using *typedef*), constants and variables (more details in Section 17.3) which exist from the point of definition and are lost on exit from the compound statement (permanent internal storage may be allocated using *static* variables, see Section 17.5). When defined, internal variables may be initialised, otherwise the value is *undefined*. In general anywhere where a statement may be used a compound statement may be used.

Program 11_2 (next page), which is a modification of Program 5_3, attempts to read a real number from the keyboard (line 13) into variable radius and tests to see if an error occurred (scanf should return a function result of 1). If an error occurred an error message is printed (line 14) otherwise the circle area is calculated (compound statement lines 16 to 25). Note the definition of the local *named constant* PI and local variables area and radius_check which exist only within the compound statement. Variable success_indicator is used to return a success/fail indicator to the operating system (see Section 4.5.1).

```
 1 /* Program 11_2 - read radius of circle from the keyboard and if OK  *
 2  *                     calculate circle area and check radius          */
 3
 4 #include <stdio.h>
 5 #include <math.h>
 6
 7 int main(void)
 8 {
 9     float radius;                                   /* radius of circle */
10     int success_indicator = -1;       /* success/fail indicator, assume fail */
11
12     printf("Enter radius of circle (real number) ? ");
13     if (scanf("%f", &radius) != 1)                      /* read radius */
14         printf("data entry error !! \a\n");                /* error ! */
15     else
16         {                                           /* radius read OK */
17         const float PI = 3.1415926f;             /* internal constant */
18         float area, radius_check;               /* internal variables */
19
20         area = PI * radius * radius;              /* calculate area */
21         printf("radius = %f, area = %f", radius, area);
22         radius_check = sqrt(area / PI);          /* calculate radius */
23         printf(", radius check = %f \n", radius_check);
24         success_indicator = 0;                    /* return success */
25         }
26     return success_indicator;              /* return success/fail */
27 }
```

Program 11_2 Using an *if* and a compound statement

11.6 Nested *if* statements

The statements which make up the body of an if can be any C statement including other if statements. Program 11_3 (next page) reads an integer number and prints information indicating that an error occurred, or the number was zero, or greater than or less than zero. The layout of the three if statements (lines 10 to 15) was deliberately made quite complex with a number of else scattered around. Does the first else belong to the first or second if? The indentation of the code suggests the second but program layout means little to the compiler. In fact this is correct because the rule which C uses is that an else belongs to the closest preceding if which has no corresponding else, i.e.:

1   the first else belongs to the second if
2   the second else belongs to the third if
3   the third else belongs to the first if.

Program 11_3 is short and it is fairly easy to sort out the flow of the code. However, an if may contain quite long compound statements (see Section 11.5) and it could be very difficult to sort out the flow. Although one would use functions to break up a large section of code (see Chapter 16) a simple change in the program logic and layout can often improve the readability.

Program 11_3a is a modification of Program 11_3 with improved layout. The == test in line 10 of Program 11_3 has been replaced with != enabling the corresponding else to be moved up the code so that it immediately follows the if.

```
 1 /* Program 11_3 - read a number and test for zero, greater or less than zero */
 2
 3 #include <stdio.h>
 4
 5 int main(void)
 6 {
 7     int i;
 8
 9     printf("Please enter a number ? ");
10     if (scanf("%d", &i) == 1)                              /* read data */
11         if (i == 0) printf("value %d was zero \n", i);     /* OK test value */
12         else
13             if (i > 0) printf("value %d was greater than zero \n", i);
14             else       printf("value %d was less than zero \n", i);
15     else printf("\nData input error \a\n");                /* error ! */
16     return 0;
17 }
```

Program 11_3 Read a number and test for zero, greater or less than zero

```
 1 /* Program 11_3a - read a number and test for zero, greater or less than zero */
 2
 3 #include <stdio.h>
 4
 5 int main(void)
 6 {
 7     int i;
 8
 9     printf("Please enter a number ? ");
10     if (scanf("%d", &i) != 1)                              /* read data */
11         printf("\nData input error \a\n");                 /* error ! */
12     else
13         if (i == 0) printf("value %d was zero \n", i);     /* OK test value */
14         else
15             if (i > 0) printf("value %d was greater than zero \n", i);
16             else       printf("value %d was less than zero \n", i);
17     return 0;
18 }
```

Program 11_3a Restructured version of Program 11_3 (above)

The general rule that an else belongs to the first if above which has no corresponding else can be overridden by 'hiding' an if inside a compound statement, e.g.:

```
if (expression1)
    {
    if (expression2) statement2                    /* this if is 'hidden'*/
    }
else statement3                                    /* this else belongs to first if */
```

Although there are no hard and fast rules about the layout of if statements a general recommendation is that single statements (such as those in lines 10 and 11 of Program 11_1) are put on the same line as the if or else; this is to remind one to put in the enclosing braces {} when expanding a single statement into a compound statement, e.g. if expanding line 10 of Program 11_1 to read the number again if i was 0:

```
if (i == 0)
    printf("value was zero = %d\n");              /* these two statements */
    scanf("%d", &i);                              /* should be enclosed in {} */
else printf("value was non-zero = %d\n");
```

If there is insufficient room for a statement to fit on the same line as the if or else it may be enclosed in braces {} in case it is ever expanded. A compound statement should be indented to emphasise the logical structure of the code (lines 16 to 25 of Program 11_2). The position of the braces {} is not critical so long as one is consistent and the program code is readable (but placing them on separate lines makes them more visible). The use of 'extra' braces {} (or blank lines) around complex structures can also aid readability, i.e. {} which are not needed by the compiler to sort out the logic but aid the reader in grouping logical sections of code. In addition, good commenting helps, e.g. a note alongside an else showing the conditions which cause execution of the else statement.

Exercise 11.3 (*see Appendix B for sample answer*)

Amend Exercise 11.2 to check for invalid data entry and to print an appropriate message when an error occurs. Test with invalid characters and end of file as well as valid data.

11.7 The conditional operator ?

The conditional operator ? is a ternary operator (it has three operands) in which the operands are three expressions. It takes the following general form:

```
expression1 ? expression2 : expression3
```

First expression1 is evaluated and if it is:

true (non-zero) expression2 is evaluated and that is the value of the whole expression
false (zero)   expression3 is evaluated and that is the value of the whole expression

For example, consider the following if statement:

```
if (x >= 0)   z = cos(x);
else          z = sin(x);
```

This may be written:

```
z = (x >= 0) ? cos(x) : sin(x);
```

The conditional operator may be used in an expression just like any other operator. For example, consider a variable bit_value where the value of bit 0 is to be printed as a binary number (0 or 1). It may be written:

```
if ((bit_value & 1) == 0) putchar('0');
else                      putchar('1');
```

or `putchar((bit_value & 1) ? '1' : '0');`

or `putchar('0' + (bit_value & 1));`

In each case the *bitwise* & (AND, see Section 9.4) operator is used to test bit 0 (the function putchar writes a character to the output stream stdout).

Use the conditional operator with care; excessive use can lead to code which is difficult to follow and maintain. In general an if statement will be more readable, and sometimes a little more thought will give a more elegant solution.

Exercise 11.4 (*see Appendix B for sample answer*)

The tuition fees charged by a college are based on the type of course (arts, science or engineering based) and the mode of study (evening, day or full time), e.g.:

mode of study	arts	science	engineering
one evening per week	$350	$500	$650
one day per week	$1000	$1200	$1400
full time	$5000	$7000	$8000

Write a program (using nested if statements) which, given the course type (a character: a arts, s science and e engineering) and the mode (a character: e evening, d day and f full time), prints the course fee. Modify the program to use the conditional operator ?.

11.8 Using diagnostic aids in <assert.h>

The assert function in header file <assert.h> tests an expression and if it evaluates to zero (*false*) displays a message about the expression, the name of the source file and the line number in the file and then calls the abort function to terminate the program, e.g.:

```
#include <assert.h>
    fflush(0);                          /* flush output streams */
    assert(i == 10);                    /* test for error condition */
```

if the value of i was *not* 10 the above would display a message of the form:

```
Assertion fail: i == 10, file x.c, line 5
Abnormal program termination
```

Remember that assert displays the message if the expression evaluates to zero (*false*) ! It is useful in identifying the file (and the line in the file) where an error occurrs, see line 18 of file stack2.c in Section 25.2. It is a good idea to call fflush to flush the output streams otherwise output may be lost when the program aborts. The debugging can be turned off (e.g. in a fully tested program) by defining the identifier NDEBUG *before* including <assert.h>, e.g. #define NDEBUG (note that the expression in assert will not be evaluated).

Problem for Chapter 11

Problem 2 for Chapter 8 found the roots of the quadratic equation. Extend the program to check for complex roots, i.e. if $(b^2 - 4ac) < 0$ evaluate and print the real and imaginary components of the complex roots. For example, try the following data:

```
a = 2.0     b = -6.0     c = 4.0     real roots = 2.0 and 1.0
a = 61.0    b = 159.0    c = 87.0    real roots = -0.781449 and -1.825108
a = 1.0     b = 2.0      c = 5.0     complex roots = -1.0 ± i2.00
a = 61.0    b = 2.0      c = 87.0    complex roots = -0.016393 ± i1.194136
a = 1.0     b = 0.0      c = 1.0     complex roots = ± i1.0
a = 10.0    b = 99.0     c = 98.0    real roots = -1.115616 and -8.784384
```

12

The *while* and *do* statements

12.1 The *while* statement

The *while* (and *do*, see next section) statement enables a sequence of statements to be executed a number of times depending upon the value, *true* or *false*, of some expression.

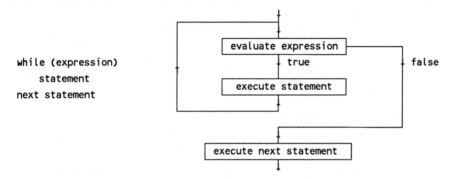

```
while (expression)
    statement
next statement
```

In the while loop the statement is executed while expression is true (non-zero), i.e.:

1   expression is evaluated
2   if the result of expression is

     true   (non-zero) statement is executed and then control returns to step 1
   or *false*   (zero) the while terminates and execution continues with next statement.

If, on entry to the while, the expression is *false* (zero) the statement is never executed.

The interest on a given capital sum over a one-year period may be calculated using the following relationship:

```
interest = capital * interest_rate
```

Program 12_1 (next page), given the interest rate per year, works out the number of years required to double a capital sum invested. The variable capital is initialised to 1.0f (line 7), the % interest rate read (line 10) and then the number of years required to double capital evaluated using the while statement (lines 11 to 15):

```
while (capital < 2.0f)          /* loop while capital < two times original */
    {
    capital = capital + capital * rate / 100.0f;     /* new capital */
    years++;                                /* increment years */
    }
```

while the value of capital is less than 2.0f the compound statement is executed adding one year's interest to capital and incrementing years. When capital has (at least) doubled the while terminates and the results printed. A run gave:

```
Enter % interest rate (integer) ? 8↲
 after 10 years, capital is 2.16 times original
```

```
 1 /* Program 12_1  for given interest rate work out time to double capital */
 2 #include <stdio.h>
 3
 4 int main(void)
 5 {
 6     int rate, years = 0;                         /* local variables */
 7     float capital = 1.0f;                        /* start capital at 1.0 */
 8
 9     printf("Enter %% interest rate (integer) ? ");          /* prompt user */
10     scanf("%d", &rate);                          /* read interest rate */
11     while (capital < 2.0f)        /* loop while capital < two times original */
12         {
13         capital = capital + capital * rate / 100.0f;      /* new capital */
14         years++;                                 /* increment years */
15         }
16     printf(" after %d years, capital is %.2f times original\n", years, capital);
17     return 0;
18 }
```

Program 12_1 For given interest rate work out number of years to double capital

The sequence of statements in Program 12_1 is:

6-7   define variables rate, years (initialised to 0) and capital (initialised to 1.0f)
9-10   prompt user for input and read an integer into variable rate
11-15   a while statement executed while capital < 2.0f
            13-14 add a years interest capital * rate / 100.0f to capital and increment years
16   print years and the increase in the value of capital.

Exercise 12.1 (*see Appendix B for sample answer*)

Economists, when discussing inflation, quote the *rule of 72*, which states that the period in which a fixed sum of money will decline to half its value is 72 / inflation_rate. Write a program which, given the yearly inflation_rate, calculates the number of years for a fixed sum to halve in value and compare the result with the value given by the *rule of 72*.

12.1.1 Program to calculate the average of a sequence of real numbers

Program 12_2 reads a sequence of real numbers from stdin until an error or *end of file* occurs, then it calculates the average value of the numbers entered. The program is essentially a while statement which attempts to read a real number using scanf:

```
while (scanf("%f", &x) == 1)                     /* read a real number */
    {
    number++;                             /* increment number of values read */
    sum = sum + x;                        /* add value to sum so far */
    }
average = sum / number;
```

In the while statement scanf("%f", &x) attempts to read a real number from stdin into x. After the read operation the while tests the function result returned by scanf:

1   the read was successful; number is incremented and x added to the sum
0   the read failed (error or eof); the while terminates and average is calculated.

```
 1 /* Program 12_2, loop reading real numbers until error (or eof)          */
 2 /*                  then calculate the average value of the number entered */
 3
 4 #include <stdio.h>                              /* standard stream I/O library */
 5
 6 int main(void)
 7 {
 8     int number = 0;                              /* number of values read */
 9     float x,                                     /* current value read */
10          sum = 0.0f,                        /* sum of values initialised to 0 */
11          average;                               /* average of the values */
12
13     printf("enter a series of real numbers (terminate with eof) ? ");
14     /* loop reading numbers until error or eof */
15     while (scanf("%f", &x) == 1)                 /* read a real number */
16         {
17         number++;                        /* increment number of values read */
18         sum = sum + x;                        /* add value to sum so far */
19         }
20
21     /* input complete, calculate average and print results */
22     average = sum / number;
23     printf("%d numbers entered, average = %f\n", number, average);
24     return 0;
25 }
```

Program 12_2 Read numbers until error or eof occurs then calculate the average

The sequence of statements in Program 12_2 is:

8   define number, an int which holds the number of values read (initialised to 0)
9   define x, a float which will hold the real numbers read from stdin
10   define sum, a float which will hold the sum of the numbers read (initialised to 0)
11   define average, a float which will hold the average of the numbers read
13   prompt user to enter real numbers terminated with end of file
15-19   loops while scanf returns 1 (one sucessful conversion)
        15 read a real number from stdin into x, terminate while if read fails
        17 number++ increment number (count of numbers read)
        18 sum = sum + x add latest number read to sum calculated so far
22   average = sum / number calculate average of the numbers entered
23   print the number of values read and their average value.

A run of Program 12_2 on an IBM PC compatible under Turbo C V3.00 was (user input in bold, end of file is CTRL/Z followed by newline - shown as ˇz ↲):

```
enter a series of real numbers (terminate with eof) ? 1 2 3 4 5 6ˇz↲
6 numbers entered, average = 3.500000
```

Exercise 12.2 (*see Appendix B for sample answer*)

Extend Program 12_2 to calculate the standard deviation of the numbers entered, i.e.:

$$\text{standard deviation} = \left(\sum_{i=1}^{n} x_i^2 \, / \, n \; - \; \left(\sum_{i=1}^{n} x_i \, / \, n \right)^2 \right)^{\frac{1}{2}}$$

where x_i are the values entered and n is the number of values entered, e.g. if x_i is 12, 6, 7, 3, 15, 10, 18 and 5 the average would be 9.5 and the standard deviation 4.87.

12.2 The *do* statement

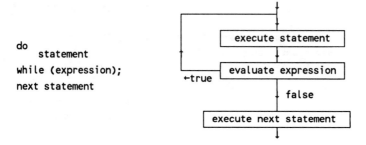

```
do
    statement
while (expression);
next statement
```

The sequence of events in the do statement is:

1   statement is executed
2   expression is evaluated
3   if the result of expression is
          true   (non-zero) then control returns to step 1
     or   false   (zero) the do terminates and execution continues with next statement.

Thus statement is executed at least once (in a while statement, the statement is never executed if expression is false (zero) on entry). Note the ; on the end of the do statement, it is required to terminate the statement.

A while or do statement is chosen to suit the algorithm, in particular whether it is natural to test before or after executing statement for the first time. For example, if the evaluation of statement produces something used in expression the do would be the natural choice, e.g. in the summation of the sine series (see Chapter 27). Consider a situation where a stream of numbers is read and processed by a function process_data and the sequence is terminated by a 0 value. It may be implemented as a while or a do statement:

```
scanf("%d", &data);              do
while (data != 0)                {
    {                                scanf("%d", &data);
    process_data(data);              process_data(data);
    scanf("%d", &data);              }
    }                            while (data != 0);
```

The difference between these is that the terminating 0 is not processed in the while whereas it is in the do. This seems inconsequential but could have a major effect if the terminating 0 was or was not part of the data stream to be processed by process_data.

12.2.1 Program to evaluate the *epsilon* of a real type

Chapter 8, which introduced real number types, discussed the number of digits of precision and the value *epsilon* which is specified thus:

```
1.0 + epsilon != 1.0
```

The value of *epsilon* is the smallest number which, when added to the value 1.0, changes the value, i.e. adding any smaller value to 1.0 still gives 1.0. A pseudo-code version of the algorithm often used to calculate the values of *epsilon* defined in <float.h> is:

```
epsilon = 1.0
do
      epsilon = epsilon / 2.0
while ( 1.0 + epsilon != 1.0 )
epsilon = 2.0 * epsilon
```

The value of *epsilon* is initialised to 1.0 then a do loop executed. On each iteration of the loop epsilon is divided by 2.0 and the expression 1.0 + epsilon != 1.0 tested, i.e.:

if   1.0 + epsilon is not equal to 1.0 the do continues
else   the do terminates (if 1.0 + epsilon equals 1.0).

When the do terminates the value of *epsilon* is the value before the last division. In fact the algorithm only yields an approximate value with the true value lying between epsilon and epsilon / 2: see Exercise 12.3.

```
 1|/* Program 12_3 - determine epsilon precision of float type        */
 2|/*         i.e. smallest number epsilon such that 1.0 + epsilon != 1.0    */
 3|
 4|#include <stdio.h>                              /* standard stream I/O library */
 5|#include <float.h>                                /* float types header */
 6|
 7|int main(void)
 8|{
 9|    float epsilon = 1.0f;
10|
11|    printf(" float epsilon from <float.h> = %g\n", FLT_EPSILON);
12|    do
13|        epsilon = epsilon / 2.0f;
14|    while ((1.0f + epsilon) != 1.0f);
15|    printf(" float epsilon calculated    = %g\n", epsilon * 2.0f);
16|    return 0;
17|}
```

Program 12_3 Determine the epsilon of the float type

Program 12_3 uses the above algorithm to determine the epsilon of the float type and prints the result together with the epsilon from <float.h>. A run on an IBM PC compatible using Turbo C V3.00 and GNU C (under MS-DOS and LINUX) was:

```
float epsilon from <float.h> = 1.19209e-07
float epsilon calculated     = 1.0842e-19
```

The calculated value of float epsilon is nothing like that specified in <float.h>; in fact it is the value of epsilon for the long double type, see Table 8.1. What has happened is that the compiler has optimised the code and the (1.0f + epsilon) != 1.0f comparison is being carried out in the floating point processor using long double precision.

Program 12_4 (below) attempts to get around the problem found with Program 12_3 by using variables to hold intermediate values, i.e. the float variable test is used in the comparison (test != 1.0f) which *should* therefore be carried out to float precision. A run of Program 12_4 on an IBM PC compatible using Turbo C V3.00 and GNU C gave:

```
float epsilon from <float.h> = 1.19209e-07
float epsilon calculated    = 1.19209e-07
```

Even Program 12_4 may not always give the correct result, e.g. when compiled using the GNU C V2.6.3 compiler with the optimise flag -O set the result was:

```
float epsilon from <float.h> = 1.19209e-07
float epsilon calculated    = 1.0842e-19
```

When optimising loops, compilers will attempt to hold variables used within the loop in processor registers (to reduce traffic to/from memory and speed up processing). Thus the calculations in the loop could still be carried out in long double and the results copied to the float variables in memory when the loop terminates.

It is possible that the local variables of compound statements may not exist in memory at all! The variables may be created in the processor registers on entry to the compound statement, used as required and discarded on exit (never being saved into memory at all). This is particularly true for RISC (Reduced Instruction Set Computers) which have a large number of processor registers. Compilers usually allow the level of optimisation to be selected; optimising code increases compilation time but can reduce execution time.

```
 1 /* Program 12_4 - determine epsilon precision of float type      */
 2 /*    i.e. smallest number epsilon such that 1.0 + epsilon != 1.0 */
 3 /*    this algorithm attempts to force the use of variables in memory */
 4 /*    it may still be optimised so switch off compiler optimising */
 5
 6 #include <stdio.h>                           /* standard stream I/O library */
 7 #include <float.h>                           /* float types header */
 8
 9 int main(void)
10 {
11     float test, epsilon, new_epsilon = 1.0f;
12
13     printf("  float epsilon from <float.h> = %g\n", FLT_EPSILON);
14     do
15         {
16         epsilon = new_epsilon;               /* save last working epsilon */
17         new_epsilon = new_epsilon / 2.0f;    /* calculate next epsilon */
18         test = 1.0f + new_epsilon;           /* calculate test value */
19         }
20     while (test != 1.0f);                     /* exit if 1.0 + new_epsilon = 1.0 */
21     printf("  float epsilon calculated    = %g\n", epsilon);
22     return 0;
23 }
```

Program 12_4 Determine the epsilon of the float type

Exercise 12.3 (*see Appendix B for sample answer*)

The algorithm of Program 12_3/4 yields an approximate value of *epsilon* which is sufficient for most applications (it is often used to calculate the values given in <float.h>). In the case of Program 12_4 the true value lies between new_epsilon and epsilon on exit from the do, i.e.:

```
new_epsilon + 1.0f    was equal to 1.0 and the do terminated
epsilon + 1.0f        was not equal to 1.0 and the do continued.
```

Modify Program 12_4 to evaluate a better value of *epsilon*. A suitable algorithm is:

```
new_epsilon = 1.0
divisor = 1.0
do
    do
        epsilon = new_epsilon
        new_epsilon = new_epsilon / (1.0 + divisor)
        test = 1.0 + new_epsilon
    while ( test != 1.0 )
    new_epsilon = epsilon
    divisor = divisor / 2.0
while (divisor > 1.0e-5)
```

In Program 12_4 epsilon was divided by the constant 2.0f on each iteration of the do. In the above algorithm epsilon is divided by 2.0 on the first pass through the inner do loop (1.0 + divisor); when the do terminates the value of epsilon will be as Program 12_4. The variable divisor is then divided by 2.0 and the inner do loop repeated. This process continues, with epsilon approaching the true value on each iteration, until divisor <= 1.0e-5 when the outer do loop terminates. A run of the modified program on an IBM PC compatible under Turbo C and GNU C V2.6.3 gave:

```
float epsilon from <float.h> = 1.19209e-07
float epsilon calculated     = 5.96056e-08
```

12.3 The *null* or empty statement

The *null* or empty statement takes the form:

```
;                                              /* null statement */
```

Often time delays are required during program execution, e.g. to display a message on the screen for ten seconds and then continue. In Program 12_5 a delay of ten seconds is generated using the function clock() from library <time.h> (see Appendix C.15). Function clock() returns the number of processor clock 'ticks' since the start of program execution. The header <time.h> contains the symbolic constant CLOCKS_PER_SEC which defines the number of processor clock 'ticks' per second. The program sequence is:

8   declare clock_start to be of type clock_t (the type returned by the function clock)
11   assign the current time to variable clock_start
12-13   a while statement which loops for ten seconds, i.e. the following calculates the
         number of seconds since the value of clock_start was assigned (in line 11):
              (clock() - clock_start) / CLOCKS_PER_SEC
         When ten seconds have elapsed the while terminates.

Note that the body of the while statement (line 13) is a *null statement* which is on a separate line and commented so that it is clearly visible. If the ; was put on the end of the while (in line 12) it may be missed when reading the program and the code on following lines thought to be under the control of the while. The function clock() is very useful for timing events independently of the processor speed, e.g. see timing the execution speed of function and macro versions of a function in Program 16_5 in Section 16.13.

```
 1 /* Program 12_5 - a ten second time delay using library routines */
 2
 3 #include <stdio.h>
 4 #include <time.h>
 5
 6 int main(void)
 7 {
 8     clock_t  clock_start;                      /* holds clock start time */
 9
10     printf("\ndelay ten seconds using library routine clock()/n");
11     clock_start = clock();
12     while (((clock() - clock_start) / CLOCKS_PER_SEC) < 10)
13         /* null statement */ ;
14     putchar('\a');
15     return 0;
16 }
```

Program 12_5 Program to delay ten seconds and sound the alarm

12.4 Infinite loops

It is sometimes necessary to lock the program into an infinite loop. For example, in a control system the program may loop continuously, reading control values and taking actions. In such a situation the program cannot stop itself, this is done externally by an operating system killing the process (e.g. CTRL/C or CTRL/Q key under UNIX or ALT/ESC under Windows 95 and OS/2 to display the *process list* then *close* the process) or by using a hardware reset button to reboot the computer. Infinite loops may be achieved in a number of ways (the for statement will be discussed in Chapter 13):

```
while (1)                do                      for (;;)
    statement                statement               statement
                         while (1);
```

In the above statement is executed until the program is stopped by some external agency (e.g. hardware reset). If the condition is omitted (as in the for) it is assumed to be true.

Problem for Chapter 12

Use the time of day functions from <time.h> to display the time on the screen (see compiler manuals or on-line help for details). Update the time display every second and ring the alarm every ten seconds. If cursor control functions are available (e.g. from <graph.h> under Microsoft C and <conio.h> under Turbo C) display the time in the centre of the screen. A problem for Chapter 15 is to draw a clock face (with second, minute and hour hands) on the screen updating it every second.

13

The *for* statement

13.1 The *for* statement

A common program requirement is to have a loop in which a control variable is incremented from an initial value to a terminal value with some statement being evaluated on each iteration. A for statement is ideal for this purpose, although it is far more flexible, being a shorthand way of writing a while statement.

```
for (expression1; expression2; expression3)
    statement
next statement
```

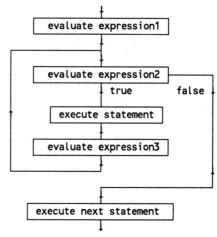

The sequence of events in the for statement is:

1   expression1 is evaluated
2   expression2 is evaluated
3   if the result of expression2 is
            true   statement is executed followed by expression3 then control returns to step 2
     or   *false*   the for terminates and execution continues with next statement.

Hence the above for statement can be considered equivalent to:

```
expression1;
while (expression2)
    {
    statement
    expression3;
    }
next statement
```

The complexity of the algorithm will determine whether a for or a while is most suitable. The general recommendation is that once the for (expression1; expression2; expression3) structure is longer than a single line a while should be used. Otherwise the for(.....) could spread over several lines, leading to unreadable code (this is particularly the case when the sequence operator , (comma) is used, see Section 13.3).

13.2 Program to evaluate capital growth at a given interest rate

```
 1 /* Program 13_1 - capital growth over time at a given interest rate         */
 2
 3 #include <stdio.h>
 4
 5 int main(void)
 6 {
 7     int years, rate, input;              /* years, interest rate and scanf result */
 8
 9     printf("\nEnter %% interest rate and years (integers) ? ");     /* prompt */
10     input = scanf("%d%d", &rate, &years);           /* read two integer numbers */
11     while(input != EOF)                              /* if EOF terminate */
12         {
13         /* if scanf reports an error read faulty character and print message */
14         if (input != 2)
15             printf("\a illegal character '%c', try again ?", getchar());
16         else
17             {                               /* read OK, calculate growth */
18             float capital = 1000;           /* assume capital of $1000 */
19             int year;                       /* for loop counter */
20
21             for (year = 1; year <= years; year++)          /* loop for years */
22                 {
23                 float interest = capital * rate / 100.f;
24                 capital = capital + interest;
25                 printf("    year = %d, interest = %6.2f, capital = %7.2f\n",
26                         year, interest, capital);
27                 }
28             printf("  After %d years at %d%%, capital = $%.2f, growth = %.2f%%",
29                     years, rate, capital, 0.1f * (capital - 1000.0f));
30             }
31         printf("\nEnter %% interest rate and years (integers) ? ");  /* prompt */
32         input = scanf("%d%d", &rate, &years);       /* read two integer numbers */
33         }
34     return 0;
35 }
```

Program 13_1 Capital growth over time period at a given interest rate

The interest on a given capital sum over a one-year period may be calculated:

```
    interest = capital * interest_rate
```

Program 13_1 evaluates, for a given interest rate, the capital growth of $1000 over a period of years. When data is read it should be verified and if an error occurs appropriate action taken (more discussion in Section 15.1). Program 13_1 verifies its input in two ways:

1   If *end of file* is entered the program terminates.
2   If scanf("%d%d", &rate, &years) fails to read two integers an error message is displayed (the character in error is extracted from stdin) and the read attempted again.

In Program 13_1 lines 11 to 33 are a while which attempts to read numbers into variables rate and years and terminates when *end of file* is entered. The program sequence is:

7   define local variables `years`, `rate` and `input`

9-10   prompt the user and attempt to read integer numbers into `rate` and `years`

              in the `printf` control string the `%%` conversion specification prints a single `%`

11-33   `while(input != EOF)` a `while` executed until `EOF` is entered

                 if the value returned by `scanf` was `EOF` (*end of file*) the `while` is terminated

          14-15   `if (input != 2)` test if error occurred on read; if so

                   15   print error message together with the character in error

                       `getchar()` reads the next character and returns it as an `int`

       else

          17-30   a compound statement which evaluates the capital growth

                18-19   local variables `capital` (initialised to $1000) and `year`

                21-27   a `for` statement, increments `year` from 1 to `years`

                   23   define local variable `interest` and calculate it

                   24   add the `interest` to the `capital`

                   25-26   print the `year`, `interest` and `capital`

                28-29   print `years`, % interest rate, capital and % growth rate

         31-32   prompt the user to enter a number and attempt to read the value into `rate`

         33   this is the end of the `while` statement started in line 11.

Consider lines 21 to 27:

```
for (year = 1; year <= years; year++)              /* loop for years */
   {
   float interest = capital * rate / 100.f;    /* interest for the year */
   capital = capital + interest;                    /* update capital */
   printf("   year = %d, interest = %6.2f, capital = %7.2f\n",
             year, interest, capital);
   }
```

This is a shorthand way of writing the following `while` statement:

```
year = 1;                                     /* initialise year to 1 */
while (year <= years)                              /* loop for years */
   {
   float interest = capital * rate / 100.f;    /* interest for the year */
   capital = capital + interest;                    /* update capital */
   printf("   year = %d, interest = %6.2f, capital = %7.2f\n",
             year, interest, capital);
   year = year + 1;                               /* increment year */
   }
```

The variable `year` is incremented from 1 to `years` and on each iteration the year's interest is calculated and added to the capital, i.e.:

1   `year` is initialised to 1

2   if `year` is > `years` the `for` or `while` terminates

3   the interest is calculated, added to the capital and the results printed

4   `year` is incremented.

Therefore Program 13_1 could have been written using a `while` instead of a `for`. In practice the precise coding used would be selected using various criteria, e.g. speed, accuracy, clarity, etc. Unless code is time critical it is better to make the code slightly longer if it is easier to read and understand.

A run of Program 13_1 gave:

```
Enter % interest rate and years (integers) ? t↲
 illegal character 't', try again ?
Enter % interest rate and years (integers) ? 8 4↲
    year = 1, interest =  80.00, capital = 1080.00
    year = 2, interest =  86.40, capital = 1166.40
    year = 3, interest =  93.31, capital = 1259.71
    year = 4, interest = 100.78, capital = 1360.49
 After 4 years at 8%, capital = $1360.49, growth = 36.05%
Enter % interest rate and years (integers) ? 10 6↲
    year = 1, interest = 100.00, capital = 1100.00
    year = 2, interest = 110.00, capital = 1210.00
    year = 3, interest = 121.00, capital = 1331.00
    year = 4, interest = 133.10, capital = 1464.10
    year = 5, interest = 146.41, capital = 1610.51
    year = 6, interest = 161.05, capital = 1771.56
 After 6 years at 10%, capital = $1771.56, growth = 77.16%
Enter % interest rate and years (integers) ? ¯z↲
```

Exercise 13.1 (*see Appendix B for sample answer*)

(a) A machine in a factory depreciates in value over time. Implement a program which, given the cost of a machine and the % yearly depreciation rate, prints the value of the machine at the end of each year for a five-year period. At the end of five years print the total % depreciation.

(b) Write a program, using nested for statements, to display the following pattern:

```
*
***
*****
*******
*********
***********
```

13.3 The sequence operator , (comma)

The , (comma) or sequence operator is a binary operator which has the lowest precedence and associates from left to right:

    expression1 , expression2

first (a) expression1 is evaluated,
then (b) expression2 is evaluated,
and (c) the overall expression has the value and type of the right hand operand.

Thus a new expression may be formed from a sequence of other expressions separated by the , (comma) operator:

    expression , expression , expression , expression , expression , expression
        →   ↑
    order of evaluation   value of whole expression

The expressions are evaluated from left to right and the type and value of the whole expression is the type and value of the right-most one. A common use for the comma operator is in while and for statements:

```
for (expression1; expression2; expression3)
    statement
```

The expressions expression1, expression2, expression3 may be sequences of expressions separated by the comma operator, e.g. consider the following for statement where the characters up and down are initialised to 'a' and 'z' respectively and then incremented and decremented:

```
char up, down;
for (up = 'a', down = 'z'; up < down; up++, down--)
    printf(" %c %c", up, down);
```

This for statement:

(a) increments up from 'a' and decrements down from 'z'

(b) terminates when up => down

(c) increments up and decrements down on each iteration.

For this to work the character codes of the alphabet a to z must be contiguous (as in ASCII). For example, a run on an IBM PC compatible gave:

```
a z b y c x d w e v f u g t h s i r j q k p l o m n
```

If the comma operator is used in a place where confusion may occur enclose the expression in brackets, e.g. convert angle from degrees to radians and print cos(angle):

```
angle = 3.14159f * angle /180.0f;
printf("%f\n", cos(angle));
```

could be written (less clearly):

```
printf("%f\n", (angle = 3.14159f * angle /180.0f, cos(angle)));
```

printf is called with two parameters (not three):

(a) the variable angle is assigned the value 3.14159f * angle /180.0f,

then (b) cos(angle) is evaluated,

and (c) the result of (b) is the overall result of the expression and this value is printed.

At each , operator is a *sequence point* where the preceding expression, including possible side effects, will have been fully evaluated (see Section 18.8). It should be emphasised that the vast majority of commas in programs are not comma operators, i.e. the commas used to separate variable names in definitions and expressions in the parameter list of a function. The general recommendation is to use the comma operator very sparingly and only in situations where it fits naturally and simplifies the code. Extensive use of comma operators in for statements that stretch over many lines leads to unreadable code.

13.4 Program to evaluate the factorial of an integer number

Program 13_2 (next page) evaluates the factorial of a positive integer number, i.e.:

N! = N * (N -1) * (N - 2) 1   N > 0 (0! = 1)

Program 13_1 verified data input by checking the function result returned by scanf for *end of file* or conversion failure. In addition to this, in line 18, Program 13_2 verifies that the number entered is >= 0 and if not an error message is displayed and the read attempted again, i.e. factorial cannot be calculated if the number is less than 0 (note that 0! = 1).

```
 1 /* Program 13_2 - Calculate the factorial of an integer number, i.e.     */
 2 /*     N! = N * (N -1) * (N - 2) ..... 1                                   */
 3
 4 #include <stdio.h>
 5
 6 int main(void)
 7 {
 8     int n, input;                      /* holds number and value returned by scanf */
 9
10     /* prompt user,  read an integer number, if EOF terminate */
11     while (printf("\nnumber >= 0 ? "), (input = scanf("%d", &n)) != EOF)
12     {
13       if (input != 1)                               /* error during read ? */
14           /* read faulty character and print message  */
15           printf("\a illegal character '%c', try again ?", getchar());
16       else
17           /* number read, if < 0 display message else calculate N! */
18           if (n < 0)  printf("\a Number %d < 0, try again ?", n);
19           else
20             {                                      /* number is OK */
21               /* calculate factorial by incrementing i from 1 to n */
22               int i;                          /* loop control variable */
23               int factorial_n = 1;            /* initialise N! to 1 */
24               for (i = 2; i <= n; i++)           /* loop i = 2 to n */
25                   factorial_n = factorial_n * i;   /* N! = N * (N-1)! * .. */
26               printf("  factorial %d = %d", n, factorial_n);
27             }
28     }
29     return 0;
30 }
```

Program 13_2 Evaluate the factorial of an integer number

If the number entered is >= 0 lines 23 to 25 evaluate the factorial:

```
    int factorial_n = 1;                      /* initialise N! to 1 */
    for (i = 2; i <= n; i++)                   /* loop i = 2 to n */
        factorial_n = factorial_n * i;        /* N! = N * (N-1)! * .. */
```

This is a shorthand way of writing the following while statement:

```
    int factorial_n = 1;                      /* initialise N! to 1 */
    i = 2;
    while(i <= n)
        {
        factorial_n = factorial_n * i;        /* N! = N * (N-1)! * .. */
        i = i + 1;                            /* increment i */
        }
```

The variable i is incremented from 2 to n (if n is less than 2 the while will terminate immediatly with n! = 1) and on each iteration the next term of the series is calculated:

1   `factorial_n` is initialised to 1
2   `i` is initialised to 2 (there is no need to multiply `factorial_n` by 1)
3   if `i` is > `n` the `for` or `while` terminates
4   the value of the next term of N! is calculated
5   `i` is incremented

Note that the factorial algorithm (lines 22 to 26) could have been written thus (in file c13\p13_3.c on the disk which accompanies this text):

```
long int factorial_n = 1;                       /* holds N!, assume 0! or 1! */
/* calculate factorial by decrementing n to 1  */
while (n > 1)
    factorial_n = factorial_n * n--;            /* N! = N * (N-1)! * .. */
```

in which `factorial_n` is initialised to 1 and `n` is decremented to 1 (this will still work for 0! and 1! but has the problem that the value of `n` is lost).

Care must be taken to ensure that the result of calculations does not exceed the range of the variables, e.g. a run of Program 13_2 using Turbo C on an IBM PC compatible:

```
number > 0 ? t↵
 illegal character 't', try again ?
number > 0 ? -3↵
 Number -3 < 0, try again ?
number > 0 ? 1↵
  factorial 1 = 1
number > 0 ? 3↵
  factorial 3 = 6
number > 0 ? 7↵
  factorial 7 = 5040
number > 0 ? 8↵
  factorial 8 = -25216
number > 0 ? ˆz↵
```

The value of 8! is 40320 yet the above run gave -25216; under Turbo C the type `int` is a signed 16-bit number with a maximum positive value 32767. Even if a 32-bit `long int` is used the program then fails when `n > 16` (see Program 13_3 in file c13\p13_3.c on the disk). In practice a `float` would probably be used.

Section 13.3 introduced the comma or sequence operator. Program 13_2 makes use of the comma operator in line 11:

```
while (printf("\nnumber >= 0 ? "), (input = scanf("%d", &n)) != EOF)
```

The expression `printf("\nnumber >= 0 ? "), (input = scanf("%d", &n)) != EOF` consists of two sub-expressions evaluated as follows:

(a) `printf("\nnumber >= 0 ? ")` prints a prompt on the screen

then   (b) `(input = scanf("%d", &n)) != EOF`

(i) `scanf` attempts to read an integer from `stdin` into variable `n`

(ii) the number of successful conversion is assigned to variable `input`

(iii) this value is compared with `EOF` using the `!=` operator.

The result of the comparison in (b) (iii) is the result of the whole expression and controls the `while`, i.e. when `scanf` returns `EOF` the `while` terminates.

Thus the five statements in Program 13_1 which prompt the user, read the numbers and test for *eof* (lines 9 to 11 and 31 to 32) have been reduced to a single statement in

Program 13_2 (line 11) which, although more efficient in terms of the code generated, is less easy to understand. Note the parentheses in the expression in line 11:

    (input = scanf("%d", &n)) != EOF

If the line had been written:

    input = scanf("%d", &n) != EOF

the program would not work. The relational operator != has a higher priority than the assignment operator = therefore the order of evaluation would be:

    input = (scanf("%d", &n) != EOF)

The expression scanf("%d", &n) != EOF compares the value returned by scanf with EOF. The result of the comparison (1 or 0) would then be assigned to input.

Exercise 13.2 (*see Appendix B for sample answer*)

A prime number is greater than 1 and is divisible only by itself and 1, e.g. 2 3 5 7 11 13 17 19 23 29 31 37 41 43 47 53 59 61 67 etc. Implement and test a program to find and print prime numbers up to 100.

Problem for Chapter 13

1 Implement and test a program, using a *for* loop, to evaluate the sine series:

$$sin(x) = x - \frac{x^3}{3!} + \frac{x^5}{5!} - \frac{x^7}{7!} + \frac{x^9}{9!} \cdots\cdots \qquad x^2 < \infty$$

The number of iterations should be entered from the keyboard together with value of x. Print your answer together with that from the sin function in <math.h>. Comment on the effect of the number of iterations and large values of x (this is discussed in Chapter 27).

2 Implement programs to draw the following patterns on the display screen:

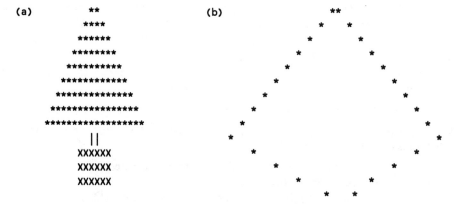

14

Further control statements

The vast majority of control structures required in program implementation can be satisfied by the if, while, do and for statements covered in the previous chapters. This chapter will describe some control statements which can be very useful in particular circumstances.

14.1 The *continue* statement

The continue statement is used within while, do and for statements. Executing a continue starts the next iteration of the smallest enclosing while, do or for. For example, if a condition occurs where the remaining statements of a loop are to be skipped and execution continued with the next loop, e.g.:

```
while (i < 10)
    {
    ......
    if (x == 0) continue;
    ......                              /* statements skipped if x is 0 */
    }
```

which could be better written:

```
while (i < 10)
    {
    ......
    if (x != 0)
        {
        ......                          /* statements executed if x is not 0 */
        }
    }
```

Use continue with care and only after consideration of alternatives (such as that shown above). If used, comment it clearly otherwise it may be missed when reading the code.

14.2 The *break* statement

The break statement is used within while, do, for and switch (see Section 14.4) statements. Executing a break terminates the statement and transfers control to the statement immediately following the body of the while, do, for or switch. For example, if an error condition occurs and the execution of a loop is to be aborted, e.g.:

```
while (i < 10)
    {
    ......
    if ((conv = scanf("%d", &x)) == EOF) break;        /* abort loop on EOF */
    ......
    }
```

Again use break with great care and comment it clearly.

14.3 The *goto* statement

The goto statement takes the following general form:

    goto label;

Control is transferred to the statement labelled with the name label, e.g.:

    label: statement

A label is an identifier followed by a colon. The identifier only exists within the body of the particular function (Chapter 16 discusses functions) so the same name can be used in different functions. Labels have *function scope* in that they may be used anywhere in the function in which they are declared (scope is discussed in Chapter 17) and have their own *name space* so the same name can be used for labels, variables and function names (not recommended as the same name used for different things can cause confusion).

Reliance on goto statements will lead to unstructured and unreadable code. There are, however, rare situations where the use of a goto will simplify the overall structure of a program. For example, consider a program which consists of a number of nested loops where an error condition within the innermost loop should abort all the loops (a break would only abort the loop containing the break):

```
while (.....)
  {
  while (.....)
     {
     .....
     if ((conv = scanf("%d", &x)) == EOF) goto abort;     /* abort on EOF */
     ......
     }
  ......
  }
......
abort: ....                                               /* come here on EOF */
......
```

It is possible to transfer into a *compound statement* but not in such a way to bypass the initialisation of variables. In practice goto should only be used after careful consideration of the alternatives, e.g. could a different structure avoid the use of goto?

14.4 The *switch* statement

A common programming requirement is to select one of a sequence of statements depending upon the value of some integer variable, e.g.:

```
if (i == 1) statement1
else
    if (i == 2) statement2
    else
        if (i == 3) statement3
        ....
        else
            if (i == 4) statement4
            ....
            else default_statement
```

The switch statement provides a more elegant means of carrying out such a selection:

```
switch (expression)
    {
    case constant1: statement1
    case constant2: statement2
    case constant3: statement3
    ......
    default: default_statement
    }
```

where expression should evaluate to an integral value (using a cast if necessary) and constant1, constant2, etc. should be integral constant expressions, i.e. which evaluate to an integral constant at compile time. The switch statement operates as follows:

evaluate expression and if its value equals:

    constant1 execution continues with the statement following the associated case label

    constant2 execution continues with the statement following the associated case label

    constant3 execution continues with the statement following the associated case label

      etc.

else

    the default is executed (if it does not exist the switch automatically terminates and execution continues with the next statement).

Notes:

1   The expression is used to select an entry point into the body of the switch statement. When a case label is selected all the following statements will be executed in turn (including the default) unless the break statement is used to terminate the switch.

2   The case labels do not have to appear in any order.

3   Several labels can be in front of a single statement, e.g. case 1: case 2: statement.

4   Several statements can be placed after a label (it need not be a compound statement).

5   The default label can be placed anywhere (but it is good practice to put it last).

In Program 14_1 (next page) switch is used to select the execution of a group of statements via a command character read from the keyboard. The program sequence is:

10-21   a while which prompts the user for input and reads the command character ch
             the while terminates on *end of file* (when scanf returns EOF)

11-21   a switch statement which selects statements to execute under the control of ch

      13-15   executed if ch == 'r', reads a new value into data

      16-17   executed if ch == 'p', prints the value of data

      18-19   executed if ch == 'c', multiplies data by 10

      20   else **default** prints a message indicating invalid character

22-23   terminates the program if *end of file* was entered.

The break statements terminate the switch after the statement(s) associated with a particular command have been executed. For example, if the break statement in line 15 had been omitted and 'r' was entered lines 13, 14 and 16 would be executed in turn until the break in line 17 terminates the switch. Missing break statements are a common fault in switch statements. Note the use of the comma operator in line 10 (which is similar to its use in Program 13_2):

```
    while (printf("\nCommand ? "), scanf(" %c", &ch) != EOF)      /* read ch */
```

The scanf(" %c", &ch) reads a character into ch, the space before the % causes scanf to skip any **white space** (spaces, tabs, newlines, etc.) in the input stream.

```
 1 /* Program 14_1 - use of the switch and break statements */
 2
 3 #include <stdio.h>
 4
 5 int main()
 6 {
 7     char ch;                        /* command character read from keyboard */
 8     int data = 1;                   /* integer value being read and printed */
 9
10     while (printf("\nCommand ? "), scanf(" %c", &ch) != EOF)      /* read ch */
11         switch (ch)
12             {
13             case 'r': printf("\n Enter value of data ? ");       /* r = read */
14                       scanf(" %d", &data);
15                       break;
16             case 'p': printf("\n value of data = %d ", data);  /* p = print */
17                       break;
18             case 'c': data = data * 10;                        /* c = calculate */
19                       break;
20             default: printf("   illegal character %c (%#x) ", ch, ch);
21             }
22     printf("program terminated on EOF\n");
23     return 0;
24 }
```

Program 14_1 Command selection using switch and break statements

Many library functions return information in the form of integer values indicating success or failure. For example, the Turbo C graphics library is initialised by calling the function initgraph (see Program 15_3 for more details):

```
    int graphdriver = DETECT, graphmode;
    initgraph(&graphdriver, &graphmode, "c:\\tc\\bgi");
```

If successful, an integer value indicating the type of graphics card found is returned in parameter graphdriver. This could be displayed on the screen as an integer number and the user would look up (in manuals) the meaning of the value to determine what graphics card is fitted. A preferable alternative is to print a meaningful message on the screen:

```
    initgraph(&graphdriver, &graphmode, "c:\\tc\\bgi");      /* initialise graphics */
    switch (graphdriver)                                     /* and print driver */
        {
        case CGA: printf("\n  CGA graphics initialised"); break;
        case EGA: printf("\n  EGA graphics initialised"); break;
        case VGA: printf("\n  VGA graphics initialised"); break;
        }
```

the *symbolic constants*, CGA, EGA and VGA are defined in <graphics.h> as integral constants corresponding to the values which may be returned in graphdriver.

Exercise 14.1 (*see Appendix B for sample answer*)

(a) The sample answer to Exercise 11.4 (see Appendix B) used a sequence of if statements with course_type as the selector. Modify the program to use a switch.

(b) A motor insurance company categorises people into age ranges and calculates the motor insurance premium based on the age range and the car group. The following fragment of code (from file c14\ex14_1b.c on the disk), given a person's age range and car group, returns the motor insurance premium:

```
enum {UNDER_TWENTIES, TWENTIES, THIRTIES, FORTIES, OVER_FORTIES};
/* calculate premium from age range and car group */
if ((age <= TWENTIES) && (group > 5)) premium = 500;
else
    if ((age <= TWENTIES) || (age == OVER_FORTIES)) premium = 460;
    else
        if (group > 3) premium = 480;       /* else THIRTIES and FORTIES */
        else            premium = 450;
```

In two separate programs, rewrite the fragment of code with switch statements using:

1 group (1 to 7) as the selector
2 age (UNDER_TWENTIES, TWENTIES, THIRTIES, FORTIES, OVER_FORTIES) as the selector.

Problem for Chapter 14

The *soundex* code phonetically groups characters as follows:

group 0: A E I O U H W Y plus all non-alphabetic characters
group 1: B F P V
group 2: C G J K Q S X Z
group 3: D T
group 4: L
group 5: M N
group 6: R

A sequence of characters is encoded as follows:

1   each character is replaced by its group digit, i.e. SMIT becomes 2503, SMITH becomes 25030 and SCHMIDT becomes 2205033
2   consecutive similar digits are replaced by a single digit, i.e. SMIT remains 2503 and SMITH and SCHMIDT become 20503
3   zeros are removed and SMIT, SMITH and SCHMIDT become 253.

The technique can be used to encode names in such a way that the effect of slight variations in spelling are reduced. For example, it could be used when taking customer orders over a noisy telephone line where the generated codes are used to key into a computer database. As each code is generated (surname, first name, house number, street name, city name, post code, etc.) it narrows down to the information on a particular customer.

Implement and test a program which reads a sequence of characters from the keyboard and generates the *soundex* code. Use the library function toupper (from <ctype.h>) to convert the characters to upper case then use a switch statement to select the group. Remember that several case labels can be in front of a single statement, e.g.:

```
case 'D': case 'T': group = 3;
```

15

More on input and output

The reading, processing and display of large amounts of numeric data are common in many mathematical, scientific and engineering applications. This chapter discusses the validation of numeric data input and introduces some simple graph plotting techniques.

15.1 Validation of numeric data input

When data is read either from the keyboard (via stdin) or a file (see Chapter 23) it should be checked for correctness and appropriate action taken if an error occurs, i.e.:

(a) validate the conversion process when reading a numeric value from a stream, then (b) validate the range of the data.

The latter is dependent upon the application, e.g. Program 13_2 checked (in line 18) that the value of a number entered was greater than or equal to 0 before attempting to evaluate its factorial. The validation of the conversion process is common to all applications and the techniques described here are applicable to all numeric input.

After an attempt has been made to read a numeric value from a stream the function result of scanf (and similar functions) should be checked to ensure that the expected number of conversions occurred, see Section 11.4. For example, the following section of code attempts to read an int value from stdin into variable n:

```
int n, converted;
while ((converted = scanf("%d", &n)) != EOF)
    if (converted != 1)                              /* error during read ? */
        /* read faulty character and print message  */
        printf("\n error at '%c'\n", getchar());
    else
        printf("%d OK ", n);
```

The expression (converted = scanf("%d", &n)) != EOF is evaluated as follows:

(a) converted = scanf("%d", &n) attempts to read an integer from stdin into variable n; the function result of scanf (the number of successful conversions) is assigned to converted

then   (b) the value of converted is checked for EOF to test for *end of file*.

If *end of file* was entered the while terminates.

If *end of file* was not entered the value of converted is tested and if it is not 1 (one successful conversion) an error occurred when attempting to read an integer, i.e.:

```
if (converted != 1)                              /* error during read ? */
    printf("\n error at '%c'\n", getchar());
```

If an error occurred a message is printed to stdout; the call to getchar() reads the next character in the input stream (where the conversion process stopped) and returns it as an int function result.

When converting a numeric value from characters (e.g. read from stdin) the conversion process terminates when a non-digit is encountered and so long as some digits have been read the stream will be error free, e.g. if 123a was entered the value 123 would be returned and the next read will fail due to the a. For example, a sequence of numbers should be:

```
10   1125    15680    79    897
```

When entering the data into the above section of code mistyping occurs, e.g.:

```
10   1125    156t80    79    897 ↲
10 OK   1125 OK   156 OK
 error at 't' ?
80 OK   79 OK   897 OK
```

The first and second numbers were correctly read as 10 and 1125 and the third incorrectly as 156 (conversion stopped at the character t and the stream was error free). An error was reported on the next read when the t character was encountered. The character was removed from stdin and the read attempted again resulting in the value 80 being read. The final two numbers were then read correctly. The overall result was that six numbers were read instead of five and the third and fourth were faulty.

The above technique which detects an error on the following read may be far too late in practice, i.e. the third number was apparently correct and may have been used in some processing (e.g. controlling a power station). When the error is detected it may not be possible to recover (the power station may have blown up!). In most applications each number should be terminated by *white space* (spaces or newlines), e.g.:

```
int n, converted;
while ((converted = scanf("%d", &n)) != EOF)
   if (converted != 1 || ! isspace(getchar()))        /* error during read ? */
      {
      /* read faulty character, print message & discard characters to \n */
      printf("\n error at '%c', try again ? ", getchar());
      do ; while (getchar() != '\n');
      }
   else
      printf("%d OK ", n);
```

If converted != 1 or the next character is **not** *whitespace* an error condition is assumed. The function getchar() returns the next character in stdin and the function isspace checks for *whitespace*, returning *true* if it is (isspace is one of the character testing functions in library <ctype.h>, see Section 20.4). If an error condition is detected an error message is printed, reporting the character in error. The statement do ; while (getchar() != '\n'); then extracts and discards all characters up to and including the following newline. Executing the above section of code with the faulty data gave:

```
10   1125    156t80    79    897 ↲
10 OK   1125 OK
  error at 't' try again  ? 15680    79    897 ↲
15680 OK   79 OK   897 OK
```

An error was detected when reading 156t80 (the number 156 was not terminated by *whitespace*) and this and all following data discarded. The user was prompted for more input which was entered correctly and accepted.

Due to limited space the programs in this book will perform little or no input validation. In practical applications, however, it is very important; the amount of code devoted to input/output is often larger than the code doing the actual processing.

Exercise 15.1 (*Sample answers are on the disk which accompanies this text*)

Write programs using the fragments of code in the previous section; test that they work as expected (sample answers are in files c15\ex15_1.c and c15\ex15_1a.c on the disk).

15.2 Plotting a graph on a text display screen

A common programming requirement is to display information on the screen in pictorial or graphical form. Program 15_1 reads a data set from the keyboard, see Fig. 15.1 (next page), and draws a graph on the display screen using ordinary character output (see Fig. 15.2, next page). The program reads the number of data values to be plotted, the minimum and maximum x and y values, followed by the x and y data. In the data set of Fig. 15.1 the first line specifies that the data contains 41 numbers, the minimum and maximum x and y values are 0 to 3.00 and 0 to 5.00 respectively; the data to be plotted then follows as a sequence of x and y pairs.

```
 1 /* Program 15_1  Display a graph on the screen  */
 2
 3 #include <stdio.h>                              /* standard stream I/O library */
 4
 5 int main(void)
 6 {
 7     float x_min, x_max, y_min, y_max, x_data, y_data;
 8     int number, x, y;
 9
10     /* read number of values and minimum and maximum values */
11     scanf("%d%g%g%g%g", &number, &x_min, &x_max, &y_min, &y_max);
12     /* print heading of graph */
13     printf("%13.2f%35s%25.2f\n", y_min, "y_data -------->", y_max);
14     printf("   x_data |------------------------"
15            "--------------------------------| y_data\n");
16
17     /* loop reading data values and displaying on the screen */
18     for (x = 0 ; x < number; x++)
19         {
20         scanf("%f%f", &x_data, &y_data);                    /* read x & y data */
21         y = (60.0f / (y_max - y_min)) * (y_data - y_min);      /* y offset */
22         printf("%9.2f%*s%*s%.2f\n", x_data                  /* print x value */
23                , y + 3, "*"                      /* print spaces then an * */
24                , 60 - y, " ", y_data);          /* print spaces then y value */
25         }
26     return 0;
27 }
```

Program 15_1 Display a graph on the display screen

```
31  0  3.00    0  5.00
0.00  0.00    0.10  0.86    0.20  1.57    0.30  2.03    0.40  2.23    0.50  2.17
0.60  1.95    0.70  1.66    0.80  1.45    0.90  1.40    1.00  1.57    1.10  1.96
1.20  2.52    1.30  3.12    1.40  3.67    1.50  4.05    1.60  4.18    1.70  4.07
1.80  3.75    1.90  3.33    2.00  2.91    2.10  2.63    2.20  2.56    2.30  2.72
2.40  3.10    2.50  3.61    2.60  4.12    2.70  4.53    2.80  4.75    2.90  4.71
3.00  4.45
```

Fig. 15.1 Sample data for Program 15_1

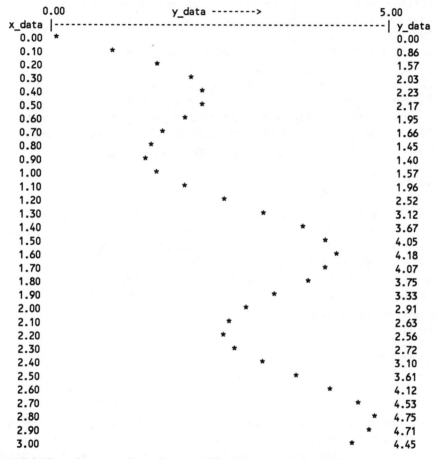

Fig. 15.2 Sample output from Program 15_1 (using data from Fig. 15.1)

Program 15_1 plots the x axis down the screen and y axis across the screen. It starts with a heading indicating the range of the y values followed by the graph; each line showing the x values on the left hand side, a plot of the y value indicated by an * and the y value on the right hand side.   The data in Fig. 15.1 was generated using the following equation (x ranging from 0 to 3 in steps of 0.1, see Program 15_2):

$$y = 4 * (1 - e^{x}) + \sin(5x)$$

The most difficult part of a graph plotting program is the 'mapping' of data onto the drawing area. Program 15_1 plots x down the screen and y across the screen:

x data values   are mapped one per line (x_min and x_max are discarded)

y data values   vary from y_min to y_max (read from the keyboard) and are mapped across the screen starting at character position 11 and finishing at character position 71 (the plot is 60 characters wide).

The sequence of statements in Program 15_1 is:

line

11	read the number of x and y pairs and the minimum and maximum x and y values
13-14	print heading for the graph (setting field widths to position the text and numbers)
18-25	a for statement reading x and y coordinates and plotting them

      20 read the x_data and y_data values

      21 calculate the 'mapping' of the y_data value across the screen

          i.e. (y_max - y_min) is 60 characters wide

      22 print the x_data value as a number (on the left hand side of the screen)

      23 plot the y_data value (an * at the appropriate position)

          the %*s prints y + 2 spaces then the string "*", i.e. y + 3 is the field width

      24 print the y_data value as a number (on the right hand side of the screen).

In line 21 the y_data value is 'mapped' into a field 60 characters wide, i.e.:

$$y = 60 * \frac{(y\_data - y\_min)}{(y\_max - y\_min)}$$

y_min and y_max are the left hand and right hand edges of the graph respectively. The values of x_min and x_max are not used; it is assumed that the x increments are all the same and are 'mapped' one to a line (x_min and x_max are used in Program 15_3).

    Note the use of %*s conversion specifications in line 22 to print the string "*" in a field width of y + 3 (y + 2 spaces are printed before the *) and the string " " in a field of 60 - y. Lines 22 to 24 could be written (less efficiently) using two for statements:

```
printf("%9.2f", x_data);              /* print x value */
for (i = 0; i < y + 2; i++)
    putchar(' ');                     /* print spaces */
putchar('*');                         /* print * */
for (i = 0; i < 60 - y; i++)
    putchar(' ');                     /* print spaces */
printf("%.2f\n", y_data);             /* print y value */
```

In practice it is much more efficient to let the purpose built library functions perform such low-level operations (as in lines 22 to 24 of Program 15_1).

    Program 15_1 is a general purpose graph plotting program which can be used to plot the results of any program where the data can be printed as a series of x and y data pairs. For example, the data of Fig. 15.1 was produced using Program 15_2 (next page):

line

12-14	a for statement incrementing i from 1 to number

         the value of x is incremented (from 0) on each loop by x_increment

      13 print the value of x and 4 * (1 - e^x) + sin(5x)

      14 print a newline every 6 loops (else ' ').

Note the use of the ? conditional operator in line 14:

```
, (i % 6) ? ' ': '\n');
```

If the result of i % 6 is non-zero ' ' is printed else (when i is 6, 12, etc.) a newline is printed (using the %c conversion specification in line 13). Thus the data is printed in columns of six pairs, see Fig. 15.1. Although the output of Program 15_2 would normally be sent to the display screen it can be redirected to a file at execution time. For example under MS-DOS, assuming the executable version of Program 15_2 is in file p15_2.exe and the program output is to go to file p15_1.dat:

C: > p15_2 > p15_1.dat ↲

Program input can similarly be redirected, e.g. to input p15_1.dat into Program 15_1:

C: > p15_1 < p15_1.dat ↲

should produce the output of Fig. 15.2. In fact the output of Program 15_2 can be *piped* directly into Program 15_1:

C: > p15_2 | p15_1 ↲

As stated above Program 15_1 is a general purpose graph plotting program which can be used to plot the results of any program where the data can be printed as a series of x and y data pairs (the field widths and conversion specifications may need to be changed to suit the data values). The data can be generated as in Program 15_2 or partial data generated and then edited with a text editor, e.g. to add the number of data values and the x and y minimum and maximum values. The data does not have to be set out as in Fig. 15.1 so long as it is in the correct order, i.e. the x and y data values can be columns of six (as in Fig. 15.1), columns of four, two, etc.

```
1 /* Program 15_2   Generate data for graph plotting Program 15_1 */
2
3 #include <stdio.h>
4 #include <math.h>
5
6 int main(void)
7 {
8     int i, number = 31;
9     float x = 0.0, x_increment = 0.1;
10
11     printf("%d  0  3.00   0  5.00\n", number);
12     for (i = 1; i <= number; i++, x = x + x_increment)
13         printf("%6.2f%6.2f%c", x, 4 - 4 * exp(-x) + sin(5 * x)
14                 , ( i % 6) ? ' ': '\n');
15     return 0;
16 }
```

Program 15_2   Used to generate data (Fig. 15.1) for graph plotting Program 15_1

15.3 Plotting a graph on a graphics display screen

The main problem with using character based output to plot pictorial information is that the quality of the result is very poor and lacks detail. The alternative is to use the pixel based graphics facilities available on the majority of modern microcomputers and workstations. Such facilities enable the drawing of lines, plotting of points, etc. at a much higher quality than is possible when using characters.

Program 15_3 (at the end of the chapter) is a modified version of Program 15_1 which uses the Turbo C graphics library <graphics.h> to plot the graph on the screen of an IBM PC compatible microcomputer. In this case the x axis is across the screen and the y axis down the screen (the 'normal' way a graph is drawn), see Fig. 15.3. The 'mapping' of the plot shown in Fig 15.3 onto the screen was designed as follows:

1   The display screen size is such that the x axis varies from 0 to x_right horizontally across the screen and the y axis from 0 to y_bottom vertically down the screen (the position 0 0 is the top left hand corner). The values of x_right and y_bottom are obtained either from graphics package functions (see Program 15_3 lines 21 and 22) or from a knowledge of the screen size.

2   The range of x data values from x_min to x_max is 'mapped' to screen coordinates 0 to x_right.

3   The range of y data values from y_min to y_max is 'mapped' to screen coordinates y_bottom to 0; the origin of the screen is the top left hand corner therefore the calculation must be done to show the graph the correct way up.

The sequence of statements in Program 15_3 is:

4   include <graphics.h> the Turbo C graphics library
5   include <dos.h> the Turbo C DOS library (required for delay)
9   define variables used by initgraph and initialise graphdriver to DETECT (see below)
14   call initgraph to initialise the graphics system (see below)
15-19   if the result of graphresult was not grOK (graphics OK) display error report
         17   print error message returned from function grapherrormsg(graphdriver)
         18   return to operating system indicating failure
20-21   get the maximum x and y screen coordinates
22   set the colour to WHITE (defined in <graphics.h>)
23-24   draw a box around the edges of the screen and text at screen coordinate 20, 20
27   read the number of x and y pairs and the minimum and maximum x and y values
29-36   a for statement reading x and y coordinates and plotting them
         31   read the x_data and y_data values
         32   calculate the 'mapping' of the x_data value across the screen
         33   calculate the 'mapping' of the y_data value down the screen
         34   if first data values moveto start of graph
         35   else draw a lineto the coordinate
              moveto moves to a specified position on the screen, lineto draws a line from
              the previous position to that specified
37   delay for 5 seconds to display the graph (delay is a DOS specific function)
38-40   close the Turbo C graphics system and terminate the program.

Program 15_3 is a general purpose graph plotting program which will accept data in the format of Fig. 15.1 (as Program 15_1).

Clearly if Program 15_3 is to give a high quality graph it needs many more x and y data points than are needed for the unrefined graph of Program 15_1, i.e. ten to twenty times more. For example, Program 15_2 could be edited to increase the number of data points from 41 to 401 with the x_increment reduced from 0.1 to 0.01.

In line 14 initgraph initialises the graphics system. The first parameter, graphdriver, specifies the graphics driver to use and the second parameter, graphmode, the mode of the driver. In the above example graphdriver is set to DETECT (defined in <graphics.h>) which will automatically detect the type of graphics card fitted (graphmode is not used in this case). The third parameter is the path name to the directory where the Turbo C graphics driver files are stored (in a string constant \\ is converted to \ hence the string "c:\\tc\\bgi" refers to the subdirectory c:\tc\bgi). In line 15 the function graphresult is called to check that the graphics was initialised correctly. If so graphresult returns the value grOk otherwise an error message is displayed (line 17) and the program terminates (line 18). In line 17 the function grapherrormsg(graphdriver) returns a pointer to a string containing an error message which is printed to stdout. Refer to the manuals and online help system for details of functions initgraph, moveto, lineto, etc.

Note that the function initgraph (line 14 of Program 15_3) expects the parameters to be *pointers*, hence the use of the & (*address of*) operator (the use of pointers when passing parameters is explained in Section 16.8).

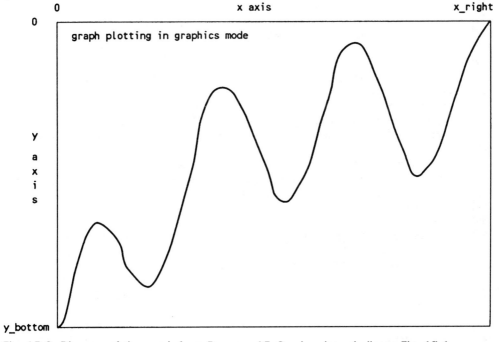

Fig. 15.3 Diagram of the graph from Program 15_3 using data similar to Fig. 15.1

Exercise 15.2 (*see Appendix B for sample answer*)

Using a graphics library write a program to bounce a ball around the display screen, e.g.:

1   Initialise the graphics system.
2   Determine the minimum and maximum screen coordinates in the x and y directions.
3   Draw a box around the edges of the screen.
4   Loop: (a) draw ball at current x and y coordinates in white, e.g. draw a circle,
            (b) calculate new x and y coordinates,
            (c) redraw ball at old coordinates in black (to erase old ball).

Either loop forever or terminate the loop when a key is hit. You will need to consult manuals to determine how to use the graphics library (Program 15_3 used Turbo C).

```
 1 /* Program 15_3  Display a graph on the screen using Turbo C graphics    */
 2
 3 #include <stdio.h>                                /* standard stream I/O library */
 4 #include <graphics.h>                    /* Turbo C graphics library functions */
 5 #include <dos.h>                                    /* MS-DOS specific header */
 6
 7 int main(void)
 8 {
 9     int graphdriver = DETECT, graphmode;                    /* for initgraph */
10     float x_right, y_bottom, x_min, x_max, y_min, y_max, x_data, y_data;
11     int i, number, x, y;
12
13     /* Initialise graphics system  */
14     initgraph(&graphdriver, &graphmode, "c:\\tc\\bgi");
15     if (graphresult() != grOk)
16         {
17         printf("initgraph failed: %s\n", grapherrormsg(graphdriver));
18         return 1;                                        /* failed, return */
19         }
20     x_right = getmaxx();                         /* get the size of the screen */
21     y_bottom = getmaxy();
22     setcolor(WHITE);                                    /* set colour white */
23     rectangle(0, 0, x_right, y_bottom);             /* draw box around screen */
24     outtextxy(20, 20, "graph plotting in graphics mode");   /* draw some text */
25
26     /* read number of values and minimum and maximum values */
27     scanf("%d%f%f%f%f", &number, &x_min, &x_max, &y_min, &y_max);
28     /* loop reading data values and displaying on the screen */
29     for (i = 0 ; i <= number; i++)
30         {
31         scanf("%f%f", &x_data, &y_data);                  /* read x and y data */
32         x = (x_right / (x_max - x_min)) * (x_data - x_min);       /* x offset */
33         y = (y_bottom / (y_max - y_min)) * (y_data - y_min);      /* y offset */
34         if (i == 0) moveto(x, y_bottom - y);         /* move to start position */
35         else         lineto(x, y_bottom - y);           /* draw next line */
36         }
37     delay(5000);                                      /* delay 5 seconds */
38     clearviewport();                                    /* clear screen */
39     closegraph();                              /* close graphics system */
40     return 0;
41 }
```

Program 15_3 Display a graph on the screen using Turbo C graphics

Problems for Chapter 15

1   Amend Exercise 15.2, bouncing ball, to have a box in the middle of the screen (length and height one third screen size would be suitable). Bounce the ball around between the edges of the screen and the edges of the box.

2   Using a graphics library and the time of day functions from <time.h> draw a clock face (with second, minute and hour hands) on the screen updating it every second.

16

Functions

There are three major reasons for breaking a program down into *functions*:

(a) to break a large program down into manageable modules,

(b) to provide libraries of common modules,

and (c) to save repeating the same code many times in the program.

For example, a large engineering program could contain many expressions which require the evaluation of the square root of a number. At each point in the program it would be possible to repeat the identical sequence of instructions but this is wasteful and error prone. By using a *function* the sequence of instructions can be written once and then *called* as required. If a function has a wider context it may be placed in a library to be accessed by other programs (possibly written by other programmers) in a way similar to the standard libraries such as <math.h> (setting up libraries is discussed in Chapter 18).

Section 16.13 discusses *preprocessor macros* which may be used to replace small functions in situations where speed and efficiency is critical, e.g. in a real time system.

16.1 Function *definition*

The function *definition*, where the body of the function is defined, takes the following general form:

```
result_type function_name(parameter_list)
{
    declarations and definitions
    statements
}
```

where:

the function *header*, `result_type function_name(parameter_list)`, declares:

(a) `result_type`   the type of the function result, e.g. `int`, `double`, etc.

(b) `function_name`   the name or identifier of the function,

(c) `parameter_list`   a list of parameters (see next section).

`{` indicates the start of *compound statement* containing function `function_name`

`declarations/definitions` list of *types*, *constants* and *variables* local to `function_name`

`statements`   the computing operations carried out in `function_name`

`}` indicates the end of the *compound statement* containing function `function_name`

The body of the function, enclosed in `{}`, is a *compound statement* (see Section 11.5). Internal variables are created on entry to the function and lost on exit and may not be accessed by other functions unless passed as parameters to another function (permanent local storage may be allocated using *static* variables, see Section 17.5). When defined local variables may be initialised, otherwise the value is *undefined*.

Although some functions are 'stand alone', in that no data is passed in or out, the majority:

(a) require data from the calling function in the form of parameters,

and (b) return a *function result*, e.g. the square root of a number (passed as a parameter).

Functions return the *function result* to the calling function via the function_name (introduced in Section 4.5). The result_type declares the type returned by the *function result* which may be any type other than an array (see Chapter 19) or a function (although *pointers* to arrays and functions can be returned, see Chapters 22 and 23). If a function does not return a *function result* result_type should be declared as void, i.e. a function may carry out some task for which no result is returned (e.g. clear the display screen). Declaring a result_type of void indicates to the compiler that no result is returned and it can check that no attempt is made to return a result or that a calling function does not attempt to use a result which does not exist. Note that if the result_type is missing int will be assumed.

16.1.1 The *parameter_list*

The majority of functions require data from the calling function in the form of parameters, e.g. the mathematical function pow(x,y) in library <math.h> has two double parameters, x and y, and returns x^y as a double function result:

The *actual parameters* are the values passed to the function when it is called (sometimes called *arguments*).

The *formal parameters* are the names used inside the function to refer to the *actual parameters*.

The parameter_list *declares* the names and types of the *formal parameters*:

```
(parameter_type parameter_name, parameter_type parameter_name, ....)
```

If a function has no parameters void should be declared as the parameter_list (indicating that there are no parameters). If the parameter_list is missing ... will be assumed indicating a variable number of parameters, see Section 28.5.

When a function is called, the number and types of the *actual parameters* passed to the function must match, in order, the number and types as declared by the *formal parameters*. Note that the order in which the *actual parameters* are evaluated before being passed is not specified although all the parameters are completely evaluated, including side effects, before the function is called (see Section 18.8).

16.2 The *return* statement

The return statement performs two operations:

1   it terminates the function and returns control to the calling function,
2   if followed by an expression it returns a *function result* to the calling function.

For example:

```
return i*j;                /* terminate and return function result */
return 25.0;               /* terminate and return function result */
return;                      /* terminate without function result */
return (2.0 * x - sin(y));  /* terminate and return function result */
```

Points to note:

1   The type of expression following return must match the result_type of the function or be capable of conversion to it.
2   If the function does not have a return statement the closing } acts as one.
3   If the result_type is other than void and a function result is not returned garbage will be passed back to the calling function resulting in *undefined behaviour* (a modern compiler will issue a warning in such a case).
4   A function with a result_type of void may not return a function result and the compiler will indicate an error if an attempt is made to return a result.
5   The expression returned can be enclosed in parentheses, i.e. to make a complex expression stand out in the program.

In general it is recommended that a function have only one return at the end of the body of the function otherwise it can become very difficult to follow the flow of the code.

16.3 A function to square a number

```
 1 /* Program 16_1 - call a function to square a number                  */
 2
 3 #include <stdio.h>                        /* standard stream I/O library */
 4
 5 /*-----------------------------------------------------------------*/
 6 /* Function to square a number                                      */
 7 /* Parameters in: number (float) value to be squared                */
 8 /* Function result: number squared                                  */
 9 /*-----------------------------------------------------------------*/
10 float square(float number)                        /* function header */
11 {
12      float answer;                        /* local variable holds result */
13
14      answer = number * number;                     /* square number */
15      return answer;                        /* return function result */
16 }                                          /* end of function square */
17
18 /*-----------------------------------------------------------------*/
19 /* function main - no parameters returns result indicating success/fail  */
20 int main(void)
21 {
22      float x, answer;                              /* local variables */
23
24      printf("\nEnter real number ? ");
25      scanf("%f", &x);                              /* read data */
26      answer = square(x);                           /* call function */
27      printf(" %f squared = %f\n", x, answer);
28      return 0;
29 }                                          /* end of function main */
```

Program 16_1 Function to square a number

Program 16_1 consists of two functions with headers as follows:

`float square(float number)` which returns the square of a number passed as a parameter
        function name is `square`
        has one `float` parameter
        returns a `float` function result
`int main(void)` which reads a number, calls `square` and prints the result.
        function name is `main`
        has no parameters
        returns an `int` function result (program success/fail indicator)

The sequence of statements in Program 16_1 is:

10-16	definition of function `square`	
	10	function header declaring one `float` parameter and returns a `float` result
	12	define variable `answer` which is local to `square`
	14	calculate x squared
	15	return `answer`
20-29	definition of function `main`	
	22	define variables local to `main`
	24-25	prompt the user for input and read number entered into x
	26	call function `square` with parameter x
		assign function result returned to variable `answer`
	27	print `answer`.

A run of Program 16_1 gave:

```
Enter real number ? 2↵
  2.000000 squared = 4.000000
```

The name used within a function for a *formal parameter* has no relationship with the name of the corresponding *actual parameter* when the function is called, i.e. they may be the same or not. The critical thing is when the function is called at execution time the order, number and types of parameters correspond, with each *formal parameter* taking the value of the corresponding *actual parameter*. To enable the compiler to check that a function call is correct it requires information regarding number and type of parameters expected and the type of *function result* returned. This information may be provided in two ways:

    (a) by *defining* the function before calling it, e.g. in Program 16_1 function `square` is
        defined (lines 10 to 16) before function `main` (where it is called in line 26)
or (b) by *declaring* a *function prototype* of the function before calling it (see next section).

When a function is called the compiler:

1   Checks that the number of parameters is correct, i.e. `square` expects one parameter.
2   If necessary, converts the types of the *actual parameters* to those required by the *formal parameters*, e.g. `sqrt` expects one parameter of type `double` thus in Program 5_1 the `float` parameter to `sqrt` (line 14) would be converted to a `double`. The conversion is carried out as though the *formal parameter* is assigned the value of the *actual parameter* using the *assignment operator* = (see Section 10.2).
3   If necessary, convert the type returned by the *function result* to that required by the calling function, e.g. in Program 5_1 the `double` result returned by `sqrt` (line 14) is assigned to the `float` variable `radius_check`.

Variables defined within functions are *local* and are not accessible outside the function (unless passed as parameters to other functions), e.g. answer defined in main of Program 16_1 (line 22) is a totally distinct variable from answer defined in square (line 12). When a function terminates, any local variables are lost and recreated when it is called again (except for *static* local variables, see Section 17.5).

Exercise 16.1 (*see Appendix B for sample answer*)

Implement a function which, when given the length of a simple pendulum in metres, returns the period of oscillation in seconds, i.e.:

period = 2π √(length / g)   where Standard Gravity g = 9.80665 metres/sec^2

Implement a function main which reads the pendulum length, calls the above function and prints the result. A pendulum of length 1 metre has a period of 2.006409 seconds.

16.4 Function *prototypes*

The previous section explained that when a function is called the compiler checks that the number and types of the *actual parameters* correspond to the *formal parameters* expected by the function. In Program 16_1 function square was *defined* before it was called in function main, i.e. the code of square was placed before the code of main in the source code file. This enabled the compiler to check that the call to square (in line 26) had one parameter of type float (or something that could be converted to float) and that the float function result was correctly assigned to variable answer (if answer had been of type int the float result from square would be converted to int before assignment).

It is not always convenient or even possible to define a function before calling it. In such cases information about a function may be provided by a *function prototype* which *declares* the name of the function, the number and types of the parameters and the type of the function result (*declarations* and *definitions* will be discussed in Chapters 17 and 18).

A *function prototype* is effectively a copy of the *header* from the *function definition* plus a terminating ; and has the following general form:

```
result_type function_name(parameter_list);
```

For example, the *function prototype* of function square would declare that it had one parameter of type float (single precision real) and returns a function result of type float:

```
float square(float number);                          /* function prototype */
```

The standard header files contain *function prototypes* for the library functions. For example, in <math.h> the *function prototype* for pow declares that it has two parameters of type double (double precision real) and returns a function result of type double:

```
double pow(double x, double y);              /* returns x to the power y */
```

Exercise 16.2 (*see Appendix B for sample answer*)

Implement and test a pair of functions which determine the factorial !N and inverse factorial 1/!N of an integer number N, i.e.:

N! = N * (N -1) * (N - 2) 1   N > 0

Implement a function main which reads an integer, calls the functions and prints the results. The function main should use *function prototypes* (see the next section if in doubt).

16.5 Function to raise a *float* to an positive *integer* exponent

```
 1 /* Program 16_2 - call function to raise a float to an integer exponent >= 0  */
 2
 3 #include <stdio.h>                             /* standard stream I/O library */
 4
 5 int main(void)
 6 {
 7     float power(float number, int exponent);            /* function prototype */
 8
 9     float x, x_to_exp;                                    /* local variables */
10     int exp;
11
12     printf("\nEnter real number and integer exponent >= 0 ? ");
13     while (scanf("%f%d", &x, &exp) == 2)                       /* read data */
14         {
15         x_to_exp = power(x, exp);                        /* call function */
16         printf(" %f to the exponent %d = %f", x, exp, x_to_exp);
17         printf("\nEnter real number and integer exponent ? ");
18         }
19     return 0;
20 }                                              /* end of function main */
21
22 /*-------------------------------------------------------------------*/
23 /* Function to raise a float to integer exponent >= 0                 */
24 /* Parameters in: number (float) value to be raise to exponent        */
25 /*                exponent (int) the value of the exponent ( > or = 0) */
26 /* Function result: number raised to exponent                         */
27 /*-------------------------------------------------------------------*/
28 float power(float number, int exponent)                /* function header */
29 {
30     float result;                           /* local variable holds result */
31     int i;                             /* local variable holds loop counter */
32
33     for (result = i = 1; i <= exponent; i++)    /* loop i from 1 to exponent */
34         result = result * number;               /* number to the exponent i */
35     return result;                              /* return function result */
36 }                                              /* end of function power */
```

Program 16_2 Function to raise a float to an positive integer exponent (>= 0)

Program 16_2 contains the functions main and power, which evaluates $number^{exponent}$ where number is a float and exponent is an int (>= 0), e.g. 3.6^4. The function main consists of:

7 float power(float number, int exponent); the *prototype* of the function power
9-10 define variables which are local to main
12 prompts the user to enter a real number and an integer exponent
13-18 a while statement executed while scanf successfully converts two numbers
    15 x_to_exp = power(x, exp);
      call power, parameters x and exp and the result assigned to x_to_exp
   16-17 print results and prompt for next input.

The function `power` (lines 28 to 36) consists of:

line

28   `float power(float number, int exponent)`, the function header

30-31   local variables used within in the function `power`

33-34   a `for` statement to evaluate `number`^exponent^

35   `return result;` returns control to `main` together with the function result.

The program terminates when `scanf` fails to convert two numbers. The function prototype in line 7 tells the compiler that function `power` has two parameters of types `float` and `int` respectively and returns a function result of type `float`. In the call to `power` in line 15 there is no need for conversion but if it had been called with two `int` parameters the compiler would know to convert the first to a `float` before passing it. The *function prototype* need only declare the types of the parameters (the names being unnecessary), i.e. line 7 of Program 16_2 could be written:

```
float power(float, int);                              /* function prototype */
```

If, when the function is defined, the *header* differs from any *prototype* an error message will be generated. For example, if line 28 of Program 16_2 was replaced with:

```
float power(float number, float exponent)            /* function header */
```

Turbo C version 3.00 would display the following message when the program is compiled:

```
Error p16_2.c 29: Type mismatch in redeclaration of 'power'
```

Unfortunately, for reasons of compatibility with the original C, ANSI C does not require a *function definition* or *function prototype* when a function is called. In such circumstances integral parameters undergo integral promotion and `float` parameters are converted to `double` (other types are passed as they are) and any function result is assumed to be of type `int`. For example, if the declaration of the *function prototype* of `power` in line 7 of Program 16_2 had been missed out the call to `power` in line 15 would give problems:

1   The number of parameters could not be checked and the compiler would assume that it was called with the correct number (two in this case).
2   The way a parameter is passed depends upon its type with integral parameters undergoing integral promotion and `float` parameters being converted to `double` (other types are passed as they are). Therefore in the call to `power` in line 15 the first parameter would be passed incorrectly (as a `double`) and the second correctly.
3   The function result would be assumed to be of type `int` and converted to a `float` to be assigned to `result` (this giving an incorrect result).

Undefined behaviour occurs if the number or types of the actual parameters disagrees with the formal parameters, e.g. the program may crash with a run-time error or at the very least the result of the function would be incorrect. It is therefore unwise to miss out *function prototypes* and considered very bad programming practice. A modern compiler will display a warning if a *function definition* or a *function prototype* is missing when a function is called, e.g. Turbo C V3.0 gave the following warning when line 7 was removed from Program 16_2 (the appropriate warning level must be enabled):

```
Warning p16_2.c 15: Call to function 'power' with no prototype in function main
```

Note that if function `power` was *defined* before function `main` (lines 28 to 36 placed before line 5) the function prototype for `power` (line 7) would be unnecessary.

Exercise 16.3 (*see Appendix B for sample answer*)

Implement a function which evaluates the reactance of a series circuit consisting of an inductor L and capacitor C at frequency f:

$$\text{reactance} = 2\pi f L - \frac{1}{2\pi f C}$$

Test the function with a suitable main, e.g. if L = 0.2 henries, C = 2 μfarads and f = 50 Hz the reactance will be -1528.717 Ω. Implement and test another function which determines the resonant frequency (the above circuit would resonate at 251.65 Hz):

$$\text{resonant frequency} = \frac{1}{2\pi \sqrt{(LC)}}$$

16.6 Function declarations in the original C

Function prototypes and the method of function definition described in Section 16.1 are new to ANSI C. In the original C the header of function power would be:

```
float power(number, exponent)          /* function header */
float number;                          /* first parameter type */
int exponent;                          /* second parameter type */
{                                      /* start of function power */
```

The () contain a list of the names of the formal parameters and the types are declared on the following lines (before the opening { of the function compound statement). The declaration of power in a function which calls it would be:

```
float power();               /* declaration of function power in old 'c' */
```

Only the function result type is specified. It is up to the programmer to ensure that the number and types of parameters are correct when the function is called.

16.7 Passing parameters using *pass by value*

C passes parameters into a function using *pass by value*:

1 **copies** of the *actual parameters* are made in temporary variables and these are passed;
2 the called function can access the **copies of the values** of the *actual parameters* via the names of the corresponding *formal parameters*.

Consider line 15 of Program 16_2:

```
x_to_exp = power(x, exp);                   /* call function */
```

When power is called copies of the values of x and exp are made into temporary variables. The function power would then access these values via the names number and exponent as declared in the parameter list in the function header in line 28:

```
float power(float number, int exponent)
```

On entry to the function power the *formal parameters* number and exponent have the same values as x and exp respectively, as passed from the function main. Such *formal parameters* can be considered as *local* variables which are given an initial value on entry to the function and may then be used like any other variable. Passing parameters by value prevents code within the function inadvertently accessing the original parameters and corrupting them, i.e. if parameter number in power is changed the value of x in main is not affected. It is therefore possible to modify function power as follows (disk file p16_2a.c):

```
float power(float number, int exponent)                    /* function header */
{
    float result;                                /* local variable holds result */
    for (result = 1; exponent >= 1; exponent--)    /* loop exponent down to 1 */
        result = result * number;                  /* number to the exponent */
    return result;                                 /* return function result */
}
```

$number^{exponent}$ is calculated with the value of exponent decrementing until it reaches 0, when the for statement terminates. The value of exp in main is unaffected. This modification enables the local variable i in function power of Program 16_2 to be removed.

If a formal parameter should not be altered within the function it should be prefixed with the *type qualifier* const. For example, the header of power could be written:

```
float power(const float number, const int exponent)        /* function header */
```

indicating that number and exponent are constants and may not be altered within power. The modified version of power would now give an error, e.g. GNU C V2.6.3:

`P16_2C.c:32: warning: decrement of read-only location`

indicating that an attempt was made to alter a const qualified object (in this case exponent).

Qualifying parameters using const will ensure that a value is not altered inadvertently within the function (e.g. by mistyping a variable name) and may allow the compiler to perform some optimisation. This is particularly important when using *pointers* (see next section) to achieve *pass by reference* (where the function can access the memory used to store the *actual parameters*, not just a copy of their values). In fact, when passing large objects (such as *structures*) if the value of a formal parameter is not to be changed within a function it is preferable to pass parameters as *pointers* to const qualified objects to remove the overhead of *pass by value* (see Section 16.12).

16.8 Passing parameters *by reference*

In general programming terms there are two ways of passing a parameter into a function:

by value: a **copy** of the value of the actual parameter is made in a temporary variable and this is passed to the function (within the function the formal parameter appears to be a local variable initialised with the value of the actual parameter).

by reference: the **address** of the actual parameter is passed to the function. The function can use the address to access and alter the memory allocated to the parameter.

Many functions perform a sequence of calculations and yield a single result which can be passed back to the calling function via the *function result*, e.g. the library functions sin, sqrt, etc. and the functions square and power in Programs 16_1 and 16_2 respectively. In many cases, however, a function needs to return more than one result and there are two techniques which can be used to achieve this:

(a) Use *pointers* as parameters to *pass by reference*. Using the & operator the **value of the address** of a variable is passed as an actual parameter and inside the function use the address, via the name of the corresponding formal parameter.

(b) Use *external variables* which can be accessed by any function in a file (or other files).

In general the former is preferred. The use of *external variables* should be carefully controlled if the concept of *information hiding* is to be maintained, see Chapters 17 and 18.

16.8.1 Introduction to *pointers*

A pointer to a particular type of object is defined as follows:

```
type *p_name;                          /* declare a pointer to type */
```

The * prefixing the identifier p_name in the declaration indicates that it is a pointer, i.e. it can hold the address of an object of the specified type (to differentiate pointers from other types it is wise to use some naming convention, e.g. use p_ to start pointer names).

The following two statements define a variable number (an int) and a variable p_to_int, a 'pointer to int' (an int *, which can hold the address of an int variable):

```
int number;                            /* define an int variable */
int *p_to_int;                         /* define a pointer to an int */

p_to_int = &number;                    /* point p_to_int to variable number */
```

The latter statement, p_to_int = &number;, assigns the *value of the address* of variable number to pointer p_to_int (the address operator & returns the *address of* an operand).

To access the object which a pointer points to (holds the address of), the pointer is prefixed by the indirection operator *, e.g.:

```
int number;                            /* define an int variable */
int *p_to_int;                         /* define a pointer to an int */

p_to_int = &number;                    /* point p_to_int to variable number */
*p_to_int = 10;        /* assign the value 10 to the int pointed at by p_to_int */
```

The last statement assigns the value 10 to the variable number, i.e. *p_to_int = 10; assigns 10 to the variable pointed at by p_to_int, which in this case points at variable number, therefore 10 is assigned to number. This is equivalent to:

```
number = 10;                    /* assign of the value 10 to the variable number */
```

A simplified view of the data area in the memory of the computer would now be:

variable	contents	comments
number	10	integer value 10
p_to_int	&number	address of variable number

Unfortunately * means two different things in the context of pointers:

1 in a definition, e.g. int *p_to_int; declares p_to_int to be a pointer to int
2 in an expression, e.g. *p_to_int = 10; the int object pointed to by p_to_int is assigned the value 10.

Thus in expressions the pointer name (e.g. p_to_int) accesses the contents of the pointer itself (an address) and the pointer name prefixed by the indirection operator (e.g. *p_to_int) accesses the contents of the object pointed to (e.g. the contents of number).

16.8.2 Using *pointers* to pass parameters *by reference*

To pass an object into a function *by reference* the address of the object is passed as the actual parameter (using the address operator &) and the corresponding formal parameter is declared as a pointer. Inside the function the name of the formal parameter is prefixed with the indirection operator * which will then access the memory allocated to the original object. Consider the following function which swaps the contents of a pair of int parameters (Section 16.13 shows how to implement this function as a *preprocessor macro*):

```
void swap_int(int *p_int1, int *p_int2)
{
    int temporary;                          /* temporary storage */
    temporary = *p_int1;            /* copy first variable into temporary */
    *p_int1 = *p_int2;               /* copy second variable into first */
    *p_int2 = temporary;            /* copy temporary variable into first */
}
```

The formal parameters p_int1 and p_int2 are pointers to type int. The function would be called as follows (where x and y are variables of type int):

```
    swap_int(&x, &y);
```

The address operator & will pass the addresses of x and y to the function swap_int (not a copy of their values). Function swap_int can then access x and y:

   *p_int1 will access the memory allocated to variable x
and *p_int2 will access the memory allocated to variable y.

Hence the following statements:

```
    temporary = *p_int1;            /* copy first variable into temporary */
    *p_int1 = *p_int2;               /* copy second variable into first */
    *p_int2 = temporary;            /* copy temporary variable into first */
```

swaps the contents of variables x and y by:

   (a) assigning the value of x to temporary
   (b) assigning the value of y to x
and (c) assigning the value of temporary (old value of x) to y.

16.9 Function to swap the values of two variables

Program 16_3 (next page) contains a slightly enhanced version of the swap_int function discussed in the previous section. The sequence of statements is:

7   define int variables x and y and initialise them
8   function prototype for swap_int
10 print values of variables x and y
11 swap_int(&x, &y); call swap_int to swap the values of variables x and y
12 print the new values of variables x and y
22 void swap_int(int *const p_int1, int *const p_int2)
      function header with two formal parameters which are pointers to type int (see below)
24 internal variable used for swapping
26 assign contents of int pointed to by p_int1 (x in this case) to temporary
27 assign contents of int pointed to by p_int2 (y in this case) to int pointed to by p_int1
      (x in this case)
28 assign contents of temporary to int pointed to by p_int2 (y in this case).

Note that the formal parameters of function swap_int (lines 8 and 22) are const qualified pointers to int, i.e. the pointer values may not be changed inside the function (although the object pointed to may be). For example, the following would generate a warning or error:

```
    p_int1 = &temporary;                    /* point p_int1 at temporary */
```

```
 1 /* Program 16_3 - calling a function using 'pass by reference' */
 2
 3 #include <stdio.h>
 4
 5 int main(void)
 6    {
 7       int x = 1, y = 2;                                    /* local variables */
 8       void swap_int(int *const p_int1, int *const p_int2);     /* prototype */
 9
10       printf("\n x = %d and y = %d ", x, y);            /* print x and y */
11       swap_int(&x, &y);                                  /* swap x and y */
12       printf("\n x = %d and y = %d ", x, y);            /* print x and y */
13       return 0;
14    }
15
16 /*-----------------------------------------------------------------*/
17 /* Function swap_int: to swap the values of two int parameters          */
18 /*  Parameters in/out: p_int1 (pointer to int) address of first variable */
19 /*                     p_int2 (pointer to int) address of second variable */
20 /*  Function result: none                                               */
21 /*-----------------------------------------------------------------*/
22 void swap_int(int *const p_int1, int *const p_int2)
23 {
24       int temporary;                                 /* temporary storage */
25
26       temporary = *p_int1;        /* copy first variable into temporary */
27       *p_int1 = *p_int2;          /* copy second variable into first */
28       *p_int2 = temporary;        /* copy temporary variable into first */
29 }
```

Program 16_3 Calling a function using *pass by reference*

A run of Program 16_3 gave:

```
x = 1 and y = 2
x = 2 and y = 1
```

16.10 Function to maintain a running mean

Program 16_4 (next page) contains a function running_mean which, when given a sequence of numbers, maintains a running average. The values of the count of numbers entered so far and the running average so far are passed to the function *by reference*.

To declare that a function parameter is to be a pointer the * operator is used, e.g. consider the function header in line 26:

```
void running_mean(const float number, int *count, float *average)    /* header */
```

This function header declares three parameters:

number   type float (const qualified), is *passed by value*
count   type int * 'pointer to int', is *passed by reference*
average   type float * 'pointer to float', is *passed by reference*

Now consider the call to function running_mean in line 13 of Program 16_4:

```
running_mean(next_number, &count_so_far, &average_so_far);
```

The compiler passes the value of the float variable next_number as the first parameter and the *addresses* of the float variables count_so_far and average_so_far as the second and third parameters respectively. Inside the function running_mean the pointers count and average are used to directly access the memory allocated to count_so_far and average_so_far (reading/writing them as required). When variables count_so_far and average_so_far are defined (lines 8 and 9) they are initialised to 0 so that the values are defined when they are accessed in the function running_mean via the pointers count and average (in lines 28 and 29). Beware of writing lines 28 and 29 as follows:

```
*average = (*average * *count + number) / ++(*count);      /* new average ?? */
```

Will the value of *count in the expression (*average * *count + number) be that before or after the increment in ++(*count)? It is not specified (see Section 10.3) and the program will work with some compilers and fail with others.

It should be noted that a much more efficient way of implementing function running_mean is to use *static* local variables inside the function to hold count_so_far and average_so_far (removing the need to pass them from the calling function), see Section 17.5.

```
 1 /* Program 16_4 - passing parameters to a function by reference    */
 2
 3 #include <stdio.h>                          /* standard stream I/O library */
 4
 5 int main(void)
 6 {
 7     void running_mean(const float number, int *count, float *average);
 8     float next_number, average_so_far = 0.0f;           /* local variables */
 9     int count_so_far = 0;
10
11     while (printf("\nEnter next number ? "), scanf("%f", &next_number) == 1)
12         {
13         running_mean(next_number, &count_so_far, &average_so_far);
14         printf("    average so far = %f", average_so_far);
15         }
16     return 0;
17 }
18
19 /*------------------------------------------------------------------------*/
20 /* Function to calculate the running average of a sequence of numbers     */
21 /* Parameters  in: number  (float) next number in the sequence           */
22 /* Parameters out: count   (float *) pointer to count of numbers entered  */
23 /*                 average (float *) pointer to average so far            */
24 /* Function result: none                                                  */
25 /*------------------------------------------------------------------------*/
26 void running_mean(const float number, int *count, float *average)  /* header */
27 {
28     *average = (*average * *count + number) / (*count + 1);   /* new average */
29     *count = *count + 1;                              /* increment count */
30 }                                              /* end of running mean */
```

Program 16_4 Passing parameters to a function by reference

Exercise 16.4 (*see Appendix B for sample answer*)

Implement and test a function, which when given a distance in metres, converts it into feet and inches (there are 3.280839895 feet/metre and 12 inches in a foot). The converted values should be passed by reference, e.g. the function header could be:

```
void metres_to_feet(const float metres, int *feet, float *inches);
```

16.11 Summary: *pass by reference*

In C actual parameters are passed into a function *by value*, i.e. copies of the *actual parameters* are made in temporary variables and these are passed. To *pass by reference* the programmer explicitly passes the address of an object as the actual parameter to the function (using the address operator &). Within the function a pointer is used to access the memory allocated to the object (using the indirection operator *). In fact, C is still passing the actual parameter by value but it is the value of the address of the object that is passed, not a copy of the value of the object itself. The function then uses the value of the address (via a pointer) to access the memory allocated to the object.

Both the calling and called functions must agree which parameters are to be passed using *pass by value* and which using *pass by reference*. When a parameter is to be passed *by reference*:

1   The calling function must remember to prefix the name of the object with the address operator & when calling the function (arrays are the exception, see Chapter 19).

2   The called function must:
    (a) declare the corresponding formal parameter to be a pointer to the type of object.
    and (b) prefix the name of the corresponding formal parameter with the indirection operator * to access the memory allocated to the object.

The use of function prototypes, introduced by ANSI C, enables compilers to check that an address is passed as an actual parameter when the corresponding formal parameter is a pointer. In addition a modern compiler will issue errors or warnings if a pointer is used in a dubious way, e.g. by forgetting to prefix the name of the formal parameter with the indirection operator *.

16.12 Efficiency: parameter passing and function result

C passes parameters into a function *by value*, i.e.:

        (a) a temporary variable of the type of the formal parameter is created on the stack,
    then (b) the value of the actual parameter is copied into the temporary variable (the value being converted if necessary).

In the case of the fundamental types (int, float, etc.) this is a small overhead. When passing large objects (such as large *structures*) the overhead in creating the temporary copy of the data members not only takes processor time but may cause stack overflow. For example, the structure student, used in Section 24.6 to hold student records, takes 52 bytes under Turbo C and 60 bytes under GNU C. It is therefore recommended to pass such objects *by reference*, i.e.

(a) a temporary pointer is created on the stack,

then (b) the *address* of the actual parameter is copied into the pointer.

Inside the function the pointer is used to access the memory allocated to the actual parameter. Clearly, when *passing by reference*, the function has access to the memory used to store the actual parameter and may corrupt its value. If the value should not be changed the formal parameter should be const qualified, see implementation file stu_lib.c in Chapter 24.

A similar problem occurs when returning a function result as the return statement creates a temporary object of the function return type and copies the function result into it. The fundamental types are normally returned in processor registers, e.g. Microsoft C on an IBM PC compatible returns a 16-bit function result (e.g. an int) in the AX register and a 32-bit function result (e.g. a long int) in the AX and DX registers. In the case of larger objects the result would be stored in memory and a *pointer* (an address) to it returned. Thus returning large structures as a function result can cause a significant processing overhead. In such cases alternatives should be considered, e.g.:

1   returning the result via a function parameter *by reference*, see Section 16.8
2   returning, as a function result, a *pointer* to an object which holds the result, see Section 22.2.

In the latter case the pointer must be to an external object, a static local object (see Section 17.5) or an object in dynamic memory (see Chapter 25). Do not return a pointer to a local automatic object as the object is destroyed on exit from the function and the pointer will be referencing something which no longer exists. See function str_ch_find in implementation file str_libp.c in Section 22.3 for an example of returning a pointer as a function result.

16.13 Using preprocessor macros to generate *inline functions*

The preprocessor #define directive can be used to define macros with parameters, e.g.:

```
#define IDENTIFIER(parm_1, parm_2, parm_3, ........) replacement_text
```

Note that there must be no spaces between IDENTIFIER and the (or the text (parm_1, parm_2, parm_3, ...) would be treated as part of replacement_text.

When the macro is called the preprocessor replaces each occurrence of the formal parameters parm_1, parm_2, etc. with the corresponding actual parameter. For example, Program 16_1 contained a function which evaluated the square of a number which could be implemented as a macro (remember not to put a ; on the end of the line, see Section 5.5):

```
#define square(a) a * a
```

The macro could be used in line 26 of Program 16_1 as though it was a function call:

```
answer = square(x);                              /* call function */
```

after preprocessing the compiler would get:

```
answer = x * x;
```

Although macros appear to be similar to functions they are expanded *inline* with the code and are therefore more efficient in terms of execution time, i.e. the overheads of parameter passing and function call and return are avoided. Program 16_5 contains code which compares the relative timings of 100000000 calls to function and macro versions of square:

23-27   finds in seconds the time for a for statement with 100000000 loops
29-33   finds the time for 100000000 loops call function square()
35-39   finds the time for 100000000 loops call macro msquare().

```
1 /* Program 16_5 - compare function and macro versions of square()          */
2
3 #include <stdio.h>                              /* standard stream I/O library */
4 #include <time.h>
5
6 /*-----------------------------------------------------------------------*/
7 /* preprocessor macro to square a number */
8 #define msquare(x) (x) * (x)
9
10 /*-----------------------------------------------------------------------*/
11 /* Function to square a number                                           */
12 float square(float number)                            /* function header */
13 {
14     return  number * number;                          /* square number */
15 }                                                   /* end of function square */
16
17 int main(void)
18 {
19     float x = 2, answer, time1;                       /* local variables */
20     time_t start_time;
21     long int i;
22
23     start_time = clock();                            /*  get time for loops */
24     for (i = 0; i < 100000000L; i++)
25        /* dummy operation */ ;
26     time1 = (float) (clock() - start_time) / CLOCKS_PER_SEC;
27     printf("time for 100000000 loops %f seconds\n", time1);
28
29     start_time = clock();                   /* get time using function calls */
30     for (i = 0; i < 100000000L; i++)
31        answer = square(x);                           /* call function */
32     printf("function square called 100000000 times %f seconds\n",
33             (clock() - start_time) / CLOCKS_PER_SEC - time1);
34
35     start_time = clock();                    /* get time using macro calls */
36     for (i = 0; i < 100000000L; i++)
37        answer = msquare(x);                          /* call macro */
38     printf("macro square called 100000000 times %f seconds\n",
39             (clock() - start_time) / CLOCKS_PER_SEC - time1);
40     return 0;
41 }                                              /* end of function main */
```

Program 16_5   Compare function and macro versions of square()

The above shows a fairly crude but effective way of timing events within a computer system (assuming that an optimising compiler does not optimise the loops out of existence and that one is not using a multi-processing environment where other processes could distort the figures). The function clock() (in <time.h>) returns the number of clock ticks since program execution began and CLOCKS_PER_SEC is the number of clock ticks per second (see Section 12.4 and Appendix C.15). A run on an IBM PC compatible Pentium P133 under MS-DOS 6.2 and DJ's port GNU C V2.6.3 gave:

```
time for 100000000 loops 4.504342 seconds
function square called 100000000 times 13.458095 seconds
macro square called 100000000 times 5.218445 seconds
```

It can be seen that for a simple function such as square the run time of the macro version is less than half that of the function version. However, the complete macro code is generated on each call so long macros should be avoided (a function call becomes more efficient in terms of memory usage).

Because the macro call is replaced using literal substitution obscure errors can occur. Consider the following use of the macro square:

```
#define square(a) a * a
     float x = 10, z;
     z = square(x + 2);
```

The value assigned to z is 32 (not 144) because the macro call is expanded to:

```
     z = x + 2 * x + 2;
```

The order of evaluation is x + (2 * x) + 2. Now consider:

```
     float x = 10, y = 200, z;
     z = y / square(x);
```

This would assign z the value 200 (not 2) because the macro call is expanded to:

```
     z = y / x * x;
```

The order of evaluation is (y / x) * x.

To overcome these problems it is highly recommended that when the formal parameters are used in macros they are enclosed in parentheses and the whole replacement_text is enclosed in parentheses, e.g. in Program 16_5 macro msquare is written:

```
#define msquare(x) ((x) * (x))
```

and the above examples of its use would then work 'as expected'. Now consider:

```
     float x = 10, z;
     z = square(++x);
```

This would result in x being incremented twice and the value 144 assigned to z. Avoid operations which have side effects in macro calls, e.g. increment and decrement operators, input/output or calls to functions which return different values on successive calls (such as the fibonacci number function in Section 17.6).

The definition of a macro may contain a call to another macro (which has already been defined). For example, a macro to cube a value:

```
#define square(a) ((a) * (a))
#define cube(a)    (square(a) * (a))
```

Because macros only deal with pure text replacement they have no knowledge of C types and the same macro can be used with any suitable type of data. For example, the above macro square could be used to square integers or floats. Consider:

```
#define swap(type, a, b) {type temp; temp = a; a = b; b = temp;}
```

This defines a macro which will swap two variables of type (the function swap_int of Program 16_3 could only swap integer values). Clearly care must be taken when calling the macro as it may only be called where a statement may be used and the actual parameters must be simple variables. For example (in file c16\p16_6.c on the disk):

```
int x = 10, z = 25;            /* from Program 16_6 in file c16\p16_6.c */
float a = 1, b = 2;

swap(int, z, x)
swap(float, a, b)
```

A run of Program 16_6 showning the values before and after calling swap gave:

```
x = 10 and z = 25
a = 1.000000 and b = 2.000000
x = 25 and z = 10
a = 2.000000 and b = 1.000000
```

Preprocessor macros as function replacements are a powerful tool but should be used with care, i.e. there is no parameter type checking/conversion and *side effects* can arise. They should only be used with small functions and where efficiency is critical, e.g. subscript calculations for multi-dimensional matrices, see files matrix2.h and matrix3.h in Chapter 26. In general implement the code using 'normal functions' and then recode critical functions using macros and see the effect. Note that C++ overcomes this problem by the use of inline functions which enable ordinary functions to be generated inline with the code in a similar way to macros (but preserving parameter type checking, etc.).

Exercise 16.5 (see Appendix B for sample answer)

Implement a function which returns the larger of a pair of integer parameters, e.g.:

```
int maximum(const int x1, const int x2)                    /* function header */
```

Test with a suitable main which calls the function with integer and real parameters; comment on the results. Rewrite the function as a preprocessor macro and repeat the tests; comment on the results (see files c16\ex16_5a.c and c16\ex16_5b.c for sample answers).

Problems for Chapter 16

1 Implement a function which determines the capacitance of a parallel plate capacitor:

$$C = \epsilon_r \epsilon_0 A / D \text{ farads}$$

    where: A   is the area of the plates in metres^2
              D   is the distance between the plates in metres
              ϵ_r is the relative permittivity of the dielectric material between the plates
              ϵ_0 is the permittivity of free space = 8.854e-12.

2 Implement a function to find the roots of a quadratic equation $ax^2 + bx + c = 0$. The function should cope with real or complex roots (see problems for Chapters 8 and 11). The function prototype should be (the roots x1 and x2 are *passed by reference*):

```
int quadratic(const float a, const float b, const float c, float *x1, float *x2);
```

The function result should return 0 for real roots (x1 and x2 are the roots) and 1 for complex roots (x1 and x2 being the real and imaginary components respectively).

17

Towards larger programs

A large program can consist of hundreds of functions and attention must now be paid to the problems of managing data storage and the flow of information between functions.

17.1 Information hiding and the scope of identifiers

An important concept in Software Engineering is *information hiding*. Program modules are kept as independent as possible by controlling the passage of information between modules, i.e. a module may only access the data and functions that it actually uses. Information hiding is facilitated in different programming languages using different techniques. In C the *scope* of a particular identifier determines where it may be used:

local scope   used within a compound statement (see Section 17.3)

function scope   used **anywhere** within the function in which they are declared; only labels have *function scope*, see Section 14.3

file scope   used within a particular file of the program (see Section 17.4).

Identifiers in *file scope* may be local to the file (have *local linkage*) or may be referenced by other files in a multi-file program (have *external linkage*), see Chapter 18.

17.2 Declarations and definitions

A variable may need to be accessed by program code in a number of separate source code files of a multi-file program. There then arises the problem of how and where storage for the variable is allocated and how code in other files can then access that storage, i.e. several files could attempt to allocate storage to variables of the same name which would cause errors when the object code of the files was linked. This leads to the separate concepts of the *declaration* and *definition* of a variable:

declaration   a specification of the name and type of the variable

definition   a declaration which *defines* (allocates storage for) the variable.

The variable *declarations* in the sample programs so far have all been *definitions* in that each defined an entity for the names to refer to, e.g. Program 5_2 line 9:

```
int main(void)
{
    float angle = 25.0f, sin_2a, cos_2a;           /* define local variables */
    ...
```

This *declares* `angle`, `sin_2a` and `cos_2a` to be of type `float`. They are also *definitions* in that the compiler would allocate storage, e.g. four bytes for each `float`. Understanding the difference between *declarations* and *definitions* becomes important in multi-file programs where a variable is *defined* in one file (with storage allocated) and *declared* in another (to allow it to access the storage allocated in the first file), see Chapter 18.

In fact we have already come across the concept of separate *declarations* and *definitions* when dealing with functions:

function prototype   *declares* the name, parameters and function result
function definition   a function header followed by the function code.

In addition, the `parameter_list` in the function header (or prototype) *declares* the names and types of the *formal parameters* (which are replaced by the *actual parameters* when the function is called).

In summary, there must be exactly one definition of each variable, function and enumerator in a program; there can be as many declarations as required.

17.3 Local identifiers and local scope

Local identifiers are those local to a compound statement and have *local scope*:

1   Within a compound statement *local identifiers* (function prototypes, variables, etc.) may be used from the point of declaration/definition up to the end of the compound statement in which they are declared or defined.
2   The *formal parameters* of a function may be used from the point of declaration up to the end of the compound statement which forms the body of the function.

Although the same identifier may be used to define local variables in different compound statements the identifiers are distinct and do not refer to the same variable. An identifier declared/defined within a compound statement will 'hide' any identifier with the same name declared/defined outside.

17.4 External identifiers and file scope

Identifiers (functions, variables, etc.) declared/defined outside functions have *file scope* and may be used from the point of declaration/definition to the end of the file in which they are declared or defined. Such identifiers are said to be *external*. In addition external identifiers may also be accessed from other files if they have *external linkage* (see Chapter 18). Because external identifiers may be accessed by any function which follows the declaration in the file they must be used with care if the concept of *information hiding* is to be maintained.

External variables are allocated storage and initialised prior to the start of program execution and maintained until the program terminates. They may be initialised with the proviso that the initial values are constants (local variables my be initialised with any meaningful expression using constants and previously declared variables and functions). External variables not explicitly initialised are initialised to zero when program execution starts.

A formal parameter declared in a function header or a local identifier declared within a compound statement will 'hide' any external identifier of the same name. Careful naming will avoid such possibly confusing situations.

```
 1 /* Program 17_1 - examples of scope of local and external variables */
 2 #include <stdio.h>
 3
 4 float a = 2, b = 10;                         /* external variables a and b */
 5 const float PI = 3.14159f;              /* external const qualified variable */
 6
 7 int main(void)
 8 {
 9     int test(float, int);                       /* function prototype */
10     int i, x = 5;                            /* variables local to main */
11     /* can use external a, b and PI and local i and x */
12
13     for (i = 1 ; i < b ; i++)
14         {
15         int x = 2, y = 10;
16         /* can use external a, b and PI, local i and own local x & y */
17
18         printf("\ni = %d, a = %f, b = %f, PI = %f, x = %d, y = %d, test = %d ",
19             i, a, b, PI, x, y, test(a, x));
20         }
21     return 0;
22 }
23
24 int i = 2;                                   /* external variable i */
25
26 int test(float b, int j)                 /* formal parameters b and j */
27 {
28     /* can use external a, PI and i and formal parameters b and j */
29   · a = a + j;                      /* altering value of external variable */
30     return (b * i);                          /* function result */
31 }
```

Program 17_1 Examples of scope of local and external variables

Program 17_1 shows some simple examples of the scope of local and external variables:

4	define external variables a and b and assign initial values
5	define external const qualified variable PI and assign it the value 3.14159f
7	start of function main
9	declare prototype of function test
10	define variables local to main
11	at this point external a, b and PI and local i and x can be used
13-20	a for statement executed while i < b

     15   define local x and y (x defined in line 10 is now 'hidden')

     18-19   print various values including result of a call to function test

24	define external variable i
26	function header for test with formal parameters b and j (the formal parameter b 'hides' the external variable b)
29	assign a new value to the external variable a
30	return a function result.

Fig. 17.1 is a diagrammatic representation of the scope of identifiers in Program 17_1.

```
float a = 2, b = 10;
const float PI = 3.14159f;


int main(void)
{
        int test(float, int);
        int i, x = 5;
        /* can use external a, b and PI and local i and x */


            for (i = 1 ; i < b ; i++)
                {
                int x = 2, y =10;
                /* can use external a, b and PI,
                    local i and own local x & y */

                printf("          ",
                        i, a, b, PI, x, y, test(a, x));
                }


        return 0;
}

int i = 2;

int test(float b, int j)
{
    /* can use external a, PI and i   *
     *   and formal parameters b and j */
    a = a + j;
    return (b * i);
}
```

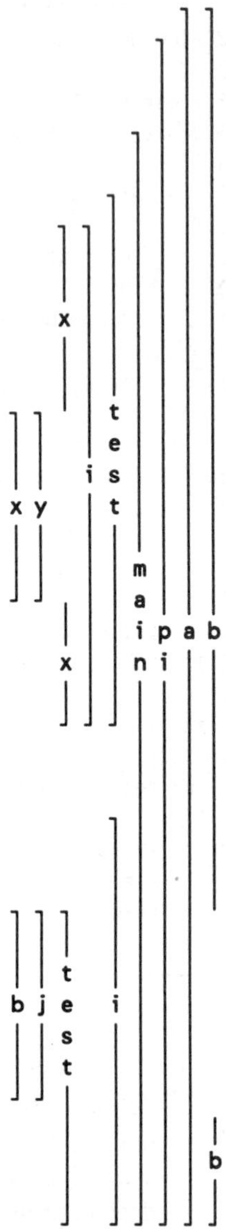

Fig. 17.1 Diagram showing the scope of local and external variables in Program 17_1

Note:

1   The variable x defined in line 10 cannot be accessed from within the compound statement in lines 14 to 20 because it is 'hidden' by the declaration of x in line 15, i.e. any references within the compound statement will access the x defined in line 15. The variables x and y defined in line 15 will be lost when the compound statement finishes and any further references will access the x defined in line 10.

2   The formal parameter b defined in the header of function test (line 26) 'hides' the external variable b defined in line 4.

Note that the external variable a which is an actual parameter to the call of function test in line 19 is altered within test in line 29. If great care is not taken such alterations to external variables can give rise to unforeseen *side effects* and is therefore not recommended (see Section 18.8 for a discussion of side effects). Work out on paper what the results of the program should be and then run the program (file c17\p17_1.c on the disk); compare the results!

It can be seen that the same identifiers may refer to different things in different parts of the program. Program 17_1 purely shows the effect of identifier scope and it is not recommended practice to use the same name to mean several different things. If a variable which is to be local to a compound statement is not defined (such as variable x in line 15 of Program 17_1) and the same name is already defined (as in line 10 of Program 17_1), run-time errors will occur which can be very difficult to find.

17.5 *Automatic* and *static* storage classes

The *storage class* of a variable determines its period of existence, i.e. the points where memory is allocated to store the variable and when it is deallocated and the contents lost. In C there are two declarable *storage classes*:

automatic   Objects are local to each invocation of a compound statement. Each time the compound statement is entered the variables are created and lost on exit.

static   Objects exist and retain their values throughout the execution of the entire program. The variables are created prior to function main being called and exist until main returns control to the operating system.

By default *external* variables have the storage class *static* and local variables the storage class *automatic*. It is possible, however, to give local variables the *static* storage class by the explicit use of the static storage class specifier.

The main problem with external variables is that all functions following the declaration/definition will have access to the values and may corrupt them. If only one function needs to maintain the values of variables between successive calls *static* local variables are more suitable as they are allocated permanent storage which is maintained until the program terminates, i.e. the permanent information is 'hidden' within the function. *Static* local variables can be explicitly initialised using constants otherwise they are automatically initialised to zero. A *static* local variable is initialised the first time control passes through its definition; it may then be changed and the updated value is available the next time the function is called.

17.6 Evaluating Fibonacci numbers using *static* local variables

The Fibonacci numbers (0 1 1 2 3 5 8 13 21 34 55 89 144 233 377 610 987 etc.) are evaluated using the following relationship:

$$F_0 = 0 \text{ and } F_1 = 1 \text{ then } F_{n+2} = F_{n+1} + F_n$$

A function which evaluates the numbers needs to store the values of F_n and F_{n+1} between successive calls and *static* local variables are the simplest way to do this. For example, the function fibonacci, in Program 17_2 (next page), contains the following (line 22):

```
    static long int fn_plus1 = 0, fn_plus2 = 1;      /* initialise f(0) & f(1) */
```

The variables fn_plus1 and fn_plus2 are local to the function but because the type is prefixed with the keyword static they are made permanent and initialised (the first time the function is called) with the values of the first two Fibonacci numbers:

fn_plus1 holds the next value of F_n to be returned by the function
fn_plus2 holds F_{n+1}.

On successive calls to fibonacci the variables are updated with the next values in the sequence, i.e.:

23 fn = fn_plus1; copy current value of F_n to local variable (will be the function result)
24 fn_plus1 = fn_plus2; evaluate F_{n+1}
25 fn_plus2 = fn + fn_plus1; evaluate F_{n+2}
26 return fn; return current value of F_n.

Because fn_plus1 and fn_plus2 are static local variables the updated values are available on the next call to the function.

```
 1 /* Program 17_2 - Evaluate Fibonacci numbers using static local variables  */
 2
 3 #include <stdio.h>                            /* standard stream I/O library */
 4
 5 int main(void)
 6 {
 7     long int fibonacci(void);                  /* function prototype */
 8     int counter;                               /* local variables */
 9
10     for (counter = 1; counter < 20 ; counter++)        /* print 20 numbers */
11         printf("%ld ", fibonacci());
12     return 0;
13 }
14
15 /*-----------------------------------------------------------------------*/
16 /* Function to return Fibonacci numbers, i.e.: 0 1 1 2 3 5 8 13 etc.      */
17 /*   evaluated thus: f(0) = 0, f(1) = 1,   f(n+2) = f(n+1) + f(n)         */
18 /* Function result: on successive calls return next Fibonacci number      */
19 long int fibonacci(void)
20 {
21     /* declare Fibonacci numbers in static local variables  */
22     static long int fn_plus1 = 0, fn_plus2 = 1;    /* initialise f(0) & f(1) */
23     long int fn = fn_plus1;                        /* set up f(n) */
24     fn_plus1 = fn_plus2;                           /* set up next f(n+1) */
25     fn_plus2 = fn + fn_plus1;                      /* set up next f(n+2) */
26     return fn;                                     /* return current f(n) */
27 }
```

Program 17_2 Evaluation of Fibonacci numbers (using static local variables)

Exercise 17.1 (*see Appendix B for sample answer*)

Modify the function running_mean (which maintains a running average) of Program 16_4 to hold the values of the count of numbers entered so far and the running average so far in local static variables (not passed by reference from the calling function). The function should have one parameter number and return the new average as the function result.

17.7 The type qualifiers *const* and *volatile*

17.7.1 The type qualifier *const*

Applying the keyword const in a definition or declaration indicates to the compiler that once the variable is initialised it is to be treated as a constant and should not be altered. If an attempt is made to alter a const qualified variable the result is implementation dependent. Some compilers issue a warning and then treat the variable like any other variable.

A local const qualified variable may be initialised with any arbitrary expression, i.e. the compiler does not need to know the value at compile time (external variables may only be initialised with constants):

```
int test(int x)
{
    const int X_TWO = x * 2;      /* initialise constant with parameter value * 2 */
    ...
```

The constant x_value is initialised (on each call to the function) with the value of the parameter x.

It is up to the programmer to ensure that a variable qualified as const in a definition in one file is similarly qualified in declarations in other files. Collecting all the declarations in a header file (discussed in Section 18.4) helps to prevent this type of error.

17.7.2 The type qualifier *volatile*

Applying the keyword volatile in a definition or declaration indicates to the compiler that the contents of the variable are subject to unpredictable alterations and references to it must not be optimised. For example, it may be a variable which will be changed by an interrupt service routine, or an I/O register which will be changed by the action of the corresponding I/O device (see Chapter 31 on low-level programming). A typical situation is where a program is in a loop waiting for an I/O device to become ready, i.e. the loop continuously tests a bit in a memory mapped I/O register. The problem is that a modern optimising compiler will notice that the loop tests the same address again and again and, on entry to the loop, makes a copy of it in a high speed CPU register. It then tests the contents of the CPU register within the loop! Using volatile tells the compiler that variable may be changed by something external to the code and prevents the compiler optimising references to it. If a volatile I/O register should not be changed by the program it can also be type qualified with const, e.g.:

```
const volatile unsigned char io_register;       /* a byte sized I/O register */
```

This declares a byte sized variable io_register which may not be altered by the program but is subject to changes from outside the program.

17.8 Summary: identifier scope

The *scope* of a particular identifier determines where it may be used:

local scope   within a compound statement *local identifiers* (formal function parameters, function prototypes, variables, etc.) may be used from the point of declaration or definition up to the end of the compound statement, see Section 17.3

function scope used **anywhere** within the function in which they are declared; only labels have *function scope*, see Section 14.3

file scope   external identifiers (functions, variables, etc.) declared/defined outside functions and *classes* have *file scope* and may be used from the point of declaration or definition to the end of the file, see Section 17.4

Identifiers (functions, variables, etc.) in *file scope* may be local to the file (said to have *local linkage*) or may be referenced by other files in a multi-file program (said to have *external linkage*), see Chapter 18.

17.9 Storage classes

The storage that is allocated for a variable (a simple variable or a structured type such as an array or structure) is dependent upon its storage class:

automatic local variable   defined within a compound statement
static local variable   defined within a compound statement
formal parameter to a function declared as a parameter in a function header
external variable   defined outside function bodies

Local variables are those declared/defined within a compound statement and *external* variables are those declared/defined outside functions.

Automatic local variables. This is the default storage class for variables defined within compound statements (see also the *static* and *register* storage classes below). The scope of automatic local variables is from the point of definition up to the end of the compound statement in which they are defined. They are allocated storage (and optionally initialised) each time control passes through the definition of the variable and deallocated on exit from the compound statement (any contents are then lost). Automatic local variables may be initialised with any meaningful expression using constants and previously declared variables and functions (every time the statement is reentered the automatic variables are recreated and reinitialised). The contents of automatic local variables not explicitly initialised will be *undefined*. These are the 'normal' working variables of the program.

Static local variables. If the definition of a local variable is prefixed with the keyword static it is allocated permanent storage the first time control passes through the definition and maintained until the program terminates. The scope of static local variables is the same as automatic local variables, i.e. from the point of definition up to the end of the compound statement in which they are defined. Static local variables may be explicitly initialised using constants otherwise they are automatically initialised to zero; initialisation being performed the first time control passes through the definition. The values stored in *static* local variables can be changed during program execution and the updated values will be available when the compound statement is reentered. These are generally used when a single function needs to retain information between successive calls and the information should be 'hidden' within the function and not accessible from outside.

Formal parameters to a function.   Storage is allocated on entry to the function and initialised with the values of the actual parameters (see also the *register* storage class below). Their scope is from the point of declaration up to the end of the function.

External variables.   Permanent storage is allocated and initialised prior to program execution and maintained until the program terminates.   External variables may be explicitly initialised using constants otherwise they are automatically initialised to zero. The scope is from the point of definition up to the end of the file. This may be extended (within the file and to other files) by declaring the variable with the keyword extern (discussed in Chapter 18).   The scope of external variables prefixed with the keyword static is limited to the file in which they are defined.

17.9.1 The storage class *register* *

The storage class *register* only applies to *automatic* local variables and the formal parameters of functions. It advises the compiler that the associated variables are heavily used and should, if possible, be stored in processor registers, e.g. to improve the loop performance:

```
register int i;
for (i = 1 ; i < 10000 ; i++)
    ....
```

The keyword *register* is purely advisory (compiler does not have to take any notice of it) and in most implementations it will be ignored if the address of the variable is taken.

In practice, *register* variables should be used sparingly within time critical routines, keeping in mind that a processor only has a few processor registers and over use can slow a program down if the compiler has to save a large number of registers when entering a function. In the main, the normal optimisation processes of a modern compiler should be left to generate efficient code. If it is found that a particular section of code is executing too slowly (e.g. in a real-time system) various approaches can be taken:

1   The algorithm should be examined to see if it can be made more efficient.
2   Small critical functions can be implemented in assembly language (see Chapter 30).
3   A faster computer could be purchased (this is often cheaper than paying a programmer to make the code more efficient).

18

Multi-file programs

Chapter 17 considered the problems of managing data storage and the flow of information between functions in programs implemented as a single source code file. This chapter will describe the techniques used to split up a program into several separate source code files, discuss the management of functions and data storage within the files and the flow of information between functions in different files.

18.1 Modular programming and multi-file programs

During the program specification and design stages logical tasks or sequences of tasks, which will become modules, are identified and specified. Once a specification of the logical steps performed by each module has been drawn up (modules can contain other modules and call other modules as required) the individual modules, which may be groups of *functions* (and *classes* in C++), can then be designed, coded and tested. Modules are kept as independent as possible by controlling the passing of information between modules and only allowing an individual module access to data that it actually uses. Errors then tend to be localised to a module or a group of modules making them much easier to find than if all modules had access to all the data (Chapter 17 discussed *information hiding* within functions using *static* local variables). Once working satisfactorily, modules can be integrated to build up to the complete package. As modules are integrated with others, errors can occur due to faulty interaction of modules. Modular programming tends to limit errors and isolate them to particular sets of modules within the package. In addition, if errors are found whilst the package is being used in its application environment, or when upgrades are required, it is easy to identify the relevant modules and modify just these.

In practice many modules provide common facilities which are required by programs in a given application area. Such modules tend to form logical groups which are implemented as libraries of functions, e.g. the standard maths library of C or a graphics library to support CAD packages. The program source code of such a library would be maintained in a separate implementation file or files and as each module is completed it is added to the file. The implementation file is then compiled into object code to be linked into the application programs as required.

In addition to aiding in the implementation and maintenance of libraries there are a number of other very good reasons for splitting a program up into separate files:

1   The code within each file is more manageable in terms of finding and editing particular sections of text.
2   If modules which are already implemented and tested are in separate files there is no likelihood of the programmer inadvertently corrupting them in an editing session.
3   It is easier to constrain the access of individual modules or groups of modules to the data sets required (*information hiding*).
4   The shorter the source code file the faster it will compile.

18.2 External linkage and external variables and functions

18.2.1 Declarations and definitions

Section 17.2 introduced the concepts of the *declaration* and *definition* of a variable:

declaration   a specification of the name and type of the variable
definition   a declaration which *defines* (allocates storage for) the variable.

When implementing multi-file programs it is important to understand the difference between *declarations* and *definitions*, i.e. a variable *defined* in one file (with storage allocated) may be *declared* in others (allowing access to storage allocated in the first file).

18.2.2 External variables and functions

External variables (defined outside functions) and functions have *file scope* and may be used from the point of definition to the end of the file. In addition, an external variable or function may be referenced by code either in the same file (prior to definition) or in another file:

functions   by declaring a *function prototype* and then calling the function as normal
variables   by declaring the variable type and name prefixed with extern.

Thus the *scope* of external identifiers may be extended beyond (or within) the file which contains its definition. For example, Program 18_1 (below) consists of two files:

Program 18_1a   contains the definition of function main and the declaration of variable data and function square
Program 18_1b   contains the definitions of variable data and function square.

```
1  /* Program 18_1a, first file of a two-file program */
2
3  #include <stdio.h>
4
5  int square(int x);                        /* declare function prototype */
6  extern int data;                          /* declare external variable */
7
8  int main(void)                              /* define function main */
9  {
10     printf("%d\n", square(data));          /* call function square */
11     return 0;
12 }
```

Program 18_1a First file (of a two-file program) containing function main

```
1  /* Program 18_1b, second file of a two-file program */
2
3  int data = 5;                            /* define external variable */
4  int square(int x)                         /* define function square */
5  {
6      return x * x;                          /* return square */
7  }
```

Program 18_1b Second file (of a two-file program) containing function square

In Program 18_1a the declaration of variable data is prefixed with the keyword extern, i.e.:

```
extern int data;                              /* declare external variable */
```

The extern in line 6 of Program 18_1a tells the compiler that this is a declaration, not a definition (the variable will be defined later in the file or in another file). The function prototype in line 5 does not need an extern (it will be assumed), however, it is common practice to put extern in front of such function prototypes to make it clear that its definition is in another file.

After compilation the object files of Programs 18_1a and 18_1b must be linked together (together with any standard libraries required) to form the executable program. For example, using the Turbo C V3.00 command line compiler:

```
tcc -w p18_1a.c p18_1b.c
```

This compiles source files p18_1a.c and p18_1b.c and links the resultant object files with the standard libraries. If a file of a multi-file program is missing the linker will give *undefined reference* errors or similar, e.g. attempting to compile and link Program 18_1a by itself (using Turbo C V3.00):

```
c:> tcc p18_1a.c ↵
Turbo Link  Version 5.0 Copyright (c) 1992 Borland International
Error: Undefined symbol _square in module p18_1a.c
Error: Undefined symbol _data in module p18_1a.c
```

When using the Turbo C/C++ IDE (integrated development environment) a project file, which contains details of the files that make up the program, has to be set up, i.e.:

1   Select **Project** then **Open project** and enter a filename to hold the new project details, e.g. p18_1.prj.
2   Select **Project** then **Add item** and enter the filenames which make up the multi-file program, e.g. p18_1a.c and p18_1b.c; when complete select **Done**

To compile and link the complete program select **Compile** then **Make**. **Make** will compile any source code files in the project that are not up to date then link the project. When work has finished on a multi-file program select **Project** then **Close project**. Each multi-file program would have its own project file which needs to be opened each time the program is worked on. The disk which accompanies this text contains project files for Turbo C V3.0 (.prj) and Borland C V4.5 (.ide) for all the multi-file programs. If one is working on a multi-file program it is important to ensure that all files are compiled for the same target environment, e.g. Turbo C V3.00 under DOS supports tiny, small, medium, compact, large and huge memory models enabling different size programs to be built. Linking programs where files have been compiled for different target environments can give odd results at run-time (assuming that they will link at all).

It is important that there must be exactly one definition of each variable, function and enumerator in a program, e.g. if extern was missing from line 6 of Program 18_1a it would become a definition and give an error at link time; under Turbo C V3.00:

```
Error: _data defined in module p18_1a.c is duplicated in module p18_1b.c
```

Beware, if a variable declaration using extern is initialised it becomes a definition, i.e.:

```
extern int data = 5;                          /* this is a definition !! */
```

It is up to the programmer to ensure that the information in declarations and definitions correspond, i.e. it is possible to define a variable as a float in one file and declare it (using extern) as an int in another or to define a const qualified object in one file and not const qualify declarations in another. For example, if line 6 of Program 18_1a was:

```
extern float data;                              /* declare external variable */
```

the resultant files would compile and link OK, even though data is defined as an int in one file and declared as a float in another. What happens when the program is executed is implementation dependent, e.g. under Turbo C V3.00 the program crashed with:

```
Floating Point Error: Domain
Abnormal Program Termination
```

The use of *header files* can avoid such situations, see Section 18.4.

Functions and variables that can be accessed by other files are said to have *external linkage*. The fact that functions and variables defined in one file can be accessed from all other files of a multi-file program clashes with the concept of *information hiding* in that modules should only have access to the functions and data sets which they require. Although C lacks the more rigorous techniques available in languages such as C++ it is possible to restrict the scope of external functions and variables to the file in which they are defined (using the *static* keyword, see next section). Such functions and variables are said to have *internal linkage*.

18.3 Internal linkage and *static* external variables and functions

Unfortunately the keyword static means two different things depending upon its context:

static local variables (see Section 17.5) are allocated permanent storage prior to program execution and maintained until the program terminates; initialisation being performed the first time control passes through the definition.

static external identifiers are external functions or variables with their scope restricted to the file in which they are defined. Such functions and variables are said to have *internal linkage*.

External variables and functions explicitly declared static are 'hidden' from code in other files thus making the program easier to understand. Code in other files cannot use the functions or alter the value of variables. In addition, if the compiler knows that access is restricted to the file it could perform some optimisation in terms of function calls or addressing the variables. Note that in C const qualifed objects have *external linkage* by default (in C++ they have *internal linkage*).

It is recommended that definitions of simple static const qualified objects (fundamental types, pointers, etc.) are placed in header files enabling the compiler to optimise the code more efficiently.

It is recommended that one uses variables with external linkage as little as possible, i.e. define all external variables as static. If a variable needs to be accessed from another file do this via a function which reads and/or sets the value of the variable. This gives a much cleaner interface allowing one to alter the data structures within a file without worrying about code in other files being affected (so long as the interface stays the same). In C++ *classes* allow an even more elegant way of implementing *information hiding*.

18.4 Constructing and using header files

Before a program can use functions and variables defined in another file it must declare them, and all such declarations must be consistent with each other and the definition. Although declarations can be within the program source code (Program 18_1a lines 5 and 6) this is tedious and a source of typing errors. The recommended technique is to construct a header file which is included in the program using the preprocessor #include directive, e.g.:

```
#include <filename>                    /* include file from 'standard' place */
#include "filename"    /* include file from current directory else 'standard' place */
```

These directives include the contents of filename at that point in the source program (filename can contain any valid C code). In the first form (filename enclosed in <>) the file is assumed to be in a 'standard' directory in the file system which the C compiler automatically searches, e.g. the header files for Turbo C are usually stored in directory \tc\include. The second form of #include (filename enclosed in "") searches the current directory for filename and then, if it is not found, the 'standard' directory. For example:

```
#include <math.h>                    /* include standard header file math.h */
#include "my_own.h"                    /* include header file my_own.h */
#include "my_func.c"                /* include C code from file my_func.c */
#include "c:\test\test1.c"        /* include C code from file c:\test\test1.c */
```

Header files are constructed by extracting function headers and the definitions of external variables from a file (using the editor) and amending as required. Many compilers have an option which will generate a header file of *function prototypes* from a C source code file without compiling, e.g. the /Zg option of the Microsoft C compiler.

Keeping header files and the files which use them synchronised is difficult. It is possible to modify a header file and associated implementation file and forget to recompile all the files which use it. Using the *project* option of integrated environments such as Turbo C V3.00 IDE may not overcome the problem; it can keep track of C source files which are modified and recompile then when the executable is built but not modified header files. Even when using more modern and sophisticated environments, such as Borland C++ V5.00 and Microsoft Visual C++ V4.00, which will keep track of modified header files one must be careful, e.g. one may modify a header file which is included by another header file. Compilers usually have a *Rebuild all* command (which recompiles all the files of a project) which is used when one suspects files may not be synchronised.

On the next page is Program 18_2b (a modification of part of Program 17_1) with associated Header file p18_2b.h. Consider Program 18_2b:

line

3   #include "p18_2b.h" includes its own header file
         this enables the compiler to check declarations in the header file against the
         corresponding definitions, e.g. if a variable declared as int is defined as float
5   function prototype of test2 (with internal linkage)
7   define external variables a and b (with external linkage, the default)
9   define static external variables c, e and i (with internal linkage)
11-17   define function test (with external linkage, the default)
         this is similar to function test in Program 17_1
19-23   define static function test2 (with internal linkage).

Note:

(a) The identifiers test (function), test2 (function), a, b, c, e and i are external.

(b) The scope of identifiers test2 (function), c, e and i is restricted to the file, i.e. they have internal linkage and are 'hidden' inside the file.

The corresponding header file p18_2.h contains:

3   declare function prototype for function test
5   define static external named constant PI (with internal linkage)
7   declaration of external variables a and b.

```
 1 /* Program 18_2b - other file of a multi-file program */
 2
 3 #include "p18_2b.h"                          /* include own header file */
 4
 5 static void test2(void);              /* declare function prototype */
 6
 7 float a = 2, b = 10;              /* define external variables a and b */
 8
 9 static int c, e, i = 2;        /* define external variables local to file */
10
11 int test(float b, int j)          /* define function wiuth external linkage */
12 {
13     /* can use external a, PI, c, e and i and formal parameters b and j */
14     a = a + j;                        /* altering value of external variable */
15     test2();                                    /* call function test2 */
16     return (b * i);                              /* function result */
17 }
18
19 static void test2(void)           /* define function with internal linkage */
20 {
21     /* can use external a, b, PI, c, e and i */
22     i = 10 * b;
23 }
```

Program 18_2b File of a multi-file program (file p18_2b.c)

```
 1 /* Header file p18_2b.h - header file for a two-file program */
 2
 3 int test(float b, int j);                    /* declare function prototype */
 4
 5 static const float PI = 3.14159f;  /* external constant with internal linkage */
 6
 7 extern float a, b;                           /* external variables a and b */
```

Header file p18_2b.h Header file of external identifiers defined in Program 18_2b

Program 18_2a (below) uses the variables and functions defined in Program 18_2b:

4   #include "p18_2b.h" include header file of Program 18_2b
6   define static external variables c and d (with internal linkage)
7   define external variable e (with external linkage)
9-23   define function main (with external linkage), similar to main in Program 17_1.

In this file the identifiers main (function), PI, a, b, c, d, e and test (function) are all external but the scope of c, d and PI is restricted to the file. The definition of the external identifiers c and e (in lines 6 and 7) will not clash with the external identifiers c and e defined in line 9 of Program 18_2b (which are static and are therefore 'hidden' within the file). In addition, although the named constant PI is defined in both Program 18_2a and 18_2b (by including header file p18_2b.h) it has internal linkage (it is declared static) and there is no clash between the two definitions.

```
 1 /* Program 18_2a - Main program file of a multi-file program */
 2
 3 #include <stdio.h>                          /* include standard I/O library */
 4 #include "p18_2b.h"                         /* include local header file */
 5
 6 static int c, d;          /* define external variables with internal linkage */
 7 float e;                                    /* define external e */
 8
 9 int main(void)
10 {
11     int i, x = 5;                           /* variables local to main */
12     /* can use external PI, a, b, c, d and e and internal i and x */
13
14     for (i = 1 ; i < b ; i++)
15         {
16         int x = 2, y =10;;
17         /* can use external PI, a, b, c, d, e, local i and own local x & y */
18
19         printf("\ni = %d, a = %f, b = %f, PI = %f, x = %d, y = %d, test = %d ",
20                 i, a, b, PI, x, y, test(a, x));
21         }
22     return 0;
23 }
```

Program 18_2a Main program file of a multi-file program (file p18_1a.c)

The same identifiers may refer to different things within files and in different files of a multi-file program. Programs 18_1 and 18_2 purely show the effect of identifier scope across multi-file programs and it is not recommended practice to use the same name to mean several different things.

As far as possible all external variables should be specified as static ('hidden' within the file) with functions providing an interface to the outside world, i.e. other files call the functions to access and manipulate the data. This gives a much cleaner interface allowing the data structures within a file to be altered without effecting code in other files (so long as the interface is not changed). Similarly any functions which do not need to be accessed from outside the file should be declared static.

18.5 Conditional selection

The conditional selection directives of the preprocessor enables the selection of sections of code which are to be passed (or not) to the compiler. The directives are:

```
#if expression             /* if expression is non-zero include the code following */
#ifdef identifier           /* if identifier is defined include the code following */
#ifndef identifier        /* if identifier is not defined include the code following */
```

If the condition is satisfied the code following (up to the next #else, #elif or #endif) is included otherwise it is skipped. The condition is terminated by:

```
#endif
```

The #else directive enables a choice of code selection, e.g.:

```
#ifdef identifier
    .....                           /* code included if identifier is defined */
#else
    .....                       /* code included if identifier is not defined */
#endif
```

The #elif directive is shorthand for else if, e.g.:

```
#ifdef identifier
    .....                           /* code included if identifier is defined */
#elif expression
    /* code included if identifier is not defined and expression is non-zero */
    .....
#endif
```

Conditional selection directives can be used as an aid to program portability. For example, a program may need to be executed on a range of target environments (host machine, operating system, etc.) and conditional selection directives can be used to include particular definitions and/or functions appropriate to the target.

In particular, when using #include, it is recommended that the same header file is not included more than once when compiling a source file. Not only is it inefficient to 'recompile' the same code more than once but identifiers may be defined more than once, which will generate compile time errors (declarations may be included many times so long as they agree, e.g. function prototypes). For example, when the header file p18_1b.h was included twice in Program 18_2a Turbo C V3.00 gave:

```
Error p18_2b.h 5: Variable 'PI' is initialised more than once
```

This indicates that PI was defined and initialised more than once when compiling the file. Include files may contain #include directives and in a large program it is possible to include the same file several times either directly or via other include files. The #ifndef directive can be used within a header file to check if it has already been included.

Fig. 18.1 (next page) shows a version of the header file p18_2b.h modified to include an #ifndef directive. When the file is first included _p18_2b_h_ is not defined so the #ifndef directive includes the text which follows; the identifier _p18_2b_h_ is then defined followed by the remainder of the file. If the file was included again _p18_2b_h_ would be defined and the #ifndef would skip the remainder of the text up to #endif. The convention for the identifier name to be used in this way is to use the name of the header file prefixed and postfixed with _ and the . replaced with _.

```
 1 /* Header file 18_2b.h - header file for a two-file program */
 2
 3 #ifndef _p18_2b_h_                      /* if _p18_2b_h_ is not defined */
 4 #define _p18_2b_h_                         /* define _p18_2b_h_ */
 5
 6 int test(float b, int j);               /* declare function prototype */
 7
 8 static const float PI = 3.14159f;  /* external constant with internal linkage */
 9
10 extern float a, b;                      /* external variables a and b */
11
12 #endif
```

Fig. 18.1 Version of header file p18_2b.h using #ifndef conditional selection directive

18.6 Random number generators *

Random number generators are commonly used in computer simulations of real life systems. The standard C library <stdlib.h> contains the following functions:

```
void srand(unsigned int seed);          /* set seed for random number sequence */
int rand(void);                 /* return random number in range 0 to RAND_MAX */
```

The function srand may be called to initialise the seed (default seed is 1) and then rand is called as often as required to get the next number in the sequence. The maximum random number possible is specified by the constant RAND_MAX (defined in <stdlib.h>).

In general, the library function rand uses the *linear congruential method* in which each number in a random sequence is calculated from its predecessor (MOD is the modulus operation, % in C):

$$\text{number}_{n+1} = (\textit{multiplier} * \text{number}_n + \textit{increment}) \text{ MOD } \textit{modulus}$$

The sequence of numbers generated by this formula is not truly random in that given a particular starting value of number_n (called the *seed*) the sequence generated is always the same (it is often called a *pseudo-random sequence*). In addition, the sequence will eventually repeat itself with a period no greater than *modulus* (and often much less).

The problem is that many standard random number generators are seriously defective and some are totally botched (page 276, Press *et al.* 1994) yielding very poor random sequences. Another major problem is that because rand returns an int the value of RAND_MAX is limited on machines where an int is 16 bits (typically RAND_MAX is 32767), i.e. one generates 1000000 random numbers and gets the same 32767 numbers thirty times. It is recommended that any rand which returns a 16-bit int should be rejected.

A weakness of linear congruential generators is that the low-order (least significant) bits are often much less random than the high-order bits. Thus to generate a value between 1 and 10 one would use the high-order bits as follows:

```
x = 1 + int(10.0 * rand()/(RAND_MAX + 1.0));
```

rather than using the low-order bits (which appears to be much simpler and faster):

```
x = 1 + rand() % 10;
```

In general it is recommended that serious applications should implement their own, proven, random number generator. Press *et al.* (1994) review a number of generators of which two will be described: a 'quick and dirty' generator (see problem 18.2) which is very fast and a better minimal standard generator (which is about ten times slower, see below).

```
1  /* Header file random.h - for random number generator    */
2
3  /* Initialise random number generator, return maximum random number    */
4  /* if seed <> 0 initialise random_seed with seed else with current time */
5  unsigned long int random_initialise(const unsigned long int seed);
6
7  /* Return next random number in sequence */
8  unsigned long int random_number(void);
```

Header file random.h For the random number generator in random0.c (below)

```
1  /* Implementation file random0.c - Minimal standard random number generator    */
2
3  #include <time.h>                          /* time and date functions library */
4  #include "random.h"                        /* 'my own' header file */
5
6  static const long int MULTIPLIER = 16807L,                    /* multiplier */
7                        MODULUS    = 2147483647L;                /* modulus */
8
9  static long int random_seed;     /* external variable holds random number seed */
10
11 /*-------------------------------------------------------------------------*/
12 /* Initialise random number generator, if seed <> 0 initialise random_seed    */
13 /*    with seed else with low-order bits (seconds) of current time            */
14 /* Function result: return maximum random number                              */
15 unsigned long int random_initialise(const unsigned long int seed)
16 {
17     if (seed) random_seed = seed;                        /* seed with value */
18     else      random_seed = (time(0) & 0x1f) + 1;        /* or time */
19     return  MODULUS - 1;                          /* return maximum random value */
20 }
21
22 /*-------------------------------------------------------------------------*/
23 /* Minimal standard random number generator from:                          */
24 /* 'Numerical recipes in C' by Press, Teukolsky, Vetterling & Flannery, 1994 */
25 /*   this version uses Schrage's algorithm to prevent 32-bit overflow        */
26 unsigned long int random_number(void)
27 {
28     const long int Q = 127773L,             /* used in Schrage's algorithm */
29                    R = 2836L;                /*  to prevent 32-bit overflow */
30
31     /* calculate random_seed = (MULTIPLIER * random_seed) % MODULUS   */
32     /*   without 32 bit overflow (using Schrage's algorithm ) */
33     random_seed = MULTIPLIER * (random_seed % Q) - R * (random_seed / Q);
34     if (random_seed < 0) random_seed = random_seed + MODULUS;
35     return random_seed;                        /* return next random number */
36 }
```

Implementation file random0.c Minimal random number generator (Press *et al.* 1994)

The *minimal standard* generator, recommended for general use (page 278, Press *et al.* 1994), uses the *simple multiplicative congruential* algorithm:

number$_{n+1}$ = *multiplier* * number$_n$ MOD *modulus*

with the values :

number$_{n+1}$ = (7^5 * number$_n$) MOD (2^{31} - 1) = 16807 * number$_n$ MOD 2147483647

which gives a generator with a period of 2^{31} - 2. Note that such a generator must not be seeded with 0; it perpetuates itself (0 will not occur for a non-zero seed). The main problem with this algorithm is that it is not possible to directly implement it on the majority of systems because the product exceeds the maximum value for a 32-bit integer.

Implementation file random0.c shows an implementation of the minimal standard generator which uses an algorithm due to Schrage (Press *et al.* 1994) to prevent 32 bit overflow. The file contains two functions random_initialise which seeds the generator and random_number which returns the next number in sequence. An external variable random_seed (line 9) is used to pass information between the functions and store information between successive calls of random_number (note that it is static so that its scope is 'local' to the file). The sequence of events in random_initialise is:

15 the function header: one parameter seed and returns a unsigned long int result
17 if seed is non-zero initialise random_seed with the value of seed
18 else initialise random_seed with the low-order bits (seconds) of the current time
19 return the maximum random value possible, i.e. *modulus* - 1.

Thus random_seed is initialised either from the value of seed (if seed is not zero) or from the low-order bits of the current time (time is defined in <time.h> and returns the calendar time, see Appendix C.15). Using the time to seed the generator is a crude but effective means of ensuring that successive runs of the program will start with different values of random_seed (unless run within the same second). The sequence in random_number is:

26   function header, no parameters and returns an unsigned long int function result
33-34   calculate random_number = 16807 * random_number % 2147483647
        using Schrage's algorithm to prevent 32-bit overflow (page 278, Press *et al.* 1994)
        intermediate results may be signed therefore long int is used for calculations
35   return the random number.

Associated with implementation file random0.c is the header file random.h which contains prototypes of the functions random_initialise and random_number. This provides an interface for programs which use the random number generator (see the test program in the file rand_tst.c on the disk which accompanies this text). It would therefore be possible for the implementation details to be changed so long as the interface was not affected, i.e. to replace the minimal generator with the 'quick and dirty' generator or a better generator (Press *et al.* 1994). It is so that random.h can be used with other generators that both functions return an unsigned long int function result, e.g. the maximum possible number generated by the 'quick and dirty' random number generator is 4294967295 decimal (the maximum for a 32-bit unsigned long int), see Problem 18.2. Note that random.h does not use condition selection; it is short and contains only function prototypes.

It is not recommended to use the standard C random number generator rand except for trivial applications (for a full discussion see Press *et al.* 1994). Compilers often have several alternative generators otherwise one should be implemented to suit the application.

18.7 Simulation of the flow of patients through a doctor's surgery *

```
 1 /* Program 18_3  Simulation of patients through a doctor's surgery          */
 2 /*   one doctor, 10 patients per day, consulting time between 2 and 10 minutes */
 3
 4 #include <stdio.h>                              /* standard stream I/O library */
 5 #include "random.h"                               /* random number functions */
 6
 7 static unsigned long int random_maximum;     /* maximum value of random number */
 8
 9 int main(void)
10 {
11     int consultation(void);                          /* function prototype */
12     int patient_waits, total_wait_time = 0, doctor_free = 0, doctor_waits;
13     int patient, patients, patient_arrives, interval, consultation_time;
14
15     random_maximum = random_initialise(0);         /* initialise with time */
16     printf("Enter appointment interval and number of patients each time ? ");
17     scanf("%d%d", &interval, &patients);
18     /* now loop working out consultation time for patients 1 to 10 */
19     for (patient = 1; patient <= 10; patient++)
20       {
21       /* work out time when patient arrives, how long they wait, etc. */
22       patient_arrives = ((patient - 1)/ patients) * interval;
23       patient_waits = doctor_free - patient_arrives;
24       consultation_time = consultation();
25       /* work out how long the patient or doctor has to wait  */
26       if (patient_waits > 0)
27           {                                 /* patient has to wait for doctor */
28           doctor_waits = 0;
29           total_wait_time = total_wait_time + patient_waits;
30           }
31       else
32           {                           /* doctor has to wait for next patient */
33           doctor_waits = -patient_waits;
34           patient_waits = 0;
35           }
36       printf(" Doctor free at %2d waits %2d, patient %2d arrives %2d "
37               "waits %2d, consults for %2d\n", doctor_free, doctor_waits,
38              patient, patient_arrives, patient_waits, consultation_time);
39       /* work out when doctor is free */
40       if (patient_waits > 0) doctor_free = doctor_free + consultation_time;
41       else                   doctor_free = patient_arrives + consultation_time;
42       }
43     printf("   mean patient wait time %f mins\n", total_wait_time / 10.0);
44     return 0;
45 }
46
47 /*----------------------------------------------------------------------*/
48 /* Function to return length of next consultation between 2 and 10 minutes    */
49 int consultation(void)
50 {
51     return 2 + (int) ((9.0 * random_number())/ (random_maximum + 1.0));
52 }
```

Program 18_3 Simulation of patients through a doctor's surgery

Program 18_3 is a very simple simulation of the flow of patients through a doctor's surgery (Program 19_4 is a more complex simulation). The model is very simple, there is one doctor who sees 10 patients in an afternoon with a consultation taking between 2 and 10 minutes. The consultation period is generated by the function consultation, lines 48 to 52, which calls random_number (described in the previous section) and returns a random consultation time in the range 2 to 10 minutes:

49 function header, no parameters and returns an int function result
51 return the next pseudo random consultation time in the range 2 to 10 minutes
    random_number returns a random number in the range 0 to random_maximum
    (int) ((9.0 * random_number())/ (random_maximum + 1.0)) gives value in range 0 to 8
    2 + (int) ((9.0 * random_number())/ (random_maximum + 1.0)), value in range 2 to 10.

The doctor's receptionist arranges appointments at set intervals of time (e.g. every 5 or 10 or 15 minutes) for a specified number of patients (e.g. 2 patients may have appointments every 10 minutes); this makes some allowance for patients being early or late or missing the appointment. The sequence of events in main of Program 18_3 is:

5   include header file "random.h" for the random number functions
11   declare function prototype for consultation, defined in lines 48 to 52
15   call random_initialise to seed the random number generator with the current time
         the function result is assigned to random_maximum
16-17   prompt user and read the appointment interval and the number of patients
19-42   a for loop processing each patient in turn
         22   work out time when patient arrives (assuming they are on time)
         23   work out how long patient has to wait for doctor to become free
                 variable doctor_free holds the time when the doctor becomes free
         24   call consultation() to determine the consultation_time
         26-35   an if statement which determines if the patient or doctor has to wait
                 27-30   patient has to wait for doctor, add time to total_wait_time
                 32-35   doctor has to wait, set up doctor_waits
         36-38   print information to display screen (see example below)
         40-41   an if statement which works out when doctor becomes free
                 40 patient had to wait, add consultation to time when doctor was free
                 41 doctor had to wait, add consultation to time when patient arrived
43   print out average patient wait time.

If the model is realistic the simulation will give some idea of how long the patients have to wait, if the doctor has time for a cup of tea, etc. A run of the program gave:

```
Enter appointment interval and number of patients each time ? 16 2↲
 Doctor free at  0 waits  0, patient  1 arrives  0 waits  0, consults for  2
 Doctor free at  2 waits  0, patient  2 arrives  0 waits  2, consults for  7
 Doctor free at  9 waits  7, patient  3 arrives 16 waits  0, consults for  2
 Doctor free at 18 waits  0, patient  4 arrives 16 waits  2, consults for  6
 Doctor free at 24 waits  8, patient  5 arrives 32 waits  0, consults for  5
 Doctor free at 37 waits  0, patient  6 arrives 32 waits  5, consults for  7
 Doctor free at 44 waits  4, patient  7 arrives 48 waits  0, consults for  7
 Doctor free at 55 waits  0, patient  8 arrives 48 waits  7, consults for  3
 Doctor free at 58 waits  6, patient  9 arrives 64 waits  0, consults for  3
 Doctor free at 67 waits  0, patient 10 arrives 64 waits  3, consults for  3
  mean patient wait time 1.900000 mins
```

18.8 Side effects

It is recommended that a single program statement or a function (composed of a number of statements) should perform a single cohesive operation. Function calls, nested assignment operators, and the increment and decrement operators cause *side effects* in that the value of variables may be changed by the evaluation of an expression.

For example, when evaluating expressions the order of evaluation is determined by the operator precedence and associativity, see Section 9.2. Except for the logical operators (see Section 11.3) the order of the evaluation of the operands is not specified, e.g.:

```
x = x * func_1(x) * func_2(x);
```

Function func_1 may be called before func_2 or vice versa (selected to be the most efficient for the architecture of the computer concerned). In the majority of cases this probably does not matter but a situation may arise where two functions are accessing and modifying a common data set and the order of evaluation is critical, i.e. a program which works on one machine fails when transported to another. In addition, if variable x is modified within one of the functions (e.g. if it is external and the function can access it) the result of the expression is totally unpredictable. This should be avoided.

A similar situation arises when a function is called in that the order in which the *actual parameters* are evaluated before being passed is not specified:

```
func_3(x, func_1(x), func_2(x));
```

Again func_1 may be called before func_2 or vice versa and the value of x passed to func_3 may be that before or after the calls (if it is modified within func_1 or func_2). However, all the parameters of a function are completely evaluated, including side effects, before a function is called (it is the order of evaluation that is not specified).

Another example is when using increment and decrement operators. There is no guarantee when an affected variable will change its value, e.g. from the discussion of Program 16_4 in Section 16.10:

```
*average = (*average * *count + number) / ++(*count);      /* new average */
```

Will the value of *count in the expression (*average * *count + number) be that before or after the increment in ++(*count)? It is not specified (see Section 10.3) and the program will work with some compilers and fail with others.

There are a number of sequence points specified in ANSI C where expressions, including possible side effects, will have been evaluated. These are:

1   When a function is called, after all the parameters have been evaluated.
2   The end of the first (left hand) operand of the &&, || and ?: operators.
3   The end of each operand of the sequence or comma operator (see Section 13.3)
    thus the expression i = 10, i++, i++; will result in i having a value of 12.
4   Completion of the evaluation of a full expression, i.e.:
    (a) evaluation of a program statement (terminated by a semicolon)
    (b) the initialisation of an automatic variable
    (c) evaluation of the controlling expressions of do, while, for and switch statements
    (d) evaluation of the expression of a return statement.

Use this knowledge to implement code that is not dependent upon the order of evaluation of an expression or expressions. Break suspect code down into separate statements so that the order of evaluation will be as required by the specification.

A major source of *side effects* occurs when functions access and alter non-local variables, e.g. a function could alter variables which had been passed by reference (Section 16.8) or external variables (Section 18.2). Problems may arise from side effects:

1   It can be difficult to understand the overall program semantics unless the code is well designed and commented.

2   External variables may be inadvertently altered, e.g. if a local variable name is misspelt and an external variable name in scope corresponds to the correct name.

In the majority of functions presented in sample programs in this book any alterations made to parameters passed by reference (e.g. swap in Program 16_3 swaps the contents of two parameters) and external variables (e.g. functions random_initialise and random_number in implementation file random0.c alter the external variable random_seed) are required for the overall operation of the function (access to random_seed should be controlled so other functions cannot alter it). Consider, however, Program 17_1 where the external variable a is an actual parameter to the call of function test (in line 19) and is also altered within function test (in line 29). This is a dangerous side effect and such practices can lead to very obscure errors. Care must therefore be taken when passing parameters by reference and access to external variables should be restricted (Section 18.3 discussed static external variables). If parameters which should not be altered are passed by reference (e.g. arrays which are always passed by reference) they should be const qualified.

18.9 ADTs - abstract data types

A type defines the characteristics of a variable: the data stored within it together with operators which may be used to operate upon that data, e.g. consider the type int:

type	data stored	operators
int	signed integer numeric data	+ - * / % | & sizeof etc.

Once the characteristics of a type have been defined variables of that type may be defined and used in a program. For example, the following fragment of code defines variables a, b and c of type int and then adds the contents of a to b and assigns the result to c:

```
int a = 1, b = 2, c;        /* define three variables of type int */
c = a + b;                  /* add a to b, assign result to c */
```

In Software Engineering terminology a, b and c would be called *instances* of the type int.

When working on large software systems programmers often implement modules which contain data structures and associated functions which operate upon that data. In Software Engineering terminology these components are collectively known as an ADT or *abstract data type* (sometimes called a *user defined type*); a concept for grouping data and associated operations into an integrated entity. For example, consider the header file random.h and associated implementation file random0.c:

data stored	operators
next random number in sequence	random_initialise, random_number

In effect random0.c implemented an *instance* of type 'random number' (in this case only a single instance is possible unless a copy is made of implementation file random0.c with the copies of the functions renamed `random2_initialise` and `random2_number`, etc.).   In the following chapters a number of ADTs will be implemented.   In general, a header file (such as random.h) will present a public interface to user programs with the data structures and function definitions hidden in an Implementation File (such as random0.c); thus supporting the software engineering concept of *information hiding*.

In summary, an *abstract data type* defines the characteristics of a particular type: the data stored within it together with functions which operate upon the data.

18.10   Summary: external identifiers, internal and external linkage

External variables (defined outside functions) and functions have *file scope* and may be used from the point of definition to the end of the file.   In addition they may have:

internal linkage   scope is restricted to the file in which they are defined (using `static`)
or   *external linkage*   they are available to all the files of a multi-file program.

Note that functions and external variables have *external linkage* by default.   Prefixing the definition with `static` restricts their scope to the file and they have *internal linkage*.   In addition `enum` and `typedef` declarations are local to a file.

Problems for Chapter 18

Problem 18.1   Implement the calculator program designed in outline in Chapter 2.   Place the main and calculation functions in one file and the input/output functions in another.

Problem 18.2   Implement and test the very fast (it only contains a single multiply and addition) 'quick and dirty' random number generator (Press *et al.* 1994) which is adequate for many uses (and is at least as good as any 32-bit *linear congruential generator*):

```
unsigned long int random_number = seed;              /* seed with suitable value */
...
random_number = 1664525UL * random_number + 1013904223UL
```

This assumes that the multiplication of two 32-bit `unsigned long int` values yields the low-order 32 bits of the true 64-bit product (which is the case on many machines); in effect one gets the *modulus* `%` 4294967296 'for free' (the maximum possible number is 4294967295 decimal).   An implementation can be checked by setting the seed to 0 which should yield the sequence (values in hexadecimal): 3c6ef35f, 47502932, d1ccf6e9, aaf95334, 6252e503, v29f2ec686, 57fe6c2d, a3d95fa8, 81fdbee7, 94f0af1a, cbf633b1, etc.

Problem 18.3   Write a program (using random.h) to simulate the rolling of a dice, i.e. rolling the dice 6000 times should, in theory, give a total of 1000 throws of each number. Extend the program to simulate a game involving a pair of dice:

the first roll of the dice is the player's *mark*
if the player's *mark* is 7 or 11 the player wins the bet immediately
else the player keeps rolling until
the *mark* is matched for a win, or the player rolls a 7 or 11 for a loss
The amount won or lost is equal to the bet unless the player wins with a
mark of 2 (*snake's eyes*) or 12 (*box cars*) when they win twice the bet

Start with a bankroll of 1000 dollars.

19

One-dimensional arrays

Many applications require the storing and processing of large sequences of data elements. For example, an experiment may require the sampling of the temperature and pressure of a liquid over a period of ten seconds with readings taken every tenth of a second. If the data from the experiment is to be processed by a computer a means is required to store two hundred values. It would be possible to define 200 separate identifiers:

```
int temperature_1, temperature_2, temperature_3 etc.
int pressure_1, pressure_2, pressure_3 etc.
```

which although possible is very clumsy and error prone. The C programming language provides three ways of grouping basic types into data structures:

An array   a fixed sized group in which the elements are of the same type
A structure   a fixed sized group in which the elements are of dissimilar types
A union   an overlap of different structures.

19.1 Defining and initialising arrays

The definition of an array has the following general form:

```
array_type   array_name[array_size];
```

where: `array_type`   is the type of the array elements
        `array_name`   is the identifier or name of the array
        `array_size`   is an integer constant specifying the number of elements in the array.

For example, to define two arrays both of 100 `int` elements:

```
int temperatures[100], pressures[100];
```

Although not recommended, for reasons of clarity, arrays may be defined along with simple variables of that type, e.g.:

```
int temperature, temperatures[100], min_temperature, max_temperature;
```

Only `temperatures` is an array, the others are simple `int` variables. It is often recommended to use *typedef* to define a new type and then define variables, e.g.:

```
typedef int Data_array[100];              /* define a new type */
Data_array temperatures, pressures;       /* and define variables */
```

When defining arrays the size or dimension of the array must be a positive integer specified by an **integer constant** or a **constant expression** which yields an integer type, e.g.:

```
int temperatures[100], pressures[100 * 2];
```

enum (see Section 7.4) and *#define* (see Section 5.5) may be used to define integer constants which can be used to specify array size, see Section 19.6. It is not possible to define dynamic arrays although dynamic arrays can be created at run time using the `malloc` and `calloc` functions (see Section 25.1).

19.1.1 Array initialisation

The contents of an array may be initialised when it is defined:

```
float voltages[5] = {3.6, 56.0, 5.0e-6, 2.0e4, 95.0};
int test_data[10] = {2, 5, 78, -9, 67, -3, 34, -9};
```

The initial values are expressions using constants. The second example initialises the first eight of the ten array elements. Any elements not explicitly initialised will be initialised to 0. If an array is not initialised the element values are *undefined* if it is internal or zero if it is external or a static internal. A simple way to initialise all the elements of an array to 0 is:

```
float array[20] = {0}                    /* initialise all elements to 0 */
```

Element array[0] is explicitly initialised to 0 and the remainder zeroed automatically.

If the size of the array is not specified the number of initialisers will be used to determine its size, e.g. in the following the array Fibonacci has fifteen elements:

```
int Fibonacci[] = {0, 1, 2, 3, 5, 8, 13, 21, 34, 55, 89, 144, 233, 377, 610};
```

The sizeof operator may be used to determine the number of bytes in an array, e.g. sizeof(Fibonacci) returns the number of bytes used to store the whole array and sizeof(Fibonacci[0]) returns the number of bytes required to store one element (note the (int) cast to convert the value returned by sizeof to an int for printing):

```
printf("%d %d", (int) sizeof(Fibonacci), (int) sizeof(Fibonacci[0]));
```

Thus sizeof(Fibonacci)/sizeof(Fibonacci[0]) yields the number of elements in the array.

19.2 Accessing the elements of an array

The elements of an array are accessed using an integer subscript or index which ranges from 0 to array_size - 1:

```
int array_index, temperatures[100], pressures[100];
temperatures[0] = 0;                     /* zero first element of the array */
temperatures[4] = 20;                    /* assign 20 to the fifth element */
value = temperatures[99];            /* assign the value of the last element */
printf("%d", temperatures[10]);          /* print the eleventh element */
```

The size of array temperatures is 100 elements hence the index range is 0 to 99, i.e. the first element is temperatures[0], second temperatures[1] and last temperatures[99]. A for statement can be used to zero all the elements of the array:

```
for (array_index = 0 ; array_index < 100 ; array_index++)
    temperatures[array_index] = 0;
```

It is very important to note that the array index starts at 0; a common error is to assume that the index range is 1 to array_size (as in Fortran). C performs no array bound checking so an invalid index will access memory outside the array. This can lead to the corruption of memory contents (program or data) or a run-time error where the program may halt with a message such as 'memory segmentation error'. Such faults can be very difficult to find, the corruption of data may show up much later in a different function which has nothing to do with the original array (possibly even after the program has been used for years when a new data set overflows an array bound).

A difference between arrays and all other types is that the name of an object generally refers to the contents of the object whereas the name of an array refers to the address of the first element in memory (in fact the name of an array is a *pointer* to the first element). This may appear to be a rather subtle point but it has major implications in the way arrays are treated, in particular how arrays are passed to functions (discussed in Section 19.4). It also prevents the assignment of one array to another, e.g.:

```
pressures = temperatures;                              /* illegal for arrays */
```

If pressures and temperatures are arrays the names refer to the address of the first elements and the statement is therefore incorrect, i.e. the start address of array pressures cannot be assigned the value of the start address of array temperatures. To assign the contents of one array to another the arrays must be copied element by element, e.g.:

```
for (array_index = 0 ; array_index < 100 ; array_indexn++)
      pressures[array_index] = temperatures[array_index];
```

Library <string.h> contains functions to manipulate arrays, e.g. memcpy to copy an array:

```
memcpy(pressures, temperatures, sizeof(temperatures));          /* copy array */
```

this performs a bitwise copy from temperatures to pressures of length sizeof(temperatures) bytes; it is up to the programmer to ensure that the destination has sufficient room to take the copied data. If the array elements are pointers (Chapter 21) or structures (Chapter 24) which contain pointers to other data structures such structures will not be copied; use a program loop and copy each element in turn together with any data structures pointed to.

19.3 Program to calculate the average of a sequence of real numbers

Exercise 9.2 calculated the average of a sequence of six real numbers. The sample answer (Appendix B) defined six variables x1, x2, x3, x4, x5 and x6 which held the numbers read. Program 19_1 reads up to ten numbers on a line by line basis and calculates the average:

(a) The program will terminate when *end of file* is entered.
(b) Less than ten numbers will be terminated by a newline.
(c) If more than ten numbers are entered on a line they will be summed in groups of ten.
(d) Invalid characters will be reported and the program will then continue.

10	define array data of 10 float elements
11	initialise index to zero (to index first element of array data)
15	prompt the user for input
16-37	a while statement calling scanf to read one real number into element data[index] (the while terminates when EOF is entered)
17-18	if scanf failed to convert one number print message and character in error
	else
21	echo number and postincrement index to index next element of array data
22-23	removes any space characters from the input stream
24	push the last character (read by line 22) back into the input stream (ready for the next call of scanf)
27	if the last character was \n (newline) or the array index == 10
29-31	sum the contents of the array data from 0 to index - 1
32-33	print the average
34-35	prompt for next input and reset index to start of array data.

```
 1 /* Program 19_1  - to calculate the average of a sequence of real numbers   */
 2 /* (a) a sequence of numbers is terminated with newline <CR>                 */
 3 /* (b) a maximum of ten numbers may be processed at one time                 */
 4 /* (c) report invalid character and terminate program on EOF                 */
 5
 6 #include <stdio.h>
 7
 8 int main(void)
 9 {
10     float data[10];                                    /* local array */
11     int index = 0;                              /* initialise array index */
12     int converted, ch, i;
13
14     /* read one real number, terminate on EOF */
15     printf("\nEnter up to ten numbers (<CR> to end) \n    ? ");
16     while ((converted = scanf("%f", &data[index])) != EOF)
17         if (converted != 1)                            /* read error */
18             printf("\n illegal character %c in input, try again\n", getchar());
19         else
20             {                                      /* number read OK */
21             printf("%6.1f ", data[index++]);
22             while ((ch = getchar()) == ' ')            /* remove spaces */
23                 /* null statement */;
24             ungetc(ch, stdin);                     /* push last character back */
25
26             /* if newline entered or index = 10 calculate average */
27             if ((ch == '\n') || (index == 10))
28                 {
29                 float sum = 0.0f;                      /* local sum */
30                 for (i = 0 ; i < index ; i++)
31                     sum = sum + data[i];
32                 printf("\n  Average of %d numbers = %f ",
33                                       index, sum / index);
34                 printf("\n\nEnter up to ten numbers (<CR> to end) \n    ? ");
35                 index = 0;                         /* initialise array index */
36                 }
37             }
38     return 0;
39 }
```

Program 19_1 Calculate the average of a sequence of real numbers

Lines 22 to 24 remove any space characters (following the number) from the stream stdin:

```
while ((ch = getchar()) == ' ')                    /* remove spaces */
    /* null statement */;
ungetc(ch, stdin);                     /* push last character back */
```

The while statement reads characters from stdin until a non-space character is found (to check if it is newline in line 27); the function ungetc pushes the last character read back into the input stream stdin ready for the next call to scanf.

Line 27 ensures that the array bounds are not exceeded, i.e. if ten numbers have been entered the average of the ten is calculated and then scanf called again.

19.4 Arrays as function parameters

In C, *actual parameters* are passed to a function *by value*, i.e. copies of the *actual parameters* are made in temporary variables and these are passed. Arrays, however, *appear* to be an exception in that they are passed *by reference*.

Section 19.2 explained that the name of an array refers to the address of the first element. Hence, when an array name appears in a function call the actual parameter is the address of the first element and a copy of the address is passed to the function (not a copy of the values stored in the array). Within the function the address is then used to access the memory allocated to the original array. Consider a function `array_write` which prints the contents of a five-element `float` array to the screen. The code to call it could be:

```
void array_write(float array[5]);          /* function prototype */
float data[5] = {1.0, 2.0, 3.0, 4.0, 5.0};   /* initialised array */

array_write(data);                          /* call function */
```

The function prototype tells the compiler that `array_write` has one parameter which is an array of type `float`. When the function is called the compiler can check that there is one parameter and that it is an array of the correct type (because arrays are passed using the address of the first element there can be no conversion of types). The statement:

```
array_write(data);                          /* call function */
```

passes the address of the first element of array `data` as the first (and only) actual parameter. The function can then use the address to directly access the contents of array `data`, e.g.:

```
void array_write(float array[5])      /* function to print an array of 5 elements */
{
    int index;
    for (index = 0 ; index < 5 ; index++)
        printf("%f ", array[index]);
}
```

The [5] following the name `array` declares that the first formal parameter is an array (otherwise it would be a variable). Inside the function the name of the formal parameter is a synonym for the name of the array in the calling function (in fact the formal parameter is a *pointer* which is initialised with the start address of the actual parameter and which may be manipulated using pointer arithmetic, see Section 21.3).

In the above example the array size was specified in the function header. In practice it can be specified or not; it makes no difference because C does no array bound checking and the function could be called with arrays of different sizes. It is up to the programmer to ensure that the bounds of the array are not exceeded. In this case the programmer must ensure that `array_write` is called with arrays of five elements or greater (only the first five elements will be printed). If the function is to process arrays of different sizes the size of the array must be passed into the function, see Program 19_2. Note that it is not possible to use the `sizeof` operator inside a function to determine the size of an array passed as a parameter, see Section 21.10.

Remember that arrays are passed *by reference* and the called function has access to memory allocated to the original array, i.e. if the contents should not be changed `const` qualify the corresponding formal parameter. In addition, because an array name refers to the address of the first element, not the contents, **arrays cannot be returned as function results** (although *pointers* to arrays may be, see Chapter 26).

19.4.1 Functions to read, write and manipulate arrays

Header file array.h contains function prototypes for array processing functions:

lines

4	array_read	which reads real numbers into a float array
5	array_write	which prints the contents of a float array
6	array_maximum	which returns the index to the element with the maximum value
7	array_minimum	which returns the index to the element with the minimum value
8	array_reverse	which reverses the elements of an array.

```
1 /* Header file array.h - for array read, write, reverse, maximum & minimum    */
2
3 /* function prototypes */
4 int array_read(float array[], const int max_index);
5 void array_write(const float array[], const int number);
6 int array_maximum(const float array[], const int number);
7 int array_minimum(const float array[], int number);
8 void array_reverse(float array[], const int number);
```

Header file array.h   For array processing functions

```
 1 /* Implementation file array.c, array read, write, reverse, maximum & minimum */
 2
 3 #include <stdio.h>                          /* include standard I/O header file */
 4 #include "array.h"                              /* include "own" header file */
 5
 6 /*-------------------------------------------------------------------------*/
 7 /* function to read up to max_number values into array,                     */
 8 /*    return  number of values read or 0 for EOF                            */
 9 int array_read(float array[], const int max_number)
10 {
11     int converted, index = 0, ch = 0;
12
13     printf("\n\nEnter up to %d numbers (<CR> to end) \n    ? ", max_number);
14     while ((converted = scanf("%f", &array[index])) != EOF)
15         if (converted != 1)                              /* read error ? */
16             printf("\n illegal character %c in input, try again\n", getchar());
17         else
18             {
19             while ((ch = getchar()) == ' ')     /* get next non-space character */
20                 /* null statement */;
21             ungetc(ch, stdin);                      /* push last character back */
22             if ((++index == max_number) || (ch == '\n'))
23                 return index;                            /* return OK */
24             }
25     return 0;                                    /* return EOF indicator */
26 }
27
28 /*-------------------------------------------------------------------------*/
```

Implementation file array.c   For array processing functions (continued on next page)

```
29 /* function to print an array of number elements, print five values per line  */
30 void array_write(const float array[], const int number)
31 {
32     int index;
33
34     for (index = 0 ; index < number ; index++)
35         printf("%c%10.3f", (index % 5) ? ' ' : '\n', array[index]);
36 }
37
38 /*--------------------------------------------------------------------*/
39 /* function to find the maximum value in an array of number elements        */
40 /*  function result: return index to element with maximum value             */
41 int array_maximum(const float array[], const int number)
42 {
43     int index,                                      /* general array index */
44         index_max = 0;                      /* index to maximum, initialise to 0 */
45
46     for (index = 1 ; index < number ; index++)
47         if (array[index] > array[index_max])        /* new maximum value ? */
48             index_max = index;                       /* if so note index */
49     return index_max;
50 }
51
52 /*--------------------------------------------------------------------*/
53 /* function to find the minimum value in an array of number elements        */
54 /*  function result: return index to element with minimum value             */
55 int array_minimum(const float array[], int number)
56 {
57     int index_min = 0;                  /* index to minimum, initialise to 0 */
58
59     for (number-- ; number > 0 ; number--)
60         if (array[number] < array[index_min])       /* new minimum value ? */
61             index_min = number;                      /* if so note index */
62     return index_min;
63 }
64
65 /*--------------------------------------------------------------------*/
66 /* function to reverse the contents of an array                             */
67 void array_reverse(float array[], const int number)
68 {
69     int up, down;                           /* up and down array index values */
70     float value;                                /* temporary data store */
71
72     for (up = 0, down = number-1 ; up < down ; up++, down--)
73         (value = array[up], array[up] = array[down], array[down] = value);
74 }
```

Implementation file array.c For array processing functions

Implementation file array.c contains the definitions of the functions prototyped in array.h; it reads its 'own' header file (line 4), which enables the compiler to check the function definitions against the prototypes.

The function `array_read`, lines 9 to 26, will read up to `max_number` real values into `array` terminating when EOF or *newline* is entered or when the array contains `max_number` values. The function returns, as a function result, the number of values in the array, or 0 for EOF:

lines

9   `int array_read(float array[], const int max_number)`
           is the function header specifying that:
                (a) it returns an `int` function result (the number of values read or 0 for EOF)
                (b) it has two parameters, the `array` and `max_number`

13   prompts the user to enter up to `max_number` numbers

14-24   a `while` statement which terminates when EOF is entered

      14   call `scanf` to read one number (terminate the `while` on EOF)
      15-16 if `scanf` failed print error message and character in error
      else
      19-20 read `stdin` input stream looking for next non-space character
      21   `ungetc` last character (ready for next scanf call)
      22   if array is full (`index == max_number`) or last character was *newline*
           23 `return` the number of values entered

25   EOF has been entered, `return` 0 to indicate EOF.

The function `array_write`, lines 30 to 36, prints the contents of an array:

30   `void array_write(const float array[], const int number)`
           is the function header specifying:
                (a) it does not return a function result
                (b) it has two parameters, the `array` and the `number` of elements

34-35   a `for` statement printing the elements of `array` from index 0 to `number-1`.

Note the use of the conditional operator `?` in line 35:

      `printf("%c%10.3f", (index % 5) ? ' ' : '\n', array[index]);`

The function `array_write` prints five numbers to a line. The `scanf` control string `"%c%10.3f"` prints a character (calculated from `index`) and a `float` (`array[index]`). The condition operator `?` selects the character, i.e. if `index % 5` is non-zero a space is printed otherwise a *newline* is printed.

The function `array_maximum`, lines 41 to 50, scans (up) an array looking for the maximum value. The sequence of statements is:

41 `int array_maximum(const float array[], const int number)`
          is the function header specifying that:
              (a) it returns an `int` function result (index to the maximum value found)
              (b) it has two parameters, the `array` and the `number` of elements

44 define `index_max` and initialise it to 0 (assume `array[0]` is the maximum)

46 a `for` statement scanning the array for the maximum value
        `index` is incremented from 1 to `number-1` when the `for` terminates
    47 if the value of array element `array[index]` is greater than `array[index_max]`
        48 set `index_max` to `index`

49 `return` `index_max` as the function result (index to the element with the maximum value).

The function `array_minimum`, lines 55 to 63, scans an array looking for the minimum value.

Although it could be written in a similar manner to array_maximum the algorithm used is different in that it searches from the end of the array:

55 int array_minimum(const float array[], int number) the function header
57 define index_min and initialise it to 0 (assume array[0] is the minimum)
59 a for statement scanning the array for the minimum value
        number is decremented from its initial value - 1 to 0 when the for terminates
    60 if the value of array element array[number] is less than array[index_min]
        61 set index_min to number (the current index)
62 return index_min as the function result (index to the element with the minimum value).

Note that the formal parameter number is used as the array index (hence it is not const qualified as in the header of function array_maximum). In line 59 the for statement is initialised by decrementing number so that it indexes the last element of the array (number is then decremented to 0 when the for terminates).

The function array_reverse, lines 67 to 74, reverses the elements of an array, the sequence of statements is:

67 void array_reverse(float array[], const int number) is the function header
69 int up, down; two array indices, i.e.:
        up increments up the array and down decrements down the array
72 a for statement which:
        (a) increments up from 0
        (b) decrements down from number-1
        (c) terminates when up = down
        (d) increments up and decrements down on each iteration
73 swaps the two array elements array[up] and array[down].

Note the use of the comma or sequence operator in lines 72 and 73:

```
for (up = 0, down = number-1 ; up < number/2 ; up++, down--)
    (value = array[up], array[up] = array[down], array[down] = value);
```

Line 72, in particular, is a very good example of the use of the sequence or comma operator where there are two array indices, up indexing up the array and down indexing down the array. Line 73 is a single statement using the comma operator which could have been written, perhaps more clearly, as the compound statement:

```
{
value = array[up];
array[up] = array[down];
array[down] = value);
}
```

Which is used is a matter of programming style but use the comma operator with restraint because excessive use can lead to code which is difficult to read and maintain.

The majority of the formal function parameters in array.c are const qualified, i.e. if the function attempts to alter a value a warning or error will be issued. This is particularly important with arrays because the function has access to the memory allocated to the array, not just a copy of its value. Only functions array_read and array_reverse need to alter the array values and the corresponding formal parameter is not const qualified.

```
 1 /* Program 19_2 - text array read, write, reverse, maximum & minimum         */
 2
 3 #include <stdio.h>                        /* include standard I/O header file */
 4 #include "array.h"                           /* include array header file */
 5
 6 int main(void)
 7 {
 8     float  data[10] = {0};                              /* data array */
 9     int number;                           /* number of elements in data */
10
11     while ((number = array_read(data, 10)) > 0)    /* read array, exit on EOF */
12         {
13         array_write(data, number);                       /* write array */
14         printf("\n maximum %f", data[array_maximum(data, number)]); /* maximum */
15         printf("\n minimum %f", data[array_minimum(data, number)]); /* minimum */
16         data[array_maximum(data, number)] = 100;         /* replace maximum */
17         data[array_minimum(data, number)] = -100;        /* replace minimum */
18         array_reverse(data, number);                     /* reverse array */
19         array_write(data, number);                       /* write array */
20         }
21     return 0;
22 }
```

Program 19_2 To test array processing functions in array.c

Program 19_2 tests the functions defined in array.c:

4   read header file array.h which contains the prototypes of the array functions
8   define array data initialised to 0
9   define number which will hold number of elements in the array data
11-20   a for statement which reads an array and processes it
        11 call array_read to read the array, terminate for on EOF (0 returned)
        13 write the contents of array data
        14 call array_maximum to find maximum value in array
        15 call array_minimum to find minimum value in array
        16 replace maximum value with 100
        17 replace minimum value with -100
        18 call array_reverse to reverse the contents of the array
        19 print array contents again
21   terminate program.

A run of Program 19_2 gave:

```
Enter up to 10 numbers (<CR> to end)
    ? 1 2 3 4 5↵
    1.000      2.000      3.000      4.000      5.000
maximum 5.000000
minimum 1.000000
    100.000      4.000      3.000      2.000   -100.000
```

The functions array_maximum and array_minimum are called twice which is inefficient. A modification would be to assign the index value returned to a variable and then use that.

Now consider the function header of `array_read`, defined in lines 9 to 26 of implementation file array.c:

```
int array_read(float array[], const int max_number)
```

The `[]` following the name `array` tells the compiler that the first formal parameter is an array (otherwise it would be a variable).

In Program 19_2 the function `array_read` is prototyped in header file array.h (read in line 4) and it is called in line 11:

```
while ((index = array_read(data, 10)) > 0)     /* read array, exit on EOF */
    {
```

the function `array_read` is called with the actual arguments `data`, the array to be passed, and 10, the size of the array `data`.

The value of the address of the first element of `data` is passed to the function `array_read` (the function prototype enables the compiler to check that the first formal parameter is an address). The function returns either the number of values read or 0 for EOF. Because arrays are passed *by reference* the values read from the keyboard by `array_read` are placed directly in array `data` defined in the function `main`.

Exercise 19.1 (*see Appendix B for sample answer*)

Extend Program 19_2, implementing and testing functions to return the average and standard deviation of the values stored in the array, see Exercise 12.1. Add a function to sort the values stored in the array into ascending order using a simple linear sort:

```
FOR   index_1 = 0  TO  ARRAY_SIZE-2
    minimum = array[index_1]
    FOR   index_2 = index_1 + 1  TO  ARRAY_SIZE - 1
        IF   array[index_2] < minimum
            minimum = array[index_2]
            SWAP   array[index_2] and array[index_1]
```

19.5 Summary: arrays as function parameters

A difference between arrays and all other types is that the name of an object generally refers to the contents of the object whereas the name of an array refers to the address of the first element in memory (the name is a *pointer* to the first element). One of the effects of this is that arrays are passed *by reference*; when an array name appears in a function call the *actual parameter* is the address of the first element and this (not a copy of the values stored in the array) is passed to the function. Within the function the address is used to access the memory allocated to the original array, e.g. line 13 of Program 19_2:

```
array_write(data, index);                        /* write array */
```

The array name `data` represents the memory address of the first element, and **the value of this address** is passed to the function. In the function header of `array_write` the first formal parameter is specified as an array therefore the function will expect an address and be able to access the memory allocated to the array via the name of the formal parameter.

When an array name is followed by a subscript enclosed in `[]` operators the complete expression refers to the contents of the specified element, e.g. line 35 of file array.c:

```
printf("%c%10.3f", (index % 5) ? ' ' : '\n', array[index]);
```

The expression array[index] refers to the contents of an element of the array and its **value** is passed to printf.

In C arrays and pointers have a very close relationship and the function header of array_write can generally be written using pointer notation without any other modification:

```
void array_write(const float *array, const int number)
```

The first formal parameter is a 'pointer to an object of type float'. Inside the function the name array can be used with subscripts as normal. The use of pointer notation in function headers is common in particular in the descriptions of library functions. There will be more discussion when pointers are described in Chapters 21 and 22. Note that when using pointer notation (as above) there is no way to tell if array is a pointer to a simple float variable or to an array of float (further discussion in Section 22.5)

To summarise, when an array name is an actual parameter in a function call it is the value of the address of the first element which is passed. The address is used inside the function to access the original array. Thus although the actual parameter is passed *by value* the overall effect is that arrays are passed *by reference*. If the contents of an array should not be altered the formal parameter should be const qualified.

Note that library <string.h> contains functions to manipulate arrays, e.g. memset to set all elements to a value, memcpy to copy an array, memchr and memcmp to search an array, etc.

19.6 Using #*define* and *enum* to specify the array size

Programs should be as portable as possible and the size of particular arrays may be dependent upon the target application. To have to edit a large program changing dozens of array sizes in declarations would be a time consuming and error prone task and some method is therefore required of associating a name with an integer constant and then using the name in declarations. There are two methods of doing this:

1   Use the preprocessor #define directive to define a *symbolic constant* (see Section 5.5).
2   Use the enumerative type to define an integer constant (see Section 7.4).

For example, using #define:

```
#define ARRAY_SIZE 100
    int temperatures[ARRAY_SIZE], pressures[ARRAY_SIZE];
```

The #define is a preprocessor directive (it is on a line by itself and not terminated by a ;) which replaces every occurrence of ARRAY_SIZE with 100 using literal substitution (see Section 5.5). After preprocessing the compiler then gets the result:

```
    int temperatures[100], pressures[100];
```

The compiler knows nothing about the symbolic constant ARRAY_SIZE, it having been replaced by the preprocessor with the replacement text 100. When transporting the program the #define directives are edited and the program recompiled. A problem with using #define is that once a symbolic constant has been defined it remains in existence for the remainder of the file (unless undefined using #undef) and functions following will have access to it (which may be acceptable or not, depending upon the program).

An alternative is to use the enumerative type to define an integer constant, for example:

```
enum {ARRAY_SIZE = 100};
int temperatures[ARRAY_SIZE], pressures[ARRAY_SIZE];
```

The identifier ARRAY_SIZE is an integer constant which is used to specify the array sizes. There are two advantages in this technique:

1 The identifier ARRAY_SIZE has the same scope as the declarations, i.e. within the compound statement where it is defined.
2 Because the compiler knows about the enumerations it can generate information to enable a debugger to print the values in symbolic form (#define is a preprocessor directive and the compiler knows nothing about the symbolic constants, only the equivalent constants).

The value of a const qualified int may not be used to specify an array size, e.g. Turbo C:

```
6      const int ARRAY_SIZE = 100;
7      int temperatures[ARRAY_SIZE];
***** X.C(7) : error C2057: expected constant expression
***** X.C(7) : error C2133: 'temperatures' : unknown size
```

const is a *type qualifier* (see Section 17.7) indicating that the object concerned has special properties; ARRAY_SIZE is a non-modifiable variable, **not** an integer constant. Note, however, that the above is legal in C++ in that the const *modifier* defines true constants.

One of the problems with using arrays in C is that the array index starts at 0 whereas most mathematical algorithms tend to assume that it starts from 1. This can lead to errors when coding the algorithm. Techniques used to overcome this problem include:

1 Increasing each array dimension by one with the array index ranging from 1 to the array size, i.e. not using the first element. This can be very wasteful of memory.
2 Store the array 'as normal' (with index starting at 0), implement the algorithm with index starting at 1 and perform arithmetic to convert between the two (see Section 26.4 on two-dimensional matrices). The arithmetic performed in the extra index calculations imposes a run-time overhead and having different parts of the program using different indexes can lead to errors.

19.7 Using an array to implement a stack ADT

Queues and stacks are data structures used for storing information:

queue is a *first in first out* data structure, i.e. if the characters ABCDEF were added to a queue (one character at a time) they would be removed in the order ABCDEF;

stack is a *last in first out* data structure, i.e. if the characters ABCDEF were added to a stack (one character at a time) they would be removed in the reverse order FEDCBA.

The functions used to store and retrieve data to/from a stack are usually called push (to *push* a data item onto the stack) and pop (to *pop* the top item off the stack), e.g. function headers could be:

```
void push(const char data);    /* push a character onto the stack */
char pop(void);                /* pop a character off the stack */
```

which would be used as follows (ch is a char):

```
push('a');                     /* push character 'a' onto the stack */
ch = pop();                    /* pop the top character off the stack into ch */
```

```
1 /* Header file stack.h - interface for stack ADT (abstract data type)        */
2
3 /* allocate a stack of specified size - return size of stack allocated        */
4 int setup_stack(const int size);
5
6 /* push character onto stack - return TRUE if OK else FALSE if stack is full   */
7 int push(const char data);
8
9 /* test if stack is empty - return TRUE if it is otherwise FALSE               */
10 int empty(void);
11
12 /* pop character (as function result) off stack (return 0 if stack empty)      */
13 char pop(void);
```

Header file stack.h Interface for stack ADT (abstract data type)

```
1 /* Program 19_3.c - test stack ADT (abstract data type) in stack.h            */
2 /* this program will attempt to push a sequence of characters onto the stack  */
3 /* and then pop them off.  The output should look like:                       */
4 /*    Test stack processing functions: f0r a stack size of 10                  */
5 /*     Pushing: ABCDEFGHIJ                                                     */
6 /*     Popping: JIHGFEDCBA                                                     */
7
8 #include <stdio.h>
9 #include "stack.h"                              /* stack processing functions */
10
11 int main(void)
12 {
13     char character = 'A';                /* character data being stacked */
14     int size = setup_stack(20);              /* request a stack size 20 */
15
16     printf("\nTest stack functions: stack size is %d\nPushing: ", size);
17     while (push(character))                 /* attempt to push char onto stack */
18         {
19         putchar(character);                     /* OK, write char pushed */
20         character++;                            /* next character to push */
21         }
22
23     printf("\nPopping: ");
24     while (! empty())                       /* while stack is not empty */
25         putchar(pop());                         /* pop and print character */
26
27     return 0;
28 }                                              /* end of program */
```

Program 19_3 Test stack ADT (abstract data type), interface in stack.h

The header file stack.h (above) provides an interface to a stack ADT (abstract data type) declaring stack processing functions which push and pop data and check for error conditions such as stack full (when pushing) and stack empty (when popping):

4 setup_stack; is called to setup stack of size; returns size of stack allocated
7 push, pushes character data onto the stack; returns 1 if successful, 0 if stack is full
10 empty, checks if stack is empty; returns *true* if so otherwise *false*
13 pop, pops of top of stack; returns character popped otherwise 0 if stack is empty.

Program 19_3 (previous page) tests the stack ADT:

9 include the header file "stack.h"
13 define character initialised to 'A'
14-16 call setup_stack requesting a stack of 20 and print size of stack allocated
17-21 a while calling push to push characters onto the stack; terminates when stack is full
19-20 if push was successful (stack not full) print character and increment the character (this assumes the character code for the alphabet is contiguous)
24-25 a while calling empty; terminates when stack is empty
25 if stack not empty call pop and print character returned.

A run of Program 19_3 on an IBM PC compatible gave:

```
Test stack functions: stack size is 10
Pushing: ABCDEFGHIJ
Popping: JIHGFEDCBA
```

Implementation file stack1.c (next page) contains stack ADT code, the data structures to store the stack data and definitions of the functions which manipulate the stack:

3 include the header file "stack.h" (to check prototypes against definitions)
6 define named constant stack_size which specifies the size of the stack
7 define the array stack_data which will hold the stack (size is fixed in this version)
8 define stack_index which will index the next free location on the stack
13-17 function setup_stack: the array size is fixed in this version so size is ignored
15 set stack_index to 0 to index the first location on the stack
16 return stack_size, the size of stack allocated
21-27 function push: attempts to push (value parameter) data onto the stack
24 if stack_index >= stack_size the stack is full
return 0 (*false*) indicating that the push failed due to the stack being full
25 move data onto top of stack and increment stack_index to index next location
26 return 1 (*true*) indicating that the push was successful
31-32 function empty tests if stack is empty
32 return *true* (1) if stack is empty, i.e. stack_index is 0
36-40 function pop: attempts to pop the top of the stack (returned as a function result)
38 if the stack is empty return 0 (error condition, see below)
39 decrement stack_index and pop top of stack (returned as the function result).

Normally before calling pop the user would call empty to see if there is data on the stack (see line 24 Program 19_3). If pop is called when the stack is empty some error action must be taken (otherwise array bounds overflow would occur in line 39). In this case 0 is returned as an error indicator (which may be checked by the user program), an alternative would be to display an error message and call exit to terminate the program.

Note that stack_data and stack_index are declared static and are hidden within the file together with the implementation details of the functions. This promotes *information hiding* which is an important concept in Software Engineering, see next section.

```
 1 /* Implementation file stack1.c - stack ADT (abstract data type) using arrays */
 2
 3 #include "stack.h"                              /* include own header file */
 4
 5 /* data hidden within the module */
 6 enum {stack_size = 10};                                  /* stack size */
 7 static char stack_data[stack_size];                    /* array for stack */
 8 static int stack_index = 0;          /* index to next free location on stack */
 9
10 /*------------------------------------------------------------------------*/
11 /* allocate a stack of specified size - return size of stack allocated    */
12 /*   Note that the size fixed in this version (set by stack_size)          */
13 int setup_stack(const int size)
14 {
15     stack_index = 0;                        /* index first free location */
16     return stack_size;                  /* return size of stack allocated */
17 }
18
19 /*------------------------------------------------------------------------*/
20 /* push character onto stack - return TRUE if OK else FALSE if stack is full  */
21 int push(const char data)
22 {
23     /* if stack is full return false else push data onto the stack */
24     if (stack_index >= stack_size) return 0;         /* yes, return false */
25     stack_data[stack_index++] = data;                 /* OK, push data */
26     return 1;                                      /* all OK return true */
27 }
28
29 /*------------------------------------------------------------------------*/
30 /* test if stack is empty - return TRUE if it is otherwise FALSE           */
31 int empty(void)
32 {   return (stack_index == 0); }            /* if stack is empty return TRUE */
33
34 /*------------------------------------------------------------------------*/
35 /* pop character (as function result) off stack (return 0 if stack empty)  */
36 char pop(void)
37 {
38     if (empty()) return 0;                   /* if stack is empty return 0 */
39     return stack_data[--stack_index];           /* OK, pop top of stack */
40 }
```

Implementation file stack1.c   A stack ADT (abstract data type) using arrays

19.8 Implementing ADTs (abstract data types)

An *abstract data type* is a logical grouping of data and associated operations into an integrated entity, in effect, the creation of a *user defined type*. When implementing ADTs an important concept is *information hiding* by which the implementation details of a type (data structures used, algorithms used, etc.) are 'hidden' within an object. To enable the outside world to use objects there must exist an interface which usually consists of a number of functions which are called to invoke tasks performed by the object (store data, write data, etc.) For example, the users of file stack1.c in Section 19.7 (which stores data in a stack data structure) have to call functions push and pop to store and retrieve data; they have no idea what underlying data structure is used to store the objects. This enables the implementation details of an ADT to be changed without having to modify programs which use it (so long as the public interface is maintained). For example, in file stack1.c the size of the array is fixed and the parameter size to function setup_stack is ignored. Section 25.2 will show how to allocate the array dynamically at run time (file stack2.c) and also how to use pointers to implement the push and pop operations (file stack3.c), the public interface (presented by header file stack.h) being unchanged.

When writing programs an *abstract data type* is defined by specifying the data to be stored together with the associated functions which operate upon the data. In procedural programming languages such as Fortran, C, Pascal, etc. the data and associated functions are distinct, the data is declared and then the functions are implemented. By using modular programming techniques data and associated functions can be grouped into modules with a public interface between the module and the outside world. For example, a module implemented in the C language would:

(a) use the static storage class specifier to 'hide' external objects and functions within the source file, see Section 18.3.

and (b) have an associated header file which declares types, function prototypes, etc. which may be used by functions in other modules, see Section 18.4, i.e. this acts as the interface between the module and the outside world.

19.9 Simulation of the flow of patients through an outpatient clinic *

Program 19_4 (following page) is a simulation of the flow of patients through an outpatient clinic. The simulation is more complex than that of Section 18.7 in that it models two doctors who see 20 patients in an afternoon with the consultation time taken randomly from the distribution 10, 11, 12, 12, 13, 13, 14, 14, 15, 15, 15, 16, 16, 16, 16, 17, 17, 17, 18, 18, 19, 19, 20, 22, 24. Thus consultations take between 10 and 24 minutes with most being near to the average of 16 minutes (unlike Program 18_3, where the consultation was a random time between 2 and 10 minutes).

The function consultation, lines 54 to 61, returns a value selected from the distribution (stored in array length, lines 57 and 58) using the random number generator functions declared in random.h (see Section 18.6). The expression in line 60 length[(int) ((25.0 * random_number()) / (random_maximum + 1.0))] gives an index in the range 0 to 25 to return a time from array length. The random number generator is seeded with the current time using a call to random_initialise (line 15).

Function main performs the simulation and is very similar to that of Program 18_3. The main difference is that, as there are two doctors, an array doctor_free holds the time when the doctors consultations finish. An if statement, lines 24 and 25, checks which doctor's consultation finishes first and sets the variable doctor to the corresponding value:

```
if (doctor_free[0] <= doctor_free[1]) doctor = 0;
else                                  doctor = 1;
```

The value of doctor is then used to index the array doctor_free when calculating the time the patient waits, etc. in line 26. This is a very simple simulation which could be extended to model more doctors, a number of patient queues, patients late or absent, etc.

```
 1 /* Program 19_4  Simulation of patients through a doctor's surgery       */
 2 /* two doctors, 20 patients per day, consulting time between 2 and 10 minutes */
 3
 4 #include <stdio.h>                              /* standard stream I/O library */
 5 #include "random.h"                             /* random number functions */
 6
 7 unsigned long int random_maximum;               /* maximum value of random number */
 8
 9 int main(void)
10 {
11    int consultation(void);                      /* function prototype */
12    int patient_waits, total_wait_time = 0, doctor_free[2] = {0}, doctor_waits;
13    int doctor, patient, patients, patient_arrives, interval, consultation_time;
14
15    random_maximum = random_initialise(0);       /* initialise with time */
16    printf("Enter appointment interval and number of patients each time ? ");
17    scanf("%d%d", &interval, &patients);
18    /* now loop working out consultation time for patients 1 to 20 */
19    for (patient = 1; patient <= 20; patient++)
20      {
21      /* work out time when patient arrives, how long they wait, etc. */
22      patient_arrives = ((patient - 1)/ patients) * interval;
23      /* which doctor is free first */
24      if (doctor_free[0] <= doctor_free[1]) doctor = 0;
25      else                               doctor = 1;
26      patient_waits = doctor_free[doctor] - patient_arrives;
27      consultation_time = consultation();
28      /* work out how long the patient or doctor has to wait  */
29      if (patient_waits > 0)
30          {                              /* patient has to wait for doctor */
31          doctor_waits = 0;
32          total_wait_time = total_wait_time + patient_waits;
33          }
34      else
35          {                              /* doctor has to wait for next patient */
36          doctor_waits = -patient_waits;
37          patient_waits = 0;
38          }
39      printf(" Doctor %d free at %2d waits %2d, patient %2d arrives %2d waits "
40          "%2d, consults for %2d\n", doctor, doctor_free[doctor], doctor_waits,
41          patient, patient_arrives, patient_waits, consultation_time);
42      /* work out when doctor is free */
43      if (patient_waits > 0)
44          doctor_free[doctor] = doctor_free[doctor] + consultation_time;
45      else
46          doctor_free[doctor] = patient_arrives + consultation_time;
47      }
48    printf("   mean patient wait time %f mins\n", total_wait_time / 10.0);
49    return 0;
50 }
```

Program 19_4 Simulation of patients through an outpatient clinic

```
51 /*-------------------------------------------------------------------*/
52 /* Function to return length of next consultation, range 10 to 24 minutes    */
53 int consultation(void)
54 {
55     /* consultation times from 10 to 24 minutes with a mean of 16 minutes */
56     int length[26] = {10,11,12,12,13,13,14,14,15,15,15,16,
57                       16,16,16,17,17,17,18,18,19,19,20,22,24};
58     /* get random number in range 0 to 25 then consultation time from array    */
59     return length[(int) ((25.0 * random_number()) / (random_maximum + 1.0))];
60 }
```

Program 19_4 Simulation of patients through an outpatient clinic

Problems for Chapter 19

Problem 19.1 Implement and test a program which uses Aristosthenes method of finding prime numbers in the range 2 to n:

1 Construct an array from 2 to n zeroing all elements.
2 Starting from 2 examine each element in turn:
      (a) if zero it is prime, print the index and mark all multiples of it,
  or (b) if marked (from a previous prime) it is not a prime.

The number 2 is the only even prime; hence half the space in the array of Problem 19.2 is effectively wasted. Rewrite the program only considering odd numbers and utilising all elements of the array, i.e. the length of the array can be n / 2.

Problem 19.2 Implement and test a queue ADT (a *first in first out* data structure). Note that Exercise 25.1 implements a queue ADT using a linked list.

Problem 19.3 Implement and test a program which sorts the elements of an array into ascending order using a bubble sort, e.g. assuming an array of number elements:

1 scan through the array:
      (a) if array[1] > array[0] swap the values
      (b) if array[2] > array[1] swap the values
      (c) if array[3] > array[2] swap the values
    etc. up to:
      (d) if array[number-1] > array[number-2] swap the values
    array[number-1] now holds the largest value
2 repeat 1 terminating at number-2
3 repeat 1 terminating at number-3

The process stops at array[0]. A pseudo-code version would be:

```
FOR   end_index = number - 1  DOWNTO  1
    FOR   index = 0  TO end_index - 1
        IF array[index + 1] < array[index]
            SWAP  array[index] and [array[index+1]
```

Exercise 30.1 describes the quicksort algorithm and its implementation.

20

Characters and strings

The processing of characters and sequences of characters is of particular importance in applications such as systems programming (editors, compilers, etc.) and commercial data processing. It still needs attention in many other application areas if only to control interaction with the user terminal, e.g. display of prompts, menus, reading commands, etc. This chapter will introduce character processing and strings (arrays of characters).

20.1 The character type *char*

Chapter 1 described how characters are represented within a computer system using a character code such as ASCII, e.g. character 'a' is 97 decimal, 'A' is 65, '0' is 48, etc. Many modern languages (e.g. Pascal) treat characters as a separate data type with their own special rules. This is not the case in C where any integral type can be used to represent characters and the data type char is, in effect, a byte size int. The ANSI C standard specifies the following minimum requirements for the data type char:

> (a) it has a minimum size of 8 bits,
> (b) its maximum value is at least +127,
> and (c) its minimum value is 0 or lower.

The following points should be noted:

1   The guaranteed range for char variables is 0 to +127 (i.e. sufficient to hold English language character sets such as ASCII or EBCDIC).
2   Whether char variables are signed or unsigned is implementation dependent (the most efficient for the particular environment is selected, see Section 20.1.2).
3   The character code is not specified so long as it can represent the C character set (see Section 6.1).
4   The character codes for the alphabet a to z and A to Z may not be contiguous (as in ASCII). To overcome this problem the library <ctype.h> (see Section 20.4) contains functions to test characters including upper (isupper) and lower (islower) case letters and digits (isdigit).

20.1.1 Character constants

Character constants are enclosed in apostrophes, e.g.:

    'a' 'A' 'b' 'B' 'z' 'Z' '1' '2' '9' 'a' '#' ')'   '\n' '\a'

C converts the character into the equivalent integer value in the target processor's character code, e.g. in ASCII 'a' becomes 97, 'A' becomes 65, '0' becomes 48, etc. Note that these are constants of type int; in C there are no constants of type char (unlike C++ where these are constants of type char).

Because character variables and constants are treated as integers they may be used directly in arithmetic expressions (unlike languages such as Pascal where integers and characters are distinct data types). For example, the following fragment of code converts a digit character (range '0' to '9') to its equivalent numeric value (range 0 to 9):

```
char ch = '5';                    /* define char variable initial value '5' */
int ch_int;                                    /* define int variable */
ch_int = ch - '0';               /* convert char to equivalent numeric value */
```

In the ASCII character code ch has the value 53 (character '5') and '0' has the value 48 therefore the statement ch_int = ch - '0'; becomes effectively ch_int = 53 - 48 = 5.

If a character constant (within ' marks) is prefixed with a \ it is an *escape sequence* which is used to represent special characters, see Table 20.1. For example, the character constant '\x1b' would represent the ASCII control character ESC (value 1b hexadecimal).

escape sequence	character represented	action taken by printf, etc.
\n	NL newline	moves to the start of the next line on page
\t	HT horizontal tab	move horizontally one tabulate position
\v	VT vertical tab	move vertically one tabulate position
\b	BS backspace	move back one character position
\r	CR carriage return	move to start of current line
\f	FF form feed	typically new page or clear screen
\a	BEL audible alert	ring terminal bell or sound buzzer
\\	\ backslash	display a \ character
\?	? question mark	display a ? character
\'	' single quote	display a ' character
\"	" double quote	display a " character
\ooo	ooo octal number	specify the numeric value of the character
\xhh	hh hexadecimal number	specify the numeric value of the character

Table 20.1 Character escape codes

20.1.2 *Signed* and *unsigned* characters

Unless otherwise specified int types are signed. The char data type, however, may be signed or unsigned depending upon the implementation. So long as the restrictions imposed upon char variables are observed this is no problem, i.e. the guaranteed range of 0 to 127 can be represented in either. In many applications it is useful to store data other than character codes in byte sized char variables and the sign of the data could well be important. In such cases the signed or unsigned type specifiers should be used:

data type	numeric range
signed char unsigned char	signed integer range -128 to +127 unsigned integer range 0 to 255

In practice one can treat these types as *signed byte* and *unsigned byte* data types. For example, one may be sampling data from an 8-bit A to D (analogue to digital) converter. It would be very wasteful of memory to store a large amount of such data in int or even short int variables (both of which may be 32-bit in a particular implementation), so unsigned char would be used.

20.2 Printing and reading characters

20.2.1 Character level I/O functions

Individual characters may be read from stdin and written to stdout by:

```
int  getchar(void);                        /* read next character from stdin */
int  putchar(int char);                    /* write character char to stdout */
```

The function getchar reads a character from the standard input stream **stdin** and returns it as an int function result. It does **not** return a char because it can return, in addition to characters, an *end of file* indicator, the value of which is outside the 0 to +127 range which the ANSI C standard guarantees can be represented by a char. This *end of file* indicator is defined in <stdio.h> as the symbolic constant EOF which can be used in IF statements to test for end of input (see Chapter 13 Program 13_1). In practice a program would read a character into an int variable, see Program 20_1 below, test for EOF and if *end of file* was not found assign the int to a char variable. If *end of file* was found the program would stop reading.

The function putchar prints characters to the standard output stream **stdout**. It returns an int function result which is either the character written, if successful, otherwise EOF to indicate that an error occurred. Functions scanf and printf can also be used for character I/O using the %c conversion specification, e.g. when characters are part of a formatted stream containing other data types:

```
char ch;                                   /* define a char */
scanf("%c", &ch);                          /* read a character from stdin */
printf("character was %c", ch);            /* write a character to stdout */
```

A useful function is ungetc which is used to 'push' a character back into an input stream:

```
int ch = 'A';
ungetc(ch, stdio);                         /* push character ch back into stdio */
```

Normally a maximum of one character may be pushed back into a stream and it is not possible to push EOF.

Text streams operate on a line by line basis with characters entered being placed in an input buffer until newline (or *end of file*) is entered. The next character can then be read by getchar (or scanf) and passed to the program. Thus successive calls to getchar can read characters until the input buffer is exhausted (terminated by \n) and the next line is read from the keyboard (see Program 20_1). Some C systems have functions which will read individual characters directly from the keyboard, e.g. MicroSoft C and Turbo C have functions getche (echo character) and getch (no echo) in <conio.h>, see Section 20.3.

Program 20_1 (next page) reads characters from stdin (the keyboard) and prints the characters to stdout together with the character codes in decimal, octal and hexadecimal:

8   define ch of type int (so that it can hold the value of EOF)
10   prompt the user to enter characters
11-15   a while which reads a character from stdin, terminates on *end of file*
        12   if character read was newline '\n'
           13   prompt the user to enter more characters
      else
           15   print character and character code in decimal, octal and hexadecimal
               the # prints a leading 0 or 0x with octal or hexadecimal conversions.

```
 1 /* Program 20_1 - read next character, exit on newline or end of file      */
 2 /*                  print character code in decimal, octal & hex            */
 3
 4 #include <stdio.h>                               /* standard stream I/O library */
 5
 6 int main(void)
 7 {
 8     int ch;                                       /* holds character read */
 9
10     printf("Please enter characters (EOF to terminate) ? ");
11     while ((ch = getchar()) != EOF)               /* read char, exit on EOF */
12         if (ch == '\n')
13             printf("Please enter characters (EOF to terminate) ? ");
14         else
15             printf(" Character %c code %3d, %#4o, %#x \n", ch, ch, ch, ch);
16     return 0;
17 }
```

Program 20_1 Character input from stdin and output to stdout

A run of Program 20_1 on an IBM PC compatible under Turbo C gave (user input in **bold** with ↲ indicating carriage return and ˆz ↲ *end of file*):

```
Please enter characters (EOF to terminate) ?  ab AB ↲
 Character a code  97, 0141, 0x61
 Character b code  98, 0142, 0x62
 Character   code  32,  040, 0x20
 Character A code  65, 0101, 0x41
 Character B code  66, 0102, 0x42
Please enter characters (EOF to terminate) ?  123!"&ˆz ↲
 Character 1 code  49,  061, 0x31
 Character 2 code  50,  062, 0x32
 Character 3 code  51,  063, 0x33
 Character ! code  33,  041, 0x21
 Character " code  34,  042, 0x22
 Character & code  38,  046, 0x26
```

20.2.2 Program to read binary numbers from the keyboard

Program 20_2 (next page) uses the character level I/O functions to read a binary number from the keyboard. The binary numbers are terminated by newline or end of file and invalid characters (not 0 or 1) are reported then ignored. The program terminates when end of file is entered. A run of the program gave:

```
Enter binary number ? 101 ↲
  Value was 5 05 0x5
Enter binary number ? 11t1u1 ↲
t ignored
u ignored
  Value was 15 017 0xf
Enter binary number ? ˆz ↲
```

```
 1 /* Program 20_2 - call a function to read binary numbers */
 2
 3 #include <stdio.h>
 4 #include <ctype.h>
 5
 6 main(void)
 7 {
 8     long int read_binary(void);                    /* function prototype */
 9     long int n;                                    /* holds number read */
10     do                                             /* read until EOF found */
11         {
12         printf("\nEnter binary number ? ");
13         n = read_binary();                         /* read number */
14         printf(" Value was %ld, %#lo, %#lx ", n, n, n);
15         }
16     while (getchar() != 0);                        /* if EOF (0) terminate */
17     return 0;
18 }
19
20 /*-------------------------------------------------------------------------*/
21 /* Function to read a binary number from the keyboard                      */
22 /*   terminate input when character read was not 0 or 1                    */
23 /*   leave last character read in the input stream with EOF as 0           */
24 /* Parameters none                                                         */
25 /* Function result: value of number read as a long int                    */
26 long int read_binary(void)                         /* function header */
27 {
28     long int n = 0;                                /* holds number while reading */
29     int ch;                                        /* holds character read */
30
31     while (((ch = getchar()) != EOF) && (ch != '\n'))
32         /* if a 0 or 1 was read add bit to number else print bad character */
33         if ((ch == '0') || (ch == '1')) n = n * 2 + (ch - '0');
34         else                            printf(" %c ignored\n", ch);
35     if (ch == EOF) ch = 0;                         /* replace EOF with 0 */
36     ungetc(ch, stdin);                             /* unget last character */
37     return n;                                      /* return number */
38 }
```

Program 20_2 Read numbers in binary from keyboard

In Program 20_2 main calls the function read_binary and then displays the value returned in decimal, octal and hexadecimal. The sequence of events in function read_binary is:

31-34   a while which terminates when newline or EOF is entered
       33-34   if character is 0 or 1 add bit to n else display invalid character.

Consider line 31:

```
while (((ch = getchar()) != EOF) && (ch != '\n'))
```

This calls getchar() to read the next character, assigns the value read to ch (an int) then tests if it was EOF or newline (if so the while terminates). When using the && or || operators C guarantees that the operands will be evaluated from left to right (after any precedence, see Section 11.3). In addition, if the final result can be determined from the value of the operand on the left, the operand on the right will not be evaluated. Thus:

(a) `ch = getchar()` returns the next character and assigns it to `ch`,

then   (b) if `ch != EOF` is evaluated and if false the `while` terminates

otherwise   (c) `(ch != '\n')` is evaluated and if false the `while` terminates

otherwise   (d) the body of the `while` is executed.

Hence the character is read and then the tests carried out. If the order of evaluation was not specified for binary logical operations the expression `(ch != '\n')` could be evaluated before `((ch = getchar()) != EOF)` and the program would not work correctly.

Exercise 20.1 (see Appendix B for sample answer)

Write and test a function `read_hex` which reads a hexadecimal number from `stdin`. Ignore invalid characters, terminate the number when newline is entered and terminate the program when end of file is entered.

20.3 Direct character I/O from the operating system

Text streams such as `stdin` operate on a line by line basis (see Section 5.3) with characters entered being placed in an input buffer until newline (or *end of file*) is entered. The next character can then be read by `getchar()` and passed to the program. Thus successive calls to `getchar()` read characters until the input buffer is exhausted (terminated by \n or EOF) and the next line is read from the keyboard (see sample run of Program 20_1). Some C systems have functions which will read individual characters directly from the keyboard and output directly to the display screen, e.g. on IBM PC compatibles Turbo C, Microsoft C and the DOS version of GNU C have a library <conio.h> which includes:

```
ch = getche()    /* read next character directly from the keyboard (with echo) */
ch = getch()     /* read next character directly from the keyboard (no echo) */
kbhit()                /* return 1 if the keyboard has been hit else 0 */
clrscr()                            /* clear the display screen */
gotoxy(x, y)                    /* move to position on the display screen */
putch(ch);                      /* write character ch to display screen */
```

These functions communicate directly with the DOS BIOS (not via the C I/O system) therefore the newline character is carriage return (value 0xd) and end of file is the CTRL/Z character (value 0x1a), see sample answer to Exercise 20.2 below.

Program 20_3 (next page) clears the screen and then loops displaying the date and time until the keyboard is hit (`gotoxy` moves the cursor to the specified column x and line y with the top left hand corner being x = 0 and y = 0 and the bottom right hand corner being x = 79 and y = 24, assuming an 80 column by 25 line screen). Note that `ctime()` returns a pointer to a string which is printed using the %s conversion specification.

Take care when mixing I/O systems, e.g. C `stdio` and direct operating system I/O. In general, so long as one works on a line by line basis all should be well, i.e. call the function `fflush(stdout)` to flush the `stdout` stream output buffers (see Appendix C12.1).

Exercise 20.2 (see Appendix B for sample answer)

Rewrite Program 20_2 to use operating system direct character I/O. Remember that the C I/O system is being bypassed and newline and end of file may not be as usual.

```
 1 /* Program 20_3 - Using console I/O functions display time until key hit */
 2
 3 #include <stdio.h>                          /* standard stream I/O library */
 4 #include <conio.h>                          /* Turbo C console I/O library */
 5 #include <time.h>                         /* standard time functions library */
 6
 7 int main(void)
 8 {
 9     time_t t;                             /* variable to hold time data */
10
11     clrscr();                                       /* clear screen */
12     while (! kbhit())                       /* terminate cn a key hit */
13         {
14         gotoxy(30, 12);                     /* goto position on screen */
15         time(&t);                             /* get date and time */
16         printf("%s", ctime(&t));              /* and display it */
17         }
18     return 0;
19 }
```

Program 20_3 Display date and time until keyboard is hit

20.4 The standard library <ctype.h>: functions to test characters

C does not specify the character code and care must be taken if programs are to be portable across a range of machines. The standard library <ctype.h> contains a range of useful functions which test a character for being within a particular set or sets. The character to be tested is passed as an int parameter and the int function result indicates *true* (non-zero) if the character is in the set otherwise *false* (zero). These functions return *true* as **non-zero** rather than 1 (the relational and logical operators return 1 for *true*). The functions include (see Appendix C2, compiler manuals or on-line help system for a full list):

```
isalpha(character)     /* a letter of the alphabet 'a' to 'z' or 'A' to 'Z' */
isupper(character)             /* an upper case letter 'A' to 'Z' */
islower(character)             /* a lower case letter 'a' to 'z' */
isdigit(character)                    /* a digit '0' to '9' */
isxdigit(character)   /* a hexadecimal digit '0' to '9', 'a' to 'f', 'A' to 'F' */
isspace(character)    /* white space: space, newline, carriage return and tabs */
ispunct(character)    /* a printing character except space, letter or digit */
isalnum(character)     /* letter or digit, i.e. isalpha or isdigit is true */
isprint(character)         /* any printing character including space */
isgraph(character)         /* any printing character except space */
iscntrl(character)                  /* a control character */
```

In addition <ctype.h> contains functions which convert to upper or lower case:

```
toupper(character)      /* if lower case letter convert to upper case */
tolower(character)      /* if upper case letter convert to lower case */
```

Program 20_4 (next page) counts digits, upper and lower case and other characters. Braces {} are not required around the sequence of if statements (lines 12 to 17) which appear to the while as a single statement, but may be added to improve readability. Lines 16 and 17 could be replaced with one line using the conditional operator ? thus:

```
                     (islower(ch)) ? lower++ : other++;
```

Don't, however, get carried away using these (and other) techniques and compress a page of code down to a few lines which are totally unreadable (in fact lines 12 to 17 can be coded using a sequence of three conditional operators). In practice one should aim to produce efficient code but not at the expense of readability.

```
 1 /* Program 20_4 - read and count characters until EOF (end of file) found */
 2
 3 #include <stdio.h>
 4 #include <ctype.h>
 5
 6 int main(void)
 7 {
 8     int digits = 0, upper = 0, lower = 0, other = 0, ch;
 9
10     printf("Please enter characters (EOF to terminate) ? ");
11     while ((ch = getchar()) != EOF)          /* read char & if EOF terminate */
12         if (isdigit(ch)) digits ++;                         /* count digits */
13         else
14           if (isupper(ch)) upper++;                      /* count upper case */
15           else
16             if (islower(ch)) lower++;                    /* count lower case */
17             else              other++;        /* count other characters */
18     printf("\nDigits %d, upper case %d, lower case %d and other %d\n",
19                     digits, upper, lower, other);
20     return 0;
21 }
```

Program 20_4 Read and count characters until EOF (end of file) found

20.5 String constants

In C, a constant enclosed in single quotes ' is a single character and a constant enclosed in double quotes " is a string or an array of char, e.g.:

```
'x'                     /* a single character constant of type int */
"hello"                 /* a string constant of five characters */
"x"                     /* a string constant of one character */
```

Strings such as "hello" and "x" are arrays of char where the element immediately after the last character is set to the null character '\0'. For example, the following table shows the internal representation of the above constants in the ASCII character code:

constant	type	internal representation (ASCII)
'x'	int	120
"hello"	array of char	104 101 108 108 111 0
"x"	array of char	120 0

It is important to note that the constants 'x' and "x" are different, the former being a single character of type int and the latter a two-element array of type char. When the C compiler comes across a string constant, such as "hello" or "x", it converts the characters into the equivalent character codes and appends '\0'.

20.6 Defining and manipulating arrays of characters

Arrays of characters may be defined and initialised like any other array, e.g.:

```
char student_name[30];
char today[10] = {'F','r','i','d','a','y','\0'};
```

If the elements of the array are initialised individually (as in the second example above) the programmer is responsible for appending the terminating null. Arrays of `char` may, however, be initialised with strings and the compiler will append the terminating null, e.g.:

```
char day_of_week[10] = "Tuesday";        /* an initialised character array */
char month_of_year[] = "May"             /* character array of 4 elements */
```

In the first example the character array `day_of_week` is initialised with the string `Tuesday` and the compiler automatically appends the terminating null `'\0'` (the array length must allow for the addition of the terminating null). In the second example the array size is not specified so it becomes the number of characters plus one (for the terminating null).

Arrays of characters may be assigned and manipulated like any other array. For example, to find the `number` of characters in an array:

```
for (number = 0 ; array[number] != '\0' ; number++)      /* look for null char */
        /* null statement */ ;
```

This assumes that the terminating null exists, otherwise unpredictable behaviour will occur (depending upon what is in the array and the memory following it).

There are a large number of functions which can be used to read, write and manipulate strings. For example, the above code which returns the length of a string can be replaced with a call to the function `strlen`. The function prototype is:

```
size_t strlen(const char string[]);
```

`strlen` returns the length of the string (not including the terminating null) as a function result of type `size_t`, which is defined in `<stdlib.h>` (typically an `unsigned int`). The formal parameter `string` represents the address of the first element of the array passed as the actual parameter, i.e. arrays are passed *by reference*. The more common way to write the function prototype is to use pointer notation, see Section 22.3:

```
size_t strlen(const char * string)
```

The parameter `string` is a pointer to (the start address of) an array of characters. Because arrays and pointers are closely related either notation may generally be used. The function could be called as follows:

```
printf(" string length %d", (int) strlen(char_array));
if (strlen(char_array) > 10) .....
```

Note the `cast` (see Section 9.5) to ensure that the second parameter of `printf` is an `int` (to suit the conversion specification `%d`).

Arrays of characters, like any other arrays, cannot be assigned using an assignment statement such as the following:

```
char_array = "hello John Doe";                          /* not allowed */
```

Although the individual elements may be set up like any other array there is a library function `strcpy` which performs this operation:

```
strcpy(char_array, "hello John Doe");           /* assign a character array */
strcpy(string1, string2);                       /* assign one char array to another */
```

In the first example the string "hello John Doe" is copied into the array char_array, in the second the contents of string2 is copied into string1. The function prototype for strcpy is:

```
char *strcpy(char destination[], const char source[]);
```

The parameters source and destination are source and destination arrays of char. The function returns a pointer to the first character of the destination string which can be used as the parameter to another function (further discussion in Section 22.3). When using strcpy it is up to the programmer to ensure that there is sufficient room in the destination array to accept the source string. An alternative function is strncpy:

```
char *strncpy(char destination[], const char source[], size_t n);
```

which copies until a null is encountered or n characters have been copied. If less than n characters are copied destination is padded with nulls '\0', otherwise, if n characters are copied the terminal null is not appended and it is up to the program to ensure that the destination is terminated correctly, e.g. by placing a null at destination[n].

To concatenate two strings there are the functions strcat and strncat. The function prototypes are:

```
char *strcat(char destination[], const char source[]);
char *strncat(char destination[], const char source[], size_t n);
```

The string source is appended to the end of any existing string in destination. strncat stops if the source contains more than n characters, e.g.:

```
strcat(char_array, " text to append ");
strncat(string1, string2, 10);
```

The first example appends string "text to append" on the end of any existing characters in char_array (removing the terminating null) and adds a terminating null to the complete string. The second example appends at most 10 characters (not counting the null) from string2 on the end of any characters in string1.

This has been a very brief introduction to string processing routines (for full details see compiler manuals or on-line help system). To use many of the string processing functions (in particular string searching) more knowledge of pointers is required (see Section 22.3). It is possible, however, to perform many basic string operations using normal array manipulation techniques (although not as efficiently as the specialised functions).

It is important that strings are terminated with a null character '\0'. If copying individual characters into a string (using array indexes or pointers) remember to put a terminating null on the end of the string when finished. It is very easy to forget this, e.g. copying one string to another up to the null but failing to copy the null. If strings contain extra characters after the expected ones a null has been forgotten.

20.7 String input and output

Strings may be printed and read using printf and scanf, e.g.:

```
printf("%s", char_array);                        /* print characters */
scanf(" %s", char_array);    /* skip white space then read chars to white space */
```

printf prints characters from a string until a terminating '\0' is found and scanf reads a string of non-white space characters and appends the terminating '\0'. In both cases the %s conversion specification expects the corresponding parameter to be an address (because the name of an array refers to the address of the first element an & is not required).

Alternatively strings may be printed and read character by character using getchar and putchar, e.g.:

```
for (index = 0; (array[index] = getchar()) != '\n' ; index++)  /* read until \n */
    putchar(array[index]);                                      /* echo character */
array[index] = '\0';                                            /* replace \n with \0 */
printf("\n%s ", array);                                         /* print the string */
```

Another method is to use the string input/output library functions gets and puts:

```
char *gets(char string[])
int puts(const char string[])
```

gets reads characters from the standard input stream stdin into the array string until newline '\n' is entered. The newline character is replaced by '\0' (its effect is similar to the code using getchar above). It returns a pointer to string or the null pointer NULL if EOF was entered (the null pointer is discussed in Section 21.5).

puts writes the string to stdout and appends a newline. It returns EOF if an error occurred otherwise some non-negative value.

For example, to terminate the program on EOF the code could be:

```
if (gets(char_array) == NULL)        /* read characters into char_array */
    exit(1);                         /* failed !, terminate */
```

A problem with using scanf and gets is that no array bounds checking is performed and if too many characters are entered the bounds will be exceeded, corrupting the program. Recommended practice is to use fgets which will perform array bounds checking:

```
char *fgets(char string[], int n, FILE *stream)
int fputs(const char string[], FILE *stream)
```

fgets reads at most n - 1 characters from stream (FILE and streams will be described in Chapter 23) into the array string. If a newline character is found, reading stops and '\n' is placed into array. A terminating '\0' is appended to the string.

fputs writes string to stream (no terminating newline).

For example, if char_array is a character array of twenty elements a string may be read from the keyboard and printed on the screen (a maximum of 19 characters being read):

```
if (fgets(char_array, 20, stdin) == NULL)      /* read characters from keyboard */
    exit(1);                                   /* failed !, terminate */
fputs(char_array, stdout);                     /* print characters to screen */
```

The main differences between gets and fgets are:

1   fgets stops reading after n - 1 characters
2   fgets includes the newline '\n' in the string (gets does not)
3   fgets can read from any input stream, e.g. a file (gets reads from stdin only).

Remember when using fgets that if n - 1 characters are read reading stops and a '\0' appended. A newline character '\n' will not be placed in the string and any characters remaining on the line will be left in the input stream. It is therefore up to the user to check for this condition if appropriate (see function str_read in implementation file str_lib.c in the next section). Similarly puts terminates the string with a newline, fputs does not.

20.8 Program using functions to process strings

Program 20_5 (next page) consists of function main which calls a number of string processing functions which are in implementation file str_lib.c (next page but one):

str_length	returns the length of a string
str_copy	copies contents of string to another (returns number of chars copied)
str_reverse	reverses the contents of a string
str_ch_find	find a character in a string (returns index to character found else -1)
str_remove_spaces	removes leading and trailing spaces from a string
str_read	reads a string from the keyboard (returns 0 on end of file)

The header file str_lib.h (below) contains the prototypes of string processing functions in implementation file str_lib.c.

```
1 /* Header file str_lib.h, string processing functions */
2
3 int str_length(const char string[]);              /* function prototypes */
4 int str_copy(char string_1[], const char string_2[]);
5 void str_remove_spaces(char string[]);
6 void str_reverse(char string[]);
7 int str_ch_find(const char string[], const char character, int index);
8 int str_read(const char prompt[], char string[], const int max_length);
```

Header file str_lib.h   For string processing functions

The sequence of statements in function main of Program 20_5 is:

5	include header file str_lib.h
9	define text_1 and text_2 as arrays of char length 20 elements
10	define index which is used as a character count and array index
12-36	a while statement which reads strings until EOF is entered
12	call str_read to read a string into text_1 maximum 20 characters returns *true* if OK else *false* if EOF was entered
14-15	print the size of the string using string_length and library function strlen the string enclosed in | (so that the start and end can be seen)
17	call str_copy to copy the contents of text_1 to text_2
18-19	print the number of characters copied and the contents of text_2
21	call str_reverse to reverse the contents of text_2
22-23	print the reversed contents of text_2
25	call str_remove_spaces to remove leading/trailing spaces from text_1
26-27	print the length of text_1 and its contents
29	print heading for character search
30	initialise index to -1 (one before the start of the array)
31-35	a while searching string text_1 the search starts from position index + 1 for next occurrence of 'a'
33	replace character 'a' at position index with an 'x'
34	print remainder of string from position index.

```
 1 /* Program 20_5 - Test string processing functions */
 2
 3 #include <stdio.h>                              /* standard I/O library */
 4 #include <string.h>                   /* C string processing functions */
 5 #include "str_lib.h"         /* include own string functions header file */
 6
 7 int main(void)
 8 {
 9     char text_1[20], text_2[20];                  /* internal variables */
10     int index;
11
12     while (str_read("\n\nEnter string ? ", text_1, 20))     /* read string */
13         {
14         printf("read    string length %3d (%3d) |%s| \n",    /* print string */
15                 str_length(text_1), (int) strlen(text_1), text_1);
16
17         index = str_copy(text_2, text_1);                  /* copy string */
18         printf("copied string  length %3d (%3d) |%s| \n",
19                 index, (int) strlen(text_2), text_2);
20
21         str_reverse(text_2);                            /* reverse string */
22         printf("reverse string length %3d (%3d) |%s| \n",
23                 str_length(text_2), strlen(text_2), text_2);
24
25         str_remove_spaces(text_1);                       /* remove spaces */
26         printf("spaces removed length %3d (%3d) |%s| \n",
27                 str_length(text_1), (int) strlen(text_1), text_1);
28
29         printf("Character 'a' found:");                 /* search for 'a' */
30         index = -1;
31         while((index = str_ch_find(text_1, 'a', index + 1)) >= 0)
32             {
33             text_1[index] = 'x';                 /* replace 'a' with 'x' */
34             printf(" |%s|", &text_1[index]);            /* and print */
35             }
36         }
37     return 0;
38 }
```

Program 20_5   Test string processing functions in Implementation file str_lib.c

Implementation file str_lib.c (next page) contains the string processing functions (notice that it includes its own header file in line 5 so that the function prototype declarations can be checked against the function definitions):

str_length	lines 9 to 16, returns the length of a string
str_copy	lines 20 to 27, copies the contents of one string to another
str_reverse	lines 31 to 38, reverses the contents of a string
str_ch_find	lines 42 to 48, find a character in a string
str_remove_spaces	lines 52 to 68, removes leading and trailing spaces from a string
str_read	lines 76 to 90, reads a string from the keyboard.

```
 1 /* Implementation file str_lib.c, string processing functions using arrays   */
 2
 3 #include <stdio.h>                                  /* standard I/O library */
 4 #include <string.h>                          /* C string processing functions */
 5 #include "str_lib.h"                          /* include 'own' header file */
 6
 7 /*-------------------------------------------------------------------------*/
 8 /* function to find length of string, not counting terminating null          */
 9 int str_length(const char string[])
10 {
11     int number = 0;                    /* initialise number of characters to 0 */
12
13     while (string[number] != '\0')               /* look for null character */
14         number++;                       /* not null increment character count */
15     return number;                        /* return number of characters */
16 }
17
18 /*-------------------------------------------------------------------------*/
19 /* function to copy a string to another, return number of characters copied   */
20 int str_copy(char string_1[], const char string_2[])
21 {
22     int index = 0;
23
24     while ((string_1[index] = string_2[index]) != '\0')      /* copy to null */
25         index++;                              /* if not null increment index */
26     return index;                    /* return number of characters copied */
27 }
28
29 /*-------------------------------------------------------------------------*/
30 /* function to reverse the contents of an array                              */
31 void str_reverse(char string[])
32 {
33     int up, down;                       /* up and down array index values */
34     char value;                              /* temporary data store */
35
36     for (up = 0, down = strlen(string) - 1 ; up < down ; up++, down--)
37         (value = string[up], string[up] = string[down], string[down] = value);
38 }
39
40 /*-------------------------------------------------------------------------*/
41 /* function to find character in string starting from position index          */
42 int str_ch_find(const char string[], const char character, int index)
43 {
44     while (string[index] != '\0')                /* look for null character */
45         if (string[index] == character) return index;   /* found character ! */
46         else                              index++;       /* increment index */
47     return -1;                               /* return -1 for fail */
48 }
```

Implementation file str_lib.c String functions using arrays and subscripts

```
49
50  /*---------------------------------------------------------------------*/
51  /* function to remove leading and trailing spaces from a string          */
52  void str_remove_spaces(char string[])
53  {
54      int index,                          /* index to first non-space character */
55          index2,                         /* index to next position to copy to */
56          index3;                         /* index to put terminating null */
57
58      /* find first non-space character, return position in index */
59      for (index = 0 ; string[index] == ' ' ; index++)
60          /* null statement */;
61
62      index2 = index3 = 0;                             /* set to start of array */
63      /* loop copying characters until null character found */
64      while (string[index] != '\0')
65          if ((string[index2++] = string[index++]) != ' ')    /* copy character */
66              index3 = index2;                /* not space note position in index3 */
67      string[index3] = '\0';                          /* put in terminating null */
68  }
69
70  /*---------------------------------------------------------------------*/
71  /* read string using fgets remove terminating \n or characters left in stdin  */
72  /* on entry prompt[]    contains prompt string to print                    */
73  /*           max_length contains maximum length of string                  */
74  /* return string read in array string[]                                    */
75  /* return function result true if all OK else false on EOF                 */
76  int str_read(const char prompt[], char string[], const int max_length)
77  {
78      int index;
79
80      printf("%s", prompt);                            /* print prompt */
81      if (fgets(string, max_length, stdin) == NULL)        /* get string */
82          return 0;                                /* if EOF return false */
83      for (index = 0 ; string[index] != '\0' ; index++)        /* look for \0 */
84          /* null statement */;
85      if (string[--index] == '\n')
86          string[index] = '\0';                        /* replace \n with \0 */
87      else
88          do ; while (getchar() != '\n');      /* else discard characters to \n */
89      return 1;                                    /* all OK return true */
90  }
```

Implementation file str_lib.c String functions using arrays and subscripts

In implementation file str_lib.c function `str_length`, lines 9 to 16, returns the length of the string (not counting the terminating null). The sequence of statements is:

9   `int str_length(const char string[])` the function header

11   define `number` and initialise it to 0 (used to index array and hold character count)

13-14   a `while` statement searching `string` for a null

          the `while` terminates when a null `'\0'` is found

         14 if the character was not null increment character count (and index) `number`

15   return number of characters in `string`.

Because C treats 0 as *false* lines 13 and 14 could be written:

```
while (string[number])                    /* look for null character */
      number++;                    /* not null increment character count */
```

The result from this function is printed in `main` of Program 20_5 together with the result returned by the standard library function `strlen` from `<string.h>`.

Function `str_copy`, lines 20 to 27, copies the contents of `string_2` to `string_1` overwriting any existing contents. It returns the number of characters copied (not counting the null `'\0'`). The sequence of statements is:

20   `int str_copy(char string_1[], const char string_2[])` the function header

21   define `index` and initialise it to 0 (used to index array and hold character count)

24-25   a `while` statement copying `string_2` into `string_1`

          the `while` terminates when a null `'\0'` is copied

         25 if the character was not null increment `index` to next character position

26   return number of characters copied.

Line 24 copies a character from `string_2` into `string_1` and terminates the `while` if the character is a `'\0'`. As in lines 13 and 14 the `!= '\0'` can be removed, i.e.:

```
while (string_1[index] = string_2[index])              /* copy to null */
```

However, a modern compiler will issue a warning, e.g. Turbo C V3.00:

`Warning str_lib.c 24: Possibly incorrect assignment in function str_copy`

This warns that there is an assignment within a conditional statement (a common error is to use = instead of ==). In this case the warning can be ignored as assignment is intended (the original version is easier to understand).

The function `str_reverse`, lines 31 to 38, reverses the characters in a string and is similar to `array_reverse` in array.c in Chapter 19. The sequence of statements is:

31 `void str_reverse(char string[])` the function header

33 `int up, down;` two array indices, i.e.:

       `up` will increment up the array and `down` will decrement down the array

36 a `for` statement which:

       (a) increments `up` from 0

       (b) decrements `down` from `strlen(string)` - 1 (last character in the string)

       (c) terminates when `up` = `down`

37 swaps the two characters `string[up]` and `string[down]`.

The function `str_ch_find`, lines 42 to 48, searches `string` from position `index` for a character. If the character is found it returns the index, else -1:

42   `int str_ch_find(const char string[], const char character, int index)` header
44-46   a `while` statement scanning `string` for a null, if found the `while` terminates
      45 if `string[index] == character` return `index` (character found)
      46 else increment `index` to next character
47   `character` not found, return -1 to indicate fail.

The function is called from `main` of Program 20_5, lines 30 to 35, searching for occurrences of the character `'a'` in string `text_1`:

```
index = -1;
while((index = str_ch_find(text_1, 'a', index + 1)) >= 0)
    {
    text_1[index] = 'x';                    /* replace 'a' with 'x' */
    printf(" |%s|", &text_1[index]);          /* and print */
    }
```

On each call one is added to the current value of `index` to start the search either from the beginning of the string (`index` is initialised to -1 in line 30) or following the last occurrence of the character (`str_ch_find` returns -1 if the character is not found). The character indexed by `index` is replaced and the remainder of the string is printed. Thus `str_ch_find` works down the string finding each occurrence of the character `'a'` and replacing it with `'x'`. Note the use of `&text_1[index]` in line 34 to pass the address of a position within `text_1`; the remainder of string from position `index` is printed. This technique can be used to pass parts of arrays into functions, i.e. in the above case the name `text_1` is the address of the first element and `&text_1[index]` is the address of the element at position `index`. The `printf` conversion specification `%s` expects the corresponding parameter to be an address.

Function `str_remove_spaces`, lines 52 to 68, removes leading and trailing spaces from a string. The sequence of statements is:

52   `void str_remove_spaces(char string[])` the function header
54-56   define `int` indices used in the function
59-60   find first non-space character in the string, return position in `index`
62   initialise indices `index2` and `index3` to the start of the array
64-66   a `while` loop which copies characters until `'\0'` is found (see notes below)
      65 copies a character (overwriting any leading spaces)
      66 if character copied was not a space note array index in `index3`
67   terminate string (`index3` contains the position of last non-space character plus 1).

Notes:
1   After executing lines 59 to 60 `index` contains the position of the first non-space character in the array.
2   Line 62 positions `index2` at the start of the array ready for copying the characters.
3   Line 62 positions `index3` at the start of the array in case the string is empty or full of spaces, i.e. line 66 would not be executed to assign a value to `index3`.
4   Line 65 overwrites any leading spaces by overwriting the character at position `index2` with the one from position `index`.
5   In line 66 `index3` is positioned at the last non-space character plus 1 which is then overwritten with `'\0'` in line 67.

The function `str_read`, lines 76 to 90, reads a string of length `max_length` from `stdin`. It returns *true* if the string was read successfully or *false* if `EOF` was entered. If the length of the string is less than max_length characters the terminating newline is replaced with '\0', else the characters remaining on the line are discarded including the newline:

76   `int str_read(const char prompt[], char string[], int max_length)`
        the function header defining three parameters:

        `prompt[]`   an array of `char` containing a message to print on the screen
        `string`   an array of `char` to accept the characters input
        `max_length`   an `int` specifying the length of `string`

80-82   display `prompt` and call `fgets` to read a string length max_length - 1 from `stdin`
        82 if EOF was entered (`fgets` returned NULL) terminate function with result *false*

83-84   search `string` for terminating '\0'
85   if previous character (to '\0') was newline
           86 replace '\n' with '\0'
        else 88 discard remaining characters from `stdin` up to and including newline.

Line 86 is executed if the input text contained less than max_length - 1 characters otherwise the input text contained too many characters and line 88 discards them (so that they do not appear when `fgets` is called again). Line 88 could be written:

```
while (getchar() != '\n')                 /* else remove characters to \n */
    /* null statement */;
```

Below is a run of Program 20_5 (newline is indicated by ↲). The second test shows the removal of leading and trailing spaces (the | show the limits of the string), the third the truncation of the input text at 19 characters and the final test an empty string (it is wise to test string processing functions with an empty string as it can often cause problems):

```
Enter string ? hello abc abc abc ↲
read      string length  17 ( 17) |hello abc abc abc|
copied string  length  17 ( 17) |hello abc abc abc|
reverse string length  17 ( 17) |cba cba cba olleh|
spaces removed length  17 ( 17) |hello abc abc abc|
Character 'a' found: |xbc abc abc| |xbc abc| |xbc|

Enter string ?       test spaces      ↲
read      string length  19 ( 19) |      test spaces      |
copied string  length  19 ( 19) |      test spaces      |
reverse string length  19 ( 19) |      secaps tset      |
spaces removed length  11 ( 11) |test spaces|
Character 'a' found: |xces|

Enter string ? abcdefghijklmnopqrstuvwxyz ↲
read      string length  19 ( 19) |abcdefghijklmnopqrs|
copied string  length  19 ( 19) |abcdefghijklmnopqrs|
reverse string length  19 ( 19) |srqponmlkjihgfedcba|
spaces removed length  19 ( 19) |abcdefghijklmnopqrs|
Character 'a' found: |xbcdefghijklmnopqrs|

Enter string ? ↲
read      string length   0 (  0) ||
copied string  length   0 (  0) ||
reverse string length   0 (  0) ||
spaces removed length   0 (  0) ||
Character 'a' found:

Enter string ? ˆZ ↲
```

Exercise 20.3 (*see Appendix B for sample answer*)

Implement and test a function which searches for a string within a string. The function prototype of a string search function could be:

```
int str_search(const char string_1[], const char string_2[], int index);
```

Starting at position `index` search `string_1` for the next occurrence of `string_2`. If found return the index else -1. Test the function (similar to lines 30 to 35 in Program 20_5).

Implement and test a function `str_compare` which compares two strings (similar to `strcmp` in the standard library):

```
int str_compare(const char string_1[], const char string_2[]);
```

the contents of `string_1` is compared with `string_2` and the following result returned:

<0   if `string_1` comes before `string_2` in the sorting sequence
0   if `string_1` equals `string_2`
>0   if `string_1` comes after `string_2` in the sorting sequence.

20.9 Array processing functions in <string.h>

Arrays of characters can be processed using the same techniques as any other array with the proviso that special attention has to be paid to the terminating null `'\0'`. The library `<string.h>` contains functions to process strings (arrays of char terminated by `'\0'`) which give enhanced performance in terms of faster processing. However, many of the functions require a knowledge of pointers (see Chapter 21), e.g. (see Appendix C14 for a full list):

```
char *strcpy(char *destination, const char *source);
```
    copy string source to string destination; return a pointer to destination
```
char *strncpy(char *destination, const char *source, size_t maxlen);
```
    copy at most maxlen characters from string source to string destination
```
char *strcat(char *destination, const char *source);
```
    concatenate string source onto the end of string destination;
```
char *strncat(char *destination, const char *source, size_t maxlen);
```
    concatenate at most maxlen characters of string source onto destination
```
int strcmp(const char *string1, const char *string2);
```
    compare string1 with string2; return:
        <0 if string1 < string2, 0 if string1 == string2 and >0 if string1 > string2
```
int strncmp(const char *string1, const char *string2, size_t maxlen);
```
    compare at most maxlen characters of string1 with string2; return:
        <0 if string1 < string2, 0 if string1 == string2 and >0 if string1 > string2
```
char *strchr(const char *string, int character);
```
    search string for character; if found return pointer to first occurrence else NULL
```
char *strrchr(const char *string, int character);
```
    reverse search string for character; if found return pointer to last occurrence else NULL

Library `<string.h>` also contains general functions to manipulate blocks of memory as arrays of characters (bytes) which are not null terminated, e.g. `memset` to set all elements to a value, `memcpy` to copy an array, `memchr` and `memcmp` to search an array, etc.:

```
void *memset(void *string, int character, size_t number);
```
    fill the first number characters of string with character

```
void *memchr(const void *string, int character, size_t number);
```
    search at most number characters of string for character;
    if found return pointer to first occurrence else NULL
```
int memcmp(const void *string1, const void *string2, size_t number);
```
    compare at most number characters of string1 with string2; return:
        <0 if string1 < string2, 0 if string1 == string2 and >0 if string1 > string2
```
void *memcpy(void *destination, const void *source, size_t number);
```
    copy at most number characters from string source to string destination;
        return a pointer to destination
```
void *memmove(void *destination, const void *source, size_t number);
```
    copy at most number characters from string source to string destination;
        return a pointer to destination. This will work even if the objects overlap

For example, memcmp compares at most number characters of string1 with string2:

```
int memcmp(const void *string1, const void *string2, size_t number);
```

The pointers string1 and string2 can point to any type of data (void * will be discussed in Section 21.7) with the comparison being carried out on a bitwise basis, e.g.:

```
if (! memcmp(x , y, sizeof(x))) printf("arrays are the same");
else                           printf("arrays are different");
```

x and y could be arrays of float, double, int, structures (see Chapter 24), etc.

It must be emphasised that memcpy, memcmp, etc. perform bitwise operations upon the memory areas pointed to. If the objects pointed to are data structures which contain pointers to other structures such structures will not be copied or compared; use a program loop which copies or tests each object in turn using appropriate operators.

In addition <stdlib.h> contains functions which convert the contents of string to a numeric value (skipping leading white space). A pointer (see Chapter 21) to the character which stopped the conversion process is placed in endptr (if endptr is NULL the address is not returned). In the case of strtol and strtoul the base of the number may be specified:

```
double   strtod(const char *string, char **endptr);
long     strtol(const char *string, char **endptr, int radix);
unsigned long strtoul(const char *string, char **endptr, int radix);
```

The following are simplified versions of the above:

```
double   atof(const char *string);
int      atoi(const char *string);
long     atol(const char *string);
```

Problem for Chapter 20

Implement and test some string processing functions. For example:

    (a) Concatenate string_1 with string_2; return result in string_1, e.g.:

```
void str_concat(char string_1[], const char string_2[]);
```

    (b) Find last occurrence of a character in a string; return index if found, else -1, e.g.:

```
int str_r_ch_find(const char string[], const char character);
```

21

Pointers

Although it is possible to implement programs in C with minimal use of pointers it is wise to have an understanding of pointers and where they may be used to advantage. Many library functions use pointer parameters and return pointers as function results.

21.1 Variables and addresses

Consider the definition of the external variables i, j, k, x, y and z:

```
int i = 10, j = 20, k[10] = {0};          /* define variables of type int */
float x = 2.0f, z[20] = {0}, y = 5.0f;    /* define variables of type float */
```

When program execution starts space will be allocated in RAM memory to store the variables:

1   Each variable will be assigned storage in memory starting at a particular address.
2   The amount of storage depends upon the size of the variable (the program can use the sizeof operator to determine the size of an object in bytes).

Assume that:

    (a) int variables are two bytes in size,
    (b) float variables are four bytes in size,
and (c) storage is allocated starting at address 1000 hexadecimal.

The above variables could be stored at the following addresses:

variable name	address hexadecimal	size decimal bytes	comment
i	1000	2	int stored in locations 1000 and 1001
j	1002	2	int stored in locations 1002 and 1003
k	1004	20	array stored in locations 1004 to 1017
x	1018	4	float stored in locations 1018 to 101B
z	101C	80	array stored in locations 101C to 106B
y	106C	4	float stored in locations 106C to 106F
	1070		next 'free' location

When a variable name is used in an expression the contents of the object are accessed (except arrays where the array name refers to the address of the first element), e.g:

```
x = y;                    /* assign the value of variable y to variable x */
```

which, using the above addresses, copies the contents of y (locations 106C to 106F) into x (locations 1018 to 101B). Variables, therefore, are areas in memory used to store information of a particular type (int, float, etc.) where the variables may be simple types (a single int) or a structured type such as an array or a structure.

A pointer is just another type of variable which is used to store the address of an object (it is said to 'point to' the object). For example, a pointer having a value 1018 would be a pointer to variable x in the above table (assuming that there is a simple one to one relationship between pointers and physical memory addresses). By using the address contained in the pointer it would be possible to access the contents of variable x.

21.2 Defining and using pointers

In C a pointer is defined as follows:

```
type *p_type;                                    /* define a 'pointer to type' */
```

Prefixing an identifier with an * defines a variable of type type *, which is a 'pointer to type', i.e. p_type can hold the address of an object of type. For example:

```
int *p_int;                                      /* define a 'pointer to int' */
```

This defines p_int to be of type int * which is a 'pointer to int'.

The address operator &, which returns the *address of* an operand, is used to set up a pointer, e.g.:

```
int *p_int;                                      /* define a 'pointer to int' */
int number;                                              /* define an int */

p_int = &number;                            /* point p_int to variable number */
```

The statement p_int = &number; assigns the *value of the address* of variable number to pointer p_int, i.e. if number was at address 1010 hexadecimal in memory this address would be assigned to p_int (assuming a simple one to one relationship between pointers and physical addresses). Once set up p_int *points to* number.

It is possible to define variables and pointers (to the same type) in a single definition (and also initialise the variables and pointers):

```
int number,                                      /* define an int variable */
    *p_int = &number;            /* define a pointer and 'point it' to number */
```

This defines number (type int, an int variable) and p_int (type int *, a 'pointer to int') initialised to point to number. Clearly the compiler must know about the variable before it can assign the address. For example, changing the order in the definition produced the following error message with Microsoft C V7.00:

```
1 int *p_int = &number, number;
***** X.C(1) : error C2065: 'number' : undefined
***** X.C(1) : error C2086: 'number' : redefinition
```

Take care not to confuse the use of & as the *address operator* with its use as the *bitwise AND operator* (Section 9.4).

To access the object to which a pointer points (holds the address of), the pointer is prefixed by the *indirection* or *dereferencing* operator *, e.g.:

```
int *p_int;                                      /* define a pointer to an int */
int number;                                      /* define an int variable */

p_int = &number;                            /* point p_int to variable number */
*p_int = 10;              /* assign the value 10 to the int pointed to by p_int */
```

The last statement assigns the value 10 to the variable number, i.e. *p_int = 10; assigns 10 to the variable pointed to by p_int, which in this case 'points to' variable number, therefore 10 is assigned to number. A pointer may be used in an arithmetic expression, e.g.:

```
int *p_int;                          /* define a pointer to an int */
int i, number = 20;                    /* define int variables */

p_int = &number;                  /* point p_int to variable number */
i = *p_int * 10;        /* multiply object pointed to by 10, assign result to i */
```

This multiplies the value of the int pointed to by p_int by 10 and assigns the result, 200, to i (could be written i = 10 * *p_int; the indirection operator having a higher precedence than the multiplier operator). Note that the following two statements have the same effect:

```
number = i;                       /* assign value of i to number */
number = *&i;                     /* assign value of i to number */
```

It is important to note that different objects have different pointer types. For example, int * 'pointer to int' is not the same type as a float * 'pointer to float' (in particular pointer arithmetic depends upon the type of object pointed to, see Section 21.3.1), e.g.:

```
int i, *p_int = &i;              /* define an int and a 'pointer to int' */
float x, *p_float;           /* define a float and a 'pointer to float' */

/* error !!  assign the value of a 'pointer to int' to a 'pointer to float' */
p_float = p_int;                          /* not allowed !!! */
```

Microsoft C V7.00 generated the following error message for the latter statement:

```
***** x.c(7) : error C2446: '=' : no conversion between 'float *' and 'int *'
```

which indicates that assigning the value of a 'pointer to an int' to a 'pointer to a float' is an error. A cast p_float = (float *) p_int; may be used, but the code is highly machine dependent and should be avoided. Assignment of variables using the pointers is legal:

```
int i = 10, *p_int = &i;                /* an int and a 'pointer to an int' */
float x, *p_float = &x;          /* a float and a 'pointer to a float' */

/* assign value of int 'pointed to' by p_int to float 'pointed to' by p_float */
*p_float = *p_int;
printf("float value %f", x);
```

The value of the int pointed to by p_int (i in this case) is converted to a float and assigned to the float pointed to by p_float (x in this case). The value 10 would be printed.

It is very important to set up a pointer to 'point to' something before it is used. If a pointer is not explicitly initialised its value is undefined if it is an automatic internal or zero if it is external or a static internal (see Section 18.9). To differentiate pointers from other types it is wise to use some naming convention, e.g. use p_ to start pointer names.

Take care when using the divide operator / with the *indirection operator* *, e.g. consider the following:

```
i = 10/*p_int;          /* divide 10 by object pointed to, assign result to i */
```

Although this looks correct the characters /* in the middle of the expression 10/*p_int will be taken as the start of a comment to be terminated by the next */. In practice the next */ may be several lines further on and a large amount of code would be commented out. This type of error can be difficult to find as the error messages often refer to lines much later in the code (following the */).

21.3 Arrays and pointers

The sample programs presented so far in this book have used an integer index or subscript to access the element of an array, e.g. to zero the contents of an array:

```
int array_index, x[100];            /* define an int and an array of int */
for (array_index = 0 ; array_index < 100 ; array_index++)
    x[array_index] = 0;                /* zero an array element */
```

Arrays and pointers have a very close relationship and it is possible, and sometimes more efficient, to use pointers to manipulate the elements of arrays.

21.3.1 Introduction to pointer arithmetic

The name of an array refers to the address of its first element (it is a constant pointer to the first element). Consider:

```
int *p_array, x[100];          /* define pointer to int and array of int */
p_array = x;                     /* point to first element of array */
p_array = &x[0];                 /* point to first element of array */
```

This defines a pointer to int and an array of int and then shows two ways of assigning the value of the address of the first element of x to pointer p_array. Once the pointer is set up it can be used instead of the array name. For example, the following statements are alternative ways of accessing the first element of x and assigning 0 to it:

```
x[0] = 0;                          /* zero first element of array */
*x = 0;                            /* zero first element of array */
*p_array = 0;                      /* zero first element of array */
p_array[0] = 0;                    /* zero first element of array */
```

Arithmetic may be performed with pointers in that integral values may be added to or subtracted from pointers and pointers of the same type can be compared and subtracted. As the name of an array is a pointer to the first element, successive elements can be accessed by adding an integer to the pointer, e.g. consider the array int x[100];:

x	refers to the address of the first element, i.e. &x[0]
x + 1	refers to the address of the second element, i.e. &x[1]
....	
x + n	refers to the address of the (n + 1)th element, i.e. &x[n]
....	
x + 99	refers to the address of the last element, i.e. &x[99]
x + 100	refers to an address beyond the end of the array.

Table 21.1 shows examples of accessing array elements using either integer indexes or a pointer with an integer offset (it is up to the programmer to ensure that the pointer stays within the array bounds when accessing the array elements). The parentheses in an expression such as *(x + n) are required because without them the indirection operator * would take effect before the +, i.e. *x + n is equivalent to x[0] + n.

An important point to note is that arithmetic on a particular type of pointer automatically takes account of the length of the object concerned. This is one of the reasons why pointers to different objects are different types, i.e. a particular pointer type has to take account (in its internal machine representation) of the object size. The following arithmetic operations are allowed with pointers:

```
pointer  +   integer  yields a pointer
integer  +   pointer  yields a pointer
pointer  -   integer  yields a pointer
pointer  -   pointer  yields an integer  (the 'distance' between the two pointers)
```

The latter must be pointers to the same array otherwise the result is undefined.

Table 21.1 shows that an array name may be used like a pointer and a pointer may be used like an array name. In fact, the compiler translates expressions using indexes into the equivalent pointer notation, i.e. x[5] becomes *(x + 5). Note, however, that an array name is a constant whereas a pointer (unless const qualified) can be changed.

element	using the array name		using a pointer name	
accessed	indexed	as a pointer	indexed	as a pointer
first	x[0]	*x	p_array[0]	*p_array
second	x[1]	*(x + 1)	p_array[1]	*(p_array + 1)
third	x[2]	*(x + 2)	p_array[2]	*(p_array + 2)
nth	x[n-1]	*(x + n - 1)	p_array[n-1]	*(p_array + n - 1)
last	x[99]	*(x + 99)	p_array[99]	*(p_array + 99)

Table 21.1 Accessing array elements using the array name or a pointer

21.3.2 Using increment and decrement operators with pointers

The increment and decrement operators may be used with pointers, e.g.:

```
p_array++                              /* point p_array to next array element */
p_array--                              /* point p_array to previous array element */
```

Program 21_1 (next page) shows several for statements loading values into an array using:

1   the array name with indexes as 'normal';
2   a pointer to the array using (a) indexes and (b) pointer arithmetic.

The sequence of statements in Program 21_1 is:

7   define array_index which will be used as a 'normal' array index
8   define the array x of type int of length 100 elements
9   define p_array a pointer to int
10   define i initialised to 0
13-14   a for statement loading the values 0 to 9 into x
        the array name x is used with array_index as an index
15-16   print the values stored in x (values 0 to 9)
19-20   a for statement loading the values 10 to 19 into x
        a pointer p_array is used with array_index as an index
21-22   print the values stored in x (values 10 to 19)
25-26   a for statement loading the values 20 to 29 into x
        a pointer p_array is incremented from x to x + 10
27-28   print the values stored in x (values 20 to 29)
31-32   a for statement loading the values 30 to 39 into x
        a pointer p_array is incremented from x to &x[10].

```
1  /* Program 21_1   Using array name and pointers to access array elements */
2
3  #include <stdio.h>
4
5  int main(void)
6  {
7      int array_index,                                /* define array index */
8          x[100],                                     /* define int array */
9          *p_array,                                   /* define pointer to int */
10         i = 0;                                      /* define working variable */
11
12     printf("\nLoad 0 to 9 into array using array name and index\n");
13     for (array_index = 0 ; array_index < 10 ; i++, array_index++)
14         x[array_index] = i;
15     for (array_index = 0 ; array_index < 10 ; array_index++)
16         printf(" %3d ", x[array_index]);
17
18     printf("\nLoad 10 to 19 into array using pointer with index\n");
19     for (p_array = x, array_index = 0 ;array_index < 10 ; i++, array_index++)
20         p_array[array_index] = i;
21     for (p_array = x, array_index = 0 ;array_index < 10 ; array_index++)
22         printf(" %3d ", p_array[array_index]);
23
24     printf("\nLoad 20 to 29 into array using pointer arithmetic\n");
25     for (p_array = x ; p_array < x + 10 ; i++, p_array++)
26         *p_array = i;
27     for (p_array = x ; p_array < x + 10 ; p_array++)
28         printf(" %3d ", *p_array);
29
30     printf("\nLoad 30 to 39 into array using pointer arithmetic\n");
31     for (p_array = x ; p_array < &x[10] ; i++, p_array++)
32         *p_array = i;
33     for (p_array = x ; p_array < &x[10] ; p_array++)
34         printf(" %3d ", *p_array);
35     return 0;
36 }
```

Program 21_1 Using the array name and pointers to access array elements

```
Load 0 to 9 into array using array name and index
   0    1    2    3    4    5    6    7    8    9
Load 10 to 19 into array using pointer with index
  10   11   12   13   14   15   16   17   18   19
Load 20 to 29 into array using pointer arithmetic
  20   21   22   23   24   25   26   27   28   29
Load 30 to 39 into array using pointer arithmetic
  30   31   32   33   34   35   36   37   38   39
```

Run of Program 21_1 Using the array name and pointers to access array elements

Consider lines 25 and 26 of Program 21_1:

```
for (p_array = x ; p_array < x + 10 ; i++, p_array++)
    *p_array = i;
```

p_array is initialised to 'point to' the first element of x and then incremented to x + 10 where the for terminates (the last element of x accessed is x[9]). Lines 31 and 32 are identical except for the specification of the terminating address, i.e.:

```
for (p_array = x ; p_array < &x[10] ; i++, p_array++)
    *p_array = i;
```

p_array is initialised to 'point to' the first element of x and then incremented to &x[10] where the for terminates (x + 10 and &x[10] are the same address). Although the array element x[10] does not exist the use of the address &x[10] is permitted (this permission extends to one element beyond the end of the array and no further), i.e.:

(a) the addressable elements are from x[0] to x[9]

and (b) the valid addresses are from &x[0] to &x[10] (one beyond the end).

Addresses evaluated outside the limits of (b) are undefined and result in unpredictable behaviour (see Section 5.9 of Ellis & Stroustrup 1990 for a full discussion).

One of the major problems with arrays in C is that indexes start at 0 whereas most algorithms tend to start from 1. A common technique used to simplify coding is to allocate an extra element and not use element 0. An alternative technique proposed in many texts is to define a pointer and point it to one element before the start of the array, e.g.:

```
/* dangerous code, p_x points before the start of x which is invalid */
int x_index,                            /* define array index */
    x[100],                             /* define int array */
    *p_x = x - 1;                       /* define pointer to int, point to x - 1 */
for (x_index = 1 ; x_index <= 10 ; x_index++)    /* fill x with 1 to 10 */
    p_x[x_index] = x_index;                       /* use p_x[] */
for (x_index = 0 ; x_index < 10; x_index++)      /* print values */
    printf(" %3d ", x[x_index]);                 /* use x[] */
```

One can either use the array name x with indices x[0] to x[9] or the array name p_x with indices p_x[1] to p_x[10]. Unfortunately, the pointer p_x is initialised to an address before the start of x, i.e. outside the limits for valid addresses. What happens depends upon the architecture of the machine concerned. On some machines the value formed will be a valid memory address and the code will work. On other machines the value formed may be an invalid address and the program could either produce incorrect results or crash with a memory segmentation fault. Such techniques cause severe problems when porting software across a range of machines (programs which work on one machine fail on another) and can be very difficult to track down. Remember the limits for valid addresses and keep to them, i.e. don't used techniques such as the above if code is to be portable.

It is therefore possible to manipulate arrays using indexes or pointer arithmetic. Which is used in practice is a matter of programming style with the aim of producing efficient, readable and maintainable code. In general, however, the recommendation is that array indexes should be used unless there are good reasons for using pointer notation (non-C programmers will certainly find it easier to read). Whether using array indexes or pointers the programmer should ensure that array bounds are not overflowed and that pointers contain valid values (remember that C performs no array bounds checking).

21.3.3 Using the indirection operator with increment and decrement

The indirection operator * can be combined with increment and decrement. Consider:

```
int x[] = { 10, 20, 30, 40, 50 },        /* define a five-element int array */
         y, *p_array;                      /* define an int and a pointer to an int */
p_array = &x[2];                           /* point to third element of x */
y = *p_array;                              /* assign y value of object pointed to */
```

The pointer p_array is initialised to 'point to' the third element of x and the variable y would be assigned the value 30. Table 21.2 shows some examples of the result of the latter statement when *p_array is replaced by various expressions.

expression	value assigned to y	contents of array after evaluation of expression	element p_array then points to
*++p_array	40	10 20 30 40 50	4
++*p_array	31	10 20 31 40 50	3
*p_array++	30	10 20 30 40 50	4
(*p_array)++	30	10 20 31 40 50	3

Table 21.2 Pointer operations with increment operator

The operators * and ++ are of the same precedence and associate from right to left, e.g.:

y = *++p_array   i.e. with parentheses y = *(++p_array)
   1   the ++ is applied to p_array incrementing it to point to the fourth element of x;
   2   the * is applied accessing the object pointed to by the pointer p_array;
   3   the value of the fourth element of the array x is assigned to y, i.e. 40.

y = ++*p_array   i.e. with parentheses y = ++(*p_array)
   1   the * is applied accessing the object pointed to by p_array (the third element of x);
   2   the ++ is applied to the object pointed to by p_array incrementing its value;
   3   the incremented value of the third element of x is assigned to y, i.e. 31.

y = *p_array++   i.e. with parentheses y = *(p_array++)
   1   the ++ is applied to p_array but because it is postfix its effect is delayed until after the expression has been evaluated;
   2   the * is applied accessing the object pointed to by the pointer p_array (the third element of x);
   3   the value of the third element of x is assigned to y, i.e. 30;
   4   p_array is then incremented, pointing it to the fourth element of x.

y = (*p_array)++   parentheses are required (operators associate from right to left)
   1   the * is applied accessing the object pointed to by the pointer p_array (the third element of x);
   2   the ++ is applied to the object pointed to by p_array but because it is postfix its effect is delayed until after the expression has been evaluated;
   3   the value of the third element of x is assigned to y, i.e. 30;
   4   the value of the third element of x is then incremented.

assignment expression	contents of array after assignment	element p_array then points to
*++p_array = 500	10 20 30 500 50	4
*p_array++ = 500	10 20 500 40 50	4

Table 21.3 Assignment operations using a pointer with increment operator

Table 21.3 shows examples of using the increment and indirection operators on the left hand side of an assignment expression, i.e. assuming p_array points to &x[2]:

*++p_array = 500
    1   the pointer is incremented to point to the fourth element of array x;
    2   the fourth element of x is assigned the value 500;
    3   the overall result of the expression is 500.

*p_array++ = 500
    1   the third element of x is assigned the value 500;
    2   the pointer is incremented to point to the fourth element of array x;
    3   the overall result of the expression is 500.

The assignment operations ++*p_array = 500 and (*p_array)++ = 500 are illegal, e.g. using Microsoft C version 7.00:

```
      5 ++*p_array = 500;
***** XXXX.C(5) : error C2106: '=' : left operand must be lvalue
      6 (*p_array)++ = 500;
***** XXXX.C(6) : error C2106: '=' : left operand must be lvalue
```

An example of using an expression such as *p_array++ is when using a loop to zero the contents of an array:

```
int *p_array, x[10];          /* define pointer to int and array of int */

p_array = x;                          /* point to first element of array */
while( p_array < x + 10 )                   /* loop until end of array */
    *p_array++ = 0;           /* zero array element and increment pointer */
```

In general, use these combined operators with great care and only after consideration of alternatives, e.g. the above would be easier to understand when written as a for statement:

```
for (p_array = x; p_array < x + 10; p_array++)     /* loop until end of array */
    *p_array = 0;                                  /* zero array element */
```

or even better using array notation:

```
for (array_index = 0 ; array_index < 10 ; array_index++)
    x[array_index] = 0;
```

Exercise 21.1 (see Appendix B for sample answer)

Implement and test a program (or obtain from disk file c21\ex21_1.c) to check that the expressions in Tables 21.2 and 21.3 are evaluated as shown. Extend the program to check that assignment operations such as ++*p_array = 500 and (*p_array)++ = 500 are illegal.

21.4 *const* qualified pointers

The const type qualifier may be applied to pointers:

```
int x[] = { 10, 20, 30, 40, 50 };          /* five-element array */
int *const p_array = x;                     /* constant pointer to array x */
```

p_array is a constant pointer to the first element of array x and may not be altered (incremented or pointed to something else) although the object pointed to may be altered. In effect p_array becomes a synonym for the array name x (which is itself a constant pointer). Now consider:

```
const int a = 20 , b = 30;                  /* two const qualified variables */
const int *p_int = &a;                      /* pointer to a constant int */
```

p_int is a pointer to a constant object and may be changed to point to another object of the same type (e.g. b in the above example) although the object pointed to may not be altered. Now consider:

```
const int a = 20 , b = 30;                  /* two const qualified variables */
const int *const p_int = &a;                /* constant pointer to a constant int */
```

p_int is a constant pointer to a constant object. Neither the pointer nor the object pointed to may be altered. If an object is declared as const qualified any pointer to it must be similarly const qualified, e.g. using Microsoft C V7.00:

```
7       const int a = 20 , b = 30;
8       int *p_int2 = &a;
***** X.C(8) : warning C4090: different 'const/volatile' qualifiers
```

This warns that a is const qualified but the pointer p_int, which 'points to' a, is not and an attempt could be made to change the value of a, e.g.:

```
*p_int2 = 110;          /* error, attempt to change the value of a const object */
```

Similarly pointers which are function parameters and pointers which are returned as function results may be const qualified (see Chapter 22).

21.5 The *null pointer*

It is often necessary to assign a value to a pointer without pointing it to some object. This is achieved by assigning the value 0, which is converted to a pointer commonly called the *null pointer* (which need not be represented by the same bit pattern as integer 0). The symbolic constant NULL which is defined in <stddef.h> is often used in place of 0 to indicate that this is a special pointer value. The null pointer is guaranteed to be different from all legal pointer values and may be assigned to any pointer type, e.g.:

```
int *p_int = NULL;              /* define pointer to int initialised to null */
```

In C NULL or 0 is the only valid integer that may be assigned to or compared with a pointer. If a pointer is not initialised to point to something it should be assigned the value NULL. If the pointer is then used the operation will either be ignored (e.g. with the function free, see Section 25.1) or the program may be stopped with a *null pointer error* (one then has some idea of the problem). Using an uninitialised pointer leads to unpredictable results.

When doing low-level system programming it is sometimes necessary to assign other integer values to pointers (e.g. to access specific physical memory locations) but the code is highly machine dependent (see Chapter 31 for some sample applications).

21.6 Pointers to pointers

A pointer is a variable which can hold the address of (or 'point to') another variable. It is therefore possible to have pointers which can 'point to' a pointer which 'points to' an object. Consider:

```
int a,                              /* define an int */
    *p_int,                         /* define pointer to int */
    **p_p_int;                      /* define pointer to pointer to int */
```

This defines three variables:

a   is an int, i.e. it can hold an integer numeric value
p_int   is a 'pointer to an int', i.e. it can hold the address of a variable of type int
p_p_int   is a 'pointer to a pointer to an int', i.e. it can hold the address of a variable of type 'pointer to an int'.

Note that p_int and p_p_int are different types, the former being a 'pointer to int' and the latter a 'pointer to a pointer to int'. Once defined the variables can be assigned values:

```
    a = 10;                         /* assign value to int variable */
    p_int = &a;                     /* point p_int to variable a */
    p_p_int = &p_int;               /* point p_p_int to pointer p_int */
```

The indirection operator * is used to access the objects pointed to:

p_p_int   references the contents of p_p_int, i.e. the address of p_int
*p_p_int   the indirection operator * references the contents of the object pointed to by p_p_int, i.e. the contents of p_int which is the address of a
**p_p_int   the double indirection operator ** references the contents of the object pointed to by the pointer pointed to by p_p_int, i.e. the contents of a which is the value 10.

In the latter case p_p_int points to p_int which points to a, thus **p_p_int accesses the contents of a. For example, the following statements all print the value of the variable a:

```
    printf("%d ", a);
    printf("%d ", *p_int);
    printf("%d ", **p_p_int);
```

The following statements print the contents of p_int (an address):

```
    printf("%p ", p_int);
    printf("%p ", *p_p_int);
```

Program 21_2 shows some more examples of the use of pointers to pointers printing the addresses of variables, changing pointers to point to different variables, etc. A run of the program under MS-DOS (compiled using DJ's port of GNU C V2.6.1) gave:

```
Addresses of variables in the programs
&a = 4018, &b = 401c, &p_int1 = 4020, &p_int2 = 4024, &p_p_int = 4028

p_p_int points to p_int1 which points to a = 10
    p_p_int = 4020, *p_p_int = 4018, **p_p_int = 10

p_p_int points to p_int2 which points to b = 20
    p_p_int = 4024, *p_p_int = 401c, **p_p_int = 20

p_p_int points to p_int2 which points to a = 10
    p_p_int = 4024, *p_p_int = 4018, **p_p_int = 10
```

```
 1 /* Program 21_2 -  Example of pointers to pointers */
 2
 3 #include <stdio.h>
 4
 5 int a = 10, b = 20,                              /* define two ints */
 6     *p_int1 = &a, *p_int2 =&b,                  /* define pointers to int */
 7     **p_p_int = &p_int1;                /* define pointer to pointer to int */
 8
 9 int main(void)
10 {
11     printf("\nAddresses of variables in the programs"
12            "\n&a = %p, &b = %p, &p_int1 = %p, &p_int2 = %p, &p_p_int = %p",
13              &a, &b, &p_int1, &p_int2, &p_p_int);
14     printf("\n\np_p_int points to p_int1 which points to a = 10 "
15            "\n    p_p_int = %p, *p_p_int = %p, **p_p_int = %d",
16                  p_p_int, *p_p_int, **p_p_int);
17
18     p_p_int = &p_int2;          /* point p_p_int to p_int2 which points to b */
19     printf("\n\np_p_int points to p_int2 which points to b = 20 "
20            "\n    p_p_int = %p, *p_p_int = %p, **p_p_int = %d",
21                  p_p_int, *p_p_int, **p_p_int);
22
23     p_int2 = &a;                                 /* point p_int2 to a */
24     printf("\n\np_p_int points to p_int2 which points to a = 10 "
25            "\n    p_p_int = %p, *p_p_int = %p, **p_p_int = %d",
26                  p_p_int, *p_p_int, **p_p_int);
27     return 0;
28 }
```

Program 21_2 Program using pointers to pointers

21.7 The generic pointer type *void* *

Many library functions can operate on a range of data types, e.g. function memchr from
<string.h> searches at most number bytes of array data for byte:

```
    void *memchr(const void *data, int byte, size_t number);
```

The parameter data and the function result are of type void *, which is the generic pointer
type 'pointer to void':

1   any pointer type can be assigned to a variable of type void *
2   a 'pointer to void' cannot itself be used to access or manipulate information; it must be
    cast to another pointer type first, see below.

For example, to use memchr to search an array of byte-sized elements for a value:

```
    char x[] = { 10, 20, 30, 40, 50 },              // five-element array
        *p_char;                                    // pointer to char
    p_char = (char *) memchr(x, 30, sizeof(x));     // search for value
    // if 30 was found display value and position
    if (p_char != 0) printf("%d found at position %d", *p_char, (int) (p_char - x));
```

The pointer returned by memchr (which points to the byte found or is NULL if not found) must be cast to char * before being assigned to p_char. A run of the program would print:

30 found at position 2:

21.8 Arrays of pointers *

Consider:

```
char s[] = "hello Sam";                         /* define array of char */
char *p_s = s;                          /* pointer to char, pointed to s */

printf("%s %s\n", s, p_s);
```

This defines s, a string (an array of char), and pointer p_s, a pointer to char, initialised to point to s; in effect p_s becomes a synonym for s. Note that there is no need in the second line to use & to take the address of s because it is already an address, i.e. the array name s is a constant pointer to the first element. The printf statement would print:

hello Sam hello Sam

Pointers are just another type of variable and one can have arrays of pointers, e.g.:

```
/* define arrays of char and then point elements of an array of pointers to them */
char s1[] = "hello", s2[] = " Joe,", s3[] = " how are you ?\n";
char *p_strings[]= {s1, s2, s3};

int main(void)
{
    int index;

    for (index = 0 ; index < 3; index++)                /* print values */
        printf("%s", p_strings[index]);
}
```

This defines strings s1, s2 and s3 and p_strings, an array of pointers to char, the elements of which are initialised to point to the strings (because arrays can only be initialised with constants that can be evaluated at compile time the objects pointed to have to be external). The printf statement would print:

hello Joe, how are you ?

21.9 Passing parameters to function *main* *

All the programs so far have defined the function main to be without parameters, e.g.:

```
int main(void)
```

The majority of C environments allow parameters to be passed from the operating system command line. For example, the program of Exercise 23.1 in Chapter 23 copies the contents of one file to another changing the characters to upper or lower case as specified by an option. The filenames and options are specified as part of the command line when the program is invoked, e.g.:

c:> **ex23_1 file_1 file_2 -lower** ⏎

The program is able to access the character strings "file_1", "file_2" and "-lower" and take appropriate action. In such a case the function header for main is:

```
int main(int argc, char *argv[])
```

which specifies two parameters:

argc   an int which contains the number of command line parameters;
*argv[] is an array of pointers to char (character strings which contain the parameters).

In the command line "ex23_1 file_1 file_2 -lower" the value of argc would be 4 and argv would appear as follows:

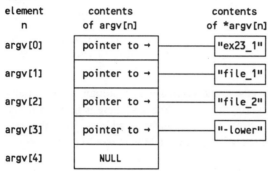

element n	contents of argv[n]	contents of *argv[n]
argv[0]	pointer to →	"ex23_1"
argv[1]	pointer to →	"file_1"
argv[2]	pointer to →	"file_2"
argv[3]	pointer to →	"-lower"
argv[4]	NULL	

Therefore the elements of argv are pointers to strings which contain the command line parameters (null terminated). By convention argv[0] points to a string which contains the name by which the program was invoked and element argv[argc] is the NULL pointer. The program can access the command line arguments and interpret them as it wishes. For example, the above command line would invoke the program ex23_1.exe which will copy file1 to file2 converting any upper case letters to lower case (option -lower). If insufficient or invalid parameters are specified the program displays an error message.

```
 1 /* Program 21_3 -  Print parameters passed from operating system to main  */
 2
 3 #include <stdio.h>
 4 #include <string.h>
 5
 6 /* function main with parameters                                          */
 7 /*    argc - number of elements in array argv                             */
 8 /*    argv - an array of pointers to strings                              */
 9 int main(int argc, char *argv[])
10 {
11     int index;
12     printf("\nNumber of parameters in command line is %d", argc);
13     for (index = 0; index < argc ; index++)
14         {
15         printf("\n parameter %d is %s ", index, argv[index]);
16         if (strcmp(argv[index],"-lower") == 0) printf("    option -lower ! ");
17         if (strcmp(argv[index],"-upper") == 0) printf("    option -upper ! ");
18         }
19     return 0;
20 }
```

Program 21_3 Print parameters passed from operating system to main

Program 21_3 reads the command line parameters and prints their values on the screen. The sequence of statements is:

9-20 define function main with parameters argc and argv
12 print number of parameters passed to main, i.e. value of argc
13-20 a for statement incrementing index from 0 to argc
    15 print current parameter
    16 if current parameter is string "-lower" print appropriate message
    17 if current parameter is string "-upper" print appropriate message.

When executed using MS-DOS and Turbo C V3.00 with the following command line:

```
p21_3 filename_1 filename_2 -lower
```

Program 21_3 gave (the program name is expanded to the full MS-DOS drive and path):

```
Number of parameters in command line is 4
 parameter 0 is D:\C_BOOK\C21\P21_3.EXE
 parameter 1 is filename_1
 parameter 2 is filename_2
 parameter 3 is -lower    option -lower !
```

Exercise 21.2 (*see Appendix B for sample answer*)

Rewrite Program 21_3 to use a pointer to argv (rather than using an array index).

21.10 Pointers and the *sizeof* operator

If the sizeof operator is used with a pointer it returns the number of bytes used to store the pointer, **not** the number of bytes in the object pointed to, e.g.:

```
int x[] = { 10, 20, 30, 40, 50 },              /* five-element array */
    *p_array = x;                              /* pointer to array */

printf("size of x = %d", (int) sizeof(x));
printf(", size of p_array = %d", (int) sizeof(p_array));
printf(", size of *p_array = %d", (int) sizeof(*p_array));
```

The three printf statements would print:

1 the number of bytes used to store the int array x, e.g. 10 if each int was two bytes
2 the number of bytes used to store a 'pointer to int'
3 the number of bytes used to store an int, i.e. the type that p_array points to.

For example, a run on an IBM PC compatible under Turbo C V3.00 gave:

```
size of x = 10, size of p_array = 4, size of *p_array = 2
```

To determine the size of an array the array name itself is required, e.g. sizeof(x). Thus it is not possible to use the sizeof operator inside a function to determine the size of an array passed as a parameter, i.e. the formal parameter is actually a *pointer* and sizeof returns the number of bytes used to store the *pointer* not the size of the array pointed at, see Section 19.4. The size of the array must be passed as a parameter or some other mechanism provided for the function to determine the array size, e.g. strings of characters are terminated by a '\0' null character.

Problem for Chapter 21

Problem 3 for Chapter 19 was to sort the elements of an array using a bubble sort. Rewrite the program to use pointers to access and manipulate the array elements.

22

Functions and pointers

22.1 Pointers as function parameters

Pointers can be passed as parameters to functions just like any other type of variable. For example, Section 16.8 described using pointers to pass function parameters *by reference* (remember that arrays are always passed by reference, see Section 19.4). The critical thing to remember is that the value of the pointer (the address) is passed *by value* so any alterations made to the pointer (formal parameter) inside the function do not affect the value of the pointer (actual parameter) in the calling function (although the object pointed to can be altered).

Because an array name is a constant pointer to the first element, arrays which are formal parameters to functions can generally be declared using either array or pointer notation. For example, in header file str_lib.h in Section 20.8 the function prototype of str_copy, which copies the contents of string_2 into string_1, was:

```
int str_copy(char string_1[], const char string_2[]);
```

The number of characters copied is returned as a function result. In general, an alternative way of writing the function header is:

```
int str_copy(char *string_1, const char *string_2);
```

The body of the function could remain as in implementation file str_lib.c in Section 20.8 or be altered to use pointer arithmetic (see Program 22_1).

22.2 Functions that return a pointer as the function result

A function can return a pointer as a function result, e.g. a prototype from Header File str_libp.h (on next page):

```
char *str_ch_find(char *string, const char character)
```

The * prefixing the function name indicates that the function returns a pointer to a char (the function searches string for a character and returns either a pointer to the character (if found) or NULL. The pointer returned may then be used to access the object either to read its value or assign a new value, e.g.:

```
char *p_char, string[] = " hello alan ";

if ((p_char = str_ch_find(string, 'a')) != NULL)
      *p_char = 'x';
printf(" %s ", string);
```

would print hello xlan on the display screen.

Do not return a pointer to an internal automatic variable defined within the function. The variable will be deallocated on function exit and the pointer will effectively be undefined (pointing to a memory area which could be allocated to something else), e.g.:

```
int *func(void)
{
    int x;
    return &x;                 /* error !!  returning a pointer to a local variable */
}
```

When compiled using GNU C V2.6.1 the above fragment of code gave the following warning (many compilers will not even issue a warning):

```
X.c: In function `func':
X.c:5: warning: function returns address of local variable
```

If a function returns a const qualified pointer (the object pointed to is a constant) the function result may only be used to read the value of the object pointed to but not to change its value, e.g.:

```
const char *find_char(void);                    /* function prototype */
char *p_char;                                   /* define pointer to char */
const char *p_const_char;          /* define const qualified pointer to char */

p_const_char = find_char();                              /* OK */
printf("%c", *p_const_char);         /* print character pointed to */
p_char = find_char();                                 /* error !! */
*p_char = 'a';                       /* assign 'a' to char pointed at */
```

The function result returned by find_char may be assigned to p_const_char but not to p_char (which is then used in the expression *p_char = 'a' to change the char pointed at by p_char). For example, the Turbo C V3.00 compiler gave the following message:

```
p_char = find_char();                                 /* error !! */
Warning x.c 11: Suspicious pointer conversion in function main
```

22.3 String processing functions using pointers

Implementation file str_libp.c (next page) is a version of implementation file str_lib.c (see Section 20.8) modified to use pointers instead of array indexes. The string parameters in the function headers are declared using pointer notation and pointers are used to manipulate characters within the functions.

The associated header file str_libp.h (below) is similar to str_lib.h (see Section 20.8) except that the function prototypes use pointer notation instead of array notation and function str_ch_find returns a char * (pointer to the char found else NULL if not found) instead of an int (returns the index to the character found else -1 if not found).

```
1 /* Header file str_libp.h, string processing functions using pointers       */
2
3 int str_length(const char *string);                        /* prototypes */
4 int str_copy(char *string_1, const char *string_2);
5 void str_remove_spaces(char *string);
6 void str_reverse(char *string);
7 char *str_ch_find(char *string, const char character);
8 int str_read(const char *const prompt, char *const string, const int length);
```

Header file str_libp.h String processing functions using pointers

```
 1 /* Implementation file str_libp.c, string processing functions using pointers */
 2
 3 #include <stdio.h>                              /* standard I/O library */
 4 #include <string.h>                      /* string manipulation library */
 5 #include "str_libp.h"                            /* own header file */
 6
 7 /*--------------------------------------------------------------------*/
 8 /* function to find length of string, not counting terminating null          */
 9 int str_length(const char *string)
10 {
11     const char *p_str = string;                 /* point at start of string */
12
13     while ( *p_str != '\0')
14         p_str++;                                 /* look for null */
15     return (int) (p_str - string);          /* return length of string */
16 }
17
18 /*--------------------------------------------------------------------*/
19 /* function to copy a string to another, return number of characters copied   */
20 int str_copy(char *string_1, const char *string_2)
21 {
22     int number = 0;
23
24     while ((*string_1++ = *string_2++) != '\0')           /* copy to null */
25         number++;                          /* if not null increment number */
26     return number;                   /* return number of characters copied */
27 }
28
29
30 /*--------------------------------------------------------------------*/
31 /* function to reverse the contents of a string                          */
32 void str_reverse(char *string)
33 {
34     char *p_up = string,                     /* points to start of string */
35         *p_down = string + strlen(string);   /* points to end of string + 1 */
36     char value;                                /* temporary data store */
37
38     while ( p_up < p_down )
39         (value = *p_up, *p_up++ = *--p_down, *p_down = value);
40 }
41
42 /*--------------------------------------------------------------------*/
43 /* function to find character in string, return pointer to character else NULL*/
44 char *str_ch_find(char *string, const char character)
45 {
46     while (*string != '\0')                 /* look for null character */
47         if (*string == character) return string;   /* found character ! */
48         else                       string++;        /* increment pointer */
49     return NULL;                                /* return NULL for fail */
50 }
```

Implementation file str_libp.c String processing functions using pointers

```
51 /*--------------------------------------------------------------------*/
52 /* function to remove leading and trailing spaces from a string       */
53 void str_remove_spaces(char *string)
54 {
55     char *p_str1,                       /* points at first non-space character */
56          *p_str2,                       /* points at next position to copy to */
57          *p_str3;                  /* points at position to put terminating null */
58
59     /* point p_str1 at first non-space character */
60     for (p_str1 = string ; *p_str1 == ' ' ; p_str1++)
61         /* null statement */;
62     /* p_str1 = string + strspn(string, " ");*/              /* alternative !! */
63
64     p_str2 = p_str3 = string;                    /* point to start of string */
65     /* loop copying characters until null character found */
66     while (*p_str1 != '\0')
67         /* copy character, if not space, note position in p_str3 */
68         if ((*p_str2++ = *p_str1++) != ' ') p_str3 = p_str2;
69     *p_str3 = '\0';                              /* put in terminating null */
70 }
71
72 /*--------------------------------------------------------------------*/
73 /* read string using fgets, remove terminating \n and any trailing characters */
74 /* on entry *prompt   contains prompt string to print                 */
75 /*          length    contains maximum length of string               */
76 /* return string read in array *string                                */
77 /* return function result true if all OK else false on EOF            */
78 int str_read(const char *const prompt, char *const string, const int length)
79 {
80     char *p_str;                             /* define pointer to char */
81
82     printf("%s", prompt);                           /* print prompt */
83     /* get string and if EOF return false */
84     if (fgets(string, length, stdin) == NULL) return 0;
85     if ((p_str = strchr(string, '\n')) != NULL)           /* look for \n */
86         *p_str = '\0';                          /* replace \n with \0 */
87     else
88         do ; while (getchar() != '\n');      /* else discard characters to \n */
89     return 1;                                   /* all OK return true */
90 }
```

Implementation file str_libp.c String processing functions using pointers

In implementation file str_libp.h the function str_length, lines 9 to 16, returns the length of the string (not counting the terminating null). The sequence of statements is:

9   int str_length(const char *string) the function header
11   declare pointer p_str and point it to the start of string
13-14   a while statement searching string for a null character '\0'
            the while terminates when a null is found
            14 if the character was not null increment the pointer p_str
15   returns the number of characters in string.

In line 15 the expression p_str - string evaluates the length of the string, i.e. string and p_str point to the start of the string and the terminating null respectively and subtracting them yields an integer which is the distance between the two (which is cast to an int). Because C treats 0 as *false* lines 13 and 14 could be written (perhaps less legibly):

```
while ( *p_str )
    p_str++;                                          /* look for null */
```

When '\0' is found (*false*) the while terminates and the number of characters in string evaluated. In Program 22_1 the result from this function is printed in main together with the result returned by the library function strlen.

Function str_copy, lines 20 to 27, copies the contents of one string (string_2) to another (string_1) overwriting any existing contents. It returns the number of characters copied. The sequence of statements is:

20   int str_copy(char *string_1, const char *string_2) the function header
22   declare number and initialise it to 0 (used to hold the character count)
24-25 a while statement copying characters from string_2 into string_1
          the while terminates when a null '\0' is copied
      25 if the character was not null increment number
26   return the number of characters copied.

Line 24 copies a character from string_2 to string_1 and terminates the while if the character is a '\0'. The != '\0' could be removed but a modern compiler will issue a warning, e.g. Microsoft C V7.00:

```
24      while (*string_1++ = *string_2++)             /* copy to null */
***** P22_1.C(24) : warning C4206: assignment within conditional expression
```

warning that there is an assignment within a conditional statement; which is intended in this case.

The function str_reverse, lines 32 to 40, reverses the characters in a string. The sequence of statements is:

32 void str_reverse(char *string) is the function header
34 define pointer p_up and point to the first element of the string
35 define pointer p_down and point it to the last element of the string plus 1, i.e. the '\0'
38 a while statement which:
    (a) increments pointer p_up up the string
    (b) decrements pointer p_down down the string
    (c) terminates when p_up = p_down (half way up the string)
39 (value = *p_up, *p_up++ = *--p_down, *p_down = value) swaps two characters
    (a) value = *p_up copies the character pointed to by p_up into value
    (b) *p_up++ = *--p_down
        (i)   decrements p_down
        (ii) copies character pointed to by p_down to character pointed to by p_up
        (iii) increments p_up
    (c) copies value into the character pointed to by p_down.

The function str_ch_find, lines 44 to 50, searches string for a character. If the character is found it returns a pointer to the character else NULL. The sequence of statements is:

44   int str_ch_find(const char *string, const char character) the function header

46-48   a while statement scanning string for a null, if found the while terminates

       47   if *string == character return string (a pointer to the character found)

       48   else increment the pointer string to point to next character

49   character not found, return NULL to indicate fail.

Function str_remove_spaces, lines 53 to 70, removes leading and trailing spaces from a string. The sequence of statements is:

lines

53   void str_remove_spaces(char *string) the function header

55-57   declare pointers to char used in the function

60-61   find first non-space character in the string, on exit p_str1 points to it

62   alternative to lines 60 and 61, discussed below

64   point p_str2 and p_str3 to start of array string

66-68   a while loop which copies characters until '\0' is found

       67-68   copies a character (overwriting any leading spaces) and

             if character copied was not a space copy pointer p_str2 to p_str3

69   terminate string (p_str3 points to last non-space character plus 1).

Notes:

1. After executing lines 60 and 61 (or line 62) p_str1 points to the position of the first non-space character in string.
2. Line 64 points p_str2 to the start of string ready for copying characters.
3. Line 64 points p_str3 to the start of string in case the string is empty or full of spaces, i.e. line 68 would not be executed to assign a value to p_str3.
4. Line 67 overwrites any leading spaces by overwriting the character pointed to by p_str2 with the one pointed to by p_str1.
5. In line 68 p_str3 is pointed to the last non-space character plus 1 which is then overwritten with '\0' in line 69.

Note that lines 60 and 61, which point p_str1 to the first non-space character, can be replaced with the statement in line 62, i.e.:

```
p_str1 = string + strspn(string, " ");
```

The prototype of the library function strspn is:

```
size_t strspn(const char *string1 , const char *string2);
```

This returns the length of the initial sub-string in string1 which consists entirely of the characters in string2, i.e.:

```
strspn(string, " ")
```

returns the number of spaces at the start of string. Therefore:

```
p_str1 = string + strspn(string, " ");
```

points p_str1 to the first non-space character in string.

The function `str_read`, lines 78 to 90, reads a string of maximum length `max_length` from stdin using function `fgets`. It returns *true* if the string read was successful otherwise *false* if EOF was entered. If the length of the string is less than `max_length` characters the terminating newline is replaced with '\0', otherwise the characters remaining on the line are removed, including the newline. The sequence of statements is:

lines

78   `int str_read(const char *const prompt, char *const string, const int length)`
      `the function header declaring three parameters:`

      `prompt`   a pointer to a message to print on the screen

      `string`   a pointer to an array of `char` to accept the characters input

      `length`   an `int` specifying the maximum length of `string`

80   define a pointer to `char`

82   display `prompt` on the screen

84   call `fgets` to read a string of maximum `length` - 1 characters from stdin
          if EOF was entered terminate function with result *false* (i.e. `fgets` returns NULL)

85-88   an `if` searching `string` for a '\n' character
      86 '\n' found, replace with '\0'
      else
      88 remove characters from stdin up to and including newline.

Note that when parameters which are pointers should not be modified they (the pointers) are `const` qualified, i.e. consider the header of `str_read`:

    `int str_read(const char *const prompt, char *const string, const int length)`

1   the pointers `prompt` and `string` may not be modified (both are `const` qualified)
2   the object `prompt` points to may not be modified (`prompt` points to a `const` qualified object)
3   the object `string` points to may be modified, i.e. line 84 reads a string into it.
4   the parameter `length` may not be modified.

Program 22_1 (next page), which tests the functions in library stu_libp.c, is similar to Program 20_5. The main difference is in the call to `str_ch_find`, i.e. lines 30 to 35 which search for occurrences of the character 'a' and replace them with 'x' characters:

```
        p_char = text_1;                        /* point at start of string */
        while ((p_char = str_ch_find(p_char, 'a')) != NULL)
            {
            *p_char = 'x';                      /* replace 'a' with 'x' */
            printf(" |%s|", p_char++);          /* and print string */
            }
```

On the first call pointer p_char points to the start of the string text_1. The function `str_ch_find` assigns p_char a pointer to the position where the character was found else NULL (the loop terminates). The character pointed to by p_char is replaced and the remainder of the string is printed. The pointer p_char is incremented and `str_ch_find` called again. Thus `str_ch_find` works down the string finding each occurrence of the character 'a'.

```
 1 /* Program 22_1 - Test string processing functions using pointers        */
 2
 3 #include <stdio.h>
 4 #include <string.h>
 5 #include "str_libp.h"                        /* string processing functions */
 6
 7 int main(void)
 8 {
 9     char text_1[20], text_2[20], *p_char;            /* internal variables */
10     int index;
11
12     while (str_read("\n\nEnter string ? ", text_1, 20))      /* read string */
13         {
14         printf("read    string length %3d (%3d) |%s| \n",    /* print string */
15                 str_length(text_1), (int) strlen(text_1), text_1);
16
17         index = str_copy(text_2, text_1);               /* copy string */
18         printf("copied string  length %3d (%3d) |%s| \n",
19                 index, (int) strlen(text_2), text_2);
20
21         str_reverse(text_2);                            /* reverse string */
22         printf("reverse string length %3d (%3d) |%s| \n",
23                 str_length(text_2), strlen(text_2), text_2);
24
25         str_remove_spaces(text_1);                      /* remove spaces */
26         printf("spaces removed length %3d (%3d) |%s| \n",
27                 str_length(text_1), (int) strlen(text_1), text_1);
28
29         printf("Character 'a' found: ");               /* search for 'a' */
30         p_char = text_1;                          /* point at start of string */
31         while ((p_char = str_ch_find(p_char, 'a')) != NULL)
32             {
33             *p_char = 'x';                          /* replace 'a' with 'x' */
34             printf(" |%s|", p_char++);              /* and print string */
35             }
36         }
37     return 0;
38 }
```

Program 22_1 Test string processing functions in library str_libp.c

A run of Program 22_1 gave:

```
Enter string ? hello abc abc ↵
read     string length  13 ( 13) |hello abc abc|
copied string  length  13 ( 13) |hello abc abc|
reverse string length  13 ( 13) |cba cba olleh|
spaces removed length  13 ( 13) |hello abc abc|
Character 'a' found:  |xbc abc| |xbc|

Enter string ?      test spaces    ↵
read     string length  19 ( 19) |     test spaces   |
copied string  length  19 ( 19) |     test spaces   |
reverse string length  19 ( 19) |   secaps tset     |
spaces removed length  11 ( 11) |test spaces|
Character 'a' found:  |xces|

Enter string ? abcdefghijklmnopqrstuvwxyz ↵
read     string length  19 ( 19) |abcdefghijklmnopqrs|
copied string  length  19 ( 19) |abcdefghijklmnopqrs|
reverse string length  19 ( 19) |srqponmlkjihgfedcba|
spaces removed length  19 ( 19) |abcdefghijklmnopqrs|
Character 'a' found:  |xbcdefghijklmnopqrs|

Enter string ? ↵
read     string length   0 (  0) ||
copied string  length   0 (  0) ||
reverse string length   0 (  0) ||
spaces removed length   0 (  0) ||
Character 'a' found:

Enter string ? ˆZ ↵
```

Section 22.1 stated that when arrays are formal parameters they may be declared using either array notation or pointer notation. In implementation file str_libp.c pointer notation is used throughout but array notation could be used. For example, str_copy could be written:

```
int str_copy(char string_1[], const char string_2[])
{
    int number = 0;
    while ((*string_1++ = *string_2++) != '\0')          /* copy to null */
        number++;                                /* if not null increment number */
    return number;                      /* return number of characters copied */
}
```

Although string_1 and string_2 are declared as arrays they can be used as pointers and manipulated using pointer arithmetic (including ++). When an array is defined its name is a constant pointer to the first address. However, when an array name is a formal parameter it is assigned the value of the actual parameter (the address of the array) and it can then be treated like a pointer variable (more discussion in next section).

Exercise 22.1 (*see Appendix B for sample answer*)

Implement and test a function which searches for a string within a string. The function prototype of a string search function could be:

```
char *str_search(char *string_1, const char *string_2);
```

Search the string pointed to by string_1 for the next occurrence of the string pointed to by string_2. If found return a pointer to the character else NULL. Write a main program which read two strings and then calls str_search to look for occurrences of one string within the other (similar to lines 36 to 41 in Program 22_1).

Implement and test a function str_compare which compares two strings (similar to strcmp in the standard library):

```
int str_compare(const char *string_1, const char *string_2);
```

the content of the string pointed to by string_1 is compared with the string pointed to by string_2 and the following result returned:

<0   if *string_1 comes before *string_2 in the sorting sequence

0   if *string_1 equals *string_2

>0   if *string_1 comes after *string_2 in the sorting sequence.

22.4 Pointers should only contain valid addresses

It must be emphasised that when a pointer is being used it should only contain a valid address or the value NULL. Consider the array:

```
int x[10];                              /* define an array of 10 elements */
```

Section 21.3.2 explained:

    (a) the addressable elements are from x[0] to x[9]

and (b) the valid addresses are from &x[0] to &x[10] (one beyond the end of the array).

Although array element x[10] does not exist the ANSI standard permits the use of the address &x[10] (mainly for use in determining the terminating conditions of loops, see Program 21_1). This permission extends to one element beyond the end of the array and no further and addresses evaluated outside the limits of (b) above are undefined and may crash the program. Consider the following version of function str_reverse:

```
void str_reverse(char *string)                          /* faulty version */
{
    char *p_up = string,                      /* points to start of string */
         *p_down = string + strlen(string) - 1;   /* points to end of string */
    char value;                                  /* temporary data store */

    while ( p_up < p_down )
        (value = *p_up, *p_up++ = *p_down, *p_down-- = value);
}
```

This is similar to str_reverse in str_libp.c with the exception that the pointer p_down is initialised to point to the last character in the string (the version in str_libp.c initialised p_down to point to the last element of the string plus 1, i.e. the terminating '\0'). The statement which swaps the characters is then slightly modified to take account of the change. The above version of str_reverse will work without problems so long as the string is not empty. If the string is empty the statement:

```
    *p_down = string + strlen(string) - 1;    /* points to end of string */
```

initialises p_down to an address before the start of string, i.e. outside the limits for valid addresses. What happens depends upon the architecture of the machine concerned. On some machines the value formed may be a valid memory address and the comparison:

```
    while ( p_up < p_down )
```

would work without problems. On other machines the value formed may be an invalid address and the program could either produce incorrect results or crash with a memory segmentation fault.

Incorrect addresses stored in pointers are a very common programming fault and can be very difficult to track down. Careful design of the algorithms is required to avoid problems such as the one described above. For example, when a program has worked without problems (for months or even years) then crashes or produces faulty results with new program data, suspect array bounds overflow as a major culprit. A problem is that an array bounds overflow may not show up until much later in the program when data sets corrupted by the overflow are used. Slight modifications to the program data may select alternate paths through the program and the error appears and disappears.

22.5 When is an actual parameter an array or a simple variable?

If an actual parameter of a function is to be an array the function header and prototype can be written in array notation:

```
    int str_copy(char string_1[], const char string_2[]);
```

or pointer notation:

```
    int str_copy(char *string_1, const char *string_2);
```

Now consider the following function header:

```
    void test(int *pointer);
```

It is not possible to determine from the function header if the function expects a pointer to a simple int variable or to the first element of an array of int.

It is therefore recommended to use array notation in function headers and prototypes when a formal parameter is to be an array, or, if using pointer notation use a suitable name for the formal parameter, e.g. string_1, p_array, etc. Similarly, if a formal parameter is to be a pointer to a simple variable use a suitable name. For example, from Program 16_3:

```
    void swap_int(int *const p_int1, int *const p_int2);
```

The parameters are const qualified pointers to simple int variables.

Problem for Chapter 22

Modify the problem for Chapter 20 to use pointers. The function prototypes could be:

```
    void str_concat(char *string_1, const char *string_2);
    char *str_r_ch_find(const char *string, const char character);
```

23

Input and output functions

In C all input and output operations are performed by library functions. The ANSI standard defines a number of basic functions (in <stdio.h>, see Appendix C.12) and most compilers provide additional non-standard libraries to access facilities which are operating system dependent, e.g. Microsoft C and Turbo C provide <conio.h> which contains prototypes of functions to directly access the console keyboard and display screen.

In C input and output takes place via a *stream* which may be connected to a disk file, the keyboard, the display screen, a serial port, or any other suitable device. Before any input/output operations can take place the stream must be connected to something, e.g. a file on disk opened for input or output. Associated with each open stream is a structure of type FILE which is defined in <stdio.h>. The structure contains information which enables the program to control the flow of information, e.g. pointer to its I/O buffer, pointer to current position in buffer, error indicator, etc. When connected the stream name is a pointer to a structure of type FILE.

23.1 Standard input/output streams

When setting up the program run-time environment prior to the start of program execution the following three standard streams are automatically opened:

```
FILE  *stdin;           /* input stream: usually connected to keyboard */
FILE  *stdout;          /* output stream: usually connected to display screen */
FILE  *stderr;          /* error output, usually connected to display screen */
```

The connection of the streams to physical devices is operating system dependent. When using interactive systems stdin is usually connected to the terminal keyboard and stdout and stderr to the display screen (could be separate windows on a window managed system). The operating system usually provides some means of redirecting the streams to other devices, e.g. under UNIX the redirection commands are (MS-DOS is similar):

```
program < data          execute program with stream stdin from file data
program > out_data       execute program with stream stdout to file out_data
program 2> err_data      execute program with stream stderr to file err_data
program >> out_data      stream stdout is appended on the end of file out_data
program < data > out_data  stdin from file data, stdout to file out_data
program1 | program2      the stdout output from program1 is piped directly into the
                         stdin input of program2.
```

If an error occurs during input/output operations a message indicating failure can be displayed on the screen. In addition C provides additional information regarding the failure which can assist in tracking down the cause of the problem.

When an error occurs many of the functions set up an integer error number in errno which is declared in <errno.h> (errno is usually an external variable set up by the C run-time system and the name should not be used for anything else). Although the value of errno can be accessed and printed the error values are operating system and compiler dependent and are meaningless without reference to manuals. When given `errno` as a parameter the function `strerror` in `<string.h>` returns a pointer to a corresponding implementation defined string which can then be printed (see line 17 of Program 23_1):

```
char *strerror(int errnum);    /* return pointer to string corresponding to errno */
```

23.2 Opening, closing, deleting and renaming files

Apart from the standard streams (`stdin`, `stdout` and `stderr`) a stream must be connected to a file or a device before it can be used (see Appendix C.12.1 for further discussion):

```
FILE *fopen(const char *filename, const char *mode);        /* open a file for I/O */
```

`fopen` returns a pointer to a structure of type `FILE` (which is then used to identify the stream in future operations) or `NULL` if an error occurred (see next section). The parameters are:

filename: a pointer to a character string which contains the filename in a format acceptable to the operating system

mode: a pointer to a character string specifying the mode of operation:
- r   opens an existing file for reading
- w   creates a new file for writing (if it already exists its contents are discarded)
- a   opens an existing file for append, information written is appended onto existing data, otherwise a new file is created for writing
- r+   opens an existing file for update (reading and writing)
- w+   creates a new file for update (reading and writing)
- a+   opens an existing file or creates a new file for update and append.

The above modes are for opening *text* streams which are used to process character based data, i.e. lines of characters terminated by *newline*. C also supports *binary* streams which are used to process data transferred in machine dependent binary form. For *binary* streams the mode should include the letter b, e.g. rb, wb, wb+, etc. (see Section 23.6).

Attempting to open a file which does not exist for reading or opening a file without the correct access rights will give an error (`fopen` returns a `NULL`). When input/output transfers are complete the file should be closed using the function `fclose`:

```
int  fclose(FILE *stream);
```

this closes the file pointed to by `stream`. If successful `fclose` returns 0 or, if an error occurred, `EOF` (see below for reporting of error conditions).

If a temporary file is required function `tmpfile` creates a temporary file of mode wb+ which is automatically deleted when closed or on program termination:

```
FILE *tmpfile(void);                                    /* open temporary file */
```

Many of the file input/output functions set up indicators in the `FILE` structure when an error or `EOF` (end of file) occurs. These can be set and tested using the following functions:

```
void clearerr(FILE *stream);                    /* clear EOF and error indicators */
int feof(FILE *stream);                  /* returns non-zero if EOF indicator is set */
int ferror(FILE *stream);                /* returns non-zero if error indicator is set */
```

Useful file maintenance functions are (both return 0 if successful):

```
int  remove(const char *filename);                            /* delete a file */
int  rename(const char *old_filename, const char *new_filename);   /* rename a file */
```

23.3 Character and string input and output

Individual characters may be read by:

```
int  fgetc(FILE *stream);                    /* read next character from stream */
int  getc(FILE *stream);              /* macro: read next character from stream */
int  getchar(void);                          /* read next character from stdin */
```

fgetc reads the next character from stream; it returns the character as an int, or EOF if end of file was found. getc is equivalent to fgetc but may be implemented as a macro (to save the overhead of a function call). getchar is a special version of getc which reads from the standard input stream stdin. The corresponding character output functions are:

```
int  fputc(int char, FILE *stream);          /* write character char to stream */
int  putc(int char, FILE *stream);    /* macro: write character char to stream */
int  putchar(int char);                      /* write character char to stdout */
```

fputc writes a character to stream, putc is equivalent but may be a macro and putchar is a version of putc which writes to stdout. The functions return the character written if successful or EOF if an error occurs.

Function ungetc 'pushes' a character back into the input stream (see line 21 of Implementation File array.c in Chapter 19), normally a maximum of one character may be pushed and it is not possible push EOF:

```
int  ungetc(int char, FILE *stream);      /* push character back into input stream */
```

The functions getchar and putchar are often defined as macros to avoid the run-time overhead of a function call for every character read or printed. The standard does, however, guarantee that even if a library function is normally implemented as a macro there will also be a 'real' function. To invoke the 'real' function the macro can be undefined using #undef or the function name enclosed in parentheses, e.g.:

```
    (putchar)(ch);                           /* call 'real' version of putchar */
```

Strings (arrays of char terminated by '\0') may be printed and read character by character using the individual character I/O functions (fgetc, getc, getchar, fputc, putc and putchar. Alternatively complete strings may be read and written using the string I/O functions (see Section 20.7 and Appendix C.12.5 for a full discussion):

```
char *fgets(char *string, int n, FILE *stream);   /* read characters from stream */
char *gets(char *string);                         /* read characters from stdin */
int  fputs(const char *string, FILE *stream);        /* write a string to stream */
int  puts(const char *string);          /* write a string plus '\n' to stdout */
```

Program 23_1 (next page) opens an input file (which must exist) then loops reading characters from the file writing them to the display screen (terminating on EOF):

3-4   include header files (<errno.h> declares errno)
9   define in_file a pointer to type FILE (defined in <stdio.h>)
12-13   prompt user to enter the name of a file and read the filename into string filename
15-19   call fopen to open file filename for reading (mode "r")
        17 failed: print message corresponding the value of errno (declared in <error.h>)
        18 terminate program indicating failure
21-22   a while reading characters from in_file (terminates on EOF)
        22 call putchar to write character to output stream stdout
23   close the input file.

The name of the file filename specified in the call to fopen in line 15 is the name which the file will have on disk (including directories, etc.). Filenames must therefore adhere to the conventions of the operating system, e.g. to separate subdirectory names MS-DOS and UNIX use \ and / respectively, e.g. c_progs\test.c or c_progs/test.c. A run of the program when an invalid filename was entered (run on an IBM PC compatible) gave:

```
Enter name of input file ? test.dat ↵
Unable to open file 'test.dat': No such file or directory
```

strerror returned a pointer to the string No such file or directory (printed using %s) which gives immediate feedback on the problem (rather than just aborting the program).

```
 1 /* Program 23_1  Open an input file, read characters and display on screen    */
 2
 3 #include <stdio.h>                                  /* standard I/O header */
 4 #include <errno.h>                                  /* required for errno */
 5
 6 int main(void)
 7 {
 8     FILE *in_file;                          /* define pointer to input file */
 9     char filename[20];
10     int ch;
11
12     printf("\nEnter name of input file ? ");
13     gets(filename);                                       /* read filename */
14     /* filename read, attempt to open input file */
15     if ((in_file = fopen(filename, "r")) == NULL)        /* open input file */
16         {
17         printf("\nUnable to open file '%s': %s", filename, strerror(errno));
18         return 1;                                        /* open failed */
19         }
20     /* file opened OK, read characters and display until EOF is read */
21     while ((ch = getc(in_file)) != EOF)                  /* read character */
22         putchar(ch);                                     /* write character */
23     fclose(in_file);                                     /* close input file */
24     return 0;
25 }
```

Program 23_1 Open a file, read characters and display on screen

Exercise 23.1 (*see Appendix B for sample answer*)

Implement a program which copies the contents of one character based file to another. The filenames should be specified in the program command line, e.g. (program is ex23_1.exe):

ex23_1 file_1 file_2 -options

copies the contents of file_1 into file_2. The options specified by -options should be:

-upper	convert lower case characters to upper case
-lower	convert upper case characters to lower case

If neither option is specified copy the file without any conversion. Test the program, specifying invalid filenames, filenames which do not exist, etc.

23.4 The *fprintf, printf* and *sprintf* functions

The following output functions provide a means of converting the internal machine representation of information into sequences of characters in a specified format:

```
int fprintf(FILE *stream, const char *format, ...);        /* print to stream */
int printf(const char *format, ...);                       /* print to stdout */
int sprintf(char *string, const char *format, ...);        /* print to "string" */
```

the ... indicates a variable number of parameters (see Section 28.5) which are processed under the control of the *control string* pointed to by format:

fprintf writes the converted output to the output stream

printf writes the converted output to the output stream stdout

sprintf places the converted output in the character array pointed to by string.

The parameter format points to an array of characters, the *control string*, which controls the format of the output. The *control string* contains ordinary characters which are copied to the output and conversion specifications which control the conversion of the corresponding parameters to the output (see Appendix C.12.6 and Table C.1 for details).

The function printf prints information to the display screen and fprintf performs a similar function to stream (e.g. a file on disk). The function sprintf is used for in memory formatting. For example, when displaying pictorial information using a graphics package it may be necessary to annotate parts of the image with numeric values (e.g. loads on a bridge). Under such circumstances it will be necessary to use the text output functions of the graphics package which are usually limited to string display (not conversion of numeric information). The function sprintf can be used to convert the information required into a string which is then displayed on the screen (see function write_number in Program 31_1).

The following code, replacing lines 38 to 41 of the sample answer to Exercise 15.2 (see Appendix B), displays the x and y coordinates of the bouncing ball on the screen:

```
do
    {
    char text[50];                        /* text displaying ball position */
    int text_x;                              /* x position of the text */
    setcolor(WHITE);                            /* draw ball in white */
    sprintf(text, "x = %3d, y = %3d ", x, y);      /* convert x and y */
    text_x = (maxx / 2) - (textwidth(text) / 2);     /* get x position */
    outtextxy(text_x, 10, text);                     /* display text */
    circle(x, y, Circle_size);
```

To display the screen position:

1   sprintf is called to convert the x and y coordinates into a string stored in text
2   the x coordinate text_x is calculated to print the text in the middle of the screen
3   outtext is called to display the text
4   then circle is called to draw the ball as in file c15\ex15_2.c.

As the ball bounces around the screen the updated x and y coordinates are shown centred horizontally towards the top of the screen. Note:

1   the text has to be erased at the end of the loop (in a similar way to the ball),
2   the delay loop needs adjusting to take account of the time taken to display the text.

The complete program is in file c15\ex15_2a.c on the disk which accompanies this book.

23.5 The *fscanf, scanf* and *sscanf* functions

The standard input functions scanf, fscanf and sscanf provide a means of converting sequences of characters into the internal machine representation of integers, reals, etc.:

```
int fscanf(FILE *stream, const char *format, ...);          /* read from stream */
int scanf(const char *format, ...);                         /* read from stdout */
int sscanf(const char *string, const char *format, ...);    /* read from "string" */
```

The parameter format points to an array of characters, the *control string*, which controls the conversion of characters from the input into values to be assigned to a variable number of parameters indicated by ... (see Section 28.5). See Appendix C.12.7 for details of the *control string* and Table D.2 for details of the *conversion specifications*. The functions return an int function indicating the number of successful conversions:

1   If no conversions occurred 0 is returned.
2   If a matching failure occurs (a non-numeric character in a decimal number) conversion stops and the number of successful conversions is returned (the faulty character is left in the input stream where the program can read it and take action, see Program 13_2).
3   If *end of file* occurs before any conversions the value EOF is returned.

Thus it is possible for all input to be verified and action taken in case of error, e.g. a message printed and the user prompted for more input (see Chapter 13 Program 13_2).

The function scanf is used to read information from the terminal keyboard and fscanf performs a similar function from stream (e.g. from a file on disk). The function sscanf is used for in memory formatting. For example, a text string may be read from an external device into an array of char and then sscanf used to extract numeric data from the string:

```
char text[50] = " 1 2 3";
int input, x, y, z;

input = sscanf(text, "%d%d%d", &x, &y, &z);
printf("converted %d ints, x=%d y=%d z=%d\n", input, x, y, z);
```

This converts the characters stored in string text into integers to be stored in variables x, y and z. When run the program prints:

```
converted 3 ints, x=1 y=2 z=3
```

See function integer_read in file stu_lib.c (in Section 24.6) for another example of the use of sscanf.

23.6 Binary (unformatted) input and output

If the contents of a file are not to be directly examined by a human it is more efficient to use binary (unformatted) input and output (rather than fprintf, fscanf, etc.):

1   binary input/output is much faster because there is no overhead of converting between the internal machine representation and the formatted character based text;
2   there is no loss of information, e.g. converting a double value (with a minimum precision of 10 figures) using %f (with a default precision of 6 figures) will lose a significant amount of information.

Unformatted input/output is usually used with binary files (some systems make no distinction between binary and text files, e.g. UNIX):

```
size_t   fread(void *p_data, size_t size, size_t number, FILE *stream);
size_t   fwrite(const void *p_data, size_t size, size_t number, FILE *stream);
```

where: p_data   is a pointer to the data to be read or written

   size   specifies the size in bytes of the object(s) to be transferred

   number   specifies the number of objects to be transferred

   stream   is a pointer to a structure of type FILE.

size_t is the unsigned integral type which the sizeof operator produces (defined in the header file <stddef.h>) and void * is the generic pointer (discussed in Section 21.7).

fread attempts to read number objects of size from stream, returning the data in the array pointed to by p_data. It returns as an int function result the number of objects read (which may be less than the number requested). After calling fread the functions feof and ferror should be called to see if an error occurred or end of file was encountered.

fwrite attempts to write number objects of size from the array pointed to by p_data to stream. It returns as an int function result the number of objects written (which will be less than number if an error occurred).

For example, consider an array x of twenty int elements:

```
int x[20];
FILE *stream;

fread(x, sizeof(x), 1, stream);          /* read whole of array x */
fread(x, sizeof(int), 20, stream);       /* read whole of array x */
```

In both cases fread (if successful) reads data into all the elements of array x, i.e.:

1   The first call reads a single object of size sizeof(x); fread should return the value 1.
2   The second call reads twenty objects of size sizeof(int); fread should return 20.

The following calls read a single element of x (see function stu_write_file in implementation file stu_lib.c in Section 24.6 for an example of binary write):

```
fread(x, sizeof(int), 1, stream);          /* read first element of x */
fread(&x[5], sizeof(int), 1, stream);      /* read sixth element of x */
```

If parameter p_data to fread or fwrite points to a data structure which contains pointers (Chapter 21) to other data structures such structures will not be read/written; perform the I/O on each data structure separately.   In addition one has to be very careful when transferring data in binary format between machines with different architectures or even different operating systems or compilers on the same machine.   There may be differences in the number of bytes used to store a type and the internal representation of information, e.g. ones complement or twos complement integers, little-endian or big-endian storage of multi-byte integers, IEEE or non-IEEE format floating point numbers, etc.

Exercise 23.2 (see Appendix B for sample answer)

Modify the file copy program of Exercise 23.1 to use fread and fwrite, enabling any type of file to be copied (remove the -upper and -lower options).

Problem for Chapter 23

Implement and test a program which compares the contents of a pair of files.

24

Structures

Whereas arrays provide a way to group elements of the same type, structures provide a way to group elements of different types. For example, consider a program used to store student records in a college or university where the data could include:

(a) student's name, a character string
(b) student's age, an integer
(c) course code, an integer
(d) year of course, an integer
(e) identification number for library card, etc., a large integer.

The course code would probably provide an index into an array of course data which would provide the course name, length (in years), level (undergraduate, postgraduate), fees, etc.

24.1 Declaring and initialising structures

The keyword `struct` introduces a structure declaration which contains a list of member declarations enclosed in braces {}. The members of a structure can be any simple data type, pointer, array or another structure. For example, a structure declaration to hold student data could be:

```
struct Student {
            char name[20];                       /* student name */
            int age;                             /* student age */
            int course_code;            /* institution's course code */
            int course_year;                  /* year of course */
            long int student_identifier;   /* library card identifier */
            };
```

A `struct` declaration *defines* a new type, i.e. the above defines a new type `struct Student` (where the identifier `Student` is called the structure *tag* or name) with member's `name`, `age`, `course_code`, `course_year` and `student_identifier`; the same names can be used for members of different structures. Note the semicolon following the closing brace `}`; one of the few places where it is necessary following a `}`. Once the new type has been defined variables of that type can be defined, e.g.:

```
    struct Student  student_1, student_2, students[100];      /* define variables */
```

This defines two variables `student_1` and `student_2` and an array `students` of 100 elements of type `struct Student`. A structure object may be initialised with constants in a similar way to an array, e.g.:

```
struct Student  student_1 = { "Smith, Sam", 19, 405, 2 },
                students[5] = { { "Doe, John", 18, 201, 1 },
                                { "Smith, Sally", 18, 65, 1 },
                                { "Jones, Daisy", 21, 345, 3} };
```

Any members not explicitly initialised will be initialised to 0, i.e. the member student_identifier in the above statements would be initialised to 0 as would students[4] and students[5]. If a structure is not initialised the member values are *undefined* if the structure is internal, or zero if it is external or a static internal.

An alternative and possibly more elegant way to define a structure is to use *typedef* (this technique will be used from now on), e.g.:

```
typedef struct {
            char name[20];                      /* student name */
            int age;                            /* student age */
            int course_code;            /* institution's course code */
            int course_year;                   /* year of course */
            long int student_identifier;    /* library card identifier */
            }
            Student;                          /* structure type name */
Student   student_1, student_2, students[100];        /* define variables */
```

defines a type Student and then defines two variables student_1 and student_2, and an array students of 100 elements of that type.

24.2 Accessing the members of a structure

To access a particular member of a structure the . (dot) structure member operator is used:

```
Student   student_1, student_2, students[100];        /* define variables */
strcpy(student_1.name, "Smith, Bert");                /* set up name */
student_1.age = 17;                                   /* set up age */
printf("student name %s, age %d ",
            student_1.name, student_1.age);         /* print student data */
strcpy(students[2].name, "Jones, Daisy");             /* set up name */
students[2].name[0] = 'x';           /* change first character of name */
student_2 = student_1;               /* copy one structure to another */
```

Consider the assignment statement:

```
students[2].name[0] = 'x';           /* change first character of name */
```

This sets the first character of member name of the third element of the array students. The . (dot), [and] operators associate from left to right, therefore:

students[2] accesses the third element of array students
students[2].name accesses the member name (which is an array) within the third element
students[2].name[0] accesses the first element of the member name.

There is a major difference in the way that C treats arrays and structures in that the name of an array refers to the address of its first element and the name of a structure refers to the whole structure. This has a number of implications:

1 A structure can be assigned to another of the same type (even if it contains arrays).
2 Structures are passed to functions *by value* (unlike arrays).
3 A function can return a structure as a function result (new in ANSI C).

Section 19.2 stated that an array cannot be assigned to another, arrays are passed *by reference* and arrays cannot be returned as a function result. The above rules for structures apply even if the structure contains an array. Thus, although it is not possible to assign the structure member name (an array) using a single statement:

```
    student_2.name = student_1.name;              /* copy name, not allowed !! */
```
it is possible to assign the whole structure:
```
    student_2 = student_1;                        /* copy one structure to another */
```
Note that assignment is the only operation that may be carried out on the whole structure, i.e. structures (as a whole) cannot be added, multiplied or even compared.

Arrays of structures (such as students in the above example) obey the normal rules for an array (although the individual elements would obey the rules for structures).

24.3 Pointers to structures

Consider a simplified version of the structure Student:
```
// define structure type to hold student information
typedef struct {
               char name[20];                     /* student name */
               int age;                           /* student age */
               } Student;
Student student,                      /* define a variable to hold student data */
         *p_student = &student;       /* define a pointer to the structure */
```
This defines type Student, variables student (type Student) and p_student (type 'pointer to type Student' initialised to point to student). The pointer can be used to access the members of the structure, e.g. to set up the age and name of the student:
```
    (*p_student).age = 20;                        /* set up student age */
    strcpy((*p_student).name, "daisy");           /* set up student name */
```
Because the dot (.) operator has a higher precedence than the indirection operator (*) the parentheses are required to force the correct association using p_student as the pointer, i.e. the expression *p_student.age is using the structure member p_student.age as though it is a pointer to something. The use of pointers with structures is very common and an equivalent simpler notation using the -> structure pointer operator is generally used:
```
    p_student->age = 30;                          /* set up student age */
    strcpy(p_student->name, "mary");              /* set up student name */
```

24.4 Structures as function parameters

Unlike arrays, structures are passed *by value* (they can be passed *by reference* by using pointers, see Section 16.8). In addition a function may return a structure as a function result. For example, if a structure of type Student is to be passed as a parameter to a function the function header could be:
```
    void stu_print(const Student student)
```
The formal parameter student is a const qualified structure of type Student.

Care must be taken when passing large structures as function parameters. It is possible to run out of storage space on the stack (the data structure used to hold temporary information) and the time taken to copy a large structure will adversely effect program execution speed. Large structures should be passed using pointers to achieve *pass by reference* (see Section 16.8). If, when passing a structure by reference, the contents should not be changed the formal parameter should be const qualified.

24.5 Structures as members of structures

A structure may be a member of another structure. For example, the course details in the above example could be expanded and placed in a separate structure:

```
/* define structure to hold course information */
typedef struct {
            char course_name[20];                    /* name of course */
            int course_code;              /* institution's course code */
            int course_year;                         /* year of course */
            }
            Course;
/* define structure type to hold student information */
typedef struct {
            char name[20];                           /* student name */
            int age;                                  /* student age */
            Course course;                       /* details of course */
            long int student_identifier;  /* library card identifier */
            }
            Student;                          /* structure type name */
Student   student_1, student_2, students[100];   /* define variables */
```

The above:

   (a) defines a type Course which will hold course information,
   (b) defines a type Student which will hold student information (including Course),
and (c) defines variables and an array of type Student.

The members of Course can be accessed using the . (dot) operator:

```
strcpy(student_1.course.course_name, "B.Sc Elec. Eng.");   /* set course name */
student_1.course.course_year = 2;                          /* set course year */
printf("course name %s ", student_1.course.course_name);  /* print course name */
```

24.6 An ADT (abstract data type) to store student records

This section describes, in outline, an ADT to store student records using the structure Student described above and a test program. The overall program consists of four files:

stu_lib.h a header file contains the declarations of the structures Course and Student and prototypes of functions from the implementation files stu_lib.c and stu_lib1.c.
stu_lib.c contains functions to manipulate individual student records (calls stu_lib1.c).
stu_lib1.c contains functions to store student records in an array data structure.
p24_1.c (Program 24_1) contains the program to test the ADT.

The files were designed to promote *information hiding*. Files stu_lib.c and stu_lib1.c contain the code which implements the ADT (data structures and functions which operate on the data) and header file stu_lib.h provides the public interface. In addition, file stu_lib.c only has access to individual student records, not to the underlying data structure which holds all the records implemented in file stu_lib1.c. This enables the underlying data structure to be changed without effecting the header file stu_lib.h and the code in p24_1.c and stu_lib.c. Chapter 25 presents two modifications of stu_lib1.c, the first using dynamic array allocation (file stu_lib.2c) and the second a linked list (file stu_lib3.c).

```
1  /* Header file stu_lib.h, for ADT defined in files stu_lib.c and stu_lib1.c */
2
3  #ifndef _stu_lib_h_                        /* if _stu_lib_h_ is not defined */
4  #define _stu_lib_h_                              /* define _stu_lib_h_ */
5
6  enum {NAME_LENGTH = 20};          /* length of student name, course name, etc. */
7
8  /* define structure to hold course information */
9  typedef struct {
10               char course_name[NAME_LENGTH];                /* name of course */
11               int course_code;             /* institution's course code */
12               int course_year;                      /* year of course */
13         }
14         Course;
15
16 /* define structure type to hold student information */
17 typedef struct {
18               char name[NAME_LENGTH];                      /* student name */
19               int age;                                     /* student age */
20               int start_year;               /* year of starting course */
21               Course course;                     /* details of course */
22               long int identifier;          /* student identifier number */
23         }
24         Student;                              /* structure type name */
25
26 /* prototypes for record processing functions in stu_lib.c & stu_lib1.c */
27 int stu_read_data(Student *student);                     /* read record */
28 int stu_store(const Student *student);                  /* store record */
29 void stu_print(const Student *student);                 /* print record */
30 void stu_all_print(void);                          /* print all records */
31 int stu_name(const Student *student, const char name[]);   /* compare names */
32 const Student *stu_find(char student_name[]);             /* find record */
33 int stu_write_file(const char filename[]);             /* write to file */
34 /* read string and integer read functions */
35 int str_read(const char prompt[], char string[], const int max_length);
36 int integer_read(const char prompt[], const int maximum);
37
38 #endif                                            /* end of condition */
```

Header file stu_lib.h For ADT defined in files stu_lib.c and stu_lib1.c

Header file stu_lib.h provides the public interface to the ADT, defining a constant, two structures and the prototypes of functions defined in files stu_lib1.c and stu_lib.c:

3	use ifndef directive to see if file has already been included (see Section 18.5)
	if identifier _stu_lib_h_ already exists skip rest of file up to line 38
4	first time file has been included, define identifier _stu_lib_h_ (see Section 18.5)
6	define NAME_LENGTH which specifies the number of characters in names
9-14	declare structure Course
17-24	declare structure Student
27-36	declare function prototypes
38	end of conditional compilation.

```
 1 /* Implementation file stu_lib1.c - ADT: store student records in an array */
 2
 3 #include "stu_lib.h"                 /* include student records header file */
 4 #include <stdlib.h>                          /* required for NULL */
 5
 6 enum {max_students = 4};                /* maximum number of students  */
 7
 8 static Student students[max_students] ={{" "}};   /* array of student records */
 9 static int number_of_students = 0;        /* indicates number of records used */
10
11 /*------------------------------------------------------------------*/
12 /* return pointer to record for next student record in the data structure   */
13 /*    if reset_to_start is TRUE reset to first student record               */
14 /*    if past end of records return NULL pointer to indicate failure        */
15 Student *stu_next(const int reset_to_start)
16 {
17     static int stu_index = 0;             /* working index into array students */
18
19     if (reset_to_start) stu_index = 0;     /* if TRUE reset to first student */
20     /* if valid index return pointer to record */
21     if (stu_index < number_of_students) return &students[stu_index++];
22     return NULL;                          /* return NULL indicating failure */
23 }
24
25 /*------------------------------------------------------------------*/
26 /* Store student record into data structure                                 */
27 /*   return 0 failed (array full), 1 stored OK or 2 replaced existing record */
28 int stu_store(const Student *student)
29 {
30     Student *p_student = stu_next(1);        /* get pointer to first record */
31     /* loop searching for record or NULL (end of records) */
32     while (p_student != NULL)
33         if (stu_name(p_student, student->name))      /* found same name ? */
34             {
35             *p_student = *student;                   /* yes, replace record */
36             return 2;                         /* return 2 indicating replace */
37             }
38         else
39             p_student = stu_next(0);          /* get pointer to next record */
40     if (number_of_students == max_students) return 0;  /* array full, error */
41     students[number_of_students++] = *student;          /* store record */
42     return 1;                                           /* return TRUE */
43 }
```

Implementation file stu_lib1.c ADT: functions to store student records in an array

The implementation file stu_lib1.c defines the following:

students (line 8) an array of type Student which will hold the student records

number_of_students (line 9) a variable which:

        (a) indicates the number of student records stored in students

  and (b) indexes the next element of array students to be used (see line 41).

stu_store (function) which is called to store (or replace) a student record in array students
    if successful it returns 1 if record was stored, 2 if an existing record was replaced
    or (*false*) if it failed, e.g. if the array students is full.
stu_next (function) which returns a pointer to a record in the array students
    if parameter reset_to_start is *true* the first record is returned else the next in sequence
    if unsuccessful (attempt to access outside records) NULL is returned.

The array and variable are *static external*. Thus they will be allocated permanent storage
but may not be accessed by functions in other files, i.e. functions in other files have no
knowledge of the underlying data structure and must call the functions stu_store and
stu_next to access the records, the concept of *information hiding*. The sequence of
statements is:

3	include the header file "stu_lib.h" which defines the structure Student, etc.
6	define max_students, the size of the array students (this is small for test purposes)
8	define the static array students type Student to hold student records
9	define number_of_students which indicates the number of records in use and is also used as an index to the next element of array students (see line 41)
15-23	define stu_next, returns either a pointer to the first record or the next (or NULL) if reset_to_start is *true* stu_index is reset to index the first record if beyond the end of the records the function returns NULL
17	define static internal stu_index which will index the record to be returned (initialised to 0). It will allocated permanent storage and retain its value from call to call of the function (but is not accessible by any other function)
19	if reset_to_start is *true* reset stu_index to index first record
21	if stu_index < number_of_students it is a valid record, return pointer to it, i.e.:

        return pointer to students[student_index]
        postincrement stu_index to index next record (ready for next call to function)

22	return NULL to indicate attempt to access beyond end of records
28-43	define stu_store which stores or replaces a record in the array students

        return 1 if stored, 2 if replacing existing record or NULL if it failed

30	call stu_next with parameter *true* to get a pointer to the *first* student record
32-39	a while statement, terminates when stu_next returns NULL

      33 if the name is the same as one being stored
          35 replace record pointed to by p_student by that pointed to by student
          36 return 2 to indicate that a record has been replaced
      else
          39 call stu_next to get pointer to the *next* record in the data structure

40	if number_of_students == max_students array is full, return 0 indicating failure
41	copy new record into the array students, postincrement number_of_students
42	return 1 indicating that the record was stored.

The function result of stu_next is a pointer to either the first record (if reset_to_start is
true) or the next in sequence as indexed by stu_index (which is static internal and
allocated permanent storage). If an attempt is made to access outside the stored records the
function returns NULL.
    The parameter to stu_store is a pointer to const Student, i.e. for efficiency it is passed
by reference and const qualified to indicate that it may not be changed within the function.

The implementation file stu_lib.c (next page but one) contains the ADT functions to manipulate individual student records. Lines 3 to 5 include standard library header files and line 6 includes the header file "stu_lib.h" which declares the structure student, etc. Line 8 is a prototype of the function stu_next (from file stu_lib1.c). This prototype is not in the header file "stu_lib.h" because the only functions which should use it are in stu_lib.c.

Function stu_name, lines 12 to 15, compares a student name with the name stored in a student record and returns *true* if they are identical. It can be used as a general utility function to search for a record on a particular student (see function stu_find below).

Function stu_read_data, lines 20 to 29, reads a student record from the keyboard. The function result (type int) indicates success (*true*) or failure (*false*). If successful the record is returned via the formal parameter student which is a pointer to type Student. Thus the parameter in the calling function is *passed by reference* (see Section 16.8).

20 function header for stu_read_data
    (a) one parameter student, pointer to type Student
    (b) returns an int function result: *true* if data read OK else *false*
23 call str_read to read the student's name, if successful
    24 call integer_read to read the student's age, if successful
        25 call str_read to read the course name, if successful
            27 success, return *true* (1)
28 failed, return *false* (0).

The function stu_print, lines 33 to 37, prints the contents of a single student record (passed as a parameter) to the display screen. The output is printed in columns (see sample run) the width of which is determined by the value of NAME_LENGTH. If the program is modified and NAME_LENGTH is altered the printed output should change accordingly. Consider the call to printf in lines 35 and 36:

```
printf("\n %-*s %2d %-*s ", NAME_LENGTH, student.name,
                student.age, NAME_LENGTH, student.course.course_name);
```

This prints the strings student.name and student.course.course_name left justified in a field of width NAME_LENGTH. The conversion specification %-*s (see Appendix C.12.6 for details):
- indicates that the string is to be printed left justified in the field (default is right)
* indicates that the field width is specified by the next parameter (must be an int)
s indicates that the object to be printed is a string.

Function stu_find, lines 42 to 49, searches the data structure for a record for a named student (name passed as a parameter) and returns a pointer to the record if found else NULL:

42   function header for stu_find (one parameter, the student name)
44   call stu_next with parameter *true* to get pointer to the first student record
46-47   a while statement, terminating when
            (a) stu_next returns NULL for end of records or (b) the record is found
            note the check for NULL is performed before attempting to call stu_name.
            Calling strcmp with a NULL pointer can cause a memory fault on some systems.
        47 not found or NULL, call stu_next to get pointer to next record
48   return p_student, either pointer to record found or NULL.

The function stu_all_print, lines 53 to 64, prints all the student records to the screen:

55   call stu_next with parameter *true* to get pointer to the first student record

57-58   print a heading (see discussion of the %-*s conversion specification above)

59-63   a while statement, terminating when stu_next returns NULL

          61 call stu_print to print the student record

          62 call stu_next to get pointer to next record in data structure.

The function stu_write_file, lines 68 to 86, writes the records to a file called filename:

70   define stream out_file, a pointer to a structure of type FILE

71   call stu_next with parameter *true* to get pointer to the first student record

74-78   call fopen to open filename for binary write (see Section 23.6)

          76-77   if open failed display error messages and return with *false*

79-83   a while statement, terminating when stu_next returns NULL

          81 call fwrite to write one record to disk (see Section 23.6)

          82 call stu_next to get pointer to next record in data structure

84-85   close output file and return *true* for successful completion.

The function performs no error checking on fwrite and should be extended to do this. Note that there is no point writing the whole array student; only a small part may be used.

The function str_read, lines 94 to 104, reads a string of maximum length max_length. It is similar to str_read in str_lib.c (Section 20.8) except that the characters are read individually using getchar rather than as a string using fgets. The function discards excess characters on the line and returns (function result) the number of characters read:

96   define index (which will index string) and ch (the character read)

99   prompt the user with the string prompt

99-101 a while reading a character, terminating when newline or EOF is entered

          100 if the character is printable and there is room in the string

             101 copy character into string, postincrement index

                 note the cast (char) ch converting ch to a char to be assigned to string

102   place terminating null '\0' on end of string

103   return index, the number of characters in string (not counting '\0').

Function integer_read, lines 108 to 131, reads an integer number in the range 1 to maximum. The function str_read is used to read a string and sscanf is used to convert a decimal integer from the string. The function sscanf conversions are similar to scanf except that the characters are read from a string (passed as a parameter), see Section 23.5 and Appendix C.12.7. The function checks for invalid characters and EOF (the program terminates). The sequence of statements is:

113-29 a do statement looping until a value in the range 1 to maximum is entered

116   call str_read to read a string into array string

117-21 call sscanf to convert one int number from array string (see Section 23.5)

          117   if sscanf failed to convert one number

             119 if EOF was entered return 0 indicating failure

             120 else print message and character in error

          122-27 else check value is in the range 1 to maximum

130   return the value read.

Parameters of type student are passed to the functions using pointers. To access the storage allocated to the original object either the -> structure pointer operator or the indirection * and dot . operators may be used, e.g. lines 24 and 25 of stu_read_data:

```
if (str_read(" student name ? ", p_student->name, NAME_LENGTH))   /* name */
    if (((*p_student).age = integer_read(" age ? ", 100)) != 0)      /* age */
```

The first statement calls str_read_data to read a string into the array student->name (which may have been written (*student).name) and the second calls integer_read and assigns the return value to (*p_student).age (which may have been written p_student->age). Because the dot . operator has a higher precedence than the indirection operator * the parentheses are required to force the correct association (see Section 24.3).

```
 1 /* Implementation file stu_lib.c - ADT: manipulate individual student records */
 2
 3 #include <stdio.h>                             /* standard function headers */
 4 #include <ctype.h>
 5 #include <string.h>
 6 #include "stu_lib.h"                    /* include student records header file */
 7
 8 Student *stu_next(const int reset_to_start);        /* prototype for stu_next */
 9
10 /*-------------------------------------------------------------------------*/
11 /* Check student name in record, return TRUE if identical              */
12 int stu_name(const Student *p_student, const char name[])
13 {
14     return (! strcmp(p_student->name, name));            /* compare the names */
15 }
16
17 /*-------------------------------------------------------------------------*/
18 /* read data into record pointed at by 'student' (name, age, course, etc.)   */
19 /*  if all OK return function result TRUE else FALSE if data entry fails     */
20 int stu_read_data(Student *p_student)
21 {
22     /* prompt for student data, read name, age, etc. */
23     if (str_read("\n\nEnter student name ? ", p_student->name, NAME_LENGTH))
24         if (((*p_student).age = integer_read(" age ? ", 100)) != 0)     /* age */
25           if(str_read(" course ? ", p_student->course.course_name, NAME_LENGTH))
26             /* extension required to read further course details, etc. */
27               return 1;                               /* return success */
28       return 0;                                       /* return fail */
29 }
30
31 /*-------------------------------------------------------------------------*/
32 /* print a student record to the screen                                */
33 void stu_print(const Student *p_student)
34 {
35     printf("\n %-*s  %2d  %-*s ", NAME_LENGTH, p_student->name,
36               p_student->age, NAME_LENGTH, p_student->course.course_name);
37 }
```

Implementation file stu_lib.c   ADT: functions to manipulate individual student records

```
38
39 /*-------------------------------------------------------------------*/
40 /* Find record for student_name, return into record pointed at by 'student'   */
41 /*  if found return const pointer to record else NULL                         */
42 const Student *stu_find(char student_name[])
43 {
44     Student *p_student = stu_next(1);          /* get pointer to first record */
45     /* loop searching NULL (end of records) or for required record */
46     while ((p_student != NULL) && (! stu_name(p_student, student_name)))
47         p_student = stu_next(0);               /* get pointer to next record */
48     return p_student;                      /* return pointer to record or NULL */
49 }
50
51 /*-------------------------------------------------------------------*/
52 /* print records for all students to the screen                               */
53 void stu_all_print(void)
54 {
55     Student *p_student = stu_next(1);          /* get pointer to first record */
56
57     printf("\n\nPrint of all student records\n  %-*s age  %-*s",   /* heading */
58             NAME_LENGTH, "student name", NAME_LENGTH, "course");
59     while (p_student != NULL)                               /* if record OK */
60       {
61        stu_print(p_student);                      /* print the student record */
62        p_student = stu_next(0);               /* get pointer to next record */
63       }
64 }
65
66 /*-------------------------------------------------------------------*/
67 /* write student data to file on disk, return TRUE if successful              */
68 int stu_write_file(const char filename[])
69 {
70     FILE *out_file;                              /* pointer to output file */
71     Student *p_student = stu_next(1);          /* get pointer to first record */
72
73     printf("\n\nWrite student records to file '%s' ", filename);
74     if ((out_file = fopen(filename, "wb")) == NULL)        /* open output file */
75       {
76        perror("\a\nUnable to open student records output file");
77        return 0;                                          /* open failed */
78       }
79     while (p_student != NULL)                               /* if record OK */
80       {
81        fwrite(p_student, sizeof(Student), 1, out_file);    /* write record */
82        p_student = stu_next(0);               /* get pointer to next record */
83       }
84     fclose(out_file);                              /* close the output file */
85     return 1;                                      /* indicate success */
86 }
```

Implementation file stu_lib.c ADT: functions to manipulate individual student records

```
87
88  /*------------------------------------------------------------------*/
89  /* read string up to \n, printable characters only !                */
90  /* on entry prompt[]     contains prompt string to print            */
91  /*          max_length   contains maximum length of string          */
92  /* return string read in array string[]                             */
93  /* return function result: number of characters in string           */
94  int str_read(const char prompt[], char string[], const int max_length)
95  {
96      int index = 0, ch;                          /* initialise index to 0 */
97
98      printf("%s", prompt);                             /* print prompt */
99      while (((ch = getchar()) != '\n') && (ch != EOF))  /* read to \n or EOF */
100         if (isprint(ch) && (index < max_length - 1))        /* if OK */
101             string[index++] = (char) ch;            /* put ch in string */
102     string[index] = '\0';                        /* terminate string */
103     return index;                             /* all OK return true */
104 }
105
106 /*------------------------------------------------------------------*/
107 /* function: read an integer number in range 1 to maximum (return 0 on EOF)  */
108 int integer_read(const char prompt[], const int maximum)
109 {
110     int converted, value = maximum + 1;
111     char string[NAME_LENGTH];
112
113     do                             /* read integer in range 1 to maximum */
114       {
115       /* read a string and call sscanf to convert it into a decimal number */
116       if (! str_read(prompt, string, NAME_LENGTH)) return 0;
117       if ((converted = sscanf(string, "%d", &value)) != 1)
118           {
119           if (converted == EOF) return 0;        /* return fail indicator */
120           printf("  non-numeric character in input string, try again ? \n");
121           }
122       else
123         if (value > maximum)                           /* range check */
124           printf("  value %1d > maximum %1d, try again ? ", value, maximum);
125           else
126             if (value < 1)                             /* range check */
127                 printf("  value %1d < minimum 1, try again ? ", value);
128       }
129     while ((value < 1) || (value > maximum));
130     return value;
131 }
```

Implementation file stu_lib.c ADT: functions to manipulate individual student records

```
 1 /* Program 24_1, test student ADT defined in files stu_lib.c and stu_lib1.c */
 2
 3 #include <stdio.h>                              /* standard I/O header */
 4 #include "stu_lib.h"                /* include student records header file */
 5
 6 int main(void)
 7 {
 8     int result;
 9     Student student;                             /* 'working' record */
10     Student const *p_student = NULL;             /* used with stu_find */
11     char student_name[NAME_LENGTH];        /* holds student name to find */
12
13     /* read data on students and store in data structure */
14     while (stu_read_data(&student))                     /* read record */
15         if ((result = stu_store(&student)) == 0)
16             printf("\n\a  Failed to store '%s'", student.name);     /* fail */
17         else
18           if (result == 1)                              /* stored it ? */
19               printf("\n  Data on '%s' stored ", student.name);     /* OK */
20           else
21               printf("\n  Data on '%s' replaced ", student.name);   /* OK */
22
23     /* search data structure for student names */
24     while (str_read("\n\nFind student name ? ", student_name, NAME_LENGTH))
25         if ((p_student = stu_find(student_name)) != NULL)
26             printf("\n    '%s' data found, age %d", student_name, p_student->age)
27         else
28             printf("\n    '%s' data not found", student_name);
29     stu_all_print();                             /* print data on all students */
30     stu_write_file("student.dat");                       /* write to file */
31     return 0;
32 }
```

Program 24_1 To test student ADT defined in files stu_lib.c and stu_lib1.c

Program 24_1 tests the student ADT defined in files stu_lib.c and stu_lib1.c:

4   include the header file "stu_lib.h" which defines the structure Student, etc.

9   define student type Student which will hold a student record

10   define p_student type Student *, a pointer to Student

11   define student_name which will hold the name of a student to search for

14-21   a while statement which terminates when stu_read_data returns 0 (*false*)

          14 call stu_read_data to read a record from the keyboard into student, if OK

               15 call stu_store to store the student record in the data structure

                    16-21 print message indicating if record was stored/replaced/failed

24-28   a while which reads a student name and searches the data structure for the record

          24   call str_read to read the name, terminate while when the string is empty

          25   call stu_find to search for the record on the student

                26-28 print message indicating if record was found or not

29   call stu_print_all to print the records of all the students

30   call stu_write_file to write student data to file student.dat.

In line 14 the formal parameter student is prefixed with the address operator & to *pass by reference* (the function expects a pointer). The address of student is passed to the function which can then use it to return the record read. In line 25 the pointer returned by stu_find is assigned to p_student which is then used in line 26 to display the student's age.

The pointer returned by stu_find is const qualified to prevent user programs using it to access the internal data structures defined within stu_lib1.c. If it was not const qualified a user program would be able to do operations such as:

```
if ((p_student = stu_find(student_name)) != NULL)
    {
    Student mary = {{"Smith, Mary"}};
    *p_student = mary;                          /* alter record ! */
```

Such operations conflict with the concept of information hiding; if a user program wishes to alter a record it should be performed via functions which make up the interface.

The program will only be able to store data on four students (the size of array students defined in file stu_lib1.c), see sample run on next page. Attempts to store more records result in an error message and the alarm sounding. After testing the array size would be increased to that required. Chapter 25 presents two modifications of stu_lib1.c, the first using dynamic array allocation (file stu_lib.2c) and the second a linked list (file stu_lib3.c).

On the next page is a run of Program 24_1 (the data file used to produce this is on the disk in file c24\p24_1.dat). Note that the program replaces the record for student Jones, Sam and fails to store the record for student Adams, Simon (the array is full). The function str_read is correctly truncating the input at the array bounds NAME_LENGTH and then stripping the surplus characters off the line (including the terminating '\n'). The final table is in columns of the correct width. Changing the value of NAME_LENGTH (in stu_lib.h) to 30 and recompiling and executing the program gave the following final result:

```
Print of all student records
    student name                 age   course
    Jones, Sam                    18   B.Sc Computer Science
    Smith, Daisy                  19   B.Sc Electrical Engineering
    Doe, John                     19   B.Sc Mechanical Engineering
    Jones, Sally                  20   B.Sc Physics and Mathematics
```

Clearly Program 24_1 is only the beginning of a student records program. Much more input verification is required. For example, records with the same student name are replaced without checking (one can have students of the same name); the course and student identifier should be checked before doing a replacement.

Parameters of type Student are passed to the functions defined in stu_lib.c and stu_lib1.c using pointers (to *pass by reference*). The reasons for this are two-fold:

1. Some functions need to return a result via a parameter, e.g. function stu_read_data returns the student record read from the keyboard.

2. For efficiency, i.e. a record of type Student on an IMB/PC compatible microcomputer takes 52 bytes under Turbo C and 60 under GNU C. If records of such size were passed by value there would be significant overhead in creating and initialising the temporary variable. If a function does not need to change the contents of a variable the associated formal parameter is const qualified, e.g. function stu_name only needs to read the student name stored within the record not write to it.

A run of Program 24_1 gave:

```
Enter student name ? Jones, Sam ↲
  age ? 8 ↲
  course ? B.Sc Computer Science ↲
Data on 'Jones, Sam' stored
Enter student name ? Smith, Daisy ↲
  age ? 19 ↲
  course ? B.Sc Electrical Engineering ↲
Data on 'Smith, Daisy' stored
Enter student name ? Doe, John ↲
  age ? 19 ↲
  course ? B.Sc Mechanical Engineering ↲
Data on 'Doe, John' stored
Enter student name ? Jones, Sam ↲
  age ? 18 ↲
  course ? B.Sc Computer Science ↲
Data on 'Jones, Sam' replaced
Enter student name ? Jones, Sally ↲
  age ? 18 ↲
  course ? B.Sc Physics and Mathematics↲
Data on 'Jones, Sally' stored
Enter student name ? Adams, Simon ↲
  age ? 18 ↲
  course ? B.Sc Business Studies ↲
 Failed to store 'Adams, Simon'
Enter student name ? ↲

Find student name ? Jones, Sam ↲
   'Jones, Sam' data found, age 18
Find student name ? Smith, George ↲
   'Smith, George' data not found
Find student name ? Doe, John ↲
   'Doe, John' data found, age 19
Find student name ? ↲

Print of all student records
   student name        age  course
   Jones, Sam           18  B.Sc Computer Scien
   Smith, Daisy         19  B.Sc Electrical Eng
   Doe, John            19  B.Sc Mechanical Eng
   Jones, Sally         20  B.Sc Physics and Ma
Write student records to file 'student.dat'
```

In C only limited success in *information hiding* can achieved without fragmenting and over-complicating the code. C++ (Bramer & Bramer 1996) contains further facilities, e.g. access to members of a data structure (such as Student) can be restricted to particular functions. User programs are able to define objects of type Student but not access the members (e.g. such as student.name in line 16 of Program 24_2). However, functions in stu_lib.c and stu_lib1.c could have full access to members. Hence if the data structure Student is modified only functions which have access to its members (may) need to be modified. Functions which cannot access the members (but only define objects of that type) need only be recompiled.

24.7 An ADT to store complex numbers

Unlike Fortran, C has no built-in type which can directly represent and operate upon complex numbers (which are required in many mathematical, scientific and engineering applications). A complex number z has two components, e.g.:

$$z = a + ib$$

where a is the real part and b is the imaginary part (i being the square root of -1). Complex numbers may be added, multiplied and divided using the following equations:

addition $(a + ib) + (c + id) = (a + c) + i(b + d)$

multiplication $(a + ib) * (c + id) = (ac - bd) + i(bc + ad)$

division $\dfrac{(a + ib)}{(c + id)} = \dfrac{(ac + bd) - i(ad - bc)}{c^2 + d^2}$

absolute value $(a + ib) = (a^2 + b^2)^{\frac{1}{2}}$

There may also be functions of complex numbers, e.g. e^x:

$$e^{(a + ib)} = e^a (\sin(b) + i\cos(b))$$

In C a complex number may be represented by two variables, an array of two elements or a structure of two members. Because a structure can be returned as a function result the use of a structure appears to be a good choice, e.g.:

```
typedef  struct {
                float real;                          /* real component */
                float imag;                          /* imaginary component */
                }
                Complex;                             /* complex number type */
Complex  x, y, z;                        /* define variables of type Complex */
```

This defines a type Complex which has two float members (used to represent the real and imaginary components of a complex number) and then declares variables of that type. Two complex numbers stored in variables x and y could be added:

```
z.real = x.real + y.real;
z.imag = x.imag + y.imag;
```

This could easily be implemented as a function which is called with two variables of type Complex, the result of which is returned as a function result of Complex, e.g.:

```
/* Function to add a pair of complex numbers, result = x + y              */
Complex c_add(Complex x, const Complex y)
{
    x.real = x.real + y.real;                    /* setup real part */
    x.imag = x.imag + y.imag;                    /* setup imaginary part */
    return x;                                    /* return function result */
}
```

Note that formal parameter x is used as a working variable within the function (structures are passed *by value* so the actual parameter will not be affected). The function could be called as follows (the variable c would be assigned the value $4.0 +i\ 6.0$):

```
Complex a = {{1.0f}, {2.0f}}, b = {{3.0}, {4.0f}}, c;    /* define variables */
c = c_add(a, b);                                         /* add complex */
```

```
/* Header file complex.h  An ADT to store complex numbers using structures      */

#ifndef _complex_h_                        /* if _complex_h_ is not defined */
#define _complex_h_                             /* define _complex_h_ */

typedef  struct {                          /* complex number type */
              float real;                      /* real component */
              float imag;                      /* imaginary component */
          } Complex;

Complex c_numb(const float real, const float imag);    /* form a complex number */
Complex c_add(const Complex x, const Complex y);         /* add, result = x + y */
Complex c_sub(const Complex x, const Complex y);      /* subtract, result = x - y */
Complex c_mult(const Complex x, const Complex y);     /* multiply, result = x * y */
Complex c_div(const Complex x, const Complex y);       /* divide, result = x / y */
float c_abs(const Complex x);                            /* absolute value */
void c_print(const char text[], const Complex x);      /* print value with text */
Complex c_exp(const Complex x);                     /* exp(x) complex exponent  */

#endif                                             /* end of condition */
```

Header file complex.h   An ADT to store complex numbers using structures

```
 1 /* Implementation file complex.c  An ADT to store complex numbers           */
 2
 3 #include <stdio.h>                            /* include required headers */
 4 #include <math.h>                             /* needed for fabs, etc. */
 5 #include "complex.h"                    /* include complex number header file */
 6
 7 /*-------------------------------------------------------------------------*/
 8 /* Function to form a complex number (type complex) from two reals         */
 9 /* returns a function result of type complex                               */
10 Complex c_numb(const float real, const float imag)
11 {
12     Complex x;
13
14     x.real = real;                            /* setup real part */
15     x.imag = imag;                            /* setup imaginary part */
16     return x;                                 /* return function result */
17 }
18
19 /*-------------------------------------------------------------------------*/
20 /* Function to add a pair of complex numbers, result = x + y               */
21 Complex c_add(const Complex x, const Complex y)
22 {
23     return c_numb(x.real + y.real, x.imag + y.imag);     /* function result */
24 }
25
```

Implementation file complex.c   An ADT to store complex numbers

```
26 /*------------------------------------------------------------*/
27 /* Function to subtract a pair of complex numbers, result = x - y        */
28 Complex c_sub(const Complex x, const Complex y)
29 {
30     return c_numb(x.real - y.real, x.imag - y.imag);     /* function result */
31 }
32
33 /*------------------------------------------------------------*/
34 /* Function to multiply a pair of complex numbers, result = x * y        */
35 Complex c_mult(const Complex x, const Complex y)
36 {
37     return c_numb(x.real * y.real - x.imag * y.imag,        /* real part */
38                   x.real * y.imag + x.imag * y.real);    /* imaginary part */
39 }
40
41 /*------------------------------------------------------------*/
42 /* Function to divide a pair of complex numbers, result = x / y         */
43 Complex c_div(const Complex x, const Complex y)
44 {
45     float y_squared = y.real * y.real + y.imag * y.imag;
46
47     return c_numb((x.real * y.real + x.imag * y.imag) / y_squared,    /* real */
48                   (x.imag * y.real - x.real * y.imag) / y_squared);   /* imag */
49 }
50
51 /*------------------------------------------------------------*/
52 /* Function to evaluate the absolute value of a complex, returns a float    */
53 float c_abs(const Complex x)
54 {
55     return ((float) sqrt(x.real * x.real + x.imag * x.imag));
56 }
57
58 /*------------------------------------------------------------*/
59 /* Function to print the value of a complex number with associated text    */
60 void c_print(const char text[], const Complex x)
61 {
62     printf("%s%2.2f %c i%2.2f", text, x.real,
63            (x.imag >= 0) ? '+' : '-' , fabs(x.imag));
64 }
65
66 /*------------------------------------------------------------*/
67 /* Function to evaluate exp(x), where x and result are complex numbers     */
68 /*    c_exp = exp(x.real) * (sin(x.imag) + i cos(x.imag))               */
69 Complex c_exp(const Complex x)
70 {
71     float exp_real = (float) exp(x.real);
72
73     return c_numb(exp_real * cos(x.imag),                   /* real part */
74                   exp_real * sin(x.imag));             /* imaginary part */
75 }
```

Implementation file complex.c   An ADT to store complex numbers

Header file complex.h and implementation file complex.c implement an ADT to manipulate complex numbers (add, subtract, multiply, print, etc.). The code within the functions is fairly simple and the comments should provide adequate explanation. The only exception is possibly lines 62 and 63 which print the real and imaginary components of a complex number:

```
printf("%s%2.2f %c i%2.2f", text, x.real,
        (x.imag >= 0) ? '+' : '-' , fabs(x.imag));
```

(a) prints the string text, e.g. name of the variable, heading, etc.,
(b) prints the float real component x.real,
(c) prints a character + or - (the sign of the imaginary component),
(d) prints an i (indicating the imaginary component follows)
(e) prints the float absolute value of the imaginary component x.imag.

Progran 24_2 (next page) performs some simple tests on the complex number ADT. The header file complex.h (which declares the type Complex and prototypes of the complex number functions) is included in line 4. Complex variables a = 1 + i2 and b = 4 + i5 are defined and initialised in lines 8 and 12 and printed in lines 11 and 13. Lines 15 to 19 perform some simple tests of the functions, e.g. line 19:

```
c_print("\n(a / b) * b = ",  c_mult(c_div(a, b), b));        /* (a / b) * b */
```

divides a by b and then multiplies the result by b, which should give the original value of a. Because c_div returns a / b as a function result it can be used as an argument to c_mult. For example, lines 21 to 26 evaluate the following expression:

$$\frac{c * d * e^{ic}}{g} - g$$

where: c = real number value 2.1
         d = complex number value -1.7 + i1.2
         g = complex number 0.2 - i0.7.

Lines 21 to 23 set up the values of c, d and g and lines 24 and 25 evaluate the expression (the result of which should be 5.41 - i1.436). A run of the program gave:

```
Complex number operations
a = 1.00 + i2.00, b = 4.00 + i5.00, c_abs(a) = 2.24
a + b = 5.00 + i7.00
a - b = -3.00 - i3.00
a * b = -6.00 + i13.00
a / b = 0.34 + i0.07
(a / b) * b = 1.00 + i2.00
    Sample calculation = 5.41 - i1.44
```

It is worth noting that a complex number ADT can be implemented in a much more elegant way in C++ (Bramer and Bramer 1996). The aggregate type *class* (an extension of the idea of *struct* in C) enables the definition of a type with associated functions and operators. Using operator *overloading* a number of meanings may be given to an operator or a function, e.g. the operator + may be *overloaded* so that it can directly operate upon complex numbers (rather than having to call a function such as c_add in Program 24_2).

```
 1 /* Progran 24_2, test complex number ADT (abstract data type)                */
 2
 3 #include <stdio.h>                         /* include standard I/O header file */
 4 #include "complex.h"                       /* include complex number header file */
 5
 6 int main(void)
 7 {
 8     Complex a = {{1.0f} , {2.0f}}, b, d, g;        /* define complex numbers */
 9     float c;
10
11     c_print("\nComplex number operations\na = ", a);        /* print a */
12     b = c_numb(4.0f, 5.0f);                                 /* set up b */
13     c_print(", b = ", b);                                   /* print b */
14     printf(", c_abs(a) = %2.2f", c_abs(a));            /* print abs(a) */
15     c_print("\na + b = ", c_add(a, b));                    /* a + b */
16     c_print("\na - b = ", c_sub(a, b));                    /* a - b */
17     c_print("\na * b = ", c_mult(a, b));                   /* a * b */
18     c_print("\na / b = ", c_div(a, b));                    /* a / b */
19     c_print("\n(a / b) * b = ",  c_mult(c_div(a, b), b));     /* (a / b) * b */
20
21     c = 2.1f;                                  /* do a sample calculation */
22     d = c_numb(-1.7f, 1.2f);
23     g = c_numb(0.2f, -0.7f);
24     a = c_mult(c_numb(c,0.0f), c_mult(d, c_exp(c_numb(0.0f, c))));
25     a = c_sub(c_div(a, g),g);
26     c_print("\n   Sample calculation = ", a);
27     return 0;
28 }
```

Progran 24_2 To test complex number ADT (abstract data type)

Exercise 24.1 (*see Appendix B for sample answer*)

Using the complex number ADT implement a program which evaluates the impedance of an RLC (resistor R, inductor L and capacitor C) series circuit at frequency f:

```
impedance Z = R + i(2πfL - 1/(2πfC))
```

e.g. if f = 50 Hz, R = 1000 Ω, H = 0.2 henries and C = 2.0 μfarads the impedance would be Z = 1000 - i1528.718 Ω.

24.8 Unions *

A union is similar to a structure in the way that it is declared and how its members are accessed, but there is a fundamental difference in the way storage is allocated:

structures each member has its own area of storage
unions   the members use the same area of storage, i.e. they overlay each other.

For example, one of the problems at the end of this chapter is to implement a set of functions to support a structured display file on a raster scan display. The display file is built up from drawing elements each of which contains information on a particular drawing primitive such as a line (type Line), circle (type Circle) and box (type Box), etc., e.g.:

```
typedef short int Gdata;                         /* type used for graphics data */

/* line: its type and start and end coordinates */
typedef struct { Gdata l_type; Gdata x1; Gdata y1; Gdata x2; Gdata y2; } Line;

/* box: if filled and top left hand and bottom right hand coordinates */
typedef struct { Gdata fill; Gdata x_lh; Gdata y_lh; Gdata x_rh; Gdata y_rh; } Box;

/* circle: if filled and coordinates of centre and radius */
typedef struct { Gdata fill; Gdata x; Gdata y; Gdata radius; } Circle;
```

Because a particular element would only store information on one primitive at any time a union is a suitable structure to hold such elements, e.g.:

```
/* define a union to hold drawing primitives  */
typedef union {
                Line line;                                      /* lines */
                Box box;                                        /* boxes */
                Circle circle;                                  /* circles */
              } Primitive;

Primitive primitive, drawing[100];
```

This defines a type `Primitive` and a variable and an array of that type. It is important to remember that only one of the members `Primitive.Line`, `Primitive.Circle` or `Primitive.Box` will exist in each object at any instant. A simple variable (such as `primitive`) is not much use but an array (such as `drawing`) could be used to store a drawing built up from lines, circles and boxes. C performs no consistency checking on what is stored in a union and it is up to the programmer to keep track of which member is in use at any instant, i.e. if information is written into `Primitive.Line` and then read as `Primitive.Circle` the resultant circle information would be incorrect. The members of a union start at the same address and the overall size of the union is the size of its longest member.

Structures can contain unions and vice versa and one can have arrays of such structures. It is because structures can contain a union that structures cannot be compared, i.e. the compiler does not know which member of a union is in use and although a comparison at the bit level may yield identical structures it could be pure chance that the data stored in different union members had the same bit pattern.

A common practice is to have a union as a member of a structure where another member of the structure is a variable which keeps track of what is stored in the union, e.g.:

```
/* define drawing primitive indicators and size of display file */
typedef enum { LINE, BOX, CIRCLE, DF_SIZE = 200 };

typedef struct {
                Gdata element_number;                    /* element number */
                Gdata color;                             /* primitive colour */
                Gdata indicator;                 /* indicates primitive type */
                Primitive primitive;                     /* primitive type */
               } Element;

Element drawing[DF_SIZE];                         /* array of drawing elements */
```

When information is stored in `drawing[index].primitive` the corresponding value `LINE`, `CIRCLE` or `BOX` is assigned to member `drawing[index].indicator`. Functions processing the elements of the array `drawing` would then check the contents of member `indicator` to see what type of information was stored in the corresponding `primitive`.

24.9 Bitfields *

Consider a process control program which contains a number of variables whose values indicate the state of control valves in the system:

```
/* variables holding information on the state of valves in a control system */
unsigned char valve_1;                          /* valve 1 open/closed */
unsigned char valve_2;                          /* valve 2 open/closed */
unsigned char valve_3;                        /* valve 3 - 4 positions */
unsigned char valve_4;                       /* valve 4 - 16 positions */
unsigned char valve_5;                      /* valve 5 - 256 positions */

valve_1 = 0;                                   /* valve 1 is closed */
valve_2 = 1;                                     /* valve 2 is open */
valve_3 = 1;                   /* valve 3 is approximately 33% open */
valve_4 = 9;                   /* valve 4 is approximately 60% open */
valve_5 = 191;                 /* valve 5 is approximately 75% open */
```

In the above example, valves 1 and 2 are either open or closed with 0 indicating closed and 1 indicating open. Valves 3, 4 and 5 have variable settings, e.g. the state of valve 4 varies between 0, closed, and 15, fully open. The variables are of type unsigned char, which is the smallest simple data type which can be defined (a char is always a byte, eight-bits). Storing a simple open/closed (binary 1/0) value in an unsigned char is very wasteful in terms of storage space, i.e. seven bits of variable valve_1 are not used. The alternative is to store a number of such values within a byte; this may be achieved by:

1   using *bitfields* within a structure;
2   using the *bitwise* operators to access particular bits within a byte or a sequence of bytes (*bitwise* operators were covered in Section 9.4).

Bitfields, which may only be declared inside a structure or union, allow the specification of very small objects of a given length in bits. If a member of a structure or union is to be a bitfield the numbers of bits is specified following the identifier:

```
/* structure to hold information on the state of valves in a control system */
typedef struct {
            unsigned int valve_1: 1;              /* valve 1 open/closed */
            unsigned int valve_2: 1;              /* valve 2 open/closed */
            unsigned int valve_3: 2;            /* valve 3 - 4 positions */
            unsigned int valve_4: 4;           /* valve 4 - 16 positions */
            unsigned int valve_5: 8;          /* valve 5 - 256 positions */
            } Valve;

Valve valves;                          /* variable holding data on valves */

valves.valve_1 = 0;                              /* valve 1 is closed */
valves.valve_2 = 1;                                /* valve 2 is open */
valves.valve_3 = 1;              /* valve 3 is approximately 33% open */
valves.valve_4 = 9;              /* valve 4 is approximately 60% open */
valves.valve_5 = 191;            /* valve 5 is approximately 75% open */
printf("size %d\n", (int) sizeof(Valve));     /* print sizeof struct Valve */
printf("valve_1 %d\n", valves.valve_1);              /* print valve data */
printf("valve_2 %d\n", valves.valve_2);
printf("valve_3 %d\n", valves.valve_3);
printf("valve_4 %d\n", valves.valve_4);
printf("valve_5 %d\n", valves.valve_5);
```

The above example shows how the information on the valves could be stored in a *bitfield* (VALVE_1 and VALVE_2 are one bit in length, VALVE_3 and VALVE_4 are two and four bits in length respectively and VALVE_5 is a byte). The bitfields are accessed and manipulated as are other members of a structure. Bitfields behave like small integers, and when used in an expression (such as a parameter in the above calls to printf) undergo integral promotion. The unit of storage used to store bitfields, the order of the bitfields within the storage unit and whether or not bitfields may cross a unit boundary are all implementation dependent (to force alignment to a storage unit boundary a zero width field is specified).

Take care in using bitfields. Although the amount of storage used to store the data may be reduced, the overhead in terms of run-time code required to pack and unpack the fields can be considerable.

An alternative approach is to use the *bitwise* operators (see Section 9.4) explicitly to pack and unpack data by accessing and manipulating particular bits or groups of bits within a variable. For example:

```
/* define bit mask for valves within an 8-bit unsigned char */
enum { VALVE_1 = 0x80, VALVE_2 = 0x40, VALVE_3 = 0x30, VALVE_4 = 0x0f };

unsigned char valves = 0, valve_5;    /* define variable to store valve positions */

valves = valves & ~VALVE_1;                         /* valve 1 is closed */
valves = valves | VALVE_2;                          /* valve 2 is open */
valves = (valves & ~VALVE_3) | (1 << 4);   /* valve 3 is approximately 33% open */
valves = (valves & ~VALVE_4) | 9;          /* valve 4 is approximately 60% open */
valve_5 = 191;                             /* valve 5 is approximately 75% open */

printf("valves size %d value %#x\n", (int)sizeof(valves), valves); /* print values */
printf("valve_1 %d\n", (valves & VALVE_1) >> 7);
printf("valve_2 %d\n", (valves & VALVE_2) >> 6);
printf("valve_3 %d\n", (valves & VALVE_3) >> 4);
printf("valve_4 %d\n", valves & VALVE_4);
printf("valve_5 %d\n", (int) valve_5);
```

Within variable valves the value of VALVE_1 is stored in bit 7, VALVE_2 in bit 6, VALVE_3 in bits 4 and 5 and VALVE_4 in bits 0 to 3. The particular bits are accessed using the bit masks defined using enum (#define could be used) together with & (and) to clear bits, | (or) to set bits and shifts to position the fields within the variable. For example, valve 3 is represented by two bits (bits 4 and 5 of valves) giving a range from 0 (closed) to 3 (open):

```
valves = (valves & ~VALVE_3) | (1 << 4);      /* valve 3 is approximately 33% open */
```

(a) the value of valves is ANDed with the complement of VALVE_3 (clearing bits 4 and 5)
(b) the value 1 (approximately 30% of 7) is shifted 4 bits left (into bits 4 and 5)
(c) the results of (a) and (b) are ORed and the result assigned to valves.

A run of the above fragment of code gave:

```
valves size 1 value 0x69
valve_1 0
valve_2 1
valve_3 1
valve_4 9
valve_5 191
```

Using *bitwise* operators may or may not be more efficient than using bitfields but it at least makes the programmer aware of the overheads in terms of the code required to do the bit manipulation, .e.g. to store a Valve the above code using *bitfields* used 3 bytes under Turbo C V3.00 and 4 bytes under GNU C V2.6.3 whereas the *bitwise* code used a byte. This forces careful design of the data structures to achieve the most efficient methods of accessing and manipulating the bits. In practice, a small change in the position or order of fields can make orders of magnitude changes in program execution times. Another alternative is to implement assembly language functions (see Chapter 30) to carry out packing and unpacking operations on groups or blocks of fields at a time.

Problems for Chapter 24

Problem 24.1 Add functions to implementation file stu_lib1.c to delete records (identified by name) and sort the records by student name (see Exercise 19.1 for linear sort). Add functions to read records from a disk file and amend records, e.g. to correct student names, course names, etc.

Problem 24.2 Extend Program 24_2 to evaluate the following functions:

The log of a complex number: $\log(a + ib) = \frac{1}{2}\log(a^2 + b^2) + i\tan^{-1}(b/a)$.

The sine of a complex number: $\sin(a + ib) = \sin(a) \cosh(b) + i \cos(a) \sinh(b)$.

The cosine of a complex number: $\cos(a + ib) = \cos(a) \cosh(b) - i \sin(a) \sinh(b)$.

To read a complex number, e.g. Complex c_read(const char prompt[]).

Extend the main to read a complex number from the keyboard (using c_read) and then call the various functions. The following relationships should be true:

$x = e^{\log(x)}$

$\sin^2(x) + \cos^2(x) = 1$ (no imaginary component).

Problem 24.3 A raster scan graphics system (used on PCs and the majority of modern workstations) organises the display screen as a two-dimensional matrix of addressable points called pixels. For example, the VGA graphics system on IBM PC compatible microcomputers consists of 480 lines each of which has 640 pixels. Associated with each pixel on the screen is one or more bits in a RAM memory; usually called the bitmap. In a single plane system (one bit/pixel) if a particular bit is set the associated pixel on the screen is illuminated, if it is zero the pixel is blank. Additional memory planes can be used to represent various levels of intensity or colour. The bitmap is scanned 50 or 60 times per second (ignoring non-interlaced displays) with the corresponding pixels on the screen illuminated in the appropriate colour.

```
        bitmap contents
00000000000000000000
00000010000000100000
00000001000001000000
00000000100010000000
00000000010100000000
00000000001000000000
00000000010100000000
00000000100010000000
00000001000001000000
00000010000000100000
00000000000000000000
```

display screen

A vector or character can be represented by setting a pattern of bits in the bitmap to 1 and, thus, illuminating the associated pixels on the display screen. The above example shows the character X stored in bitmap memory and the resultant display. So long as the character is built up from sufficient pixels and the adjacent pixels (vertical and horizontal) on the display screen are sufficiently close together the eye will perceive a continuous shape rather than a number of separate points. The more pixels the finer the quality of the resultant image (assuming that the quality of the display screen is sufficient in terms of dot size, etc.). For example, professional workstations, used for advanced CAD design work, typically have a 19- or 21-inch screen with a minimum of 1000 * 1000 pixels and 256 to 16 million colours.

When using a raster scan display system it is possible for the programmer to manipulate individual pixels and groups of pixels either directly by addressing the appropriate memory locations or by calling functions in a graphics library. Applications such as image processing, television picture manipulation, etc., would use pixel-based 'bitmapped' graphics. In other application areas, however, the pictorial information is not naturally in a bitmapped pixel-based form. For example, engineers may wish to draw pictures of resistors, capacitors, ICs, bridges, engines, jumbo jets, etc. Although these tend to be application specific they can all be built using simple drawing primitives such as lines, polygons, circles, arcs, etc. There are many graphics packages which enable the user to write a program in terms of such drawing primitives by calling functions which convert the primitive into the equivalent bitmapped form, i.e. a line would be converted into a series of illuminated pixels on the screen (Program 15_3 used the Turbo C V3.00 graphics library; other compilers offer libraries with similar facilities).

A major problem for a programmer working in terms of drawing primitives is that once the object has been 'drawn' into the bitmap it is no longer recognisable to the program as a line, circle, arc, etc., it is just a series of pixels in a bitmap. If the program needs to delete a particular line or change the colour of a particular circle other information than that in the bitmap is required (it may be possible using image processing techniques to extract lines and circles from the bitmap but this is not easy!). Another data structure, in addition to the bitmap, is therefore required to hold information on the primitives which make up the drawing (Bramer & Sutcliffe 1981).

Implement a set of functions to support a structured display file of primitives which have been drawn to the screen. The functions will sit 'on top' of the normal raster graphics library functions (such as the Turbo C graphics library (graphics.h) and maintain a graphical display file of the information on the screen. The display file could be an array of drawing elements (such as Element described in Section 24.8) where each element contains data on a primitive together with support information:

1   The element number: an integer number given so that a particular element may be identified at a later time, e.g. if it is to be deleted.
2   The element colour: the colour in which the primitive will be drawn.
3   The primitive indicator: indicates if the primitive is a line, circle, etc.
4   The data on the primitive, e.g. screen coordinates, line type and thickness, etc.

The functions implemented should include basic drawing functions (to draw primitives on the screen and update the display file) and file maintenance functions, e.g. to delete an element (redraw element on the screen in black and then delete from display file) and redraw all elements (deleting can result in 'holes' being left in the drawing).

25

Dynamic storage allocation

Section 18.9 discussed the allocation and storage of variables:

automatic internal variable: defined within a compound statement: allocated storage on entry to the compound statement and deallocated on exit from the compound statement.

static internal variable: defined within a compound statement: allocated and initialised prior to program execution and maintained until program termination.

formal parameter to a function: declared as a parameter in a function header: allocated on function entry and initialised with the values of the actual parameter.

external variable: defined outside a function body: allocated and initialised prior to program execution and maintained until the program terminates.

The allocation and deallocation of the above variables is set up by the compiler and linker and, once defined, the size of such a variable may not be changed. In many applications the actual size required to store a data set may not be known until run time. In implementation file stack1.c in Section 19.7, for example, the array to store the stack was defined in line 6 (char stack_data[stack_size]; where stack_size = 10) although the actual size was not known until function setup_stack was called at run time. If the size required at run time was greater than stack_size the program would fail when 10 characters had been pushed onto the stack (push would return 0 indicating the stack was full). It would be possible to define a larger array but this would waste storage if the stack required was small. It would be preferable if storage space of the required size could be acquired dynamically at run time and then released when no longer required.

25.1 Functions to allocate memory dynamically

The library <stdlib.h> contains functions which support dynamic memory allocation:

```
void *malloc(size_t size);                    /* allocate one object of 'size' */
void *calloc(size_t number, size_t size);   /* allocate 'number' objects of 'size' */
void *realloc(void *pointer, size_t size);   /* reallocate 'pointer' to 'size' */
void free(void *pointer);                      /* deallocate 'pointer' */
```

The type size_t is defined in <stdlib.h> and is typically an unsigned int (this is the type returned by the sizeof operator, see Section 9.6).

The function malloc allocates storage (from within the run-time system) for an object of size bytes and returns a pointer to the object, or NULL if the allocation failed. The pointer returned is type void * (see Section 21.7) which must be cast to the required data type before it can be used. The storage allocated is not initialised. For example, to allocate storage for a 100-element float array:

```
float *p_array;                              /* define 'pointer to float' */

p_array = (float *) malloc(100 * sizeof(float));   /* allocate array */
if (p_array == NULL) printf("allocation failed ");   /* failed */
else               printf("allocation OK ");          /* OK */
```

Note the cast, (float *), which converts the pointer returned by malloc to a pointer to float. Once storage is allocated it can be accessed via the pointer p_array as normal.

The function calloc allocates storage for number objects of size bytes and returns a pointer to the objects or, if it fails, NULL. The storage allocated is initialised to zeros. For example, to allocate the 100-element float array:

```
p_array = (float *) calloc(100, sizeof(float));     /* allocate array */
```

The main difference between malloc and calloc is that calloc initialises the storage to zeros (this imposes a run-time overhead so use malloc if the storage does not need initialising).

The function realloc changes the size of the storage area pointed to by pointer, to number bytes (which may be smaller or larger than already allocated). It returns a pointer to the reallocated storage or, if it fails, NULL if the reallocation failed. The current allocation may be extended (if possible) or new storage allocated; in any case the original contents are preserved and the extra storage is not initialised. For example, to reallocate the storage to a 200-element array of float (in this case assert from <assert.h> is called to display a message and abort the program if the reallocation failed, i.e. p_array == NULL see Section 11.8):

```
p_array = (float *) realloc(p_array, 200 * sizeof(float));     /* reallocate */
assert(p_array != NULL);                    /* if NULL display message and abort */
printf("reallocation OK ");                                          /* OK */
```

Once storage is finished with it can be deallocated using free, e.g.:

```
free(student);                                        /* deallocate storage */
```

Passing uninitialised pointers or calling free twice with the same pointer value will result in *undefined behaviour*, which may result in a system crash or carrying on with corrupt information. Passing a NULL pointer to free will do nothing. Storage can be allocated and deallocated in any order but beware of fragmenting the memory. It is possible to end up in a situation where there is a large number of small 'free' areas in memory and allocation fails when storage is requested for something large. It must be emphasised that it is up to the programmer to free memory when it is finished with. A common fault is to forget and one ends up running out of memory. For example, consider the following function:

```
void func(int array_size)
{
    float *p_x = (float *) malloc(array_size * sizeof(float)),
          *p_y = (float *) malloc(array_size * sizeof(float));
    if ((p_x == NULL) || (p_y == NULL))
        printf("allocation failed ");                                /* failed */
    else
        printf("allocation OK ");                                    /* OK */
    free(p_x);                                              /* don't forget */
    free(p_y);                                       /* to deallocate storage */
}
```

Two arrays of size array_size are used as working storage within the function. On entry two pointers to float are defined and initialised to point to memory allocated using malloc. The pointers are then checked to ensure that the allocation succeeded; if so they may be used as required. When complete the function calls free to deallocate storage (it is safe to call free even if the allocation failed because the pointers will contain NULL and free will ignore the call).

25.2 Using dynamic storage allocation to implement a stack

```
 1 /* Implementation file stack2.c  Stack ADT using dynamic array allocation    */
 2
 3 #include "stack.h"                              /* include own header file */
 4 #include <stdlib.h>                             /* required for malloc */
 5 #include <assert.h>                             /* assert for diagnostics */
 6
 7 /* data hidden within the module  */
 8 static short int stack_size = 0;                          /* stack size */
 9 static char *stack_data;                   /* pointer to char array for stack */
10 static int stack_index = 0;            /* index to next free location on stack */
11
12 /*---------------------------------------------------------------------*/
13 /* allocate a stack of specified size - return size of stack allocated      */
14 int setup_stack(const int size)
15 {
16     /* allocate array of specified size to hold chars */
17     stack_data = (char *) malloc(size * sizeof(char));
18     assert(stack_data != NULL);              /* if allocation failed abort */
19     stack_size = size;                 /* OK set stack_size to size allocated */
20     stack_index = 0;                          /* index first free location */
21     return stack_size;                    /* return size of stack allocated */
22 }
23
24 /*---------------------------------------------------------------------*/
25 /* push character onto stack - return TRUE if OK else FALSE if stack is full  */
26 int push(const char data)
27 {
28     /* if stack is full return false else push data onto the stack */
29     if (stack_index >= stack_size) return 0;             /* yes, return false */
30     stack_data[stack_index++] = data;                    /* OK, push data */
31     return 1;                                       /* all OK return true */
32 }
33
34 /*---------------------------------------------------------------------*/
35 /* test if stack is empty - return TRUE if it is otherwise FALSE         */
36 int empty(void)
37 {   return (stack_index == 0); }              /* if stack is empty return TRUE */
38
39 /*---------------------------------------------------------------------*/
40 /* pop character (as function result) off stack (return 0 if stack empty)    */
41 char pop(void)
42 {
43     if (empty()) return 0;                   /* if stack is empty return 0 */
44     return stack_data[--stack_index];               /* OK, pop top of stack */
45 }
```

Implementation file stack2.c A stack ADT using dynamic array allocation

A problem with file stack1.c (Section 19.7), which used an array to implement a stack ADT, was that the user had no control over the stack size at run time (although this was passed as a parameter to setup_stack). Implementation file stack2.c (previous page) is a modified version of stack1.c which allocates the array dynamically:

8	define stack_size which will hold the size of the stack (initialised to 0)
9	define a 'pointer to char' which will point to the array allocated
10	define stack_index which will index the next free location on the stack
14-22	function setup_stack: allocates a stack of size characters

    17 call malloc to allocate a char array of size

    18 call assert to see if malloc allocated the storage, abort program if it failed
        remember assert will abort the program if stack_data != NULL is *false*

    19 allocation worked, assign size to stack_size

    20 set stack_index to 0 to index the first location on the stack

    21 return stack_size, the size of stack allocated or 0 if allocation failed.

The remainder of the file is identical to file stack1.c in Section 19.7 (also stack.h and Program 19_3 which tests the stack functions need no modification).

Implementation file stack3.c (next page) is a version of the stack processing functions which uses a pointer to access and manipulate the stack (rather than an array index):

8	define stack_size which will hold the size of the stack (initialised to 0)
9	define stack_start which will point to the start of the array allocated
10	define stack_pointer which will point to the next free location on the stack
14-23	function setup_stack: allocates a stack of size characters

    16 if stack_start != 0 delete existing stack; this allows setup_stack to be called
        as required to delete any old stack and allocate a new stack

    18 call malloc to allocate a char array of size

    19 call assert to see if malloc allocated the storage, abort program if it failed

    20 allocation worked, assign size to stack_size

    21 set stack_pointer to point to the first location on the stack

    22 return stack_size, the size of stack allocated or 0 if allocation failed

27-33   function push: attempts to push data onto the stack

    30 if stack_pointer >= stack_start + stack_size the stack is full
        return 0 (*false*) indicating that the push failed due to the stack being full

    31 move data onto top of stack, increment stack_pointer to point to next location
        *stack_pointer accesses the object pointed to by stack_pointer
        the ++ then increments stack_pointer

    32 return 1 (*true*) indicating that the push was successful

37-38   function empty tests if stack is empty

    38 return *true* (1) if stack is empty, i.e. stack_pointer equals stack_start

42-46   function pop: attempts to pop the top of the stack (returned as a function result)

    44 if the stack is empty return 0, error condition !

    45 decrement stack_pointer and pop top of stack (returned as function result).

Header file stack.h and Program 19_3 which tests the stack functions need no modification. Both stack2.c and stack3.c call assert to abort the program if the memory allocation failed; this would loose any other data the program had been processing. An alternative would be for setup_stack to return 0 enabling the calling program to take any action required.

```
 1 /* Implementation file stack3.c    A stack ADT using pointer notation        */
 2
 3 #include "stack.h"                                  /* include own header file */
 4 #include <stdlib.h>                                      /* for malloc, etc. */
 5 #include <assert.h>                                  /* assert for diagnostics */
 6
 7 /* data hidden within the module */
 8 static short int stack_size = 0;                                /* stack size */
 9 static char *stack_start = 0,                      /* pointer to start of stack */
10          *stack_pointer = 0;     /* pointer to next free location on stack */
11
12 /*--------------------------------------------------------------------------*/
13 /* allocate a stack of specified size - return size of stack allocated       */
14 int setup_stack(const int size)
15 {
16     if (stack_start != 0) free(stack_start);          /* delete any old stack */
17     /* allocate array of specified size to holds chars */
18     stack_start = (char *) malloc(size * sizeof(char));
19     assert(stack_start != NULL);             /* if allocation failed abort */
20     stack_size = size;                    /* OK set stack_size to size allocated */
21     stack_pointer = stack_start;                /* point to start of stack */
22     return stack_size;                      /* return size of stack allocated */
23 }
24
25 /*--------------------------------------------------------------------------*/
26 /* push character onto stack - return TRUE if OK else FALSE if stack is full  */
27 int push(const char data)
28 {
29     /* if stack is full return false else push data onto the stack */
30     if (stack_pointer >= stack_start + stack_size) return 0;
31     *stack_pointer++ = data;                          /* OK, push data */
32     return 1;                                    /* all OK return true */
33 }
34
35 /*--------------------------------------------------------------------------*/
36 /* test if stack is empty - return TRUE if it is otherwise FALSE             */
37 int empty(void)
38 {   return (stack_pointer == stack_start); }    /* if stack empty return TRUE */
39
40 /*--------------------------------------------------------------------------*/
41 /* pop character (as function result) off stack (return 0 if stack empty)    */
42 char pop(void)
43 {
44     if (empty()) return 0;                       /* if stack is empty return 0 */
45     return *--stack_pointer;                            /* OK, pop data */
46 }
```

Implementation file stack3.c   A stack ADT using pointer notation

Implementation file stu_lib2.c is a version of stu_lib1.c (from Section 24.6) modified to allocate the array to hold student records dynamically. The sequence of statements is:

7   define p_students a pointer to type Student

8   define number_of_students indicates number of records stored in the data structure

14-22   define function stu_next, this is similar to stu_next in stu_lib1.c except that
            references to the array students have been replaced with the pointer p_students

27-64   define function stu_store as follows:

29   define new_students, the number of new students to allocate storage for

30   define max_students holds the size of the array pointed to by p_students

31-41   look for existing record and replace it if found (as in stu_lib1.c)

43-61   if number_of_students == max_students the array is full - reallocate !!

      46   if max_students == 0 (on first call to stu_store)

           48   call calloc to allocate storage for the student records

     else

           51-52   call realloc to extend existing storage

      55   if allocation failed terminate and return function result 0

      58   assign pointer to new storage area to students

      59   assign max_students the size of the updated array

      60   sound alarm to indicate success (this can be removed when fully tested)

62   copy record into array pointed to by p_students, postincrement number_of_students

63   return *true* for success.

In stu_lib2.c, once the storage for the array has been allocated the pointer p_students can be used with array indexes as in file stu_lib1.c.

```
 1 /* Implementation file stu_lib2.c - ADT: store records in a dynamic array    */
 2
 3 #include "stu_lib.h"                      /* include student records header file */
 4 #include <stdio.h>                                          /* I/O library */
 5 #include <stdlib.h>                          /* required for malloc, NULL, etc. */
 6
 7 static Student *p_students = 0;        /* pointer to array of student records */
 8 static int number_of_students = 0;        /* indicates number of records used */
 9
10 /*-----------------------------------------------------------------------*/
11 /* return pointer to record for next student record in the data structure    */
12 /*    if reset_to_start is TRUE reset to first student record                */
13 /*    if past end of records return NULL pointer to indicate failure         */
14 Student *stu_next(const int reset_to_start)
15 {
16     static int stu_index = 0;              /* working index into array students */
17
18     if (reset_to_start) stu_index = 0;       /* if TRUE reset to first student */
19     /* if valid index return pointer to record */
20     if (stu_index < number_of_students) return &p_students[stu_index++];
21     return NULL;                               /* return NULL indicating failure */
22 }
23
```

Implementation file stu_lib2.c ADT: functions to store records in a dynamic array

```
24 /*---------------------------------------------------------------------*/
25 /* Store student record into data structure                           */
26 /*   return 0 allocation failed, 1 stored OK or 2 replaced existing record   */
27 int stu_store(const Student *student)
28 {
29     const int new_students = 4;      /* new students to allocate storage for */
30     static int max_students = 0;              /* size of array allocated */
31     Student *p_student = stu_next(1);      /* get pointer to first record */
32
33     /* loop searching for record or NULL (end of records) */
34     while (p_student != NULL)
35         if (stu_name(p_student, student->name))      /* found same name ? */
36             {
37             *p_student = *student;                /* yes, replace record */
38             return 2;                    /* return 2 indicating replace */
39             }
40         else
41             p_student = stu_next(0);      /* get pointer to next record */
42
43     if (number_of_students == max_students)      /* array full, allocate */
44         {
45         Student *p_new_students;              /* pointer to new storage */
46         if (max_students == 0)                         /* first call ? */
47             /* yes, call calloc to allocate initial storage for student data */
48             p_new_students = (Student *) calloc(new_students, sizeof(Student));
49         else
50             /* no, call realloc to extend storage for student data */
51             p_new_students = (Student *) realloc(p_students,
52                 (max_students + new_students) * sizeof(Student));
53
54         /* calloc/realloc OK ? if not return 0 */
55         if (p_new_students == NULL) return 0;
56
57         /* OK set up pointer to storage and set up new size of array */
58         p_students = p_new_students;                      /* pointer */
59         max_students = max_students + new_students;       /* new size */
60         putchar('\a');                                    /* ring alarm */
61         }
62     p_students[number_of_students++] = *student;      /* store record */
63     return 1;                                         /* return TRUE */
64 }
```

Implementation file stu_lib2.c   ADT: functions to store records in a dynamic array

In stu_lib2.c the array is initially allocated four elements (line 48) and then extended by four elements (lines 51 and 52) as required; the alarm is sounded on each allocation to indicate success. When fully tested the size can be increased to a more reasonable size (e.g. 10 elements) and the sounding of the alarm removed.

The interface presented to the outside world by stu_lib2.c is identical to stu_lib1.c in Section 24.6. Therefore the files which use it need no modification, i.e. Program 24_1, header file stu_lib.c and implementation file stu_lib.c needed no modification to use stu_lib2.c. A run of Program 24_1 using stu_lib2.c is presented at the end of the chapter.

25.3 Linked lists

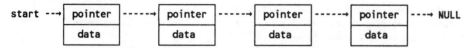

A linked list is a data structure where each element contains, in addition to any data, a pointer to the next element in the list. A pointer, start in the above diagram, points to the first element and the pointer of the final element points to NULL (which indicates the end of the list). Linked lists can be single linked (as above) or double linked with each element containing a link to the previous as well as the following element. Operations which can be carried out on linked lists include:

Create first element create an element (using malloc or calloc)
                    point start to the element, point pointer of the element to 0

Insert element   create new element (using malloc or calloc)
               if inserting at start of list
                    copy start to pointer of new element
                    point start to a new element
               else
                    if adding on end of list
                         point pointer of last element in existing list to a new element
                         point pointer of new element to NULL
                      else (inserting in middle of list)
                         copy pointer of previous element to pointer of new element
                         point pointer of previous element to new element

Delete element   if first element
                    copy pointer of element being deleted to start
               else
                    copy pointer of element being deleted to pointer of previous element
               delete element using free.

Implementation file stu_lib3.c (below) is an implementation of the student records system of Section 24.6 using a linked list to store the records.

```
1 /* Implementation file stu_lib3.c - ADT: store records using a linked list    */
2
3 #include <stdio.h>                                  /* standard headers */
4 #include <stdlib.h>
5 #include "stu_lib.h"                      /* include student records header file */
6
7 /* define a type to hold the student records in a linked list */
8 typedef struct S {
9                  struct S *p_next;                    /* pointer to next record */
10                 Student student;                 /* current student record */
11                 }
12               Link;
13
14 static Link *p_students_start = NULL,     /* pointer to first record in list */
15              *p_students_last = NULL;     /* pointer to last record in list */
```

Implementation file stu_lib3.c ADT: store student records using a linked list

```
16
17  /*-------------------------------------------------------------------*/
18  /* return pointer to record for next student record in the data structure  */
19  /*    if reset_to_start is TRUE reset to first student record         */
20  /*    if past end of records return NULL pointer to indicate failure  */
21  Student *stu_next(const int reset_to_start)
22  {
23      static Link *p_next_student = NULL;  /* pointer to current record in list */
24      static Student *p_student;
25
26      if (reset_to_start) p_next_student = p_students_start; /* reset pointer ? */
27      if (p_next_student == NULL) return NULL;    /* if end of list return NULL */
28      p_student = &(p_next_student->student);             /* point to record */
29      p_next_student = p_next_student->p_next;         /* point to next record */
30      return p_student;                            /* return pointer to record */
31  }
32
33  /*-------------------------------------------------------------------*/
34  /* Store student record into data structure                          */
35  /*    return 0 allocation failed, 1 stored OK or 2 replaced existing record  */
36  int stu_store(const Student *student)
37  {
38      Link *p_new_record;                    /* will point to new record created */
39      Student *p_student = stu_next(1);         /* get pointer to first record */
40
41      /* loop searching for record or NULL (end of records) */
42      while (p_student != NULL)
43          if (stu_name(p_student, student->name))       /* found same name ? */
44              {
45              *p_student = *student;                  /* yes, replace record */
46              return 2;                         /* return 2 indicating replace */
47              }
48          else
49              p_student = stu_next(0);         /* get pointer to next record */
50
51      /* not found create new record, if fail return 0 */
52      if ((p_new_record = (Link *) calloc(1, sizeof(Link))) == NULL) return 0;
53
54      /* if first record set up p_students_start else set up p_students_last */
55      if (p_students_start == NULL) p_students_start = p_new_record;
56      else                          p_students_last->p_next = p_new_record;
57      p_students_last = p_new_record;            /* point last to new record */
58      p_new_record->p_next = NULL;                /* point new to NULL */
59      p_new_record->student = *student;                /* store record */
60      return 1;                                    /* return success */
61  }
```

Implementation file stu_lib3.c ADT: store student records using a linked list

In stu_lib3.c lines 8 to 12 define a type, Link, which is a structure one of whose members is a pointer to the same type, i.e. a pointer to the next record in the linked list. This is achieved by using the tag s for the structure and then using it in the declaration of the first member, pointer p_next. The second member of the structure is of type Student (defined in "stu_lib.h") which holds the student record. Once defined the type Link is used to:

line 14 define p_students_start which will point to the first record in the linked list

line 15 define p_students_last which will point to the last record in the linked list.

The function stu_next, lines 21 to 31, returns either a pointer to the first record (if reset_to_start is true), the next in sequence or NULL if beyond the end of the records:

21   function header with one parameter reset_to_start, returns a pointer to Student
        if reset_to_start is *true* p_next_student is reset to point to the first record
        if beyond the end of records (at end of linked list) a NULL pointer is returned
23   define p_next_student which will point to the Link record to be returned
24   define p_student which will point to the Student data in the Link record
26   if reset_to_start is *true* reset p_next_student to point to first Link record
27   if p_next_student is equal to NULL it is past the end of the records, return NULL
28   copy address of Student data into p_student
29   point p_next_student to next Link record in the linked list
30   return p_student printer to the Student record.

The function stu_store, lines 36 to 61, attempts to create a new record and append it onto the end of the linked list. If student data is replaced in an existing record it returns 2, if a new record is created successfully it returns 1 and if memory allocation fails it returns 0. The sequence of statements is:

36   the function header with one parameter, student points to the record to be stored
38   define p_new_record, a pointer which will point to the new Link record
39-49   look for existing student record and replace it if found (as in stu_lib1.c)
52   call calloc to allocate one Link record (calloc zeros the storage)
        return 0 if allocation fails
55-56   allocation successful, set up pointers to the new record
        55 if new record is first in linked list, point p_students_start to it
        56 else point pointer of last record in linked list to new record
57   point p_students_last (pointer to last record) to new record
58   set pointer p_next in new record to NULL (this is the last record in the list)
59   copy student data into new record
60   return 1 for success.

Program 24_1, header file stu_lib.h and implementation file stu_lib.c (in Section 24.6) need no modifications to use stu_lib3.c. This illustrates the importance of having a clearly defined loosely coupled interface between a library and the programs which use it. Thus the underlying implementation may be changed extensively without effecting the code of functions which use it, so long as the interface, in terms of function names, parameters passed, results returned, etc., remains unchanged. A run of Program 24_1 is shown on the next page.

Exercise 25.1 (*see Appendix B for sample answer*)

Implement and test a queue ADT (a *first in first out* data structure) using a linked list.

A run of Program 24_1 using stu_lib2.c and stu_lib3.c gave:

```
Enter student name ? Jones, Sam ↵
   age ? 8 ↵
   course ? B.Sc Computer Science ↵
Data on 'Jones, Sam' stored
Enter student name ? Smith, Daisy ↵
   age ? 19 ↵
   course ? B.Sc Electrical Engineering ↵
Data on 'Smith, Daisy' stored
Enter student name ? Doe, John ↵
   age ? 19 ↵
   course ? B.Sc Mechanical Engineering ↵
Data on 'Doe, John' stored
Enter student name ? Jones, Sam ↵
   age ? 18 ↵
   course ? B.Sc Computer Science ↵
Data on 'Jones, Sam' replaced
Enter student name ? Jones, Sally ↵
   age ? 18 ↵
   course ? B.Sc Physics and Mathematics↵
Data on 'Jones, Sally' stored
Enter student name ? Adams, Simon ↵
   age ? 18 ↵
   course ? B.Sc Business Studies ↵
Data on 'Adams, Simon' stored
Enter student name ?  ↵
Find student name ? Jones, Sam ↵
     'Jones, Sam' data found, age 18
Find student name ? Smith, George ↵
     'Smith, George' data not found
Find student name ? Doe, John ↵
     'Doe, John' data found, age 19
Find student name ?  ↵
Print of all student records
   student name          age  course
   Jones, Sam            18   B.Sc Computer Scien
   Smith, Daisy          19   B.Sc Electrical Eng
   Doe, John             19   B.Sc Mechanical Eng
   Jones, Sally          20   B.Sc Physics and Ma
   Adams, Simon          18   B.Sc Business Studi
Write student records to file 'student.dat'
```

Problems for Chapter 25

1   Add a function to stu_lib3.c to delete a record (identified by name); note that special care must be taken when deleting the first or last record in the linked list. Add a function to sort the records by student name (see Exercise 19.1 for linear sort).

2   Implement the stack functions of Section 25.2 using a linked list.

26

Multi-dimensional arrays

26.1 Declaring and accessing multi-dimensional arrays

In C one can have arrays of any type and an array is itself just another type of object. It is therefore possible to define a type which is an array and then an array of that type, e.g.:

```
enum {ROWS = 2, COLUMNS = 3};
typedef float Row[COLUMNS];              /* type Row is a one-dimensional array */
Row matrix[ROWS];                        /* variable matrix is an array of type Row */
```

The array matrix is made up of two elements of type Row each of which is an array of three float elements. Alternatively matrix could be defined:

```
enum {ROWS = 2, COLUMNS = 3};
float matrix[ROWS][COLUMNS] ;            /* a two-dimensional array */
```

Alternatively one can define a new type Matrix and then variables of that type, e.g.:

```
enum {ROWS = 2, COLUMNS = 3};
typedef float Matrix[ROWS][COLUMNS];   /* type Matrix is a two-dimensional array */
Matrix matrix1, matrix2, matrix3;       /* define variables of type Matrix */
```

The contents of an array may be initialised with simple constants when it is defined:

```
enum {ROWS = 2, COLUMNS = 3};
float matrix[ROWS][COLUMNS] = { { 2, -1, 0} ,      /* initialise row 0 */
                               {-1,  0, 3} };      /* initialise row 1 */
```

Any elements not explicitly initialised will be initialised to 0. If an array is not initialised the element values are *undefined* if the array is local or zero if it is external or a static local. The simplest way to initialise all the elements of an array to zero is to explicitly initialise the first element matrix[0][0] to 0 then the remainder will be zeroed automatically:

```
enum {ROWS = 2, COLUMNS = 3};
float matrix[ROWS][COLUMNS] = {{0}};  /* two-dimensional array initialised to 0 */
```

The elements of a multi-dimensional array are accessed using integer subscripts, e.g. :

```
matrix[0][0] = 0.0f;                     /* zero first column of first row */
matrix[0][1] = 0.0f;                     /* zero second column of first row */
matrix[1][0] = 0.0f;                     /* zero first column of second row */
matrix[ROWS - 1][COLUMNS - 1] = 0.0f;    /* zero last column of last row */
```

Take care not to inadvertently use the comma operator when specifying array subscripts:

```
matrix[0,1] = 0.0f;                                              /* invalid */
```

This looks fine to a Pascal programmer and the expression matrix[0,1] is valid C code, i.e. the subscript [0,1] contains the comma operator and is evaluated as [1] which will access the array element matrix[1], the second row of matrix. In this case the assignment statement is invalid and would produce an error message, e.g. Microsoft C version 7.00:

```
25      matrix[0,1] = 0.0f;
***** X.C(25) : error C2106: '=' : left operand must be lvalue
```

Some compilers produce warnings when the comma operator is used in an array subscript, others just carry on and produce erroneous results, the cause of which can be very difficult to track down.

C stores multi-dimensional arrays in memory such that the rightmost subscript(s) varies fastest, i.e. a two-dimensional two row by three column matrix would be stored in memory as a sequence of three rows each two columns wide:

matrix[0] [0]	matrix[0] [1]	matrix[0] [2]	matrix[1] [0]	matrix[1] [1]	matrix[1] [2]

Thus a two-dimensional matrix is stored in memory as a one-dimensional array with C performing the subscript calculation (i * COLUMNS) + j to access the memory location storing element matrix[i][j] (where COLUMNS is the number of columns in the declaration matrix[ROWS][COLUMNS]). It is therefore important when sequentially accessing elements of a multi-dimensional array that the rightmost subscript(s) varies fastest (to access the memory sequentially thus taking maximum advantage of cache memories); e.g. to zero an array:

```
enum {ROWS = 2, COLUMNS = 3};
float matrix[ROWS][COLUMNS] ;                        /* a two-dimensional array */
int row_index, column_index;

for (row_index = 0; row_index < ROWS ; row_index++)
    for (column_index = 0; column_index < COLUMNS ; column_index++)
        matrix[row_index][column_index] = 0.0f;              /* zero element */
```

rather than (which accesses in row order):

```
for (column_index = 0; column_index < COLUMNS ; column_index++)
    for (row_index = 0; row_index < ROWS ; row_index++)
        matrix[row_index][column_index] = 0.0f;              /* zero element */
```

Accessing elements in the wrong order can be very inefficient leading to excessive traffic between the cache and main memory or even excessive paging in a virtual memory system, e.g. when processing with large arrays of 10000 * 10000 elements. Note that this is the opposite to Fortran which stores multi-dimensional arrays such that the leftmost subscript varies fastest, i.e. matrix[0] [0], matrix[1] [0], matrix[0] [1], matrix[1] [1], etc.

26.2 Multi-dimensional arrays as function parameters

When multi-dimensional arrays are passed as function parameters the number of elements in the right most indices must be specified in the function header, i.e. to access element matrix[i][j] the number of columns in the declaration matrix[ROWS][COLUMNS] must be known to perform the subscript calculation (i * COLUMNS) + j (the value of ROWS is not needed in this case).

For example, if the above two row by three column matrix is to be passed into a function the function header could appear:

```
void matrix_print(float array[2][3])
```

or:
```
void matrix_print(float array[][3])
```

with the number of elements in the left most index not specified. When the function is called the actual argument is just the array name, e.g.:

```
matrix_print(matrix);
```

Remember an array cannot be returned as a function result (see Section 19.4), although a pointer to an array may be, see implementation file matrix2.c in Section 26.4.

26.3 Functions to read, write and multiply a two-dimensional matrix

In order to multiply two matrices, c = a * b, the number of columns in the first matrix a must equal the number of rows in the second matrix b. The product matrix c will have the number of rows of a and the number of columns of b, i.e. if a is a_rows by a_columns and b is b_rows by b_columns the size of c will be a_rows by b_columns. The individual elements of c are given by:

$$c_{ij} = \sum_{k=1}^{n} a_{ik} * b_{kj} \qquad \text{where } n = \text{number of columns in matrix a (and rows in b)}$$

For example:

$$\begin{bmatrix} 2 & -1 & 0 \\ -1 & 0 & 3 \end{bmatrix} * \begin{bmatrix} 4 & 1 \\ 2 & 0 \\ -3 & 2 \end{bmatrix} = \begin{bmatrix} 6 & 2 \\ -13 & 5 \end{bmatrix}$$

Matrix multiplication is not commutative, i.e. a * b ≠ b * a. For example

$$\begin{bmatrix} 4 & 1 \\ 2 & 0 \\ -3 & 2 \end{bmatrix} * \begin{bmatrix} 2 & -1 & 0 \\ -1 & 0 & 3 \end{bmatrix} = \begin{bmatrix} 7 & -4 & 3 \\ 4 & -2 & 0 \\ -8 & 3 & 6 \end{bmatrix}$$

Even the product of square matrices is generally not commutative, e.g.:

$$\begin{bmatrix} 1 & 0 \\ -1 & 2 \end{bmatrix} * \begin{bmatrix} -1 & 0 \\ 0 & 2 \end{bmatrix} = \begin{bmatrix} -1 & 0 \\ 1 & 4 \end{bmatrix}$$

$$\begin{bmatrix} -1 & 0 \\ 0 & 2 \end{bmatrix} * \begin{bmatrix} 1 & 0 \\ -1 & 2 \end{bmatrix} = \begin{bmatrix} -1 & 0 \\ -2 & 4 \end{bmatrix}$$

The following pages show header file matrix1.h and implementation file matrix1.c which contain functions to read, write and multiply two-dimensional matrices (line numbers in implementation file matrix1.c):

matrix_read   lines 8 to 23, reads the size of the matrix and then the matrix values
matrix_print   lines 25 to 36, prints the name, size and values of a matrix
matrix_multiply   lines 38 to 63, multiplies matrices a and b and returns the result in c.

```
 1 /* Header matrix1.h - header for 2D matrix read, write & multiply functions  */
 2 /*      arrays stored as normal C two-dimensional arrays                 */
 3
 4 /* define maximum matrix size and new type to hold a two-dimensional matrix  */
 5 enum {MAX_ROWS = 10, MAX_COLUMNS = 10};
 6 typedef float Matrix[MAX_ROWS][MAX_COLUMNS];
 7
 8 /* Read matrix name, number of rows and columns and then the matrix values  */
 9 void matrix_read(const char name,
10                    Matrix matrix, int *const rows, int *const columns);
11
12 /* print matrix name, size and the contents of matrix[rows,columns]      */
13 void matrix_print(const char name,
14                    const Matrix matrix, const int rows, const int columns);
15
16 /* multiply matrix a[a_rows][a_columns] by matrix b[b_rows][b_columns]    */
17 int matrix_multiply(const Matrix a, const int a_rows, const int a_columns,
18                    const Matrix b, const int b_rows, const int b_columns,
19                    Matrix c, int *const p_c_rows, int *const p_c_columns);
```

Header file matrix1.h For two-dimensional matrix read, write and multiply

```
 1 /* Implementation file matrix1.c, 2D matrix read, write & multiply functions */
 2 /*      arrays stored as normal C two-dimensional arrays                 */
 3
 4 #include <stdlib.h>
 5 #include <stdio.h>
 6 #include "matrix1.h"                           /* include own header file */
 7
 8 /*-----------------------------------------------------------------------*/
 9 /* Read matrix data - number of rows and columns and then the matrix values  */
10 void matrix_read
11   (const char name, Matrix matrix, int *const p_rows, int *const p_columns)
12 {
13     int row, column;
14
15     printf("\nEnter number of rows and columns in matrix %c ? ", name);
16     scanf("%d%d", p_rows, p_columns);              /* read row and column size */
17     for (row = 0 ; row < *p_rows ; row++)          /* now read matrix values */
18         {
19         printf("\nEnter row %d of %c (%d values) ? ", row, name, *p_columns);
20         for (column = 0 ; column < *p_columns ; column++)
21             scanf("%f", &matrix[row][column]);
22         }
23 }
24
25 /*-----------------------------------------------------------------------*/
```

Implementation file matrix1.c Two-dimensional matrix read, write and multiply

```
26 /* print matrix name, size and the contents of matrix[rows,columns]           */
27 void matrix_print
28    (const char name, const Matrix matrix, const int rows, const int columns)
29 {
30     int row, column;
31
32     printf("\nMatrix %c[%1d,%1d] values are:\n", name, rows, columns);
33     for (row = 0 ; row < rows ; printf("\n") , row++)
34       for (column = 0 ; column < columns ; column++)
35         printf("   %c[%1d,%1d] = %8.2f", name, row, column, matrix[row][column]);
36 }
37
38 /*------------------------------------------------------------------------*/
39 /* multiply matrix a[a_rows][a_columns] by matrix b[b_rows][b_columns]     */
40 /*  return result in matrix c[c_rows][c_columns]                           */
41 /*  function result is TRUE if multiply OK, else FALSE if failed           */
42 int matrix_multiply(const Matrix a, const int a_rows, const int a_columns,
43                     const Matrix b, const int b_rows, const int b_columns,
44                     Matrix c, int *const p_c_rows, int *const p_c_columns)
45 {
46     int i, j, k;                                    /* matrix indexes */
47
48     /* the number of rows in a must equal the number of columns in b */
49     if (a_columns != b_rows) return 0;              /* return, error ! */
50     /* OK, evaluate c as a matrix size c[a_rows][b_columns] */
51     *p_c_rows = a_rows;
52     *p_c_columns = b_columns;
53     for (i = 0 ; i < *p_c_rows ; i++)
54        for (j = 0 ; j < *p_c_columns ; j++)
55           {
56              c[i][j] = 0.0f;                        /* evaluate element c[i][j] */
57              for (k = 0 ; k < a_columns ; k++)
58                  /* evaluate c[i][j] = c[i][j] + a[i][k] * b[k][j] */
59                  c[i][j] += a[i][k] * b[k][j];
60           }
61     return 1;                                       /* return true for OK */
62 }
```

Implementation file matrix1.c Two-dimensional matrix read, write and multiply

In header file matrix1.h the sequence of statements is:

lines
5   use enum to define int constants which specify the maximum matrix size
6   define a new type Matrix, i.e. a float matrix size MAX_ROWS by MAX_COLUMNS
         this will be used to declare variables and formal parameters in function headers
8-19   declare function prototypes of the matrix manipulation functions.

In line 5 the constants MAX_ROWS and MAX_COLUMNS specify the maximum size of the matrices. The actual size used to hold data can be less than this with the size being passed between functions by integer variables, e.g. a_rows, a_columns, etc. Note that formal function parameters which should not be altered within the functions are const qualified.

Implementation file matrix1.c contains the definitions of the matrix manipulation functions. Function `matrix_read`, lines 10 to 23, reads the matrix name (one character), size and the values to be stored in the matrix:

10-11 `void matrix_read`
        `(const char name, Matrix matrix, int *const p_rows, int *const p_columns)`
      is the function header, the formal parameters are:
      `name`   (a const qualified `char`) holds the matrix name to be printed on the screen
      `matrix` (an array of type `Matrix`) returns the matrix values read
      `p_rows` (a const qualified pointer to an `int`) returns the number of rows read
      `p_columns` (a const qualified pointer to an `int`) returns the number of columns read
        (the pointers are used to *pass by reference*, further discussion below)
15-16 prompt user to enter the number of rows and columns and read the values
17-22 a `for` statement to read the rows of the matrix
     19   prompt user to enter a row of the matrix
     20-21   a `for` statement which reads the matrix values.

Because the size of the matrix (read in line 16) needs to be returned to the calling function, the formal parameters `p_rows` and `p_columns` are pointers and the corresponding actual parameters are *passed by reference*, i.e. using the `&` operator in lines 11 and 12 in `main` of Program 26_1 (see next page).

Function `matrix_print`, lines 27-36, prints the name, size and values stored in a matrix. The sequence of statements is:

27-28 `void matrix_print`
        `(const char name, const Matrix matrix, const int rows, const int columns)`
      is the function header, the formal parameters are:
      `name`   (a const qualified `char`) holds the matrix name to be printed on the screen
      `matrix` (a const qualified array of type `Matrix`) holds the matrix to be printed
      `rows`   (a const qualified `int`) holds the number of rows in `matrix`
      `columns` (a const qualified `int`) holds the number of columns in `matrix`
32   print the name and size of the matrix
33-35 prints the values of the matrix.
      Note the use of the comma operator in line 33 to print a newline after every row.

Function `matrix_multiply`, lines 42 to 62, multiplies two matrices a and b and returns the result in matrix c:

42-44 `int matrix_multiply(const Matrix a, const int a_rows, const int a_columns,`
                     `const Matrix b, const int b_rows, const int b_columns,`
                     `Matrix c, int *const p_c_rows, int *const p_c_columns)`
      is the function header, the formal parameters are:
      `a`   (a const qualified array of type `Matrix`) holds the first matrix
      `a_rows` and `a_columns`   (const qualified `int`) holds the size of matrix a
      `b`   (a const qualified array of type `Matrix`) holds the second matrix
      `b_rows` and `b_columns`   (const qualified `int`) holds the size of matrix b
      `c`   (an array of type `Matrix`) returns the result of a `*` b
      `p_c_rows` and `p_c_columns` (const qualified pointers to `int`) returns the size of c
          the pointers are used to *pass by reference*, as in `matrix_read`

49   check if matrices can be multiplied, i.e. a_columns != b_rows
            if not return FALSE (zero) to indicate matrices cannot be multiplied
51-60   multiply matrices
        51-52   set up size of matrix c
        53-60   multiply a and b to give c
                note the use of the *compound assignment operator* += in line 59
                this is where the efficiency of such an operator can be used to good effect
                i.e. the subscript c[i] [j] need only be evaluated once
                line 58 contains a comment describing the operation performed in line 59
                matrix2.c shows how a pointer to c[i] [j] can make it even more efficient
61   return TRUE (non zero) to indicate multiply worked OK.

On return the function result of matrix_multiply can be checked for success or failure, see
Program 26_1.c (below). Input validation is not performed in matrix1.c (which would be
required in a real application) or checking for array subscript bounds overflow. In practice
array bounds checking would probably be included during program testing but may then be
removed to achieve faster run times (conditional selection directives are useful in this
context, see Section 18.5).

```
1  /* Program 26_1.c, test 2D matrix read, write and multiply in matrix1.c */
2
3  #include <stdio.h>
4  #include "matrix1.h"                              /* include matrix functions */
5
6  int main(void)
7  {
8      int a_rows, a_columns, b_rows, b_columns, c_rows, c_columns;
9      Matrix a, b, c;                               /* define matrices */
10
11     matrix_read('a', a, &a_rows, &a_columns);     /* read new a and b */
12     matrix_read('b', b, &b_rows, &b_columns);
13     matrix_print('a', a, a_rows, a_columns);      /* print a and b */
14     matrix_print('b', b, b_rows, b_columns);
15
16     printf("\nMultiply b * a");                   /* multiply b * a */
17     if (! matrix_multiply(
18          b, b_rows, b_columns, a, a_rows, a_columns, c, &c_rows, &c_columns))
19        printf("\nMatrix multiply failed a_rows <> b_columns\a\n");
20     else
21        {
22        matrix_print('c', c, c_rows, c_columns);         /* print c */
23        c[0] [0] = 100.0f;                    /* change element c[0] [0] */
24        c[1] [1] = 200.0f;                    /* change element c[1] [1] */
25        c[2] [2] = 300.0f;                    /* change element c[2] [2] */
26        matrix_print('c', c, c_rows, c_columns);         /* print c */
27        }
28     return 0;
29  }
```

Program 26_1 Test two-dimensional matrix read, write and multiply functions

Program 26_1 contains the main function to test the matrix read, write and multiply functions implemented in matrix1.c. The sequence of statements is:

4	include matrix.h header file for the matrix functions
8	define int variables to hold the size of the matrices
9	define matrices a, b and c (in fact pointers which will point to the arrays)
11-14	read data into matrices a and b and print the values read
17-18	multiply a by b to give matrix c
19	print error message if multiply failed (matrix_multiply returned *false* 0)
22	else if multiply was OK print c
23-25	assign new values to matrix[0] [0], [1] [1] and [2] [2]
26	print updated c.

A run of Program 26_1 gave (the input data for this run is in file c26\p26.dat on the disk):

```
Enter number of rows and columns in matrix a ? 2 3↵
Enter row 0 of a (3 values) ? 2 -1 0↵
Enter row 1 of a (3 values) ? -1 0 3↵
Enter number of rows and columns in matrix b ? 3 2↵
Enter row 0 of b (2 values) ? 4 1↵
Enter row 1 of b (2 values) ? 2 0↵
Enter row 2 of b (2 values) ? -3 2↵

Matrix a[2,3] values are:
  a[0,0] =    2.00   a[0,1] =   -1.00   a[0,2] =    0.00
  a[1,0] =   -1.00   a[1,1] =    0.00   a[1,2] =    3.00

Matrix b[3,2] values are:
  b[0,0] =    4.00   b[0,1] =    1.00
  b[1,0] =    2.00   b[1,1] =    0.00
  b[2,0] =   -3.00   b[2,1] =    2.00

Multiply b * a
Matrix c[3,3] values are:
  c[0,0] =    7.00   c[0,1] =   -4.00   c[0,2] =    3.00
  c[1,0] =    4.00   c[1,1] =   -2.00   c[1,2] =    0.00
  c[2,0] =   -8.00   c[2,1] =    3.00   c[2,2] =    6.00

Matrix c[3,3] values are:
  c[0,0] =  100.00   c[0,1] =   -4.00   c[0,2] =    3.00
  c[1,0] =    4.00   c[1,1] =  200.00   c[1,2] =    0.00
  c[2,0] =   -8.00   c[2,1] =    3.00   c[2,2] =  300.00
```

26.4 Dynamically allocating multi-dimensional arrays

The problem with the built-in multi-dimensional array handling is that the compiler has to know (at compile time) the number of elements in the right most indices when arrays are passed as function parameters. For example, in file matrix1.c functions matrix_read, matrix_write and matrix_multiply know that type Matrix is a 10 by 10 array. This enables the subscript calculation (i * 10) + j to access the memory location storing element matrix[i] [j] to be performed within the function. The size of the actual array stored in the type Matrix is then passed to/from functions via parameters, e.g. parameters rows and columns in the case of function matrix_print. When using the built-in multi-dimensional array handling in C there is no way of specifying the array size at run time (as in Fortran).

Mathematical and scientific applications need to process two-dimensional arrays ranging from a small two by two to large 10000 by 10000. Allocating the largest possible size (ten by ten for type Matrix in matrix1.c) is very inefficient. One either wastes storage (a two by three matrix would only use six elements of the 100 allocated to a variable of type Matrix) or, sooner or later, one has an application where the data is too large to fit the allocated size.

The usual way to get around the problem is to dynamically allocate (using malloc, calloc, etc.) a one-dimensional array of sufficient size to hold the multi-dimensional array and then perform the subscript calculations oneself. For example, function matrix_read could read the number of rows and columns and then call malloc to allocate storage:

```
float *matrix_read(const char name, int *const p_rows, int *const p_columns)
{
    float *matrix;                              /* pointer to new matrix */
    int row, column;                            /* row and column indexes */
    printf("\nEnter number of rows and columns in matrix %c ? ", name);
    scanf("%d%d", p_rows, p_columns);           /* read row and column size */
    matrix = (float *) malloc(*p_rows * *p_columns * sizeof(float));    /* allocate */
```

This defines variable matrix (a pointer to float), reads the size of the new matrix and then calls malloc to allocate a float array size *p_rows by *p_columns (the result of malloc is cast to float * and assigned to matrix). The remainder of the function is then:

```
    for (row = 0 ; row < *p_rows ; row++)              /* now read matrix values */
        {
        printf("\nEnter row %d of %c (%d values) ? ", row + 1, name, *p_columns);
        for (column = 0 ; column < *p_columns ; column++)
            scanf("%f", matrix + (row * *p_columns) + column);
        }
    return matrix;                              /* return pointer to new matrix */
}
```

In the call to scanf the expression matrix + (row * *p_columns) + column yields a pointer to element [row] [column] (as an offset from the pointer matrix). This code is performing a similar subscript calculation to that performed automatically when using the built-in C multi-dimensional arrays. The return returns (as a function result) a pointer to the new matrix. This function could be used as follows:

```
    int a_rows, a_columns;                      /* holds size of new matrix */
    float *a;                                   /* pointer to new matrix */
    a = matrix_read('a', &a_rows, &a_columns);  /* read new matrix a */
```

In the above code the majority of pointer names start with p_, the exceptions are pointers to arrays (matrix and a). This is to maintain consistency with 'normal' array names which, although constant pointers to the first element, have not started with p_. This practice will be followed in the remainder of the chapater.

The following pages show header file matrix2.h and implementation file matrix2.c which contains 2D matrix functions using the above technique. Note that subscripts start from 1 (1 is subtracted from the row and column values when performing subscript calculations). This gives a more natural interface (in that most mathematical algorithms start subscripts from 1) making the slight overhead in subscript calculations worthwhile.

In header file matrix2.h line 6 defines a new type Matrix which is a float * (pointer to float) and lines 8 to 29 declare function prototypes of the matrix manipulation functions.

Function `matrix_create` allocates an array of size `rows` * `columns`. To access a particular element `[row]` `[column]` the following function could be used:

```
/* return pointer to element matrix[row][column] subscripts start from [1][1] */
float *matrix(Matrix matrix, const int row, const int column, const int columns)
   {    return matrix + ((row - 1) * columns) + (column - 1);  }
```

This returns a `float` * pointing to element `[row]` `[column]` of the matrix pointed to by `matrix`; 1 has to be subtracted from `row` and `column` (subscripts start from 1). The problem is that accessing matrix elements should be as efficient as possible and the function call adds a significant overhead (creating/initialising the parameters and function call/return). In such a case (where efficiency is critical) it is worthwhile implementing it using a preprocessor macro (see Section 16.13), i.e. lines 16 and 17 of matrix1.h.

```
#define matrix(matrix, row, column, columns) \
          ((matrix) + ((row) - 1) * (columns) + (column) - 1)
```

The () are required to force the correct expansion of the macro when used in expressions such as (see discussion in Section 16.13):

```
*matrix(a, i - 2, j - 2, a_columns) = 100.0f;    /* change contents of element */
```

```
 1 /* Header matrix2.h - header for 2D matrix read, write and multiply functions */
 2 /*       dynamically allocate 2D matrix stored using a pointer to an 1D array  */
 3 /*       to simplify use matrix subscripts start from [1][1]                   */
 4
 5 /* define type Matrix, i.e. float * - a pointer to an array of float elements */
 6 typedef float *Matrix;
 7
 8 /* create a Matrix size rows by columns, return pointer to new matrix         */
 9 Matrix matrix_create(const int rows, const int columns);
10
11 /* free memory allocated to the matrix                                        */
12 void matrix_delete(Matrix matrix);
13
14 /* return pointer to element matrix[row][column] subscripts start from [1][1] */
15 /*  use preprocessor macro - more efficient being expanded inline             */
16 #define matrix(p_matrix, row, column, columns) \
17             ((p_matrix) + ((row) - 1) * (columns) + (column) - 1)
18
19 /* Read matrix data - number of rows and columns and then the matrix values   */
20 Matrix matrix_read(const char name, int *const p_rows, int *const p_columns);
21
22 /* function to print name and the contents of a matrix[rows,columns]          */
23 void matrix_print
24    (const char name, const Matrix matrix, const int rows, const int columns);
25
26 /* multiply matrix a[a_rows][a_columns] by matrix b[b_rows][b_columns]         */
27 Matrix matrix_multiply(const Matrix a, const int a_rows, const int a_columns,
28                        const Matrix b, const int b_rows, const int b_columns,
29                        int *const p_c_rows, int *const p_c_columns);
```

Header file matrix2.h 2D matrix functions using dynamic memory allocation

```
 1 /* Implementation file matrix2.c, 2D matrix read, write & multiply functions */
 2 /*       dynamically allocate 2D matrix stored using a pointer to an 1D array */
 3 /*       to simplify use matrix subscripts start from [1][1]                  */
 4
 5 #include <stdio.h>                              /* standard I/O header */
 6 #include <stdlib.h>                             /* for calloc, etc. */
 7 #include "matrix2.h"                            /* include own header file */
 8
 9 /*---------------------------------------------------------------------*/
10 /* create a Matrix size rows by columns, return pointer to new float matrix   */
11 Matrix matrix_create(const int rows, const int columns)
12   { return (float *) malloc((rows * columns) * sizeof(float)); }
13
14 /* free memory allocated to the matrix                                        */
15 void matrix_delete(Matrix matrix)
16   { free(matrix); }
17
18 /*---------------------------------------------------------------------*/
19 /* Read matrix data - number of rows and columns and then the matrix values   */
20 /* return pointer to new matrix (function result) & size in rows and columns  */
21 Matrix matrix_read(const char name, int *const p_rows, int *const p_columns)
22 {
23     int row, column;
24     Matrix matrix;                             /* pointer to new matrix */
25
26     printf("\nEnter number of rows and columns in matrix %c ? ", name);
27     scanf("%d%d", p_rows, p_columns);          /* read row and column size */
28     matrix = matrix_create(*p_rows, *p_columns);      /* create new matrix */
29
30     for (row = 1 ; row <= *p_rows ; row++)            /* now read matrix values */
31         {
32         printf("\nEnter row %d of %c (%d values) ? ", row, name, *p_columns);
33         for (column = 1; column <= *p_columns ; column++)
34             scanf("%f", matrix(matrix, row, column, *p_columns));
35         }
36     return matrix;                             /* return pointer to new matrix */
37 }
38
39 /*---------------------------------------------------------------------*/
40 /* function to print name and the contents of a matrix[rows,columns]          */
41 void matrix_print
42   (const char name, const Matrix matrix, const int rows, const int columns)
43 {
44     int row, column;
45     printf("\nMatrix %c[%1d,%1d] values are:\n", name, rows, columns);
46     for (row = 1; row <= rows ; printf("\n") , row++)
47         for (column = 1; column <= columns ; column++)
48             printf("  %c[%1d,%1d] = %8.2f",
49                 name, row, column, *matrix(matrix, row, column, columns));
50 }
```

Implementation file matrix2.c 2D matrix functions using dynamic memory allocation

```
51
52 /*--------------------------------------------------------------*/
53 /* multiply matrix a[a_rows][a_columns] by matrix b[b_rows][b_columns]    */
54 /*  function result: return pointer to new matrix if OK or NULL if failed  */
55 /*     if OK update c_rows and c_columns with size of new matrix           */
56 Matrix matrix_multiply(const Matrix a, const int a_rows, const int a_columns,
57                   const Matrix b, const int b_rows, const int b_columns,
58                   int *const p_c_rows, int *const p_c_columns)
59 {
60     int i, j, k;                                /* matrix indexes */
61     Matrix c;                              /* pointer to new matrix */
62
63     /* the number of rows in a must equal the number of columns in b */
64     if (a_columns != b_rows) return NULL;            /* error, return NULL */
65     /* OK, evaluate c as a matrix size c[a_rows][b_columns] */
66     *p_c_rows = a_rows;
67     *p_c_columns = b_columns;
68     c = matrix_create(*p_c_rows, *p_c_columns);       /* create new matrix */
69     for (i = 1 ; i <= *p_c_rows ; i++)
70       for (j = 1 ; j <= *p_c_columns ; j++)
71         {                                     /* evaluate element c[i][j] */
72         float *p_cij = matrix(c, i, j, *p_c_columns);    /* point to c[i][j] */
73         *p_cij = 0.0f;
74         for (k = 1; k <= a_columns ; k++)
75             /* evaluate c[i][j] = c[i][j] + a[i][k] * b[k][j] */
76             *p_cij += *matrix(a, i, k, a_columns) * *matrix(b, k, j, b_columns);
77         }
78     return c;                              /* return pointer to new matrix */
79 }
```

Implementation file matrix2.c 2D matrix functions using dynamic memory allocation

Implementation file matrix2.c contains the definitions of the 2D matrix manipulation functions using dynamic memory allocation. Function matrix_create, lines 11 to 12, creates a matrix and returns (as a function result) a pointer to the allocated storage:

11 header, create matrix size rows by columns
12 call malloc to create a float array size rows * columns
      and return (as function result) a pointer to the new array allocated.

Note that no check is performed to ensure that malloc allocated the required storage; in a real application this would be required, i.e. to check the result of malloc for being NULL.

Function matrix_delete, lines 15 and 16, calls free to deallocate the storage allocated to matrix. It is important that the user program calls matrix_delete when a matrix is finished with, see Program 26_2. A common fault is to forget to free allocated storage (e.g. when calling matrix_multiply a number of times) and one ends running out of storage.

Function matrix_read, lines 21 to 37, is similar to that in matrix1.c except that matrix_create is called to allocate storage, macro matrix is called to perform subscript calculations and subscripts start from 1 (in the for statements, etc.):

24   define local variable matrix which will point to new matrix
26-27   prompt user to enter the number of rows and columns and read the values
28   call matrix_create to allocate storage for new matrix
30-35   a for statement to read the rows of the matrix
      32   prompt user to enter a row of the matrix
      33-34   a for statement which reads element [row] [column]
36   return the value of matrix, a pointer to the new matrix.

Function matrix_print, lines 41 to 50, is similar to that in matrix1.c except that macro matrix is called to perform subscript calculations and the subscripts start from 1.

Function matrix_multiply, lines 56 to 79, multiplies two matrices a and b and returns a pointer (as a function result) to the new matrix:

64   check if matrices can be multiplied, i.e. a_columns != b_rows
      if not return NULL to indicate matrices cannot be multiplied
66-77   multiply matrices a and b
      66-68   set up size of new matrix and call matrix_create to allocate storage
      70-77   multiply a and b
78   return pointer to new matrix.

Note the use of the pointer p_cij which is defined in line 72 and pointed to element matrix[i][j]. This saves evaluating matrix(c, i, j, *p_c_columns) every time line 76 is executed within the for statement in lines 74 to 76.

Program 26_2 (next page), which is similar to Program 26_1, tests the 2D matrix functions in matrix2.h and matrix2.c. The sequence of statements is:

lines
5   include matrix2.h header file for the matrix functions
9   define int variables to hold the size of the matrices
10   define a, b and c to be of type Matrix, i.e. float *
12-13   call function matrix_read to read matrix data, assign results to a and b
14-15   print values stored in a and b
17-18   multiply a by b, assign result to matrix c
      19   print error message if multiply failed (i.e. matrix_read returned NULL)
    else
      22   if multiply was OK print c
      23-25   assign new values to c[1][1], c[2][2] and c[3][3]
            remember subscripts start from [1][1]
      26   print updated c
      27-28   print the contents of matrix c as a one-dimensional array
      29   deallocate matrix c
31-32   deallocate matrices a and b.

The printf statement in lines 27 and 28 shows how the matrix c is actually stored in memory (see sample run on next page), i.e. it is stored as a one-dimensional array and the functions in matrix2.h and matrix2.c provide an interface to enable user programs to manipulate it as a two-dimensional array.

```
 1 /* Program p26_2.c - test 2D matrix read, write and multiply in matrix2.c   */
 2 /*    note that in matrix2.c user subscripts start from [1][1]               */
 3
 4 #include <stdio.h>
 5 #include "matrix2.h"                                    /* matrix functions */
 6
 7 int main(void)
 8 {
 9     int i, a_rows, a_columns, b_rows, b_columns, c_rows, c_columns;
10     Matrix a, b, c;
11
12     a = matrix_read('a', &a_rows, &a_columns);          /* read new a and b */
13     b = matrix_read('b', &b_rows, &b_columns);
14     matrix_print('a', a, a_rows, a_columns);            /* print a and b */
15     matrix_print('b', b, b_rows, b_columns);
16     printf("\nMultiply b * a");                         /* multiply b * a */
17     if (NULL == (c = matrix_multiply(                   /* failed ? */
18             b, b_rows, b_columns, a, a_rows, a_columns, &c_rows, &c_columns)))
19         printf("\nMatrix multiply failed a_rows <> b_columns\a\n");
20     else
21         {
22         matrix_print('c', c, c_rows, c_columns);            /* print c */
23         *matrix(c, 1, 1, c_columns) = 100.0f;       /* change c[1][1] */
24         *matrix(c, 2, 2, c_columns) = 200.0f;       /* change c[2][2] */
25         *matrix(c, 3, 3, c_columns) = 300.0f;       /* change c[3][3] */
26         matrix_print('c', c, c_rows, c_columns);            /* print c */
27         for (i = 0; i < c_rows * c_columns; i++)        /* and 1D array */
28             printf("%6.2f ", c[i]);                     /* storing c */
29         matrix_delete(c);                               /* delete c */
30         }
31     matrix_delete(a);                                   /* delete a */
32     matrix_delete(b);                                   /* delete b */
33     return 0;
34 }
```

Program 26_2 test 2D matrix functions using dynamic memory allocation

A run of Program 26_2 gave (remember subscripts start from [1][1]):

```
Enter number of rows and columns in matrix a ? 2 3↵
Enter row 1 of a (3 values) ? 2 -1 0↵
Enter row 2 of a (3 values) ? -1 0 3↵
Enter number of rows and columns in matrix b ? 3 2↵
Enter row 1 of b (2 values) ? 4 1↵
Enter row 2 of b (2 values) ? 2 0↵
Enter row 3 of b (2 values) ? -3 2↵

Matrix a[2,3] values are:
   a[1,1] =    2.00   a[1,2] =   -1.00   a[1,3] =    0.00
   a[2,1] =   -1.00   a[2,2] =    0.00   a[2,3] =    3.00
Matrix b[3,2] values are:
   b[1,1] =    4.00   b[1,2] =    1.00
   b[2,1] =    2.00   b[2,2] =    0.00
   b[3,1] =   -3.00   b[3,2] =    2.00
```

```
Multiply b * a
Matrix c[3,3] values are:
    c[1,1] =      7.00    c[1,2] =     -4.00    c[1,3] =      3.00
    c[2,1] =      4.00    c[2,2] =     -2.00    c[2,3] =      0.00
    c[3,1] =     -8.00    c[3,2] =      3.00    c[3,3] =      6.00

Matrix c[3,3] values are:
    c[1,1] =    100.00    c[1,2] =     -4.00    c[1,3] =      3.00
    c[2,1] =      4.00    c[2,2] =    200.00    c[2,3] =      0.00
    c[3,1] =     -8.00    c[3,2] =      3.00    c[3,3] =    300.00
100.00  -4.00    3.00    4.00 200.00    0.00  -8.00    3.00 300.00
```

The final line of the output shows how the matrix c is stored as a one-dimensional array.

26.5 Two-dimensional arrays using an array of pointers to row data

The main problem with the above 2D matrix technique is the time taken to perform the subscript calculation matrix + (row * columns) + column (requiring a multiplication and two additions). An alternative technique is to use two arrays:

1   a 1D array to hold the 2D matrix as a sequence of rows (as in matrix2.c)
2   a 1D array of pointers which point to the start of each row in the above array.

For example, the 3 row by 2 column array b used in the above program test run would appear so (subscripts from [0] [0]):

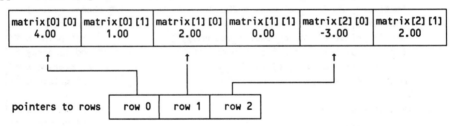

Assuming the array holding the pointers to the rows is called matrix the subscript calculation now becomes:

        matrix[row] + column

matrix[row] yields the address of the start of the row and matrix[row] + column yields the address of element matrix[row] [column]. Using this technique there is one array access and one addition to obtain the address of a particular matrix element (which should be faster than a multiplication and two additions).

   Header file matrix3.h (next page) and implementation file matrix3.c (next page but one) contain the code using this technique. In header file matrix3.h the type Matrix is defined (in line 8) as float ** (a pointer to a pointer to float); a variable of this type will point to the start of an array of pointers of type float *, each element of which points to the start of a row in an array which holds the matrix data (as a sequence of float elements in row order). The remainder of the file is similar to Header File matrix2.h except for the preprocessor macro matrix, line 18, which returns a pointer to element matrix[row] [column]; note that it does not need the parameter columns (as did the version in matrix2.c), this not being required to do the subscript calculation.

```
 1 /* Header file matrix3.h - for 2D matrix read, write and multiply functions */
 2 /* This version dynamically allocates two arrays:                           */
 3 /*   (a) a 1D array to hold the 2D matrix as a sequence of rows              */
 4 /*   (b) a 1D array of pointers which point to the start of each row in (a)  */
 5 /* to simplify use matrix subscripts start from [1][1]                       */
 6
 7 /* type Matrix, i.e. float ** - a pointer to an array of pointers to float   */
 8 typedef float **Matrix;
 9
10 /* create a Matrix size rows by columns, return pointer to new matrix        */
11 Matrix matrix_create(const int rows, const int columns);
12
13 /* free memory allocated to the matrix                                       */
14 void matrix_delete(Matrix matrix);
15
16 /* return pointer to element matrix[row][column] subscripts start from [1][1] */
17 /*     use preprocessor macro - more efficient being expanded inline          */
18 #define matrix(matrix, row, column) ((matrix)[(row)] + (column))
19
20 /* Read matrix data - number of rows and columns and then the matrix values  */
21 Matrix matrix_read(const char name, int *const p_rows, int *const p_columns);
22
23 /* function to print name and the contents of a matrix[rows,columns]         */
24 void matrix_print
25    (const char name, const Matrix matrix, const int rows, const int columns);
26
27 /* multiply matrix a[a_rows][a_columns] by matrix b[b_rows][b_columns]        */
28 Matrix matrix_multiply(const Matrix a, const int a_rows, const int a_columns,
29                        const Matrix b, const int b_rows, const int b_columns,
30                        int *const p_c_rows, int *const p_c_columns);
```

Header file matrix3.h 2D matrix functions using dynamic memory allocation

In implementation file matrix3.c (next page) function matrix_create, lines 13 to 27, creates a matrix and returns (as a function result) a pointer to the allocated storage:

13   header, create matrix size rows by columns
17   allocate array matrix of type float size rows * columns + 1 to hold matrix data
19   allocate array row_array of type float * size rows + 1 which will point to row data
21-25   a for which points the row_array pointers to the row data in matrix
        23   point pointer row_array[i] to start of row i in matrix
        24   increment matrix to point at start of next row
26   returns a pointer to the array of pointers to the rows.

To enable row and column subscripts to start from 1 an extra element is allocated to both arrays (this saves having to subtract 1 when doing subscript calculations), i.e. in the following subscript calculation the first element of both arrays is never accessed:

    matrix[row] + column

Function matrix_delete, lines 30 to 34, deletes a matrix:

32   call free to deallocate array which holds the matrix data
33   calls free to deallocate the array of pointers to the row data.

```
 1 /* Implementation file matrix3.c, 2D matrix read, write & multiply functions */
 2 /* This version dynamically allocates two arrays:                            */
 3 /*   (a) a 1D array to hold the 2D matrix as a sequence of rows              */
 4 /*   (b) a 1D array of pointers which point to the start of each row in (a)  */
 5 /* to simplify use matrix subscripts start from [1][1]                       */
 6
 7 #include <stdlib.h>
 8 #include <stdio.h>
 9 #include "matrix3.h"                             /* include own header file */
10
11 /*-----------------------------------------------------------------------*/
12 /* create a Matrix size rows by columns, return pointer to new row array   */
13 Matrix matrix_create(const int rows, const int columns)
14 {
15     int i;
16     /* create array (size rows * columns) to hold matrix elements */
17     float *matrix = (float *) malloc((rows * columns + 1) * sizeof(float));
18     /* create array (size rows) of pointers to point to start of each row */
19     float **row_array = (float **) malloc((rows + 1) * sizeof(float *));
20     /* point row array at start of each row */
21     for (i = 1; i <= rows; i++)
22         {
23         row_array[i] = matrix;            /* set up pointer to start of row */
24         matrix+= columns;                  /* point at start of next row */
25         }
26     return row_array;                      /* return pointer to row array */
27 }
28
29 /* free memory allocated to the matrix                                      */
30 void matrix_delete(Matrix matrix)
31 {
32     free(matrix[1]);                       /* delete array holding column data */
33     free(matrix);            /* delete array of pointers pointing to columns */
34 }
35
            remainder of file similar to matrix2.c (except for calls to matrix)
```

Implementation file matrix3.c 2D matrix functions using dynamic memory allocation

The remainder of matrix3.c is similar to matrix2.c except the calls to matrix have three parameters instead of four.   The files matrix3.h and matrix3.c are on the disk which accompanies this text together with Program 26_3.c which can be used to test them. This program is similar to Program 26_2.c except that the number of parameters in the calls to matrix is reduced from four to three and lines 27 and 28 become:

```
        for (i = 0; i <= c_rows*c_columns; i++)          /* and 1D array */
            printf("%6.2f ", *(c[1] + i));                /* storing c */
```

Remember c[0] is not used. The final line of a run under Turbo C V3.00 gave:

```
  0.00 100.00  -4.00    3.00    4.00 200.00    0.00  -8.00    3.00 300.00
```

The first element of the array pointed to by c[1] is not used!

26.6 Efficiency considerations when manipulating matrices

Multi-dimensional matrices are used in many mathematical, engineering and scientific applications. The matrices concerned are often very large and many operations are performed upon them. In addition to making the matrix manipulation functions easy to use, efficiency in accessing individual matrix elements and implementing algorithms is of major importance if optimum run times are to be achieved. The previous sections have shown various techniques for implementing two-dimensional matrices. On the disk which accompanies this text are files time1.c, time2.c and time3.c (in directory c26) which were used to compare matrix1.c, matrix2.c, etc. when performing multiple loops carrying out matrix multiply and subscript operations. The loops were timed using the clock() function in a similar way to Program 16_5 in Chapter 16. The following table presents some results (in seconds) making calls to matrix_multiply and matrix using DJ's port of GNU V2.6.3 on an IBM PC compatible Pentium P133.

	matrix1	matrix2	matrix3
matrix multiply	4.8	15.2	17.2
matrix index	2.7	5.6	4.2

It can be seen that matrix1.c, using the built-in two-dimensional array handling of C, is the fastest (one would expect that the compiler would use the most efficient handling technique to suit the architecture of the machine concerned). The matrix index test shows clearly that the subscript calculation technique used in matrix3.c (matrix[row] + column) is more efficient than that used in matrix2.c (matrix + (row * columns) + column). The matrix_multiply test shows that matrix2.c was faster than matrix3.c; probably due to the time taken to create and initialise the matrices in matrix_create and delete them in matrix_delete. The above tests were run using a number of compilers on a number of machines. In general, the results were similar to the above but on a few systems matrix3 was faster on both tests. In addition, different compilers on the same machine gave varying results (halving the overall run times in some cases). This shows that efficiency gains are not easy to achieve, a simple change in an algorithm or the way a complex data set is structured or a change of compiler or processor can make orders of magnitude difference in run times.

Problem for Chapter 26

1 Implement the algorithms of matrix2.c and matrix3.c in assembly language. Compare the performance (using the programs in files time2.c and time3.c) with the C versions.

2 Extend Program 26_1 to evaluate the transpose of a matrix $c_{ji} = a_{ij}$ interchanging the rows and columns of a matrix, e.g.:

$$X = \begin{bmatrix} 1 & 0 \\ -6 & 5 \\ 3 & 2 \end{bmatrix} \qquad X^T = \begin{bmatrix} 1 & -6 & 3 \\ 0 & 5 & 2 \end{bmatrix}$$

Additional functions could be implemented to evaluate the determinant of a square matrix, inverse of a square matrix, etc.

Evaluating mathematical series

The summation of an infinite series or the evaluation of algorithms which involve an infinite number of iterations are common in many mathematical, scientific and engineering applications. The chapter introduces programming techniques for solving such problems.

27.1 Truncating infinite series

Consider the Taylor series for the sine function `sin(x)` (where x is an angle in radians):

$$\sin(x) = x - \frac{x^3}{3!} + \frac{x^5}{5!} - \frac{x^7}{7!} + \frac{x^9}{9!} \cdots \cdots \qquad x^2 < \infty$$

Although the series is infinite, in practice it is terminated after calculating a certain number of terms (five or ten or fifty or ten thousand) when it is deemed (somehow) that the summation has achieved a value which is sufficiently accurate. The terms omitted (which are infinite in number) introduce an error into the result caused by the truncation of an infinite process. This is acceptable so long as the contribution from the remaining terms in the truncated series is less than the required accuracy.

Series such as the sine function are well suited to evaluation using `while`, `do` or `for` statements. The problem facing the programmer is when to terminate the iterative process. For example, using a simple `for` statement with one hundred loops could either result in doing too many loops (if the result is sufficiently accurate after ten iterations) or too few (the series needs to be summed for ten thousand loops). A technique commonly used is to terminate the iterative process when the absolute value of a particular term becomes less than the accuracy required, i.e.:

  | value of nth term | < ACCURACY   terminate the iteration.

When evaluating the sine series, the iterative process is terminated when the contribution of x^n / n! becomes so small that it can be ignored (typically ACCURACY is between 10^{-6} and 10^{-9}). This technique is suitable for terminating the sine series where the result is in the range -1.0 to +1.0. Problems can occur, however, when the summation results in a very small number (the result is of the same order of magnitude as ACCURACY) or a very large number (looking for changes of 10^{-6} in a figure of 10^9). An alternative technique is to examine the contribution of the current term relative to the summation so far:

  | value of nth term / sum of series so far | < ACCURACY   terminate iterations.

This fails if the sum becomes zero, i.e. division by 0 occurs. An alternative is:

  | value of nth term | < | ACCURACY * sum of series so far | terminate iterations.

A more exacting requirement may be that one of the above criteria is satisfied for a minimum of ten (or more) iterations, then the process terminates. The precise techniques used depend on how well conditioned and convergent the formulas are; refer to a text on numerical methods for a full discussion (Press *et al.* 1994).

27.2 Program to evaluate the sine function sin(x)

```
 1 /* Program 27_1 - test sin(x) function */
 2
 3 #include <stdio.h>
 4 #include <math.h>
 5
 6 int main()
 7 {
 8     float sinf(const float x);                    /* function prototype of sinf */
 9     float x;                                      /* evaluate sin(x) */
10
11     while (printf("\nAngle (radians) ? ") , scanf("%f", &x) == 1)
12         printf(" sin = %20.8f, library = %12.8f ", sinf(x), sin(x));
13     return 0;
14 }
15
16 /*-----------------------------------------------------------------------*/
17 /* Function to evaluate sin(x) by summing the series (** is power):      */
18 /* sin(x) = x - (x**3 / 3!) + (x**5 / 5!) - (x**7 / 7!) + ..            */
19 float sinf(const float x)
20 {
21     const float ACCURACY = 1.0e-8f;               /* accuracy required */
22     float xsq = x * x,                            /* x squared */
23           sin_x = x,                              /* sum of sin(x) series */
24           n = 3.0f,                               /* start iterations at 3rd term */
25           term_n = x;                             /* value of nth term of series */
26
27     /*printf("              n              term_n              sin_x ");*/
28     do
29         {
30         term_n = -(term_n * xsq / (n * (n - 1)));  /* evaluate nth term */
31         sin_x = sin_x + term_n;                    /* add term */
32         n = n + 2;                                 /* next n */
33         /*printf("\n sin(%6.1f) %3d %24f %20f", x, n, term_n, sin_x);*/
34         }
35     while (fabs(term_n) > ACCURACY);               /* finished ? */
36     return sin_x;                                  /* yes, return result */
37 }
```

Program 27_1 Program to evaluate sin(x) and check using the library function

Program 27_1 evaluates the sine series:

$$\sin(x) = x - \frac{x^3}{3!} + \frac{x^5}{5!} - \frac{x^7}{7!} + \frac{x^9}{9!} \ldots \ldots \qquad x^2 < \infty$$

where n! is factorial n, see Program 13_2. Although each term of the series could be calculated independently, use can be made of the fact that each term has a simple relationship to the previous, i.e.:

$$\text{term}_n = \pm \frac{x^n}{n!} = -\text{term}_{n-1} * \frac{x^2}{n*(n-1)}$$

In function sinf the following float (single precision real) variables are used:

xsq   holds the value of x^2
sin_x   holds the current value of the sum of the series sin(x)
n   holds the number of the term being calculated (a float in case it becomes large)
term_n holds the value of the nth term of the series.

The sequence of statements in Program 27_1 is:

line
8   declare prototype of the function sinf
11-12   prompt the user to enter angle, read the value into variable x, if converted OK
           12 call sinf and the maths library function sin to evaluate sin(x)
19   header for function sinf, one float parameter, returns a float function result
21   define ACCURACY (const qualified) and initialise its value to required accuracy
22   define xsq and initialise its value to x^2 (which is used in every term and is constant within the iteration loop; evaluating x^2 outside the loop makes the code more efficient - a good optimising compiler would do a similar thing)
23   define sin_x and initialise its value to x (the value of the first term of the series)
24   define n and initialise its value to 3 (the next term to be calculated)
25   define term_n and initialise its value to x (the value of the first term of the series)
27   a printf statement used for debugging (commented out)
28-35   a do statement which sums the series sin(x)
          30 term_n = -(term_n * xsq / (n * (n -1)))
               calculates the value of the nth term in the series
          31 sin_x = sin_x + term_n adds the nth term to the sum of the series
          32 n = n + 2; increments n by 2 ready to calculate the next term
          33 a printf statement used for debugging (commented out)
               prints x, n, term_n and sin_x (the sum of the series so far)
          35 while (fabs(term_n) > ACCURACY); terminates the sum - see below
36   return function result.

The summation of the series is stopped (in line 35) when the absolute value of a particular term becomes less than or equal to the accuracy required:

```
while (fabs(term_n) > ACCURACY);                              /* finished ? */
```

The maths function fabs is used to determine the float absolute value of term_n (the absolute value is required because negative values may be evaluated).

The value of ACCURACY can be set to give the required accuracy for the application. Line 33 prints information to enable the convergence of the series to be viewed while executing the program (commented out in this version).

Below is shown a sample run of the program (using Turbo C V3.0 on an IBM PC compatible). The results show that when the angle is below 5.0 radians the value returned by sinf is the same as that returned by the maths function sin(x) to approximately six or seven figures. When the angle is 10 radians the accuracy of the sum is approximately two to three figures and when the angle is above 20 radians the results are complete nonsense! The series is valid for all angles assuming that the calculations are performed to infinite accuracy and the problem with the results is due to rounding errors in floating point calculations (which will be discussed in the next section).

```
Angle (radians) ? .5   sin =          0.47942552, library =    0.47942554
Angle (radians) ? 1    sin =          0.84147096, library =    0.84147098
Angle (radians) ? 2    sin =          0.90929741, library =    0.90929743
Angle (radians) ? 5    sin =         -0.95892441, library =   -0.95892427
Angle (radians) ? 10   sin =         -0.54420567, library =   -0.54402111
Angle (radians) ? 15   sin =          0.66512936, library =    0.65028784
Angle (radians) ? 20   sin =          1.52592909, library =    0.91294525
Angle (radians) ? 25   sin =         -5.36588192, library =   -0.13235175
Angle (radians) ? 30   sin =      -24048.72656250, library =   -0.98803162
Angle (radians) ? 40   sin =   523443136.00000000, library =    0.74511316
Angle (radians) ? 50   sin = -8887603298304.00000000, library =   -0.26237485
```

27.3 Rounding errors

In C real numbers are stored in floating point form, i.e. a fractional part and an exponent. For example, decimal floating point numbers are in the form $f*10^e$ where f is the fraction in the range $0.1 \leq f < 1.0$ and e is the exponent, e.g. 7392.0 would be $0.7392 * 10^4$ and 0.0007392 would be $0.7392 * 10^{-3}$. Note, however, that computer systems tend to use base 2 or 16 for floating point numbers, e.g. $f*2^e$, but the following discussion still applies.

When computation is being carried out the fractional part of a decimal floating point must be within the range $0.1 \leq f < 1$ and if at any time the leading digit becomes 0 then the fractional part is shifted one place left and the exponent decremented, e.g. $0.0023*10^4$ becomes $0.23*10^2$. This process of getting the fractional part in the correct range is called **normalisation**.

Now suppose that two floating point numbers which are accurate to four significant figures are to be added:

$$z = 1.246 + 0.03290 = 0.1246*10^1 + 0.3290*10^{-1}$$

Before the add can take place the floating point number exponents must be aligned, i.e. one of the numbers unnormalized:

$$z = 0.1246*10^1 + 0.00329*10^1$$

This gives the result $0.1278*10^1$ assuming four-figure accuracy. Note that the digits of the fraction shifted out of the capacity of the system have been lost. Furthermore, no rounding was carried out when the digits were lost. Many computer systems do not round in this situation so it is a likely source of error in the program. Now consider subtraction:

$$z = 26.31 - 19.76 = 0.2631*10^2 - 0.1976*10^2 = 0.0655*10^2$$

this has resulted in a leading zero so it will be shifted:

$$z = 0.6550*10^1$$

Notice two things:

1 The last digit of the result has no significance whatever. The zero has been inserted in the shifting process because something has to be placed in that position in storage.
2 There can easily be more than one leading zero in such sums. For example if $0.3471*10^5$ is subtracted from $0.3472*10^5$ the answer is $0.0001*10^5$ which when normalised is $0.1000*10^2$. The last three digits have no meaning.

Thus when subtracting it is possible to end up with numbers with far less significant figures than the calculation started with. However, succeeding operations will act on these results as though all the figures were significant. This is a major source of run-time inaccuracy.

Now consider Program 27_1 which evaluates sin(x). As the signs of the terms alternate rounding errors can result from the subtraction process (as described above). In addition, if x is large the values of x^n can become a very large number. Below is a listing of a run of Program 27_1 for an angle of 25.0 radians with the /* ---- */ in lines 27 and 33 removed (so that the results of each iteration are printed):

Angle (radians) ? 25

	n	term_n	sin_x
sin(25.0)	5	-2604.166748	-2579.166748
sin(25.0)	7	81380.210938	78801.046875
sin(25.0)	9	-1211015.000000	-1132214.000000
sin(25.0)	11	10512283.000000	9380069.000000
sin(25.0)	13	-59728880.000000	-50348812.000000
sin(25.0)	15	239298400.000000	188949584.000000
sin(25.0)	17	-712197632.000000	-523248064.000000
sin(25.0)	19	1636483584.000000	1113235456.000000
sin(25.0)	21	-2990649856.000000	-1877414400.000000
sin(25.0)	23	4450371584.000000	2572957184.000000
sin(25.0)	25	-5497000448.000000	-2924043264.000000
sin(25.0)	27	5726042112.000000	2801998848.000000
sin(25.0)	29	-5097971712.000000	-2295972864.000000
sin(25.0)	31	3923931392.000000	1627958528.000000
sin(25.0)	33	-2637050624.000000	-1009092096.000000
sin(25.0)	35	1560754432.000000	551662336.000000
sin(25.0)	37	-819723968.000000	-268061632.000000
sin(25.0)	39	384630240.000000	116568608.000000
sin(25.0)	41	-162209104.000000	-45640496.000000
sin(25.0)	43	61817492.000000	16176996.000000
sin(25.0)	45	-21393096.000000	-5216100.000000
sin(25.0)	47	6752871.000000	1536771.000000
sin(25.0)	49	-1952148.125000	-415377.125000
sin(25.0)	51	518746.843750	103369.718750
sin(25.0)	53	-127143.835938	-23774.117188
sin(25.0)	55	28833.417969	5059.300781
sin(25.0)	57	-6067.638672	-1008.337891
sin(25.0)	59	1188.055786	179.717896
sin(25.0)	61	-216.988571	-37.270676
sin(25.0)	63	37.054058	-0.216618
sin(25.0)	65	-5.929029	-6.145647
sin(25.0)	67	0.890780	-5.254867
sin(25.0)	69	-0.125902	-5.380769
sin(25.0)	71	0.016771	-5.363998
sin(25.0)	73	-0.002109	-5.366107
sin(25.0)	75	0.000251	-5.365856
sin(25.0)	77	-0.000028	-5.365884
sin(25.0)	79	0.000003	-5.365881
sin(25.0)	81	-0.000000	-5.365882
sin(25.0)	83	0.000000	-5.365882
sin(25.0)	85	-0.000000	-5.365882
sin =		-5.36588192, library =	-0.13235175

The final value of the sin of an angle must be in the range -1.0 to 1.0 but the above listing shows values of terms as large as 5726042112.0. As the float calculations are only carried out to six or seven figures of accuracy the last four figures of the number are meaningless. We are therefore attempting to get a result in the range -1.0 to 1.0 using values that are not accurate to hundreds or even thousands.

27.3.1 Using higher precision types to overcome rounding errors

One way to *reduce* the effect of rounding errors is to increase the precision and range of the variables and constants used. This, however, has an overhead in that the extra computation involved increases the run-time of the program. In many applications there is often a trade-off between the accuracy desired and the run-time acceptable.

Increasing precision, however, only reduces the problem; it does not eliminate it. Consider the following results produced using float, double and long double versions of the sin(x) function of Program 27_1 (in file c27\p27_1a.c on the disk). Note that even long double (19 decimal digits of precision) is only effective up to about 30 radians.

angle x	sin(x) =	float	double	long double	library
1.0		0.841471	0.841471	0.841471	0.841471
2.0		0.909297	0.909297	0.909297	0.909297
5.0		-0.958924	-0.958924	-0.958924	-0.958924
10.0		-0.544206	-0.544021	-0.544021	-0.544021
15.0		0.665129	0.650288	0.650288	0.650288
20.0		1.525929	0.912945	0.912945	0.912945
25.0		-5.365882	-0.132351	-0.132352	-0.132352
30.0		-24048.726562	-0.988053	-0.988032	-0.988032
40.0		523443136.000000	-0.605842	0.744634	0.745113
50.0		-8887603298304.000000	9991.828290	13.111824	-0.262375

27.3.2 Modification of the algorithm to overcome rounding errors

A change to the algorithm may be possible, e.g.:

1 Modify the way that the mathematical equation is mapped into program code. For example, try to avoid situations where numbers with similar values are subtracted.
2 Using different mathematical equations and/or algorithms over different ranges of the input values, e.g. the exponential integral (see the problem at the end of the chapter).

For example, because the sin(x) function is periodic, a simple approach is to subtract 2π from the angle until its value is in the range 0 to 2π (for angles greater than 0), e.g. assuming an angle x in radians and TWO_PI equals 2π:

```
x = x - TWO_PI * (int) (x / TWO_PI);        /* get x in range 0 to 2pi */
```

The expression (int) (x / TWO_PI) evaluates, as an integer, how many times 2π goes into the angle x. This integer value is then multiplied by 2π and subtracted from the angle x; the result being an angle in the range 0 to 2π. The problem is that casting the floating result of x / TWO_PI to an int may result in integer overflow. This can be overcome by using the maths library function floor:

```
double floor(double x);        /* returns the largest integer below x */
```

which returns as a double function result the largest integer below x (the effect is similar to an int cast but avoids the danger of overflow). Hence the statement can be rewritten (and it also works for negative angles):

```
x = x - TWO_PI * floor(x / TWO_PI);                    /* get x in range 0 to 2pi */
```

Fig. 27.1 shows a modified version of the sinf function of Program 27_1 using the above technique (in file c27\p27_1b.c on the disk).

```
 1 float sinf(float x)
 2 {
 3     const float ACCURACY = 1.0e-8f;                        /* accuracy required */
 4     const float TWO_PI = 2.0f * 3.141592653589793238462643f;  /* constant 2pi */
 5     float xsq,                                                  /* x squared */
 6           sin_x,                                     /* sum of sin(x) series */
 7           n = 3.0f,                            /* start iterations at 3rd term */
 8           term_n;                               /* value of nth term of series */
 9
10     x = x - TWO_PI * floor(x / TWO_PI);              /* get x in range 0 to 2pi */
11     xsq = x * x;                                       /* calculate x squared */
12     sin_x = x;                                          /* initialise sin(x) */
13     term_n = x;                                          /* initialise term */
14     /*printf("                 n                    term_n                  sin_x ");*/
15     do
16         {
17         term_n = -(term_n * xsq / (n * (n - 1)));       /* evaluate nth term */
18         sin_x = sin_x + term_n;                              /* add term    */
19         n = n + 2;                                            /* next n */
20         /*printf("\n sin(%6.1f) %3d %24f %20f", x, n, term_n, sin_x);*/
21         }
22     while (fabs(term_n) > ACCURACY);                     /* finished ? */
23     return sin_x;                               /* yes, return result */
24 }
```

Fig. 27.1 Modified version of sin(x) to cope with large angles

The following results were produced using float, double and long double versions of Fig. 27.1 (it is a run of the program in file c27\p27_1b.c on the disk):

angle x	sin(x) = float	double	long double	library
10.0	-0.544021	-0.544021	-0.544021	-0.544021
50.0	-0.262379	-0.262375	-0.262375	-0.262375
100.0	-0.506368	-0.506366	-0.506366	-0.506366
1000.0	0.826864	0.826880	0.826880	0.826880
10000.0	-0.305349	-0.305614	-0.305614	-0.305614
100000.0	0.038530	0.035749	0.035749	0.035749
1000000.0	-0.375923	-0.349994	-0.349994	-0.349994

The double and long double results are as accurate as the maths library function to the six figures displayed. The error in the float is due to rounding errors in the evaluation of the angle in the range 0 to 2π (line 10 of Fig. 27.1).

The above discussion has necessarily been very brief; refer to a text on numerical methods for a full discussion of such problems and the techniques used to overcome them (Press *et al.* 1994).

27.4 Evaluation of square root using Newton-Raphson method

```
 1 /* Program 27_2 - test sqrt(x) function */
 2
 3 #include <stdio.h>
 4 #include <math.h>
 5
 6 int main()
 7 {
 8     double sq_root(const double x);                    /* function prototype */
 9     double number;                          /* hold number to find square root of */
10
11     while (printf("\nNumber > 0 ? ") , scanf("%lf", &number) == 1)
12         printf("  square root = %20.8f, library = %12.8f ",
13                     sq_root(number), sqrt(number));
14     return 0;
15 }
16
17 /*----------------------------------------------------------------*/
18 /* Function: square root using Newton-Raphson method of successive      */
19 /*       approximations, i.e. next approximation  = x - f(x) / f'(x)    */
20 /*  For sqrt(number)  f(x) = x ** 2 - number   and f'(x) = 2 * x        */
21 /*   thus f(x) / f'(x) = (x - number / x) / 2                           */
22 double sq_root(const double x)
23 {
24     const double ACCURACY = 1.0e-8;                   /* accuracy required */
25     double root,                       /* holds calculated value of square root */
26             term;                            /* holds f(x)/f'(x) term */
27
28     root = x;                                /* initial 'guess' at root */
29     do
30         {
31         term = (root - (x / root)) / 2.0;             /* f(x) / f('(x) */
32         root = root - term;                           /* new root */
33         }
34     while (fabs(term) > fabs(ACCURACY * root));        /* finished ? */
35     return root;                                       /* return result */
36 }
```

Program 27_2 Evaluation of the square root of a number using Newton-Raphson method

Program 27_2 evaluates the square root of a real number using the Newton-Raphson method of successive approximations, i.e. to find the root of the equation $f(x) = 0$:

$$x_{n+1} = x_n - \frac{f(x_n)}{f'(x_n)}$$

where x_n is the last approximation of the root

x_{n+1} is the next approximation of the root

$f(x_n)$ is the value of the function $f(x)$ at x_n

$f'(x_n)$ is the value of the first derivative of $f(x)$ at x_n.

A do statement is very suitable for solving an iterative problem such as this (it is often the technique used by the library routine sqrt):

1   An informed 'guess' of the initial value of x_n is made (how, depends upon f(x) and one would usually refer to a mathematical text).

2   The next approximation x_{n+1} = x_n - $f(x_n)$ / $f'(x_n)$ is evaluated.

3   The value of x_n is replaced with x_{n+1} and step 2 repeated.

Steps 2 and 3 are repeated until the value of x_{n+1} is sufficiently accurate when the iteration is terminated. Like the initial 'guess' of x_n, the method for terminating the iterations depends upon f(x) and how well the process converges. The techniques described in Section 27.1 are suitable, i.e. terminate the iteration when the absolute value of $f(x_n)$ / $f'(x_n)$ becomes less than some value of accuracy:

    | $f(x_n)$ / $f'(x_n)$ | < ACCURACY   then terminate the iteration.

Program 27_2 uses a value relative to x_{n+1}:

    | $f(x_n)$ / $f'(x_n)$ | < | ACCURACY * x_{n+1} | then terminate the iteration.

Both techniques will fail if f'(x) becomes zero, i.e. division by zero occurs.

    To solve a problem such as finding the square root of number, i.e. x = (number)$^{1/2}$, the equation must be in the form:

    f(x) = 0

Thus to determine square root x = (number)$^{1/2}$ the form of f(x) is:

    f(x)   = x^2 - number = 0

hence   f'(x) = 2 * x

In this case $f(x_n)$ / $f'(x_n)$ can be rewritten as:

    $f(x_n)$ / $f'(x_n)$ = ½ (x - (number / x))

The sequence of events in Program 27_2 is:

6-15	function main
8	declare prototype of function sq_root
9	define variable number which will hold the value whose square root is required
11-13	prompt the user to enter a number > 0, read the value into variable number,
	12-13 call sq_root and the maths library function sqrt and print results
22-36	function sq_root: evaluates the square root of a double parameter, returns a double
22	function header indicating one double parameter x, returns a double function result
24	define ACCURACY (const qualified) and initialise its value to 1.0e-8
25	define variable root which will hold the value of x_n
26	define variable term which will hold the value of $f(x_n)$ / $f'(x_n)$
28	assign root = x; the initial 'guess' at the root
29-34	a do statement evaluating successive approximations of root
	31 evaluate $f(x_n)$ / $f'(x_n)$ and assign the result to variable term
	32 evaluate next approximation of root
	34 terminate the do when absolute value of term is ≤ ACCURACY * root
35	return the function result.

Program 27_2 will fail if a negative value is entered for number, i.e. the square root of a negative number has imaginary components. The input should therefore be verified as a positive number (Program 13_2 shows a method).

Program 28_2 (in Section 28.3) contains a generalised function newton which uses the Newton-Raphson method of successive approximation to determine the root of a function $f(x) = 0$. Pointers to the functions $f(x)$ and $f'(x)$ are passed to newton which then calls them as required. The function main calls newton twice to find the roots of $f(x) = \cosh(x) + \cos(x) - 3 = 0$ and $f(x) = x^2 - 25 = 0$.

Exercise 27.1 (see Appendix B for sample answer)

Implement and test a program which evaluates $\sin^{-1}(x)$ using the series:

$$\sin^{-1}(x) = x + \frac{x^3}{2.3} + \frac{1.3x^5}{2.4.5} + \frac{1.3.5x^7}{2.4.6.7} + \frac{1.3.5.7x^9}{2.4.6.8.9} \qquad x^2 < 1$$

which returns an angle in radians $-\pi/2 < \sin^{-1}(x) < \pi/2$.

Problem for Chapter 27

The exponential integral for a parameter x is defined:

$$E_1(x) = \int_1^\infty \frac{e^{-xt}}{t} dt \qquad\qquad x > 0$$

Implement and test a function to evaluate the exponential integral using the series:

$$E_1(x) = -\tau - \ln(x) - \sum_{n=1}^\infty \frac{(-1)^n x^n}{n\,n!} \qquad\qquad x > 0$$

where Euler's constant $\tau = 0.5772156649$. If $x = 1$ the above should give E1(1) = 0.219383934. If x becomes large the results become inaccurate depending upon the number of significant digits used (typically when using double with 15 significant digits it fails when $x > 10$), e.g. using double with Turbo C/C++ V3.00 on an IBM PC compatible gave E1(50) = -0.35630926 when the correct value is E1(50) = 3.783264e-24. This is due to rounding errors in the summation which involves subtracting numbers many orders of magnitude larger than the result (similar to the sine series with large angles), i.e. when $x = 50$ the summation involves terms of the order of 10^{19} when the end result is of the order of 10^{-24}; Turbo C V3.00 performs double calculations to approximately 15 figures of accuracy.

The above algorithm fails due to rounding errors for large values of x. An alternative is to use the asymptotic expansion for the exponential integral:

$$E_1(x) \approx \frac{e^{-x}}{x}\left(1 + \sum_{n=1}^\infty \frac{(-1)^n n!}{x^n}\right) \qquad\qquad x > 0$$

Implement and test a function using this algorithm. Compare the results with that from the previous algorithm. This algorithm will give 'floating point overflow' errors for small values of x but works for larger values when the previous algorithm fails (for further discussion see Press et al. 1994).

28

Advanced use of functions

28.1 Recursive functions

In C a function may be used recursively in that it may call itself either directly (from within itself) or indirectly (from a function which it has called). For example, the factorial of a number may be evaluated using the series (see Program 13_2):

$$N! = N * (N - 1) * (N - 2) * (N - 3) \ldots\ldots 1 \qquad\qquad N > 0$$

or using the recursive relationship:

```
N! = N * (N - 1)!      for N > 1
   = 1                 for N = 0 or 1
```

The function factorial in Program 28_1 is recursive. Consider lines:

```
22 if (n <= 1)  return 1;            if n is <= 1 the recursion is terminated
23 return (n * factorial(n - 1));    the function calls itself to evaluate (n-1)!.
```

```
1 /* Program 28_1  Evaluate factorial using a recursive function          */
2 /*     N! = N * (N -1)! down to !1  = 1                                  */
3
4 #include <stdio.h>
5
6 int main(void)
7 {
8      long int factorial(long int n);                  /* function prototype */
9
10     int n;                                           /* holds number */
11
12     /* read an integer number, terminate on EOF */
13     while(printf("\nNumber > 0 ? ") , (scanf(" %d", &n)) == 1)
14         printf(" number = %d,  factorial = %ld \n", n, factorial(n));
15     return 0;
16 }
17
18 /*------------------------------------------------------------------*/
19 /* Factorial of an integer number:  n! = n * (n -1)! down to !1  = 1    */
20 long int factorial(long int n)
21 {
22      if (n <= 1)  return 1;                           /* return 1! */
23      return (n * factorial(n - 1));                   /* return n! */
24 }
```

Program 28_1 Evaluate factorial using a recursive function

Recursive functions should only be used when alternative non-recursive algorithms are not available or are more complex, e.g. evaluating factorial by recursion is very inefficient and a simple loop should be used as in Program 13_2. Recursion entails a high overhead in terms of parameter passing, creation of internal automatic variables (a new set of auto variables is created on each call), etc. The overhead is not only in terms of execution time but if the function has a large number of internal variables or the recursion is very deep the program can run out of stack space.

Exercise 28.1 (see Appendix B for sample answer)

A good example of where recursion can be used very effectively is the quicksort algorithm. In a given array an element x is selected and the other elements are partitioned into two subsets; one containing elements with a value less than x and the other with values greater than x. The partitioning process is then applied to the two subsets. An algorithm is:

1   Select an element in the array and assign its value to x. Although the element may be selected randomly the usual technique is to select the middle element.
2   Scan up the array until element array[up] >= x.
3   Scan down the array until element array[down] <= x.
4   Exchange elements array[up] and array[down].
5   Return to step 2 to continue the process of scanning up and down until up > down.

When the scan is complete the array will be partitioned into two sets; a lower set with values less than or equal to x and an upper set with values greater than or equal to x. The upper and lower sets are then sorted using the algorithm. The algorithm lends itself to a recursive solution (the recursion terminates when arrays of two elements have been sorted).

28.2 Pointers to functions

Although functions are not variables they do have an address (associated with the function name) and it is possible to define pointers to functions. Consider:

```
double *function(double);                    /* declare function prototype */
```

This is a prototype for a function with one double parameter and which returns a pointer to a double as a function result. Now consider:

```
double (*p_function)(double);                    /* define a pointer */
```

This defines a variable p_function which is a 'pointer to a function with one double parameter and which returns a double function result'. Because unary * has a lower precedence than () the parentheses are required around (*p_function) to force the proper association, i.e. 'pointer to function'. Consider:

```
double (*p_function)(double);        /* define a pointer to a function */
double result;                       /* define a double */

p_function = sin;                    /* point to sin function */
result = p_function(0.5);            /* evaluate sin(0.5) */
```

This defines p_function (a pointer to a function) which is assigned to 'point to' the maths function sin. The function is then called via the pointer, i.e. the last two statements are equivalent to:

```
result = sin(0.5);                       /* evaluate sin(0.5) */
```

The pointer p_function can be set up to point to any function of the correct type, i.e. 'a function with one double parameter and which returns a double function result'. Thus it would be able to 'point to' many of the mathematical functions in the standard library, e.g. cos, sqrt, tan, etc. An alternative way to declare the pointer p_function is:

```
/* define a pointer to a function: double parameter returning a double */
typedef double (*P_function)(double);            /* define type P_function */
P_function p_func1, p_func2;                /* define two pointers to functions */
```

This defines a type P_function which is a 'pointer to a function with one double parameter and which returns a double function result'. It is then used to define a pair of pointers.

28.3 Passing pointers to functions as function parameters

A pointer to a function may be passed as a function parameter just like any other pointer. Program 28_2 (next page) contains a general purpose function newton which uses the Newton-Raphson method of successive approximation to determine the root of a function $f(x) = 0$ (Section 27.4 described the technique in outline). Pointers to $f(x)$ and $f'(x)$ are passed to newton which can then call them as required. The function main calls newton twice to find the roots of $f(x) = \cosh(x) + \cos(x) - 3 = 0$ and $f(x) = x^2 - 25 = 0$:

9   prototype of function func_1 which evaluates $f(x) = \cosh(x) + \cos(x) - 3$
10   prototype of function fdiv_1 which evaluates the first derivative of func_1
11   prototype of function func_2 which evaluates $f(x) = x^2 - 25$
12   prototype of function fdiv_2 which evaluates the first derivative of func_2
14-15   prototype of function newton (further discussion below)
20   initial 'guess' of root of $f(x) = \cosh(x) + \cos(x) - 3 = 0$
21   call newton to find root of $f(x) = \cosh(x) + \cos(x) - 3$
           22-23   print root found or error message
26   initial 'guess' of root of $f(x) = x^2 - 25 = 0$
27   call newton to find root of $f(x) = x^2 - 25$
           28-29   print root found or error message.

The sequence of statements in function newton, lines 61 to 76, is:

61-62   `int newton(double *p_x, double (*p_f)(double), double (*p_fdiv)(double),`
                      `int max_loop, const double accuracy, const int print)`
           a function header specifying the following parameters:
           double *p_x   on entry *p_x contains 'guess' and on exit returns root found
           (*p_f)(double)   pointer to the function $f(x)$
           (*p_fdiv)(double)   pointer to the function $f'(x)$
           int max_loop   specifies the maximum number of iterations
           const double accuracy specifies the required accuracy
           const int print   if *true* information is printed during the iterations
           the function returns a *true* if the root is found within max_loop iterations
66-73   a do evaluating successive approximations of the root x_n
           69 evaluate $f(x_n) / f'(x_n)$ and assign the result to variable term
           70 evaluate next approximation of x_n
           73 terminate do when $|term / x_n| <=$ accuracy or --max_loop becomes 0
75   return max_loop: if > 0 root has been found thus returning *true*.

```
 1│/* Program 28_2 - Passing pointers to functions as function parameters       */
 2│/*   Function newton uses the Newton-Raphson method of finding roots          */
 3│/*   parameters passed includes the functions f(x) and f'(x)                  */
 4│#include <stdio.h>
 5│#include <math.h>
 6│
 7│int main()
 8│{
 9│    double func_1(double);                    /* f(x) = cosh(x) + cos(x) - 3 = 0 */
10│    double fdiv_1(double);                    /* f'(x) = sinh(x) - sin(x)        */
11│    double func_2(double);                          /* f(x) = x*x -25 = 0 */
12│    double fdiv_2(double);                          /* f'(x) = 2x         */
13│    /* prototype for the function newton */
14│    int newton(double *, double (*)(double), double (*)(double),
15│                      int, const double, const int);
16│
17│    double x;                                 /* holds value of root of f(x) */
18│
19│    printf("\nFind root of f(x) = cosh(x) + cos(x) - 3 = 0");
20│    x = 1.0;                                  /* initial 'guess' at root */
21│    if (newton( &x, func_1, fdiv_1, 100, 1.0e-8, 0))
22│          printf("\n   root x = %g, test of f(x) = %g ", x, func_1(x));
23│    else  printf("\n   failed to find root ");
24│
25│    printf("\n\nFind root of f(x) = x * x - 25 = 0");
26│    x = 1.0;                                  /* initial 'guess' at root */
27│    if ( newton( &x, func_2, fdiv_2, 100, 1.0e-8, 1))
28│          printf("\n   root x = %g, test of f(x) = %g ", x, func_2(x));
29│    else  printf("\n   failed to find root ");
30│    return 0;
31│}
32│
33│/*-----------------------------------------------------------------------*/
34│/* function f(x) = cosh(x) + cos(x) - 3 = 0                              */
35│double func_1(double x)
36│{    return (cosh(x) + cos(x) - 3.0); }
37│
38│/* first derivative f'(x) = sinh(x) - sin(x) */
39│double fdiv_1(double x)
40│{    return (sinh(x) - sin(x));  }
41│
42│/*-----------------------------------------------------------------------*/
43│/* function f(x) = x*x -25 = 0                                           */
44│double func_2(double x)
45│{    return (x*x - 25.0);  }
46│
47│/* f'(x) = 2x */
48│double fdiv_2(double x)
49│{    return (2.0 * x);  }
50│
```

Program 28_2 Passing pointers to functions as function parameters

```
51 /*------------------------------------------------------------------------*/
52 /* Using Newton-Raphson method find a root of the equation f(x)           */
53 /* Parameters in:  *p_x            pointer to first approximation of root */
54 /*                  (*p_f)(x)      pointer to function f(x)               */
55 /*                  (*p_fdiv)(x)   pointer to function f'(x)              */
56 /*                  max_loop       maximum number of iterations           */
57 /*                  accuracy       required accuracy                      */
58 /*                  print          if TRUE print information to screen     */
59 /*            out: *p_x            return root found                      */
60 /* function result: >0 (true) if root found, 0 (false) if max_loop exceeded */
61 int newton(double *p_x, double (*p_f)(double), double (*p_fdiv)(double),
62                int max_loop, const double accuracy, const int print)
63 {
64     double term;
65
66     do
67         {
68         /* calculate next term f(x) / f'(x) then subtract from current root  */
69         term = (*p_f)(*p_x) / (*p_fdiv)(*p_x);
70         *p_x = *p_x - term;                              /* new root */
71         if (print) printf("\n   x = %20g term = %20g", *p_x , term);
72         }
73     while ((fabs(term / *p_x) > accuracy) && (--max_loop));
74     if (print) printf("\n root = %g, f(x) = %g ", *p_x , (*p_f)(*p_x));
75     return max_loop;
76 }
```

Program 28_2 Passing pointers to functions as function parameters

Consider the prototype of function newton in lines 14 and 15 of Program 28_2:

```
int newton(double *, double (*)(double), double (*)(double), int, double, int);
```

The second and third parameters, double (*)(double), are declared to be 'pointers to a function with a double parameter and which returns a double'. The parentheses around (*) are required to force the proper association, i.e. unary * has a lower precedence than ().

The function newton would be used as a general purpose function to test if the Newton-Raphson method was suitable for finding the root of a particular function. Specifying max_loops prevents the technique looping forever (and returns *false* if it fails) and using the print facility would show how well the technique converged. A run gave:

```
Find root of f(x) = cosh(x) + cos(x) - 3 = 0
   root x = 1.85792, test of f(x) = 7.64363e-16
Find root of f(x) = x * x - 25 = 0
   x =                   13 term =                  -12
   x =              7.46154 term =              5.53846
   x =              5.40603 term =              2.05551
   x =              5.01525 term =             0.390779
   x =              5.00002 term =            0.0152244
   x =                    5 term =          2.31782e-05
   x =                    5 term =          5.37232e-11
 root = 5, f(x) = 0
   root x = 5, test of f(x) = 0
```

28.4 Returning pointers to functions as a function result

Consider the following (rather complicated) function prototype:

```
double (*get_func(int i))(double);              /* complicated function prototype */
```

This prototype declares a function `get_func` which has a single `int` parameter and returns, as a function result, a pointer to a function which has a single `double` parameter and returns a `double` function result. The use of `typedef` can simplify the declaration:

```
typedef double (*P_function)(double);           /* define a 'pointer to a function' */
P_function get_func(int i);                      /* function prototype returning above type */
```

A common programming requirement is the selection, by the user, of a command from a menu of commands followed by the execution of associated statements or functions. For example, in Program 14_1, a character entered from the keyboard was used, via a `switch` statement, to select statements to execute. Program 28_3 (next page) is more sophisticated in that a `menu` array is used to hold commands to be displayed on the screen with associated functions. The function `get_command` displays the menu on the screen and prompts the user for a keyboard hit. A menu command is selected on the first character of the command string (`toupper` makes the character read upper case). The function returns either a pointer to the function associated with the command or `NULL` if an `<ESC>` character was entered:

8	define `P_function` 'pointer to a function with no parameters and no function result'
11-14	define `Menu`, a structure to hold the commands and associated function pointers
	`command` a 20 character string which indicates the command to be executed
	`p_command` a pointer to a function to be executed when the command is selected
16	define external `data`, holds the value to be processed by the functions selected
20	prototype of function `get_command`
21-23	prototypes of the functions to be executed via a command from the menu
26-29	define array `menu` with commands and pointers to functions
	each element of `menu` is a 20-character command string and an associated pointer
30	define `p_function`, a pointer to a function
34-37	a `do` statement calling `get_command` to obtain a 'pointer to a function'
	if the pointer returned is `NULL` the `do` terminates otherwise the function is called
44-62	definitions of functions to read, print and square the value of the variable `data`
69	header for `get_command`; returns a 'pointer to a function' (line 70 is an alternative)
76-77	increment `index` from 0 until a `NULL` pointer is found (menu terminator)
	77 print menu command string on the screen
80-82	print `"Enter command character:"` followed by the first character of each command
86-92	a `while` loop reading characters into `ch` until an `<ESC>` character is entered
	88-90 search `menu` for a command beginning with character `ch`
	90 found command, return associated pointer to function
	91 character not in commands, ring bell.
93	return `NULL` indicating that an `<ESC>` character was entered

The function `getch` (see Section 20.3) reads characters directly from the keyboard. Thus commands are entered character by character rather than on a line terminated by *newline*.

Note that some compilers generate errors when attempting to initialise `menu` (lines 26 to 28) with the addresses of functions. Making `menu` external by moving lines 21 to 29 before `main` (line 18) will generally overcome the problem.

```
 1 /* Program 28_3 - menu selection returning a pointer to a function */
 2
 3 #include <stdio.h>                                    /* standard headers */
 4 #include <ctype.h>
 5 #include <conio.h>                           /* Turbo C console I/O header */
 6
 7 /* define: a pointer to a function with no parameters and no function result */
 8 typedef void (*P_function)(void);
 9
10 /* define structure which holds command string and pointer to a function */
11 typedef struct {
12                 char command[20];                /* menu command to print */
13                 P_function p_command;    /* pointer to corresponding function */
14               } Menu;
15
16 float data;                          /* used to hold data value read and printed */
17
18 int main(void)
19 {
20     P_function get_command(Menu menu[]);             /* function prototypes */
21     void read_data(void);
22     void print_data(void);
23     void square_data(void);
24
25     /* define menu: initialise with command strings and function pointers */
26     Menu menu[4] = {{"Read value" , read_data} ,           /* menu data */
27                     {"Print value", print_data},
28                     {"Square value", square_data},
29                     {"", NULL}                    };       /* terminator */
30     P_function p_function;
31
32     clrscr();
33     /* loop reading and executing a command until a control character is read */
34     do
35         if ((p_function = get_command(menu)) != NULL)
36             p_function();                             /* call function */
37     while (p_function != NULL);
38     return 0;
39 }
40
41 /*-------------------------------------------------------------------*/
42 /* functions to perform the commands entered                         */
43
44 void read_data(void)                                     /* read value */
45 {
46     clrscr();
47     printf("\n\nPlease enter data value (float) ? ");
48     scanf("%f", &data);
49 }
50
```

Program 28_3 Menu selection returning a pointer to a function (using Turbo C)

```
51 void print_data(void)                                        /* print value */
52 {
53     clrscr();
54     printf("\n\nValue of data = %f ", data);
55 }
56
57 void square_data(void)                                     /* square value */
58 {
59     clrscr();
60     data = data * data;
61     printf("\n\nData value squared ");
62 }
63
64 /*----------------------------------------------------------------*/
65 /* Function which displays a menu and returns a command selected         */
66 /*  The array menu contains command strings and function pointers        */
67 /*  Selection is on first character of command string                    */
68 /*  return a pointer to appropriate function else NULL (control character) */
69 P_function get_command(Menu menu[])
70 /*void (*get_command(Menu menu[]))(void)*/              /* alternative header */
71 {
72     int ch, index;
73
74     /* print menu command strings on the screen */
75     printf("\n\nCommand menu is:");
76     for (index = 0 ; menu[index].p_command != NULL ; index++)
77         printf("\n     %s", menu[index].command);
78
79     /* print user prompt and first characters of command strings */
80     printf("\nPlease enter command character (or <ESC> to exit): ");
81     for (index = 0 ; menu[index].p_command != NULL ; index++)
82         printf("%c ", menu[index].command[0]);
83     putchar('?');
84
85     /* read characters until a command or <ESC> entered */
86     while ((ch = toupper(getch())) != 27)
87         {
88         for (index = 0 ; menu[index].p_command != NULL ; index++)
89             if (ch == menu[index].command[0])
90                 return menu[index].p_command;          /* return command */
91         putchar('\a');                              /* illegal character ! */
92         }
93     return NULL;                                 /* <ESC> character entered ! */
94 }
```

Program 28_3 Menu selection returning a pointer to a function (using Turbo C)

It is very important that a function which returns a pointer to a function should return something indicating failure if a selection fails. Either return NULL (which can be checked by the calling program) or a pointer to an error function which will print an error message and take appropriate action. If a valid pointer is not returned the program will crash when the pointer is used for a function call (this includes NULL).

28.5 Functions with a variable number of parameters

Although the vast majority of functions implemented will have a fixed number of parameters it is sometimes necessary to write a function which will be passed a different number of parameters on different calls. Consider, for example, printf from <stdio.h>:

```
printf("%d %f %c ", int_value, float_value, char_value);
```

The function printf can be called with a varying number of parameters and uses the conversion specifications in the control string to determine the number of parameters following the control string. The function header of printf is:

```
int printf(const char *format, ...);
```

where format is a pointer to the control string and ... indicates a variable number of parameters.

When implementing a function with a variable number of parameters there must be at least one named parameter in the function header (which is used as a starting point to access the unnamed parameters specified by ...). For example, consider the following function header:

```
void my_func(int v, ...);
```

The standard header <stdarg.h> contains a set of macro definitions (see Section 16.13) which specifies how a program can access a sequence of parameters in a variable length parameter list. The implementation of the header is system dependent but typically looks something like:

```
typedef void *va_list;
#define va_start(ap, v)    ((void) (ap = (va_list) &v + sizeof(v)))
#define va_arg(ap, type)   (*((type *) (ap++)))
#define va_end(ap)         ((void) (ap = NULL))
```

Where v is the name of the parameter to the left of the variable parameter list , ...) and:

va_list	is a type which is used to define a pointer ap; the pointer will be used to access each parameter in turn
va_start	initialises pointer ap to point to the parameter following v
va_arg	returns the next parameter and increments ap to point to the next type specifies the type of parameter expected, va_arg uses this to: (a) return the correct type (note the (cast) in va_arg) and (b) to be able to increment ap to point to the next parameter
va_end	terminates the process and performs any cleanup operations necessary.

In addition to being used by the above macros the parameter v would provide the called function with the number (and possibly type) of the variable number of unnamed parameters, in a similar way to printf using the number of conversion specifications in the control string.

Program 28_4 (at the end of the chapter) contains a function str_concat which will concatenate a variable number of strings. The function header in line 26 is:

```
char *str_concat(int number, ...)
```

The parameter number specifies the number of strings to be concatenated. The parameter number would be followed by number strings which are to be appended (concatenated) onto the end of the first string (which must not be a constant). On termination str_concat returns a pointer to the first string. For example, str_concat is called twice in main in lines 13 and 16, i.e.:

```
str_concat(6, string_1, " add 1 ", "add_2 ", "add 3 ", "add 4 ", "add 5");
p_str = str_concat(5, string_2, "alan ", "simon ", "george ", "henry ");
```

The sequence of statements in function str_concat is:

26   char *str_concat(int number, ...) the function header
28   va_list ap; define the pointer ap which will point to the unnamed parameters
29-30   define two pointers to char
32   va_start(ap, number); initialise ap to point to the parameter following number
33   p_str = va_arg(ap, char *); point p_str to the next parameter (the first string)
        char * specifies the type of parameter expected, i.e. 'pointer to char'
34   print the first string
37-42   a while statement concatenating number - 1 strings onto the first
       39   p_str2 = va_arg(ap, char *); point p_str2 to start of next string
             (the type parameter is char * - 'pointer to char')
       40   print the string
       41   concatenate the string onto the end of the existing string (pointed to by p_str)
43   va_end(ap); perform any cleanup operations necessary
44   terminate the function and return pointer to the start of the first string.

The named actual parameters (preceding the ...) are checked and converted to the type expected by the corresponding formal parameters (see Section 16.4). The unnamed parameters, however, specified by ... cannot be checked (the compiler has no idea what the function is expecting). The unnamed parameters are therefore treated as if a function prototype is not available, i.e. integral parameters undergo integral promotion and float parameters are converted to double. Clearly great care is required in accessing the parameters, i.e. an incorrect type specified in va_arg would not only return rubbish but could corrupt the stack and crash the program. A run of Program 28_4 gave:

```
Parameters are "string_1" " add 1 " "add_2 " "add 3 " "add 4 " "add 5"
Result is: "string_1 add 1 add_2 add 3 add 4 add 5"

Parameters are "" "alan " "simon " "george " "henry "
Names are :"alan simon george henry "
```

Once tested and operational the printf statements in lines 34 and 40 would be removed.

Problem for Chapter 28

Implement a simple equivalent of function printf, e.g.:

```
int simple_printf(const char *format, ...);
```

Use conversion specifications in format to determinate the number and type of parameters (like printf). Implement the function to print integer decimal (%d), integer hexadecimal (%x), float (%f), character (%c) and strings (%s).

```
 1 /* Program 28_4   Function with a variable number of parameters */
 2
 3 #include <stdio.h>
 4 #include <stdarg.h>
 5 #include <string.h>
 6
 7 int main(void)
 8 {
 9     char *str_concat(int number, ...);                    /* function prototype */
10
11     char *p_str, string_1[100] = "string_1", string_2[100] = "";
12
13     str_concat(6, string_1, " add 1 ", "add_2 ", "add 3 ", "add 4 ", "add 5");
14     printf("\nResult is: \"%s\" ", string_1);
15
16     p_str = str_concat(5, string_2, "alan ", "simon ", "george ", "henry ");
17     printf("\nNames are :\"%s\"", p_str);
18     return 0;
19 }
20
21 /*-------------------------------------------------------------------*
22  * Function to concatenate a variable number of strings             *
23  *   on entry number (first parameter) specifies number of strings  *
24  *   followed by number strings                                     *
25  * Return pointer to first string                                   */
26 char *str_concat(int number, ...)
27 {
28     va_list ap;                              /* pointer to the parameters */
29     char *p_str,                             /* will point to first string */
30          *p_str2;                            /* will point to following strings */
31
32     va_start(ap, number);                    /* point ap to first string */
33     p_str = va_arg(ap, char *);              /* get pointer to first string */
34     printf("\n\nParameters are \"%s\"", p_str);        /* and print it */
35
36     /* concatenate number -1 strings on the end of *p_str */
37     while( --number)
38         {
39         p_str2 = va_arg(ap, char *);         /* get pointer to next string */
40         printf(" \"%s\"", p_str2);                     /* and print it */
41         strcat(p_str, p_str2);                         /* concatenate */
42         }
43     va_end(ap);                                        /* cleanup */
44     return p_str;                            /* return pointer to first string */
45 }
```

Program 28_4 Function with a variable number of parameters

29

Accessing operating system facilities

The C standard libraries contain an extensive set of functions which provide a general programming environment to aid program portability. There are occasions when operations specific to a target operating system or hardware need to be performed:

1 To provide faster and more efficient access to system and I/O facilities than is possible via standard library functions, i.e. by making calls directly to the operating system or even driving the hardware directly (see Chapter 31 for further discussion).
2 To access facilities which are specific to a particular system, e.g. graphics facilities such as those used in Section 15.3 to plot a graph on the display screen.

Many compilers provide extra libraries to support different operating systems or target computers, e.g. the Turbo C graphics library `<graphics.h>` to drive IBM PC compatible graphics cards. In particular, the UNIX programming environment comes with extensive support libraries which provide user programs with access to system facilities. In addition, assuming the correct calling conventions are used, C programs may call modules written in other languages, e.g. many mathematical packages are implemented in Fortran but may be called from other languages including C (Chapter 30 will discuss calling functions written in other languages from C). If a library function is not available the host operating system must be called directly.

29.1 Hardware and software interrupts

An interrupt stops the execution of the current program and transfers control to an operating system function (usually called an interrupt service routine) which processes the interrupt and then returns control to the interrupted program.

Hardware interrupts are generated by a hardware device (memory management unit, timer, I/O device, etc.) to request service, e.g. a fault has occurred or an I/O operation is complete and the program may access the data.

Software interrupts are generated by programs (user or system) to request a service provided by the operating system kernel (the base level functions of the system).

29.1.1 Interrupt instructions

In a sophisticated multiprogramming environment a user program is only allowed to access memory allocated to its own instructions and data and any access outside this generates a memory segmentation fault. Interrupt instructions provide a mechanism by which a program can stop execution, transfer control to the operating system to carry out some function, and then resume. For example, the Intel 8086 family has the INT instruction:

```
INT      operand
```

and the Motorola MC68000 family has the TRAP instruction:

```
TRAP     operand
```

In both cases the value of operand specifies the interrupt number and the particular operating system function to be invoked. Additional information is passed to the operating system via processor registers (which may contain pointers to further data areas in the user program). When the operating system has completed the required operation it places information in the CPU registers and resumes the user program by executing a *return from interrupt* instruction, e.g. IRET on the Intel 8086 and RTE on the Motorola MC68000.

29.2 Accessing MS-DOS operating system facilities

The MS-DOS operating system, used on IBM PC compatible microcomputers, is accessed via the INT instruction. It is possible to write an assembly language function which loads relevant values into the processor registers, executes INT and then returns register values to the calling function. The majority of C compilers which run under MS-DOS provide such a function, e.g. both Turbo C and Borland C have the function int86. When int86 is called information is passed to MS-DOS via the 16-bit processor registers, ax, bx, cx, dx, si and di or their byte equivalents (the 16-bit register ax can be addressed as two 8-bit registers ah (the high byte) and al (the low byte)). Under Turbo C and Borland C the function prototype of int86 is declared in header file <dos.h> as follows:

```
int int86(int int_number, union REGS *in_registers, union REGS *out_registers);
```

where:

int_number	the interrupt number to invoke the required MS-DOS function
in_registers	the values to be passed to MS-DOS via processor registers
out_registers	the value of the processor registers as returned by MS-DOS.

The declaration of union REGS is of the form:

```
/* Intel 8086 family word registers (16-bit), cflag is the carry flag */
struct WORD_REGS { unsigned int ax, bx, cx, dx, si, di, cflag; };

/* Intel 8086 family byte registers (8-bit) */
struct BYTE_REGS { unsigned char al, ah, bl, bh, cl, ch, dl, dh; };

/* Intel 8086 general purpose registers: union overlays word and byte registers */
union REGS {
            struct WORD_REGS x;                    /* word registers */
            struct BYTE_REGS h;                    /* byte registers */
        };
```

This declares the types struct WORD_REGS (a structure of seven unsigned int 16-bit members) and struct BYTE_REGS (a structure of eight unsigned char 8-bit members). The union REGS overlays struct WORD_REGS and struct BYTE_REGS. Using a variable of type union REGS a CPU register may be accessed as a 16-bit value or a pair of 8-bit values, e.g.:

```
union REGS cpu_registers;                  /* define variable to hold cpu registers */

cpu_registers.x.ax = 2;                         /* set cpu register ax to 2 */
cpu_registers.h.al = 1;                          /* set low byte al to 1 */
cpu_registers.h.ah = 0;                         /* set high byte ah to 0 */
printf("bx = %d", cpu_registers.x.bx);              /* print value of bx */
```

Program 29_1 (next page but one) contains two screen control functions, scroll_text which scrolls a section of the text screen and cursor_text_to which positions the screen cursor. The standard IBM PC compatible display default text mode is 80 characters per line and 25 lines high with sixteen colours (video mode 3, see Tischer 1994). Various screen control functions are available (invoked via interrupt 10 hexadecimal) including:

Scrolling a window on the display screen. The following are specified and int86 called:

ah   equals 6 for scroll up and 7 for scroll down
al   equals the number of lines to scroll (0 means the window is cleared)
bh   attribute byte to put into the blanked characters, i.e. sets the screen colours:
     bits 0 to 3 specify the blue, green and red values of the foreground text colour
     bit 4 specifies the foreground intensity (0 normal, 1 intense)
     bits 5 to 7 specify the blue, green and red values of the background colour
     bit 7 specifies blink off (0) or on (1)
ch and cl   row and column position of top left hand corner of text window
dh and dl   row and column position of lower right hand corner of text window.

Setting the cursor position. The following are specified and int86 called:

ah   equals 2 for set cursor position
bh   equals the page number (several text pages are supported, 0 is default page)
dh   equals the row or line on the page (the top line is row 0)
dl   equals the column or character position (the first character is column 0).

The sequence of statements in Program 29_1 is:

3   include <dos.h> which contains the prototype of int86 and the declaration of union REGS
8-9 function prototypes for scroll_text and cursor_text_to
10 call scroll_text to clear the whole screen to green background and black foreground text will now be displayed in black on a green background
11 call cursor_text_to to position the text cursor at bottom left hand corner of screen
12 print message on bottom line of the screen
13 call scroll_text to scroll the text up 24 lines (message is now at top of screen)
14 call scroll_text to clear a window in the centre of the screen to blue background
15 call cursor_text_to to position the cursor at the centre of the text screen
16 print character 'x' in the middle of the screen.

Function scroll_text, lines 26 to 38, scrolls a section of the screen as specified by:

up_down is 0 for scroll up and 1 for scroll down (line 30 adds 6 to this value to set up ah)
x_left and y_top specifies the top left hand column and row of the area to scroll
x_right and y_bottom specifies the lower left hand column and row of the area to scroll
attribute specifies the attribute byte to be loaded into the scrolled characters.

Function cursor_text_to, lines 42 to 50, positions the cursor at screen coordinate x_column, y_row. See Section 30.1 for an assembly language version of this function and Section 31.2 for a similar function which accesses the video RAM memory directly using pointers.

    The functions use the standard coordinates of the screen (top left hand corner is (0, 0) and bottom right hand corner is (79, 24)). MS-DOS screen handling functions supplied with compilers may use a different coordinate system, e.g. the Turbo C cursor position function gotoxy (in <conio.h>) assumes that the top left hand corner is coordinate (1, 1).

    The register values returned by the third parameter of int86 (lines 37 and 49) are not used in this program. Other MS-DOS functions use them to return status information and data (see Section 29.3.4 which describes the use of PC serial ports under MS-DOS).

```
1  /* Program 29_1 MS-DOS functions to scroll the screen and position the cursor */
2
3  #include <dos.h>                              /* MS-DOS specific header file */
4  #include <stdio.h>                            /* standard I/O header file */
5
6  int main(void)
7  {
8      void scroll_text(int, int, int, int, int, int, int);       /* prototypes */
9      void cursor_text_to(const int x_column, const int y_row);
10     scroll_text(1, 0, 0,  79, 25, 0, 0x20);            /* clear screen to green */
11     cursor_text_to(0, 24);                     /* cursor to bottm L.H. corner */
12     printf("Text at bottom of screen");                        /* print text */
13     scroll_text(0, 0, 0,  79, 25, 24, 0x20);          /* scrool 24 lines up */
14     scroll_text(1, 20, 5, 59, 18, 0, 0x10);           /* scroll block to blue */
15     cursor_text_to(39 , 12);                  /* cursor to middle of screen */
16     putchar('x');                                     /* print a character */
17     return 0;
18 }
19
20 /*------------------------------------------------------------------------*/
21 /* scroll text screen up or down setting attribute byte as specified        */
22 /* on entry:  up_down    0 is scroll up, 1 is scroll down                    */
23 /*            x_left, y_top & x_right & y_bottom specify window coordinates  */
24 /*            lines      number of lines to scroll                           */
25 /*            attribute set IBM PC compatible attribute byte                 */
26 void scroll_text(int up_down, int x_left, int y_top,
27                  int x_right, int y_bottom, int lines, int attribute)
28 {
29     union REGS registers;                   /* variable to hold 8086 registers */
30     registers.h.ah = (unsigned char) ( 6 + up_down);   /* scroll up 6, down 7 */
31     registers.h.al = (unsigned char) lines;            /* scroll whole window */
32     registers.h.bh = (unsigned char) attribute;                /* attribute byte */
33     registers.h.cl = (unsigned char) x_left;      /* start column, x position */
34     registers.h.ch = (unsigned char) y_top;       /* start row, y position */
35     registers.h.dl = (unsigned char) x_right;     /* end column, x position */
36     registers.h.dh = (unsigned char) y_bottom;    /* end row, y position */
37     int86(0x10, &registers, &registers);      /* interrupt 10 hexadecimal */
38 }
39
40 /*------------------------------------------------------------------------*/
41 /* position text cursor, note that top left hand corner is column 0 row 0   */
42 void cursor_text_to(const int x_column, const int y_row)
43 {
44     union REGS registers;                   /* variable to hold 8086 registers */
45     registers.h.ah = 2;                 /* command, set text cursor position */
46     registers.h.bh = 0;                                       /* set page 0 */
47     registers.h.dl = (unsigned char) x_column;     /* column, x position */
48     registers.h.dh = (unsigned char) y_row;             /* row, y position */
49     int86(0x10, &registers, &registers);      /* interrupt 10 hexadecimal */
50 }
```

Program 29_1 MS-DOS functions to scroll the screen and position the cursor (Trubo C)

29.3 Using the RS232 serial port via MS-DOS

29.3.1 Introduction to asynchronous serial communications

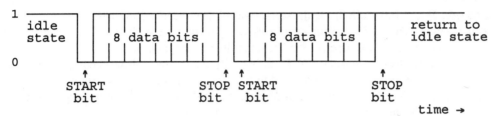

Fig. 29.1 Format of data on an asynchronous serial line

In an asynchronous serial communications system a byte of data is transferred between the transmitter and receiver bit by bit over a single communications line. Bit 0 is transmitted, then bit 1, through to bit 7. When the first byte is finished, the next byte, if any, can be sent. The data is transferred at an agreed rate of a number of bits per second, which is called the baud rate. To separate the data bytes a **START bit** is transmitted before the first data bit and one or two **STOP bits** are transmitted after the last data bit.

Fig. 29.1 shows the format of the data on a serial line when two 8-bit (byte) characters are transmitted (plus one START bit and one STOP bit in each case). When no data is being transmitted the line is in the idle state at logical 1, which corresponds to a nominal voltage level of -6 volt. When the serial interface is ready to transmit a data byte, it first transmits a START bit of logical 0 (nominal level +6 volt). The START bit serves to separate the idle state from the first data bit which could be 0 or 1. The data bits are then transmitted, bit 0 first, one after the other. After the data bits, one or two STOP bits, at logical 1, are transmitted. If, after the STOP bit(s), more data is available, the next START bit is transmitted, otherwise the line returns to the idle state. Thus if another data byte is to be immediately transmitted (as in Fig. 29.1), the STOP bit(s) serve to separate the last data bit from the START bit of the next data byte.

To check for errors when transmitting characters over a noisy communications channel, a parity check bit can be generated which can replace bit 7 of the character or be appended on the end of it to form a 9-bit code. Thus for each data byte transmitted, 10, 11 or 12 bits are actually transmitted (START + data bits + parity bit + STOP bit(s)). Typical baud rates are from 50 to 38.4K baud (bits/second). If, for example, the baud rate is 1200, each bit takes 0.8333 milliseconds to transmit with 120 bytes per second transferred if one STOP bit is used.

29.3.2 The EIA RS232C standard

The EIA RS232C standard was originally developed to foster data communications via public telephone networks. It defines the interface between a DTE (Data Terminal Equipment, i.e. a user terminal), and a DCE (Data Communications Equipment, i.e. a modem), using serial binary data interchange. The nominal signal levels are -6 volt for logical 1 (sometimes called MARK), but any level between -3 and -12 volt is accepted, and +6 volt for logical 0 (sometimes called SPACE), but any level between +3 and +12 volt is accepted. Signal levels between -3 and +3 volt are not valid and data would probably be corrupt.

The facilities of particular serial I/O ports vary with the computer concerned and the following refers to IBM PC and compatible microcomputers (using the standard RS232 25-way D type connector):

TXD (pin 2) and RXD (pin 3) are the serial transmit and receive data lines.

$\overline{\text{RTS}}$ **(Request To Send - output on pin 4)** is typically used as the **receive handshaking output** which the PC asserts to indicate that it can accept data.

$\overline{\text{CTS}}$ **(Clear To Send - input on pin 5)** is typically the hardware handshaking input to the PC. The external device asserts $\overline{\text{CTS}}$ to indicate that it is ready to accept data.

$\overline{\text{DSR}}$ **(Data Set Ready - input on pin 6)** indicates that the remote device (e.g. printer) is switched on and ready.

Signal ground (pin 7) is the common signal level reference (often ground).

$\overline{\text{DCD}}$ **(Data Carrier Detect - input on pin 8).** Can be used when the external device is able to send/receive characters (e.g. a modem would negate $\overline{\text{DCD}}$ if the data carrier was lost due to a telephone line fault).

$\overline{\text{DTR}}$ **(Data Terminal Ready - output on pin 20)** indicates that the PC is switched on.

The $\overline{\text{RTS}}$, $\overline{\text{CTS}}$, $\overline{\text{DSR}}$, $\overline{\text{DCD}}$ and $\overline{\text{DTR}}$ are all active low. In such a case, if the signal is negated the line is at logical 1 (a -6 volt level), and if it is asserted or active the value is logical 0 (a +6 volt level). For example, if a printer attached to the PC is not ready to accept data the $\overline{\text{CTS}}$ line will be logical 1, otherwise, if it is ready $\overline{\text{CTS}}$ will be at logical 0.

An additional problem occurs with IBM PC compatibles in that the connectors used are often 9-way D type connectors instead of the standard RS232 25-way D type. For example, Fig. 29.2 shows how to connect two IBM PC compatible microcomputers 'back to back' using a *null* modem with either 9-way or 25-way D type connectors (the signals emulate the handshaking of a modem). Programs used to transfer files between PCs typically use the connections shown in Fig. 29.2.

RS232C Signal name	25 pin	9 pin	cable connections	9 pin	25 pin	RS232C Signal name
data common	7	5		5	7	data common
RxD data	3	2		2	3	RxD data
TxD data	2	3		3	2	TxD data
$\overline{\text{RTS}}$ output	4	7		7	4	$\overline{\text{RTS}}$ output
$\overline{\text{CTS}}$ input	5	8		8	5	$\overline{\text{CTS}}$ input
$\overline{\text{DSR}}$ input	6	6		6	6	$\overline{\text{DSR}}$ input
$\overline{\text{DCD}}$ input	8	1		1	8	$\overline{\text{DCD}}$ input
$\overline{\text{DTR}}$ output	20	4		4	20	$\overline{\text{DTR}}$ output

Fig. 29.2 Serial port connection of two IBM PC compatible computers via a *null* modem

29.3.3 Handshaking with serial communications systems

When data is being transferred via a communications system it is possible for the transmitter to send information faster than the receiver can process it with the result that data can become lost. To prevent this a *handshaking protocol* is used in which the receiver signals the transmitter that it is *ready for data*.

Hardware handshaking makes use of the $\overline{\text{RTS}}$, $\overline{\text{CTS}}$, $\overline{\text{DCD}}$ and/or $\overline{\text{DTR}}$ lines of the serial interface. A common technique is to connect the $\overline{\text{RTS}}$ output of one computer to the $\overline{\text{CTS}}$ input of another (as in Fig. 29.2). When the receiver is ready for data it asserts $\overline{\text{RTS}}$ and the transmitter checks $\overline{\text{CTS}}$ before attempting to transmit.

Software handshaking is usually the XON/XOFF protocol in which the receiver transmits the XOFF character (transmit off, ASCII DC3 or CTRL/S) to stop the transmitter and the XON (transmit on, ASCII character DC1 or CTRL/Q) to restart transmission.

29.3.4 Accessing the serial ports via MS-DOS

The BIOS provides four functions, via interrupt 14 hexadecimal, for controlling the serial ports (MS-DOS devices COM1: to COM4:). In all cases ah contains the function number (0 to 4) and dx the serial port (note that COM1: is port 0, COM2: port 1, etc.). A brief description of each function is presented below (consult an MS-DOS text for full details).

Initialise serial port (function 0). The data word format is specified in al:

bits 1, 0   data word length: 10 is seven bits and 11 is eight bits
bit 2   number of stop bits: 0 is one stop bit, 1 is two stop bits
bits 4, 3   parity: 00 none, 01 odd, 10 none, 11 even
bits 7,6,5   baud rate: from 000 for 110 baud to 111 for 9600 baud.

Transmit character (function 1). Character to transmit is in al. On return, bit 7 of ah will be set if an error occurred and the remainder of ah contains the status (see function 3).

Receive a character (function 2). When called this function waits for a character to be received. The character is returned in al and bit 7 of ah indicates if an error occurred (bits 1, 2, 3 and 4 indicate the status, see function 3).

Read serial port status (function 3). Returns the values of the line status register and modem status register of the serial port in al and ah:

ah bit	line status register
7	time out
6	TSRE transmitter shift register empty (all data transmitted)
5	THRE transmitter holding register empty (ready for next data to transmit)
4	BI break detected (a break signal received, line held at logical 0)
3	FE framing error (character not properly framed by start and stop bits)
2	PE parity error (parity bit of character received was not as expected)
1	OE overrun error (another character received before last character read)
0	DR received data ready (character received and may be read)

al bit	modem status register
7	DCD Data Carrier Detect
6	RI ring indicator
5	DSR Data Set Ready (current level)
4	CTS Clear To Send (current level)
3	DDCD delta DCD (DCD changed since last checked)
2	TERI trailing edge ring indicator
1	DDSR delta DSR (DSR changed since last checked)
0	DCTS delta CTS (CTS changed since last checked)

Table 29.1 PC serial port line status and modem status registers

```
 1 /* Program 29_2  A terminal emulator using MS-DOS functions              */
 2
 3 #include <stdio.h>                              /* standard I/O header */
 4 #include <conio.h>                     /* MS-DOS direct console I/O header */
 5 #include "rs_lib.h"                    /* RS232 serial line functions header */
 6
 7 int main(void)
 8 {
 9     int io_port = 0, kb_char = 0, rs_char;       /* define various variables */
10
11     printf("Simple terminal emulator, hit <ESC> to terminate \n\n");
12     rs_initialise(io_port);                        /* initialise io_port */
13     rs_putstring(io_port, "testing line \x0d\x0a");       /* send characters */
14
15     /* loop: transmit keyboard characters and display received characters */
16     while (kb_char != 27)                    /* terminate when <ESC> entered */
17        {
18        if (kbhit())      /* if keyboard hit transmit character to serial port */
19           {
20           kb_char = getch();                     /* read keyboard character */
21           /* if character is <CR> send <CR> <LF> else transmit it */
22           if (kb_char == 0x0d) rs_putstring(io_port, "\x0d\x0a");
23           else               rs_putch(io_port, kb_char);
24           }
25        /* if character received from serial port display it */
26        if (rs_received(io_port))                    /* if character received */
27           {
28           rs_char = rs_getch(io_port);                     /* read it */
29           /* if carriage return do newline else display printable characters */
30           if (rs_char == 0x0d) {putch(10); putch(13);}
31           else             if (rs_char >= ' ') putch(rs_char);
32           }
33        }
34     rs_terminate(io_port);                          /* close io_port */
35     return 0;
36 }
```

Program 29_2 An RS232 serial line terminal emulator

```
 1 /* Header file rs_lib.h - prototypes for PC RS232 serial line functions */
 2
 3 void rs_initialise(const int io_port);                    /* initialise */
 4 void rs_terminate(const int io_port);                     /* terminate */
 5 void rs_putch(const int port, const int character);        /* put char */
 6 void rs_putstring(const int io_port, const char *string);  /* put string */
 7 int rs_received(int io_port);                            /* check char */
 8 char rs_getch(const int io_port);                         /* get char */
 9 int rs_status(const int io_port);                        /* get status */
```

Header file rs_lib.h For RS232 serial line functions

The header file rs_lib.h (previous page) contains prototypes of functions defining in implementation file rs_lib1.c which use the MS-DOS serial line functions described above). Program 29_2 (previous page) is a serial line terminal emulator which calls the functions in rs_lib1.c. These files work with Turbo V3, Borland V4.5 and Microsoft V8 (Visual C/C++ V1.5) compilers; when using compilers under Windows (e.g. Borland, Visual, etc.) ensure that the project type is an MS-DOS .EXE file and then run under DOS. For example, if two IBM PC compatible microcomputers running the program are connected 'back to back' (as in Fig. 30.2) characters typed on the keyboard of one machine should appear on the screen of the other (and vice versa).

3-5   include header files including "rs_lib.h"
12   call rs_initialise to initialise io_port (the value of io_port is initialised to 0 in line 8 but could be read from the command line, see Section 21.9)
13   transmit a string to serial line io_port
16-33   a while loop which exits when <ESC> is hit on the keyboard
        18-24   if the keyboard has been hit
                20   read the character from the keyboard
                22   if the character is <CR> transmit <CR> <LF> (carriage return, line feed)
                23   else transmit the character down the serial line
        26-32   if a character has been received from the serial line
                28   read the character into rs_char
                30   if the character is <CR> call putch to print a newline
                31   else if the character code is printable print the character
34   call rs_terminate to close the serial line.

In implementation file rs_lib1.c (next page) the serial line functions specify the serial port as parameter io_port (port 0 is com1: etc.). Thus a program can drive a number of serial ports simultaneously.

Function rs_initialise, lines 8 to 17, initialises the serial port to 9600 baud, 8 data bits, no parity and one stop bit. Function rs_status, lines 22 to 30, returns the line status and modem status register values (modem status in bits 0 to 7 and line status in bits 8 to 15). Function rs_putch, lines 34 to 46, transmits a character then checks for any error (if the character should be echoed to the screen remove the comments in line 38). Function rs_putstring, lines 50 to 54, calls rs_putch to transmit a string of characters. Function rs_received, lines 58 to 67, checks to see if a character has been received from the serial line (line 63 checks for a receive error and line 66 checks the DR bit in the line status register returning non zero (*true*) if a character has been received. Function rs_getch, lines 71 to 81, reads a character from a serial line; lines 75 and 76 wait for a character to be received and lines 77 to 80 read and return the character. Function rs_terminate, lines 85 to 88, does nothing but is added for completeness (required for libraries rs_lib2.c and rs_lib3.c which directly control the serial port, see Section 31.5).

In practice, depending upon the particular BIOS being used, there may be problems with hardware handshaking. Initialisation, function 0, normally asserts the output handshaking lines $\overline{RTS}$ and $\overline{DTR}$. Transmit character, function 1, normally checks the input handshaking line $\overline{CTS}$ (which is connected to the $\overline{RTS}$ line of the other machine). Check the documentation on the BIOS for details. An alternative technique is to address the hardware serial ports and control the handshaking lines directly (see Section 31.5).

```
 1 /* Implementation file rs_lib1.c -  PC serial line fuctions calling MS-DOS   */
 2
 3 #include <dos.h>                            /* MS-DOS specific header file */
 4 #include <stdio.h>                          /* standard I/O header file */
 5
 6 /*-------------------------------------------------------------------*/
 7 /* Serial port: initialise io_port                                   */
 8 void rs_initialise(const int io_port)
 9 {
10     union REGS registers;                  /* variable to hold 8086 registers */
11
12     registers.h.ah = 0;                             /* command, initialise */
13     /* set baud rate to 9600, 8 data bits, no parity and 1 stop bit */
14     registers.h.al = 0xe3;                          /* baud rate to 9600  */
15     registers.x.dx = io_port;                          /* for port */
16     int86(0x14, &registers, &registers);        /* interrupt 14 hexadecimal */
17 }
18
19 /*-------------------------------------------------------------------*/
20 /* Serial port: return status of io_port                             */
21 /*    line status in top byte (ah), modem status in lower byte (al)  */
22 int rs_status(const int io_port)
23 {
24     union REGS registers;                  /* variable to hold 8086 registers */
25
26     registers.h.ah = 3;                             /* command, read status */
27     registers.x.dx = io_port;                          /* from port */
28     int86(0x14, &registers, &registers);        /* interrupt 14 hexadecimal */
29     return registers.x.ax;                             /* return status */
30 }
31
32 /*-------------------------------------------------------------------*/
33 /* Serial port: transmit character to io_port                        */
34 void rs_putch(const int io_port, const int character)
35 {
36     union REGS registers;                  /* variable to hold 8086 registers */
37
38     /*putch(character);*/                      /* echo character if required */
39     registers.h.ah = 1;                        /* command, send character */
40     registers.h.al = (unsigned char) character;           /* character */
41     registers.x.dx = io_port;                             /* to port */
42     int86(0x14, &registers, &registers);        /* interrupt 14 hexadecimal */
43     if (registers.h.ah & 0x80)
44         printf("\nTransmit error on serial port %d, status %#x ",
45                 io_port, registers.h.ah);
46 }
47
48 /*-------------------------------------------------------------------*/
```

Library rs_lib1.c   PC serial line functions calling MS-DOS functions

```
49 /* Serial port: transmit a string of characters to io_port            */
50 void rs_putstring(const int io_port, const char *string)
51 {
52     while (*string != '\0')
53         rs_putch(io_port, *string++);
54 }
55
56 /*--------------------------------------------------------------------*/
57 /* Serial port: return TRUE if character available from serial line    */
58 int rs_received(int io_port)
59 {
60     int status;
61
62     status = rs_status(io_port);                        /* get status */
63     if (status & 0xe00)                           /* receive error ?? */
64         printf("\n\aRead error on serial line %d, status = %#x\n",
65                    io_port, status & 0xe00);
66     return (status & 0x100);       /* test DR bit in line status register */
67 }
68
69 /*--------------------------------------------------------------------*/
70 /* Serial port: read character from io_port                            */
71 char rs_getch(const int io_port)
72 {
73     union REGS registers;            /* variable to hold 8086 registers */
74
75     while (! rs_received(io_port))
76         /* wait for character received */ ;
77     registers.h.ah = 2;                     /* command, read character */
78     registers.x.dx = io_port;                          /* from port */
79     int86(0x14, &registers, &registers);      /* interrupt 14 hexadecimal */
80     return registers.h.al;                      /* return character */
81 }
82
83 /*--------------------------------------------------------------------*/
84 /* Serial port: terminate io_port executing any close down operations  */
85 void rs_terminate(const int io_port)
86 {
87     /* no code in this case */
88 }
```

Implementation file rs_lib1.c   PC serial line functions calling MS-DOS functions

29.4 Using a Microsoft compatible mouse under MS-DOS

The majority of IBM PC compatible microcomputers come equipped with a Microsoft compatible mouse which can be used to point to objects on the display screen. A program can read the position of the mouse and determine which, if any, of its buttons are pressed.

Before the mouse can be used a *device driver* must be installed. The driver interfaces with the mouse hardware and provides facilities, via interrupt 33 hexadecimal, to enable programs to control the mouse and read its position. The driver may be loaded from within the MS-DOS system configuration file CONFIG.SYS:

```
device = mouse.sys
```

When the mouse is being used a cursor, which tracks mouse movement, may be displayed on the screen (this is in addition to the text cursor which indicates where the next character will be displayed). The mouse software uses a coordinate system which is related to the display coordinates of the screen. For example, when the display is in the default text mode the mouse uses a coordinate system of 640 points horizontal by 200 points vertical (refer to a mouse manual for full details). Dividing the mouse coordinates by eight maps to the default text coordinates of 80 characters across the screen by 25 lines high.

The mouse driver provides a number of functions for controlling the mouse and reading its status. A function is selected by setting ax to the function number and executing an int86 with 33 hexadecimal specified as the interrupt number. The functions include:

Reset mouse and determine status (function 0). Setting ax to 0 and calling int86 will reset the mouse software (if installed) and position the mouse cursor in the centre of the display screen. On return ax will be 0 if the mouse is not available otherwise it will be -1 and bx will contain the number of mouse buttons.

Display mouse cursor (function 1). By default the mouse cursor is not displayed. Setting ax to 1 and calling int86 will display the mouse cursor on the screen at its current position (in a text mode two cursors are displayed; the 'normal' text cursor and the mouse cursor which will move when the mouse is moved).

Remove mouse cursor (function 2). Setting ax to 2 and calling int86 will remove the mouse cursor from the screen. Note that the mouse cursor should be removed before attempting to draw to the screen. If this is not done and the cursor is physically displayed on the screen part of the displayed image will disappear the next time the cursor is blinked off.

Read mouse cursor position and button status (function 3). Setting ax to 3 and calling int86 will return the mouse cursor position in cx (horizontal) and dx (vertical) and the button values in bx (the left hand button is bit 0 and the right hand button is bit 1; a bit being set indicates that the corresponding button is pressed).

Set cursor position (function 4). Setting ax to 3, cx to the horizontal coordinate, dx to the vertical coordinate and calling int86 will set the mouse cursor position (the coordinates must be valid values).

Determine mouse motion (function 11). Setting ax to 3 and calling int86 will return an indication of mouse movement since the last call (to this function). A horizontal count (positive is move right and negative is move left) is returned in cx and a vertical count (positive is move down and negative is move up) in dx. A 0 in both counts indicates the mouse has not moved.

For example, prototypes of functions to interface to the mouse could be (see the problems at the end of the chapter):

```
/* Initialise Microsoft mouse, if fail return 0 else if OK number of buttons  */
int msm_init_mouse(void);
/* switch mouse cursor off (on_off = 0) or on (on_off = 1)                     */
void msm_onoff_cursor(const int on_off);
/* Read mouse cursor position into x_pos & y_pos and button values            */
void msm_read_cursor(int &x_pos, int &y_pos, int &lh_button, int &rh_button);
```

29.5 Invoking processes

A common requirement in advanced programs is to be able to execute one program (the child) from within another (the parent). The facilities available vary with the operating system and compiler. This section will present a **brief** review of common facilities (see Kernighan and Pike 1984 for more discussion of UNIX facilities).

The function execlp (and variations in <process.h>) overlays the current process with the named program, e.g. to print a file under MS-DOS (see file c29\p29_3.c on disk):

```
execlp("print", "print", "p29_3.c", NULL);     /* attempt to invoke print */
printf("execlp 'print p29_3.c' failed\n");              /* failed !! */
```

The first parameter is the filename of the command (i.e. PRINT.EXE in the above example) and the second and subsequent parameters are the command and command line parameters to be passed to the child process (as in the array argv, see Section 28.5). If successful the parent process is terminated and the child process loaded and executed otherwise execlp returns to the parent process (if the file print.exe does not exist for example) and errno (see Appendix C.3) contains an error indicator. Under UNIX the command to obtain a long directory listing would be (in file c29\p29_4.c on disk):

```
execlp("ls", "ls", "-l", NULL);                  /* attempt to invoke ls */
printf("execlp 'ls -l' failed\n");                       /* failed !! */
```

execlp (and similar) is used when the parent process is to be terminated. There are many occasions when the parent process either wishes to resume execution when the child terminates or to run concurrently with the child (assuming a multiprocessing environment such as UNIX). MS-DOS C compilers usually have a function spawnlp (plus variations, see compiler manuals), e.g. to use the MS-DOS command del to delete files:

```
/* spawn a process to delete files */
error = spawnlp(P_WAIT, "del", "del", "*.old", "/N", NULL);
if (error == 0) printf("spawnlp 'del *.old/N' successful\n");
else            perror("spawnlp 'del *.old/N' failed \n");
```

The first parameter is mode, which indicates the state the parent process should take when the child is invoked and the remainder are as for execpl. In the above example the mode is P_WAIT which suspends the parent process until the child terminates (the modes available depend upon the compiler and operating system, see compiler manuals). When the child terminates the parent process resumes and spawnlp returns, as a function result, the exit status of the child process (in this case indicating if del was successful).

Under UNIX the function fork makes an exact copy of the process and executes it concurrently with the parent. The only difference between the two processes is that fork returns the child process ID to the parent and zero to the child (if fork fails -1 is returned and errno set). The child can then call execlp to carry out the required task. For example,

```
int pid;
if((pid = fork()) < 0)                              /* create new process */
    printf("Fork failed\n");
else
    if (pid == 0) printf("The child\n");
    else          printf("The parent, child pid %d", pid);
```

The child and parent then execute in parallel (if there is only one processor they are time-shared). Open files are shared between parent and child. Initially, the child will have a copy of the parent's memory, but it will be a separate copy. Interprocess communication can be achieved using the function `pipe` to create an interprocess input/output mechanism and then the low-level I/O functions `read` and `write` used to pass information (see UNIX systems manuals for details). If required the parent can wait for a child to terminate:

```
pid_child = wait(&status);
```

Wait returns the process ID of the terminating child process (this can be checked against the value returned by `fork`) and `status` contains information about the child's exit status.

Using `fork`, `execlp`, etc. is fairly complicated and the function `system` (available under UNIX and many other systems) has a single parameter, a command line exactly as typed at the keyboard (without the newline), e.g. to list all .c files under MS-DOS:

```
system("dir *.c");                              /* call system */
printf("parent program resumed");
```

The parent process is suspended and the command line `dir *.c` is passed to the MS-DOS command interpreter which, assuming all is well, executes the `dir` command (see file c29\p29_5.c on disk). When the command interpreter terminates, the parent process is resumed with `system` returning the return code from the command processor.

Problems for Chapter 29

Problem 29.1 Connect two IBM PC compatible computers 'back to back' (as in Fig. 29.2). Using the functions from Program 29_2 implement a file transfer program, e.g.:
(a) Read characters from the serial port saving them to a named file on disk (on the other machine use a command such as `copy file com1:` to transmit a file).
(b) Extend the program so that one machine acts as a host and the other a slave (under the command of the host). The user should be able to enter commands on the host to read and write files from/to corresponding files on the slave. The same program should be able to act as either host or slave.
(c) Extend the program to check for errors on the serial line. Parity can be used to check characters and a checksum or CRC check performed on block transfers. Use a random number generator to generate errors, e.g. corrupt the odd character.

Problem 29.2 Implement and test functions to interface to a Microsoft compatible mouse (see Section 29.4). Test using the default text screen mode reading the cursor position and printing a character at that position when the left hand button is pressed. Terminate the program when the right hand button is pressed.

Problem 29.3 Using the mouse functions and a suitable graphics library implement a painting system. A section of the screen should be reserved as a command area with facilities to select a drawing colour, different brushes, lines, etc.

Problem 29.4 Using an operating system which supports multiprocessing (e.g. UNIX on workstations, LINUX on PCs) write a C program which opens a pipe (Kernighan & Pike, 1984), forks a process (check the fork works) and the child process opens a file and sends the contents via the pipe to the parent which saves it to another file.

30

Using assembly language from C

On occasion there may be a requirement to use assembly language from a C program:

1. to speed up time critical functions (however, it is often cheaper to buy a faster computer than rewriting the code in assembly language);
2. to access machine specific hardware facilities for which library functions do not already exist.

In practice 99% of a program will be implemented in C with assembly language limited to critical areas (Hintz 1992). Assembly language code may be implemented:

1. As independent assembly language source code files which have to be assembled and then linked to the calling program by the linker.
2. As in-line code, where assembly language statements are included within the C program (the C compiler calls a suitable assembler when it comes across such statements). Not all C compilers support this facility.

This chapter introduces the techniques used to interface assembly language functions to C; it assumes a knowledge of the target assembly language and an understanding of parameter passing on the system stack.

30.1 Separate assembly language functions

When implementing a function in assembly language it is important to obey the rules imposed by the C compiler which will be used to compile the calling functions:

1. Memory allocation: where code and data is placed.
2. Parameter passing: the order in which parameters are passed and their size in bytes.
3. Register usage: which processor registers must **not** be changed, which may be used but must be restored to their original values and which may be freely used.

Refer to the appropriate compiler manuals for full details.

30.1.1 Turbo C and Microsoft C under the MS-DOS operating system

The rules for interfacing assembly language functions when using the Turbo C V3.00 and Microsoft C V7.00 compilers under MS-DOS include the following:

1. Program code is placed in the segment _TEXT and variables in the segment _DATA.
2. Actual parameters are passed on the stack from right to left, i.e. the last parameter is pushed first (the _fastcall calling convention should not be used).
3. The AX, BX, CX, DX, ES and flags registers can be freely used (all others should be saved and restored).
4. A 16-bit function result (char, int or near pointer) is returned in AX.
   A 32-bit function result is returned in DX (high-order) and AX (low-order).
   If the return value is longer than 32 bits store it in memory and return a pointer to it.

```
 1 ; position text cursor, note that top left hand corner is column 0 row 0
 2 ; The C prototype should be:
 3 ;    void _cdecl _far cursor_text_to(const int x_column, const int y_row);
 4 ; i.e.: _cdecl to use the C calling convention and _far to use a 32-bit CALL
 5 ;
 6         PUBLIC  _cursor_text_to         ;declare symbol to use in other modules
 7 _TEXT   SEGMENT WORD PUBLIC 'CODE'      ;place code in _TEXT segment
 8         ASSUME  CS: _TEXT               ;use CS to access the following code
 9 ;
10 _cursor_text_to PROC FAR
11         push    bp                      ;save bp
12         mov     bp,sp                   ;move sp into bp
13         mov     ah,2                    ;command, set text cursor position
14         mov     bh,0                    ;set page 0
15         mov     dl, [bp + 6]            ;column, x position
16         mov     dh, [bp + 8]            ;row, y position
17         int     10h                     ;interrupt 10 hexadecimal
18         pop     bp                      ;restore bp
19         ret                             ;return to calling function
20 _cursor_text_to ENDP                    ;end of _cursor_text_to
21 _TEXT   ENDS
22         END
```

File text_to.asm Version of function _cursor_text_to, see Program 29_1

File test_to.asm shows an assembly language version of the function cursor_text_to described in Program 29_1. The sequence of statements is:

6 the name _cursor_text_to is declared to be PUBLIC so that it can be accessed from other modules (note that C compilers place a _ before function names)

7 the following code is within the segment _TEXT

8 the segment register CS will be used to access the code

10 start of function _cursor_text_to (PROC defines the start of a procedure/function) PROC FAR indicates that the function will be called with a 32-bit CALL instruction

11-12 save register BP (it must be preserved) and copy the stack pointer SP into BP

13-14 and set up AH for function 2 (see Section 29.2) and set up BH to page 0

15-16 load the parameters x_column and y_row into DL and DH

17 call MS-DOS via interrupt number 10 hexadecimal (see Section 29.2)

18 restore BP

19 return to calling function (the type of return corresponds to PROC FAR in line 10)

20 end of function.

The function may be assembled using the majority of PC assemblers including the Microsoft Macro Assembler MASM or the Turbo Assembler TASM, e.g.:

MASM /MX text_to.asm text_to.obj   using the Microsoft assembler
TASM /mx text_to.asm   using the Turbo assembler.

The /MX and /mx options specify that symbols are case sensitive (otherwise the assembler converts symbols such as _cursor_text_to to upper case).

In the C program which calls cursor_text_to the function prototype should be specified as follows:

```
void _cdecl _far cursor_text_to(const int x_column, const int y_row);
```

The keywords _cdecl and _far instruct the compiler:

_cdecl: to use the C calling convention (in case _fastcall, _pascal, etc. is the default).

_far: to use a CALL instruction with a 32-bit address (to match the PROC FAR). Hence whatever memory model is the default, the function will be called correctly.

In file c30\p30_1.c on the disk is a version of Program 29_1 modified to use text_to.asm. This program will have to be linked to the object file text_to.obj, e.g. using Turbo C V3.00:

```
tcc p30_1.c text_to.obj
```

30.1.2 Whitesmiths C cross compiler for a MC68000 target microcomputer

The rules defining the Whitesmiths C interface to 68000 assembly language are complex (Whitesmiths 1986, Bramer & Bramer 1991) and include (only integral data is considered):

1   Executable code is generated into the **.text** segment.
2   Literal and global (external) data is generated into the **.data** segment.
3   Short integers are 16-bit words, integers and long integers are 32-bit long words.
4   Function calls are performed thus:
   (a) in a function call parameters are moved onto the stack **right to left**, i.e. the last argument is moved onto the stack first;
   (b) when used as function arguments character and short data is sign extended to a long word (integer and long integer data is already long word);
   (c) the function is called via jsr _func (_ prefixes the function name);
   (d) the function may use registers D0, D1, D2, D6, D7, A0, A1 and A2 without problems, if any others are used they must be **preserved** (by using MOVEM);
   (e) the function result (if any) is returned in D7.

Fig. 30.1 (next page) contains two functions which enable a C program to access the Motorola MC68000 MOVEP (Move Peripheral Data) instruction which transfers two or four bytes of data between a specified processor **data register** and **alternate byte locations in memory** (Bramer & Bramer 1991). In a C program the function movep_l_to_memory would be declared using the prototype:

```
int movep_l_to_memory(int value, iobyte *address);
```

This function moves value (a 32-bit int) to alternate locations starting at the specified address. The type iobyte is used to access byte-sized memory mapped I/O registers:

```
typedef volatile unsigned char iobyte;    /* I/O device register is a volatile byte */
```

The function movep_l_to_memory could be called as follows:

```
movep_l_to_memory(250000, (iobyte *) 0x680025);
```

The value 250000 is loaded into alternate bytes starting at address 0x680025. Note the cast (iobyte *) which converts the integer to a 'pointer to iobyte', this is highly machine dependent (see Section 31.1). Before movep_l_to_memory is called the value 0x680025 is pushed onto the stack followed by the value 250000. When movep_l_to_memory is called the 32-bit return address is pushed onto the stack and the first instruction of movep_l_to_memory executed. The sequence of statements is (referring to line numbers alongside Fig. 30.1):

9 move the address value 0x680025 off the stack into register AO

10 move the value 250000 off the stack into DO

11 move the 32-bit value in DO to alternate memory locations starting at address 0x680025

12 copy the value in DO to D7 (the function result is returned in D7)

13 execute RTS (return from subroutine) to return to calling function.

The calling function would then remove the parameters from the stack.

```
 1 * MOVEP.S  Assembly language functions to support Whitesmiths C cross compiler
 2 *    Using Whitesmiths AS68K cross assembler to MC68000 target computer
 3              .text                       * start code section
 4              .even                       * align to even address
 5 *
 6 * Function to perform a long word sized MOVEP to memory, C prototype is:
 7 *    int movep_l_to_memory(int value, iobyte *address);
 8 _movep_l_to_memory:
 9              movea.l    8(a7),a0         * get address into AO
10              move.l     4(a7),d0         * get value into DO
11              movep.l    d0,0(a0)         * move value from DO to address (AO)
12              move.l     d0,d7            * return value written
13              rts                         * return with function result in D7
14 *
15 * Function to perform a long word sized MOVEP from memory, C prototype is:
16 *    int movep_l_from_memory(iobyte *address);
17 _movep_l_from_memory:
18              movea.l    4(a7),a0         * get address into AO
19              movep.l    0(a0),d7         * move value from (AO) into D7
20              rts                         * return with function result in D7
21 *
22 * declare global identifiers (external identifiers for C programs)
23              .globl     _movep_l_to_memory
24              .globl     _movep_l_from_memory
```

Fig. 30.1 Assembly language functions to support Whitesmiths C cross compiler

30.2 In-line assembly language statements

Some compilers allow assembly language statements to be placed in-line with C statements. For example, Turbo and Microsoft C use the _asm keyword which invokes an in-line assembler. An _asm statement may appear wherever a C statement may be used, e.g.:

```
_asm      mov    ah,2                /* command, set text cursor position */
_asm      mov    bh,0                             /* set page 0 */
```

Alternatively an _asm block may be enclosed in braces {}. An _asm statement can freely use the AX, BX, CX and DX registers (save and restore any others) and can refer to any C symbols which are in scope (C symbols are variable and function names and labels; not symbolic constants). Thus it is possible to write a function letting C handle the parameter passing (which is quite complex) and then drop into assembly language.

Program 30_2 (next page) shows functions scroll_text and _cursor_text_to with the parameter passing handled by C and the internals of the functions in assembly language (as in file text_to.asm). Note that the C formal function parameters are accessed by name

(BYTE PTR lets the assembler know that values required are byte sized). Program 30_2 can be compiled with Turbo C V3.00, Borland V4.5 and Microsoft V7.00/8.00 using the DOS command line compilers or under Windows with the target specified as a DOS .EXE file.

```
 1 /*-----------------------------------------------------------------*/
 2 /* scroll text screen up or down setting attribute byte as specified        */
 3 void scroll_text(int up_down, int x_left, int y_top,
 4                  int x_right, int y_bottom, int lines, int attribute)
 5 {
 6     _asm {
 7         mov   ah,6
 8         add   ah, BYTE PTR up_down       /* command, scroll up (6) or down (7) */
 9         mov   al, BYTE PTR lines                   /* scroll whole window */
10         mov   bh, BYTE PTR attribute                  /* attribute byte */
11         mov   cl, BYTE PTR x_left            /* start column, x position */
12         mov   ch, BYTE PTR y_top                /* start row, y position */
13         mov   dl, BYTE PTR x_right             /* end column, x position */
14         mov   dh, BYTE PTR y_bottom               /* end row, y position */
15         int   0x10                        /* interrupt 10 hexadecimal */
16     }
17 }
18
19 /*-----------------------------------------------------------------*/
20 /* position text cursor, note that top left hand corner is column 0 row 0      */
21 void cursor_text_to(const int x_column, const int y_row)
22 {
23     _asm {
24         mov   ah,2                    /* command, set text cursor position */
25         mov   bh,0                                      /* set page 0 */
26         mov   dl, BYTE PTR x_column            /* column, x position */
27         mov   dh, BYTE PTR y_row                    /* row, y position */
28         int   0x10                        /* interrupt 10 hexadecimal */
29     }
30 }
```

Program 30_2 C functions using in-line assembly statements (main as Program 29_1)

30.3 Interfacing other high-level languages with C

The interfacing of other high-level languages to C is dependent upon the operating system, compiler and linker being used. Of particular importance is:

1   How memory is allocated to store to code and data, and the types and sizes of the data objects, e.g. a language may have data types which do not exist in other languages.

2   How function parameters are passed and the function result returned. C pushes parameters onto the stack from right to left (so that a variable number of parameters can be accessed). Fortran and Pascal generally push the parameters from left to right.

For example, a Microsoft C function can be called from Microsoft Pascal and Fortran (and vice versa). The use of the keywords _cdecl, _pascal and _fortran indicates which calling convention is to be used (see compiler manuals for full details).

31

Low-level hardware programming

It is sometimes necessary to access specified locations in the physical memory map of a computer system directly, e.g.:

1   to perform RAM memory tests, e.g. at power up;
2   to directly manipulate the video memory of a graphics display (see Section 31.2);
3   to access memory mapped I/O registers (see Section 31.3).

Accessing physical memory is dependent upon:

The computer architecture: e.g. using linear addressing (as in the Motorola MC68000 family) or using segment addressing (as in the 16-bit addressing of Intel 8086 family).

The operating system:
  (a) A simple operating system, such as MS-DOS, allows any program unlimited access to physical memory. A sophisticated multi-tasking operating system, such as UNIX, Windows 95 or OS/2, restricts the program to its own address space.
  (b) In a multi-tasking environment the memory addresses used by the program are logical addresses within the program memory map, not actual physical addresses.

The compiler: which provides library facilities to suit the host operating system.

31.1 Setting up pointers to 'point to' locations in physical memory

Consider:

```
int *mem_pointer;                          /* define a 'pointer to int' */

mem_pointer = 0x1000;                      /* assign an integer to the pointer */
```

A 'pointer to an int' is defined and then assigned the integer value 0x1000. This is a highly machine dependent assignment and a modern compiler will issue a warning, e.g. using Turbo C on an IBM PC compatible:

```
mem_pointer = 0x1000;                      /* assign an integer to the pointer */
Warning x.c 5: Nonportable pointer conversion in function main
```

To assure the compiler that you know what you are doing the integer should be cast to the correct pointer type and the warning will disappear, e.g.:

```
mem_pointer = (int *) 0x1000;              /* assign an integer to the pointer */
```

The compiler converts the integer value 0x1000 into the equivalent value for a 'pointer to int'.

When using pointers to physical memory locations it is very important to have an understanding of the architecture of the machine concerned, the internal format of the pointers (the addressing mode used for the pointer) and a knowledge of exactly what one is trying to achieve. Compilers often have library functions to manipulate addresses to suit the host operating system and machine architecture.

31.2 Directly accessing video RAM of an IBM PC compatible computer

Section 29.2 introduced functions to manipulate the screen of an IBM PC compatible microcomputer by means of ROM BIOS functions accessed via MS-DOS calls. A faster, but more difficult and potentially dangerous, method of manipulating such information is to directly access the RAM memory which holds the video information. An IBM PC compatible computer generally operates in a default text mode of 80 characters per line and 25 lines high with sixteen colours; video mode 3, for full details consult a specialist text (Tischer 1994). In this case the video RAM used to store the text starts at address B800:0000 (where B800 is the segment register value and 0000 is the offset value). When using Borland and Microsoft compilers a pointer to this address may be defined:

```
typedef unsigned char _far byte;          /* define a memory location as a byte */

byte *video_start = (byte *) 0xB8000000L;          /* define start of PC video RAM */
```

This defines the type byte and the pointer video_start (a 'pointer to byte') initialised to the address of the start of the video RAM. The _far indicates that a 32-bit pointer should be used (consult compiler manuals to see how such pointers are defined). Once initialised the pointer can be used to directly read and write the video RAM. It should be noted that each character position on the screen consists of two bytes in video RAM; the character to be displayed and the attribute byte which specifies the colours (see Section 29.2 for details). Thus to access a character at screen position x_column, y_row the address is:

```
character address = video_start + y_row * 160 + x_column * 2
```

Program 31_1 contains a number of functions which access the video RAM directly to clear the screen and write characters. This works with Turbo V3, Borland V4.5 and Microsoft V8 (Visual C/C++ V1.5) compilers; when using compilers under Windows (e.g. Borland, Visual, etc.) ensure that the project type is an MS-DOS .EXE file and then run under DOS. The program starts by defining two pointers:

5   define the type byte
7   define video_start which holds the start address of the video RAM
8   define video_text which holds the address to write the next character to
       (initialised to the start of the video RAM).

The function main, lines 10 to 25, tests the screen functions:

12-16   prototypes of the screen manipulation functions
18   call clear_screen to clear the text screen to a green background (attribute 0x20)
19-20   set character position to 39, 12 and write an 'x' (white on blue)
21-22   set character position to 33, 14 and write a string (red on cyan)
23   write the number 1024 (green on red).

Function clear_screen, lines 29 to 39, clears the whole of the text screen to spaces setting up the attribute byte as specified by a parameter:

31   define pointer video_mem initialised to the start address of the video RAM
34-39   a while loop clearing the screen
      36 set the character to space, incrementing video_mem
      37 set up the attribute byte, incrementing video_mem.

The pointer video_mem accesses RAM from address video_start (the start of the video RAM) to video_start + (160 * 25) - 1 (the address of last character on the screen);

remember the screen is 80 characters wide by 25 lines high and each character position consists of two bytes.

The function write_char, lines 43 to 47, writes a character to the address specified by video_text (which is incremented to point to the next character position). Function write_string, lines 51 to 58, writes a string of characters. Function position_text, lines 61 to 68, sets up the address corresponding to the screen position x_column, y_row in pointer video_text. Function write_number, lines 72 to 77, writes the numeric value of integer parameter number to the screen; function sprintf (see Section 23.4) is called to convert the numeric value into a string and then write_string called to display it on the screen.

Note that the above functions take no account of the end of a line on the screen (wrapping around to the start of the next line) and, more importantly, no account of the end of the screen (thus it is possible to overwrite RAM following). In practice the functions should check for valid addresses before writing data.

In addition, the character position referred to has nothing to do with the MS-DOS screen cursor (which will not move) and is just used to position the characters to be written. For details of how to move the actual screen cursor consult a specialist technical text (Tischer 1994) or call the MS-DOS cursor move function.

In practice such screen manipulation functions would probably be implemented in assembly language (to be called from C programs) to achieve the best possible execution speed (which is essential for such interactive operations).

```
 1 /* Program 31_1 - directly accessing IBM PC compatible video RAM         */
 2
 3 #include <stdio.h>
 4
 5 typedef unsigned char _far byte;        /* define a memory location as a byte */
 6
 7 byte *video_start = (byte *) 0xB8000000L;    /* define start of PC video RAM */
 8 byte *video_text  = (byte *) 0xB8000000L;    /* address to display character */
 9
10 int main()
11 {
12     void clear_screen(int attribute);                      /* prototypes */
13     void position_text(const int x_column, const int y_row);
14     void write_char(const char ch, const int attribute);
15     void write_string(const char *string, const int attribute);
16     void write_number(const int number, const int attribute);
17
18     clear_screen(0x20);              /* clear the screen to green background */
19     position_text(39, 12);           /* position cursor in middle of screen */
20     write_char('x', 0x17);                       /* write x, white on blue */
21     position_text(33, 14);              /* and display a string below it */
22     write_string("hello john doe", 0x34);              /* red on cyan */
23     write_number(1024, 0x42);                          /* green on red */
24     return 0;
25 }
26
27 /*------------------------------------------------------------------------*/
```

Program 31_1   Directly accessing IBM PC compatible video RAM

```
28 /* clear the screen to spaces setting attribute bytes to specified value      */
29 void clear_screen(int attribute)
30 {
31     byte *video_mem = video_start;          /* pointer initialised to video RAM */
32
33     /* clear 25 lines of 80 characters (character plus attribute byte) */
34     while (video_mem < video_start + 160 * 25)
35         {
36         *video_mem++ = ' ';                        /* set character to space */
37         *video_mem++ = (byte) attribute;                   /* set attribute */
38         }
39 }
40
41 /*-------------------------------------------------------------------------*/
42 /* write character ch with attribute at current cursor position            */
43 void write_char(const char ch, const int attribute)
44 {
45     *video_text++ = ch;                              /* write character */
46     *video_text++ = (byte) attribute;                   /* set attribute */
47 }
48
49 /*-------------------------------------------------------------------------*/
50 /* write string with attribute at current cursor position                  */
51 void write_string(const char *string, const int attribute)
52 {
53     while (*string != '\0')
54         {
55         *video_text++ = *string++;                   /* write character */
56         *video_text++ = (byte) attribute;                /* set attribute */
57         }
58 }
59
60 /*-------------------------------------------------------------------------*/
61 /* position text on screen, note that top left hand corner is column 0 row 0 */
62 void position_text(const int x_column, const int y_row)
63 {
64     /* set up address to write next character to,                        *
65      * i.e. each character is two bytes (character plus attribute)        *
66      *  and there are 80 characters on a line (in y direction)           */
67     video_text = video_start + y_row * 160 + x_column * 2;
68 }
69
70 /*-------------------------------------------------------------------------*/
71 /* write a number to the screen                                            */
72 void write_number(const int number, const int attribute)
73 {
74     char text[100];
75     sprintf(text," %d ", number);
76     write_string(text, attribute);
77 }
```

Program 31_1   Directly accessing IBM PC compatible video RAM

31.3 Accessing input/output device registers

Each I/O device interface contains a number of registers which pass data and status/control information between a program running in the processor and the I/O device circuits. There are two techniques for accessing I/O device registers:

(a) by means of special I/O instructions;

or (b) by having the I/O registers appear as part of the primary memory map.

In both cases, before any I/O programming can be carried out, the I/O addresses and the format of the information within them must be known (from hardware manuals).

Special I/O instructions. Some processors have a set of special instructions for accessing I/O device registers. Each register is assigned an I/O port number (built into the hardware of the interface) and this is used as an operand in I/O instructions. For example, the Intel 8086 family of microprocessors uses the I/O instructions IN and OUT, thus:

```
IN    AL,n        read contents of I/O port n to register AL
OUT   n,AL        output contents of register AL to port n
```

Memory mapped I/O registers appear as part of the primary memory map of the computer. In general, any instructions which are used to read and write memory can be used to access the I/O registers. Although the registers are mapped as part of the memory address space of the computer, they are **not** normal memory for program and data storage.

31.4 Polled and interrupt I/O programming

Before a program can transfer data to an I/O device it must ensure that the device is not busy (e.g. a printer may be in the process of printing a character). The simplest I/O programming technique is to use a polling loop, in which the program polls or examines the interface status register to determine if the device is ready for a data transfer. If the device is busy the program loops back to check the status register again. If the status register indicates that the device is ready for more data the next data transfer is performed.

In the case of interrupt I/O normal program execution runs in parallel with an I/O data transfer. When the I/O device interface is ready for the next data transfer it sends a signal to the processor which interrupts the current program being executed, and transfers control to an **interrupt service routine** (which is similar in format to a normal C function). The interrupt service routine code performs the data transfer to the I/O device and terminates with an instruction which resumes execution of the program that had been interrupted. The drawbacks with interrupt driven I/O systems are that the interface is more complex and it is more difficult to write and test the I/O driver programs than when using polled I/O techniques (Bramer & Bramer 1991).

31.5 Directly accessing the serial ports of an IBM PC compatible

The serial ports of IBM PC compatible computers are generally based on the Intel 8250 ACE (Asynchronous Communications Element) interface chip or equivalent. Up to four serial ports may be attached (ports 0 to 3 which are called COM1: to COM4: at MS-DOS command level, see Section 29.3) and are accessed via IN and OUT instructions. Each port consists of a number of registers which are accessed at sequential port I/O addresses from the following base address:

port number	0 (COM1:)	1 (COM2:)	2 (Com3:)	3 (COM4:)
base address	0x3F8	0x2F8	0x3E8	0x2E8

The main registers of the 8250 are (to simplify the description the divisor latch is omitted):

register name	offset from base	register function
DataReg	0 write	transmitter buffer: holds next character to transmit
	0 read	receiver buffer: holds character received
IntEna	1	Interrupt enable: bits enable various interrupts
IntIdent	2	Interrupt identification: bits identify interrupt cause
LineCtrl	3	Line control: bits set parity, word length, etc.
ModCtrl	4	Modem control: bits set RTS, DTR, etc. see below
LineStatus	5	Line status: state of DR, THRE, etc. see Table 29.1
ModStatus	6	Modem status: state of CTS, DSR, etc. see Table 29.1

Thus the line control register of serial port 1 is at I/O port address 0x2FB (0x2F8 + 3). When using Microsoft C the I/O ports can be accessed either from _asm assembly language statements (see Chapter 30) or via the functions (declared in header file <conio.h>):

```
int _far_ _cdecl inp(unsigned int io_port);              /* read a byte from io_port */
int _far_ _cdecl outp(unsigned int io_port, int data);   /* write a byte to io_port */
```

inp returns the byte read from the specified port and outp writes a byte to the specified port (it returns as a function result the byte written to the port), e.g. using serial port 0:

```
char ch;                             /* define a character */
ch = inp(0x3f8);             /* read a byte from serial port 0 receiver buffer */
outp(0x3f8, 'x');     /* write character 'x' to serial port 0 transmitter buffer */
```

Note that before:

1   A byte is read from the receiver buffer the DR bit in the line status register (see Table 29.1) should be tested to ensure that a character has been received.
2   A byte is written to the transmitter buffer (called the holding register) the THRE bit in the line status register (see Table 29.1) should be tested to ensure that it is empty. In addition it is normal to check the hardware handshaking line $\overline{CTS}$ to ensure that the receiver is ready for data (see Section 29.3.3 on hardware handshaking).

Bits in the modem control register are used to control the status of the hardware handshaking output lines $\overline{RTS}$ and $\overline{DTR}$ (see Fig. 29.2) and the interrupt enable to the 8259 PIC:

bit	modem control register (reset all other bits to 0)
3	OUT2 interrupt enable (set to pass 8250 interrupt signals to 8259 PIC)
1	RTS Request to Send output line (set to 1 to assert the output)
0	DTR Data Terminal Ready output line (set to 1 to assert the output)

```
1  /* Implementation file rs_lib2.c - IBM-PC directly controlling the 8250 ACE   */
2
3  #include <dos.h>                          /* MS-DOS specific header file */
4  #include <conio.h>                        /* direct console I/O functions */
5  #include <stdio.h>                        /* standard I/O header file */
6
7  /*-------------------------------------------------------------------*/
8  /* define 8250 port base addresses for RS232 ports 0 to 3 (com1: to com4:)   */
9  static const short int RS_BASES[] = {0x3f8, 0x2f8, 0x3e8, 0x2e8 };
10
11 /* 8250 register offsets from base address */
12 enum {DataReg, IntEna, IntIdent, LineCtrl, ModCtrl, LineStatus, ModStatus};
13
14 /* 8250 bits in line status, modem status and modem control registers */
15 enum {DR = 0x100, THRE = 0x2000, CTS = 0x10, DTR = 0x1, RTS = 0x2};
16
17 /*-------------------------------------------------------------------*/
18 /* Serial port: initialise io_port, sets DTR and RTS to high             */
19 void rs_initialise(const int io_port)
20 {
21     union REGS registers;              /* variable to hold 8086 registers */
22
23     registers.h.ah = 0;                            /* command, initialise */
24     /* set baud rate to 9600, 8 data bits, no parity and 1 stop bit */
25     registers.h.al = 0xe3;                        /* baud rate to 9600   */
26     registers.x.dx = io_port;                        /* for port */
27     int86(0x14, &registers, &registers);      /* interrupt 14 hexadecimal */
28     /* set DTR and RTS in modem control reg */
29     outp(RS_BASES[io_port] + ModCtrl, DTR + RTS);
30 }
31
32 /*-------------------------------------------------------------------*/
33 /* Serial port: terminate io_port, sets DTR and RTS to low             */
34 void rs_terminate(const int io_port)
35 {
36     /* set all bits 0 in modem control register */
37     outp(RS_BASES[io_port] + ModCtrl, 0);
38 }
39
40 /*-------------------------------------------------------------------*/
41 /* Serial port: return status of io_port                               */
42 /*    line status in top byte (ah), modem status in lower byte (al)    */
43 int rs_status(const int io_port)
44 {
45     int status = inp(RS_BASES[io_port] + LineStatus);     /* read line status */
46     /* shift line status to top byte and then read modem status */
47     status = (status << 8) + inp(RS_BASES[io_port] + ModStatus);
48     return status;                            /* and return value */
49 }
```

Implementation file rs_lib2.c IBM-PC directly controlling the 8250 ACE

```
50
51 /*----------------------------------------------------------------------*/
52 /* Serial port: transmit character to io_port                          */
53 void rs_putch(const int io_port, const int character)
54 {
55     while (! ((rs_status(io_port) & THRE) && (rs_status(io_port) & CTS)))
56         /* wait for transmitter holding register empty and CTS */ ;
57     /*putch(character);*/                    /* echo character if required */
58     outp(RS_BASES[io_port], character);              /* transmit character */
59 }
60
61 /*----------------------------------------------------------------------*/
62 /* Serial port: transmit a string of characters to io_port             */
63 void rs_putstring(const int io_port, const char *string)
64 {
65     while (*string != '\0')
66         rs_putch(io_port, *string++);
67 }
68
69 /*----------------------------------------------------------------------*/
70 /* Serial port: return TRUE if character available from serial line     */
71 int rs_received(int io_port)
72 {
73     int status = rs_status(io_port);                     /* get status */
74     if (status & 0xe00)                               /* receive error ?? */
75         printf("\n\aRead error on serial line, status = %#x\n", status & 0xe00);
76     return (status & DR);          /* test DR bit in line status register */
77 }
78
79 /*----------------------------------------------------------------------*/
80 /* Serial port: read character from io_port                            */
81 char rs_getch(const int io_port)
82 {
83     while (! rs_received(io_port))
84         /* wait for character received */ ;
85     return ((char) inp(RS_BASES[io_port]));               /* read character */
86 }
```

Implementation file rs_lib2.c IBM-PC directly controlling the 8250 ACE

The interface to implementation file rs_lib2.c is identical to that of rs_lib1.c in Chapter 29 (thus the header file rs_lib.h and Program 29_2 need no modification). Whereas rs_lib1.c controlled the RS232 serial ports via MS-DOS system calls the functions in rs_lib2.c control the 8250 ACE serial chip directly. The sequence of statements is:

9   define const qualified array RS_BASES which holds the serial port base addresses
12   define the offsets of the 8250 registers from the base address
15   define bits within the 8250 registers.

Function rs_initialise, lines 19 to 30, calls the MS-DOS serial port function 0 to initialise the baud rate, etc. of the specified port and then asserts the hardware handshaking output lines $\overline{\text{RTS}}$ and $\overline{\text{DTR}}$ (line 29), i.e.

```
outp(RS_BASES[io_port] + ModCtrl, DTR + RTS);
```

This writes a byte value DTR + RTS to port RS_BASES[io_port] + ModCtrl (base address specified by io_port). Asserting $\overline{\text{RTS}}$ (probably connected to $\overline{\text{CTS}}$ of the remote device) indicates that characters can now be received.

Function rs_terminate, lines 34 to 38, terminates communication by clearing all the bits in the modem control register. In particular $\overline{\text{RTS}}$ and $\overline{\text{DTR}}$ are negated indicating to the remote device that characters can no longer be received.

Function rs_status, lines 43 to 49, returns the line status (line 45) and modem status (line 47) register values (modem status in bits 0 to 7 and line status in bits 8 to 15).

Function rs_putch, lines 53 to 59, waits for transmitter holding register empty (THRE bit set in line status register) and $\overline{\text{CTS}}$ asserted (in the modem status register), and then transmits a character (to echo the character to the screen remove the comments in line 57). Function rs_putstring, lines 63 to 67, calls rs_putch to transmit a string of characters.

Function rs_received, lines 71 to 77, checks to see if a character has been received from the serial line. Line 74 checks for a receive error and line 76 checks the DR bit in the line status register returning non-zero (*true*) if a character has been received.

Function rs_getch, lines 81 to 86, reads a character from a serial line; lines 83 and 84 wait for a character to be received and line 85 reads the receiver data buffer.

31.6 Interrupt control of the serial ports of an IBM PC compatible

Interrupt I/O enables normal program execution to continue in parallel with the I/O of one or more devices. When a particular I/O device interface is ready for a data transfer it sends a signal to the processor which interrupts the program being executed, and transfers control to an **interrupt service routine** (which is similar in format to a normal C function). The interrupt service routine code performs the data transfer to the I/O device and terminates with an instruction which resumes execution of the program that had been interrupted (e.g. IRET in the 8086 family and RTE in the MC68000 family).

When an interrupt occurs, some mechanism is required to transfer control to the corresponding interrupt service routine. The majority of modern processors use a vector table in primary memory which contains the addresses of the interrupt service routines. When an interrupt occurs, the corresponding entry (the routine address) is obtained from the vector table and placed in the processor's Program Counter Register (PC). Program execution then continues with the first instruction of the interrupt service routine. The size of the vector table, its position in memory and precisely how it is used depends upon the processor concerned (see Bramer & Bramer 1991 for a description of the MC68000). The support provided by C compilers for interrupt I/O varies with the compiler and host operating system. For example, Turbo C and Microsoft C under MS-DOS:

```
void _dos_setvect (int int_numb, void _interrupt (_far * int_function)());
```

This loads the vector table entry for interrupt number int_numb with the address of the interrupt service routine int_function. The interrupt service function would be defined:

```
void _interrupt _far int_function(void)
{
    /* function body to process data transfer */
}
```

The keyword _interrupt tells the compiler that this is an interrupt service routine. The compiler will generate the appropriate entry and exit sequences including saving and restoring registers and terminating the function with an IRET (interrupt return) instruction (instead of RET). The keyword _far indicates that it will be 'called' (when an interrupt occurs) using a full 32-bit address.

The following points are important when writing interrupt service routines (refer to manuals for more details):

1   The cause of the interrupt should be cleared within the service function (or it will interrupt again immediately on exit; if the system 'locks up' this is a likely cause).
2   Interrupts are disabled when the service function is called. If the function is long the cause of the interrupt should be cleared and _enable (under Microsoft C) called to enable interrupts.
3   Take care calling functions from within service routines; in particular functions which call the operating system (MS-DOS is not reentrant). Refer to manuals.
4   External variables (in the host C program) can be accessed from within the service routine (it is wise to declare them with the Turbo C and Microsoft C _far attribute to ensure 32-bit addressing).

In an IBM PC compatible computer there are a number of possible interrupt sources which are assigned various levels of priority (this is set within the hardware). For example, the 8253 Timer/Counter (which drives the DOS time and date function) is at level 0, the RS232 serial ports 0 and 2 (COM1: and COM3:) are at level 4 and ports 1 and 3 are at level 3. An 8259 PIC (Programmable Interrupt Controller) controls which interrupt levels are enabled at any time and arbitrates between the different priorities (see a manual on the 8259 PIC for full details).

31.6.1 Replacing the IBM/PC 8253 timer/counter interrupt

IBM/PC compatible minicomputers contain an Intel 8253 counter/timer chip which DOS uses to maintain the time and date. The device is normally programmed to interrupt approximately 18.2 times per second (this can be changed - see problem at end of chapter) and is serviced by a DOS interrupt routine. Program 31_2 (next page) replaces the DOS interrupt routine with its own and, using a counter decremented in the routine, displays a character on the screen every second:

8   define constant count_one_second initialised to 18 (approximately 18.2)
10   declare function prototype of interrupt service routine
11   define pointer old_vector which will hold address of DOS interrupt service routine
12   define one_second which is decremented on every interrupt - initialised to 18
19   get address of DOS timer interrupt service routine into old_vector
        the timer interrupt level is 0 and the vector is 0x08
20   set timer interrupt vector to the new interrupt service routine int_8253_routine
22-30   a while loop which terminates when the keyboard is hit
            24 if one_second is 0 a second has elapsed
                26 reset one-second counter
                27 display a character (should display 12345678901234567890123 etc.)
                28 ring alarm every 10 seconds
31   reset timer interrupt vector to DOS interrupt service routine

38-42   interrupt service routine
      40   decrement one second counter
      41   call DOS interrupt service routine
          to maintain the DOS time/date and terminate the interrupt.

```
 1 /* Program 31_2 - test IBM/PC 8253 timer/counter interrupts           */
 2 /* Display a character every second and ring alarm every ten seconds   */
 3
 4 #include <conio.h>                              /* Turbo C++ DOS headers */
 5 #include <dos.h>
 6
 7 /* assume that the PC timer is interrupting 18.2 times per second */
 8 enum {count_one_second = 18};                        /* count for 1 second */
 9
10 void _interrupt _far int_8253_routine(void);         /* function prototype */
11 void (_interrupt _far *old_vector)(void);     /* define 'pointer to function' */
12 volatile int one_second = count_one_second;   /* 0 when one second has elapsed */
13
14 int main(void)
15 {
16     unsigned char ch = 0;                   /* char to display every second */
17
18     /* Replace existing timer interrupt routine with int_8253 */
19     old_vector = _dos_getvect(0x08);         /* get current timer vector 0x08 */
20     _dos_setvect( 0x08, int_8253_routine);    /* set vector for 8253 timer */
21     /* loop displaying a character every second until the keyboard hit */
22     while (! kbhit())
23         {
24             if (! one_second)                          /* second elapsed ? */
25                 {
26                 one_second = count_one_second;         /* yes, reset counter */
27                 putch('0' + ++ch % 10);                /* print character */
28                 if ((ch % 10) == 0) putch('\a')  ;  /* alarm every 10 seconds */
29                 }
30         }
31     _dos_setvect( 0x08, old_vector);       /* reset timer interrupt vector 0x08 */
32     return 0;
33 }
34
35 /*----------------------------------------------------------------------*/
36 /* 8253 Timer interrupt service routine, called on every timer interrupt  */
37 /*  Decrement second counter and call DOS routine to maintain time and date  */
38 void _interrupt _far int_8253_routine(void)
39 {
40     one_second--;                              /* decrement second counter */
41     old_vector();                        /* call DOS timer interrupt routine */
42 }
```

Program 31_2   Using IBM/PC 8253 timer/counter interrupts

So long as a function is defined as an interrupt service routine (keywords _interrupt _far) the C compiler will look after saving and restoring any registers and terminating the service routine correctly. In this case there is no need to program the 8259 PIC (DOS will have set it up to enable timer interrupts and the DOS interrupt service routine called in line 41 will terminate the interrupt). Note that variable one_second is declared volatile to indicate to the compiler that it may be changed unpredictably (e.g. by the interrupt service routine) and references to it must not be optimised (e.g. in the loop lines 22 to 30). The problem at the end of this chapter is to reprogram to 8253 counter/timer to interrupt 1000 times/second (one may wish to read an analogue to digital converter 1000 times/second).

36.6.2 Driving the IBM/PC serial ports using interrupts

It is sometimes necessary for a program to directly control a serial port using interrupts. Generally the DOS device driver does not use interrupts and characters may be lost or the program is time critical. In outline, the steps which must be taken to set up interrupts for the serial port receiver are:

1   The address of the existing interrupt service routine is saved (to be restored on exit).
2   The address of the new interrupt service routine is loaded into the correct vector (interrupt level 4 is vector 12 and interrupt level 3 is vector 11).
3   Receiver interrupts are enabled in the 8250 Interrupt Enable Register (setting bit 0 enables receiver interrupts).
4   The correct interrupt level must be enabled in the Operations Control Word 1 (OCW1) of the 8259 PIC (Programmable Interrupt Controller) which controls system wide interrupts for PC. For level 4 interrupts bit 4 is cleared and for level 3 bit 3 is cleared (the other bits should not be changed).
5   The OUT2 bit must be set in the 8250 Modem Control Register (this enables circuitry which passes the interrupt signal from the 8250 to the 8259 PIC).

Consult technical manuals on the PC, the 8250 ACE and the 8259 PIC for full details. When a receive interrupt occurs (a character has arrived from a remote device) the interrupt service routine is called:

1   The character is read from the 8250 Receiver Data Buffer (which clears the cause of the interrupt) and placed into a suitable data structure (e.g. a ring buffer). Functions waiting for data will be polling the data structure to see if any characters have arrived.
2   The interrupt must be acknowledged at the correct level in the Operations Control Word 2 (OCW2) of the 8259 PIC. The values written for level 4 and level 3 interrupts are 0x64 and 0x63 respectively (OCW2 bit EOI = 1, ST = 1, R = 0 and L0 to L2 is the interrupt level, see 8259 PIC manuals).

So long as the function is defined as an interrupt service routine (keywords _interrupt _far) the C compiler will look after saving and restoring any registers and terminating the service routine correctly. When the program terminates the interrupts must be disabled:

1   Interrupts are disabled in the 8250 Interrupt Enable Register (writing 0 disables all interrupts).
2   The OUT2 bit is cleared in the 8250 Modem Control Register.
3   The correct interrupt level must be disabled in the Operations Control Word 1 (OCW1) of the 8259 PIC. For level 4 interrupts bit 4 is set and for level 3 bit 3 is set (the other bits should not be changed).
4   The address of the original interrupt service routine (saved when enabling interrupts) is restored.

Implementation file rs_lib3.c is a version (for either Turbo C or Microsoft C under DOS) of the PC serial line function library with the receiver using interrupts.

```c
 1 /* Implementation file rs_lib3.c - IBM-PC interrupt-driven 8250 ACE functions */
 2
 3 /*--------------------------------------------------------------------*/
 4 /* Functions for the 8250 RS232 serial interface                      */
 5 /* Receiver is interrupt driven                                       */
 6 /*  (a)  single character buffer only; needs extending to a ring buffer */
 7 /*          with RTS/CTS hardware handshaking when 70% full           */
 8 /*  (b) the receiver functions will only work for one port at a time  */
 9 /*        interrupt handler, etc. needs extending to cope with more   */
10 /* The PC uses an 8259 PIC (Programmable Interrupt Controller) see manuals */
11
12 #include <dos.h>                         /* MS-DOS specific header file */
13 #include <conio.h>                       /* direct console I/O functions */
14 #include <stdio.h>                       /* standard I/O header file */
15
16 /*--------------------------------------------------------------------*/
17 /* define 8250 port base addresses for RS232 ports 0 to 3 (com1: to com4:)  */
18 static const short int RS_BASES[] = {0x3f8, 0x2f8, 0x3e8, 0x2e8 };
19
20 /* I/O port addresses for 8259 PIC (Programmable Interrupt Controller)  */
21 /*    OCW1 operation control word2 and OCW2 operation control word 2   */
22 enum {PIC_OCW1 = 0x21, PIC_OCW2 = 0x20};
23
24 /* 8250 register offsets from base address */
25 enum {DataReg, IntEna, IntIdent, LineCtrl, ModCtrl, LineStatus, ModStatus};
26
27 /* 8250 bits in line status, modem status and modem control registers */
28 enum {DR = 0x100, THRE = 0x2000, CTS = 0x10, DTR = 0x1, RTS = 0x2, OUT2 = 0x8};
29
30 void _interrupt _far new_rs232( void );               /* function prototype */
31 void (_interrupt _far *old_rs232)( void );     /* define 'pointer to function' */
32
33 /* define default interrupt parameters for serial ports, edit as required   */
34 /* com1: & com3: use interrupt level 4 and com2: & com4: interrupt level 3   */
35 /* define vector number, 8259 PIC 'interrupt enable' and 'end of interrupt ' */
36 static const int RS_VECT[] = {12, 11, 12, 11},            /* interrupt vector */
37                  RS_INTENABLE[] = {0xef, 0xf7, 0xef, 0xf7},    /* int enable */
38                  RS_EOI[] = {0x64, 0x63, 0x64, 0x63};              /* EOI */
39
40 static short int _far rs_port;                   /* holds serial port number */
41
42 static volatile unsigned char _far rs_data = 0,       /* character buffer */
43                               rs_stat_data = 0;       /* and its status */
44
45 /*--------------------------------------------------------------------*/
```

Implementation file rs_lib3.c IBM-PC interrupt-driven 8250 ACE functions

```
46 /* Serial port: initialise io_port, set 9600 baud, 8 data bits, one stop bit  */
47 /*    enable interrupts and set DTR and RTS active                             */
48 void rs_initialise(const int io_port)
49 {
50     union REGS registers;                        /* variable to hold 8086 registers */
51
52     registers.h.ah = 0;                                    /* command, initialise */
53     /* set baud rate to 9600, 8 data bits, no parity and 1 stop bit */
54     registers.h.al = 0xe3;                                 /* baud rate to 9600   */
55     registers.x.dx = io_port;                                    /* for port */
56     int86(0x14, &registers, &registers);         /* interrupt 14 hexadecimal */
57
58     rs_port = io_port;                                    /* note port number */
59     /* set up vector to interrupt handler and enable interrupts */
60     old_rs232 = _dos_getvect(RS_VECT[io_port]);        /* get current vector */
61     _dos_setvect( RS_VECT[io_port], new_rs232 );            /* set new vector */
62
63     outp(RS_BASES[io_port] + IntEna, 1);         /* enable receiver interrupts */
64     /* enable interrupt level in 8259 PIC OCW1 (operation control word 1) */
65     outp(PIC_OCW1, inp(PIC_OCW1) & RS_INTENABLE[io_port]);
66     /* OUT2 must be set in modem control reg to send interrupt to 8259 PIC */
67     outp(RS_BASES[io_port] + ModCtrl, DTR + RTS + OUT2);   /* set DTR RTS OUT2 */
68 }
69
70 /*------------------------------------------------------------------------*/
71 /* Serial port: terminate io_port, sets DTR and RTS to low                  */
72 void rs_terminate(const int io_port)
73 {
74     /* disable interrupt level in 8259 PIC OCW1 (operation control word 1) */
75     outp(PIC_OCW1, inp(PIC_OCW1) | ~RS_INTENABLE[io_port]);
76     outp(RS_BASES[io_port] + IntEna, 0);       /* disable all serial interrupts */
77     outp(RS_BASES[io_port] + ModCtrl, 0);      /* clear modem control register */
78     _dos_setvect( RS_VECT[io_port], old_rs232 );            /* reset old vector */
79 }
80
81 /*------------------------------------------------------------------------*/
82 /* Serial port: handler for receive interrupt on serial port rs_port        */
83 /*    read receiver buffer to clear interrupt and send EOI (end of interrupt) */
84 /*    to 8259 OCW2 (operation control word 2) to acknowledge the interrupt   */
85 void _interrupt _far new_rs232(void)
86 {
87     /* read line status - if character in buffer indicate overrun error */
88     rs_stat_data = (char) inp(RS_BASES[rs_port]  + LineStatus);
89     if (rs_data) rs_stat_data = (char) (rs_stat_data | 0x2);
90     rs_data = (char) inp(RS_BASES[rs_port]);                /* read character */
91     /* 8259 PIC end of interrupt: bit EOI = 1, SL = 1, R = 0, L0-L2 = level */
92     outp(PIC_OCW2, RS_EOI[rs_port]);               /* send EOI to 8259 OCW2 */
93 }
94
95 /*------------------------------------------------------------------------*/
```

Implementation file rs_lib3.c IBM-PC interrupt-driven 8250 ACE functions

```
 96  /* Serial port: return TRUE is character available from serial.line        */
 97  int rs_received(int io_port)
 98  {
 99      if (rs_stat_data & 0xe)                              /* receive error ?? */
100          printf("\n\aRead error on serial line %d, status = %#x\n",
101                  rs_port, rs_stat_data & 0xe);
102      rs_stat_data = 0;                                       /* clear status */
103      return rs_data;                             /* return > 0 if character ready */
104  }
105
106  /*----------------------------------------------------------------------*/
107  /* Serial port: read character from io_port (ignored in this version)    */
108  char rs_getch(const int io_port)
109  {
110      char ch;
111      while (! rs_received(io_port))
112          /* wait for character received */ ;
113      ch = rs_data;                                  /* get character received */
114      rs_data = 0;
115      return ch;                                          /* read character */
116  }
117
118  /*----------------------------------------------------------------------*/
119  /* Serial port: return status of io_port                                 */
120  /*    line status in top byte (ah), modem status in lower byte (al)      */
121  int rs_status(const int io_port)
122  {
123      int status = inp(RS_BASES[io_port] + LineStatus);    /* read line status */
124      /* shift line status to top byte and then read modem status */
125      status = (status << 8) + inp(RS_BASES[io_port] + ModStatus);
126      return status;                                     /* and return value */
127  }
128
129  /*----------------------------------------------------------------------*/
130  /* Serial port: transmit character to io_port                            */
131  void rs_putch(const int io_port, const int character)
132  {
133      while (! ((rs_status(io_port) & THRE) && (rs_status(io_port) & CTS)))
134          /* wait for transmitter holding register empty and CTS */ ;
135      /*putch(character);*/                        /* echo character if required */
136      outp(RS_BASES[io_port], character);             /* transmit character */
137  }
138
139  /*----------------------------------------------------------------------*/
140  /* Serial port: transmit a string of characters to io_port               */
141  void rs_putstring(const int io_port, const char *string)
142  {
143      while (*string != '\0')
144          rs_putch(io_port, *string++);
145  }
```

Implementation file rs_lib3.c IBM-PC interrupt-driven 8250 ACE functions

In implementation file rs_lib3.c the program sequence is:

18 define the I/O port base addresses of the 8250 serial ports
22 define the I/O port addresses for the 8259 PIC (Programmable Interrupt Controller)
25 define the 8250 serial register offsets from the base addresses
28 define the bits within the 8250 registers of the serial ports to be used in the program
30 declare a function prototype for new_rs232 (the interrupt service routine)
31 define pointer old_rs232 which will hold the address of the old interrupt service routine
36 define RS_VECT which holds the vectors for the ports
37 define RS_INTENABLE which holds the interrupt enable values for OCW1 of the 8259 PIC
38 define RS_EOI which holds the 'end of interrupt' values for the OCW2 of the 8259 PIC
    the above are arrays with elements corresponding to serial ports 0 to 3
    if the port hardware is altered the corresponding elements should be modified
40 define rs_port which holds the serial port number (for interrupt service routine)
42 define rs_data which holds the character received from the serial line
43 define rs_stat_data which holds the receiver status associated with the character.

Function rs_initialise, lines 48 to 68, initialises the serial port and enables interrupts:

50-56 call MS-DOS function 0 to initialise the baud rate, word length, etc.
60   save existing interrupt service routine address for vector in old_rs232
61   set up interrupt service routine address for vector to function new_rs232
63   enable receiver interrupts in the 8250 Interrupt Enable Register (set bit 0)
65   set up OCW1 in the 8259 PIC to enable interrupts at the required level
67   set DTR, RTS and OUT2 in the 8250 Modem Control Register.

Function rs_terminate, lines 72 to 79, disables interrupts:

75 set up OCW1 in the 8259 PIC to disable interrupts at the required level
76 clear the 8250 Interrupt Enable Register (disabling all interrupts)
77 clear the 8250 Modem Control Register (clears OUT2 and negates DTR and RTS)
78 restore the old interrupt service routine address for vector (saved in line 60).

Function new_rs232, lines 85 to 93, is the interrupt service routine which processes serial line receiver interrupts (for only one port at a time specified by rs_port):

85 function header with the keywords _interrupt _far
88 read the 8250 line status register into rs_stat_data (note the cast (char))
89 if rs_data is non-zero (last character has not been read) indicate data overrun
90 read the 8250 receiver buffer into rs_data (note the cast (char))
92 indicate 'end of interrupt' in the OCW2 (operations control word 2) of 8259 PIC.

Function rs_received, lines 97 to 104, returns *true* if a character has been received:

99   test rs_stat_data for a receive error and if error display status with message
102 clear the status indicator rs_stat_data
103 return *true* (non-zero) if a character has been received in rs_data.

Function rs_getch, lines 108 to 116, returns a character received:

111-12 a while which waits for a character to be received
113   copy the character received from rs_data into ch
114   clear rs_data (indicating that the character has been read)
115   return ch (the character received).

The functions rs_status, rs_putch and rs_putstring are unchanged from rs_lib2.c.

Note that rs_lib1.c and rs_lib2.c could be used to control several serial ports concurrently (as specified by the parameter io_port passed to every function). As written, rs_lib3.c can only handle receive interrupts from one serial port at any time, i.e. the interrupt service routine can only process interrupts from the port specified by the external variable rs_port. To extend the library to handle more than one port concurrently the interrupt service routine would need to check which port caused the interrupt (by looking at the Line Status Registers) and using separate data buffers for each port.

Problems for Chapter 31

Problem 31.1

Program 31_2 showed how to intercept the timer interrupts on an IBM/PC compatible microcomputer. This is rather restrictive in that interrupts only occur at the rate set by DOS (normally 18.2/second). Implement and test a program to reprogram the 8253 counter/timer to interrupt 1000 times/second - use it to display a character on the screen every second as in Program 31_2. Note:

1. (a) the 8253 has a 16-bit counter clocked at 1193180Hz
   (b) the counter is preloaded with 65535 (the maximum value), hence it interrupts
      1193180/65535 = 18.2067597467 times/sec
   (c) to interrupt at 1000 times per second load the counter with the value:
      ```
      counter    = 1193180L / interrupts_per_second
                 = 1193180L / 1000 = 1193
      ```
   (d) load the 16-bit counter as two 8-bit values, least significant byte then most significant byte, to I/O address 0x40 as follows (also disable/enable interrupts):
      ```
      disable();                                    /* disable interrupts */
      outp(0x40, (unsigned int) counter % 256);     /* load counter 0 LSB */
      outp(0x40, (unsigned int) counter / 256);     /* load counter 0 MSB */
      enable();                                      /* enable interrupts */
      ```

2. (a) In the interrupt service routine the DOS interrupt service routine must be called 18.2 times per second (to maintain the DOS time)
   (b) otherwise the interrupt service routine should terminate the interrupt as follows:
      ```
      outp(0x20, 0x60);    /* send EOI (end of interrupt) to 8259 OCW2 level 0 */
      ```

Problem 31.2

Implementation file rs_lib3.c only buffers one character at a time (in rs_data). Extend the program to use a ring buffer (e.g. rs_data and rs_stat_data becoming arrays of length 1024 bytes) with hardware handshaking (e.g. when the buffer is 70% full stop the transmitter and when 30% full restart it, see Section 29.3.3). Extend the program to control two serial ports concurrently.

Build an RS232 communications bus and use it to simulate a CSMA/CD (carrier sense multiple access / collision detect) Medium Access Control protocol (similar to that used in the Ethernet bus). Fig. 31.1 shows a simple circuit to connect a number of machines. When the TxD (transmit) output of the IBM/PC compatible microcomputers is in the idle state (logical 1, see Section 29.3) the resistor 'pulls up' the outputs of the 7405 open collector gates maintaining an idle state input into the RxD (receiver) inputs of the PCs. If any of the TxD outputs go to the active state (logical 0) the bus goes to 0 and this value is fed to all the RxD (receiver) lines. A station waiting to transmit can listen to the bus to see if it is in use. What is transmitted is immediately fed back into the receiver; hence a transmitter can check for a collision by reading what it has just transmitted.

Implement a Logical Link Layer protocol to provide error free transmission of data frames between PCs, either connected 'back to back' (see Fig. 29.2) or using the RS232 bus. The protocol should cope with data transmission errors, lost data frames, lost acknowledgements, etc. (refer to a book on communications and networks for details of data link protocols). The software should generate errors for the protocol to correct.

Implement a program, using the above protocol, to transfer files between PCs. One machine acts as a slave, the other the host. A user of the host machine should be able to transfer files reporting any errors. Transfer ASCII text initially then extend the program to handle any type of data (character stuffing will probably have to be used). Remember to be very careful when transferring data in binary format between machines with different architectures or even different operating systems or compilers on the same machine. There may be differences in the number of bytes used to store a type and the internal representation of information, e.g. ones complement or twos complement integers, little-endian (Intel 8086 family) or big-endian (Motorola 68000 family) storage of multi-byte integers, IEEE or non-IEEE format floating point numbers, etc.

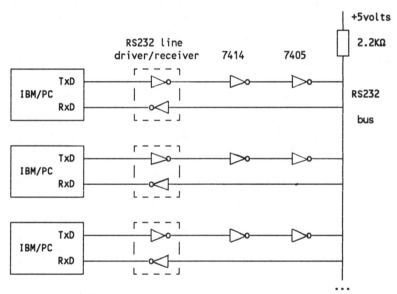

Fig. 31.1 A simple RS232C bus used to simulate CSMA/CD protocol

Appendix A

The ASCII character code

Dec	Hex	Char		Dec	Hex	Char		Dec	Hex	Char		Dec	Hex	Char
0	00	NUL		32	20	SP		64	40	@		96	60	`
1	01	SOH		33	21	!		65	41	A		97	61	a
2	02	STX		34	22	"		66	42	B		98	62	b
3	03	ETX		35	23	#		67	43	C		99	63	c
4	04	EOT		36	24	$		68	44	D		100	64	d
5	05	ENQ		37	25	%		69	45	E		101	65	e
6	06	ACK		38	26	&		70	46	F		102	66	f
7	07	BEL		39	27	'		71	47	G		103	67	g
8	08	BS		40	28	(		72	48	H		104	68	h
9	09	HT		41	29	)		73	49	I		105	69	i
10	0A	LF		42	2A	*		74	4A	J		106	6A	j
11	0B	VT		43	2B	+		75	4B	K		107	6B	k
12	0C	FF		44	2C	,		76	4C	L		108	6C	l
13	0D	CR		45	2D	-		77	4D	M		109	6D	m
14	0E	SO		46	2E	.		78	4E	N		110	6E	n
15	0F	SI		47	2F	/		79	4F	O		111	6F	o
16	10	DLE		48	30	0		80	50	P		112	70	p
17	11	DC1		49	31	1		81	51	Q		113	71	q
18	12	DC2		50	32	2		82	52	R		114	72	r
19	13	DC3		51	33	3		83	53	S		115	73	s
20	14	DC4		52	34	4		84	54	T		116	74	t
21	15	NAK		53	35	5		85	55	U		117	75	u
22	16	SYN		54	36	6		86	56	V		118	76	v
23	17	ETB		55	37	7		87	57	W		119	77	w
24	18	CAN		56	38	8		88	58	X		120	78	x
25	19	EM		57	39	9		89	59	Y		121	79	y
26	1A	SUB		58	3A	:		90	5A	Z		122	7A	z
27	1B	ESC		59	3B	;		91	5B	[		123	7B	{
28	1C	FS		60	3C	<		92	5C	\		124	7C		
29	1D	GS		61	3D	=		93	5D	]		125	7D	}
30	1E	RS		62	3E	>		94	5E	^		126	7E	~
31	1F	US		63	3F	?		95	5F	_		127	7F	DEL

In the above table the columns are decimal and hexadecimal numeric ASCII character code value followed by the character. The characters below 32 decimal (20 hexadecimal) are non-printing control characters, e.g.:

BEL	bell: rings the keyboard bell or buzzer
BS	backspace: move back one character width
HT	horizontal tabulate: move horizontally to next tabulate position
LF	line feed: move page vertically one character height
CR	carriage return: move to start of current line
ESC	escape: used in many systems as a program control character
SP	space: move horizontal by one character width

Appendix B Answers to the exercises

The answers to the exercises are on the disk which accompanies this book. The file naming convention is that the answer to Exercise 5.1 will be in file c5\ex5_1.c, Exercise 12.3 in c12\ex12_3.c, etc.

Exercise 4.1 (page 22) Print name and address on the screen.

```
/* Exercise 4_1a - to print name and address to display screen */

#include <stdio.h>                              /* preprocessor directive */

int main(void)                                 /* start of function main */
{
    printf("Brian Bramer\n");                       /* print message */
    printf("DeMontfort University\n");              /* print message */
    printf("Leicester, UK\n");                      /* print message */
    return 0;                                  /* terminate program */
}
```

File ex4_1.c   To print name and address to display screen

File ex4_1.c (in file c4\ex4_1.c on the disk which accompanies this book) shows a sample answer to Exercise 4.1. It contains three calls to printf to print the name and address. An alternative is to use one call to printf (in file c4\ex4_1b.c):

```
printf("Brian Bramer\n"
       "DeMontfort University\n"
       "Leicester, UK\n");
```

The string joining feature of ANSI C joins the three strings to form a single string which is passed to printf. The three lines could therefore be written (in file c4\ex4_1c.c):

```
printf("Brian Bramer\nDeMontfort University\nLeicester, UK\n");
```

Exercise 5.1 (page 33)

1   If the #include <math.h> is missing the program will either crash on the call to sqrt or return incorrect results, e.g. a run using Turbo C Version 3.00 printed the following:

```
radius = 2.000000, area = 12.566370, radius check = -32736.000000
```

If the compiler failed to warn of missing math function prototypes when compiling the warnings are probably switched off. Switch them on!

2   Replace line 15 of Program 5.1 with the following:

```
printf(" converted %d \n", printf(", radius check = %f \n", radius_check));
```

The int function result returned by the first call to printf is used as the parameter to another call to printf to display the number of characters printed (%d is the int conversion specification). This is an instance of a general rule of C that anywhere where it is permissible to use the value of a variable (of some type) an expression (of the same type) may be used. The modified program should then print:

```
radius = 2.000000, area = 12.566370, radius check = 2.000000
converted 27
```

i.e. printf(", radius check = %f \n", radius_check) printed 27 characters.

Exercise 5.2 (page 39) Modify Program 5_3.

```
 1 /* Exercise 5_2 - read radius of circle/sphere calculate circle area,          *
 2  *  sphere area & sphere volume and recalculate radius from sphere volume     */
 3
 4 #include <stdio.h>
 5 #include <math.h>
 6
 7 int main(void)
 8 {
 9     const float pi = 3.1415926f;
10     float radius, circle_area, sphere_area, sphere_volume, radius_check;
11
12     printf("Enter radius of circle (real number) ? ");
13     scanf("%f", &radius);                                /* read radius */
14     circle_area = pi * radius * radius;                  /* circle area */
15     printf("radius = %f, \n    circle area   = %f", radius, circle_area);
16     sphere_area  = circle_area * 4.0f;                      /* sphere area */
17     sphere_volume = sphere_area * radius / 3.0f;         /* sphere volume */
18     printf("\n    sphere area   = %f", sphere_area);
19     printf("\n    sphere volume = %f\n", sphere_volume);
20     /* recalculate radius from sphere volume */
21     radius_check = pow(3.0f * sphere_volume / (4.0f * pi), 1.0f / 3.0f);
22     printf("    radius check  = %f \n", radius_check);
23     return 0;
24 }
```

File ex5_2.c Calculate circle area, sphere area and volume and recalculate radius

In the evaluation of lines 16 and 17 in file ex5_2.c the results of previous calculations are used. This saves execution time but must be used with care, e.g. if an equation is altered it then affects all following calculations which use its result. In line 21 the maths function pow(x, 1.0/3.0) is used to evaluate the cube root.

   If the & is removed from before the variable name radius in the call to scanf in line 13 of Exercise 5.2 the value of radius will be passed instead of its address (which scanf needs to return the value read from the keyboard). What happens is implementation dependent, the program may continue with incorrect data or may even crash. The GNU V2.6.3 compiler issues a warning if the & is missing, e.g.:

```
X.c: In function 'main':
X.c:13: warning: format argument is not a pointer (arg 2)
```

When a ; was added to the end of the #define PI 3.1415926f in line 6 of Program 5_4 Turbo C V3.00 gave:

```
Error x.c 16: Illegal use of floating point in function main
Error x.c 18: Function call missing ) in function main
Error x.c 18: Expression syntax in function main
Warning x.c 19: Possible use of 'radius_check' before definition in function main
```

The preprocessor has *literally replaced* all occurrences of the *symbolic constant* PI with 3.2425926f; giving error messages in the lines which used PI (although the error is in the #define in line 6). This type of error is very difficult to find because the lines where the compiler finds the errors look fine to the programmer.

Exercise 6.1 (page 46) Batch file for the MS-DOS operating system.

MS-DOS batch file to execute a program and indicate success or failure.

```
rem Exercise 6.1 - execute program and indicate success or failure
%1
IF ERRORLEVEL 1 GOTO fail
    rem program successful
    goto exit
:fail
    rem program failed
exit
```

The name of the program is passed as the first parameter %1 of the batch file. After program execution the ERRORLEVEL value is tested for being success, 0, or failure (the ERRORLEVEL value is returned to the operating system by the C statement return n;). The control statement IF ERRORLEVEL 1 GOTO fail branches to label fail if ERRORLEVEL is greater than or equal to 1.

Exercise 7.1 (page 52) Cost of decorating a room.

```
 1 /* Exercise 7_1  Calculate cost of decorating a room using two techniques   */
 2
 3 #include <stdio.h>
 4
 5 int main(void)
 6 {
 7     int length, width, height, area, cost;
 8
 9     printf("Enter the length width and height of room (whole metres) ? ");
10     scanf("%d%d%d", &width, &length, &height);
11     /* calculate area of walls */
12     area = (2 * length * height) + (2 * width * height);
13     /* calculate cost at  10 * (wall area - 1/3) */
14     cost = 10 * (area - area / 3 );
15     printf("area = %d, cost = %d\n", area, cost);
16     /* calculate cost at 10 * 2/3 of wall area */
17     cost = 10 * (2 * area / 3 );
18     printf("area = %d, cost = %d\n", area, cost);
19     return 0;
20 }
```

File ex7_1.c Calculate cost of decorating a room using two techniques

File ex7_1.c uses two techniques to calculate the cost of decorating a room:

line 14 £10 times the area of the room less one third
line 17 £10 times two thirds the area of the room

A run gave (user input in **bold** with the Enter or carriage return key shown as ⏎):

```
Enter the length width and height of room (whole metres) ?  10 10 2⏎
area = 80, cost = 540
area = 80, cost = 530
```

The difference in the results is because the result of integer division is truncated to the nearest integer, i.e. 200 - 200 / 3 = 54 and 2 * 80 / 3 = 53. This shows how careful one must be when performing integer arithmetic (operators are discussed in Chapter 9).

Exercise 8.1 (page 58) Calculate area of a triangle.

```
 1  /* Exercise 8_1  Given length of sides calculate area of a triangle */
 2
 3  #include <stdio.h>
 4  #include <math.h>
 5
 6  int main(void)
 7  {
 8      float a, b, c, s, area;
 9
10      printf("Enter length of triangle sides (three reals) ? ");
11      scanf("%f%f%f", &a, &b, &c);                        /* read data */
12      s = (a + b + c) / 2.0f;                            /* calculate s */
13      area = sqrt(s * (s - a) * (s - b) * (s - c));      /* then area */
14      printf(" area of triangle = %f\n", area);          /* print results */
15      return 0;
16  }
```

File ex8_1.C Given length of sides calculate area of a triangle

A run of the program in file ex8_1.c gave:

```
Enter length of triangle sides (three reals) ? 1 1 1.414 ↲
  area of triangle = 0.500000
```

Exercise 9.1 (page 63) Converts time in seconds to hours, minutes and seconds.

```
 1  /* Exercise ex9_1a - convert time in seconds to hours, minutes & seconds */
 2
 3  #include <stdio.h>
 4
 5  int main(void)
 6  {
 7      int seconds, hours, minutes;                    /* local variables */
 8      printf("Enter time since midnight in seconds (integer) ? ");
 9      scanf("%d", &seconds);
10      minutes = seconds / 60;                    /* convert time to minutes */
11      seconds = seconds % 60;                    /* the remainder is the seconds */
12      hours = minutes / 60;                      /* convert time to hours */
13      minutes = minutes % 60;                    /* the remainder is the minutes */
14      printf(" time %02d:%02d:%02d \n", hours, minutes, seconds);
15      return 0;
16  }
```

File ex9_1a.c Converts time in seconds to hours, minutes & seconds

The program in file ex9_1a.c converts time to hours, minutes and seconds. A run gave:

```
Enter time since midnight in seconds (integer) ? 7263 ↲
  time 02:01:03
```

The program in file ex9_1b.c (next page) converts metres to feet and inches. A run gave:

```
Enter distance in metres ? 1 ↲
  is 3  feet 3.370079 inches
```

```
 1 /* Exercise 9_1b  Given a distance in metres, convert it into feet and inches */
 2
 3 #include <stdio.h>                           /* standard stream I/O library */
 4
 5 int main(void)
 6 {
 7     const float FEET_PER_METRE = 3.280839895f;        /* constant feet/metre */
 8     float distance;
 9
10     printf("Enter distance in metres ? ");
11     scanf("%f", &distance);                     /* read distance in metres */
12     distance = distance * FEET_PER_METRE;          /* convert to feet */
13     printf("  is %d  feet %f inches\n",
14             (int) distance, 12.0f * (distance - (int) distance));
15     return 0;
16 }
```

File ex9_1b.c Given a distance in metres, convert it into feet and inches

Exercise 9.2 (page 67) Calculate average of up to six numbers.

Program (in file ex9_2.c below) to calculate the average of six numbers. A run gave:

Enter up to six numbers terminated with a $? **1.0 2.0 3.0 $**⏎
  Average of 3 numbers = 2.000000

Consider line 14 of File ex9_2.c:

    number = scanf("%f%f%f%f%f%f", &x1, &x2, &x3, &x4, &x5, &x6);

scanf attempts to read six float values.   The number of successful conversions is assigned to number. Note that line 11 initialises the six float variables to 0 to ensure that any values not converted are 0. Line 16 then calculates the average of the six numbers:

```
 1 /* Exercise 9.2 - to calculate the average of a sequence of real numbers    *
 2  *     maximum six numbers, input terminated by an invalid character         */
 3
 4 #include <stdio.h>
 5
 6 int main(void)
 7 {
 8     float x1, x2, x3, x4, x5, x6, average;
 9     int number;
10
11     x1 = x2 = x3 = x4 = x5 = x6 = 0.0f;                 /* initialise to 0 */
12     printf("\nEnter up to six numbers terminated with a $ ? ");
13     /* read up to six numbers, getting number converted correctly */
14     number = scanf("%f%f%f%f%f%f", &x1, &x2, &x3, &x4, &x5, &x6);
15     /* calculate average (will crash if number = 0) */
16     average = (x1 + x2 + x3 + x4 + x5 + x6) / number;
17     printf("\n  Average of %d numbers = %f ", number, average);
18     return 0;
19 }
```

File ex9_2.c Calculate the average of up to six numbers

Exercise 10.1 (page 71) Assembly listing of Program 10_1.

An examination of an assembly listing should enable one to check that conversions between types are as expected, e.g. two lines of Program 10_1 assembled using Turbo C V3.00:

```
;     float_value = float_value + int_i;
;
mov          ax,word ptr DGROUP:_int_i              copy int_i
mov          word ptr [bp-2],ax
FILD         word ptr [bp-2]                        convert to float
FADD         dword ptr DGROUP:_float_value          add float_value
FSTP         dword ptr DGROUP:_float_value          result to float_value
;
;     double_value = double_value - float_value;
;
FLD          dword ptr DGROUP:_float_value          copy float_value
FSUBR        qword ptr DGROUP:_double_value         add double_value
FSTP         qword ptr DGROUP:_double_value         result to double_value
```

Exercise 10.2 (page 75) Calculate weekly, monthly and annual pay bills.

```
1 /* Exercise 10_2  Calculate weekly, monthly and annual pay bills */
2
3 #include <stdio.h>
4
5 int main(void)
6 {
7     int a_staff, b_staff, c_staff, d_staff, e_staff;
8     float a_pay, b_pay, c_pay, d_pay, e_pay, weekly, monthly, annual;
9
10    printf("Enter the number of staff in grades A, B, C, D and E ? ");
11    scanf("%d%d%d%d%d", &a_staff, &b_staff, &c_staff, &d_staff, &e_staff);
12    printf("Enter pay rates for A & B (monthly) and C, D & E (weekly) ? ");
13    scanf("%f%f%f%f%f", &a_pay, &b_pay, &c_pay, &d_pay, &e_pay);
14    weekly = c_staff * c_pay + d_staff * d_pay + e_staff * e_pay;
15    monthly = a_staff * a_pay + b_staff * b_pay;
16    annual = 52 * weekly + 12 * monthly;
17    printf("Weekly pay bill for weekly paid staff = %.2f\n"
18           "Monthly pay bill for monthly paid staff = %.2f\n"
19           "Total annual pay bill for all staff = %.2f\n",
20           weekly, monthly, annual);
21    return 0;
22 }
```

File ex10_2.c Calculate weekly, monthly and annual pay bills

A run of the program gave:

```
Enter the number of staff in grades A, B, C, D and E ? 2 4 20 15 10↵
Enter pay rates for A & B (monthly) and C, D & E (weekly) ? 1000 700 200 150 100↵
Weekly pay bill for weekly paid staff = 5250.00
Monthly pay bill for monthly paid staff = 4800.00
Total annual pay bill for all staff = 330600.00
```

Exercise 11.1 (page 77) Modifications to Program 11.1.

Removing the ; on the end of line 10 gave the following error using Microsoft C V7.00:

```
    13      else
***** P11_1.C(13) : error C2143: syntax error : missing ';' before 'else'
```

Replacing the == operator in line 10 with = gives the following warning with Microsoft C:

```
    11      if (ch = EOF)
***** P11_1.C(11) : warning C4206: assignment within conditional expression
```

indicating that the conditional expression of the if contains an assignment; which might be correct or not (discussed in Section 11.2).

Exercise 11.2 (page 79) Calculate parking prices.

```
 1 /* Exercise 11_2  calculate car park prices */
 2
 3 #include <stdio.h>
 4
 5 int main(void)
 6 {
 7     const int CAR = 1, TRUCKS = 3, BUSES = 5;              /* parking costs */
 8     char vehicle_type;
 9     int time, cost;
10
11     printf("Enter vehicle type (c - car, t - truck and b - buses) \n     and "
12           "time parked (hours) ? ");
13     scanf("%c%d", &vehicle_type, &time);                  /* read data */
14     /* work out cost depending upon vehicle type and cost per hour */
15     if (vehicle_type == 'c') cost = time * CAR;
16     else if (vehicle_type == 't') cost = time * TRUCKS;
17         else if (vehicle_type == 'b') cost = time * BUSES;
18     printf(" cost for %d hours = %d \n", time, cost);
19     return 0;
20 }
```

File ex11_2.c Calculate parking prices depending upon vehicle type and time

A run of the program in file ex11_2.c gave:

```
Enter vehicle type (c - car, t - truck and b - buses)
    and time parked (hours) ? t 6↲
  cost for 6 hours = 18
```

The main problem is that no input verification is performed, see next exercise.

Exercise 11.3 (page 83) Calculate parking prices, with data input verification

File ex11_3.c (next page) contains data input verification:

1   The function result of scanf is checked in line 13 to ensure that two conversions were performed; if not an error message is printed in line 14.
2   The value of variable cost is initialised to 0 in line 9. If the vehicle_type is incorrect all the if conditions in lines 17 to 19 will be false and the value of cost will be unchanged. The value of cost is then checked in line 20 and a message printed if data was invalid else the cost is printed (line 21).

```
 1 /* Exercise 11_3  calculate car park prices - check data entry */
 2
 3 #include <stdio.h>
 4
 5 int main(void)
 6 {
 7     const int CAR = 1, TRUCKS = 3, BUSES = 5;                /* parking costs */
 8     char vehicle_type;
 9     int time, cost = 0;                   /* initialise cost for data error check */
10
11     printf("Enter vehicle type (c - car, t - truck and b - buses) and "
12            "time parked (hours) ? ");
13     if (scanf("%c%d", &vehicle_type, &time) != 2)            /* read data */
14         printf("error on data input \n");
15     else
16        { /* work out cost depending upon vehicle type and cost per hour */
17          if (vehicle_type == 'c') cost = time * CAR;
18          else if (vehicle_type == 't') cost = time * TRUCKS;
19              else if (vehicle_type == 'b') cost = time * BUSES;
20          if (cost == 0) printf("Invalid vehicle type %c\n", vehicle_type);
21          else            printf("  cost for %d hours = %d \n", time, cost);
22        }
23     return 0;
24 }
```

File ex11_3.c   Calculate parking prices - with data input verification

Exercise 11.4 (page 84) Calculate college tuition fees.

```
 1 /* Exercise 11_4  Calculate college tuition fees */
 2
 3 #include <stdio.h>
 4
 5 int main(void)
 6 {
 7     char course_type, mode;
 8     int fees = 0;                      /* initialise fees to check for data error */
 9
10     printf("Enter course type (a - arts, s - science and e - engineering) and "
11            "\n    mode (e - evening, d - day and f - full time) ? ");
12     scanf("%c %c", &course_type, &mode);                    /* read data */
13     printf("\n%c%c\n", course_type, mode);
14     /* work out cost depending course type and attendance mode */
15     if (course_type == 'a')                             /* arts courses */
16        {
17          if (mode == 'e') fees = 350;
18          else if (mode == 'd') fees = 1000;
19              else if (mode == 'f') fees = 5000;
20        }
21     else
```

File ex11_4.c Calculate college tuition fees (continued on next page)

```
22          if (course_type == 's')                        /* science courses */
23             {
24               if (mode == 'e') fees = 500;
25               else if (mode == 'd') fees = 1200;
26                   else if (mode == 'f') fees = 7000;
27             }
28          else
29             if (course_type == 'e')                     /* engineering courses */
30                {
31                  if (mode == 'e') fees = 650;
32                  else if (mode == 'd') fees = 1400;
33                      else if (mode == 'f') fees = 8000;
34                }
35       if (fees == 0) printf("Data input error \n");
36       else            printf("  course fees = %d \n", fees);
37       return 0;
38 }
```

File ex11_4.c Calculate college tuition fees

File ex11_4.c uses a number of nested if statements to test the various conditions. File ex11_4a.c is a modified versions of ex11_4.c which uses the conditional operator ?, e.g. lines 15 to 34 of file ex14_4.c are reduced to:

```
    if (course_type == 'a')                              /* arts courses */
        fees = (mode == 'e') ? 350: ((mode == 'd') ? 1000: 5000);
    else if (course_type == 's')                         /* science courses */
            fees = (mode == 'e') ? 500: ((mode == 'd') ? 1200: 7000);
        else if (course_type == 'e')                     /* engineering courses */
                fees = (mode == 'e') ? 650: ((mode == 'd') ? 1400: 8000);
```

Exercise 12.1 (page 86) 'Rule of 72' effect of inflation on a fixed sum.

```
 1 /* Exercise 12_1  'Rule of 72' effect of inflation on a fixed sum */
 2 #include <stdio.h>
 3
 4 int main(void)
 5 {
 6     float rate, sum = 1.0f;
 7     int years = 0;
 8
 9     printf("Enter %% inflation rate ? ");
10     scanf("%f", &rate);                                /* read data */
11     while (sum > 0.5f)                          /* loop while the sum > 0.5 */
12         {
13           years++;                                 /* increment the years */
14           sum = sum * (100.0f - rate) /  100.0f;          /* new sum */
15         }
16     printf("  actual years %d, rule of 72 = %.1f\n", years, 72.0f / rate);
17     return 0;
18 }
```

File ex12_1.c 'Rule of 72' effect of inflation on a fixed sum

File ex12_1.c (previous page) contains a while statement (lines 11 to 15) which is executed while the value of sum is greater than 0.5; on each iteration of the loop years is incremented and the effect of inflation_rate on sum calculated. On loop termination (sum <= 0.5), the number of actual years is printed together with the value from the 'rule of 72'. A run gave:

```
Enter % inflation rate ? 10↲
  actual years 7, rule of 72 = 7.2
```

Exercise 12.2 (page 88) Average and standard deviation.

```
 1 /* Exercise 12_2, loop reading real numbers until error (or eof)   */
 2 /*                 calculate average and standard deviation         */
 3
 4 #include <stdio.h>                              /* standard stream I/O library */
 5 #include <math.h>                                /* standard maths library */
 6
 7 int main(void)
 8 {
 9     int number = 0;                              /* number of values read */
10     float x,                                     /* current value read */
11          sum = 0.0f,                             /* sum of values */
12          sum_squares = 0.0f,              /* sum of squares of value */
13          average,                               /* average of the values */
14          standard_deviation;          /* standard deviation of the values */
15
16     printf("enter a series of real numbers (terminate with eof) ? ");
17     /* loop reading numbers until error or eof */
18     while (scanf("%f", &x) == 1)
19         {
20         number++;                              /* increment number of values read */
21         sum = sum + x;                              /* add value to sum */
22         sum_squares = sum_squares + x * x;              /* add value squared */
23         }
24
25     /* input complete, calculate average & standard deviation, print results */
26     average = sum / number;
27     standard_deviation = sqrt( (sum_squares / number) - (average * average));
28     printf("%d numbers entered, average = %f, standard deviation = %f\n",
29             number, average, standard_deviation);
30     return 0;
31 }
```

File ex12_2.c Calculate average and standard deviation of a sequence of numbers

The sequence of statements in file ex12_2.c is:

9-14   define various variables - sum and sum_squares initialised to 0
18-23   a while reading numbers into x until EOF or error
        20-22   increment count of number read and add x to sums so far
26-29   calculate the average and standard deviation and print results.

Exercise 12.3 (page 91) Determine epsilon precision of float type.

```
 1 /* Exercise 12_3 - determine epsilon precision of float type          */
 2 /*      i.e. smallest number epsilon such that 1.0 + epsilon != 1.0    */
 3 /*      this algorithm attempts to force the use of variables in memory */
 4 /*      it uses an extended algorithm to get a more accurate value of epsilon */
 5
 6 #include <stdio.h>                          /* standard stream I/O library */
 7 #include <float.h>                          /* float types header */
 8
 9 int main(void)
10 {
11     float test, epsilon, new_epsilon = 1.0F, divisor = 1.0F;
12
13     printf("  float epsilon from <float.h> = %g\n",+FLT_EPSILON);
14     do
15        {
16        /* repeat calculations until  1.0 + new_epsilon = 1.0   */
17        do
18           {
19           epsilon = new_epsilon;                    /* save current epsilon */
20           new_epsilon = new_epsilon / (1.0F + divisor);      /* new epsilon */
21           test = 1.0F + new_epsilon;              /* calculate test value */
22           }
23        while (test != 1.0F);
24        new_epsilon = epsilon;                      /* restore last value */
25        divisor =  divisor / 2.0F;                /* calculate next divisor */
26        }
27     while (divisor > 1.0e-5F);
28     printf("  float epsilon calculated     = %g", epsilon);
29     test = (1.0f + epsilon);                         /* test value */
30     if (test != 1.0f) printf(" - OK !");
31     test = (1.0f + epsilon *.95f);
32     if (test == 1.0f) printf(" - OK !");
33     return 0;
34 }
```

File ex12_3.c   Determine epsilon precision of float type

In file ex12_3.c new_epsilon is divided by 2.0 on the first pass through the inner do loop (in line 20 new_epsilon is divided by 1.0 + divisor where divisor is 1.0F); when the do terminates the value of new_epsilon will be as Program 12_3. The variable divisor is then divided by 2.0 (line 25) and the inner do loop repeated. This process continues, with new_epsilon approaching the true value on each iteration, until divisor <= 1.0e-5 when the outer do loop terminates. Lines 29 to 32 perform a fairly simple check on the value evaluated. A run of the modified program on an IBM PC compatible under Turbo C and GNU C gave:

```
float epsilon from <float.h> = 1.19209e-07
float epsilon calculated     = 5.96056e-08 - OK ! - OK !
```

Exercise 13.1 (page 96) Programs using the for statement.

```
1 /* Exercise 13_1a - depreciation of value of a machine in a factory */
2 #include <stdio.h>
3
4 int main(void)
5 {
6     int rate, year;                    /* depreciation rate and for loop counter */
7     float value = 1000;                        /* assume machine value of $1000 */
8
9     printf("\nEnter %% depreciation rate (integer) ? ");      /* prompt user */
10    scanf("%d", &rate);                        /* read an integer number */
11    for (year = 1; year < 6; year++)                   /* loop for 5 years */
12        {
13            float depreciation = value * rate / 100.f;
14            value = value - depreciation;
15            printf("   year = %d, depreciation = %6.2f, value = %7.2f\n",
16                    year, depreciation, value);
17        }
18    printf("  After 5 years at %d%%, value = $%.2f, depreciation = "
19            "%.2f%%", rate, value, 0.1f * (1000.0f - value));
20    return 0;
21 }
```

File 13_1a.c Evaluate the depreciation of value of a machine in a factory

```
1 /* Exercise 13_1b  Draw a pattern on the screen using nested for statements */
2
3 #include <stdio.h>
4
5 int main(void)
6 {
7     int outer_loop, inner_loop;                          /* for loop counters */
8
9     for (outer_loop = 1; outer_loop < 13; outer_loop = outer_loop + 2)
10        {
11            for (inner_loop = 0; inner_loop < outer_loop; inner_loop++)
12                printf("*");
13            printf("\n");
14        }
15    return 0;
16 }
```

File 13_1b.c Draw a pattern on the screen using nested for statements

The program in file ex13_1b.c uses a pair of nested for statements to draw the pattern. Note that lines 9 to 14 could be replaced with (in file ex13_1b2.c):

```
    for (outer_loop = 1; outer_loop < 13; outer_loop += 2, printf("\n"))
        for (inner_loop = 0; inner_loop < outer_loop; inner_loop++)
            printf("*");
```

the expression outer_loop += 2, printf("\n") uses the comma operator, see Section 13.3.

Exercise 13.2 (page 100) Program to find prime numbers.

```
 1 /* Exercise 13_2 - Search positive integers for prime numbers          */
 2 /*  A prime integer is > 1 and is divisible only by itself and 1        */
 3 /*   e.g. 2 3 5 7 11 13 17 19 23 29 31 37 41 43 47 53 59 61 67 etc.     */
 4
 5 #include <stdio.h>                            /* standard stream I/O library */
 6
 7 int main(void)
 8    {
 9    unsigned long int maximum,                     /* number to search up to */
10                      n, i;                /* loop counters in for statements */
11
12    printf("\nFind prime numbers up to ? ");
13    scanf("%ld", &maximum);
14    /* search odd unsigned integers from 3 to maximum  */
15    for (n = 3 ; n <= maximum ; n = n + 2)
16       {
17       /* attempt to divide number n by odd integer i ranging from 3 to n/2 */
18       /*  exit if division occurs without remainder or when i >= n/2       */
19       for (i = 3 ; (n % i != 0) && (i < (n/2)) ; i = i + 2)
20             /* null statement */;
21       if (i >= n/2) printf("%ld is a prime\n", n);
22       else          printf("%ld is not prime, divisible by %ld\n", n, i);
23       }
24    return 0;
25 }
```

File ex13_2.c Program to search positive integers for prime numbers

A prime number is greater than 1 and is divisible only by itself and 1. File ex13_2.c uses two for statements to search for prime numbers up to some specified maximum:

15-23   `for (n = 3 ; n <= maximum ; n = n + 2)`
        is a for statement which increments the number n from 3 to maximum in steps of
        2 (the numbers 1 and 2 are ignored and even numbers cannot be prime because
        they can be divided by 2), i.e. 3 5 7 9 11 13 etc.

19-20   `for (i = 3 ; (n % i != 0) && (i < (n/2)) ; i = i + 2)`
        is a for statement which divides the number n by all the odd integers in the
        range 3 to n/2 (there is no need to go beyond n/2), i.e.:
        (a) i (which is divided into n) is initialised to 3
        (b) if the remainder of n/i is zero the for terminates (n is not a prime)
        (c) if i >= n/2 the for terminates
        (d) otherwise i is incremented by 2

21-22   prints a message indicating if the number n was a prime or not.

A run gave:

```
Find prime numbers up to ?  14↵
3 is a prime
5 is a prime
7 is a prime
9 is not prime, divisible by 3
11 is a prime
13 is a prime
```

Exercise 14.1 (page 105) Programs using the switch statement.

Part (a) File ex14_1a.c is a modification of file ex11_4.c in which the if statements have been replaced with:

```
switch (course_type)
  {
  case 'a': fees = (mode == 'e') ? 350: ((mode == 'd') ? 1000: 5000);
            break;                                    /* arts courses */
  case 's': fees = (mode == 'e') ? 500: ((mode == 'd') ? 1200: 7000);
            break;                                    /* science courses */
  case 'e': fees = (mode == 'e') ? 650: ((mode == 'd') ? 1400: 8000);
            break;                                    /* engineering courses */
  }
```

Part (b) The code in file c14\ex14_1b.c, given a person's age range and car group, returns the motor insurance premium using a sequence of if statements.   File ex14_1b1.c uses a switch statement with group (1 to 7) as the selector:

```
/* calculate premium from age range and car group */
switch (group)
    {
    case 1: case 2: case 3:
        if ((age <= TWENTIES) || (age == OVER_FORTIES)) premium = 460;
        else                                            premium = 450;
        break;
    case 4: case 5:
        if ((age <= TWENTIES) || (age == OVER_FORTIES)) premium = 460;
        else                                            premium = 480;
        break;
    case 6: case 7: if (age <= TWENTIES) premium = 500;
                    else
                           if (age == OVER_FORTIES) premium = 460;
                           else                     premium = 480;
    }
```

File ex14_1b2.c uses a switch statement with age (UNDER_TWENTIES, TWENTIES, THIRTIES, FORTIES, OVER_FORTIES) as the selector:

```
/* calculate premium from age range and car group */
switch (age)
    {
    case UNDER_TWENTIES: case TWENTIES: if (group > 5) premium = 500;
                                        else           premium = 460;
                                        break;
    case THIRTIES: case FORTIES:  if (group > 3) premium = 480;
                                  else           premium = 450;
                                  break;
    case OVER_FORTIES: premium = 460;
    }
```

Exercise 15.1 (page 108)

Files c15\ex15_1.c and c15\ex15_1a.c on the disk contain sample answers to this exercise.

Exercise 15.2 (page 113) Graphics display of a bouncing ball.

File ex15_2.c (below and on next page) displays a bouncing ball using the Turbo C graphics package. The program sequence is:

10	define integral constants for size of circle and size of ball movement.
11	declare variables used by initgraph
12-14	declare variables used in ball movement
15-16	declare variables used in time period calculations
19	call initgraph to initialise the graphics system (see below)
20-24	if the result of graphresult was not grOK (graphics OK) display error report
	22 grapherrormsg(graphdriver) returns a pointer to an error message string
26-28	count the number of loops a while performs in one second (see below)
32-33	read the maximum x and y coordinates
34-35	set colour to white and draw a box around the edges of the screen
38-53	a do statement loops until the keyboard is hit
	kbhit is a Turbo C function which returns *true* when a key is hit
40-41	draw circle at current position in white
42-43	delay for a period of time (see below)
45-48	if the ball has hit the edge of the screen reverse its movement
49-50	redraw circle position in black (to erase the circle drawn in lines 41 and 42)
51-52	calculate next drawing position.

When a key is hit the do terminates and line 55 closes the graphics system.

The purpose of the delay (lines 42 and 43, a for loop counting i from zero to time_count/20), is to slow down the movement of the ball so that it moves at a reasonable pace. Because machines execute instructions at different speeds time_count is evaluated (lines 26 to 28) by counting the number of while loops performed in one second (Program 12_5 describes the clock function). The magnitude of time_count is proportional to the speed of the processor concerned and when used in the delay loop gives a similar speed of ball movement on all machines (it is not exactly the same because the remainder of the do statement takes different times to execute on different machines and the effect of other processes under a multi-processing environment, e.g. UNIX, OS/2, Windows 95, etc.).

In line 19 initgraph initialises the graphics system. The first parameter specifies the graphics driver and the second parameter specifies the mode of the driver. In this program graphdriver is set to DETECT (defined in <graphics.h>) which will automatically detect what sort of graphics card is fitted (graphmode is not used in this case). The third parameter is the pathname to the directory containing the Turbo C graphics driver files. The function initgraph returns information indicating any error condition or, if successful, what driver was found. In the case of an error graphresult() != grOk the function grapherrormsg(graphdriver) returns a pointer to a string containing an error message (which is printed by printf using the %s conversion specification).

```
1 /* Exercise 15.2 - Bouncing ball program using Turbo C graphics library */
2
3 #include <graphics.h>          /* Turbo C graphics library functions */
4 #include <conio.h>             /* Turbo C console I/O functions */
5 #include <stdio.h>                /* standard I/O library */
6 #include <time.h>                 /* standard time library */
7
```

```
 8  int main(void)
 9  {
10      enum {Circle_size = 20, Move_size = 5 };              /* define constants */
11      int graphdriver = DETECT, graphmode, i;
12      int x = 150, y = 100,              /* current position of ball on the screen */
13          x_move = Move_size, y_move = Move_size,           /* x & y movements */
14          maxx, maxy;                                       /* screen size */
15      long int time_count = 0;                     /* holds loop time counter */
16      clock_t  clock_start;                        /* holds clock start time */
17
18      /* Initialise graphics system */
19      initgraph(&graphdriver, &graphmode, "c:\\tc\\bgi");
20      if (graphresult() != grOk)
21          {
22          printf("initgraph failed: %s ", grapherrormsg(graphdriver) );
23          return 1;                                /* failed, return */
24          }
25      /* count loops for one second, used to time bouncing ball on the screen */
26      clock_start = clock();
27      while (((clock() - clock_start) / CLOCKS_PER_SEC) < 1)
28          time_count++;
29      printf("\ntime_count = %ld ", time_count);
30
31      /* get the size of the screen and draw a box around the edges */
32      maxx = getmaxx();
33      maxy = getmaxy();
34      setcolor(WHITE);                             /* set colour white */
35      rectangle(0, 0, maxx, maxy);                 /* draw box around screen */
36
37      /* loop bouncing ball around the screen */
38      do
39          {
40          setcolor(WHITE);                         /* draw ball in white */
41          circle(x, y, Circle_size);
42          for (i = 0 ; i < time_count/20 ; i++)     /* show ball on screen */
43              /* null for delay */;
44          /* if next move would be outside screen change direction */
45          if (x + x_move >= maxx - Circle_size) x_move = -Move_size;
46          if (x + x_move <= Circle_size) x_move = Move_size;
47          if (y + y_move >= maxy - Circle_size) y_move = -Move_size;
48          if (y + y_move <= Circle_size) y_move = Move_size;
49          setcolor(BLACK);                         /* delete old ball */
50          circle(x, y, Circle_size);
51          x = x + x_move;                          /* calculate new x & y */
52          y = y + y_move;
53          }
54      while (! kbhit());
55      closegraph();
56      return 0;
57  }
```

File ex15_2.c Bouncing ball program using Turbo C graphics

Exercise 16.1 (page 119) Calculate period of oscillation of a simple pendulum.

```
 1 /* Exercise 16_1 - Calculate period of oscillation of a simple pendulum */
 2
 3 #include <stdio.h>                           /* standard stream I/O library */
 4 #include <math.h>                            /* standard maths library */
 5
 6 /*-------------------------------------------------------------------------*/
 7 /* Function to calculate the period of oscillation of a simple pendulum     */
 8 /* Parameters in: length (float) of pendulum in metres                      */
 9 /* Function result: period of oscillation in seconds                        */
10 /*-------------------------------------------------------------------------*/
11 float pendulum(float length)                         /* function header */
12 {
13     const float G = 9.80665f,                         /* g in m/sec/sec */
14               TWO_PI = 2.0f * 3.1415926f;                    /* 2 pi */
15     float period;                                    /* holds period */
16
17     period = TWO_PI * sqrt( length / G);          /* calculate period */
18     return period;                          /* return function result */
19 }
20
21 /*-------------------------------------------------------------------------*/
22 /* function main - no parameters returns result indicating success/fail     */
23 int main(void)
24 {
25     float length, time_period;                  /* internal variables */
26
27     printf("\nEnter length of pendulum in metres ? ");
28     scanf("%f", &length);                                /* read data */
29     time_period = pendulum(length);                 /* call pendulum */
30     printf(" period of oscillation = %f seconds\n", time_period);
31     return 0;
32 }
```

File ex16_1.c Calculate period of oscillation of a simple pendulum

File ex16_1.c contains two functions pendulum and main

11-19 definition of function pendulum, one float parameter returns float function result
    13-14 define local constants G and TWO_PI
    15   define local variable period
    17   calculate period of oscillation
    18   return function result
23-32 definition of function main, tests function pendulum
    29 call function pendulum.

The local constants and variables are not really needed (they are only used once) and function pendulum would, in practice, be written:

```
float pendulum(float length)                         /* function header */
{
    return 2.0f * 3.1415926f * sqrt( length / 9.80665f);  /* calculate period */
}
```

Exercise 16.2 (page 119)

```
 1 /* Exercise 16_2  Functions to evaluate factorial and inverse factorial */
 2
 3 #include <stdio.h>
 4
 5 /*-----------------------------------------------------------------------*/
 6 /* function main - no parameters returns result indicating success/fail    */
 7 int main(void)
 8 {
 9     float factorial(int number);                    /* function prototypes */
10     float inverse_factorial(int number);
11     int number;                                      /* local variable */
12
13     while (printf("Enter number >= 0 ? "), scanf("%d", &number) == 1)
14        printf("   factorial = %.2f, inverse = %g\n",
15               factorial(number), inverse_factorial(number));
16     return 0;
17 }
18
19 /*-----------------------------------------------------------------------*/
20 /* function to evaluate the factorial of a number passed as a parameter    */
21 /* parameters in:   number (integer) to find factorial of                  */
22 /* function result: factorial as a float                                   */
23 float factorial(int number)
24 {
25     float result = 1.0f;                            /* local variable */
26     while (number > 1)                              /* evaluate factorial */
27        result = result * number--;                  /* decrement number to 1 */
28     return result;
29 }
30
31 /*-----------------------------------------------------------------------*/
32 /* function to evaluate inverse factorial of a number passed as a parameter */
33 /* parameters in:   number (integer) to find inverse factorial of           */
34 /* function result: inverse factorial as a float                            */
35 float inverse_factorial(int number)
36 {
37     return 1.0f / factorial(number);                /* call factorial function */
38 }
```

File ex16_2.c Functions to evaluate factorial and inverse factorial

File ex16_2.c contains three functions factorial (lines 23 to 29), which evaluates the factorial of a number, inverse_factorial (lines 35 to 38), which calls factorial to get the inverse factorial of a number, and main (lines 7 to 17) which tests factorial and inverse_factorial. Note that factorial and inverse_factorial are prototyped in lines 9 and 10 in main. A run of the program gave:

```
Enter number >= 0 ? 7↵
   factorial = 5040.00, inverse = 0.000198
Enter number >= 0 ? 20↵
   factorial = 2432902298041581568.00, inverse = 4.11032e-19
```

Exercise 16.3 (page 122) Reactance of LC series circuit & resonant frequency.

```
 1 /* Exercise 16_3   Reactance of LC series circuit & resonant frequency */
 2
 3 #include <stdio.h>                              /* standard stream I/O library */
 4 #include <math.h>                               /* standard maths library */
 5
 6 int main(void)
 7 {
 8     float lc_reactance(float c, float l, float f);     /* function prototype */
 9     float lc_resonance(float c, float l);              /* function prototype */
10
11     /* variables to hold reactance, inductance, capacitance and frequency */
12     float reactance, l, c, f;
13
14     printf("Series LC circuit\n enter inductance (henries), "
15            "capacitance (farads) and frequency (Hz)\n               ? ");
16     scanf("%f%f%f", &l, &c, &f);
17     reactance = lc_reactance(c, l, f);                 /* determine reactance */
18     printf("\nreactance of series LC circuit = %f\n", reactance);
19     printf("resonant frequency = %f\n", lc_resonance(c, l));
20     return 0;
21 }
22
23 /*--------------------------------------------------------------------------*/
24 /* reactance of series circuit capacitance c, inductance l at frequency f   */
25 float lc_reactance(float c, float l, float f)
26 {
27     const float TWO_PI = 3.1415926f * 2.0f;            /* constant 2 pi */
28     return TWO_PI * f * l - (1.0f / (TWO_PI * f * c));  /* return reactance */
29 }
30
31 /*--------------------------------------------------------------------------*/
32 /* resonant frequency of series circuit capacitance and inductance l        */
33 float lc_resonance(float c, float l)
34 {
35     return 1.0f/ (3.1415926f * 2.0f * sqrt(l * c));    /* resonant frequency */
36 }
```

File ex16_3.c Reactance of LC series circuit & resonant frequency

File ex16_3.c contains three functions:

6-21   definition of function main
        8-9 prototypes of functions lc_reactance and lc_resonance
           the compiler uses these to check the function calls in lines 17 and 19
25-29   definition of function lc_reactance
        which calculates the reactance of an LC circuit
33-36   definition of function lc_resonance
        which calculates the resonant frequency of an LC circuit.

The functions are quite short and are candidates for being implemented as preprocessor macros (see Section 16.13). The advantage of using functions is that once tested they can be used in any program.

Exercise 16.4 (page 128) Function which passes parameter by reference.

```
1  /* Exercise 16_4 - function which returns results via reference parameters    */
2
3  #include <stdio.h>                                /* standard stream I/O library */
4
5  int main(void)
6  {
7      /* function prototype for function metres_to_feet */
8      void metres_to_feet(float metres, int *feet, float *inches);
9      float distance, x_inches;                            /* local variables */
10     int x_feet;
11
12     printf("\n Enter distance in metres (real number) ? ");
13     scanf("%f", &distance);                              /* read distance */
14     metres_to_feet(distance, &x_feet, &x_inches);        /* call function */
15     printf("   is %d feet %f inches\n",  x_feet, x_inches);
16     return 0;
17 }
18
19 /*------------------------------------------------------------------*/
20 /* Function to convert distance in metres to feet and inches        */
21 /* Parameters in: metres (float) distance in metres                 */
22 /* Parameters out: feet   (float) distance in feet                  */
23 /*                 inches (float)          and inches               */
24 /* Function result: none                                            */
25 /*------------------------------------------------------------------*/
26 void metres_to_feet(float metres, int *feet, float *inches)     /* header */
27 {
28     const float FEET_PER_METRE = 3.280839895;    /* converts metres to feet */
29     float float_feet = metres * FEET_PER_METRE;      /* convert to feet */
30
31     *feet = (int) float_feet;                    /* get whole number of feet */
32     *inches = (float_feet - *feet) * 12.0f;       /* get number of inches */
33 }
```

File ex16_3.c Function which returns results via reference parameters

To *pass by reference* the formal parameters feet and inches to function metres_to_feet in file ex16_4.c are float * (pointers to float). Using the deference operator * with the pointer names (lines 31 and 32) accesses the memory allocated to the actual parameters when the function is called (x_feet and x_inches in line 14). Formal parameter metres is passed by value - any changes made inside the function would not affect the corresponding actual parameter (distance in line 14). The function prototype in function main (line 8) informs the compiler that the second and third parameters are pointers and when the function is called (line 14) the address operator & is used to pass an address. Function metres_to_feet could be simplified as follows (in file ex16_4a.c):

```
void metres_to_feet(float metres, int *feet, float *inches)        /* header  */
{
    metres = metres * 3.280839895f;                /* convert distance to feet */
    *feet = (int) metres;                          /* get whole number of feet */
    *inches = (metres - *feet) * 12.0f;             /* get number of inches */
}
```

Exercise 16.5 (Page 132) Find larger of two numbers using a function and a macro.

```
 1 /* Exercise 16_5a - function to return the maximum of two numbers */
 2
 3 #include <stdio.h>
 4
 5 /* return maximum of two numbers of type integer */
 6 int maximum(const int x1, const int x2)
 7 {
 8     if (x1 >= x2) return x1;
 9     return x2;
10 }
11
12 int main(void)
13 {
14     int i1 = 10, i2 = 20;
15     float a1 = 50.5f, a2 = 100.3f, x1 = .5f, x2 = .3f;
16
17     printf("maximum int of %d and %d is %d\n", i1, i2, maximum(i1, i2));
18     printf("maximum float of %.2f and %.2f is %.2f\n",
19             a1, a2, (float) maximum(a1, a2));
20     /* but has real difficulty with fractional components */
21     printf("maximum float of %.2f and %.2f is %.2f\n",
22             x1, x2, (float) maximum(x1, x2));
23     return 0;
24 }
```

File ex16_5a.c Function to return the maximum of two numbers

File ex16_5a.c contains a function maximum which returns the larger of two int numbers passed as parameters. The function main tests function maximum by calling it with int and float parameters. A run gave:

```
maximum int of 10 and 20 is 20
maximum float of 50.50 and 100.30 is 100.00
maximum float of 0.50 and 0.03 is 0.00
```

The function maximum works correctly with int parameters and gives an approximate answer with the float parameters 50.5 and 100.3 (which will be passed as 50 and 100). The function fails completely with the fractional float parameters 0.5 and 0.3 which will be passed as 0. File ex16_5b.c implements maximum as the macro:

```
/* return maximum of two numbers of any fundamental type */
#define maximum(x1, x2) ((x1) >= (x2) ? (x1) : (x2))
```

The remainder of File c16_5b.c is similar to File ex16_5a.c above. A run gave:

```
maximum int of 10 and 20 is 20
maximum float of 50.00 and 100.00 is 100.00
maximum float of 0.50 and 0.30 is 0.50
```

Implementing functions as macros gives one flexibility in the parameters that can be passed (but parameter type checking is lost).

Exercise 17.1 (page 139) Running mean function using static local variables

```
 1 /* Exercise 17_1   Running mean function using static local variables        */
 2
 3 #include <stdio.h>                                    /* standard I/O library */
 4
 5 int main(void)
 6 {
 7     float running_mean(const float number);              /* function prototype */
 8     float next_number, average_so_far;                   /* local variables */
 9
10     while (printf("\nEnter next number ? "), scanf("%f", &next_number))
11         {
12         average_so_far = running_mean(next_number);
13         printf("    average so far = %f", average_so_far);
14         }
15     return 0;
16 }
17
18 /*------------------------------------------------------------------*/
19 /* Function to calculate the running average of a sequence of numbers         */
20 /* Parameters  in: number  (float) next number in the sequence               */
21 /* Function result: average calculated so far                                 */
22 /*------------------------------------------------------------------*/
23 float running_mean(const float number)
24 {
25     static float average = 0.0f;                    /* static local variables */
26     static int count = 0;
27
28     average = (average * count + number) / (count + 1);     /* new average */
29     count = count + 1;                                   /* increment count */
30     return average;
31 }                                                   /* end of running mean */
```

Exercise 17.1 Running mean function using static local variables

The sequence of statements in function running_mean in Exercise 17.1 is:

25 define static local variable average initialised to 0
26 define static local variable count initialised to 0
28 calculate new running mean, assign result to average
29 increment count of function calls
30 return new running mean.

The static local variables average and count are allocated storage and initialised on the first call of running_mean. Any modifications made are retained on function exit and are then available the next time the function is called. Normal *automatic* local variables are allocated storage and initialised on each call to a function and deallocated on function exit. Local variables declared static are generally used when a single function needs to retain information between successive calls and the information should be 'hidden' within the function and not accessible from outside.

Exercise 19.1 (page 168) Array read, write, average, standard deviation and sort.

```
 1 /* Exercise 19_1 Array read, write, average, standard deviation and sort */
 2
 3 #include <stdio.h>
 4 #include <math.h>
 5
 6 int main(void)
 7 {
 8     int array_read(float array[], const int max_index);         /* prototypes */
 9     void array_write(const float array[], const int number);
10     float array_average(const float array[], const int number);
11     float array_standard_deviation(const float array[], const int number);
12     void array_sort(float array[], const int number);
13     float  data[10] = {0};                                      /* data array */
14     int index;                                    /* number of elements in data */
15
16     index = array_read(data, 10);                          /* read array data */
17     array_write(data, index);                                  /* write array */
18     printf("\nArray average = %f, standard_deviation = %f\nSorted:",
19             array_average(data, index), array_standard_deviation(data, index));
20     array_sort(data, index);                                    /* sort array */
21     array_write(data, index);                                  /* write array */
22     return 0;
23 }
24
25 /*--------------------------------------------------------------------------*/
26 /* function to find the average of the values stored in an array            */
27 float array_average(const float array[], const int number)
28 {
29     float sum = 0.0f;                                     /* sum of values */
30     int index = 0;                                        /* array index */
31
32     while (index < number)
33         sum = sum + array[index++];                       /* add value to sum */
34     return  sum / number;                                 /* return average */
35 }
36
37 /*--------------------------------------------------------------------------*/
38 /* function to find the standard deviation of the values in an array        */
39 float array_standard_deviation(const float array[], const int number)
40 {
41     float sum_squares = 0.0f,                        /* sum of squares of value */
42           average = array_average(array, number);    /* average of the values */
43     int index = 0;                                        /* array index */
44
45     for (index = 0; index < number; index++)
46         sum_squares += array[index] * array[index];   /* add square of value */
47     return sqrt((sum_squares / number) - (average * average));    /* result */
48 }
49
```

File ex19_1.c Array read, write, average, standard deviation and sort functions

```
50 /* function to sort the contents of an array                            */
51 void array_sort(float array[], const int number)
52 {
53     int index_1, index_2;                         /* array index values */
54
55     /* look at each element of the array in turn */
56     for (index_1 = 0 ; index_1 < number - 1; index_1++)
57         {
58         float minimum = array[index_1];           /* holds minimum value */
59         /* scan remainder of array looking for minimum value */
60         for (index_2 = index_1 + 1 ; index_2 < number ; index_2++)
61             if (array[index_2] < minimum)
62                 {
63                 minimum = array[index_2];          /* found new minimum */
64                 array[index_2] = array[index_1];        /* swap values */
65                 array[index_1] = minimum;
66                 }
67         }
68 }
                *** array_read and array_write as in Program  19_1  ****
```

File ex19_1.c Array read, write, average, standard deviation and sort functions

File ex19_1.c contains the following array manipulation functions (plus main):

27-35 function array_average returns the average of the values in array length number
29-30 define and initialise local variables sum and index
32-34 while loop to sum contents of array and return average value
39-48 array_standard_deviation returns the standard deviation of the values in array
41-43 define local variables, call function array_average to obtain average of the values
45-46 for loop to sum the squares of the values stored in the array
47   return the standard deviation
51-68 function void array_sort sorts the contents of array
56-67 a for incrementing index_1 from 0 to number-2
      58   declare minimum and initialise it to the value of array[index_1]
      60-66 a for incrementing index_2 from index_1+1 to number-1
           61 if array[index_2] < current minimum
               62-66 reset minimum and swap array[index_1] and array[index_2].

In array_sort the outer for loop, line 56, does not need to look at the last element; it contains the maximum value when the for terminates. In line 42 function array_standard_deviation calls array_average; it would be more efficient to calculate the average in the for loop in lines 45 and 46 (see file ex19_1a.c). Do not write lines 45 to 46 as follows (index may be incremented before or after its use in array[index]):

```
    while (index < number)
        sum_squares += array[index++] * array[index];   /* add square of value */
```

A run of the program gave:

```
Enter up to 10 numbers (<CR> to end) ? 12 6 7 3 15 10 18 5↲
        12.000       6.000       7.000       3.000      15.000
        10.000      18.000       5.000
Array average = 9.500000, standard_deviation = 4.873397
         3.000       5.000       6.000       7.000      10.000
        12.000      15.000      18.000
```

Exercise 20.1 (page 182) Function to read a number in hexadecimal.

```
 1 /*-------------------------------------------------------------------*/
 2 /* Function to read a number in hexadecimal from the keyboard        */
 3 /*   terminate input when character read was not 0 - 9 or A - F      */
 4 /*   leave last character read in the input stream with EOF as 0     */
 5 /* Parameters none                                                   */
 6 /* Function result: value of number read as a long int              */
 7 long int read_hex(void)                            /* function header */
 8 {
 9     long int n = 0;                     /* holds number while reading */
10     int  ch;                            /* holds character read */
11
12     while (((ch = toupper(getchar())) != EOF) && (ch != '\n'))
13        /* if 0 - 9 or A - F was read add to number else print bad character */
14        if (isdigit(ch)) n = n * 16 + (ch - '0');
15        else
16            if ((ch >= 'A') && (ch <= 'F')) n = n * 16 + (ch - 'A') + 10;
17            else                           printf(" %c ignored\n", ch);
18     if (ch == EOF) ch = 0;                     /* replace EOF with 0 */
19     ungetc(ch, stdin);                         /* unget last character */
20     return n;                                  /* return number */
21 }
```

File ex20_1.c Function to read a number in hexadecimal

In file ex20_1.c function read_hex reads a number in hexadecimal from the keyboard, reporting invalid characters and terminating when EOF or newline is entered:

12-17 a while read characters, terminates on EOF or \n
       the function toupper (from <ctype.h>) converts characters to upper case
     14 if the character is a digit (0 to 9) add value to number
     16 else if character is A to F (value 10 to 15) add to number
     17 else print error message and character in error.

Exercise 20.2 (page 182) Using direct console I/O.

File ex20_2.c contains a modified version of function read_binary from Program 20_2 in which lines 31 to 35 have been replaced with:

```
/* loop until end of file (character 0x1a) or carriage return is read */
while (((ch = getch()) != 0x1a) && (ch != '\r'))
   /* if 0 or 1 was read add to number and echo else ignore bad character */
   if ((ch == '0') || (ch == '1'))
       {
       n = n * 2 + (ch - '0');
       putch(ch);
       }
if (ch == 0x1a) ch = 0;                     /* replace EOF with 0 */
```

Function getch (from <conio.h>) reads a character directly from the MS-DOS keyboard input (it does not echo to the screen). Being directly from MS-DOS the end of line character is '\r' (carriage return) and end of file is 0x1a (CTRL/Z). If the character is 0 or 1 the value is added to number and it is echoed otherwise it is ignored.

Exercise 20.3 (page 195) Functions to search and compare strings.

The sequence of statements in function main is:

11   call gets to read the first string text_1

14   call gets to read the second string text_2

16   initialise index to first element of array - 1

19-20   a while calling str_search to search for next occurrence of text_2 in text_1

          the while terminates when text_2 is not found (-1 returned)

       20 if text_2 is found print value of index and text_1 from index

           &text_1[index] passes the address of a particular element

21-27   a sequence of if statements calling str_compare

       22 print message if text_1 equals text_2

       25 print message if text_1 less than text_2

       27 print message if text_1 greater than text_2.

Lines 11 and 14 are examples of the use of gets. Remember that gets performs no bound checking and in practice fgets should be used!

```
1  /* Exercise 20_3 - string search and compare functions */
2
3  #include <stdio.h>
4
5  int main(void)
6  {
7      int str_search(const char string_1[], const char string_2[], int index);
8      int str_compare(const char string_1[], const char string_2[]);
9      char text_1[30], text_2[30];                  /* strings to search */
10
11     while (printf("\n\nEnter first string ? "), gets(text_1) != NULL)
12         {
13         printf("Enter second string ? ");
14         if (gets(text_2) != NULL)               /* read string, exit if EOF */
15             {
16             int index = -1;                     /* search from index = 0 */
17
18             printf("Index positions of %s = ", text_2);
19             while ((index = str_search(text_1, text_2, ++index)) >= 0)
20                 printf("\n%d %s ", index, &text_1[index]);
21             if (str_compare(text_1, text_2) == 0)
22                 printf("\n\n%s and %s are identical ", text_1, text_2);
23             else
24                 if (str_compare(text_1, text_2) < 0)
25                     printf("\n\n%s < %s ", text_1, text_2);
26                 else
27                     printf("\n\n%s > %s ", text_1, text_2);
28             }
29         }
30     return 0;
31 }
```

File ex20_3.c String search and compare functions (continued on next page)

```
32
33 /*------------------------------------------------------------------*/
34 /* search string for a string                                      */
35 /* on entry string_1[]   contains string to search                 */
36 /*          string_2[]   contains string to search for             */
37 /*          index        index to position to start search         */
38 /* return function result: index position if found -1 if not found */
39 int str_search(const char string_1[], const char string_2[], int index)
40 {
41     while(string_1[index] != '\0')                      /* look for '\0' */
42         {
43         if (string_1[index] == string_2[0])       /* first character found ? */
44             {
45             int i = 0;                              /* yes, check rest of string_2 */
46
47             do
48                 if (string_2[++i] == '\0') return index;    /* string_2 found */
49             while (string_1[index + i] == string_2[i]);
50             }
51         index++;                                    /* not found, try again */
52         }
53     return -1;                                      /* not found, return fail */
54 }
55
56 /*------------------------------------------------------------------*/
57 /* Compare two strings (similar to library function strcmp)          */
58 /*   return 0 if equal, >0 if string1 > string2 , <0 if string1 < string2  */
59 int str_compare(const char string_1[], const char string_2[])
60 {
61     int index = -1;
62
63     /* loop looking for terminating nulls */
64     do
65         {
66         index ++;                                   /* index to next character */
67         if (string_1[index] > string_2[index]) return 1;    /* return > 0 */
68         /* character in string_1 <= string_2, if not the same return < 0 */
69         if (string_1[index] < string_2[index]) return -1;   /* return < 0 */
70         /* strings identical so far, check next character */
71         }
72     while ((string_1[index] != '\0') && (string_2[index] != '\0'));
73     /*printf("\n %s %s", string_1, string_2);*/
74     return 0;                                       /* strings are identical return 0 */
75 }
```

File ex20_3.c   String search and compare functions (continued from previous page)

Discussion of program continued on next page

The sequence of statements in string_search is:

39   `int str_search(const char string_1[], const char string_2[], int index)`
    is the function header with the formal parameters:
    string_1 the character array to search
    string_2 the character array to search for
    index the index position to start search from.
    The function returns the index if the string is found or -1 if not found

41-52 while which terminates when '\0' is found in string_1
    43 check if current character in string_1 is the first character in string_2
        44-50   characters the same, compare rest of string_2
              48 if terminator of string_2 has been found return result index
              49 continue do if characters in string_1 and string_2 are the same
      51 string_2 not found, test next character in string_1

53 string_2 not found, return with -1.

In function str_compare the do statement, lines 64 to 72, tests in turn each character in string_1 against the corresponding character in string_2:

1   line 67: if string1[index] > string2[index], if the value of the character in string1 > string2 the function returns with value > 0

2   line 69: if string1[index] < string2[index], if the value of string1 < string2 the function returns with value < 0

3   otherwise the characters are the same and the loop tests the next character after incrementing index

4   line 74 is executed if string_1 and string_2 are identical and 0 is returned.

Exercise 21.1 (page 205) Pointers and the increment operator.

Below is a fragment of code from file ex21_1.c; a for statement is executed six times with the various valid combinations of the indirection and increment operators operating upon the array x. On every iteration the array x is recreated and initialised and the pointer p_array pointed at the third element. The switch statement selects the operation to be performed (case 7 and case 8 which would generate errors, are commented out).

```
for (i = 1 ; i < 7 ; i++ )
{
    int x[] = { 10, 20, 30, 40, 50 },          /* five element array */
        *p_array = &x[2],                      /* pointer to third element */
        array_index;                           /* general index */
    printf("\n *p = %d, ", *p_array);
    switch (i)
    {
        case 1: printf("*++p    = %d, ", *++p_array); break;
        case 2: printf("++*p    = %d, ", ++*p_array); break;
        case 3: printf("*p++    = %d, ", *p_array++); break;
        case 4: printf("(*p)++ = %d, ", (*p_array)++); break;
        case 5: printf("*++p = 500, "); *++p_array = 500; break;
        case 6: printf("*p++ = 500, "); *p_array++ = 500; break;
        /*case 7: printf("++*p = 500, "); ++*p_array = 500; break;
        case 8: printf("(*p)++ = 500, "); (*p_array)++ = 500; break;*/
    }
    printf("p - x = %d, array = ", p_array - x);
    for (array_index = 0 ; array_index < 5 ; array_index++)
        printf(" %3d", x[array_index]);
}
```

Exercise 21.2 (page 211) Passing parameters to a C program.

```
 1 /* Exercise 21_2 -   Print parameters passed from operating system to main */
 2
 3 #include <stdio.h>
 4 #include <string.h>
 5
 6 /*---------------------------------------------------------------------------*/
 7 /* function main with parameters                                            */
 8 /*    argc - number of elements in array argv                               */
 9 /*    argv - an array of pointers to strings                                */
10 int main(int argc, char *argv[])
11 {
12     char **p_to_argv;
13
14     printf("\nNumber of parameters in command line is %d", argc);
15     for (p_to_argv = argv ; *p_to_argv != NULL ; p_to_argv++)
16        {
17        printf("\n parameter is %s ", *p_to_argv);
18        if (strcmp(*p_to_argv,"-lower") == 0)
19            printf("   option -lower found ! ");
20        if (strcmp(*p_to_argv,"-upper") == 0)
21            printf("   option -upper found ! ");
22        }
23     return 0;
24 }
```

File ex21_2.c Print parameters passed from operating system to main

The sequence of statements in file ex21_2.c is:

10-24   define function main with parameters argc and argv
12   define p_to_argv a pointer which points to a pointer to char
14   print the number of parameters, i.e. value of argc
15-22   a for statement incrementing p_to_argv from argv until a NULL is found
       17 print current parameter (%s expects a pointer to a string)
       18 if current parameter is string -lower
          19 print appropriate message
       20 if current parameter is string -upper
          21 print appropriate message.

Thus p_to_argv is a pointer to argv, whose elements point to the strings from the command line:

*p_to_argv   accesses a particular element of argv
**p_to_argv   would access the character that the pointer argv points to.

Thus the first character of the parameter may be printed:

    printf("\n first character of parameter is %c ", *p_to_argv[0]);

or:

    printf("\n first character of parameter is %c ", **p_to_argv);

Exercise 22.1 (page 221) Functions to search and compare strings (using pointers).

```
 1|/* Exercise 22_1 - string search and compare functions */
 2|
 3|#include <stdio.h>
 4|
 5|int main(void)
 6|{
 7|    char *str_search(char *string_1, char *string_2);
 8|    int str_compare(const char *string_1, const char *string_2);
 9|    char text_1[30], text_2[30];                    /* strings to search */
10|
11|    while (printf("\n\nEnter first string ? "), gets(text_1) != NULL)
12|        {
13|        printf("Enter second string ? ");
14|        if (gets(text_2) != NULL)               /* read string, exit if EOF */
15|            {
16|            char *p_char = text_1;
17|
18|            printf("Index positions of %s = ", text_2);
19|            while ((p_char = str_search(p_char, text_2)) != NULL)
20|                printf("\n %s ", p_char++);
21|            if (str_compare(text_1, text_2) == 0)
22|                printf("\n\n%s and %s are identical ", text_1, text_2);
23|            else
24|                if (str_compare(text_1, text_2) < 0)
25|                    printf("\n\n%s < %s  ", text_1, text_2);
26|                else
27|                    printf("\n\n%s > %s  ", text_1, text_2);
28|            }
29|        }
30|    return 0;
31|}
```

File ex22_1.c String search and compare functions (continued on next page)

The sequence of statements in string_search is:

38   char *str_search(char *string_1, char *string_2)
            is the function header with the formal parameters:
            string_1 points to the string to search
            string_2 points to the string to search for.
        If string2 is found a pointer to its position in string_1 is returned else NULL
40-52   while which terminates when '\0' is found in string_1
            42 check if current character in string_1 is the first character in string_2
                43-50   characters the same, compare rest of string_2
                        48 if terminator of string_2 return pointer to position in string_1
                        49 continue do if characters in string_1 and string_2 are the same
            51 string_2 not found, increment pointer to test next character in string_1
53 string_2 not found, return NULL.

The function str_compare compares two strings string_1 and string_2 and returns 0 if they are equal, >0 if string1 > string2 and <0 if string1 < string2. The do statement, lines 64 to 72, tests in turn each character in string_1 against the corresponding character in string_2:

1 line 67: if (*string_1 > *string_2) if the value of character pointed to by string1 is greater than that pointed to by string2 , return with value > 0

2 line 69: if (*string_1 != *string_2) (characters are not equal) return with value < 0

3 otherwise the characters are the same and the loop tests the next character

4 line 73 is executed if string_1 and string_2 are identical and 0 is returned.

```
32
33 /*-------------------------------------------------------------------*/
34 /* search string for a string                                       */
35 /* on entry string_1     points to string to search                 */
36 /*           string_2    pointer to string to search for            */
37 /* return function result: pointer if found, NULL if not found       */
38 char *str_search(char *string_1, char *string_2)
39 {
40     while(*string_1 != '\0')                              /* look for '\0' */
41        {
42        if (*string_1 == *string_2)              /* first character found ? */
43           {
44           char *p_char1 = string_1,
45                *p_char2 = string_2;          /* yes, check rest of string_2 */
46
47           do
48               if (*++p_char2 == '\0') return string_1;   /* string_2 found */
49           while (*++p_char1 == *p_char2);
50           }
51        string_1++;                                /* not found, try again */
52        }
53     return NULL;                            /* not found, return fail */
54 }
55
56 /*-------------------------------------------------------------------*/
57 /* Compare two strings (similar to library function strcmp)          */
58 /*   return 0 if equal, >0 if string1 > string2 , <0 if string1 < string2  */
59 int str_compare(const char *string_1, const char *string_2)
60 {
61     int index = -1;
62
63     /* loop looking for terminating nulls */
64     do
65        {
66        index ++;                              /* index to next character */
67        if (*string_1 > *string_2) return 1;              /* return > 0   */
68        /* character in string_1 <= string_2, if not the same return < 0 */
69        if (*string_1 != *string_2) return -1;            /* return < 0   */
70        /* strings identical so far, check next character */
71        }
72     while ((*string_1++ != '\0') && (*string_2++ != '\0'));
73     return 0;                          /* strings are identical return 0 */
74 }
```

File ex22_1.c String search and compare functions (continued from previous page)

Exercise 23.1 (page 226) Program to copy one text file to another.

```
 1 /* Exercise 23_1    Text file copy program, e.g. to copy file_1 to file_2:    */
 2 /*    ex23_1  file_1 file_2 -options                                           */
 3 /* options: -upper and -lower to convert characters to upper and lower case    */
 4
 5 #include <stdio.h>
 6 #include <string.h>
 7 #include <ctype.h>
 8
 9 int main(int argc, char *argv[])
10 {
11     FILE *in_file, *out_file;               /* input and output file pointers */
12     int ch,                                 /* holds character being transferred */
13         convert = 0;        /* if = 1 convert to upper case, = 2 to lower case */
14
15     if (argc < 3)                           /* check for filenames in command line */
16         {
17         printf("\nInsufficent parameters ");
18         return 1;
19         }
20
21     /* open input file, first parameter of command line */
22     printf("\nOpening input file '%s' ", argv[1]);
23     if ((in_file = fopen(argv[1], "r")) == NULL)
24         {
25         perror(" failed");                  /* open fail, print error message */
26         return 1;
27         }
28
29     /* open output file, second parameter of command line */
30     printf("\nOpening output file '%s' ", argv[2]);
31     if ((out_file = fopen(argv[2], "w")) == NULL)
32         {
33         perror(" failed");                  /* open fail, print error message */
34         fclose(in_file);                            /* close the input file */
35         return 1;
36         }
37
38     printf("\nFiles opened OK");
39     if (argc == 4)                                  /* check for options */
40         if(strcmp(argv[3], "-upper") == 0)
41             {
42             printf("\nConverting text to upper case ");
43             convert = 1;                            /* set upper case indicator */
44             }
45         else
46             if(strcmp(argv[3], "-lower") == 0)
47                 {
48                 printf("\nConverting text to lower case ");
49                 convert = 2;                        /* set lower case indicator */
50                 }
```

```
52      while ((ch = getc(in_file)) != EOF)                    /* read character */
53      {
54      if (convert)
55          ch = (convert == 1) ? toupper(ch) : tolower(ch);
56          putc(ch, out_file);                                /* write character */
57      }
58
59      fclose(in_file);                                    /* close the input file */
60      fclose(out_file);                                   /* close output file */
61      printf("\nCopy complete");
62
63      return 0;
64  }
```

File ex23_1.c   Program to copy a text file

The sequence of statements in file ex23_1.c is:

15-19   check that sufficient parameters were entered on command line, if not terminate
22-27   attempt to open input file, if fail print message and terminate
30-36   attempt to open output file, if fail print message, close input file and terminate
39   if command line contains four parameters
       40-44   check for option -upper
       46-50   check for option -lower
52-57   a while reading characters from in_file until EOF is found
       54 if converting to upper or lower case
           55 select toupper or tolower to convert the character
       56 write the character to the output file
59-63   close files and terminate.

Exercise 23.2 (page 229) Program to copy one file to another (binary or text file).

The code in file ex23_2.c for a binary file copy program is similar to file ex23_1.c with the following modifications:

1   Lines 12 and 13 are removed and replaced with:

    `unsigned char size, data[100];`   `/* holds byte data being transferred */`

2   The fopen calls (lines 23 and 31) open the files in binary mode (mode "rb" and "wb").

3   Lines 39 to 50 are removed.

4   Lines 52 to 57 (which copy the file contents) are replaced with:

```
while (! feof(in_file))                          /* copy data until EOF found */
{
    size = fread(data, 1, 100, in_file);         /* read a block of data */
    if (ferror(in_file))                         /* read error ? */
        { perror("\nerror reading file"); break; }    /* yes, abort ! */
    fwrite(data, 1, size, out_file);             /* write block out */
    if (ferror(out_file))                        /* write error ? */
        { perror("\nerror writing file"); break; }    /* yes, abort ! */
}
```

This reads and writes 100 byte blocks of the file until EOF is found. Error checks are performed on read and write with break used to abort the while if an error occurs.

Exercise 24.1 (page 249) Impedance of an RLC circuit using complex number ADT.

```
 1 /* Exercise 24_1  Evaluate the impedance of an RLC circuit */
 2 #include <stdio.h>
 3 #include "complex.h"                          /* complex number ADT */
 4
 5 int main(void)
 6 {
 7     const float TWO_PI = 2.0f * 3.1415926f;
 8     float f, r, l, c;      /* frequency, resistance, inductance & capacitance */
 9     Complex z;                              /* holds impedance of circuit */
10
11     printf("Enter R (ohms) L (Henries) C (Farads) and frequency (Hz) ? ");
12     scanf("%f%f%f%f", &r, &l, &c, &f);
13     z = c_numb(r, (TWO_PI * f * l) - 1.0f / (TWO_PI * f * c));
14     c_print("   impedance = ", z);
15     return 0;
16 }
```

File ex24_1.c Evaluate the impedance of an RLC circuit

Exercise 25.1 (page 264) A queue ADT using a linked list.

File ex25_1.c contains the queue ADT. Lines 8 to 13 define a type Qelement which holds the queue element data and a pointer to the next element. Lines 15 and 16 define pointers p_front and p_end which point to the front and end of the queue respectively (the first and last elements), both initialised to NULL (indicating an empty queue).

```
 1 /* Exercise 25_1  A queue ADT (abstract data type) using a linked list  */
 2
 3 #include <stdio.h>
 4 #include <stdlib.h>
 5 #include <assert.h>
 6
 7 /* declare structure to store a queue element and pointer to next Qelement */
 8 typedef struct S
 9          {
10             int element;                         /* holds element data */
11             int priority;                        /* priority of element */
12             struct S *p_next;           /* holds pointer to next element */
13          } Qelement;
14
15 static Qelement *p_front = NULL;             /* pointer to front of queue */
16 static Qelement *p_end = NULL;                /* pointer to end of queue */
17
18 /* function to see if queue is empty, return 1 (true) if empty else 0 (false) */
19 int queue_empty(void)
20 {
21     return (p_front == 0);
22 }
23
```

File ex25_1.c A queue ADT (abstract data type) using a linked list (continued over page)

```
24 /* function to add an element on the end of the queue */
25 void queue_add(const int element, const int priority)
26 {
27     /* create new element to add to queue, point p_element to it */
28     Qelement *p_element = (Qelement *) malloc(sizeof(Qelement));
29     p_element->element = element;                   /* setup element data */
30     p_element->priority = priority;
31     p_element->p_next = NULL;                   /* point last element to null */
32     /* if queue is empty point p_front to the new element */
33     if (p_front == NULL) p_front = p_element;
34     /* else point p_next of last element in queue to new element  */
35     else            p_end->p_next = p_element;
36     p_end = p_element;                   /* point p_end to new element */
37 }
38
39  /* function to remove an element from the front of the queue */
40 int queue_remove(void)
41 {
42     if (p_front != NULL)                   /* if queue is not empty */
43     {
44     /* return value of element at front of queue then delete it */
45     int element = p_front->element;       /* get element at front of queue */
46     Qelement *p_element = p_front;            /* point to front of queue */
47     p_front = p_front->p_next;   /* point p_front to next element in queue */
48     free(p_element);                     /* delete old front of queue */
49     return element;                           /* return element */
50     }
51     printf("\nqueue_remove attempted on an empty queue\n\a");
52     fflush(NULL);                           /* flush output streams */
53     assert(0);                           /* error, abort program */
54 }
55
56 int main(void)                                   /* to test queue ADT */
57 {
58     int i;
59     printf("adding elements    ");
60     for (i = 0; i < 10; printf(" %2d", i), i++)
61         queue_add(i,1);                       /* add element to queue */
62     printf("\nremoving elements ");
63     for (i = 0; i < 5; i++)
64         printf(" %2d", queue_remove());       /* remove element from queue */
65     printf("\nadding elements    ");
66     for (i = 25; i < 31; printf(" %2d", i), i++)
67         queue_add(i,1);                       /* add element to queue */
68     printf("\nremoving elements ");
69     while (!queue_empty())
70         printf(" %2d", queue_remove());       /* remove element from queue */
71     queue_remove();                           /* should cause error ! */
72     return 0;
73 }
```

File ex25_1.c A queue ADT (abstract data type) using a linked list

File ex25_1.c contains functions to test for an empty queue and to add and remove elements :

19-22   function queue_empty returns 1 (true) if queue is empty else 0 (false)
25-37   function queue_add adds an element onto the end of the queue
      28-31   create new Qelement, initialise it with value of element and priority
               point p_next to NULL to indicate end of queue
      33   if queue is empty point p_front to new element
      35   else point p_next of last element in queue to new element
      36   point p_end (pointer to end of queue) to new element
40-53   function queue_remove removes an element from the front of the queue
      42-50   if queue is not empty
              45 get value of element at front of queue (to be returned in line 49)
              46 point p_element at element at front of queue (for free in line 48)
              47 point p_front to next element in queue (new first element)
              48 free old element which was at front of queue
              49 return value of element which was at front of queue
      51-53   if queue is empty display message, flush streams and abort program
56-73   function main which tests the queue ADT
      60-61   add the element values 0 1 2 3 4 5 6 7 8 9 to the queue
      63-64   remove element values 0 1 2 3 4 from the queue
      66-67   add element values 25 26 27 28 29 30 to the queue
      69-70   remove element values 5 6 7 8 9 25 26 27 28 29 30 from queue.
      71   call queue_remove(); queue is empty and this should give an error

A run of File ex25_1.c gave:

```
adding elements     0  1  2  3  4  5  6  7  8  9
removing elements   0  1  2  3  4
adding elements     25 26 27 28 29 30
removing elements    5  6  7  8  9 25 26 27 28 29 30
queue_remove attempted on an empty queue
Assertion fail: 0, file ex25_1.c, line 53
Abnormal program termination
```

Exercise 27.1 (page 293) Evaluate sin⁻¹(x).

File ex27_1.c contains the code to evaluate sin⁻¹(x) using the series:

$$\sin^{-1}(x) = x + \frac{x^3}{2.3} + \frac{1.3x^5}{2.4.5} + \frac{1.3.5x^7}{2.4.6.7} + \frac{1.3.5.7x^9}{2.4.6.8.9} \qquad x^2 < 1$$

The series for sin⁻¹(x) is summed for a given x using a do ... while statement:

```
xsq = x * x;                                    /* x squared */
asin_x = term_n = x;                    /* value of first term of series */
n = 3;                                  /* start summing series from n = 3 */
do
    {
    term_n = (term_n * (n - 2) * xsq / (n - 1));        /* nth term */
    asin_x = asin_x + term_n / n;                       /* add term */
    n = n + 2;                                          /* next n */
    }
while (fabs(term_n) > ACCURACY);                        /* finished ? */
```

On each iteration of the do the value of the next term in the series is evaluated and added to the sum so far. When the absolute value of the term is less than the accuracy require the do terminates.

Exercise 28.1 (page 295) Implement a function using the quicksort algorithm.

```
 1  /*-------------------------------------------------------------------------*/
 2  /* function (recursive) to sort the contents of an array - use quicksort      */
 3  /*   sort array contents from array[left] to array[right]                     */
 4  void array_qsort(float array[], const int left, const int right)
 5  {
 6      void array_write(const float array[], const int number);
 7      int up, down;                                    /* array index values */
 8      float x, temporary;                              /* working variables */
 9
10      x = array[(left + right) / 2];         /* pick element half way between */
11      up = left;                                  /* scan up the array from left */
12      down = right;                            /* scan down the array from right */
13      /* scan up and down array */
14      do
15         {
16         while (array[up] < x) up++;                       /* find element >= x */
17         while (array[down] > x) down--;                   /* find element <= x */
18
19         if (up <= down)
20            {                              /* exchange array[up] and array[down] */
21            temporary = array[up];
22            array[up] = array[down];
23            array[down] = temporary;
24            up++;
25            down--;
26            }
27         }                           /* continue process of scanning up and down */
28      while (up <= down);
29      /* printf("\nPartitioned array "); */          /* print partitioned array */
30      /* array_write(&array[left], right - left + 1); */
31
32      /* scan complete array partitioned into two sets: lower <= x & upper >= x */
33      if (left < down)  array_qsort(array, left, down);       /* sort lower set */
34      if (up < right) array_qsort(array, up, right);          /* sort upper set */
35  }
```

File ex28_1.c Sort an array using quicksort (file contains main and other functions)

The print statements in lines 29 and 30 (commented out) can be used to show the progress of the sort. A run of the program gave:

```
Enter up to 10 numbers (<CR> to end)
   ? 1 3 2  4 3 4 5 1 3 8↵
      1.000       3.000       2.000       4.000       3.000
      4.000       5.000       1.000       3.000       8.000
Sorted array
      1.000       1.000       2.000       3.000       3.000
      3.000       4.000       4.000       5.000       8.000
```

Appendix C The standard library

The ANSI C standard defines a standard library which contains a range of functions and macros to support programs implemented in C.   A number of *standard header files* contain *type definitions* (see Section 17.8), *macro definitions* (see Section 26.1) and *function prototypes declarations* (see Section 15.3):

<assert.h>	<ctype.h>	<errno.h>	<float.h>	<limits.h>
<locale.h>	<math.h>	<setjmp.h>	<signal.h>	<stdarg.h>
<stddef.h>	<stdio.h>	<stdlib.h>	<string.h>	<time.h>

A *standard header file* is included in the program using the preprocessor directive:

```
#include <name.h>
```

This appendix briefly describes most of the functions (refer to system and compiler manuals for full details).   In addition many C compilers provide a range of extra facilities, e.g. low-level system dependent I/O, graphics support, etc.

C.1 Diagnostics <assert.h> See Section 11.8.

The assert macro is used to aid diagnostics in a program:

```
void assert(int expression);
```

if expression is zero when assert is called a diagnostic message such as:

```
Assertion failed: expression, file filename, line number
```

will be printed on stderr and then abort() called to terminate program execution.

C.2 Character tests <ctype.h> See Section 20.4.

The header file <ctype.h> declares a set of functions for testing a character parameter:

```
int isalpha(int);          /* a letter of the alphabet 'a' to 'z' or 'A' to 'Z' */
int isupper(int);                      /* an upper case letter 'A' to 'Z'*/
int islower(int);                      /* a lower case letter 'a' to 'z' */
int isdigit(int);                              /* a digit '0' to '9' */
int isxdigit(int);      /* a hexadecimal digit '0' to '9', 'a' to 'f' or 'A' to 'F' */
int isspace(int);         /* white space: space, newline, carriage return and tabs */
int ispunct(int);             /* printing character except space, letter or digit */
int isalnum(int);             /* letter or digit, i.e. isalpha or isdigit is true */
int isprint(int);                     /* any printing character including space */
int isgraph(int);                      /* any printing character except space */
int iscntrl(int);                               /* a control character */
```

The character is passed to the function as an int (promoted as required) and the function returns *true* (non-zero) if the condition is satisfied otherwise *false* (zero).   These functions are typically implemented as macros (examine the file ctype.h for details) but are also available as true functions (see Section 26.4).

In addition <ctype.h> contains the following functions which convert to upper or lower case:

```
int toupper(int);          /* if lower case letter convert to upper case */
int tolower(int);          /* if upper case letter convert to lower case */
```

If the character in not an upper or lower case letter it is returned intact.

C.3 Errors <errno.h> See Section 23.1.

The header file <errno.h> defines the identifier errno together with macros which are used to report error conditions. If an error condition occurs when executing a library function, the function sets up a system dependent integer error number in errno (errno is usually an external variable of type int). For example, two values commonly used by the mathematical functions in <math.h> are:

```
#define EDOM    33                      /* Maths function domain error, see <math.h> */
#define ERANGE  34                      /* Maths function range error, see <math.h> */
```

The numeric values defined by the macros are system dependent. The program can call the function perror (in <stdio.h>) and strerror in <string.h> to print a meaningful message associated with the value.

C.4 Implementation defined floating point limits <float.h> See Section 8.2.

<float.h> contains macros which define implementation dependent floating point constants. The following are the minimum; larger values may be used in practice:

```
#define FLT_RADIX     2                     /* radix of exponent representation */
#define FLT_ROUNDS                /* floating point rounding mode for addition */
#define FLT_DIG       6                    /* float decimal digits of precision */
#define FLT_MANT_DIG  24             /* number of FLT_RADIX digits in mantissa */
#define FLT_EPSILON   1E-5      /* smallest number x such that 1.0 + x ≠ 1.0 */
#define FLT_MIN       1E-37       /* minimum normalised floating point number */
#define FLT_MAX       1E+37                /* maximum floating point number */
#define FLT_MAX_EXP          /* maximum n such that $FLT\_RADIX^n$ is representable */
#define FLT_MIN_EXP            /* minimum n such that $10^n$ is a normalised number */
#define DBL_DIG       10                 /* double decimal digits of precision */
#define DBL_MANT_DIG                 /* number of FLT_RADIX digits in mantissa */
#define DBL_EPSILON   1E-9      /* smallest number x such that 1.0 + x ≠ 1.0 */
#define DBL_MIN       1E-37       /* minimum normalised floating point number */
#define DBL_MAX       1E+37                /* maximum floating point number */
#define DBL_MAX_EXP          /* maximum n such that $FLT\_RADIX^n$ is representable */
#define DBL_MIN_EXP            /* minimum n such that $10^n$ is a normalised number */
```

C.5 Implementation defined limits <limits.h> See Section 7.1.

<limits.h> contains macros which define implementation dependent integral limits. The following values are the minimum magnitudes; larger values may be used in practice:

```
#define CHAR_BIT     8                        /* number of bits in a character */
#define CHAR_MAX     127 or 255                 /* maximum value of a char */
#define CHAR_MIN     (-128) or 0                /* minimum value of a char */
#define SCHAR_MAX    127                    /* maximum value of signed char */
#define SCHAR_MIN    (-128)           /* minimum value of signed character */
#define UCHAR_MAX    255                 /* maximum value of unsigned char */
#define SHRT_MAX     32767                 /* maximum value of short int */
#define SHRT_MIN     -32767                /* minimum value of short int */
#define USHRT_MAX    65535         /* maximum value of unsigned short int */
#define INT_MAX      32767                       /* maximum value of int */
#define INT_MIN      -32767                      /* minimum value of int */
#define UINT_MAX     65535               /* maximum value of unsigned int */
#define LONG_MAX     2147483647              /* maximum value of long int */
#define LONG_MIN     -2147483647             /* minimum value of long int */
#define ULONG_MAX    4294967295     /* maximum value of unsigned long int */
```

C.6 Localisation `<locale.h>`

The header file `<locale.h>` contains program constructs which can be used to set or access properties suitable for the current locale, i.e. application or country specific. See compiler manuals for details.

C.7 Mathematical functions `<math.h>`

The `<math.h>` header file contains the following prototypes for the mathematical functions:

```
double  acos(double x);                  /* cos⁻¹(x) range 0 to π, x range -1 to 1 */
double  asin(double x);                /* sin⁻¹(x) range -π/2 to π/2, x range -1 to 1 */
double  atan(double x);                     /* tan⁻¹(x) range -π/2 to π/2 */
double  atan2(double y, double x);          /* tan⁻¹(y/x) range -π to π */
double  ceil(double x);                 /* smallest integer greater than x */
double  cos(double x);                        /* cosine of x (radians) */
double  cosh(double x);                     /* hyperbolic cosine of x */
double  exp(double x);                    /* exponential function eˣ */
double  fabs(double x);                     /* absolute value |x| */
double  floor(double x);                  /* largest integer below x */
double  fmod(double x, double y);             /* remainder of x/y */
double  frexp(double x, int *exponent);   /* splits x into mantissa (range [½, 1]) */
                               /* & exponent of 2: x = mantissa * 2ᵉˣᵖᵒⁿᵉⁿᵗ */
double  ldexp(double x, int exponent);          /* returns x * 2ᵉˣᵖᵒⁿᵉⁿᵗ */
double  log(double x);                    /* natural logarithm ln(x), x > 0 */
double  log10(double x);                  /* base 10 logarithm log₁₀(x), x > 0 */
double  modf(double x, double *ipart);    /* breaks x into integral and fractional */
                                        /* parts, i.e. x = ipart + fraction */
double  pow(double x, double y);          /* returns xʸ, a domain error occurs */
                                        /* if x < 0 and y is not an integer */
double  sin(double x);                          /* sine of x (radians) */
double  sinh(double x);                     /* hyperbolic sine of x */
double  sqrt(double x);               /* square root of x, √x where x ≥ 0 */
double  tan(double x);                      /* tangent of x (radians) */
double  tanh(double x);                   /* hyperbolic tangent of x */
```

The *domain* of a mathematical function is the set of parameter values for which it is defined. If a function is called with a parameter not within its *domain* a *domain error* occurs, errno (defined in `<errno.h>`) is assigned the value EDOM and the function returns with an implementation defined value.

A *range error* occurs when the result of a function cannot be defined as a double; errno is assigned the value ERANGE and the function returns the value HUGH_VAL (defined in `<math.h>`) with the correct sign. If *underflow* (value too small to be represented) occurs zero is returned and errno may be assigned the value ERANGE (system dependent).

C.8 Nonlocal jumps `<setjmp.h>`

The header file `<setjmp.h>` enables the program to make non-local jumps, i.e. *goto* another function. See compiler manual for details.

C.9 Signal handling `<signal.h>`

The header `<signal.h>` contains constructs which enable the handling of errors and other exceptional conditions. Typically the following system dependent values are defined:

```
#define SIGINT  2                                              /* interrupt */
#define SIGILL  4                                   /* illegal instruction */
#define SIGFPE  8                   /* floating point trap, e.g. division by 0 */
#define SIGSEGV 11                              /* memory access violation */
#define SIGTERM 15                             /* asynchronous termination */
#define SIGABRT 22              /* abnormal termination, initiated by abort() */
```

When a signal occurs the system calls a signal handling function, which has one `int` parameter which is assigned the signal value (a handling function can process a number of signals). The function `signal` is used to specify the handling function for a signal:

```
void (*signal(int signal, void (*function)(int))) (int);
```

The prototype specifies that function `signal` has two parameters:

signal   an integer number specifying the signal number, e.g. `SIGINT`, `SIGPE`, etc.;
function   a pointer to the signal handling function

and it returns a pointer to the previous handling function for the signal.

A number of handlers are usually supplied including `SIG_DFL` which takes implementation dependent default action and `SIG_IGN` which ignores the signal.

In the following code the function call `signal(SIGFPE, fp_err)` instructs the system to call function `fp_err` with the parameter `SIGFPE` when a floating point error occurs, e.g.:

```
void fp_err(int signal)                       /* floating point error signal handler */
{
    printf("floating point error ! \a");
}
int main(void)
{
    float x = 1, y = 0;
    signal(SIGFPE, fp_err);                  /* set up handler for floating point error */
    x = x / y;                                /* floating point divide by 0 */
    printf("%f", x);
    return 0;
}
```

When x / y is evaluated a division by 0 occurs and function `fp_err` is called (with the parameter `SIGFPE`) and a message displayed. When `fp_err` terminates execution is resumed following the instruction where the error occurred. To test a signal handling function the function `raise` sends the specified signal to the environment:

```
int raise(int signal);
```

If a handler is not specified by the program, implementation-defined default behaviour is taken when a signal occurs. By using `signal` a program may implement its own error processing, enabling orderly error recovery or program termination (the normal error processing may crash the program without orderly closing down files, etc.).

C.10 Variable number of parameters `<stdarg.h>`

The header file `<stdarg.h>` enables the programmer to write functions with a variable number of parameters (such as `printf` and `scanf`). See Section 28.5 for full details.

C.11 Common definitions `<stddef.h>`

The header file `<stddef.h>` contains a number of system dependent, commonly used definitions and macros. For example, the definition of `size_t`, `NULL`, etc.

C.12 Standard input and output `<stdio.h>` See Chapter 23.

In C input and output takes place via a *stream* which may be connected to a disk file, the keyboard, the display screen, a serial port, or any other suitable device. Before any input/output operations can take place the stream must be connected to something, e.g. a file on disk opened for input or output. Associated with each open stream is a structure of type `FILE` (defined in `<stdio.h>`) which contains information which enables the program to control the flow of information, e.g. pointer to its I/O buffer, pointer to current position in buffer, error indicator, etc. A stream is connected to a device with an *open* operation and disconnected with a *close* operation. When connected the stream name is pointer to a structure of type `FILE`. When setting up the program run-time environment prior to the start of program execution the following three standard streams: `stdin`, `stdout` and `stderr` are automatically opened (see Section 27.1).

C.12.1 Operations on files See Section 23.2.

    FILE *fopen(const char *filename, const char *mode);

opens a file returning a stream (pointer to `FILE`) or `NULL` if an error occurred:

filename: a pointer to a character string which contains the filename in a format acceptable to the operating system.

mode: a pointer to a character string specifying the mode of operation:
  r   opens an existing file for reading
  w   creates a new file for writing (if it already exists its contents are discarded)
  a   opens an existing file for append, information written is appended onto existing data, otherwise a new file is created for writing
  r+ opens an existing file for update (reading and writing)
  w+ creates a new file for update (reading and writing)
  a+ opens an existing file or creates a new file for update and append.

The above modes are for opening *text* streams which are used to process character-based data, i.e. lines of characters terminated by *newline*. The run-time system may need to convert between the external representation of text files and the format acceptable to C, e.g. *newline* may be represented externally by the combination carriage return and line feed. C also supports *binary* streams which are used to process data transferred in machine dependent binary form. For *binary* streams the mode should include the letter b, e.g. rb, wb, wb+, etc.

    FILE *freopen(const char *filename, const char *mode, FILE *stream);

freopen takes the existing `stream` and associates it with a new file (closing any currently open file), e.g. it is useful to reassign `stdin`, `stdout` and `stderr`.

    int fclose(FILE *stream);

fclose flushes any unwritten data, discards any unread data and closes the file. If successful 0 is returned otherwise `EOF` if an error occurred.

    int fflush(FILE *stream);

fflush writes any buffered data to an output `stream` (it is ignored for an input stream). If successful 0 is returned or `EOF` is returned if a write error occurred. `fflush(NULL)` flushes all output streams.

```
int  remove(const char *filename);
```
removes `filename` from the file system, returns 0 if successful.

```
int  rename(const char *old_filename, const char *new_filename);
```
renames a file, returns 0 if successful.

```
FILE  *tmpfile(void);
```
creates a temporary file of mode `wb+`; removed when closed or on program termination.

```
int  setvbuf(FILE *stream, char *buffer, int mode, size_t size);
```
sets up a buffer of `size` for `stream`; `mode` indicates the form of the buffering,

> `_IONBF` unbuffered: minimum internal storage is used in an attempt to send or receive data as soon as possible.
>
> `_IOLBF` line buffered: characters are processed on a line by line basis.
>
> `_IOFBF` fully buffered: buffers are flushed when full.

`setvbuf` must be called before any reading or writing is carried out and `fflush` may be called at any time to flush the buffers.

C.12.2 I/O status and error functions See Section 23.2.

Many of the input/output functions set up indicators in the `FILE` structure when an error or `EOF` (end of file) occurs which can be set and tested using the following functions:

```
void clearerr(FILE *stream);              /* clear EOF and error indicators */
int feof(FILE *stream);            /* returns non-zero if EOF indicator is set */
int ferror(FILE *stream);          /* returns non-zero if error indicator is set */
```

When an error occurs many of the functions set up an integer error number in `errno` (declared in `<errno.h>`). The function `perror` prints a program specified `string` together with an implementation defined error message corresponding to `errno` to the stream `stderr`:

```
void perror(const char *string);          /* print string then error message */
```

C.12.3 File positioning functions

Unless otherwise specified file I/O is sequential. For example, if the sequence read, flush, write, flush, read, flush, write, flush, read is performed, each successive operation operates upon the record following the one just processed, i.e. the last read reads data following the end of the information just written (`fflush` must be called between each read/write cycle). The file positioning functions allow the user explicitly to set the position indicator in the file where the next read/write operation is to be performed.

```
long ftell(FILE *stream);
```
returns the current file position or `-1L` if an error occurs:

> **binary stream**: the position is the number of bytes from the start of the file
>
> **text stream**: the position is in some internal format and may only be used on a subsequent call to `fseek`

```
void rewind(FILE *stream);
```
sets the file position indicator to 0

```
int fgetpos(FILE *stream, fpos_t *position);
```
stores the current file position for `stream` in the object (type `fpos_t`) pointed to by `position` (the value can be used later by `fsetpos`). If successful it returns 0 else non-zero.

```
int fsetpos(FILE *stream, const fpos_t *position);
```
sets the file position for stream to position. If successful it returns 0 else non-zero.

```
int fseek(FILE *stream, long offset, int place);
```
sets the file position for stream to offset bytes from place, which may be:

    SEEK_SET beginning of file
    SEEK_CUR current position in file
    SEEK_END end of file

For a text stream offset must be 0 or a value returned by ftell (in which case place must be SEEK_SET). If successful it returns 0 else non-zero.

C.12.4 Character input and output. See Section 20.2.

Individual characters may be read and written by:

```
int  fgetc(FILE *stream);                    /* read next character from stream */
int  getc(FILE *stream);              /* macro: read next character from stream */
int  getchar(void);                           /* read next character from stdin */
int  fputc(int char, FILE *stream);          /* write character char to stream */
int  putc(int char, FILE *stream);    /* macro: write character char to stream */
int  putchar(int char);                      /* write character char to stdout */
```

The function ungetc is used to 'push' a character back into the input stream:

```
int  ungetc(int char, FILE *stream);     /* push character back into input stream */
```

Normally a maximum of one character may be pushed back into a stream and it is not possible to push EOF.

C.12.5 String input and output See Section 20.7.

Null terminated strings (arrays of char) may be printed and read using:

```
char *fgets(char *string, int n, FILE *stream);   /* read characters from stream */
char *gets(char *string);                          /* read characters from stdin */
```

string is a pointer to an array of characters:

fgets reads at most n - 1 characters from stream into the array of characters pointed to by string. Reading stops when the newline character is found ('\n' is placed in the string) or when n - 1 characters have been read. A terminating '\0' is appended.

gets reads characters from the standard input stream stdin into the character array pointed to by string until newline '\n' is entered. The newline is replaced by '\0'.

If successful both functions return a pointer to string or the null pointer NULL if EOF was entered. The function gets performs no array bound checking and it is recommended that fgets is used in practice. Note that fgets puts the newline character into the string whereas gets does not.

The string output functions are:

```
int  fputs(const char *string, FILE *stream);     /* write a string to stream */
int  puts(const char *string);             /* write a string plus '\n' to stdout */
```

string points to an array of characters which may be a string constant:

puts writes string (terminated by '\0') to stdout and appends a newline. It returns EOF if an error occurred otherwise some non-negative value.

fputs writes string (terminated by '\0') to stream (a newline is not appended).

See implementation file str_lib.c in Chapter 20 for examples of the string I/O functions.

C.12.6 The *fprintf, printf* and *sprintf* function See Section 23.4.

The standard output functions printf, fprintf and sprintf provide a means of converting the internal machine representation of information into sequences of characters in a format as specified by the program.

```
int fprintf(FILE *stream, const char *format, ...);      /* print to stream */
int printf(const char *format, ...);                     /* print to stdout */
int sprintf(char *string, const char *format, ...);      /* print to "string" */
```

the ... indicates a number of parameters which are processed under the control of the *control string* pointed to by format:

fprintf writes the converted output to the output stream
printf   writes the converted output to the output stream stdout
sprintf places the converted output in the character array pointed to by string.

The function printf is used to print information to the display screen and fprintf performs a similar function to stream (e.g. a file on disk). The function sprintf is used for conversions within the program (see Section 27.5).

The parameter format points to an array of characters, the *control string*, which controls the format of the output. The *control string* contains ordinary characters which are copied to the output and conversion specifications which control the conversion of the corresponding parameters to the output. The *conversion specifications* start with a % and end with a conversion character (e.g. c, s, d, f, p, etc). Between the % and the conversion character there may be (in the following order):

Flags (in any order) which specify:
- left justification in the field (default is right justify)
+ sign is printed (+ is suppressed by default)
space if the first character is not a sign a space will be prefixed
0 numeric conversions are padded with leading zeros (leading zeros are suppressed by default)
specifies alternate output form:

o	(octal) the first digit will be a 0
x or X	(hexadecimal) a 0x or 0X will prefix a non-zero result
e, E, f, g or G	the output will always have a decimal point
g or G	trailing zeros will not be removed.

A number specifying the minimum field width:
The converted parameter will be printed with a minimum field width as specified. If the converted parameter will not fit, the field will be extended as necessary. If the converted parameter has fewer characters than specified it will be padded on the left or right (left by default, right by specifying the - flag). The padding character is normally space unless the zero padding flag is specified.

A period (.) followed by a number specifying the precision:

s	string: specifies the maximum number of characters to be printed
d	the number of digits to be printed (prefixed with zeros as required)
e, E or f	the number of digits to be printed after the decimal point
or G	the number of significant digits.

The *field width* or *precision* may be specified as * in which case the numeric value of the next parameter is used (must be an int).

The functions printf, fprintf and sprintf return, as an int function result, the number of characters converted, or a negative value if an error occurred.

Table C.1 shows the printf conversion specifications (if the character following the % is not a conversion specification undefined behaviour occurs).

conversion specification	parameter type	converted to
%c	int	single character (after conversion to unsigned char)
%s	char *	characters for a string terminated by '\0' or until the number of characters specified have been converted
%d or %i	int, short, char	signed decimal notation
%u	int, short, char	unsigned decimal notation
%o	int, short, char	unsigned octal notation (without leading 0)
%x or %X	int, short, char	unsigned hexadecimal notation (without leading 0x or 0X) using abcdef for x & ABCDEF for X
%ld %lu %lx %lo	long int	as above but for long int
%f	float, double	signed decimal real number in form [-]mmm.ddd number of ds specified by precision (default 6), a precision of 0 suppresses the decimal point
%e or %E	float, double	signed decimal real number in form [-]m.dddde±xx or [-]m.dddddE±xx, the number of ds is specified by the precision (default 6), a 0 precision suppresses the decimal point
%g or %G	float, double	%e or %E is used if the exponent is less than -4 or greater than the precision otherwise %f is used
%Lf %Le %Lg	long double	as above but for long double real
%p	void *	a pointer in implementation dependent format
%n	int *	the number of characters converted so far are written into the parameter
%		printed as a %

Table C.1 *printf* conversion specifications for integral data types

The information printed by the %p conversion specification is a hexadecimal address, the representation of which is implementation dependent, e.g. depending upon factors such as the architecture of the computer (does it have composite address space like the Motorola 68000 or does it use memory segmentation like the Intel 8086 series), is a memory management unit being used (the addresses printed may be actual physical addresses or addresses within the logical address space of the program), etc. The interpretation of the address printed using %p requires care (see compiler manuals) but can sometimes be useful in tracking down problems with pointers. A linker map can be used to determine the addresses of external identifiers.

C.12.7 The *fscanf, scanf* and *sscanf* functions See Section 23.5.

The standard input functions scanf, fscanf and sscanf provide a means of converting sequences of characters into the internal machine representation of integers, reals, etc.:

```
int fscanf(FILE *stream, const char *format, ...);        /* read from stream */
int scanf(const char *format, ...);                       /* read from stdin */
int sscanf(const char *string, const char *format, ...);  /* read from "string" */
```

the ... indicates a number of parameters which are pointers to variables which will receive the converted values. The conversion process is under the control of the *control string* pointed to by format:

fscanf   read from input stream converting as specified by format
scanf   read from input stream stdin converting as specified by format
sscanf   read from string converting as specified by format.

The function scanf is used to read information from the terminal keyboard and fscanf performs a similar function from stream (e.g. from a file on disk). The function sscanf is used for conversions within the program (see Section 27.6).

The parameter format points to an array of characters, the *control string*, which controls the conversion of characters from the input into values to be assigned to parameters indicated by .... The control string may contain:

1   **Spaces** which cause the input stream to be read up to the next non-**white space** character (**white space** is the C term for spaces, tabs and newlines).
2   Characters other than **white space** and conversion specifications; the next character in the input stream must match this character.
3   **Conversion specifications** beginning with % and followed by:
    (a) an optional assignment suppression character *
    (b) an optional number specifying the maximum scan width
    (c) the conversion character(s), see Table C.2.

If converted successfully the value is returned in the variable which is pointed to by the corresponding parameter. If assignment suppression is indicated the corresponding field is skipped (e.g. %*d will skip an integer decimal number in the input stream).

conversion specification	parameter type	converted to
%c	char *	characters are read into the array of char up to the field width (default is 1) '\0' is not appended, white space is not skipped
%s	char *	characters are read into the array of char leading white space is skipped, characters are then read until white space is found, '\0' is then appended
%d	int *	optionally signed decimal integer
%i	int *	optionally signed decimal, octal (with leading 0) or hexadecimal (leading 0x or 0X) integer
%u	int *	unsigned decimal integer
%o	int *	optionally signed octal int (optional leading 0)
%x or %X	int *	optionally signed hexadecimal int (optional 0x)
%hd %hu %ho %hx	short int *	as above, but for data type short int
%ld %lu %lo %lx	long int *	as above, but for data type long int
%f %e %g	float *	signed decimal real number type float: optional sign, string of numbers possibly containing a decimal point, an optional exponent (e or E) followed by an (optionally signed) integer
%lf %le %lg	double *	signed decimal real number type double
%Lf %Le %Lg	long double *	signed decimal real number type long double
%p	void *	pointer in format as printed by printf
%n	int *	returns the number of characters read so far, no input read, conversion count not incremented
[...]	char *	characters matching those in the scanset ... are read into the array of char, reading stops when a character not in ... is read, '\0' is then appended. []...] includes] in the set
[^...]	char *	characters not matching those in the scanset ... are read into the array of char, reading stops when a character in ... is read, '\0' is then appended. [^]...] includes] in the set

Table C.2 *scanf* conversion specifications

The functions return an int function indicating the number of successful conversions:

1   If no conversions occurred 0 is returned.
2   If a matching failure occurs (e.g. a non-numeric character in a decimal number) conversion stops and the number of successful conversions returned (the faulty character is left in the input stream where the program can read it and take action, see Program 13_2).
3   If *end of file* occurs before any conversions the value EOF is returned.

Thus it is possible for all input to be verified and action taken in case of error, e.g. an error message printed and the user prompted for more input (see Chapter 13 Program 13_2).

C.12.8   Binary (unformatted) input and output   See Section 23.6.

Unformatted input/output is usually used with binary files (some systems make no distinction between binary and text files):

```
size_t   fread(void *p_data, size_t size, size_t number, FILE *stream);
size_t   fwrite(const void *p_data, size_t size, size_t number, FILE *stream);
```

where:

p_data   is a pointer to the data to be read or written
size   specifies the size of the object(s) to be transferred
number   specifies the number of objects to be transferred
stream   is a pointer to a structure of type FILE.

fread attempts to read number objects of size size from stream returning the data in the array pointed to by p_data. It returns as an int function result the number of objects read (which may be less than the number requested). After calling fread the functions feof and ferror should be called to see if end of file was encountered or an error occurred.

fwrite attempts to write number objects of size size from the array pointed to by p_data to stream. It returns as an int function result the number of objects written (which will be less than number if an error occurred).

See Section 23.6 for examples of use.

C.13   Utility functions   <stdlib.h>

C.13.1   Dynamic memory allocation   See Section 25.1.

```
void *malloc(size_t size);                    /* allocate one object of size bytes */
void *calloc(size_t number, size_t size);
            /* allocate an array of number objects of size bytes, initialised to 0 */
void *realloc(void *pointer, size_t size);
                    /* reallocate storage pointed to by pointer, make it size bytes */
void free(void *pointer);            /* deallocate storage pointed to by pointer */
```

If successful malloc, calloc and realloc return a pointer to the storage area allocated (which must be *cast* to the required type), otherwise NULL is returned.

C.13.2   Pseudo random number generation   See Section 18.6.

```
int     rand(void);              /* returns the next pseudo random number */
void    srand(unsigned seed);           /* seeds the random number generator */
```

The default seed is 1 and the number range returned by rand is [0, RAND_MAX] (RAND_MAX is defined as a symbolic constant in <stdlib.h>).

C.13.3 Searching and sorting

```
void qsort(void *array, size_t number, size_t size,
           int (*compare)(const void *, const void *));
```

Using the *quicksort* algorithm (see Chapter 28 Exercise 28.1) sorts array of number elements (each of size bytes) into ascending order using the comparison function compare(). The function compare() has two parameters both of which are pointers to elements of array. The function returns an int less than, equal to or greater than zero depending upon whether the element pointed to by the first parameter is considered less than, equal to or greater than the element pointed to by the second.

```
void *bsearch(const void *key, const void *array, size_t number, size_t size,
              int (*compare)(const void *, const void *));
```

Using a binary search searches array of number elements (each of size bytes) for an element which matches the object pointed to by key. The elements in array must be in ascending order with respect to the comparison function compare() (specification as for qsort above).

C.13.4 Integer arithmetic

```
int   abs (int x);                          /* returns absolute value |x| */
long labs(long x);                          /* returns absolute value |x| */
div_t  div(int numerator, int denom);       /* divide numerator by denom */
ldiv_t ldiv(long numerator, long denom);    /* divide numerator by denom */
```

div and ldiv return the quotient and remainder in a structure:

```
typedef struct {
            int quot;                       /* quotient */
            int rem;                        /* remainder */
        }
            div_t;
```

C.13.5 String conversion

The following functions convert the contents of string to a numeric value (skipping leading white space). The address of the character which stopped the conversion process is placed in endptr (if endptr is NULL the address is not returned). In the case of strtol and strtoul the base of the number may be specified:

```
double  strtod(const char *string, char **endptr);
long    strtol(const char *string, char **endptr, int radix);
unsigned long strtoul(const char *string, char **endptr, int radix);
```

The following are simplified versions of the above:

```
double  atof(const char *string);
int     atoi(const char *string);
long    atol(const char *string);
```

C.13.6 Communicating with the environment

```
void    abort(void);                    /* abnormal termination of program */
int     atexit(atexit_t function);      /* on abnormal termination execute function */
void    exit(int status);               /* normal termination of program */
char    *getenv (const char *name);     /* get environment string for name */
int     system(const char *command);    /* pass command to operating system */
```

Function atexit may be used to specify up to 32 functions which will be called on program termination, e.g. to disable interrupts, close down I/O devices, etc.

C.14 String processing functions `<string.h>` See Section 20.9.

```
char *strcpy(char *destination, const char *source);
```
copy string source to string destination; return a pointer to destination
```
char *strncpy(char *destination, const char *source, size_t maxlen);
```
copy at most maxlen characters from string source to string destination, return a pointer to destination. If the length of source ≥ maxlen the string in destination will not be null terminated (the programmer must watch out for this!).
```
char *strcat(char *destination, const char *source);
```
concatenate string source onto the end of string destination;
return a pointer to destination
```
char *strncat(char *destination, const char *source, size_t maxlen);
```
concatenate at most maxlen characters of string source onto the end of string destination; return a pointer to destination
```
int strcmp(const char *string1, const char *string2);
```
compare string1 with string2; return:
<0 if string1 < string2, 0 if string1 == string2 and >0 if string1 > string2
```
int strncmp(const char *string1, const char *string2, size_t maxlen);
```
compare at most maxlen characters of string1 with string2; return:
<0 if string1 < string2, 0 if string1 == string2 and >0 if string1 > string2
```
char *strchr(const char *string, int character);
```
search string for character; if found return pointer to first occurrence else NULL
```
char *strrchr(const char *string, int character);
```
reverse search string for character; return pointer to last occurrence else NULL
```
size_t strspn(const char *string1, const char *string2);
```
returns the length of the initial substring in string1 which consists entirely of the characters in string2
```
size_t strcspn(const char *string1, const char *string2);
```
returns the length of the initial substring in string1 which consists entirely of the characters *not* in string2
```
char *strpbrk(const char *string1, const char *string2);
```
search string1 for *any* character in string2; if *any* found return pointer to first occurrence else NULL
```
char *strstr(const char *string1, const char *string2);
```
search string1 for string2; if found return pointer to first occurrence else NULL
```
size_t strlen(const char *string);
```
returns the length of string (excluding terminating '\0')
```
char *strerror(int errnum);
```
many library functions set up an integer error number in errno (declared in `<errno.h>`) if an error occurs. strerror returns a pointer to an implementation defined string corresponding to errno (function perror can be used to print the error to stderr)
```
char *strtok(char *string1, const char *string2);
```
searches for tokens in string1 using the characters in string2 as delimiters or token separators. If not found NULL is returned. If a token is found:
  (a) the character immediately following the token is overwritten with '\0',
  (b) the remainder of string1 stored within the system,
  (c) the address of the first character of the token is returned.

Subsequent calls with string1 equal to NULL search the saved part of the original string1 for the next token. If found the address of string (within the system) that contains the next token is returned. If a token is not found NULL is returned.

There are also functions strcoll and strxfrm which process characters using the current *locale* as set up by functions defined in `<locale.h>` (see compiler manuals for details).
    The above functions (starting with str) are for processing strings terminated with a

null, '\0'. The following functions are used to manipulate blocks of memory, of a specified size, as arrays of characters which are not null terminated, e.g. records read from a database which contain character arrays which are not null terminated.

```
void *memchr(const void *string, int character, size_t number);
```
 search at most number characters of string for character; if found return pointer to first occurrence else NULL

```
int memcmp(const void *string1, const void *string2, size_t number);
```
 compare at most number characters of string1 with string2; return:
   <0 if string1 < string2, 0 if string1 == string2 and >0 if string1 > string2

```
void *memcpy(void *destination, const void *source, size_t number);
```
 copy at most number characters from string source to string destination;
  return a pointer to destination

```
void *memmove(void *destination, const void *source, size_t number);
```
 copy at most number characters from string source to string destination;
  return a pointer to destination. This will work even if the objects overlap

```
void *memset(void *string, int character, size_t number);
```
 fill the first number characters of string with character

C.15 Date and time functions <time.h>

The <time.h> header file defines the following:

```
/* two arithmetic types for representing times */
typedef long clock_t;                                   /* typical definition */
typedef long time_t;                                    /* typical definition */

/* a symbolic constant which defines the number of clock ticks per second */
#define CLOCKS_PER_SEC 18.2           /* typical value for an IBM PC compatible */

/* structure which holds the components of a calendar time */
struct tm
{
  int    tm_sec;                    /* seconds after the minute, range [0, 61] */
  int    tm_min;                     /* minutes after the hour, range [0, 59] */
  int    tm_hour;                      /* hours after midnight, range [0. 23] */
  int    tm_mday;                        /* day of the month, range [0, 31] */
  int    tm_mon;                       /* months since January, range [0, 11] */
  int    tm_year;                                       /* years since 1900 */
  int    tm_wday;                          /* days since Sunday, range 0, 6] */
  int    tm_yday;                     /* days since January 1st, range [0, 365] */
  int    tm_isdst;                              /* daylight savings time flag */
};

clock_t  clock(void);                   /* returns clock ticks since start of execution */
double   difftime(time_t time2, time_t time1);  /* returns time2 - time1 in seconds */
time_t   time(time_t *timer);                    /* returns calendar time in *timer */
char *   asctime(const struct tm *tpointer);      /* converts *tpointer to string; */
                                                  /* Fri Nov 20 05:25:17 1992\n\0 */
struct tm *localtime(const time_t *timer);        /* converts *timer to structure */
char *ctime(const time_t *time);                  /* converts *timer to string, is */
                                        /* equivalent to asctime(localtime(timer)) */
struct tm *gmtime(const time_t *timer);           /* converts *timer to structured */
                                                  /* Greenwich Mean Time */
time_t mktime(struct tm *tpointer);               /* converts *tpointer to time */
size_t strftime(char *s, size_t maxsize, const char *fmt, const struct tm *tpointer);
                         /* converts *tpointer into a string, see compiler manual */
```

Appendix D Table of C operators

precedence		operators		associativity	arity	page
highest ↑	15	member selection	->	left/right	2	232
	15	member selection	.	left/right	2	231
	15	subscripting	[]	left/right	2	159
	15	function call	()	left/right	2	115
	15	value construction	()	right/left	2	61
	15	post inc/decrement	lvalue++ lvalue--	right/left	1	71
	14	not.	!	right/left	1	79
	14	complement	~	right/left	1	64
	14	unary plus/minus	+ -	right/left	1	62
	14	dereference	*	right/left	1	198
	14	address of	&	right/left	1	198
	14	pre inc/decrement	++lvalue --lvalue	right/left	1	71
	14	type cast	()	right/left	1	65
	14	size of type/object	sizeof	right/left	1	65
	13	multiplicative	* / %	left/right	2	62
	12	add/subtract	+ -	left/right	2	62
	11	bitwise shifts	<< >>	left/right	2	64
	10	relational	< <= > >=	left/right	2	77
	9	equality	== !=	left/right	2	77
	8	bitwise AND	&	left/right	2	64
	7	bitwise XOR	^	left/right	2	64
	6	bitwise OR	|	left/right	2	64
	5	logical AND	&&	left/right	2	79
	4	logical OR	||	left/right	2	79
	3	conditional	?:	right/left	3	83
	2	assignment	= += -= *= /= %=	right/left	2	74
	2	assignment	&= ^= |= <<= >>=	right/left	2	74
lowest	1	sequence	,	left/right	2	96

page indicates page of book where operator is discussed.
Arity indicates number of operands

References

Bramer, B, 1990, 'Using a common host system to develop software products for a variety of target computer environments', IEE Computer-Aided Engineering Journal, Vol. 7 No. 5, October, pp. 129-134.

Bramer, B & Bramer, S M S, 1991, 'MC68000 Assembly Language Programming', second edition, Edward Arnold.

Bramer, B & Bramer, S M S, 1996, 'C + + for Engineers', Edward Arnold.

Bramer, B & Sutcliffe, D C, 1981, ' The use of display file techniques with raster scan displays', Proceedings of Eurographics '81, North Holland.

Ellis, M A & Stroustrup, B, 1990, 'The annotated C++ reference manual', Addison Wesley.

Hintz, K J, 1992, 'Merging C and assembly language in microcontroller applications', Journal of Microcomputer Applications, Vol. 15, July, pp. 267-278.

Kernighan, B & Pike, R, 1984, 'The UNIX programming environment', Prentice-Hall.

Kernighan, B & Ritchie, D, 1978, 'The C programming language', Prentice Hall.

Kernighan, B & Ritchie, D, 1988, 'The C programming language, ANSI C', 2nd edition, Prentice Hall.

Martin, J & Odell, J J, 1995, 'Object-oriented methods: a foundation', Prentice Hall.

Press, W H, Teukolsky, S A, Vetterling, W T & Flannery, B P, 1994, 'Numerical recipes in C', 2nd edition, Cambridge University Press.

Stroustrup, B, 1993, 'The C++ language', 2nd edition, Addison Wesley (published 1991 and revised in 1993).

Tischer, M, 1994, 'PC intern systems programming', Abacus.

Whitesmiths 1986, 'Interface manual for the MC68000', Ver. 3.1, Whitesmiths Ltd.

Index

_asm directive in Turbo and Microsoft C, 322, 323

- printf justification control, 237, **387**
- subtraction arithmetic operator, 62
- unary arithmetic operator, 62
-- decrement operator, 71, 97, 98
-- decrement operator and pointers, 201, 213, 216
-> member selection operator, 232, 239
-> structure pointer operator, 262

! unary logical not operator, 79, 80
!= test for not equal operator, 77, 81, 82, 87

?: conditional expression, 83, 111, 184, 248, 363, 375

/ division arithmetic operator, 62
/* --- */ comments, 22, 41, 92

^ bitwise exclusive or operator, 64, 252

~ unary complement operator, 64, 252

[] subscript operator, 159

* dereference operator, 198
* multiply arithmetic operator, 62

\a alarm character, 77, 92, 242
\n newline character, 31, 42

& address of operator, 198
& bitwise and operator, 64, 252
&& logical and operator, 79, 181, 355, 369, 373

printf alternate output form, 50, **387**
#define preprocessor directive, 38, 129, 169, 275
#define versus enum, 169
#else preprocessor directive, 149
#endif preprocessor directive, 149
#if preprocessor directive, 149
#include preprocessor directive, 18, 21, 30, 33
#undef preprocessor directive, 39

% modulus arithmetic operator, 62, 150, 151, 355
%c print character, 50, 180, **388**
%c read character, 50, **389**
%d print decimal integer, 33, 50, 51, 180, **388**
%d read decimal integer, 50, 51, **389**
%e print real float/double in E format, 55, **388**
%e read real float/double in E format, 56, **389**

%f print real float/double, 31, 32, 55
%f read real float, 35, 56, **389**
%g print real float/double, 35, 55, **388**
%g read real float/double, 56, **389**
%hd read decimal short integer, 50, **389**
%ld print decimal long integer, 50, **388**
%ld read decimal long integer, 50, **389**
%Le print real long double in E format, 55, 388
%Lf print real long double, 55, **388**
%lf read real double, 56, **389**
%Lf read real long double, 56, **389**
%Lg print real long double, 55, **388**
%lo print octal long integer, **388**
%lx print hexadecimal long integer, **388**
%n return characters converted, **388, 389**
%o print octal integer, 50, 51, 180, **388**
%o read octal integer, 50, **389**
%p print pointer, 207, **388**
%p read pointer, **389**
%s print string, **186**, 213, 226, 231, 237, **388**
%s read string, **186**, **389**
%u print unsigned decimal integer, 50, **388**
%u read unsigned decimal integer, 50, **389**
%x print hexadecimal integer, 50, 51, 180, **388**
%x read hexadecimal integer, 50, **389**

+ addition arithmetic operator, 62
+ unary arithmetic operator, 62
+_ increment operator, 94
++ decrement operator, 97
++ increment operator, 71, 108, 114, 127
++ increment operator and pointers, 201, 213, 216, 370, 373
+= compound assignment operator, 74

< test for less than operator, 86
< test for less than or equal to operator, 77
<< bitwise left shift operator, 64, 252
<= test for less than or equal to operator, 77
<assert.h> diagnostic aid, 84, 256, 257, 259, 378, **380**
<conio.h> Turbo and Microsoft console I/O library, 179, 182, 183, 223, 300, 307, 312, 357, 367
<ctype.h> standard library, 183, 374, **380**
<errno.h> standard library, 223, 226, **381**
<float.h> floating point header file, 54, **381**
<graphics.h> graphics library, 104, 114
<graphics.h> Turbo C graphics library, 357
<limits.h> header file, 48, 66, **381**
<locale.h> standard library, **382**
<math.h> maths library header file, 32, 344, **382**
<setjmp.h> nonlocal jumps library, **382**
<signal.h> signal handling library, **383**
<stdarg.h> standard library, 302, 304, **383**

\<stddef.h\> common definitions header file, **384**

\<stdio.h\> standard I/O header file, 32, 223, **384**

\<stdlib.h\> utility functions library, 104, 150, **390**

\<string.h\> string processing functions, 188, 189, 195, **392**

\<time.h\> date and time functions, 91, 151, 152, 183, 357, **393**

= assignment operator, 68, 347
= = test for equality operator, **77**, 82

\> test for greater than operator, 77, 82
\> = test for greater than or equal to operator, 77
\> \> bitwise right shift operator, 64, 252

| bitwise or operator, 64, 252
|| logical or operator, 79

Abstract data type
  complex numbers, 245
  introduction, 9, **156**
  queue ADT, 176, 264, 376
  stack ADT, 170, 171, 257
  student records, 233
Accessing MS-DOS system facilities, 306
Accessing operating system facilities, 305
Accessing physical memory, 324
Actual parameters (see functions), 36
ADT abstract data type, **156**
Alarm character, 92, 242
ANSI C standard, 1
Applications software, 3
argc and argv, passing parameters to main, 209
Arrays
  & address of operator, 200
  accessing the elements, 159
  const qualified, 165, 166, 170
  defining and initialising, 158
  efficiency considerations in matrix manipulation, 283
  function parameters, 162, 168
  implementing a stack, 257
  initialising, 159
  introduction, 23, 158
  maximum and minimum of an array, 163
  multi-dimensional array allocation, 273, 280
  multi-dimensional arrays, 266
  multiplying arrays, 269
  name, 158
  of pointers, 209, 371, 374, 375
  of structures, 300
  pointers, 200, 202
  pointers to access array elements, 202
  randomly accessing, 174, 175
  read and write contents of an array, 163
  reading, writing and manipulating, 163
  read, write and multiply arrays, 269
  reverse the contents of an array, 163, 213

Arrays
  size specified using #define or enum, 169
  sorting using a bubble sort, 176
  sorting using a linear sort, 168
  sorting using quicksort, 379
  stack ADT, 170
  strings, 184
  transpose, 283
  valid addresses using &, 221
ASCII character code, 6, 342
Assembler, 6, 19
Assembly language
  calling from C, 319
  calling Intel 8086 family from C, 319
  calling Motorola MC68000 family from C, 321
  in-line assembly language statements, 322
  listing of a C program, 348
  when to use, 6
assert from \<assert.h\> diagnostic aid, 84, 256, 257, 259, 378, **380**
Assignment operators, 68, 347
Associativity and precedence of operators, 61, 394
Asynchronous serial communications, 309, 311, 328, 330
Automatic local variables, 137, 140

Backslash newline sequence, 42
Batch file for MS-DOS operating system, 345
Binary (unformatted) file input/output, 228, **390**
Binary number input, 181, 367
Binary number system, 4
Bitfields, 251
Bitfields versus bitwise operators, 252
Bitmapped graphics, 253
Bitwise operators, 64, 252
Bitwise operators versus bitfields, 252
Blocks (compound statements), 80
Boolean or logical data, 48, **76**
break statement, 101, 375
Bubble sort, 176, 211, 365

C character set, 40
C compiler, 19
C preprocessor, 18
C program, assembly language listing, 348
Calling assembly language functions from C, 319
Calling other language functions from C, 323
calloc, allocate storage, 255, 260, 262, 390
Case sensitivity in C, 16, 24, 40
Casts, 65, 103, 185, 208, 238, 255, 289, 302, 321, 324, 326, 339
char type (also see character data type), 177
Character codes, 342
Character data type
  arrays of (also see strings), 177
  character manipulation functions, 183, **380**
  constants, 177, 184
  input/output, 179, 180, 225, **386**
  introduction, 6, 177
  signed and unsigned characters, 178

Characters
  \a alarm character, 92, 242
  \n newline, 31
  input/output, 92, 179
  low-level input/output, 179
  ungetc character, 161, 163, 179, 225, **386**
Clear screen under MS-DOS, 308
Clearing the display screen, 183
Command selection from a menu, 104, 299
Comments, 9, 21, 30, 41
Common definitions header file <stddef.h>, **384**
Comparing strings, 195, 221, 368, 372
Compiler
  compile time errors, 19, 43
  compile time warnings, 43, 343
  cross compiler, 4, 40, 321
  introduction, 7, 19
  listing with errors and warnings, 43
Compiling and linking, 20
Complex numbers, 245, 253, 376
Compound statements, 80
Computer hardware, 2
Conditional compilation, 149
Conditional selection directives, 149
Conditional statements
  if statement, 76
  nested if statements, 81
  switch statement, 102, 104, 370
const type qualifier
  const qualified function parameters, **123**, 222
  discussion, 139
  named constants, 37
  use with pointers, 206
Constants
  character constants, 177, 184
  defining using #define, 38
  defining using enum, 52
  integer number constants, 49
  introduction, 23
  real number constants, 53
  string constants, 184
Continue statement, 101
Conversion between types, **55**
Conversion operators, 65
Conversion specifications (see printf and scanf), 31
Cross compilers, 4, 40, 321
Cursor control
  calling MS-DOS function, 308
  text display screen, 183

Data abstraction, see Abstract data types, 9
Data definitions, 17
Data hiding, 133
Data types
  char, 23, 48
  double, 23, **53**
  float, 23, **53**
  int, 23, **48**
  long double, 23, **53**
  long int, 23, **48**

Data types
  short int, **48**
  signed integral types, **48**
  unsigned integral types, **48**
Date and time functions in <time.h>, 183, **393**
Debugging
  <assert.h> diagnostic aid, 84, 256, 378, **380**
  compile time errors and warnings, 45
  execution time errors, 46
  introduction, 19
Decimal number system, 4
Declarations
  and definitions, 133, 143
  declaration of a variable, 133
  function prototypes, 119
  introduction, 25
Definitions
  definition of a variable or function, 133, 143
  introduction, 17, 25
Direct input from operating system, 182, 183, 367
Display file for raster graphics display, 253
do .. while loop control statement, **88**, 92, 285, 290, 291
do .. while statement and break, 101
Documentation, 9, 41
double real type, **53**
Dynamic multi-dimensional arrays, 273, 280
Dynamic storage allocation, 255, 260

Editor, 18
Efficiency considerations in matrix manipulation, 283
Efficiency in function parameter passing, **128**
Efficiency in returing a function result, **129**
EIA RS232C Standard, 309
End of file, 29, 37, 87
Enumerative data type, 51, 158, 169, 266
Environment of program, **391**
EOF, end of file, 29, 87
Epsilon
  definition of, 54, 89
  evaluation of float type, 89, 90, 91, 353
Error handling, 223, **381**
Errors
  compile time, 19, 43
  execution time, 19, 45
  link time, 19, 43
  run time, 19
  semantic, 43
  syntactic, 43
Evaluating mathematical series
  exponential integral, 293
  higher precision types, 289
  introduction, 284
  Newton-Raphson method, 291
  rounding errors, 287
  sine function, 285
  square root, 291
Execution time errors, 19, 45

Expressions
  introduction, 25, 59
  mathematical equations, 26
  operands, 25
  operators, 25
  order of evaluation, 61, 65
External linkage, 143, 157
External scope, 134
External variables, 141

fabs function, 286, **382**
fclose, close a file, 224, 226, 239, 374, 375, 384
fflush I/O function, 70, 84, 378, **384**
fgets function, read a string, 187, 225, 386
Files
  binary file copy, 375
  deleting, **385**
  flushing streams, 70, 84, 378, **384**
  opening and closing, 226, 239, 374, 375, **384**
  operations on, 374, 375, **384**
  positioning functions, **385**
  renaming, **385**
  temporary file, **385**
FILE, file I/O structure, 223, 226, 239
float real type, **53**
Floating point numbers, 5
floor function, 290
fopen, open a file, 226, 239, 374, 375, 384
for loop control statement, 92, **93**
for statement and break, 101
for statement and the sequence operator, 97
for vers while statement, 93
Forking a process under UNIX, 317
Formal parameters (see functions), 36
Format control (see printf and scanf), 31
fprintf, general file output function, **227**, **387**
fputs function, print a string, 187, 225, 386
fread, binary read function, **228**, 375, **390**
free, deallocate storage, 255, 390
freopen, reopen a file, 384
fscanf, general file input function, **228**, **388**
Function result
  introduction, 26, 115
  of main, 29
  of printf, 387
  of scanf, 37, 80
Functions
  actual parameters, 36, **116**
  arguments, 26
  array read, write, average, standard deviation and sort, 168, 365
  arrays as parameters, 162
  assembly language on an IBM PC compatible, 320, 323
  calling, 26, **115**
  calling assembly language functions, 319
  calling other languages, 323
  complex number operations, 253
  complex numbers, 246, 376
  const qualified parameters, **123**, 125

Functions
  convert metres to feet and inches, 128, 347
  declarations in the original C, 122
  definition of, **115**
  dynamic memory allocation, 260
  efficiency in parameter passing, **128**
  efficiency in returning a result, **129**
  Factorial and inverse factorial, 119, 360
  factorial using recursion, 294
  Fibonacci numbers, 137
  formal parameters, **116**, 134, 141
  function name, **115**
  function result, **116**
  function result of main, 29
  functions vers preprocessor macros, 129, 275
  hardware interrupts, 332
  internal and external linkage, 143, 157
  introduction, 23, 26, **115**
  linked list, 262
  maximum and minimum of an array, 163
  maximum of a pair of numbers, 132, 363
  Motorola 68000 assembly language, 322
  MS-DOS screen and cursor control, 308
  MS-DOS serial port control, 312
  MS-DOS system facilities, 308
  multi-dimensional arrays, 269
  multiplying arrays, 269
  parameter list, 26, 115, **116**
  parameter passing by reference, 36, **123**, 128, 243, 362
  parameter passing by value, 36, **122**
  parameter promotion, 121
  pass by reference, 36, **123**, 128, 362
  pass by reference - a summary, 128
  pass by value, 35, **122**
  passing parameters to function main, 209
  passing pointers as parameters, 212, 222
  passing pointers to functions as parameters, 297
  period of oscillation of a simple pendulum, 119, 359
  pointer to a function as a function result, 300
  pointers as a function result, 212
  pointers to functions, 295
  prototypes, 33, 116, **119**
  prototypes and definitions, 133, 143
  raise a float to integer exponent, 120, 285
  random number generation, 151, 153, 157, 174
  reactance of LC circuit, 122, 361
  read a binary number, 181, 367
  read a hexadecimal number, 182, 367
  read and write contents of an array, 163
  reading, writing and manipulating arrays, 163
  recursive functions, 294, 379
  result type, **115**
  return statement, 25, **116**
  returning a result by reference, 129
  reverse the contents of an array, 163, 213
  running mean, 127, 139
  scope of formal parameters, 134
  sin and cos, 34

Functions
  sqrt square root, 32, 33
  square a number, 117
  stack ADT, 171, 257
  string processing, 188, 189
  string processing using pointers, 213
  structure manipulation, 233, 239
  structures as a function result, 232
  structures as parameters, 232
  swap two variables, 125, 126, 132
  variable number of parameters, 302, 303, 304, **383**
fwrite, binary write function, **228**, 239, 375, **390**

Generic pointer void *, 208, 255
getch read a character function, 179, 182
getchar read a character function, 179
getche read a character function, 179, 182
gets function, read a string, 187, 225, 386
goto statement, 102
Graphics display of a bouncing ball, 113
Graphics display of a graph, 114
Graphics display of bouncing ball, 357
Graphics, raster graphics, 253

Handshaking with serial communications, 310
Header files
  and #define, 38
  example, 147, 233, 234, 246, 248, 312
  introduction, 17
  using and constructing, 146, 149, 153, 163, 167
Hexadecimal number input, 182, 367
Hexadecimal values, 388, 389
High-level languages, 7

IBM PC compatible computer
  8253 timer/counter using interrupts, 334
  accessing serial ports directly, 328, 330
  accessing serial ports via MS-DOS, 311, 314
  accessing the video RAM memory, 325
  asynchronous serial communications, 310
  clearing the display screen, 325
  connecting two PCs via serial ports, 310
  display a bouncing ball in graphics mode, 357
  display a graph in graphics mode, 114
  display screen clearing, 307
  display screen scrolling, 307
  integral types, numeric ranges, 67
  interrupt control of serial ports, 332
  null modem connections, 310
  plot a graph using characters, 108
  setting the text cursor position, 320
  terminal emulator, 312
  text cursor position setting, 307
  video attribute byte, 307
Identifiers
  case sensitivity, 40
  const qualified, 139
  external, 134, 141
  formal parameters of functions, 116, 141

Identifiers
  introduction, 16, 25
  local scope, 134
  rules for constructing, 24, 40
  scope, 140
  static external, 145, 147, 151, 173, 376
  static local, 137, 138, 140, 145, 364
  storage allocation of variables, 140
  volatile qualified, 139, 334, 336
if conditional statement, **76**, 81, 82, 94, 98, 355
In-line assembly language statements in C, 322
Infinite program loops, 92
Infinite series, 284
Information hiding, 133, **156**, 243
Input/output
  accessing I/O device registers, 328
  asynchronous serial communications, 309
  binary (Unformatted) file I/O, 228, **390**
  characters, 92, 180, 225, **386**
  direct control of I/O devices, 328
  direct via operating system, 183, 367
  eof() test for end of file, 87
  extract and discard characters, 191
  file positioning functions, **385**
  flushing streams, 70, 84, 378, **384**
  get next character, 179
  hardware and software interrupts, 305
  IBM PC compatible serial communications, 311, 328, 330
  inp and outp I/O port functions, 329
  integral data types, 50, **388**
  integral types, 51
  interrupt I/O programming, 328, 332
  interrupt vectors setting, 332
  introduction, 29
  memory mapped I/O registers, 328
  Microsoft compatible mouse under MS-DOS, 315
  operations on files, **384**
  piping program output into another program, 111
  pointer values, 207, **388**, **389**
  polled I/O programming, 328, 330
  printf and similar functions, 227, **387**
  putback a character, 179
  real data types, 31, 35, 55, 56, **389**
  real types, 70
  redirecting standard input and output, 20, 111
  scanf and similar functions, 228, **388**
  standard I/O streams, 111, 223
  status and error functions, 223, **385**
  stderr standard error stream, 29
  stdin standard input stream, 29
  stdout standard output stream, 29
  strings, 186, 213, 225, 226, 231, 237, **386**, 388, 389
  test for end of file, 180
  testing the state of the stream, 79
  ungetc character, 161, 163, 179, 225, **386**
  validation of input data, 106
inp, read from I/O port function, 329, 330

Instructions
  and data storage, **4**, 229
  internal representation, 6
int integer data type, 48
int86 function under MS-DOS, 306, 308
Integer arithmetic functions, **391**
Integer numbers, 4, 23
Integral types
  boolean or logical data, 48, 77
  characters, 177
  constants, 49
  conversion between siged and unsigned, 60
  implementation defined limits, 48, 66, 381
  input/output, 50, 51, **388**
  introduction, 48
  numeric data types, 48
  numeric types, 23
  signed, 23, 48
  signed and unsigned characters, 178
Integrated environments, 19
Intel 8086 family
  assembly language from C, 319
  INT instruction, 305
  IRET instruction, 306
Internal linkage, 143, 157
Interrupting an executing program, 20
Interrupts
  hardware and software interrupts, 305
  hardware interrupts, 328, 332
  int86 function, 306, 308
  interrupt instructions, 305
  interrupt service routine, 305, 328, 332, 334,
    335
  interrupt vector, 332
  setting up interrupt vectors under MS-DOS,
    332
Invoking processes, 317

Keyboard
  input using scanf, 35
  testing for a key hit, 183

Labels and goto statement, 102
Link time errors, 19, 43
Linked lists, 262
Linker, 19
Local scope, 134
Logical operators, 79
Logical or boolean data, 48, **76**
long double real type, **53**
long int integer data type, 48
Loop control statements
  break statement, 101, 375
  continue statement, 101
  do ... while statement, 88
  for statement, 93
  goto statement, 102
  infinite loops, 92
  while statement, 85
Low-level languages, 6
Lvalue, left value, 26, 44, 205, 267

Machine code, 6
Macros with parameters, 129
Main function, passing parameters to, 209
malloc, allocate storage, 255, 390
Mathematical equations, 26, 34
Mathematical series, 284
Maths library header file <math.h>, 32, **382**
Memory mapped input/output registers, 328
Memory processing functions, 195, 208
Microsoft compatible mouse under MS-DOS,
  315
Modular programming, 9, 142
Modulus operator %, 62
Motorola MC68000 family
  assembly language from C, 322
  RTE instruction, 306
  TRAP instruction, 305
Mouse control from MS-DOS, 315
MS-DOS operating system
  batch file to execute a program, 345
  binary file copy program, 375
  display screen clearing, 307, 325
  display screen scrolling, 307
  editing and compiling, 20
  file copy program, 226, 374
  int86 function facilities, 306
  interrupt vector setting, 332
  invoking processes, 317
  Microsoft compatible mouse, 315
  passing parameters to a C program, 210, 371
  setting the text cursor position, 320
  text cursor position setting, 307
  video RAM memory accessing, 325
Multi-dimensional arrays, 266
Multi-file programs, 142

Named constants, const qualifier, 37, 38
Nested for statements, 96, 355
Newline character, 31
Newton-Raphson method of successive
  approximations, 291, 297
Null character string terminator, 185
NULL pointer, 187
Null statement, 91

Object-oriented programming, 10
Object, in C is a storage area, 44
Operands, introduction, 25
Operating system
  accessing facilities via system calls, 305
  direct input/output, 183, 367
Operators
  - subtraction operator, 62
  - unary arithmetic operator, 62
  -- decrement operator, 71, 97, 98
  -- decrement operator and pointers, 201, 213,
    216
  -> member selection operator, 232, 239
  -> structure pointer operator, 262
  ! logical not operator, 79, 80
  != test for not equal operator, 77, 81, 82, 87

Operators
?: conditional expression, 83, 111, 184, 248, 363, 375
/ division operator, 62
. member selection operator, 232
. structure member operator, 231
^ bitwise exclusive or operator, 64, 252
~ unary complement operator, 64, 252
[] subscript operator, 159
* dereference operator, 198
* multiply operator, 62
& address of operator, 198
& bitwise and operator, 64, 252
&& logical and operator, 79, 181, 355
% modulus operator, 62, 150, 151, 355
+ addition operator, 62
+ unary arithmetic operator, 62
+ + decrement operator, 97
+ + increment operator, 71, 94, 108, 114, 127
+ + increment operator and pointers, 201, 213, 216, 370, 373
< test for less than operator, 77, 86
< < bitwise left shift operator, 64, 252
< = test for less than or equal to operator, 77
= assignment operator, 68, 347
= = test for equality operator, 77, 82
> test for greater than operator, 77, 82
> = test for greater than or equal to operator, 77
> > bitwise right shift operator, 64, 252
| bitwise or operator, 64, 252
|| logical or operator, 79
arithmetic operators, 62
arithmetic overflow and underflow, 62, 70
binary operators, 62
cast operator, 103, 185, 208, 238, 255, 289, 302, 321, 324, 326, 339
casting or conversion operators, 65
compound assignment operators, 74
introduction, 25, 59
logical && (and) operator, 369, 373
order of evaluation, 61, 63, 65
precedence and associativity, 61, 394
relational, 77
sizeof operator, 65, 159, 197, 211
unary operators, 62
, sequence operator, 96, 98, 166, 190, 354
Order of evaluation in expressions, 61
Output of text (also see I/O streams), 26
outp, write to I/O port function, 329, 330
Overflow and underflow in arithmetic operations, 62, 70

Parameters of functions (see functions), 123
Pass by reference (see functions), 36
Pass by value (see functions), 35
Passing function parameters (see functions), 115
Passing parameters to main, 209
perror, print string and error message, 226, 381, 385

Piping output from one program into another, 111
Pointers
-> member selection operator, 232, 239
. (structure member) operator, 232
* and -- and + + operators, 204
* dereference operator, 198
& address of operator, 198
arrays, 200
arrays of pointers, 209, 371, 374, 375
as a function result, 212
as function parameters, 212, 222
casting to a pointer type, 208, 324, 326
const qualified, 222
defining and using, 198
generic pointer void *, 208, 255
increment and decrement operators, 201, 213, 216, 370, 373
introduction, 124, 197
NULL pointer, 187, 212, 213
pass by reference, 124
pointer arithmetic, 200, 201
printing value of, 207, **388**
reading value of, **389**
sizeof operator, 211
string processing, 213
structures, 232
the null pointer, **206**
to different types, 199
to functions, 295
to locations in physical memory, 324
to pointers, 207
valid addresses, 221
Precedence and associativity of operators, 61, 394
Preprocessor
#define and #undef directives, 38, 39, 129, 275
#if, #else and #endif directives, 149
#include directive, 18, 21
directives, 17
directives longer than a line, 42
functions vers preprocessor macros, 129, 275
introduction, 17, 18
macro parameters, 129
macro to find maximum of two numbers, 132, 363
macro to square/cube a number, 131
macro to swap two variables, 132
side effects in macros, 131
Preprocessor directives
#define, 234, 246
#endif, 234, 246
#ifndef, 234, 246
Prime numbers, 100, 176, 355
Print decimal integer, 51
Print hexadecimal integer, 51
Print octal integer, 51
printf
- justification control, 237, **387**
alternate output form, 50, **387**
+ print sign, **387**

printf
  control string, 31
  conversion specifications, 31, 50, 55, **388**
  field width control, **387**
  function result, 343, **387**
  general output function, **227, 387**
  introduction, 31
  number of characters converted, 33
  padding with leading zeros, **387**
  parameters, **387**
  printing integral data types, 50, **388**
  printing pointers, 207
  printing real data types, 31, 55
  printing real numbers, 31, 55
  printing strings, 31
Printing (also see I/O streams), 26
Printing variables
  characters, 179
  integral data types, 50, **388**
  integral types, 51
  real data types, 31, 55
Procedural programming, 9
Processes, invoking, 317
Program
  area of a rectangle, 21, 22
  area of a triangle, 58, 346
  array read, write, average, standard deviation
      and sort, 168, 365
  assembly language for Motorola 68000, 322
  assembly language listing of a C program, 348
  assembly language on an IBM PC compatible,
      320, 323
  average of a sequence of real numbers, 67,
      87, 160, 347
  binary copy one file to another, 375
  calculator program, 157
  capital growth over time period, 94
  car parking fees, 79, 349
  check for input errors, 83, 350
  circle area & check radius, 32
  circle area and sphere volume, 39, 344
  college tution fees, 84, 350
  command selection from a menu, 104, 299
  comments, 21, 41
  compiler listing with errors, 43
  complex numbers, 249, 376
  conversion between types, 70
  convert metres to feet and inches, 63, 128,
      347, 362
  convert seconds to hours, minutes, 63, 346
  copy one file to another, 226, 374
  Cost of decorating a room, 52, 345
  date and time display, 183
  depreciation of value of a machine, 96, 354
  design, coding and testing, 8
  direct input from operating system, 182, 183,
      367
  display bouncing ball, 113, 357
  display clock on screen, 114
  display time, 92, 114
  documentation, 41
  draw a pattern on the screen, 96, 354

Program
  dynamic allocation of storage, 260
  epsilon of float type, 89, 90, 91, 353
  execution, 19
  factorial and inverse factorial, 119, 360
  factorial of an integer number, 98
  factorial using recursion, 294
  Fibonacci numbers, 137
  file open and read characters, 226
  function using pass by reference, 128, 362
  functions with a variable number of
      parameters, 304
  generate data for graph plotting, 111
  graph in graphics mode, 114
  graph using characters, 108
  graphics display of bouncing ball, 357
  hardware interrupts, 332
  header file, 147, 167
  IBM/PC 8253 timer/counter using interrupts,
      334
  impedance of an RLC circuit, 249, 376
  increment and decrement operators, 72
  input verification, 81
  integral sizes and ranges, 66
  interest rate - time to double capital, 86
  inverse sine, 293, 378
  linked list, 262
  maximum and minimum of an array, 167
  maximum of a pair of numbers, 132, 363
  Motor insurance premiums, 105, 356
  MS-DOS screen and cursor control, 308
  MS-DOS system facilities, 308
  MS-DOS terminal emulator, 312
  multi-dimensional arrays, 269
  multi-file programs, 142
  multiplying arrays, 269
  operator precedence and associativity, 62
  oscillation of spring, 75
  parameters passed from operating system,
      210, 371
  passing pointers to functions as function
      parameters, 297
  payroll calculation, 75, 348
  period of oscillation of pendulum, 119, 359
  plot a graph in graphics mode, 114
  plot a graph using characters, 108
  pointer to a function as a function result, 300
  pointers to access array elements, 202
  pointers to pointers, 208
  preprocessor macros, 38, 130, 275
  prime numbers, 100, 176, 355
  print a message to the display screen, 21
  print name and address to display screen, 22,
      343
  printf using, 57
  quadratic equation, 58, 84
  queue ADT, 176, 264, 376
  raise a float to integer exponent, 120
  random number generation, 150, 151, 153,
      157, 174, 175
  reactance of LC circuit, 75, 122, 361
  read a binary number, 181, 367

Program
  read a hexadecimal number, 182, 367
  read and test a number, 77
  read and write contents of an array, 167
  read character & print character code, 180
  read float and test for conversion OK, 80
  read real numbers to error or eof, 87
  reading, writing and manipulating arrays, 163
  reverse the contents of an array, 167
  rule of 72 effect of inflation, 86, 351
  running mean, 127, 139, 364
  scanf to read a real value, 35
  scope of local and external variables, 135
  simple calculator, 157
  simulation of a dice game, 157
  simulation of a doctor's surgery, 153, 174
  simulation of rolling a dice, 157
  sin(2A) and cos(2A), 34
  sine function, 285
  sort an array, 176, 211, 295, 379
  Soundex code, 105
  square a number (function), 117
  square root of a number, 27
  stack ADT, 171, 257
  standard deviation, 88, 352
  static local variables, 138, 139, 364
  string processing, 188
  string processing using pointers, 213
  structures, 233
  student records, 233, 242
  surface areas and volume of a cylinder, 47
  swap the values of two variables, 126
  switch and break statements, 104, 370
  tan(2A), 39
  temperature conversion, 52, 58
  test number for 0, positive or negative, 82
  testing, 15
  time delay using <time.h>, 92
  variable number of function parameters, 303
  verfiying numeric input, 108
Program flow and loop control
  break statement, 101, 375
  continue statement, 101
  do ... while statement, 88
  for statement, 93
  goto statement, 102
  if statement, 76
  nested if statements, 81
  switch statement, 102, 104, 370
  while statement, 85
Prototypes of functions, 33, 116
putchar print a character function, 179
puts function, print a string, 187, 225, 386

Quadratic equation
  precision of calculations, 54
  program, 58, 84
Queue program, 176, 264, 376
Quicksort, 295, 379

Random number generation, 150, 153, 157, 174, 175, **390**
Raster graphics, 253
Re-usability, 8
Reading variables
  characters, 179
  integral data types, 50
  integral types, 51
  real data types, 35, 56, **389**
  real types, 70
Real numbers, 5, 23
Real types
  constants, 53
  conversion between types, 55
  double, 23, **53**
  float, 23, **53**
  input/output, 31, 35, 55, 56, 70, **389**
  introduction, 53
  long double, 23, **53**
  overflow, 70
  precision and ranges, 54, 381
realloc, reallocate storage, 255, 260, 390
Recursive functions, 294, 379
Redirecting standard input and output, 20, 111
Redirecting standard input and putput, 111
register storage class specifier, 141
Relational operators, 77
Remainder in integer division, 62
remove, delete a file, 224, 385
rename, rename a file, 224, 385
Rounding errors, 287
Run-time errors, 19, 45, 344

scanf
  control string, 35
  conversion specifications, 35, 36, 50, 56, **389**
  EOF end of file, 37, 80, **390**
  field width control, **389**
  function result, 37, **390**
  general keyboard input function, **228, 388**
  introduction, 35
  parameters, 36, **388**
  reading characters, 50
  reading integral data types, 50
  reading real data types, 35, 56, **389**
  reading real numbers, 56
  white space, 36, **389**
Scope
  discussion, 133, 134, 140
  external scope, 134
  file scope, 140
  function scope, 140
  local scope, 134, 140
Screen control functions under MS-DOS, 308
Searching and sorting functions, **391**
Searching strings, 188, 189, 195, 213, 221, 368, 372
Semantic errors, 43
Sequence or comma operator, 96, 166, 354
Sequence points, 97, 155

Serial communications
  EIA RS232C standard, 309
  handshaking, 310
  IBM PC compatible computer, 311, 328, 330
  introduction, 309
short int integer data type, 48
Side effects in expression evaluation, 72, 137, **155**
Side effects in macros, 131
signed and unsigned characters, 178
Signed integer numbers, 5
Signed integral types, 23, 48
Simulation of a doctor's surgery, 153, 174
Simulation of a game using a pair of dice, 157
Simulation of rolling a dice, 157
Sine function for large angles, 290
Sine series, 284, 285
sizeof operator
  arrays, 159
  examples of use, 66
  introduction, 65
  use with pointers, 66, 211
Software Engineering, system requirements, 8
Sorting and searching functions, **391**
Sorting array contents, 168, 176, 211, 295, 365, 379
Soundex code, 105
sprintf, output to a string, **227**, 326, **387**
Square root
  evaluating using Newton-Raphson method, 291
  maths function sqrt, 32, 33
Sscanf, input from a string, **228**, 238, **388**
Stack
  implemented using an array, 170
  processing functions, 171
Standard deviation evaluation, 88, 168, 352, 365
Standard input/output streams, 111, 223
Standard libraries, 17, **380**
Statements
  assignment, 25, 68, 347
  introduction, 17, 25
static external variables, 145, 147, 151, 173, 376
static local variables, 137, 138, 140, 145, 364
static storage class specifier, 137, 138, 145, 147, 151, 173, 364, 376
stderr standard error stream, 29
stdin standard input stream, 29, 179
stdout standard output stream, 29
Stepwise refinement, 10
Stopping an executing program, 20
Storage allocation, 255
Storage class specifiers
  register, 141
Static external variables, 145, 147, 151, 173, 376
Static local variables, 137, 138, 140, 145, 364
Static storage class specifier, 137, 138, 145, 147, 151, 173, 364, 376
Stderr standard error stream, 29

Stdin standard input stream, 29, 179
Stdout standard output stream, 29
Stepwise refinement, 10
Stopping an executing program, 20
Storage allocation, 255
Storage class specifiers
  register, 141
  static, 137, 138, 145, 147, 151, 173, 364, 376
Storage of instructions and data, **4**, 229
strchr function, search string for a character, **392**
strcpy function, copy a string, 185, 231, **392**

Strings
  comparing, 195, 221, 368, 372
  concatenating, 186, 196, 222
  constants, 184
  conversion functions, **391**
  copying using strcpy, 185
  function to concatenate a number of strings, 303
Strings
  functions to process strings, 188, 189, 213, 368, 372
  initialisation, 185
  input/output, 186, 225, **386**
  introduction, **184**
  length of using strlen, 185
  null character, 185
  printing, **188**, **189**
  printing with printf, **186**, 213, 226, 231, 237, **388**
  processing functions, 195, **392**
  processing using pointers, 213
  reading with scanf, **186**, **389**
  searching, 188, 189, 195, 196, 213, 221, 222, 368, 372
  sprintf output function, 227, 387
  sscanf input function, 228, 388
  terminating, 185
strlen function, length of string, 185, 188, 189, 192, **392**
Structured English, 14
Structures
  accessing members, 231
  arrays of, 300
  bitfields, 251
  declaring and initialising, 230
  function parameters, 232
  function result, 232
  initialisation, 230
  introduction, 230
  passed by reference to functions, 243
  pointers, 232
  structures within structures, 233
  type FILE, 223
  unions, 249, 306
switch conditional control statement, **102**, 104, 370
switch statement and break, 101, 102, 104, 370

Symbolic constants, #define directive, 38
Syntax errors, 43
System analysis, 9
System implementation languages, 1, 7
Systems software, 3

Testing of software, 15
Testing the state of I/O streams, 79
Time and date, 183
Time delays, 357
Time functions in <time.h>, 91, 151, 152, 357, **393**
Timing events
 and delays, 91
 using interrupts, 334
 within a program, 130
tmpfile, open a temporary file, 224, 385
Truncating infinite series, 284
Twos complement numbers, 5
Type conversion
 between integral types, 60
 between real types, 55, 60
Type conversion
 between signed and unsigned types, 60
 cast or conversion operators, 65
 conversion across assignment, 69
 introduction, 59
 the integral promotions, 60
 the usual arithmetic conversions, 60, 69
 undefined behaviour, 71
typedef, defining new type names, **43**
Types
 char, **177**
 derived types, 23
 double, **53**
 float, **53**
 fundamental types, 23
 introduction, 23
 long double, **53**
 pointers, 197
 string, 184
 typedef, defining new type names, 43

Unformatted (binary) file input/output, 228
Unformatted file input/output, **390**
ungetc, 'push' character back into a stream, 161, 163, 179, 225, **386**
Unions, 249, 306
UNIX operating system
 editing and compiling, 20
 forking a process, 317
 invoking processes, 317
unsigned integral types, 23, 48
User defined types, **156**
Validation of numeric data input, 106
Variable number of function parameters, 302
Variables
 actual parameters, 116
 addresses, 197
 allocation of storage, 140
 arrays, 158
Variables
 automatic local, 137, 140
 const qualified, 139
 declarations and definitions, 133, 143
 external, 134, 141
 formal parameters, 116
 formal parameters of functions, 141
 initialisation of variables, 140
 internal and external linkage, 143, 157
 introduction, 24
 local scope, 134
 register storage class, 141
 static external, 145, 147, 151, 173, 376
 static local, 137, 138, 140, 145, 364
 volatile qualified, 139, 334, 336
void *, the generic pointer, 208, 255
volatile type qualifier, 139, 321, 334, 336

while loop control statement, **85**, 94, 95, 98, 99, 101
while statement and break, 101, 375
White space, 36

, (comma) sequence operator, 96, 98, 166, 190, 354

OWNERSHIP OF COPYRIGHT